GRAPHICS GEMS IV

This is a volume in

The Graphics Gems Series

A Collection of Practical Techniques
for the Computer Graphics Programmer

Series Editor

Andrew Glassner
Xerox Palo Alto Research Center
Palo Alto, California

GRAPHICS GEMS
IV

Edited by Paul S. Heckbert
Computer Science Department
Carnegie Mellon University
Pittsburgh, Pennsylvania

AP PROFESSIONAL

Boston   San Diego   New York
London   Sydney   Tokyo   Toronto

This book is printed on acid-free paper ∞

AP PROFESSIONAL
955 Massachusetts Avenue, Cambridge, MA 02139

An imprint of ACADEMIC PRESS, INC.
A Division of HARCOURT BRACE & COMPANY

United Kingdom Edition published by
ACADEMIC PRESS LIMITED
24–28 Oval Road, London NW1 7DX

Library of Congress Cataloging-in-Publication Data
Graphics gems IV / edited by Paul S. Heckbert.
   p. cm. -- (The Graphics gems series)
  Includes bibliographical references and index.
  ISBN 0-12-336156-7 (with Macintosh disk). —ISBN 0-12-336155-9
(with IBM disk)
  1. Computer graphics. I. Heckbert, Paul S., 1958– .
II. Title: Graphics gems 4. III. Title: Graphics gems four.
IV. Series.
T385.G6974 1994
006.6'6--dc20   93-46995
                 CIP

Printed in the United States of America

94 95 96 97 MV 9 8 7 6 5 4 3 2 1

◇ Contents

◊ Author Index

Format: *author, institution, chapter number:* p. *start page.*
   Author's full address is listed on the first page of each chapter.

 # Foreword

Andrew S. Glassner

We make images to communicate. The ultimate measure of the quality of our images is how well they communicate information and ideas from the creator's mind to the perceiver's mind. The efficiency of this communication, and the quality of our image, depends on both what we want to say and to whom we intend to say it.

I believe that computer-generated images are used today in two distinct ways, characterized by whether the intended receiver of the work is a person or machine. Images in these two categories have quite different reasons for creation, and need to satisfy different criteria in order to be successful.

Consider first an image made for a machine. For example, an architect planning a garden next to a house may wish to know how much light the garden will typically receive per day during the summer months. To determine this illumination, the architect might build a 3D model of the house and garden, and then use computer graphics to simulate the illumination on the ground at different times of day in a variety of seasons. The images generated by the rendering program would be a by-product, and perhaps never even looked at; they were only generated in order to compute illumination. The only criterion for judgment for such images is an appropriate measure of *accuracy*.

Nobody will pass judgment on the *aesthetics* of these pictures, since no person with an aesthetic sense will ever see them. Accuracy does not require beauty. For example, a simulation may not produce images that are individually correct, but instead average to the correct answer. The light emitted by the sun may be modeled as small, discrete chunks, causing irregular blobs of illumination on the garden. When these blobs are averaged together over many hours and days, the estimates approach the correct value for the received sunlight. No one of these pictures is accurate individually, and probably none of them would be very attractive.

When we make images for people, we have a different set of demands. We almost always require that our images be *attractive* in some way. In this context, attractive does not necessarily mean beautiful, but it means that there must be an aesthetic component influenced by composition, color, weight, and so on. Even when we intend to act as analytic and dispassionate observers, humans have an innate sense of beauty that cannot be denied. This is the source of all ornament in art, music, and literature: we always desire something beyond the purely functional. Even the most utilitarian objects, such as hammers and pencils, are *designed* to provide grace and beauty to our eyes and offer comfort to our hands. When we weave together beauty and utility, we create elegance. People are more interested in beautiful things than neutral things, because they stimulate our senses and our feelings.

So even the most utilitarian image intended to communicate something to another person must be designed with that person in mind: the picture must be composed so that it is balanced in terms of form and space, the colors must harmonize, the shapes must not jar. It is by occasionally violating these principles that we can make one part of the image stand out with respect to the background; ignoring them produces images that have no focus and no balance, and thus do not capture and hold our interest. Their ability to communicate is reduced. Every successful creator of business charts, wallpaper designs, and scientific visualizations knows these rules and works with them.

So images intended for people must be attractive. Only then can we further address the idea of accuracy. What does it mean for an image intended for a person to be "accurate"?

Sometimes "accuracy" is interpreted to mean that the energy of the visible light calculated to form the image exactly matches the energy that would be measured if the modeled scene (including light sources) really existed, and were photographed; this idea is described in computer graphics by the term *photorealism*. This would certainly be desirable, under some circumstances, if the image were intended for a machine's analysis, but the human perceptual apparatus responds differently than a flatbed scanner. People are not very good at determining absolute levels of light, and we are easily fooled into thinking that the brightest and least chromatic part of an image is "white."

Again we return to the question of what we're trying to communicate. If the point of an image is that a garden is well-lit and that there is uniform illumination over its entire surface, then we do not care about the radiometric accuracy of the image as much as the fact that it conveys that information; the whole picture could be too bright or too dark by some constant factor and this message will still be carried without distortion. In the garden image, we expect a certain variation due to the variety of soil, rocks, plants, and other geometry in the scene. Very few people could spot the error in a good but imprecise approximation of such seemingly random fluctuation. In this type of situation, if you can't see the error, you don't care about it. So not only can the illumination be off by a constant factor, it can vary from the "true" value quite a bit from point to point and we won't notice, or if we do notice, we won't mind.

If we want to convey the sense of a scene viewed at night, then we need to take into account the entire observer of a night scene. The human visual system *adapts* to different light levels, which changes how it perceives different ranges of light. If we look at a room lit by a single 25-watt light bulb, and then look at it again when we use a 1000-watt bulb, the overall illumination has changed by a constant factor, but our perception of the room changes in a non-linear way. The room lit by the 25-watt bulb appears dark and shadowy, while the room lit by the 1000-watt bulb is stark and bright. If we display both on a CRT using the same intensity range, even though the underlying radiance values were computed with precision, both images will appear the same. Is this either *accurate* or *photorealistic*?

Sometimes some parts of an image intended for a person must be accurate, depending on what that image is intended to communicate. If the picture shows a new object intended for possible manufacture, the precise shape may be important, or the way it reflects light may be critical. In these applications we are treating the person as a machine; we are inviting the person to analyze one or more characteristics of the image as a predictor of a real object or scene. When we are making an image of a smooth and glossy object prior to manufacture in order to evaluate its appearance, the shading must match that of the final object as accurately as possible. If we are only rendering the shape in order to make sure it will fit into some packing material, the shading only needs to give us information about the shape of the object; this shading may be arbitrarily inaccurate as long as we still get the right perception of shape. A silver candlestick might be rendered as though it were made of concrete, for example, if including the highlights and caustics would interfere with judging its shape. In this case our definition of "accuracy" involves our ability to judge the structure of shapes from their images, and does not include the optical properties of the shape.

My point is that images made for machines should be judged by very different criteria than images made for people. This can help us evaluate the applicability of different types of images with different objective accuracies. Consider the picture generated for an architect's client, with the purpose of getting an early opinion from the client regarding whether there are enough trees in the yard. The accuracy of this image doesn't matter as long as it looks good and is roughly correct in terms of geometry and shading. Too much precision in every part of the image may lead to too much distraction; because of its perceived realism and implied finality, the client may start thinking about whether a small shed in the image is placed just right, when it hasn't even been decided that there will be a shed at all. Precision implies a statement; vagueness implies a suggestion.

Consider the situation where someone is evaluating a new design for a crystal drinking glass; the precision of the geometry and the rendering will matter a great deal, since the reflections and sparkling colors are very important in this situation. But still, the numerical accuracy of the energy simulation need not be right, as long as the relative accuracy of the image is correct. Then there's the image made as a simulation for analysis by a machine. In this case the image must be accurate with respect to whatever criteria will be measured and whatever choice of measurement is used.

Images are for communication, and the success of an image should be measured only by how well it communicates. Sometimes too little objective accuracy can distort the message; sometimes too much accuracy can detract from the message. The reason for making a picture is to communicate something that must be said; the image should support that message and not dominate it. The medium must be chosen to fit the message.

To make effective images we need effective tools, and that is what this book is intended to provide. Every profession has its rules of thumb and tricks of the trade; in computer graphics, these bits of wisdom are described in words, equations, and programs. The

Graphics Gems series is like a general store; it's fun to drop in every once in a while and browse, uncovering unusual items with which you were unfamiliar, and seeing new applications for old ideas. When you're faced with a sticky problem, you may remember seeing just the right tool on display. Happily, our stock is in limitless supply, and as near as your bookshelf or library.

◊ Preface

This book is a cookbook for computer graphics programmers, a kind of "Numerical Recipes" for graphics. It contains practical techniques that can help you do 2D and 3D modeling, animation, rendering, and image processing. The 52 articles, written by 54 authors worldwide, have been selected for their usefulness, novelty, and simplicity. Each article, or "Gem," presents a technique in words and formulas, and also, for most of the articles, in C or C++ code as well. The code is available in electronic form on the IBM or Macintosh floppy disk in the back pocket of the book, and is available on the Internet via FTP (see address below). The floppy disk also contains all of the code from the previous volumes: *Graphics Gems I, II,* and *III.* You are free to use and modify this code in any way you like.

A few of the Gems in this book deserve special mention because they provide implementations of particularly useful, but non-trivial algorithms. Gems IV.6 and IV.8 give very general, modular code to polygonize parametric and implicit surfaces, respectively. With these two and a polygon renderer, you could probably display 95% of all computer graphics models! Gem I.5 finds 2D Voronoi diagrams or Delaunay triangulations. These data structures are very widely used for mesh generation and other geometric operations. In the area of interaction, Gem III.1 provides code for control of orientation in 3D. This could be used in interactive 3D modelers. Finally, Gem I.8 gives code to find collisions of polyhedra, an important task in physically based modeling and animation.

This book, like the previous three volumes in the *Graphics Gems* series, lies somewhere between the media of textbook, journal, and computer bulletin board. Textbooks explain algorithms very well, but if you are doing computer graphics programming, then they may not provide what you need: an implementation. Similarly, technical journals seldom present implementations, and they are often much more theoretical than a programmer cares for. The third alternative, computer bulletin boards such as the USENET news group *comp.graphics.algorithms,* occasionally contains good code, but because they are unmoderated and unedited, they are so flooded with queries that it is tedious to find useful information. The *Graphics Gems* series is an attempt at a middle ground, where programmers worldwide can contribute graphics techniques that they have found useful, and the best of these get published. Most of the articles are written by the inventors of the techniques, so you will learn their motivations and see their programming techniques firsthand. Also, the implementations have been selected for their portability; they are not limited to UNIX, IBM, or Macintosh systems. Most of them will compile and run, perhaps with minor modifications, on any computer with a C or C++ compiler.

Assembling this book has been a collaborative process involving many people. In the Spring of 1993, a call for contributions was distributed worldwide via electronic mail and word of mouth. Submissions arrived in the Summer of 1993. These were read by me and many were also read by one or more of my outside reviewers: Eric Haines, Andrew Glassner, Chandrajit Bajaj, Tom Duff, Ron Goldman, Tom Sederberg, David Baraff, Jules Bloomenthal, Ken Shoemake, Mike Kass, Don Mitchell, and Greg Ward. Of the 155 articles submitted, 52 were accepted for publication. These were revised and, in most cases, formatted into LaTeX by the authors. Coordinating the project at Academic Press in Cambridge, Massachusetts, were Jenifer Niles and Brian Miller. Book composition was done by Rena Wells at Rosenlaui Publishing Services in Houston, Texas, and the cover image was made by Eben Ostby of Pixar, in Richmond, California. I am very thankful to all of these people and to the others who worked on this book for helping to make it a reality. Great thanks also to the *Graphics Gems* series editor, Andrew Glassner, for inviting me to be editor for this volume, and to my wife, Bridget Johnson-Heckbert, for her patience.

There are a few differences between this book and the previous volumes of the series. Organizationally, the code and bibliographies are not collected at the back of the book, but appear with the text of the corresponding article. These changes make each Gem more self-contained. The book also differs in emphasis. Relative to the previous volumes, I have probably stressed novelty more, and simplicity less, preferring an implementation of a complex computer graphics algorithm over formulas from analytic geometry, for example.

In addition to the *Graphics Gems* series, there are several other good sources for practical computer graphics techniques. One of these is the column "Jim Blinn's Corner" that appears in the journal *IEEE Computer Graphics and Applications*. Another is the book *A Programmer's Geometry*, by Adrian Bowyer and John Woodwark (Butterworth's, London, 1983), which is full of analytic geometry formulas. A mix of analytic geometry and basic computer graphics formulas is contained in the book *Computer Graphics Handbook: Geometry and Mathematics* by Michael E. Mortensen (Industrial Press, New York, 1990). Another excellent source is, of course, graphics textbooks.

Code in this book is available on the Internet by anonymous FTP from `princeton.edu` (`128.112.128.1`) in the directory `pub/GraphicsGems/GemsIV`. The code for other *Graphics Gems* books is also available nearby. Bug reports should be submitted as described in the `README` file there.

Paul Heckbert, March 1994

◊ About the Cover

The cover: "Washday Miracle" by Eben Ostby. Copyright © 1994 Pixar.

When series editor Andrew Glassner called me to ask if I could help with a cover image for *Graphics Gems IV*, there were four requirements: the image needed to tell a story; it needed to have gems in it; it should be a computer-generated image; and it should look good. To these parameters, I added one of my own: it should tell a story that is different from the previous covers. Those stories were usually mystical or magical; accordingly, I decided to take the mundane as my inspiration.

The image was created using a variety of tools, including Alias Studio; Menv, our own internal animation system; and Photorealistic RenderMan. The appliances, table, and basket were built in Alias. The gems were placed by a stochastic "gem-placer" running under Menv. The house set was built in Menv. Surface descriptions were written in the RenderMan shading language and include both procedural and painted textures.

For the number-conscious, this image was rendered at a resolution of 2048 by 2695 and contains the following:

16 lights
643 gems
30,529 lines or 2,389,896 bytes of model information
4 cycles: regular, delicate, Perma-Press, and Air Fluff

Galyn Susman did the lighting design. Andrew Glassner reviewed and critiqued, and made the image far better as a result. Matt Martin made prepress proofs. Pixar (in corpora Karen Robert Jackson and Ralph Guggenheim) permitted me time to do this.

Eben Ostby
Pixar

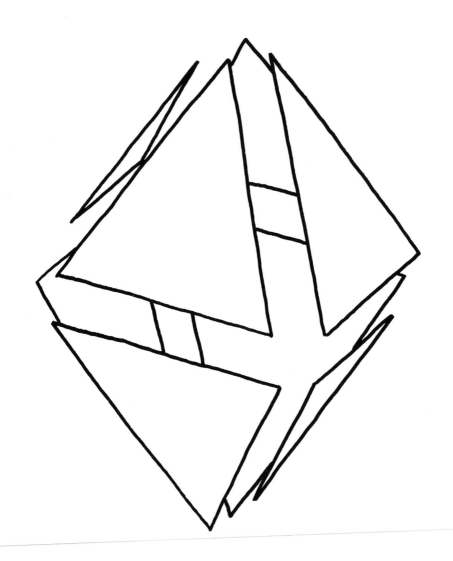

Polygons and Polyhedra

This part of the book contains five Gems on polygons and three on polyhedra. Polygons and polyhedra are the most basic and popular geometric building blocks in computer graphics.

I.1. Centroid of a Polygon, *by Gerard Bashein and Paul R. Detmer.*
Gives formulas and code to find the centroid (center of mass) of a polygon. This is useful when simulating Newtonian dynamics. Page 3.

I.2. Testing the Convexity of a Polygon, *by Peter Schorn and Frederick Fisher.*
Gives an algorithm and code to determine if a polygon is convex, non-convex (concave but not convex), or non-simple (self-intersecting). For many polygon operations, faster algorithms can be used if the polygon is known to be convex. This is true when scan converting a polygon and when determining if a point is inside a polygon, for instance. Page 7.

I.3. An Incremental Angle Point in Polygon Test, *by Kevin Weiler.*

I.4. Point in Polygon Strategies, *by Eric Haines.*
Provide algorithms for testing if a point is inside a polygon, a task known as point inclusion testing in computational geometry. Point-in-polygon testing is a basic task when ray tracing polygonal models, so these methods are useful for 3D as well as 2D graphics. Weiler presents a single algorithm for testing if a point lies in a concave polygon, while Haines surveys a number of algorithms for point inclusion testing in both convex and concave polygons, with empirical speed tests and practical optimizations. Pages 16 and 24.

I.5. Incremental Delaunay Triangulation, *by Dani Lischinski.*

Gives some code to solve a very important problem: finding Delaunay triangulations and Voronoi diagrams in 2D. These two geometric constructions are useful for triangular mesh generation and for nearest neighbor finding, respectively. Triangular mesh generation comes up when doing interpolation of surfaces from scattered data points, and in finite element simulations of all kinds, such as radiosity. Voronoi diagrams are used in many computational geometry algorithms. Page 47.

The final three Gems of this part of the book concern polyhedra: polygonal models that are intrinsically three-dimensional.

I.6. Building Vertex Normals from an Unstructured Polygon List, *by Andrew Glassner.*

Solves a fairly common rendering problem: if one is given a set of polygons in raw form, with no topological (adjacency) information, and asked to do smooth shading (Gouraud or Phong shading) of them, one must infer topology and compute vertex normals. Page 60.

I.7. Detecting Intersection of a Rectangular Solid and a Convex Polyhedron, *by Ned Greene.*

Presents an optimized technique to test for intersection between a convex polyhedron and a box. This is useful when comparing bounding boxes against a viewing frustum in a rendering program, for instance. Page 74.

I.8. Fast Collision Detection of Moving Convex Polyhedra, *by Rich Rabbitz.*

A turn-key piece of software that solves a difficult but basic problem in physically based animation and interactive modeling. Page 83.

 **I.1**

Centroid of a Polygon

Gerard Bashein[1]
Department of Anesthesiology and
Center for Bioengineering, RN-10
University of Washington
Seattle, WA 98195
gb@locke.hs.washington.edu

Paul R. Detmer[1]
Department of Surgery and
Center for Bioengineering, RF-25
University of Washington
Seattle, WA 98195
pdetmer@u.washington.edu

This Gem gives a rapid and accurate method to calculate the area and the coordinates of the center of mass of a simple polygon.

Determination of the center of mass of a polygonal object may be required in the simulation of planar mechanical systems and in some types of graphical data analysis. When the density of an object is uniform, the center of mass is called the centroid. The naive way of calculating the centroid, taking the mean of the x and y coordinates of the vertices, gives incorrect results except in a few simple situations, because it actually finds the center of mass of a massless polygon with equal point masses at its vertices. As an example of how the naive method would fail, consider a simple polygon composed of many small line segments (and closely spaced vertices) along one side and only a few vertices along the other sides. The means of the vertex coordinates would then be skewed toward the side having many vertices.

Basic mechanics texts show that the coordinates $(\overline{x}, \overline{y})$ of the centroid of a closed planar region R are given by

$$\overline{x} = \frac{\iint_R x\, dx\, dy}{A} = \frac{\mu_x}{A} \tag{1}$$

$$\overline{y} = \frac{\iint_R y\, dx\, dy}{A} = \frac{\mu_y}{A} \tag{2}$$

where A is the area of R, and μ_x and μ_y are the first moments of R along the x- and y-coordinates, respectively.

In the case where R is a polygon given by the points (x_i, y_i), $i = 0, \ldots, n$, with $x_0 = x_n$ and $y_0 = y_n$, (Roberts 1965) and later (Rokne 1991), (Goldman 1991), and others have shown a rapid method for calculating its area based upon Green's theorem in a plane.

[1]Supported by grants HL42270 and HL41464 from the National Institutes of Health, Bethesda, MD.

$$A = \frac{1}{2} \sum_{i=0}^{n-1} a_i, \quad \text{where } a_i = x_i y_{i+1} - x_{i+1} y_i$$

Janicki *et al.* have also shown that the first moments μ_x and μ_y of a polygon can also be found by Green's theorem (Janicki *et al.* 1981), which states that given continuous functions $M(x, y)$ and $N(x, y)$ having continuous partial derivatives over a region R, which is enclosed by a contour C,

$$\int_C (M dx + N dy) = \iint_R \left(\frac{\partial N}{\partial x} - \frac{\partial M}{\partial y} \right) dx \, dy \tag{3}$$

To evaluate the numerator of (1), let $M = 0$ and $N = \frac{1}{2} x^2$. Then the right side of (3) equals μ_x, and the first moment can be calculated as

$$\mu_x = \frac{1}{2} \int_C x^2 dy$$

Then, representing the line segments between each vertex parametrically and summing the integrals over each line segment yields

$$\mu_x = \frac{1}{6} \sum_{i=0}^{n-1} (x_{i+1} + x_i) \cdot a_i$$

Similarly, to evaluate the numerator of (2), let $M = -\frac{1}{2} y^2$ and $N = 0$, and evaluate the left side of (3). The result becomes

$$\mu_y = \frac{1}{6} \sum_{i=0}^{n-1} (y_{i+1} + y_i) \cdot a_i$$

The form of the equations given above is particularly suited for numerical computation, because it takes advantage of a common factor in the area and moments, and because it eliminates one subtraction (and the consequent loss of accuracy) from each term of the summation for the moments. The loss of numerical accuracy due to the remaining subtraction can be reduced if, before calculating the centroid, the coordinate system is translated to place its origin somewhere close to the polygon.

The techniques used above can be generalized to find volumes, centroids, and moments of inertia of polyhedra (Lien and Kajiya 1984).

The following C code will calculate the x- and y-coordinates of the centroid and the area of any simple (non–self-intersecting) convex or concave polygon. The algebraic signs of both the area (output by the function) and first moments (internal variables only) will be positive when the vertices are ordered in a counterclockwise direction in the x–y plane, and negative otherwise. The coordinates of the centroid will have the correct signs in either case. The method of computation is algebraically equivalent to breaking the polygon into component triangles, finding their signed areas and centroids, and combining the results. Non-simple polygons will have the contributions of their overlapping regions to the area and moments summed algebraically according to the direction (clockwise or counterclockwise) of each traversal of each region.

◇ **C Code** ◇

```
/*********************************************************************
polyCentroid: Calculates the centroid (xCentroid, yCentroid) and area
of a polygon, given its vertices (x[0], y[0]) ... (x[n-1], y[n-1]). It
is assumed that the contour is closed, i.e., that the vertex following
(x[n-1], y[n-1]) is (x[0], y[0]).  The algebraic sign of the area is
positive for counterclockwise ordering of vertices in x-y plane;
otherwise negative.

Returned values:  0 for normal execution;  1 if the polygon is
degenerate (number of vertices < 3);  and 2 if area = 0 (and the
centroid is undefined).
*********************************************************************/
int polyCentroid(double x[], double y[], int n,
                 double *xCentroid, double *yCentroid, double *area)
    {
    register int i, j;
    double ai, atmp = 0, xtmp = 0, ytmp = 0;
    if (n < 3) return 1;
    for (i = n-1, j = 0; j < n; i = j, j++)
        {
        ai = x[i] * y[j] - x[j] * y[i];
        atmp += ai;
        xtmp += (x[j] + x[i]) * ai;
        ytmp += (y[j] + y[i]) * ai;
        }
    *area = atmp / 2;
    if (atmp != 0)
        {
        *xCentroid =  xtmp / (3 * atmp);
        *yCentroid =  ytmp / (3 * atmp);
        return 0;
        }
    return 2;
    }
/***** end polyCentroid *****/
```

◇ **Bibliography** ◇

(Goldman 1991) Ronald N. Goldman. Area of planar polygons and volume of polyhedra. In James Arvo, ed., *Graphics Gems II*, pages 170–171. Academic Press,
Boston, MA, 1991.

(Janicki *et al.* 1981) Joseph S. Janicki *et al.* Three-dimensional myocardial and ven-
tricular shape: A surface representation. *Am. J. Physiol.*, 241:H1–H11, 1981.

(Lien and Kajiya 1984) S. Lien and J. T. Kajiya. A symbolic method for calculating the
integral properties of arbitrary nonconvex polyhedra. *IEEE Computer Graphics
& Applications*, 4(10):35–41, 1984.

(Roberts 1965) L. G. Roberts. Machine perception of three-dimensional solids. In
J. P. Tippet *et al.*, eds., *Optical and Electro-Optical Information Processing*. MIT
Press, Cambridge, MA, 1965.

(Rokne 1991) Jon Rokne. The area of a simple polygon. In James Arvo, ed., *Graphics
Gems II*, pages 5–6. Academic Press, Boston, MA, 1991.

◊ I.2

Testing the Convexity of a Polygon

Peter Schorn

Institut für Theoretische Informatik
ETH, CH-8092 Zürich, Switzerland
schorn@inf.ethz.ch

Frederick Fisher

2630 Walsh Avenue
Kubota Pacific Computer, Inc.
Santa Clara, CA
fred@kpc.com

◊ Abstract ◊

This article presents an algorithm that determines whether a polygon given by the sequence of its vertices is convex. The algorithm is implemented in C, runs in time proportional to the number of vertices, needs constant storage space, and handles all degenerate cases, including non-simple (self-intersecting) polygons.

Results of a polygon convexity test are useful to select between various algorithms that perform a given operation on a polygon. For example, polygon classification could be used to choose between point-in-polygon algorithms in a ray tracer, to choose an output rasterization routine, or to select an algorithm for line-polygon clipping or polygon-polygon clipping. Generally, an algorithm that can assume a specific polygon shape can be optimized to run much faster than a general routine.

Another application would be to use this classification scheme as part of a filter program that processes input data, such as from a tablet. Results of the filter could eliminate complex polygons so that following routines may assume convex polygons.

◊ Issues in Solving the Problem ◊

The problem whose solution this article describes started out as a posting on the USENET bulletin board 'comp.graphics' which asked for a program that could decide whether a polygon is convex. Answering this question turned into a contest, managed by Kenneth Sloan, which aimed at the construction of a correct and efficient program. The most important issues discussed were:

- Correctness, especially in degenerate cases. Many people quickly succeeded in writing a program which could handle *almost* all cases. The challenge was a program which works in all, even degenerate, cases. Some degenerate examples are depicted in Figure 1.

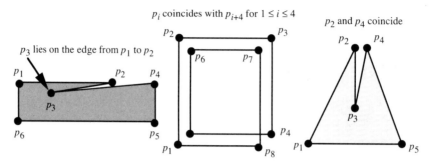

Figure 1. Some degenerate cases.

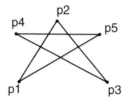

Figure 2. Non-convex polygon with a right turn at each vertex.

Although the first two examples might be considered convex (their interior is indeed convex), a majority of the participants in the discussion agreed that these cases should be considered not convex. Further complications are "all points collinear" and "repeated points."

- What is a convex polygon? This question is very much related to correctness and a suitable definition of a convex polygon was a hotly debated topic. When one thinks about the problem for the first time, a common mistake is to require a right turn at each vertex and nothing else. This leads to the counterexample in Figure 2.

- Efficiency. The program should run in time proportional to the number of vertices. Furthermore, only constant space for the program was allowed. This required a solution to read the polygon vertices from an input stream without saving them.

- Imprecise arithmetic. The meaning of "three points are collinear" becomes unclear when the coordinates of the points are only approximately correct or when floating-point arithmetic is used to test for collinearity or right turns. This article assumes exact arithmetic in order to avoid complications.

◇ What Is a Convex Polygon? ◇

Answering this question is an essential step toward the construction of a robust program. There are at least four approaches:

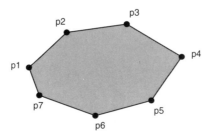

Figure 3.   An undisputed convex polygon.

- The cavalier attitude: I know what a convex polygon is when I see one. For example the polygon in Figure 3 is clearly convex.
- The "what works for me" approach: A polygon P is convex if my triangulation routine (renderer, etc.) which expects convex polygons as input can handle P.
- The "algorithm as definition" approach: A polygon is convex if my convexity testing program declares it as such.
- A more abstract, mathematical approach starting with the definition of a convex set: A set S of points is convex $\Leftrightarrow$

$$(p \in S) \wedge (q \in S) \Rightarrow \forall \lambda : 0 \leq \lambda \leq 1 : \lambda \cdot p + (1 - \lambda) \cdot q \in S$$

This roughly means that a set of points S is convex iff for any line drawn between two points in the set S, then all points on the line segment are also in the set.

In the following we propose a different, formal approach, which has the following advantages:

- It captures the intuition about a convex polygon.
- It gives a reasonable answer in degenerate cases.
- It distinguishes between clockwise- and counterclockwise orientations.
- It leads to a correct and efficient algorithm.

Classification: Given a sequence $P = p_1, p_2, \ldots, p_n$ of points in the plane such that

1. n is an integer and $(n > 0)$.
2. Consecutive vertices are different. $p_i \neq p_{i+1}$ for $1 \leq i \leq n$ (we assume $p_{n+1} = p_1$).
3. We restrict consideration to sequences where p_1 is lexicographically the smallest, i.e., $p_1 < p_i$ for $2 \leq i \leq n$ where $p < q \Leftrightarrow (p_x < q_x) \vee ((p_x = q_x) \wedge (p_y < q_y))$.
4. All convex polygons are monotone polygons, that is the x-coordinate of the points increases monotonically and then decreases monotonically. p_j is the "rightmost vertex."
   $\exists j : 1 < j \leq n : p_i < p_{i+1}$ for $1 \leq i < j$ and $p_{i+1} < p_i$ for $j \leq i \leq n$

Then if $p_i = [X_i, Y_i]$, and

$$d(i) = (X_{i-1} - X_i) \cdot (Y_i - Y_{i+1}) - (Y_{i-1} - Y_i) \cdot (X_i - X_{i+1})$$

P denotes a left- (counterclockwise) convex polygon $\Leftrightarrow$

$$(\forall i : 1 \leq i \leq n : d(i) \leq 0) \wedge (\exists i : 1 \leq i \leq n : d(i) < 0)$$

P denotes a right- (clockwise) convex polygon $\Leftrightarrow$

$$(\forall i : 1 \leq i \leq n : d(i) \geq 0) \wedge (\exists i : 1 \leq i \leq n : d(i) > 0)$$

P denotes a degenerate-convex polygon $\Leftrightarrow$

$$\forall i : 1 \leq i \leq n : d(i) = 0$$

P denotes a non-convex polygon $\Leftrightarrow$

$$(\exists i : 1 \leq i \leq n : d(i) < 0) \wedge (\exists i : 1 \leq i \leq n : d(i) > 0)$$

This classification of vertex-sequences agrees with our intuition for convex polygons (see Figure 3). For clockwise convex polygons there is a right turn at each vertex, and for counterclockwise convex polygons there is a left turn at each vertex. If the points satisfy condition 4 but lie on a line, the polygon is classified as degenerate-convex.

For purposes of simplifying the classification, conditions 2, 3, and 4 constrain the possible polygons. However, the classification can be extended to sequences not satisfying conditions 2, 3, or 4. Any sequence can easily meet conditions 2 and 3 if we remove consecutive duplicate points and perform a cyclic shift, moving the lexicographically smallest point to the beginning of the sequence. If condition 4 cannot be met, the sequence denotes a non-convex polygon.

◇ Implementation in C ◇

The following C program shows how the classification scheme can be turned into a correct and efficient implementation. The program accepts lines which contain two numbers, denoting the x- and y-coordinates of a point (see the function `GetPoint`). Duplicate points are removed on the fly (see the function `GetDifferentPoint`).

Since we do not want to store more than a constant number of points, we cannot perform a cyclic shift of the input vertices in order to assure condition 3. Instead, the program counts how often the lexicographic order of the input vertices changes. If this number exceeds two, the input polygon is definitely not convex.

In addition to the four cases distinguished in the classification scheme, the program introduces a fifth case (`NotConvexDegenerate`) for polygons whose vertices all lie on a line but do not satisfy condition 4.

◇   **Program to Classify a Polygon's Shape**   ◇

```c
#include <stdio.h>

typedef enum { NotConvex, NotConvexDegenerate,
               ConvexDegenerate, ConvexCCW, ConvexCW } PolygonClass;

typedef struct { double x, y; } Point2d;

int WhichSide(p, q, r)          /* Given a directed line pq, determine */
Point2d       p, q, r;          /* whether qr turns CW or CCW.         */
{
    double result;
    result = (p.x - q.x) * (q.y - r.y) - (p.y - q.y) * (q.x - r.x);
    if (result < 0) return -1;  /* q lies to the left  (qr turns CW).  */
    if (result > 0) return  1;  /* q lies to the right (qr turns CCW). */
    return 0;                   /* q lies on the line from p to r.     */
}

int Compare(p, q)               /* Lexicographic comparison of p and q */
Point2d     p, q;
{
    if (p.x < q.x) return -1;   /* p is less than q.                   */
    if (p.x > q.x) return  1;   /* p is greater than q.                */
    if (p.y < q.y) return -1;   /* p is less than q.                   */
    if (p.y > q.y) return  1;   /* p is greater than q.                */
    return 0;                   /* p is equal to q.                    */
}

int GetPoint(f, p)              /* Read p's x- and y-coordinates from f */
FILE     *f;                    /* and return true, iff successful.     */
Point2d *p;
{
    return !feof(f) && (2 == fscanf(f, "%lf%lf", &(p->x), &(p->y)));
}

int GetDifferentPoint(f, previous, next)
FILE     *f;                    /* Read next point into 'next' until it */
Point2d previous, *next;        /* is different from 'previous' and     */
{                               /* return true iff successful.          */
    int eof;
    while((eof = GetPoint(f, next)) && (Compare(previous, *next) == 0));
    return eof;
}

/* CheckTriple tests three consecutive points for change of direction
 * and for orientation.
 */
#define CheckTriple                                                     \
        if ( (thisDir = Compare(second, third)) == -curDir )            \
            ++dirChanges;                                               \
        curDir = thisDir;                                               \
        if ( thisSign = WhichSide(first, second, third) ) {             \
```

```
                    if ( angleSign == -thisSign )                              \
                        return NotConvex;                                      \
                    angleSign = thisSign;                                      \
                }                                                              \
            first = second; second = third;

/* Classify the polygon vertices on file 'f' according to: 'NotConvex'  */
/* 'NotConvexDegenerate', 'ConvexDegenerate', 'ConvexCCW', 'ConvexCW'.  */
PolygonClass ClassifyPolygon(f)
FILE                        *f;
{
    int          curDir, thisDir, thisSign, angleSign = 0, dirChanges = 0;
    PolygonClass result;
    Point2d      first, second, third, saveFirst, saveSecond;

    if ( !GetPoint(f, &first) || !GetDifferentPoint(f, first, &second) )
        return ConvexDegenerate;
    saveFirst = first;  saveSecond = second;
    curDir = Compare(first, second);
    while( GetDifferentPoint(f, second, &third) ) {
        CheckTriple;
    }
    /* Must check that end of list continues back to start properly. */
    if ( Compare(second, saveFirst) ) {
        third = saveFirst; CheckTriple;
    }
    third = saveSecond;  CheckTriple;

    if ( dirChanges > 2 ) return angleSign ? NotConvex : NotConvexDegenerate;
    if ( angleSign  > 0 ) return ConvexCCW;
    if ( angleSign  < 0 ) return ConvexCW;
    return ConvexDegenerate;
}

int main()
{
    switch ( ClassifyPolygon(stdin) ) {
        case NotConvex:           fprintf( stderr,"Not Convex\n");
                                  exit(-1); break;
        case NotConvexDegenerate: fprintf( stderr,"Not Convex Degenerate\n");
                                  exit(-1); break;
        case ConvexDegenerate:    fprintf( stderr,"Convex Degenerate\n");
                                  exit( 0); break;
        case ConvexCCW:           fprintf( stderr,"Convex Counter-Clockwise\n");
                                  exit( 0); break;
        case ConvexCW:            fprintf( stderr,"Convex Clockwise\n");
                                  exit( 0); break;
    }
}
```

◇   **Optimizations**   ◇

The previous code was chosen for its conciseness and readability. Other versions of the code were written which accept a vertex count and pointer to an array of vertices. Given this interface, it is possible to obtain good performance measurements by timing a large number of calls to the polygon classification routine.

Variations of the code presented have resulted in a two to four times performance increase, depending on the polygon shape. Optimizations for a particular machine or programming language will undoubtedly produce different results. Some considerations are:

- Convert each of the routines to macro definitions.
- Instead of keeping track of the first, second, and third points, keep track of the previous delta (second − first), and a current delta (third − second). This will speed up parts of the algorithm: The macro `Compare` needs only compare two numbers with zero, instead of four numbers with each other; the routine for getting a different point calculates the delta as it determines if the new point is different; the cross product calculation uses the deltas directly instead of subtracting vertices each time; the comparison for the `WhichSide` routine may be moved up to the `CheckTriple` routine to save a comparison at the expense of a little more code; and preparing to examine the next point requires three moves instead of four.
- Checking for less than three vertices is possible, but generally slows down the other cases.
- Every time the variable `dirChanges` is incremented, it would be possible to check if the number is now greater than two. This will slow down the convex cases, but makes it possible to exit early for polygons which violate classification condition 4. If it is important to distinguish between `NotConvex` and `NotConvexDegenerate`, this optimization may not be used.

◇   **Reasonably Optimized Routine to Classify a Polygon's Shape**   ◇

```
/*

. . . code omitted which reads polygon, stores in an array, and calls
        classifyPolygon2()
*/

typedef double  Number;          /* float or double */

#define ConvexCompare(delta)                                           \
    ( (delta[0] > 0) ? -1 :      /* x coord diff, second pt > first pt */\
```

```
                (delta[0] < 0) ?  1 :      /* x coord diff, second pt < first pt */\
                (delta[1] > 0) ? -1 :      /* x coord same, second pt > first pt */\
                (delta[1] < 0) ?  1 :      /* x coord same, second pt > first pt */\
                0 )                        /* second pt equals first point */

#define ConvexGetPointDelta(delta, pprev, pcur )                         \
    /* Given a previous point 'pprev', read a new point into 'pcur' */   \
    /* and return delta in 'delta'.                              */      \
    pcur = pVert[iread++];                                               \
    delta[0] = pcur[0] - pprev[0];                                       \
    delta[1] = pcur[1] - pprev[1];                                       \

#define ConvexCross(p, q) p[0] * q[1] - p[1] * q[0];

#define ConvexCheckTriple                                                \
    if ( (thisDir = ConvexCompare(dcur)) == -curDir ) {                  \
            ++dirChanges;                                                \
            /* The following line will optimize for polygons that are */ \
            /* not convex because of classification condition 4,      */ \
            /* otherwise, this will only slow down the classification. */ \
            /* if ( dirChanges > 2 ) return NotConvex;                */ \
    }                                                                    \
    curDir = thisDir;                                                    \
    cross = ConvexCross(dprev, dcur);                                    \
    if ( cross > 0 ) { if ( angleSign == -1 ) return NotConvex;          \
                    angleSign = 1;                                       \
                }                                                        \
    else if (cross < 0) { if (angleSign == 1) return NotConvex;          \
                        angleSign = -1;                                  \
                    }                                                    \
    pSecond = pThird;                /* Remember ptr to current point. */ \
    dprev[0] = dcur[0];              /* Remember current delta.        */ \
    dprev[1] = dcur[1];                                                  \

classifyPolygon2( nvert, pVert )
int     nvert;
Number  pVert[][2];
/* Determine polygon type. return one of:
 *      NotConvex, NotConvexDegenerate,
 *      ConvexCCW, ConvexCW, ConvexDegenerate
 */
{
    int     curDir, thisDir, dirChanges = 0,
            angleSign = 0, iread, endOfData;
    Number  *pSecond, *pThird, *pSaveSecond, dprev[2], dcur[2], cross;

    /* if ( nvert <= 0 ) return error;         if you care */

    /* Get different point, return if less than 3 diff points. */
    if ( nvert < 3 ) return ConvexDegenerate;
    iread = 1;
    while ( 1 ) {
        ConvexGetPointDelta( dprev, pVert[0], pSecond );
```

```
        if ( dprev[0] || dprev[1] ) break;
        /* Check if out of points. Check here to avoid slowing down cases
         * without repeated points.
         */
        if ( iread >= nvert ) return ConvexDegenerate;
    }

    pSaveSecond = pSecond;

    curDir = ConvexCompare(dprev);          /* Find initial direction */

    while ( iread < nvert ) {
        /* Get different point, break if no more points */
        ConvexGetPointDelta(dcur, pSecond, pThird );
        if ( dcur[0] == 0.0  &&  dcur[1] == 0.0 ) continue;

        ConvexCheckTriple;                  /* Check current three points */
    }

    /* Must check for direction changes from last vertex back to first */
    pThird = pVert[0];                      /* Prepare for 'ConvexCheckTriple' */
    dcur[0] = pThird[0] - pSecond[0];
    dcur[1] = pThird[1] - pSecond[1];
    if ( ConvexCompare(dcur) ) {
        ConvexCheckTriple;
    }

    /* and check for direction changes back to second vertex */
    dcur[0] = pSaveSecond[0] - pSecond[0];
    dcur[1] = pSaveSecond[1] - pSecond[1];
    ConvexCheckTriple;                      /* Don't care about 'pThird' now */

    /* Decide on polygon type given accumulated status */
    if ( dirChanges > 2 )
        return angleSign ? NotConvex : NotConvexDegenerate;

    if ( angleSign > 0 ) return ConvexCCW;
    if ( angleSign < 0 ) return ConvexCW;
    return ConvexDegenerate;
}
```

◇ **Acknowledgments** ◇

We are grateful to the participants of the electronic mail discussion: Gavin Bell, Wayne Boucher, Laurence James Edwards, Eric A. Haines, Paul Heckbert, Steve Hollasch, Torben Ægidius Mogensen, Joseph O'Rourke, Kenneth Sloan, Tom Wright, and Benjamin Zhu.

◇ I.3

An Incremental Angle Point in Polygon Test

Kevin Weiler

Autodesk Inc.
2320 Marinship Way
Sausalito, CA 94965
kjw@autodesk.com

This algorithm can determine whether a given test point is inside of, or outside of, a given polygon boundary composed of straight line segments. The algorithm is not sensitive to whether the polygon is concave or convex or whether the polygon's vertices are presented in a clockwise or counterclockwise order. Extensions allow the algorithm to handle polygons with holes and non-simple polygons. Only four bits of precision are required for all of the incremental angle calculations.

◇   Introduction   ◇

There are two commonly used algorithms for determining whether a given test point is inside or outside of a polygon.

The first, the semi-infinite line technique, extends a semi-infinite line from the test point outward, and counts the number of intersections of the edges of the polygon boundary with the semi-infinite line. An odd number of intersections indicates the point is inside the polygon, while an even number (including zero) indicates the point is outside the polygon.

The second, the incremental angle technique, uses the angle of the vertices of the polygon relative to the point being tested, where there is a total angle of 360 degrees all the way around the point. For each vertex of the polygon, the difference angle (the incremental angle) between the angle of that vertex of the polygon and the angle of the next vertex of the polygon, as viewed from the test point, is added to a running sum. If the final sum of the incremental angles is plus or minus 360 degrees, the polygon surrounds the test point and the point is inside of the polygon. If the sum is 0 degrees, the point is outside of the polygon.

What is less commonly known about the incremental angle technique is that only four bits of precision are required for all of the incremental angle calculations, greatly simplifying the necessary calculations. The angle value itself requires only two bits of precision, lending itself to a quadrant technique where the quadrants are numbered from 0 to 3. The incremental or delta angle requires an additional sign bit to indicate clockwise or counterclockwise direction, for a total of three bits to represent the incremental angle itself. The accumulated angle requires four bits total: three to represent the magnitude, ranging from 0 to 4, plus a sign bit.

The following algorithm describes a four-bit precision incremental angle point in polygon test. Extensions for polygons with holes and for degenerate polygons are also described.

The algorithm described was inspired by the incremental angle surrounder test sometimes used for the Warnock hidden surface removal algorithm. That surrounder algorithm determines if a polygon surrounds rectangular screen areas by partitioning the space around the rectangular window using an eight neighbor partitioning technique (Newman and Sproull 1973, pp. 520–521, 526–527), (Rogers 1985, pp. 249–251). If one shrinks the central rectangular window of that partitioning scheme down to a point (shrinking the rectangular partitions directly above and below and to the left and right of the window down to lines), the partitioning becomes a quadrant style division of the space around the point. This reduces the precision of angle calculations needed and simplifies the algorithm to the point in polygon test presented here.

Further discussion and comparisons of point in polygon techniques can be found in Eric Haines' article in this volume (Haines 1994).

◇ **Preliminaries** ◇

For sake of completeness, before describing the algorithm, simple type definitions used in the following code as well as a typical definition for a polygon representation are given below.

```
        /* type for quadrant id's, incremental angles, accumulated angle values */
typedef short quadrant_type;

        /* type for result value from point in polygon test */
typedef enum pt_poly_relation {INSIDE, OUTSIDE} pt_poly_relation;

        /* polygon vertex definition */
typedef struct vertex_struct {
  double x,y;                     /* coordinate values */
  struct vertex_struct *next;   /* circular singly linked list from poly */
  } vertex, *vertex_ptr;

        /* polygon definition */
typedef struct polygon_struct {
  vertex_ptr last;                /* pointer to end of circular vertex list */
  } polygon, *polygon_ptr;

        /* polygon vertex access */
#define polygon_get_vertex(poly, vertex) \
    ((vertex == NULL) ? poly->last->next : vertex->next)
```

The quadrant and return result types are self-explanatory.

Polygon vertices are regarded as structures that allow direct access of the X and Y coordinate values in C via `vertex->x` and `vertex->y` structure member dereferencing.

Polygons are treated here as objects that have a single access routine: `polygon_get_vertex(poly, vertex)`, where `poly` specifies a pointer to the polygon. If `vertex` is NULL, the function will return a pointer to an arbitrary vertex of the polygon. Otherwise, if `vertex` is a pointer to a given vertex of the polygon, the function will return a pointer to the next vertex in the ordered circular list of vertices of the polygon. Given the list representation of the polygons as described here, polygon vertices are regarded as unique even if their coordinate values are not.

◇ The Algorithm ◇

The basic idea of the algorithm, as previously stated, is to accumulate the sum of the incremental angles between the vertices of the polygon as viewed from the test point, and then see if the angles add up to the logical equivalent of a full 360 degrees, meaning the point is surrounded by the polygon.

The algorithm is presented here in four small pieces. First, a macro to determine the quadrant angle of a polygon vertex is presented. Second, a macro to determine x-intercepts of polygon edges is presented. Third, a macro to adjust the angle delta is presented. Fourth, the main point in polygon test routine is presented.

First, the angle can be calculated using only two bits of precision with a simple quadrant technique to determine the two-bit value of the angle, where x and y are the coordinates of the test point (Figure 1).

```
    /* determine the quadrant of a polygon point relative to the test point */
  #define quadrant(vertex, x, y) \
    ( (vertex->x > x) ? ((vertex->y > y) ? 0 : 3) : ( (vertex->y > y) ? 1 : 2) )
```

This classifies the space around the test point into four quadrants. Since the test used to determine the quadrant uses greater-than operations, the quadrant boundaries, shown as solid lines in the diagram, lie just above and to the right of the axes centered on the coordinates of the test point, as shown with dotted lines in the figure.

In some situations it is important to determine whether the polygon edge passes to the right of or to the left of the test point. This can be determined from the x-intercept value of the polygon edge where it intersects the infinite horizontal line passing through the y value of the test point. The x-intercept can be calculated with:

```
    /* determine x-intercept of a polygon edge
       with a horizontal line at the y value of the test point */
  #define x_intercept(pt1, pt2, yy) \
    (pt2->x - ( (pt2->y - yy) * ((pt1->x - pt2->x) / (pt1->y - pt2->y)) ) )
```

It should be noted that this x-intercept code is not a general implementation as it ignores division by zero, which occurs when the y coordinate difference is zero. The

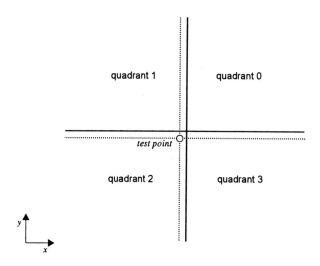

Figure 1. Quadrants.

implementation is adequate for our purposes here, however, as it will never be called under this condition.

The incremental angle itself is calculated simply by subtracting the quadrant value (angle) of one polygon vertex from the quadrant value of the next vertex. There are a few problems with this approach that must be fixed. First, because of the quadrant numbering scheme, incremental angles that cross between quadrant 0 and quadrant 3 have values of 3 instead of the proper value of 1 and the signs are also reversed. This can be fixed with a simple substitution of values. Second, an incremental angle that passes from a given quadrant to the diagonal quadrant will have its sign reversed if it passes to the right of the test point. This must be tested for by checking the x-intercept of any delta which has a value of plus or minus 2. If it passes to the right of the test point, its sign is reversed and thus must be adjusted. These adjustments are illustrated in Figure 2 and the code below. Only one of the two sets of diagonals is shown in the diagram.

```
#define adjust_delta(delta, vertex, next_vertex, xx, yy)          \
  switch (delta) {                                                 \
          /* make quadrant deltas wrap around */                  \
    case  3:    delta = -1; break;                                 \
    case -3:    delta =  1; break;                                 \
          /* check if went around point cw or ccw */              \
    case  2: case -2: if (x_intercept(vertex, next_vertex, yy) > xx)   \
                  delta = - (delta);                               \
              break;                                               \
  }
```

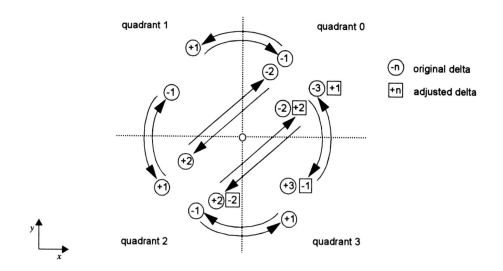

Figure 2. Adjusting delta.

A side effect of the quadrant numbering scheme is that, when adjusted, the sign of the delta value indicates whether the angle moves in a clockwise or counterclockwise direction, depending on the orientation of the coordinate axis being used. The sign of the final accumulated angle therefore also indicates the orientation of the polygon.

With these support macros and definitions out of the way, the point in polygon algorithm itself becomes simple.

In its initialization section, the algorithm prepares for traversal of the polygon points by finding the first vertex and calculating its angle from the test point, and zeroing the running sum angle. Then the algorithm loops on all of the other points (vertices) in the polygon. During the loop, the next vertex is found, its angle calculated, and the delta angle is calculated. The delta is then adjusted as necessary and added to the running sum. The loop then prepares for the next iteration. When all the points of the polygon have been seen and the loop terminated, the value of the running sum is checked. If it is equal to plus or minus 4, the angle covers a full 360 degrees and the point is inside of the polygon boundary. Otherwise the angle value is 0 and the test point is outside of the boundary of the polygon.

If the test point is actually on the polygon boundary itself, the result returned by the algorithm could be inside or outside depending on whether the actual interior of the polygon was to the right or left of the test point.

It is interesting to compare this incremental angle approach with the semi-infinite line approach. When examined closely, operation by operation, the incremental angle algorithm presented here is very similar to the semi-infinite line technique. In general, the incremental angle method takes a constant amount of time per vertex regardless of axis crossings of the polygon edges (the exception is when the vertices of the polygon edge are in diagonal quadrants, which takes the same amount of time for both approaches). The semi-infinite line technique performs more operations when its preferred axis is crossed, and fewer operations when the other axis is crossed. To put it a different way, the semi-infinite line technique has both deeper and shallower code branch alternatives than the incremental angle technique presented depending on whether its preferred axis is crossed or not. Because of this variable behavior, worst case scenarios can be constructed to make either algorithm perform better than the other.

Performance comparisons done by Haines (Haines 1994) give statistics that show the incremental angle technique presented here to be slower than the semi-infinite line technique. Some of this performance difference will be reduced if the C compiler performs case statement optimizations which utilize indexed jump tables.

```
        /* determine if a test point is inside of or outside of a polygon */
        /* polygon is "poly", test point is at "x","y" */
pt_poly_relation
point_in_poly(polygon_ptr poly, double x, double y)
{
  vertex_ptr   vertex, first_vertex, next_vertex;
  quadrant_type quad, next_quad, delta, angle;

            /* initialize */
  vertex = NULL;      /* because polygon_get_vertex is a macro */
  vertex = first_vertex = polygon_get_vertex(poly,vertex);
  quad = quadrant(vertex, x, y);
  angle = 0;
              /* loop on all vertices of polygon */
  do {
    next_vertex = polygon_get_vertex(poly,vertex);
              /* calculate quadrant and delta from last quadrant */
    next_quad = quadrant(next_vertex, x, y);
    delta = next_quad - quad;
    adjust_delta(delta,vertex,next_vertex,x,y);
              /* add delta to total angle sum */
    angle = angle + delta;
              /* increment for next step */
    quad = next_quad;
    vertex = next_vertex;
    } while (vertex != first_vertex);

            /* complete 360 degrees (angle of + 4 or -4 ) means inside */
  if ((angle == +4) || (angle == -4)) return INSIDE; else return OUTSIDE;
}
```

◇ Extension for Polygons with Holes ◇

In order to determine whether a test point is inside of or outside of a polygon which has holes, the point in polygon test needs to be applied separately to each of the polygon's boundaries. It is preferable to start with the outermost boundary of the polygon, since the polygon's area is in most applications likely to be smaller than the total area in which the test point might lie. If the test point is outside of this polygon boundary, then it is outside of the entire polygon. If it is inside, then each hole boundary needs to be checked. If the test point is inside any of the hole boundaries, then the test point is outside of the entire polygon and checking can stop immediately. If the test point is outside of every hole boundary (as well as being inside the outermost boundary), then the point is inside of the polygon. Note that because the point in polygon test presented is insensitive to whether the polygon boundaries are clockwise or counterclockwise, both the outermost polygon boundary and the hole boundaries may be of any orientation. For polygons with holes, however, the algorithm must be told which boundary is the outermost boundary (some polygon representations encode this information in the orientation of the boundaries).

◇ Extensions for Non-Simple Polygons ◇

Non-simple polygons (polygons which self-intersect, with boundaries which touch, cross, or overlap themselves) are handled by the algorithm with minor modifications to the final test of the accumulated angle. The final angle value test:

```
if ((angle == +4) || (angle == -4)) return INSIDE; else return OUTSIDE;
```

must be modified to handle non-simple polygons properly in all cases. Two different rules are commonly used to determine the interior of non-simple polygons (there are also others, but they are less common because their implementations are more difficult). Both rules allow the non-simple polygon to completely surround the point an arbitrary number of times.

With the first rule, the odd winding number rule, if the number of surroundings is odd, then the point is inside. An even number indicates the point is outside the polygon. The code for this is:

```
if (angle & 4) return INSIDE; else return OUTSIDE; /* odd number windings rule */
```

where an odd number of surroundings means that the 4-bit in the angle value will be set since a valid angle value, unless it is 0, will be a multiple of 4.

The second rule, the non-zero winding number rule, accepts any number of surroundings to mean the point is in the interior of the polygon. With this rule, the final angle value test becomes:

```
if (angle != 0) return INSIDE; else return OUTSIDE; /* non-zero winding rule */
```

Of course, the accumulated angle value can no longer be contained within a four-bit number under these conditions, but this characteristic is probably little more than a curiosity anyway, except for its original effect of reducing angle calculations to simple quadrant testing.

◇   **Bibliography**   ◇

(Haines 1994) Eric Haines. Point in Polygon Strategies. In Paul Heckbert, editor, *Graphics Gems IV*, 24–46. Academic Press, Boston, 1994.

(Newman and Sproull 1973) William Newman and Robert Sproull. *Principles of Interactive Computer Graphics*, 1st edition. McGraw-Hill, New York, 1973.

(Rogers 1985) David Rogers. *Procedural Elements for Computer Graphics*. McGraw-Hill, New York, 1985.

 **I.4**

Point in Polygon Strategies

Eric Haines

3D/Eye Inc.
1050 Craft Road
Ithaca, NY 14850
erich@eye.com

Testing whether a point is inside a polygon is a basic operation in computer graphics. This Gem presents a variety of efficient algorithms. No single algorithm is the best in all categories, so the capabilities of the better algorithms are compared and contrasted. The variables examined are the different types of polygons, the amount of memory used, and the preprocessing costs. Code is included in this article for several of the best algorithms; the Gems IV distribution includes code for all the algorithms discussed.

◇   **Introduction**   ◇

The motivation behind this Gem is to provide practical algorithms that are simple to implement and are fast for typical polygons. In applied computer graphics we usually want to check a point against a large number of triangles and quadrilaterals and occasionally test complex polygons. When dealing with floating-point operations on these polygons we do not care if a test point exactly on an edge is classified as being inside or outside, since these cases are normally extremely rare.

In contrast, the field of computational geometry has a strong focus on the order of complexity of an algorithm for all polygons, including pathological cases that are rarely encountered in real applications. The order of complexity for an algorithm in computational geometry may be low, but there is usually a large constant of proportionality or the algorithm itself is difficult to implement. Either of these conditions makes the algorithm unfit for use. Nonetheless, some insights from computational geometry can be applied to the testing of various sorts of polygons and can also shed light on connections among seemingly different algorithms.

Readers that are only interested in the results should skip to the "Conclusions" section.

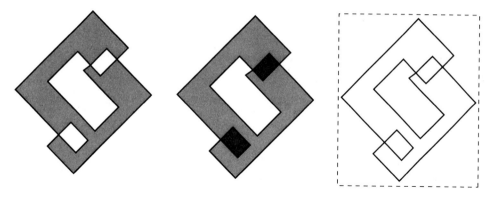

Figure 1. Jordan curve.   **Figure 2.** Winding number.   **Figure 3.** Bounding box.

◇ **Definitions** ◇

In this Gem a polygon is defined by an ordered set of vertices which form edges making a closed loop. The first and last vertices are connected by an edge, i.e., they are not the same. More complex objects, such as polygons with holes for font lettering, can be built from these polygons by applying the point in polygon test to each loop and concatenating the results.

There are two main types of polygons we will consider in this Gem: general and convex. If a number of points are to be tested against a polygon, it may be worthwhile determining whether the polygon is convex at the start so you are able to use a faster test. General polygons have no restrictions on the placement of vertices. Convex polygon determination is discussed in another Gem in this volume (Schorn and Fisher 1994). If you do not read this other Gem, at least note that a polygon with no concave angles is not necessarily convex; a good counterexample is a star formed by five vertices.

One definition of whether a point is inside a region is the *Jordan Curve Theorem*, also known as the parity or even-odd test. Essentially, it says that a point is inside a polygon if, for any ray from this point, there is an odd number of crossings of the ray with the polygon's edges. This definition means that some areas enclosed by a polygon are not considered inside (Figure 1).

If the entire area enclosed by the polygon is to be considered inside, then the *winding number* is used for testing. This value is the number of times the polygon goes around the point. In Figure 2 the darkly shaded areas have a winding number of two. Think of the polygon as a loop of string pulled tight around a pencil point; the number of loops around the point is the winding number. If a point is outside, the polygon does not wind around it and so the winding number is zero. Winding numbers also have a sign, which corresponds to the direction the edges wrap around the point. The winding number test can be converted to the parity test; an odd winding number is equivalent to the parity test's inside condition.

In ray tracing and other applications the original polygon is three-dimensional. To simplify computation it is worthwhile to project the polygon and test point into two dimensions. One way to do this is simply to ignore one coordinate. The best coordinate to drop is the one that yields the largest area for the 2D polygon formed. This is easily done by taking the absolute value of each coordinate of the polygon plane's normal and finding the largest; the corresponding coordinates are ignored (Glassner 1989). Precomputing some or all of this information once for a polygon uses more memory but increases the speed of the intersection test itself.

Point in polygon algorithms often benefit from having a bounding box around polygons with many edges. The point is first tested against this box before the full polygon test is performed; if the box is missed, so is the polygon (Figure 3). Most statistics generated in this Gem assume this bounding box test was already passed successfully.

In ray tracing, (Worley and Haines 1993) points out that the polygon's 3D bounding box can be treated like a 2D bounding box by throwing away one coordinate, as done above for polygons. By analysis of the operations involved, it can be shown to be more profitable in general to first intersect the polygon's plane and then test whether the point is inside the 2D bounding box, rather than first testing the 3D bounding box and then the plane. Other bounding box variants can be found in (Woo 1992).

◇ General Algorithms ◇

This section discusses the fastest algorithms for testing points against general polygons. Three classes of algorithms are compared: those which use the vertex list as their only data structure, those which do preprocessing and create an alternate form of the polygon, and those which create additional efficiency structures. The advantages of a vertex list algorithm is that no additional information or preprocessing is needed. However, the other two types of algorithms offer faster testing times in many cases.

Crossings Test

The fastest algorithm without any preprocessing is the crossings test. The earliest presentation of this algorithm is (Shimrat 1962), though it has a bug in it, corrected by (Hacker 1962). A ray is shot from the test point along an axis (+X is commonly used), and the number of crossings is computed for the even-odd test (Figure 4). One way to think about this algorithm is to consider the test point to be at the origin and to check the edges against this point. If the Y coordinates of a polygon edge differ in sign, then the edge can cross the test ray. In this case, if both X coordinates are positive, the edge

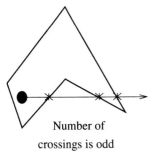

Number of
crossings is odd

Figure 4. Crossings test.

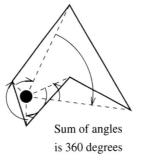

Sum of angles
is 360 degrees

Figure 5. Angle
summation.

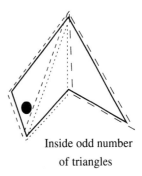

Inside odd number
of triangles

Figure 6. Triangle fan.

and ray must intersect and a crossing is recorded. Else, if the X signs differ, then the X intersection of the edge and the ray is computed and if positive a crossing is recorded.

What happens when the test ray intersects one or more vertices of the polygon? This problem can be ignored by considering the test ray to be a half-plane divider, with one of the half-planes including the ray's points (Preparata and Shamos 1985, Glassner 1989). In other words, whenever the ray would intersect a vertex, the vertex is always classified as being infinitesimally above the ray. In this way, no vertices are considered intersected and the code is both simpler and speedier.

MacMartin pointed out that for polygons with a large number of edges there are generally runs of edges that have Y coordinates with the same sign (Haines 1992). For example, a polygon representing Brazil might have a thousand edges, but only a few of these will straddle a given latitude line and there are long runs of contiguous edges on one side of this line. So a faster strategy is to loop through just the Y coordinates as fast as possible; when they differ then retrieve and check the X coordinates.

Either the even-odd or winding number test can be used to classify the point. The even-odd test is done by simply counting the number of crossings. The winding number test is computed by keeping track of whether the crossed edge passes from the Y- to the Y+ half-plane (add 1) or vice versa (subtract 1). The final value is then the number of counterclockwise windings about the point.

The slowest algorithm for testing points is by far the pure angle summation method. It's simple to describe: sum the signed angles formed at the point by each edge's endpoints (Figure 5). The winding number can then be computed by finding the nearest multiple of 360 degrees. The problem with this pure scheme is that it involves a large number of costly math function calls.

However, the idea of angle summation can be used to formulate a fast algorithm for testing points; see Weiler's Gem in this volume (Weiler 1994). There is a strong connection between Weiler's algorithm and the crossings test. Weiler avoids expensive trigonometry computations by adding or subtracting one or more increments of 90 degrees as the loop vertices move from quadrant to quadrant (with the test point at the origin). The crossings test is similar in that it can be thought of as counting movements of 360 degrees when an edge crosses the test ray. The crossings test tends to be faster because it does not have to categorize and record all quadrant-to-quadrant movements but only those which cross the test ray. Weiler's formulation is significant for the way it adds to the understanding of underlying principles.

Triangle Fan Tests

In *Graphics Gems*, (Badouel 1990) presents a method of testing points against convex polygons. The polygon is treated as a fan of triangles emanating from one vertex and the point is tested against each triangle by computing its barycentric coordinates. As (Berlin 1985) points out, this test can also be used for non-convex polygons by keeping a count of the number of triangles that overlap the point; if odd, the point is inside the polygon (Figure 6). Unlike the convex test, where an intersection means that the test is done, all the triangles must be tested against the point for the non-convex test. Also, for the non-convex test there may be multiple barycentric coordinates for a given point, since triangles can overlap.

The barycentric test is faster than the crossings test for triangles but becomes quite slow for polygons with more edges. However, (Spackman 1993) notes that pre-normalizing the barycentric equations and storing a set of precomputed values gives better performance. This version of the algorithm is twice as fast as the crossings test for triangles and is in general faster for polygons with few edges. The barycentric coordinates (which are useful for interpolation and texture mapping) are also computed.

A faster triangle fan tester, proposed by (Green 1993), is to store a set of half-plane equations for each triangle and test each in turn. If the point is outside any of the three edges, it is outside the triangle. The half-plane test is an old idea, but storing the half-planes instead of deriving them on the fly from the vertices gives this scheme its speed at the cost of some additional storage space. For triangles this scheme is the fastest of all of the algorithms discussed so far. It is also very simple to code and so lends itself to assembly language translation. Theoretically the Spackman test should usually have a smaller average number of operations per test, but in practice the optimized code for the half-plane test is faster.

Both the half-plane and Spackman triangle testers can be sped up further by sorting the order of the edge tests. Worley and Haines (Spackman 1993) note that the half-plane triangle test is more efficient if the longer edges are tested first. Larger edges tend to cut off more exterior area of the polygon's bounding box and so can result in earlier exit from testing a given triangle. Sorting in this way makes the test up to 1.7 times faster, rising quickly with the number of edges in the polygon. However, polygons with a large number of edges tend to bog down the sorted edge triangle algorithm, with the crossings test being faster above around 10 edges.

A problem occurs in general triangle fan algorithms when the code assumes that a point that lies on a triangle edge is always inside that triangle. For example, a quadrilateral is treated as two triangles. If a point is exactly on the edge between the two triangles it will be classified as being inside both triangles and so will be classified as being outside the polygon (this problem does not happen with the convex test).

The code presented for these algorithms does not fully address this problem. In reality, a random point tested against a polygon has an infinitesimal chance of landing exactly on any edge. For rendering purposes this problem can be ignored, with the result being one misshaded pixel once in a great while. A more robust solution (which will slow down the test) is to note whether an edge is to include the points exactly on it or not. Also, an option which has not been explored is to test shared interior edges only once against the point and share the results between the adjacent triangles.

Grid Method

An even faster, and more memory intensive, method of testing for points inside a polygon is lookup grids. The idea is to impose a grid inside the bounding box containing the polygon. Each grid cell is categorized as being fully inside, fully outside, or indeterminate. The indeterminate cells also have a list of edges that overlap the cell, and also one corner (or more) is determined to be inside or outside.

To test a point against this structure is extremely quick in most cases. For a reasonable polygon many of the cells are either inside or outside, so testing consists of a simple look-up. If the cell contains edges, then a line segment is formed from the test point to the cell corner and is tested against all edges in the list (Antonio 1992). Since the state of the corner is known, the state of the test point can be found from the number of intersections (Figure 7). Salesin and Stolfi suggest an algorithm similar to this as part of their ray tracing acceleration technique (Salesin and Stolfi 1989).

Care must be taken when a polygon edge exactly (or even nearly exactly) crosses a grid corner, as this corner is then unclassifiable. Rather than coping with the topological and numerical precision problems involved, one simple solution is to just start generating the grid from scratch again, giving slightly different dimensions to the bounding box. Also, when testing the line segment against the edges in a list, exact intersections of an edge endpoint must be counted only once.

One additional enhancement partially solves this problem. Each grid cell has four sides. If no polygon edges cross a side, then that side will be fully inside or outside the polygon. A horizontal or vertical test line segment can then be generated from the test

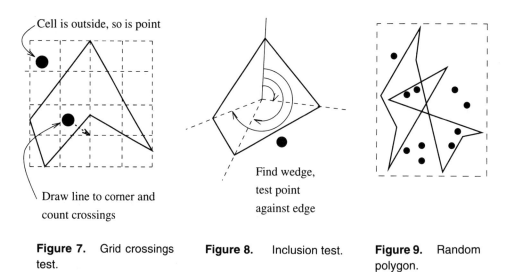

Figure 7. Grid crossings test.

Figure 8. Inclusion test.

Figure 9. Random polygon.

point to this cell side and the faster crossings test can be used against the edges in the cell. In addition, this crossings test deals with endpoint intersection more robustly.

Note: the grid test code is in the Gems IV code distribution, but has been left out of the book because of its length.

Pixel Based Testing

One interesting case that is related to gridding is that of pixel-limited picking. When a dataset is displayed on the screen and a large amount of picking is to be done on a still image, a specialized test is worthwhile. Hanrahan and Haeberli note that the image can be generated once into a separate buffer, filling in each polygon's area with an identifying index (Hanrahan and Haeberli 1990). When a pixel is picked on this fixed image, it is looked up in this buffer and the polygon selected is known immediately.

◇ Convex Polygons ◇

Convex polygons can be intersected faster due to their geometric properties. For example, the crossings test can quit as soon as two Y-sign difference edges are found, since this is the maximum that a convex polygon can have. Also, note that more polygons can use this faster crossings test by checking only the change in the Y direction (and not X and Y as for the full convexity test); see (Schorn and Fisher 1994). For example, a block letter "E" has at most two Y intersections for any test point's horizontal line (and so is called *monotone* in Y), so it can use the faster crossings test.

The triangle fan tests can exit as soon as any triangle is found to contain the point. These algorithms can be enhanced by both sorting the edges of each triangle by length and also sorting the testing order of triangles by their areas. Relatively larger triangles are more likely to enclose a point and so end testing earlier. Note that this faster test can be applied to any polygon that is decomposed into non-overlapping triangles; convex polygons always have this property when tessellated into a triangle fan.

The exterior algorithm prestores the half-plane for each polygon edge and tests the point against this set. If the point is outside any edge, then the point must be outside the entire convex polygon. This algorithm uses less additional storage than the triangle fan and is very simple to code. The order of edges tested affects the speed of this algorithm; testing edges in the order of which cuts off the most area of the bounding box earliest on is the best ordering. Finding this optimal ordering is non-trivial, but doing the edges in order is often the worst strategy, since each neighboring edge usually cuts off little more area than the previous. Randomizing the order of the edges makes this algorithm up to 10% faster overall for regular polygons.

The exterior algorithm looks for an early exit due to the point being outside the polygon, while the triangle fan convex test looks for one due to the point being inside. For example, for 100 edge polygons, if all points tested are inside the polygon the triangle fan is 1.7 times faster; if all test points are outside the exterior test is more than 16 times faster (but only 4 times faster if the edges are not randomized). So when the polygon/bounding box area ratio is low the exterior algorithm is usually best; in fact, performance is near constant time as this ratio decreases, since after only a few edges most points are categorized as outside the polygon.

A hybrid of the exterior algorithm and the triangle fan is to test triangles and exit early when the point is outside the polygon. A point is outside the polygon if it is outside any exterior triangle edge. This strategy combines the early exit features of both algorithms and so it is less dependent on bounding box fit. Our code uses sorting by triangle area instead of randomizing the exterior edge order, so it favors a higher polygon/bounding box area ratio.

A method with O(log n) performance is the inclusion algorithm (Preparata and Shamos 1985). The polygon is preprocessed by adding a central point to it and is then divided into wedges. The angles from an anchor edge to each wedge's edges are computed and saved, along with half-plane equations for the polygon edges. When a point is tested, the angle from the anchor edge is computed and a binary search is used to determine the wedge it is in, and then the corresponding polygon edge is tested against it (Figure 8). Note that this test can be used on any polygon that can be tessellated into a non-overlapping star of triangles. This algorithm is slower for polygons with few edges because the startup cost is high, but the binary search makes for a much faster test when there are many edges. However, if the bounding box is much larger than the polygon the exterior edge test is faster.

◇ **Statistics** ◇

The timings given in Tables 1–3 were produced on an HP 720 RISC workstation; timings had similar performance ratios on an IBM PC 386 with no FPU. The general non-convex algorithms were tested using two sorts of polygons: those generated with random points and regular (i.e., equal length sides and vertex angles) polygons with a random rotation applied. Random polygons tend to be somewhat unlikely (no one ever uses 1000-edge random polygons for anything except testing), while regular polygons are more orderly than a "typical" polygon; normal behavior tends to be somewhere in between. Test points were generated inside the bounding box for the polygon. Figure 9 shows a typical 10-sided random polygon and some test points. Convex algorithms were tested with only regular polygons, and so have a certain bias to them.

Test points were generated inside the box bounding the polygon; looser fitting boxes yield different results. Timings are in microseconds per polygon. They are given to two significant figures, since their accuracy is roughly ±10%. However, the best way to get useful timings is to run the code on the target machine; there is a testbed program provided in the Gems IV code distribution which can be used to try new algorithms and generate timings under various test conditions. Also, of course, hacking the code for a particular machine and compiler can make a significant difference.

◇ **Discussion** ◇

The crossings test is generally useful, but we can do better. Testing triangles using either sorted triangle fan algorithm is more than twice as fast, though for polygons with many edges the crossings test is still faster.

Given enough resolution (and enough memory!), gridding gives near constant time performance for most normal polygons, though it performs a bit slower when entirely random polygons are tested. Interestingly, even for polygons with just a few edges the gridding algorithm outperforms most of the other tests.

Testing times can be noticeably decreased by using an algorithm optimized for convex testing when possible. For example, the convex sorted half-plane test is 1.4 times faster for 10-sided polygons than its general case counterpart. For convex polygons with many edges the inclusion test is extremely efficient because of its $O(\log n)$ behavior.

Other algorithms remain to be discovered and tested; for example, a practical general polygon algorithm with better than $O(n)$ performance and low storage costs would fill a useful niche.

Table 1. General Algorithms, Random Polygons

Algorithm	Number of edges per polygon						
	3	4	10	20	50	100	1000
Crossings	2.8	3.1	5.7	10	25	48	470
Half Plane w/edge sort	1.1	1.7	5.7	12	32	65	650
Half Plane, no sort	1.2	2.0	6.3	14	36	72	740
Spackman w/edge sort	1.3	2.1	6.0	13	32	66	670
Spackman, no sort	1.4	2.2	6.4	14	35	70	720
Barycentric	2.4	4.0	13	29	76	150	1600
Weiler angle	3.7	4.3	8.7	16	39	77	760
Trigonometric angle	42	51	110	210	520	1030	10300
Grid (100x100)	1.8	1.9	1.9	1.9	2.2	2.5	9.2
Grid (20x20)	2.0	2.0	2.2	2.5	3.6	5.5	38

Table 2. General Algorithms, Regular Polygons

Algorithm	Number of edges per polygon						
	3	4	10	20	50	100	1000
Crossings	2.6	2.7	4.3	7.2	16	32	300
Half Plane w/edge sort	1.3	1.8	4.6	9.2	23	45	460
Half Plane, no sort	1.3	2.1	6.7	14	37	74	760
Spackman w/edge sort	1.5	2.1	5.4	10	26	51	510
Spackman, no sort	1.5	2.3	5.8	11	28	55	550
Barycentric	2.5	4.2	13	26	68	140	1400
Weiler angle	3.5	4.0	7.9	15	35	70	690
Trigonometric angle	39	51	120	230	560	1200	11100
Grid (100x100)	1.8	1.8	1.8	1.8	1.8	1.8	1.9
Grid (20x20)	2.0	2.0	2.0	2.0	2.0	2.1	2.8

Table 3. Convex Algorithms, Regular Polygons

Algorithm	Number of edges per polygon						
	3	4	10	20	50	100	1000
Inclusion	5.5	5.7	6.3	6.6	7.1	7.6	9.9
Hybrid Sorted Half Plane	1.3	1.6	3.3	6.1	14	28	280
Sorted Half Plane	1.2	1.6	3.4	6.2	15	29	280
Unsorted Half Plane	1.2	1.9	5.7	12	30	61	620
Random Exterior Edges	1.3	1.7	3.8	7.1	17	33	320
Ordered Exterior Edges	1.3	1.7	3.8	7.3	18	35	350
Convex Crossings	2.5	2.5	3.6	5.6	12	22	220

◇ **Conclusions** ◇

- If no preprocessing nor extra storage is available, use the **Crossings** test.
- If a little preprocessing and extra storage is available:

  - For general polygons

    * with few sides, use the **Half-Plane** or **Spackman** test.
    * with many sides, use the **Crossings** test.

  - For convex polygons

    * with few sides, use the **Hybrid Half-Plane** test.
    * with many sides, use the **Inclusion** test.
    * But if the bounding box/polygon area ratio is high, use the **Exterior Edges** test.

- If preprocessing and extra storage is available in abundance, use the **Grid Test** (except for perhaps triangles).

Of course, some of these conclusions may vary with machine architecture and compiler optimization.

◇ **C Code** ◇

ptinpoly.h

```
/* ptinpoly.h - point in polygon inside/outside algorithms header file.
 */

/* Define CONVEX to compile for testing only convex polygons (when possible,
 * this is faster). */
/* #define CONVEX */

/* Define HYBRID to compile triangle fan test for CONVEX with exterior edges
 * meaning an early exit (faster - recommended).
 */
/* #define HYBRID */
```

```
/* Define DISPLAY to display test triangle and test points on screen. */
/* #define DISPLAY */

/* Define RANDOM to randomize order of edges for exterior test (faster -
 * recommended). */
/* #define RANDOM */

/* Define SORT to sort triangle edges and areas for half-plane and Spackman
```

```
 * tests (faster - recommended). */
/* #define SORT */

/* Define WINDING if a non-zero winding number should be used as the criterion
 * for being inside the polygon.  Only used by the general crossings test and
 * Weiler test.  The winding number computed for each is the number of
 * counterclockwise loops the polygon makes around the point.
 */
/* #define WINDING */

/* =========================== System Related ============================ */

/* Define your own random number generator; change as needed. */
/* SRAN initializes random number generator, if needed. */
#define SRAN()          srand48(1)
/* RAN01 returns a double from [0..1) */
#define RAN01()         drand48()
double  drand48() ;

/* ========== Half-Plane stuff =========================================== */

typedef struct {
    double      vx, vy, c ;     /* edge equation  vx*X + vy*Y + c = 0 */
#ifdef CONVEX
#ifdef HYBRID
    int         ext_flag ;      /* TRUE == exterior edge of polygon */
#endif
#endif
} PlaneSet, *pPlaneSet ;


#ifdef  CONVEX
#ifdef  SORT
/* Size sorting structure for half-planes */
typedef struct {
    double      size ;
    pPlaneSet   pps ;
} SizePlanePair, *pSizePlanePair ;
#endif
#endif


#ifdef  CONVEX
pPlaneSet       ExteriorSetup() ;
void    ExteriorCleanup() ;
#ifdef  SORT
int     CompareSizePlanePairs() ;
#endif
#endif
pPlaneSet       PlaneSetup() ;
void    PlaneCleanup() ;
```

ptinpoly.c

```
/* ptinpoly.c - point in polygon inside/outside code.

   by Eric Haines, 3D/Eye Inc, erich@eye.com

   This code contains the following algorithms:
        crossings - count the crossing made by a ray from the test point
        half-plane testing - test triangle fan using half-space planes
        exterior test - for convex polygons, check exterior of polygon
*/

#include <stdio.h>
#include <stdlib.h>
#include <math.h>
#include "ptinpoly.h"

#define X         0
#define Y         1
#define TRUE      1

#ifndef HUGE
#define HUGE      1.79769313486232e+308
#endif

#define MALLOC_CHECK( a )         if ( !(a) ) {                               \
                                      fprintf( stderr, "out of memory\n" ) ; \
                                      exit(1) ;                               \
                                  }

/* ====== Crossings algorithm ========================================= */

/* Shoot a test ray along +X axis.  The strategy, from MacMartin, is to
 * compare vertex Y values to the testing point's Y and quickly discard
 * edges which are entirely to one side of the test ray.
 *
 * Input 2D polygon _pgon_ with _numverts_ number of vertices and test point
 * _point_, returns 1 if inside, 0 if outside.  WINDING and CONVEX can be
 * defined for this test.
 */
int CrossingsTest( pgon, numverts, point )
double  pgon[][2] ;
int     numverts ;
double  point[2] ;
{
#ifdef  WINDING
register int    crossings ;
#endif
register int    j, yflag0, yflag1, inside_flag, xflag0 ;
register double ty, tx, *vtx0, *vtx1 ;
#ifdef  CONVEX
```

```
register int     line_flag ;
#endif

    tx = point[X] ;
    ty = point[Y] ;

    vtx0 = pgon[numverts-1] ;
    /* get test bit for above/below X axis */
    yflag0 = ( vtx0[Y] >= ty ) ;
    vtx1 = pgon[0] ;

#ifdef  WINDING
    crossings = 0 ;
#else
    inside_flag = 0 ;
#endif
#ifdef  CONVEX
    line_flag = 0 ;
#endif
    for ( j = numverts+1 ; --j ; ) {

        yflag1 = ( vtx1[Y] >= ty ) ;
        /* check if endpoints straddle (are on opposite sides) of X axis
         * (i.e., the Y's differ); if so, +X ray could intersect this edge.
         */
        if ( yflag0 != yflag1 ) {
            xflag0 = ( vtx0[X] >= tx ) ;
            /* check if endpoints are on same side of the Y axis (i.e., X's
             * are the same); if so, it's easy to test if edge hits or misses.
             */
            if ( xflag0 == ( vtx1[X] >= tx ) ) {

                /* if edge's X values both right of the point, must hit */
#ifdef  WINDING
                if ( xflag0 ) crossings += ( yflag0 ? -1 : 1 ) ;
#else
                if ( xflag0 ) inside_flag = !inside_flag ;
#endif
            } else {
                /* compute intersection of pgon segment with +X ray, note
                 * if >= point's X; if so, the ray hits it.
                 */
                if ( (vtx1[X] - (vtx1[Y]-ty)*
                   ( vtx0[X]-vtx1[X])/(vtx0[Y]-vtx1[Y])) >= tx ) {
#ifdef  WINDING
                    crossings += ( yflag0 ? -1 : 1 ) ;
#else
                    inside_flag = !inside_flag ;
#endif
                }
            }
#ifdef  CONVEX
            /* if this is second edge hit, then done testing */
```

```
                    if ( line_flag ) goto Exit ;

                    /* Note that one edge has been hit by the ray's line. */
                    line_flag = TRUE ;
#endif
            }

            /* Move to next pair of vertices, retaining info as possible. */
            yflag0 = yflag1 ;
            vtx0 = vtx1 ;
            vtx1 += 2 ;
        }
#ifdef  CONVEX
    Exit: ;
#endif
#ifdef  WINDING
        /* Test if crossings is not zero. */
        inside_flag = (crossings != 0) ;
#endif

        return( inside_flag ) ;
}


/* ======= Triangle half-plane algorithm ================================= */

/* Split the polygon into a fan of triangles and for each triangle test if
 * the point is inside of the three half-planes formed by the triangle's edges.
 *
 * Call setup with 2D polygon _pgon_ with _numverts_ number of vertices,
 * which returns a pointer to a plane set array.
 * Call testing procedure with a pointer to this array, _numverts_, and
 * test point _point_, returns 1 if inside, 0 if outside.
 * Call cleanup with pointer to plane set array to free space.
 *
 * SORT and CONVEX can be defined for this test.
 */

/* Split polygons along set of x axes - call preprocess once. */
pPlaneSet       PlaneSetup( pgon, numverts )
double  pgon[][2] ;
int     numverts ;
{
int     i, p1, p2 ;
double  tx, ty, vx0, vy0 ;
pPlaneSet       pps, pps_return ;
#ifdef  SORT
double  len[3], len_temp ;
int     j ;
PlaneSet        ps_temp ;
#ifdef  CONVEX
pPlaneSet       pps_new ;
pSizePlanePair p_size_pair ;
```

```
#endif
#endif

    pps = pps_return =
            (pPlaneSet)malloc( 3 * (numverts-2) * sizeof( PlaneSet )) ;
    MALLOC_CHECK( pps ) ;
#ifdef  CONVEX
#ifdef  SORT
    p_size_pair =
        (pSizePlanePair)malloc( (numverts-2) * sizeof( SizePlanePair ) ) ;
    MALLOC_CHECK( p_size_pair ) ;
#endif
#endif

    vx0 = pgon[0][X] ;
    vy0 = pgon[0][Y] ;

    for ( p1 = 1, p2 = 2 ; p2 < numverts ; p1++, p2++ ) {
        pps->vx = vy0 - pgon[p1][Y] ;
        pps->vy = pgon[p1][X] - vx0 ;
        pps->c = pps->vx * vx0 + pps->vy * vy0 ;
#ifdef  SORT
        len[0] = pps->vx * pps->vx + pps->vy * pps->vy ;
#ifdef  CONVEX
#ifdef  HYBRID
        pps->ext_flag = ( p1 == 1 ) ;
#endif
        /* Sort triangles by areas, so compute (twice) the area here. */
        p_size_pair[p1-1].pps = pps ;
        p_size_pair[p1-1].size =
                        ( pgon[0][X] * pgon[p1][Y] ) +
                        ( pgon[p1][X] * pgon[p2][Y] ) +
                        ( pgon[p2][X] * pgon[0][Y] ) -
                        ( pgon[p1][X] * pgon[0][Y] ) -
                        ( pgon[p2][X] * pgon[p1][Y] ) -
                        ( pgon[0][X] * pgon[p2][Y] ) ;
#endif
#endif
        pps++ ;
        pps->vx = pgon[p1][Y] - pgon[p2][Y] ;
        pps->vy = pgon[p2][X] - pgon[p1][X] ;
        pps->c = pps->vx * pgon[p1][X] + pps->vy * pgon[p1][Y] ;
#ifdef  SORT
        len[1] = pps->vx * pps->vx + pps->vy * pps->vy ;
#endif
#ifdef  CONVEX
#ifdef  HYBRID
        pps->ext_flag = TRUE ;
#endif
#endif
        pps++ ;
        pps->vx = pgon[p2][Y] - vy0 ;
        pps->vy = vx0 - pgon[p2][X] ;
```

```
            pps->c = pps->vx * pgon[p2][X] + pps->vy * pgon[p2][Y] ;
#ifdef  SORT
            len[2] = pps->vx * pps->vx + pps->vy * pps->vy ;
#endif
#ifdef  CONVEX
#ifdef. HYBRID
            pps->ext_flag = ( p2 == numverts-1 ) ;
#endif
#endif

            /* Find an average point that must be inside of the triangle. */
            tx = ( vx0 + pgon[p1][X] + pgon[p2][X] ) / 3.0 ;
            ty = ( vy0 + pgon[p1][Y] + pgon[p2][Y] ) / 3.0 ;

            /* Check sense and reverse if test point is not thought to be inside  ·
             * first triangle.
             */
            if ( pps->vx * tx + pps->vy * ty >= pps->c ) {
                /* back up to start of plane set */
                pps -= 2 ;
                /* Point is thought to be outside, so reverse sense of edge
                 * normals so that it is correctly considered inside.
                 */
                for ( i = 0 ; i < 3 ; i++ ) {
                    pps->vx = -pps->vx ;
                    pps->vy = -pps->vy ;
                    pps->c  = -pps->c ;
                    pps++ ;
                }
            } else {
                pps++ ;
            }

#ifdef  SORT
            /* Sort the planes based on the edge lengths. */
            pps -= 3 ;
            for ( i = 0 ; i < 2 ; i++ ) {
                for ( j = i+1 ; j < 3 ; j++ ) {
                    if ( len[i] < len[j] ) {
                        ps_temp = pps[i] ;
                        pps[i] = pps[j] ;
                        pps[j] = ps_temp ;
                        len_temp = len[i] ;
                        len[i] = len[j] ;
                        len[j] = len_temp ;
                    }
                }
            }
            pps += 3 ;
#endif
    }

#ifdef  CONVEX
```

```
#ifdef  SORT
    /* Sort the triangles based on their areas. */
    qsort( p_size_pair, numverts-2,
            sizeof( SizePlanePair ), CompareSizePlanePairs ) ;

    /* Make the plane sets match the sorted order. */
    for ( i = 0, pps = pps_return
        ; i < numverts-2
        ; i++ ) {

        pps_new = p_size_pair[i].pps ;
        for ( j = 0 ; j < 3 ; j++, pps++, pps_new++ ) {
            ps_temp = *pps ;
            *pps = *pps_new ;
            *pps_new = ps_temp ;
        }
    }
    free( p_size_pair ) ;
#endif
#endif

    return( pps_return ) ;
}


#ifdef  CONVEX
#ifdef  SORT
int CompareSizePlanePairs( p_sp0, p_sp1 )
pSizePlanePair  p_sp0, p_sp1 ;
{
    if ( p_sp0->size == p_sp1->size ) {
        return( 0 ) ;
    } else {
        return( p_sp0->size > p_sp1->size ? -1 : 1 ) ;
    }
}
#endif
#endif


/* Check point for inside of three "planes" formed by triangle edges. */
int PlaneTest( p_plane_set, numverts, point )
pPlaneSet       p_plane_set ;
int      numverts ;
double  point[2] ;
{
register pPlaneSet      ps ;
register int    p2 ;
#ifndef CONVEX
register int     inside_flag ;
#endif
register double tx, ty ;

    tx = point[X] ;
```

```
    ty = point[Y] ;

#ifndef CONVEX
    inside_flag = 0 ;
#endif

    for ( ps = p_plane_set, p2 = numverts-1 ; --p2 ; ) {

        if ( ps->vx * tx + ps->vy * ty < ps->c ) {
            ps++ ;
            if ( ps->vx * tx + ps->vy * ty < ps->c ) {
                ps++ ;
                /* Note: we make the third edge have a slightly different
                 * equality condition, since this third edge is in fact
                 * the next triangle's first edge.  Not fool-proof, but
                 * it doesn't hurt (better would be to keep track of the
                 * triangle's area sign so we would know which kind of
                 * triangle this is).  Note that edge sorting nullifies
                 * this special inequality, too.
                 */
                if ( ps->vx * tx + ps->vy * ty <= ps->c ) {
                    /* point is inside polygon */
#ifdef CONVEX
                    return( 1 ) ;
#else
                    inside_flag = !inside_flag ;
#endif
                }
#ifdef  CONVEX
#ifdef  HYBRID
                /* check if outside exterior edge */
                else if ( ps->ext_flag ) return( 0 ) ;
#endif
#endif
                ps++ ;
            } else {
#ifdef  CONVEX
#ifdef  HYBRID
                /* check if outside exterior edge */
                if ( ps->ext_flag ) return( 0 ) ;
#endif
#endif

                /* get past last two plane tests */
                ps += 2 ;
            }
        } else {
#ifdef  CONVEX
#ifdef  HYBRID
            /* check if outside exterior edge */
            if ( ps->ext_flag ) return( 0 ) ;
#endif
#endif
            /* get past all three plane tests */
```

```
                ps += 3 ;
        }
    }

#ifdef CONVEX
    /* for convex, if we make it to here, all triangles were missed */
    return( 0 ) ;
#else
    return( inside_flag ) ;
#endif
}

void PlaneCleanup( p_plane_set )
pPlaneSet        p_plane_set ;
{
    free( p_plane_set ) ;
}


/* ======= Exterior (convex only) algorithm ============================== */

/* Test the edges of the convex polygon against the point.  If the point is
 * outside any edge, the point is outside the polygon.
 *
 * Call setup with 2D polygon _pgon_ with _numverts_ number of vertices,
 * which returns a pointer to a plane set array.
 * Call testing procedure with a pointer to this array, _numverts_, and
 * test point _point_, returns 1 if inside, 0 if outside.
 * Call cleanup with pointer to plane set array to free space.
 *
 * RANDOM can be defined for this test.
 * CONVEX must be defined for this test; it is not usable for general polygons.
 */

#ifdef  CONVEX
/* make exterior plane set */
pPlaneSet ExteriorSetup( pgon, numverts )
double  pgon[][2] ;
int     numverts ;
{
int     p1, p2, flip_edge ;
pPlaneSet        pps, pps_return ;
#ifdef  RANDOM
int     i, ind ;
PlaneSet         ps_temp ;
#endif

    pps = pps_return =
            (pPlaneSet)malloc( numverts * sizeof( PlaneSet )) ;
    MALLOC_CHECK( pps ) ;

    /* take cross product of vertex to find handedness */
    flip_edge = (pgon[0][X] - pgon[1][X]) * (pgon[1][Y] - pgon[2][Y] ) >
```

```
                                (pgon[0][Y] - pgon[1][Y]) * (pgon[1][X] - pgon[2][X] ) ;

        /* Generate half-plane boundary equations now for faster testing later.
         * vx & vy are the edge's normal, c is the offset from the origin.
         */
        for ( p1 = numverts-1, p2 = 0 ; p2 < numverts ; p1 = p2, p2++, pps++ ) {
            pps->vx = pgon[p1][Y] - pgon[p2][Y] ;
            pps->vy = pgon[p2][X] - pgon[p1][X] ;
            pps->c = pps->vx * pgon[p1][X] + pps->vy * pgon[p1][Y] ;

            /* check sense and reverse plane edge if need be */
            if ( flip_edge ) {
                pps->vx = -pps->vx ;
                pps->vy = -pps->vy ;
                pps->c  = -pps->c ;
            }
        }

#ifdef  RANDOM
        /* Randomize the order of the edges to improve chance of early out. */
        /* There are better orders, but the default order is the worst. */
        for ( i = 0, pps = pps_return
            ; i < numverts
            ; i++ ) {

            ind = (int)(RAN01() * numverts ) ;
            if ( ( ind < 0 ) || ( ind >= numverts ) ) {
                fprintf( stderr,
                    "Yikes, the random number generator is returning values\n" ) ;
                fprintf( stderr,
                    "outside the range [0.0,1.0), so please fix the code!\n" ) ;
                ind = 0 ;
            }

            /* swap edges */
            ps_temp = *pps ;
            *pps = pps_return[ind] ;
            pps_return[ind] = ps_temp ;
        }
#endif
        return( pps_return ) ;
}


/* Check point for outside of all planes. */
/* Note that we don't need "pgon", since it's been processed into
 * its corresponding PlaneSet.
 */
int ExteriorTest( p_ext_set, numverts, point )
pPlaneSet       p_ext_set ;
int     numverts ;
double  point[2] ;
{
register PlaneSet       *pps ;
```

```
register int    p0 ;
register double tx, ty ;
int      inside_flag ;

    tx = point[X] ;
    ty = point[Y] ;

    for ( p0 = numverts+1, pps = p_ext_set ; --p0 ; pps++ ) {

        /* Test if the point is outside this edge. */
        if ( pps->vx * tx + pps->vy * ty > pps->c ) {
            return( 0 ) ;
        }
    }
    /* If we make it to here, we were inside all edges. */
    return( 1 ) ;
}

void ExteriorCleanup( p_ext_set )
pPlaneSet       p_ext_set ;
{
    free( p_ext_set ) ;
}
#endif
```

◇ **Bibliography** ◇

(Antonio 1992) Franklin Antonio. Faster line segment intersection. In David Kirk, editor, *Graphics Gems III*, pages 199–202. Academic Press, Boston, 1992.

(Badouel 1990) Didier Badouel. An efficient ray-polygon intersection. In Andrew Glassner, editor, *Graphics Gems*, pages 390–393. Academic Press, Boston, 1990.

(Berlin 1985) Jr. Edwin P. Berlin. Efficiency considerations in image synthesis. In *SIGGRAPH '85 State of the Art in Image Synthesis seminar notes*, July 1985.

(Glassner 1989) A. Glassner, editor. *An Introduction to Ray Tracing*. Academic Press, London, 1989.

(Green 1993) Chris Green. Simple, fast triangle intersection. *Ray Tracing News* 6(1), E-mail edition, anonymous ftp from princeton.edu:/pub/Graphics/RTNews, 1993.

(Hacker 1962) R. Hacker. Certification of algorithm 112: position of point relative to polygon. *Communications of the ACM*, 5:606, 1962.

(Haines 1992) Eric Haines, editor. Fastest point in polygon test. *Ray Tracing News* 5(3), E-mail edition, anonymous ftp from princeton.edu:/pub/Graphics/RTNews, 1992.

(Hanrahan and Haeberli 1990) Pat Hanrahan and Paul Haeberli. Direct WYSIWYG painting and texturing on 3d shapes. *Computer Graphics (SIGGRAPH '90 Proceedings)*, 24(4):215–223, August 1990.

(Preparata and Shamos 1985) F. P. Preparata and M. I. Shamos. *Computational Geometry: An Introduction*. Springer-Verlag, New York, NY, 1985.

(Salesin and Stolfi 1989) David Salesin and Jorge Stolfi. The ZZ-buffer: A simple and efficient rendering algorithm with reliable antialiasing. In *Proc. 2nd Intl. Conf. on Computer Graphics (PIXIM '89)*, pages 451–465, Paris, France, 1989.

(Schorn and Fisher 1994) Peter Schorn and Frederick Fisher. Testing the convexity of a polygon. In Paul Heckbert, editor, *Graphics Gems IV*, 7–15. Academic Press, Boston, 1994.

(Shimrat 1962) M. Shimrat. Algorithm 112: position of point relative to polygon. *Communications of the ACM*, 5:434, 1962.

(Spackman 1993) John Spackman. Simple, fast triangle intersection, part ii. *Ray Tracing News* 6(2), E-mail edition, anonymous ftp from princeton.edu:/pub/Graphics/RTNews, 1993.

(Weiler 1994) Kevin Weiler. An incremental angle point in polygon test. In Paul Heckbert, editor, *Graphics Gems IV*, 16–23. Academic Press, Boston, 1994.

(Woo 1992) Andrew Woo. Ray tracing polygons using spatial subdivision. In *Proceedings of Graphics Interface '92*, pages 184–191, May 1992.

(Worley and Haines 1993) Steve Worley and Eric Haines. Bounding areas for ray/polygon intersection. *Ray Tracing News* 6(1), E-mail edition, anonymous ftp from princeton.edu:/pub/Graphics/RTNews, 1993.

I.5

Incremental Delaunay Triangulation

Dani Lischinski

580 ETC Building
Cornell University
Ithaca, NY 14853
danix@graphics.cornell.edu

◇ Introduction ◇

This Gem gives a simple algorithm for the incremental construction of the Delaunay triangulation (DT) and the Voronoi diagram (VD) of a set of points in the plane. A triangulation is called *Delaunay* if it satisfies the empty circumcircle property: the circumcircle of a triangle in the triangulation does not contain any input points in its interior. DT is the straight-line dual of the *Voronoi diagram* of a point set, which is a partition of the plane into polygonal cells, one for each point in the set, so that the cell for point p consists of the region of the plane closer to p than to any other input point (Preparata and Shamos 1985, Fortune 1992).

Delaunay triangulations and Voronoi diagrams, which can be constructed from them, are a useful tool for efficiently solving many problems in computational geometry (Preparata and Shamos 1985). DT is optimal in several respects. For example, it maximizes the minimum angle and minimizes the maximum circumcircle over all possible triangulations of the same point set (Fortune 1992). Thus, DT is an important tool for high-quality mesh generation for finite elements (Bern and Eppstein 1992). It should be noted, however, that standard DT doesn't allow edges that must appear in the triangulation to be specified in the input. Thus, in order to mesh general polygonal regions the more complicated *constrained* DT should be used (Bern and Eppstein 1992).

The incremental DT algorithm given in this Gem was originally presented by Green and Sibson (Green and Sibson 1977), but the implementation is based entirely on the quad-edge data structure and the pseudocode from the excellent paper by Guibas and Stolfi (Guibas and Stolfi 1985). I will briefly describe the data structures and the algorithm, but the reader is referred to Guibas and Stolfi for more details.

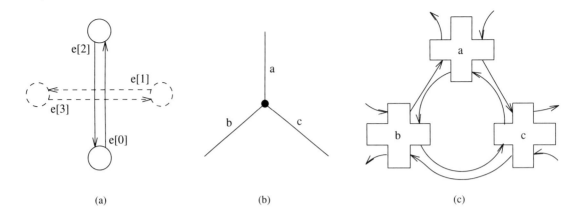

(a) (b) (c)

Figure 1. The quad-edge data structure.

◇ **The Quad-Edge Data Structure** ◇

The quad-edge data structure (Guibas and Stolfi 1985) was designed for representing general subdivisions of orientable manifolds. It is similar to the winged-edge data structure (Baumgart 1975), but it simultaneously represents both the subdivision and its dual. Each quad-edge record groups together four directed edges corresponding to a single undirected edge in the subdivision and to its dual edge (Figure 1a). Each directed edge has two pointers: a **next** pointer to the next counterclockwise edge around its origin, and a **data** pointer to geometrical and other nontopological information (such as the coordinates of its origin.)

Figures 1b and 1c illustrate how three edges incident on the same vertex are represented using the quad-edge data structure: the vertex itself corresponds to the inner cycle of pointers in Figure 1c. The remaining three cycles correspond to the three faces meeting at the vertex.

Aside from a primitive to create an edge (**MakeEdge**), a single topological operator **Splice** is defined that can be used to link disjoint edges together as well as to break two linked edges apart. This operator is its own inverse and together with **MakeEdge** it can be used to construct any subdivision.

◇ **The Incremental Algorithm** ◇

The incremental DT algorithm starts with a triangle large enough to contain all of the points in the input. Points are added into the triangulation one by one, maintaining the invariant that the triangulation is Delaunay. Figure 2 illustrates the point insertion process. First, the triangle containing the new point p is located (2a). New edges are created to connect p to the vertices of the containing triangle (2b). The old edges of the triangle are inspected to verify that they still satisfy the empty circumcircle condition.

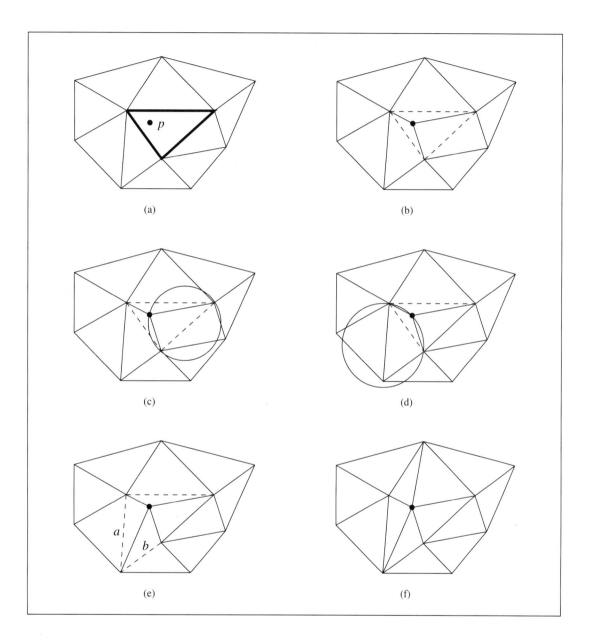

Figure 2.   Inserting a point into the triangulation. Dashed lines indicate edges that need to be inspected by the algorithm.

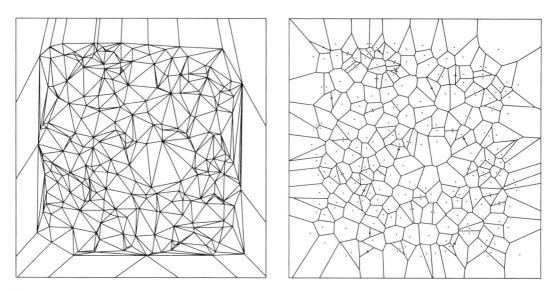

Figure 3. The DT (left) and the VD (right) of 250 random points uniformly distributed in the unit square.

If the condition is satisfied (2c) the edge remains unchanged. If it is violated (2d) the offending edge is flipped, that is, replaced by the other diagonal of the surrounding quadrilateral. In this case two more edges become candidates for inspection (edges a and b in Figure 2e.) The process continues until no more candidates remain, resulting in the triangulation shown in Figure 2f.

In the worst case the insertion of a point can require $O(n)$ edges to be flipped. However, in practice the average number of edges tested per insertion is small (< 9). Guibas, Knuth, and Sharir have shown that if the insertion order is randomized, the expected time is $O(1)$ per insertion (Guibas *et al.* 1990).

Locating the containing triangle can be done in an optimal $O(\log n)$ time, but this requires maintaining complicated data structures. Alternatively, the triangle can be located by starting from an arbitrary place in the triangulation and moving in the direction of p until the containing triangle is reached. This requires $O(n)$ time, but if the inserted points are uniformly distributed, the expected number of operations to locate a point is only $O(n^{1/2})$. A simple improvement is always to resume the search from the triangle that was found last: in this way, when the points to be located are near each other, the containing triangles are determined quickly.

Figure 3 shows the DT and the corresponding VD produced by this algorithm from 250 random points in the unit square. Note that because the quad-edge data structure represents both the triangulation and its dual, the topology of the Voronoi diagram is readily available from the DT constructed by the algorithm. To have a complete VD one only needs to compute the circumcenters of all the triangles (i.e., the locations of the Voronoi vertices).

◇ **Robustness** ◇

In order to produce a practical implementation of a geometric algorithm, one typically needs to address two problems: geometric degeneracies and numerical errors. For DT, four or more cocircular points in the input constitute a geometric degeneracy, and the resulting DT is not unique. In such a case this algorithm will produce one of the possible triangulations as output.

Dealing with numerical errors is more difficult. Various applications in which the need for DT or VD arises differ in the nature of their input and in their output accuracy requirements. Therefore, it is very difficult to come up with a single efficient solution to the problem. Karasick, Lieber, and Nackman suggest a solution that uses rational arithmetic as well as survey other approaches (Karasick *et al.* 1991).

In this implementation all the computations are performed using standard floating-point arithmetic. Epsilon tolerances are used to determine whether two points coincide and whether a point falls on an edge. No other special measures to ensure robustness were taken. Nevertheless, largely because of the simplicity of the algorithm, the implementation has proven to be very robust.

◇ **C++ Code** ◇

The code listed below is the C++ implementation of the quad-edge data structure and the incremental Delaunay triangulation algorithm. In addition, the disk that comes with this book contains code for 2D vectors, points, and lines, and a test program. This program constructs and displays a triangulation, allowing the user to add more points into the triangulation interactively by clicking a mouse button at the place of insertion. The code should compile and execute on SGI graphics workstations.

```cpp
#include <geom2d.h>

class QuadEdge;

class Edge {
    friend QuadEdge;
    friend void Splice(Edge*, Edge*);
  private:
    int num;
    Edge *next;
    Point2d *data;
  public:
    Edge() { data = 0; }
    Edge* Rot();
    Edge* invRot();
    Edge* Sym();
    Edge* Onext();
    Edge* Oprev();
```

```
        Edge* Dnext();
        Edge* Dprev();
        Edge* Lnext();
        Edge* Lprev();
        Edge* Rnext();
        Edge* Rprev();
        Point2d* Org();
        Point2d* Dest();
        const Point2d& Org2d() const;
        const Point2d& Dest2d() const;
        void  EndPoints(Point2d*, Point2d*);
        QuadEdge* Qedge()   { return (QuadEdge *)(this - num); }
};

class QuadEdge {
    friend Edge *MakeEdge();
  private:
    Edge e[4];
  public:
    QuadEdge();
};

class Subdivision {
  private:
    Edge *startingEdge;
    Edge *Locate(const Point2d&);
  public:
    Subdivision(const Point2d&, const Point2d&, const Point2d&);
    void InsertSite(const Point2d&);
    void Draw();
};

inline QuadEdge::QuadEdge()
{
    e[0].num = 0, e[1].num = 1, e[2].num = 2, e[3].num = 3;
    e[0].next = &(e[0]); e[1].next = &(e[3]);
    e[2].next = &(e[2]); e[3].next = &(e[1]);
}


/*********************** Edge Algebra *************************************/

inline Edge* Edge::Rot()
// Return the dual of the current edge, directed from its right to its left.
{
    return (num < 3) ? this + 1 : this - 3;
}


inline Edge* Edge::invRot()
// Return the dual of the current edge, directed from its left to its right.
{
    return (num > 0) ? this - 1 : this + 3;
}
```

```
inline Edge* Edge::Sym()
// Return the edge from the destination to the origin of the current edge.
{
    return (num < 2) ? this + 2 : this - 2;
}

inline Edge* Edge::Onext()
// Return the next ccw edge around (from) the origin of the current edge.
{
    return next;
}

inline Edge* Edge::Oprev()
// Return the next cw edge around (from) the origin of the current edge.
{
    return Rot()->Onext()->Rot();
}

inline Edge* Edge::Dnext()
// Return the next ccw edge around (into) the destination of the current edge.
{
    return Sym()->Onext()->Sym();
}

inline Edge* Edge::Dprev()
// Return the next cw edge around (into) the destination of the current edge.
{
    return invRot()->Onext()->invRot();
}

inline Edge* Edge::Lnext()
// Return the ccw edge around the left face following the current edge.
{
    return invRot()->Onext()->Rot();
}

inline Edge* Edge::Lprev()
// Return the ccw edge around the left face before the current edge.
{
    return Onext()->Sym();
}

inline Edge* Edge::Rnext()
// Return the edge around the right face ccw following the current edge.
{
    return Rot()->Onext()->invRot();
}

inline Edge* Edge::Rprev()
// Return the edge around the right face ccw before the current edge.
{
    return Sym()->Onext();
}
```

```
/************** Access to Data Pointers ********************************/

inline Point2d* Edge::Org()
{
    return data;
}

inline Point2d* Edge::Dest()
{
    return Sym()->data;
}

inline const Point2d& Edge::Org2d() const
{
    return *data;
}

inline const Point2d& Edge::Dest2d() const
{
    return (num < 2) ? *((this + 2)->data) : *((this - 2)->data);
}

inline void Edge::EndPoints(Point2d* or, Point2d* de)
{
    data = or;
    Sym()->data = de;
}

/******************** Basic Topological Operators *********************/

Edge* MakeEdge()
{
    QuadEdge *ql = new QuadEdge;
    return ql->e;
}

void Splice(Edge* a, Edge* b)
// This operator affects the two edge rings around the origins of a and b
// and, independently, the two edge rings around the left faces of a and b.
// In each case, (i) if the two rings are distinct, Splice will combine
// them into one; (ii) if the two are the same ring, Splice will break it
// into two separate pieces.
// Thus, Splice can be used both to attach the two edges together and
// to break them apart. See Guibas and Stolfi (1985, p. 96) for more details
// and illustrations.
{
    Edge* alpha = a->Onext()->Rot();
    Edge* beta  = b->Onext()->Rot();

    Edge* t1 = b->Onext();
    Edge* t2 = a->Onext();
    Edge* t3 = beta->Onext();
    Edge* t4 = alpha->Onext();
```

```
    a->next = t1;
    b->next = t2;
    alpha->next = t3;
    beta->next = t4;
}

void DeleteEdge(Edge* e)
{
    Splice(e, e->Oprev());
    Splice(e->Sym(), e->Sym()->Oprev());
    delete e->Qedge();
}

/************* Topological Operations for Delaunay Diagrams *****************/

Subdivision::Subdivision(const Point2d& a, const Point2d& b, const Point2d& c)
// Initialize a subdivision to the triangle defined by the points a, b, c.
{
    Point2d *da, *db, *dc;
    da = new Point2d(a), db = new Point2d(b), dc = new Point2d(c);
    Edge* ea = MakeEdge();
    ea->EndPoints(da, db);
    Edge* eb = MakeEdge();
    Splice(ea->Sym(), eb);
    eb->EndPoints(db, dc);
    Edge* ec = MakeEdge();
    Splice(eb->Sym(), ec);
    ec->EndPoints(dc, da);
    Splice(ec->Sym(), ea);
    startingEdge = ea;
}

Edge* Connect(Edge* a, Edge* b)
// Add a new edge e connecting the destination of a to the
// origin of b, in such a way that all three have the same
// left face after the connection is complete.
// Additionally, the data pointers of the new edge are set.
{
    Edge* e = MakeEdge();
    Splice(e, a->Lnext());
    Splice(e->Sym(), b);
    e->EndPoints(a->Dest(), b->Org());
    return e;
}

void Swap(Edge* e)
// Essentially turns edge e counterclockwise inside its enclosing
// quadrilateral. The data pointers are modified accordingly.
{
    Edge* a = e->Oprev();
    Edge* b = e->Sym()->Oprev();
    Splice(e, a);
```

```
        Splice(e->Sym(), b);
        Splice(e, a->Lnext());
        Splice(e->Sym(), b->Lnext());
        e->EndPoints(a->Dest(), b->Dest());
}


/*************** Geometric Predicates for Delaunay Diagrams *****************/

inline Real TriArea(const Point2d& a, const Point2d& b, const Point2d& c)
// Returns twice the area of the oriented triangle (a, b, c), i.e., the
// area is positive if the triangle is oriented counterclockwise.
{
        return (b.x - a.x)*(c.y - a.y) - (b.y - a.y)*(c.x - a.x);
}


int InCircle(const Point2d& a, const Point2d& b,
                const Point2d& c, const Point2d& d)
// Returns TRUE if the point d is inside the circle defined by the
// points a, b, c. See Guibas and Stolfi (1985) p.107.
{
        return (a.x*a.x + a.y*a.y) * TriArea(b, c, d) -
               (b.x*b.x + b.y*b.y) * TriArea(a, c, d) +
               (c.x*c.x + c.y*c.y) * TriArea(a, b, d) -
               (d.x*d.x + d.y*d.y) * TriArea(a, b, c) > 0;
}


int ccw(const Point2d& a, const Point2d& b, const Point2d& c)
// Returns TRUE if the points a, b, c are in a counterclockwise order
{
        return (TriArea(a, b, c) > 0);
}


int RightOf(const Point2d& x, Edge* e)
{
        return ccw(x, e->Dest2d(), e->Org2d());
}


int LeftOf(const Point2d& x, Edge* e)
{
        return ccw(x, e->Org2d(), e->Dest2d());
}


int OnEdge(const Point2d& x, Edge* e)
// A predicate that determines if the point x is on the edge e.
// The point is considered on if it is in the EPS-neighborhood
// of the edge.
{
        Real t1, t2, t3;
        t1 = (x - e->Org2d()).norm();
        t2 = (x - e->Dest2d()).norm();
        if (t1 < EPS || t2 < EPS)
            return TRUE;
        t3 = (e->Org2d() - e->Dest2d()).norm();
```

```
        if (t1 > t3 || t2 > t3)
            return FALSE;
        Line line(e->Org2d(), e->Dest2d());
        return (fabs(line.eval(x)) < EPS);
}


/************* An Incremental Algorithm for the Construction of *************/
/*********************** Delaunay Diagrams ******************************/

Edge* Subdivision::Locate(const Point2d& x)
// Returns an edge e, such that either x is on e, or e is an edge of
// a triangle containing x. The search starts from startingEdge
// and proceeds in the general direction of x. Based on the
// pseudocode in Guibas and Stolfi (1985, p. 121).
{
    Edge* e = startingEdge;

    while (TRUE) {
        if (x == e->Org2d() || x == e->Dest2d())
            return e;
        else if (RightOf(x, e))
            e = e->Sym();
        else if (!RightOf(x, e->Onext()))
            e = e->Onext();
        else if (!RightOf(x, e->Dprev()))
            e = e->Dprev();
        else
            return e;
    }
}


void Subdivision::InsertSite(const Point2d& x)
// Inserts a new point into a subdivision representing a Delaunay
// triangulation, and fixes the affected edges so that the result
// is still a Delaunay triangulation. This is based on the
// pseudocode from Guibas and Stolfi (1985, p. 120), with slight
// modifications and a bug fix.
{
    Edge* e = Locate(x);
    if ((x == e->Org2d()) || (x == e->Dest2d()))  // point is already in
        return;
    else if (OnEdge(x, e)) {
        e = e->Oprev();
        DeleteEdge(e->Onext());
    }

    // Connect the new point to the vertices of the containing
    // triangle (or quadrilateral, if the new point fell on an
    // existing edge).
    Edge* base = MakeEdge();
    base->EndPoints(e->Org(), new Point2d(x));
    Splice(base, e);
    startingEdge = base;
```

```
    do {
        base = Connect(e, base->Sym());
        e = base->Oprev();
    } while (e->Lnext() != startingEdge);

    // Examine suspect edges to ensure that the Delaunay condition
    // is satisfied.
    do {
        Edge* t = e->Oprev();
        if (RightOf(t->Dest2d(), e) &&
            InCircle(e->Org2d(), t->Dest2d(), e->Dest2d(), x)) {
                Swap(e);
                e = e->Oprev();
        }
        else if (e->Onext() == startingEdge)  // no more suspect edges
            return;
        else  // pop a suspect edge
            e = e->Onext()->Lprev();
    } while (TRUE);
}


/*****************************************************************************/
```

◇ **Bibliography** ◇

(Baumgart 1975) B. G. Baumgart. A polyhedron representation for computer vision. In *1975 National Computer Conference*, volume 44 of *AFIPS Conference Proceedings*, pages 589–596. AFIPS Press, Arlington, VA, 1975.

(Bern and Eppstein 1992) Marshall Bern and David Eppstein. Mesh generation and optimal triangulation. In F. K. Hwang and D.-Z. Du, editors, *Computing in Euclidean Geometry*, pages 23–90. World Scientific, Singapore, 1992.

(Fortune 1992) Steven Fortune. Voronoi diagrams and Delaunay triangulations. In F. K. Hwang and D.-Z. Du, editors, *Computing in Euclidean Geometry*, pages 193–233. World Scientific, Singapore, 1992.

(Green and Sibson 1977) P. J. Green and R. Sibson. Computing Dirichlet tessellations in the plane. *Computer Journal*, 21(2):168–173, 1977.

(Guibas and Stolfi 1985) Leonidas Guibas and Jorge Stolfi. Primitives for the manipulation of general subdivisions and the computation of Voronoi diagrams. *ACM Transactions on Graphics*, 4(2):74–123, 1985.

(Guibas *et al.* 1990) L. J. Guibas, D. E. Knuth, and M. Sharir. Randomized incremental construction of Delaunay and Voronoi diagrams. In *Proc. 17th Int. Colloq. — Automata, Languages, and Programming*, volume 443 of *Springer-Verlag LNCS*, pages 414–431. Springer-Verlag, Berlin, 1990.

(Karasick *et al.* 1991) Michael Karasick, Derek Lieber, and Lee R. Nackman. Efficient Delaunay triangulation using rational arithmetic. *ACM Transactions on Graphics*, 10(1):71–91, 1991.

(Preparata and Shamos 1985) Franco P. Preparata and Michael Ian Shamos. *Computational Geometry*. Springer-Verlag, New York, 1985.

◊ I.6

Building Vertex Normals from an Unstructured Polygon List

Andrew Glassner

Xerox PARC
3333 Coyote Hill Road
Palo Alto, CA 94304
glassner@parc.xerox.com

◊ Abstract ◊

Many polygonal models are used as piecewise-flat approximations of curved models, and are thus "smooth-shaded" when displayed. To apply Gouraud or Phong shading to a model one needs to compute a surface normal at every vertex; often this simply involves averaging the surface normal of each polygon sharing that vertex.

This Gem provides a general-purpose procedure that computes vertex normals from any list of polygons. I assume that the polygons describe a simple manifold in 3D space, so that every local neighborhood is a flat sheet. I also assume that the structure is a *mesh*; that is, there are no "T" vertices, isolated vertices, or dangling edges. Except for the addition of normals at the vertices, the input model is unchanged.

I infer the topology of the model by building a data structure that allows quick access to all the polygons that have a vertex in the same region of space. To find the normal for a selected vertex, one needs only search the region surrounding the vertex and then average the normals for all polygons that share that vertex.

◊ Overview ◊

Polygons continue to be a popular primitive for approximating curved surfaces. To make polygonal models look smooth we can use Gouraud or Phong shading, often supported by hardware. Both of these techniques require a normal at each vertex of each polygon.

Typically a vertex normal is computed by combining the normals of all the polygons that share that vertex. A number of different strategies for this computation are presented in (Glassner 1990), but they all require that the polygons be identified first. When the polygons are generated in a mesh, it is easy to find all the polygons that share a vertex.

Some shape-generation programs are not so cooperative and instead generate polygons according to a less organized scheme. The result is a big list of polygons, each identified by a list of explicit vertices. The trick then becomes finding which vertices are held in common by which polygons.

This Gem presents a piece of code that will run through all the polygons, identify shared vertices to infer the topology of the model, and average together the appropriate polygons to build vertex normals. Two vertices are labeled identical if they have very similar coordinates, to within a small tolerance.

I found it useful to provide a simple form of *edge preservation* for meshes, an idea originally introduced by Gouraud (Foley *et al.* 1990). If two adjacent polygons are sufficiently far from flat, then they are not averaged together at a common vertex. The use of edge preservation and its tolerance are selectable by the client (the calling routine).

The general idea is first to initialize the package, and then feed in a sequence of polygons in any order. When all the polygons are in, call a routine to compute all the normals. You then use the normals somehow (perhaps writing the resulting, augmented polygons to a file), and then free up the memory the package allocated.

◇ **The Algorithm** ◇

The algorithm used here is very simple. A few data structures guide the way.

First is the *Polygon*, which contains explicit storage for each vertex and its normal, and some bookkeeping information such as the polygon's own normal, its number of vertices, and so on.

The central organization comes from a hash table, which is made up of a linked list of *HashNode* structures. Each of these structures represents one vertex; it points to the polygon containing the vertex, identifies it by number, and provides its status, which is one of *waiting, working,* or *done* (explained ahead).

Polygons are entered one by one into the database. The client passes in a pointer to a list of vertices (an array of *Point3* structures), which is then copied, so the client can free or re-use that memory. When a polygon is entered, its normal is computed using Newell's method (Sutherland *et al.* 1974) (Tampieri 1992), and its vertices are inserted into the hash table. Each vertex is marked as *waiting*.

To compute normals, the system scans the list stored at each entry of the hash table and identifies all the polygons that have a particular vertex in common (to within the *fuzz* tolerance). The normals of all the participating polygons are averaged together and stored with the associated vertices.

The test for equality uses a parameter called *fuzz*, to accomodate floating-point errors when the model is made. If the Manhattan distance between two vertices doesn't exceed *fuzz*, then they are considered the same.

Note that if we identify (i.e., merge) two vertices that are nearby to be the same then we might be tempted to use just one piece of storage to hold the vertex and its normal, rather than replicate that vertex at each polygon. The reason I don't do this is to support *edge preservation*. This is a technique where two adjacent polygons are *not* averaged together if they diverge from coplanarity by more than a given criterion. For example, if a number of polygons all come together at the tip of a narrow cone, then we probably don't want to smooth the vertex at the tip, though we want to smooth the other vertices of the cone. So the vertex at the tip will have a different normal for each constituent polygon. Edge preservation is disabled by default; you can enable it (and supply its comparison threshold) with a function call.

Note that as with any hashing scheme, two spatially distinct vertices can hash to the same table entry, so we may need to pass through each hash-table list multiple times to pick up each vertex.

The general flow of the algorithm is a pair of small loops in a larger loop. The outer loop scans all the hash buckets. If the entry is NULL then it moves to the next; if it is non-NULL then it is processed. Processing starts up a loop that continues as long as there are any vertices in the list at this entry that are marked as *waiting* (I simply scan the list and look for any such vertex). The first vertex found that is *waiting* is set to *working*; this becomes the vertex for which we want to compute a normal. We initialize a new vertex normal with the normal of the polygon containing this vertex.

We now continue scanning the list. If we find another vertex that is acceptably close to this one spatially, then we examine it. If edge preservation is disabled, we mark that vertex also as *working* and add its polygon's normal in to the accumulating vertex normal. If edge preservation is enabled, we check the angle between the new polygon and the original one and mark it *working* and add in the new polygon's normal only if the angle is sufficiently large.

When we reach the end of the list, we normalize the vertex normal. We then pass through the list again, searching for nodes with the status *working*. For each such node, we copy the vertex normal into the normal pointer for that vertex for that polygon, and set the node to *done*.

When we reach the end of the list, we return to scan for any more vertices that are still *waiting*. If every node in the list is *done*, we move on to the next hash-table entry.

◇ **Use** ◇

You supply input to the package by filling up data structures of type *Polygon*, which the package augments with vertex normals.

A simple demonstration program is supplied with the code; it makes a mesh of quadrilaterals and triangles and writes them to the standard output with vertex normals. The `main` routine initializes the package, inserts polygons, enables edge preservation, builds normals, saves the polygons, and frees the package's memory. The mesh is a function $z = y|1 - 2x|$ over the unit square; so at $y = 0$ it's flat, and at $y = 1$ it's a sharp crease. In the driver I turn on edge preservation with a minimum dot value of 0.0 (corresponding to 90°), so the crease is smooth up to $y = 0.5$, when it becomes crisp.

To use the package, call `initAllTables`, which returns a pointer to a data structure of type *Smooth*.

To insert polygons, fill in an array of *Point3* structures with the vertex locations, and pass this array, the vertex count, and the *smooth* pointer to `includePolygon`. This routine also allows you to attach a *user* pointer of arbitrary type to the polygon. I have found this useful for keeping color and texture information with the polygon.

To enable edge preservation, you can call `enableEdgePreservation` at any time after initialization and before computing normals. Pass it the *smooth* pointer and the value of the smallest dot product (i.e., the cosine of the largest angle) which you are willing to call "flat." If you later want to turn off this option, call `disableEdgePreservation`.

The fuzz tolerance for comparisons is set by a call to `setFuzzFraction`.

When all your polygons are in, call `makeVertexNormals`, passing in the *smooth* pointer. The result is that *Smooth* field *polygonTable* now points to a copy of your polygon list, only each polygon now contains its own surface normal (stored in *normal*) and an array of normals (stored in *normals* as an array of *Vector3* structures) corresponding to each vertex. The *next* field points to the next polygon so you can read them all back by following this link. The polygons are stored in this list in the same order in which you included them. When you're done with all the polygons, call `freeAll` with the pointer to *smooth* to release the storage used by the system.

You may want to play with the hashing function; I used a very simple one. First I round each vertex to three digits of precision (this is controlled by the `QSIZE` constant). I then scale the three coordinates by three different small primes. You can try any hash function you like, but it must always return a non-negative value. The size of the hash table is given by the `HASH_TABLE_SIZE` constant.

◇ Discussion ◇

This algorithm can be sensitive to small variations in the input. For example, if two adjacent polygons share a vertex, but one stores the X coordinate of that vertex as 3.999999 and the other stores it as 4.0, then the two vertices might fall into different buckets. This could be fixed by multiple hashing: use two different, overlapping hashing functions, and run through both hash tables for each vertex (being careful not to duplicate included polygons).

The algorithm could be improved by making `QSIZE` also dependent on the overall bounding box of the model.

Some applications may find it useful to access the internal data structure which contains the inferred topology of the model before returning that memory to the operating system.

◇ **C Code** ◇

Header File

```
/* smooth.h */
/* header file for polygon smoothing */
/* Andrew S. Glassner / Xerox PARC */

#include <stdio.h>
#include <math.h>

#ifdef STANDALONE_TEST

#define NEWTYPE(x) (x *)malloc((unsigned)(sizeof(x)))

typedef struct Point3Struct {
   double x, y, z;
   } Point3;
typedef Point3 Vector3;
typedef int boolean;
#define TRUE  1
#define FALSE 0

Vector3 *V3Normalize(Vector3 *v);
Vector3 *V3Add(Vector3 *a, Vector3 *b, Vector3 *c);
double V3Dot(Vector3 *a, Vector3 *b);
#else
#include "GraphicsGems.h"
#endif

/********* MACROS and CONSTANTS *********/

/* new array creator */
#define NEWA(x, num) (x *)malloc((unsigned)((num) * sizeof(x)))

#define MARKWAITING    0
#define MARKWORKING    1
#define MARKDONE       2

/* fuzzy comparison macro */
#define FUZZEQ(x,y)  (fabs((x)-(y))<(smooth->fuzz))

/* hash table size; related to HASH */
#define HASH_TABLE_SIZE       1000

/* quantization increment */
#define QSIZE   1000.0

#define QUANT(x)      (((int)((x)*QSIZE))/QSIZE)
#define ABSQUANT(x)   (((int)((fabs(x))*QSIZE))/QSIZE)
#define HASH(pt)      ( \
                      (int)(((3*ABSQUANT(pt->x)) + \
```

```
                              (5*ABSQUANT(pt->y)) + \
                              (7*ABSQUANT(pt->z))) * \
                    HASH_TABLE_SIZE)) % HASH_TABLE_SIZE


/********* STRUCTS AND TYPES *********/

typedef struct Polygonstruct {
    Point3      *vertices;  /* polygon vertices */
    Vector3     *normals;   /* normal at each vertex */
    Vector3     normal;     /* normal for polygon */
    int         numVerts;   /* number of vertices */
    void        *user;      /* user information */
    struct      Polygonstruct *next;
    } Polygon_def;
typedef Polygon_def *Polygon;

typedef struct HashNodestruct {
    Polygon   polygon;      /* polygon for this vertex */
    int       vertexNum;    /* which vertex this is */
    int       marked;       /* vertex status */
    struct    HashNodestruct *next;
    } HashNode_def;
typedef HashNode_def *HashNode;

typedef struct SmoothStruct {
    HashNode  hashTable[HASH_TABLE_SIZE];
    Polygon   polygonTable;
    Polygon   polyTail;
    double    fuzz;         /* distance for vertex equality */
    double    fuzzFraction; /* fraction of model size for fuzz */
    boolean   edgeTest;     /* apply edging test using minDot */
    float     minDot;       /* if > this, make sharp edge; see above */
    } Smooth_def;
typedef Smooth_def *Smooth;

/********* public procs ************/
Smooth    initAllTables();
void      includePolygon(int numVerts, Point3 *verts, Smooth smooth, void *user);
void      makeVertexNormals(Smooth smooth);

/********* public option contorl procs ************/
void      setFuzzFraction(Smooth smooth, float fuzzFraction);
void      enableEdgePreservation(Smooth smooth, float minDot);
void      disableEdgePreservation(Smooth smooth);
```

Smoothing Code

```
/* smooth.c - Compute vertex normals for polygons.
   Andrew S. Glassner / Xerox PARC
```

The general idea is to 1) initialize the tables, 2) add polygons one by one,
3) optionally enable edge preservation, 4) optionally set the fuzz factor,
5) compute the normals, 6) do something with the new normals, then 7) free
the new storage. The calls to do this are:

```
1) smooth = initAllTables();
2) includePolygon(int numVerts, Point3 *verts, Smooth smooth);
3) (optional) enableEdgePreservation(Smooth smooth, float minDot);
4) (optional) setFuzzFraction(smooth Smooth, float fuzzFraction);
5) makeVertexNormals(smooth);
6) YOUR CODE
7) freeSmooth(smooth);
```

Edge preservation is used to retain sharp creases in the model. If it is
enabled, then the dot product of each pair of polygons sharing a vertex
is computed. If this value is below the value of 'minDot' (that is,
the two polygons are a certain distance away from flatness), then the
polygons are not averaged together for the vertex normal.

If you want to re-compute the results without edge preservation, call
  disableEdgePreservation(smooth);

The general flow of the algorithm is:
```
  1. currentHash = scan hashTable
  2. while (any unmarked) {
      3. firstVertex = first unmarked vertex.  set to MARKWORKING
      4. normal = firstVertex->polygon->normal
      5. scan currentHash.  If vertex = firstVertex
          6. normal += vertex->polygon->normal
          7. set vertex to MARKWORKING
          (end of scan)
      8. set normal to unit length
      9. scan currentHash.  If vertex set to MARKWORKING
          10. set vertex->normal = normal
          11. set to MARKDONE
          (end of scan)
      (end while)
```

The HASH macro must always return a non-negative value, even for negative inputs.
The size of the hash table can be adjusted to taste.
The fuzz for comparison needs to be matched to the resolution of the model.
```
*/
```

```
#include "smooth.h"
```

```
void      addVertexToTable(Point3 *pt, Polygon polygon, int vNum, Smooth smooth);
void      makePolyNormal(Polygon polygon);
void      writeSmooth(FILE *fp, int numPolys);
HashNode getFirstWaitingNode(HashNode node);
void      processHashNode(HashNode headNode, HashNode firstNode, Smooth smooth);
int       hashPolys(boolean phase);
void      writeGeom(int numPolys);
void      freeSmooth(Smooth smooth);
```

```
boolean  compareVerts(Point3 *v0, Point3 *v1, Smooth smooth);
void     computeFuzz(Smooth smooth);

/********* ENTRY PROCS *********/

/* add this polygon to the tables */
void includePolygon(int numVerts, Point3 *verts, Smooth smooth, void *user) {
int i;
Point3 *vp, *ovp;
    Polygon polygon = NEWTYPE(Polygon_def);
    polygon->next = NULL;
    if (smooth->polyTail != NULL) {
      smooth->polyTail->next = polygon;
    } else {
        smooth->polygonTable = polygon;
    };
    smooth->polyTail = polygon;
    polygon->vertices = NEWA(struct Point3Struct, numVerts);
    polygon->normals = NEWA(struct Point3Struct, numVerts);
    polygon->user = user;
    vp = polygon->vertices;
    ovp = verts;
    polygon->numVerts = numVerts;

    for (i=0; i<numVerts; i++) {
        vp->x = ovp->x;
        vp->y = ovp->y;
        vp->z = ovp->z;
        addVertexToTable(vp, polygon, i, smooth);
        vp++;
        ovp++;
        };
    makePolyNormal(polygon);
    }

void enableEdgePreservation(Smooth smooth, float minDot) {
    smooth->edgeTest = TRUE;
    smooth->minDot = minDot;
    }

void disableEdgePreservation(Smooth smooth) {
    smooth->edgeTest = FALSE;
    }

void setFuzzFraction(Smooth smooth, float fuzzFraction) {
    smooth->fuzzFraction = fuzzFraction;
    }

/******** PROCEDURES ********/

/* set all the hash-table linked lists to NULL */
Smooth initAllTables() {
int i;
```

```
Smooth smooth = NEWTYPE(Smooth_def);
    for (i=0; i<HASH_TABLE_SIZE; i++) smooth->hashTable[i] = NULL;
    smooth->polygonTable = NULL;
    smooth->polyTail = NULL;
    smooth->edgeTest = FALSE;
    smooth->minDot = 0.2;
    smooth->fuzzFraction = 0.001;
    smooth->fuzz = 0.001;
    return(smooth);
    }

/* hash this vertex and add it into the linked list */
void addVertexToTable(Point3 *pt, Polygon polygon, int vNum, Smooth smooth) {
int hash = HASH(pt);
HashNode newNode = NEWTYPE(HashNode_def);
    newNode->next = smooth->hashTable[hash];
    smooth->hashTable[hash] = newNode;
    newNode->polygon = polygon;
    newNode->vertexNum = vNum;
    newNode->marked = MARKWAITING;
    }

/* compute the normal for this polygon using Newell's method */
/* (see Tampieri, Gems III, p. 517) */
void makePolyNormal(Polygon polygon) {
Point3 *vp, *p0, *p1;
int i;
    polygon->normal.x = 0.0; polygon->normal.y = 0.0; polygon->normal.z = 0.0;
    vp = polygon->vertices;
    for (i=0; i<polygon->numVerts; i++) {
        p0 = vp++;
        p1 = vp;
        if (i == polygon->numVerts-1) p1 = polygon->vertices;
        polygon->normal.x += (p1->y - p0->y) * (p1->z + p0->z);
        polygon->normal.y += (p1->z - p0->z) * (p1->x + p0->x);
        polygon->normal.z += (p1->x - p0->x) * (p1->y + p0->y);
        };
    (void) V3Normalize(&(polygon->normal));
    }

/* scan each list at each hash table entry until all nodes are marked */
void makeVertexNormals(Smooth smooth) {
HashNode currentHashNode;
HashNode firstNode;
int i;
    computeFuzz(smooth);
    for (i=0; i<HASH_TABLE_SIZE; i++) {
        currentHashNode = smooth->hashTable[i];
        do {
            firstNode = getFirstWaitingNode(currentHashNode);
            if (firstNode != NULL) {
                processHashNode(currentHashNode, firstNode, smooth);
                };
```

```
                } while (firstNode != NULL);
            };
        }

void computeFuzz(Smooth smooth) {
Point3 min, max;
double od, d;
Point3 *v;
int i;
Polygon poly = smooth->polygonTable;
    min.x = max.x = poly->vertices->x;
    min.y = max.y = poly->vertices->y;
    min.z = max.z = poly->vertices->z;
    while (poly != NULL) {
        v = poly->vertices;
        for (i=0; i<poly->numVerts; i++) {
            if (v->x < min.x) min.x = v->x;
            if (v->y < min.y) min.y = v->y;
            if (v->z < min.z) min.z = v->z;
            if (v->x > max.x) max.x = v->x;
            if (v->y > max.y) max.y = v->y;
            if (v->z > max.z) max.z = v->z;
            v++;
            };
        poly = poly->next;
        };
    d = fabs(max.x - min.x);
    od = fabs(max.y - min.y);  if (od > d) d = od;
    od = fabs(max.z - min.z);  if (od > d) d = od;
    smooth->fuzz = od * smooth->fuzzFraction;
    }


/* get first node in this list that isn't marked as done */
HashNode getFirstWaitingNode(HashNode node) {
    while (node != NULL) {
        if (node->marked != MARKDONE) return(node);
        node = node->next;
        };
    return(NULL);
    }


/* are these two vertices the same to with the tolerance? */
boolean compareVerts(Point3 *v0, Point3 *v1, Smooth smooth) {
    float q0, q1;
    q0 = QUANT(v0->x); q1 = QUANT(v1->x); if (!FUZZEQ(q0, q1)) return(FALSE);
    q0 = QUANT(v0->y); q1 = QUANT(v1->y); if (!FUZZEQ(q0, q1)) return(FALSE);
    q0 = QUANT(v0->z); q1 = QUANT(v1->z); if (!FUZZEQ(q0, q1)) return(FALSE);
    return(TRUE);
    }


/* compute the normal for an unmarked vertex */
void processHashNode(HashNode headNode, HashNode firstNode, Smooth smooth) {
    HashNode scanNode = firstNode->next;
```

```
    Point3 *firstVert = &(firstNode->polygon->vertices[firstNode->vertexNum]);
    Point3 *headNorm = &(firstNode->polygon->normal);
    Point3 *testVert, *testNorm;
    Point3 normal;
    float ndot;

    firstNode->marked = MARKWORKING;
    normal.x = firstNode->polygon->normal.x;
    normal.y = firstNode->polygon->normal.y;
    normal.z = firstNode->polygon->normal.z;

    while (scanNode != NULL) {
        testVert = &(scanNode->polygon->vertices[scanNode->vertexNum]);
        if (compareVerts(testVert, firstVert, smooth)) {
            testNorm = &(scanNode->polygon->normal);
            ndot = V3Dot(testNorm, headNorm);

                if ((!(smooth->edgeTest)) || (ndot > smooth->minDot)) {
                V3Add(&normal, testNorm, &normal);
                scanNode->marked = MARKWORKING;
                };
            };
        scanNode = scanNode->next;
        };

    V3Normalize(&normal);

    scanNode = firstNode;
    while (scanNode != NULL) {
        if (scanNode->marked == MARKWORKING) {
            testNorm = &(scanNode->polygon->normals[scanNode->vertexNum]);
            testNorm->x = normal.x;
            testNorm->y = normal.y;
            testNorm->z = normal.z;
            scanNode->marked = MARKDONE;
            testVert = &(scanNode->polygon->vertices[scanNode->vertexNum]);
            };
        scanNode = scanNode->next;
        };
    }

/* free up all the memory */
void freeSmooth(Smooth smooth) {
HashNode headNode;
HashNode nextNode;
Polygon poly;
Polygon nextPoly;
int i;
    for (i=0; i<HASH_TABLE_SIZE; i++) {
        headNode = smooth->hashTable[i];
        while (headNode != NULL) {
            nextNode = headNode->next;
            free(headNode);
```

```
                  headNode = nextNode;
                  };
            };
      poly = smooth->polygonTable;
      while (poly != NULL) {
            nextPoly = poly->next;
            freePoly(poly);
            poly = nextPoly;
            };
      smooth->polygonTable = NULL;
      free(smooth);
      }

freePoly(polygon) Polygon polygon; {
      if (polygon->vertices != NULL) free(polygon->vertices);
      if (polygon->normals != NULL) free(polygon->normals);
      polygon->next = NULL;
      free(polygon);
      }
```

Sample Driver

```
/* test.c - sample driver for polygon smoother */
/* makes a mesh height field of quadrilaterals and triangles */
/* Andrew S. Glassner / Xerox PARC */

#include "smooth.h"

#ifdef STANDALONE_TEST
/* from Graphics Gems library ; for standalone compile */

/* normalizes the input vector and returns it */
Vector3 *V3Normalize(Vector3 *v) {
  double len = sqrt(V3Dot(v, v));
  if (len != 0.0) { v->x /= len;  v->y /= len; v->z /= len; }
  return(v);
  }

/* return vector sum c = a+b */
Vector3 *V3Add(Vector3 *a, Vector3 *b, Vector3 *c) {
  c->x = a->x+b->x;  c->y = a->y+b->y;  c->z = a->z+b->z;
  return(c);
  }

/* return the dot product of vectors a and b */
double V3Dot(Vector3 *a, Vector3 *b) {
  return((a->x*b->x)+(a->y*b->y)+(a->z*b->z));
  }
#endif
```

```
/* make a square height field of quadrilaterals and triangles */
main(int ac, char *av[]) {
int xres, yres;
Smooth smooth;
  if (ac < 3) { printf("use: test x y\n"); exit(-1); };  /* abrupt, I know */
  xres = atoi(*++av);
  yres = atoi(*++av);
  smooth = initAllTables();              /* initialize */
  buildMesh(smooth, xres, yres);         /* build the mesh (calls includePolygon) */
  enableEdgePreservation(smooth, 0.0);   /* 90 degree folds or more stay crisp */
  makeVertexNormals(smooth);             /* build the normals */
  savePolys(smooth);                     /* save the result in a file */
  freeSmooth(smooth);                    /* take only normals, leave only footprints */
  }

/* z=f(x,y) */
double fofxy(double x, double y) {
   double h;
   h = 2.0 * (0.5 - x); if (h < 0) h = -h; h = h * y;
   return(h);
   }

buildMesh(Smooth smooth, int xres, int yres) {
int x, y;
Point3 *vlist;
double dx, dy, lx, ly, hx, hy;
  vlist = NEWA(struct Point3Struct, 4);
  dx = 1.0/((double)(xres));
  dy = 1.0/((double)(yres));
  for (y=0; y<yres; y++) {
    ly = y * dy;
    hy = (y+1) * dy;
    for (x=0; x<xres; x++) {
       lx = x * dx;
       hx = (x+1) * dx;
       if ((x+y)%2 == 0) addTriangles(lx, ly, hx, hy, vlist, smooth);
                else addQuadrilateral(lx, ly, hx, hy, vlist, smooth);
     };
   };
  free(vlist);
  }

addTriangles(double lx, double ly, double hx, double hy,
          Point3 *vlist, Smooth smooth) {
Point3 *p = vlist;
   /* make the first triangle */
   p->x = lx;  p->y = ly;  p->z = fofxy(p->x, p->y); p++;
   p->x = hx;  p->y = ly;  p->z = fofxy(p->x, p->y); p++;
   p->x = lx;  p->y = hy;  p->z = fofxy(p->x, p->y); p++;
   includePolygon(3, vlist, smooth, NULL);  /* add the polygon */
   /* make the other triangle */
   p = vlist;
   p->x = hx;  p->y = ly;  p->z = fofxy(p->x, p->y); p++;
```

```
   p->x = hx;   p->y = hy;   p->z = fofxy(p->x, p->y); p++;
   p->x = lx;   p->y = hy;   p->z = fofxy(p->x, p->y); p++;
   includePolygon(3, vlist, smooth, NULL);   /* add the polygon */
   }


addQuadrilateral(double lx, double ly, double hx, double hy,
                 Point3 *vlist, Smooth smooth) {
Point3 *p = vlist;
   p->x = lx;   p->y = ly;   p->z = fofxy(p->x, p->y); p++;
   p->x = hx;   p->y = ly;   p->z = fofxy(p->x, p->y); p++;
   p->x = hx;   p->y = hy;   p->z = fofxy(p->x, p->y); p++;
   p->x = lx;   p->y = hy;   p->z = fofxy(p->x, p->y); p++;
   includePolygon(4, vlist, smooth, NULL);   /* add the polygon */
   }


savePolys(Smooth smooth) {
Polygon poly = smooth->polygonTable;
int i, k;
Point3 *v, *n;
   printf("NQUAD\n");    /* header for point/normal format */
   while (poly != NULL) {
      for (i=0; i<4; i++) {
         k = i;    /* we always write 4 points so double 3rd triangle vertex */
         if (i >= poly->numVerts) k = poly->numVerts-1;
         v = &(poly->vertices[k]);
         n = &(poly->normals[k]);
         printf("%f %f %f %f %f %f\n", v->x, v->y, v->z, n->x, n->y, n->z);
         };
      printf("\n");
      poly = poly->next;
      };
   }
```

◇ **Bibliography** ◇

(Foley *et al.* 1990) James Foley, Andries van Dam, Steven Feiner, and John Hughes. *Computer Graphics Principles and Practice*, second edition. Addison-Wesley, Reading, 1990.

(Glassner 1990) Andrew S. Glassner. Computing surface normals for 3d models. In Andrew S. Glassner, editor, *Graphics Gems*, chapter 10.12. Academic Press, Boston, 1990.

(Sutherland *et al.* 1974) I. E. Sutherland, R. F. Sproull, and R. A. Schumacker. A characterization of ten hidden-surface algorithms. *AMC Computing Surveys*, 6(1):1–55, 1974.

(Tampieri 1992) Filippo Tampieri. Newell's method for computing the plane equation of a polygon. In David Kirk, editor, *Graphics Gems III*, chapter V.5. Academic Press, Boston, 1992.

I.7

Detecting Intersection of a Rectangular Solid and a Convex Polyhedron

Ned Greene
Apple Computer and University of California at Santa Cruz
One Infinite Loop, MS 301-3J
Cupertino, CA 95014
greene@apple.com

This Gem presents a fast method for determining whether a rectangular solid intersects a convex polyhedron. Our algorithm is based on the observation that a rectangular solid R intersects a convex polyhedron P if and only if (a) the projections of R and P intersect in all three axis-aligned orthographic views (i.e., front, side, and top views), and (b) R does not lie entirely "outside" the plane of any face of P. After finding the equations of certain lines and planes associated with P, we can determine whether these criteria are satisfied by simply evaluating inequalities. The method is well suited to culling a geometric model organized in an octree to a viewing frustum. For this application, determining whether a bounding box intersects a viewing frustum requires evaluating between one and thirty inequalities. The method can also be applied to detecting the intersection of a rectangular solid and a 3D planar polygon.

$$\diamond \quad \textbf{Introduction} \quad \diamond$$

Beginning with some definitions, we will refer to a convex polyhedron simply as a polyhedron and to an axis-aligned rectangular solid simply as a box. The term "bounding box" will specifically refer to a "tight," axis-aligned rectangle in 2D or rectangular solid in 3D. Axis-aligned orthographic views, the familiar front, side, and top views of engineering drawings, will be referred to simply as orthographic views.

Various computer graphics techniques associate bounding boxes in the shape of rectangular solids with clusters of geometric primitives to enhance efficiency, the idea being that performing a single operation on a bounding box often eliminates the need to process primitives inside the box individually. When culling a geometric model to a viewing frustum, for example, if a bounding box lies outside the frustum, the primitives it contains also lie outside and need not be considered individually. This observation underlies simple, fast procedures for culling models represented in spatial hierarchies.

For example, if geometric primitives are organized in an octree of bounding boxes, parts of the model which lie entirely outside a viewing frustum can be efficiently culled by testing for box-frustum intersection during recursive subdivision of the octree (Garlick et al. 1990).

Since box-polyhedron intersection tests may be performed hundreds or thousands of times in the course of producing a single image of a scene, devising an efficient intersection algorithm is worthwhile. One intuitive approach to the problem combines a test for intersecting bounding boxes, tests to see if a vertex of one solid lies inside the other, and tests to see if an edge of one solid intersects a face of the other. While this method is very straightforward, the expense of finding geometric intersections makes it quite costly. Alternatively, we could employ algorithms for detecting intersection of convex polyhedra that are described in the computational geometry literature, for example, the method of Chazelle and Dobkin (Chazelle and Dobkin 1987). However, such methods are typically complicated, designed with asymptotic performance in mind, and poorly suited to simple problems like deciding whether a box intersects a viewing frustum.

Our approach is both simple and efficient. It does not require finding geometric intersections, but rather, after finding the equations of certain lines and planes associated with a polyhedron, box-polyhedron intersection can be determined by simply comparing bounding boxes and evaluating inequalities. The algorithm performs most efficiently when comparing numerous bounding boxes to the same polyhedron, but even when performing a single intersection test, efficiency compares favorably to other methods.

We precede our analysis of box-polyhedron intersection with a discussion of primitive operations that our algorithm performs — determining whether a box intersects a plane, whether a rectangle intersects a line, and whether a rectangle intersects a polygon.

◇ **Box-Plane and Rectangle-Line Intersection** ◇

One of the fundamental operations performed by our box-polyhedron intersection algorithm is determining whether a box intersects a plane, and if not, which side of the plane the box lies on. The problem is illustrated in Figure 1, an orthographic projection in which the viewpoint has been chosen so that plane P is perpendicular to the screen. Vector N is normal to P, pointing into P's positive half-space.[1] Box B1 lies in P's negative half-space, box B2 lies in P's positive half-space, and box B3 intersects P. These are the three cases that we wish to distinguish in general.

The first step in distinguishing these cases is to establish which of a box's vertices lies farthest in the "positive direction" (the direction of normal N), call this the *p-vertex*,

---

[1] Recall that a plane defined by equation $Ax+By+Cz+D=0$ has normal (A,B,C) and divides space into a *positive half-space* satisfying the equation $Ax+By+Cz+D>0$ and a *negative half-space* satisfying the equation $Ax+By+Cz+D<0$.

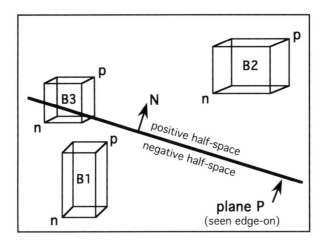

Figure 1.

and which of the box's vertices lies farthest in the "negative direction," call this the *n-vertex*. P- and n-vertices are easily identified, since the p-vertex corresponds to the octant of the plane's normal, and the n-vertex lies at the opposite corner. When an edge or face of the box is parallel to the plane, the octant rule does not specify a unique vertex, but in these cases it doesn't matter which of the obvious candidates is selected. In Figure 1 p-vertices are labeled **p** and n-vertices are labeled **n**. Note that the p- and n-vertices associated with a particular plane have the same relative positions on all axis-aligned bounding boxes, so they need to be identified only once.

Once p- and n-vertices have been identified, distinguishing the three cases of box-plane intersection is very simple. Box B lies entirely in plane P's negative half-space if and only if its p-vertex lies in P's negative half-space, B lies entirely in P's positive half-space if and only if its n-vertex lies in P's positive half-space, and if neither of these relationships holds, B intersects P (Haines and Wallace 1991). It follows that we can determine whether a box lies in a particular half-space by evaluating one plane equation, and that the three cases of box-plane intersection can be distinguished by evaluating one or two plane equations as follows:

```
Given an axis-aligned rectangular solid R with n-vertex (xn,yn,zn) and
p-vertex (xp,yp,zp), and plane P with equation Ax+By+Cz+D=0,

if (A*xp + B*yp + C*zp + D < 0) { R lies entirely in P's negative half-space }
else if (A*xn + B*yn + C*zn + D > 0) { R lies entirely in P's positive half-space }
else{ R intersects P }
```

The two-dimensional problem of determining whether an axis-aligned rectangle intersects a line, lies entirely in the line's negative half-plane, or lies entirely in the line's positive half-plane is entirely analogous, requiring the evaluation of one or two line equations.

```
Given an axis-aligned rectangle R with n-vertex (xn,yn) and p-vertex (xp,yp),
and line L with equation Ax+By+C=0,

if (A*xp + B*yp + C < 0) { R lies entirely in L's negative half-plane }
else if (A*xn + B*yn + C > 0) { R lies entirely in L's positive half-plane }
else{ R intersects L }
```

◇ Rectangle-Polygon Intersection ◇

We now consider another subproblem, determining whether an axis-aligned rectangle R and a convex polygon P, both lying in the same plane, intersect. It can easily be shown that R intersects P if and only if (a) R intersects P's bounding box and (b) R does not lie entirely "outside"[2] any of the infinite lines defined by P's edges, which we will refer to as *edge-lines*. The problem is illustrated in Figure 2 where P's bounding box B is drawn in dashed lines and P's edge-lines are drawn in dotted lines (e.g., E). Applying the intersection criteria to rectangles R1, R2, and R3 of Figure 2, R1 is found not to intersect P because it does not intersect P's bounding box, R2 is found not to intersect P because it lies outside of edge-line E, and R3 is found to intersect P because it satisfies both intersection criteria.

The rectangle-line intersection method described in the preceding section is an efficient way to evaluate criterion (b). Using this method we can determine whether a rectangle lies outside an edge-line by substituting the coordinates of the rectangle's n-vertex into the edge-line's equation. For example, to show that R2 lies outside edge-line E we would substitute the coordinates of R2's lower left vertex (the n-vertex for E) into the line equation for E.

The rectangle-polygon intersection problem is germane because our algorithm looks for box-polyhedron intersection in orthographic views,[3] and in these views a box always projects to an axis-aligned rectangle and the silhouette of a convex polyhedron is always a convex polygon. These conditions apply, for example, in Figure 3 where the panels labeled "front," "side," and "top" are orthographic views of a box and a polyhedron in the shape of a viewing frustum. Once the polygonal silhouette of the polyhedron has been identified in an orthographic view,[4] determining whether box-polyhedron intersection occurs in that view reduces to the rectangle-polygon intersection problem described above. Incidentally, Figure 3 illustrates that intersection of a box and a polyhedron in

---

[2]By "outside" we mean on the side opposite polygon P.

[3]Remember that *axis-aligned* is implied in this term.

[4]Finding a convex polyhedron's silhouette edges is particularly straightforward in an orthographic view. In a view down an axis, call it the u-axis, if the u components of the outward-pointing normals of two adjacent faces have opposite signs, their common edge is a silhouette edge.

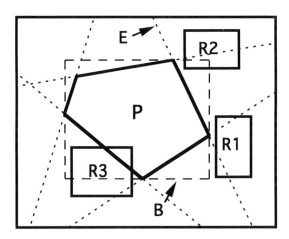

Figure 2. Testing for intersection between a polygon P and various rectangles R_i.

all three orthographic views does not guarantee intersection in 3D, as is apparent in the upper right panel.

It follows from the rules for rectangle-polygon intersection that the projections of a box B and a polyhedron P intersect in all three orthographic views if and only if (1) B intersects P's bounding box and (2) the projection of B does not lie outside any of the edge-lines of P's silhouette in any of the three orthographic views. Our box-polyhedron intersection algorithm uses this formulation to establish intersection in orthographic views, as elaborated in the following section.

◇ Box-Polyhedron Intersection ◇

Our box-polyhedron intersection algorithm is based on the observation that for any two convex polyhedra A and B which do not intersect, there exists a *separating plane* lying between them that is (1) parallel to a face of A, (2) parallel to a face of B, or (3) parallel to an edge of A and an edge of B.[5]

Applying this observation to a rectangular solid R and a convex polyhedron P, we will say that a separating plane which is parallel to a face of R is of *type 1*, a separating plane which is parallel to a face of P is of *type 2*, and a separating plane which is parallel to an edge of R and an edge of P is of *type 3*. If a separating plane of type 1, 2, or 3 exists, R and P do not intersect; otherwise they do.

---

[5]My thanks to an anonymous reviewer for pointing this out and suggesting the ensuing line of exposition. As a starting point for a proof, consider two non-interpenetrating convex polyhedra whose surfaces are in contact, e.g., a vertex touches a face, an edge touches an edge, an edge touches a face, etc. For any possible configuration, a plane of type 1, 2, or 3 separates the polyhedra except for the point, line segment, or polygon of contact.

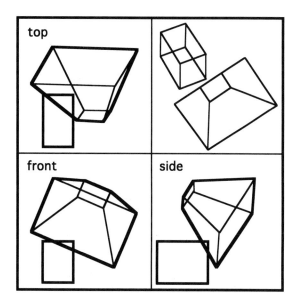

Figure 3. Four views of a rectangular solid and a polyhedron in the shape of a viewing frustum. The front, side, and top views are axis-aligned orthographic views.

We can easily see whether a type 1 plane exists by determining whether P's bounding box intersects R. If so, a type 1 plane does not exist; if not, a type 1 plane does exist, demonstrating that R and P do not intersect, and we are done.

We can see whether a type 2 plane exists by comparing each face-plane of P with the corresponding n-vertex of R using the method presented in the section on box-plane intersection. If any of these n-vertices is outside of its respective face-plane, there exists a type 2 separating plane demonstrating that R and P do not intersect and we are done.

The remaining problem is to determine whether a separating plane of type 3 exists. Since a type 3 plane is parallel to an edge of R, it projects to a "separating line" lying between the projections of R and P in one of the orthographic views. It follows that a type 3 plane exists if and only if the projections of R and P do not intersect in at least one of the three orthographic views. Combining this observation with intersection criterion (2) from the preceding section, the existence of a type 3 plane can be decided by determining whether the projection of R lies outside an edge-line of P in at least one orthographic view.[6] If so, a type 3 plane exists, establishing that R and P do not intersect; if not, a type 3 plane does not exist and we conclude that R and P intersect because no type 1, 2, or 3 separating plane exists.

---

[6]Note that we have already established that R intersects P's bounding box, satisfying intersection criterion (1) from the preceding section.

Incidentally, the conditions for box-polyhedron intersection can be stated very concisely as follows: Box R intersects polyhedron P if and only if (a) the projections of R and P intersect in all three orthographic views, and (b) R does not lie entirely outside the plane of any face of P. In this formulation the requirement that R intersects P's bounding box is subsumed by condition (a). The analogous intersection conditions for a box R and a 3D planar polygon P are as follows: R and P intersect if and only if the projections of R and P intersect in all three orthographic views and R intersects the plane of P.

◇ Summary of the Algorithm ◇

Let's reiterate the algorithm as it is applied in practice with efficient execution in mind. Assuming for the moment that polyhedron P will be compared to numerous boxes, we begin with the following preliminary steps: 1) for each face of P we find the plane equation and identify which box corner is the n-vertex; 2) for each silhouette edge of P in the three orthographic views we find the line equation and identify which box corner is the n-vertex;[7] and 3) we find P's bounding box. If P will be compared to only a small number of boxes, lazy evaluation of this information may be more efficient.

Now box-polyhedron intersection testing proceeds as follows. If box R does not intersect P's bounding box, we conclude that R does not intersect P and we are done. Next we consider P's face-planes one by one, seeing if R lies entirely outside any of these planes. If so, we conclude that R does not intersect P and we are done. Finally, we consider P's edge-lines[8] one by one, seeing if R's projection lies entirely outside any of these lines in the appropriate orthographic view. If so, we conclude that R does not intersect P and we are done. Otherwise, it has been established that intersection does occur.

To estimate the computational expense of the algorithm we examine the cost of the primitive operations. We can determine whether two 3D bounding boxes intersect by evaluating between one and six simple inequalities of the form "is a < b?" Determining whether a box lies entirely outside a face-plane requires evaluating one plane equation. Determining whether a box's projection lies entirely outside an edge-line requires evaluating one line equation. So when comparing a box to a polyhedron with F faces and E silhouette edges in orthographic views, each box-polyhedron intersection test requires evaluating between one and six simple inequalities, evaluating between zero and F plane equations, and evaluating between zero and E line equations. Summing up, between 1 and 6 + E + F inequalities must be evaluated to show that B and P do not intersect, and all 6 + E + F inequalities must be evaluated to show that B and

---

[7] Pick either of the two vertices which coincide in the orthographic view.

[8] I.e., the lines defined by P's silhouette edges in the three orthographic views.

P do intersect. For a viewing frustum, E is at most 18 and F is 6, so the maximum number of inequalities which must be evaluated to decide box-frustum intersection is 30. Our cost estimate should also amortize the cost of finding line and plane equations and identifying n-vertices over the number of intersection tests performed.

There are many variations on this basic algorithm. To avoid evaluating all $6 + E + F$ inequalities whenever intersection occurs, a test can be added to see if the polyhedron lies entirely inside the box or vice versa. When culling geometry to a viewing frustum it may be useful to know which of the frustum's face-planes a box intersects, because they correspond to clipping planes. These refinements are included in the procedure outlined in the following section which we use to cull an octree to a viewing frustum.

◇ **Pseudocode** ◇

Given a collection of axis-aligned rectangular solids and a convex polyhedron P, the following procedure classifies each rectangular solid R as entirely outside, entirely inside, or partially inside P, and in the latter case reports which face-planes of P are intersected by R. The procedure can be streamlined for applications which only need to detect intersection.

```
/* Routine for Detecting Box-Polyhedron Intersection */

/* Preliminary Step */
Determine P's bounding box.
Find the plane equation of each face of P (these are face-planes).
Determine which vertex of an axis-aligned rectangular solid is the "n-vertex"
    and which is the "p-vertex" for each face-plane of P.
Determine the silhouette edges of P's projection in the three orthographic
    views, and find the line equation of each of these edges (these are edge-lines).
Determine which vertex of an axis-aligned rectangular solid is the "n-vertex"
    for each edge-line of P.

For each rectangular solid R {
    /* Bounding Box Tests */
    if R does not intersect P's bounding box, R is entirely outside P, done with R
    if P's bounding box is entirely inside R, R is partially inside P and R
        intersects all face-planes, done with R

    /* Face-Plane Tests */
    for each face-plane F {
        if R is entirely outside F, R is entirely outside P, done with R
        if R is entirely inside F, set a flag indicating that R does not intersect F
        else R intersects F, set a flag indicating that R intersects F
    }
    if R was entirely inside all face-planes, R is entirely inside P, done with R
```

```
/* Edge-Line Tests */
for each edge-line E
    if the projection of R is entirely outside E (in the appropriate
        orthographic projection), R is entirely outside P, done with R

R is partially inside P and it is known which face-planes R intersects
}
```

◇   **Bibliography**   ◇

(Chazelle and Dobkin 1987) B. Chazelle and D. Dobkin. Intersection of convex objects in two and three dimensions. *Journal of the ACM*, 34(1):1–27, Jan. 1987.

(Garlick et al. 1990) B. Garlick, D. Baum, and J. Winget. Interactive viewing of large geometric data bases using multiprocessor graphics workstations. Siggraph '90, Course Notes, Vol. 28 (Parallel Algorithms and Architectures for 3D Image Generation), pp. 239–245.

(Haines and Wallace 1991) E. Haines and J. Wallace. Shaft culling for efficient ray-traced radiosity. SIGGRAPH '91, Course Notes, Vol. 12 (Frontiers in Rendering), pp. 2.1–2.28.

◇ I.8

Fast Collision Detection of Moving Convex Polyhedra

Rich Rabbitz

Martin Marietta, 138-202
Moorestown, NJ 08057
rrabbitz%pgn138fs@serling.motown.ge.com

◇ Introduction ◇

Traditional animation systems do not consider the possibility of two objects colliding. Two objects crossing the same path are simply allowed to move through each other, creating an unrealistic effect. A more realistic approach would be to detect when two objects collide and apply the laws of physics to compute an impulse. As a minimum capability, an animation system should allow the animator to visualize when two objects collide. This would allow the empirical simulation of an impulse.

This Gem combines ideas from (Baraff 1990) and (Gilbert *et al.* 1988) to form an efficient algorithm for collision detection in an environment where the basic modeling primitives are represented as convex polyhedra. The main collision detection algorithm calls a distance algorithm that can be tailored to compute efficiently the minimum distance between two convex polyhedra in R^3, or between two convex polygons in R^2. C code is provided. Readers not interested in a summary of the algorithm can skip straight to the code.

◇ Background ◇

This section reviews some necessary equations and definitions from convex analysis. For completeness a brief summary is given of the results presented in (Gilbert *et al.* 1988) and (Rockafellar 1970), where more detailed discussions can be obtained.

All geometry will be defined in Euclidean space. The inner product of points $W, Q \in R^n$ is denoted by $\langle W, Q \rangle = \sum_{i=1}^{n} w_i q_i$. The Euclidean norm is denoted $\|W\| = \sqrt{\langle W, W \rangle}$. An object can be represented by the space it occupies with a compact set $S \subset R^n$. Then, the minimum distance between two objects is defined by

$$d(S_1, S_2) = \min \|W - Q\|, \quad W \in S_1, \quad Q \in S_2 \tag{1}$$

In R^n a set of points S is convex if any two points $W, Q \in S$ form a line segment that is entirely contained in S. It is a closed convex set if it is finitely bounded. For our purposes all convex sets are assumed to be closed. The affine and convex hulls of a set of points $S \in R^n$ are defined by

$$\text{aff}(S) = \left\{ \sum_{i=1}^{r} \lambda_i Q_i, \text{ where } \sum_{i=1}^{r} \lambda_i = 1, \quad Q_i \in S, \quad \lambda_i \in R \right\} \tag{2}$$

$$\text{conv}(S) = \left\{ \sum_{i=1}^{r} \lambda_i Q_i, \text{ where } \sum_{i=1}^{r} \lambda_i = 1, \quad \lambda_i \geq 0, \quad Q_i \in S, \quad \lambda_i \in R \right\} \tag{3}$$

In R^n a point W is linearly dependent on a set of points $S = \{Q_1, \ldots, Q_m\}$ if there exist some real scalar numbers $\lambda_1, \ldots, \lambda_m$ such that $W = \lambda_1 Q_1 + \cdots + \lambda_m Q_m$. If we impose the additional condition that $\lambda_1 + \cdots + \lambda_m = 1$, then W is affinely dependent on S. If we add the constraint that all $\lambda_i \geq 0$, then W is convexly dependent on S. A set of points $S = \{Q_1, \ldots, Q_m\}$ is affinely independent if no single point Q_i of S is affinely dependent on all the other members of S. If V is a finite set of points, the convex hull of V is called a **convex polytope**. For the sake of brevity, when we refer to polytope, it implies convex polytope.

In R^n a hyperplane H is defined by $\{Q \in R^n : \langle Q, \mathbf{A} \rangle = \beta\}$, where $\mathbf{A} \neq \mathbf{0}$ is normal to H. H is an affine subspace of R^n of dimension $n - 1$. H divides R^n into two half-spaces. These half-spaces can be open or closed. The two closed half-spaces corresponding to H are defined as $H- = \{Q \in R^n : \langle Q, \mathbf{A} \rangle \leq \beta\}$, and $H+ = \{Q \in R^n : \langle Q, \mathbf{A} \rangle \geq \beta\}$.

If S is a compact convex set, $S \cap H \neq \varnothing$, and S is contained in one of the closed half-spaces determined by H, then H is a supporting hyperplane of S. The supporting function $H_S : R^n \mapsto R$ of S is defined by

$$H_S(\mathbf{A}) = \max\{\langle Q, \mathbf{A} \rangle : Q \in S\}, \quad \mathbf{A} \in R^n \tag{4}$$

We denote the contact function $C_S(\mathbf{A}) : R^n \mapsto S$ as a solution to (4) where $C_S(\mathbf{A})$ satisfies

$$H_S(\mathbf{A}) = \langle C_S(\mathbf{A}), \mathbf{A} \rangle, \quad C_S(\mathbf{A}) \in S \tag{5}$$

for all $\mathbf{A}$ in R^n. $C_S(\mathbf{A})$ defines a point farthest in S in the direction of $\mathbf{A}$. If $\{Q_1, \ldots, Q_r\}$, where $Q_i \in V$ is a finite set of points in R^n the support and contact functions for the conv(V) are similarly defined by

$$H_{\text{conv}(V)}(\mathbf{A}) = \max\{\langle Q_i, \mathbf{A} \rangle, \quad i = 1, \ldots, r\}, \quad \mathbf{A} \in R^n \tag{6}$$

and

$$C_{\text{conv}(V)}(\mathbf{A}) = Q_j, \quad j = \min\{i : \langle \mathbf{A}, Q_i \rangle = H_{\text{conv}(V)}(\mathbf{A}), \quad 1 \leq i \leq r\} \tag{7}$$

A result of Equations (4), (5), (6), and (7) is that compact convex sets and polytopes can be described in terms of their support properties. This result is particularly useful when dealing with functions such as the sum or difference of two sets. For example, we can describe the set difference $S = S_1 - S_2$ in terms of its support and contact functions by

$$H_S = H_{S_1}(\mathbf{A}) + H_{S_2}(-\mathbf{A}) \tag{8}$$

$$C_S = C_{S_1}(\mathbf{A}) - C_{S_2}(-\mathbf{A}) \tag{9}$$

Let S_1 and S_2 be non-empty sets in R^n. Then S_1 and S_2 are said to be **separated** if there exists a hyperplane H such that S_1 and S_2 belong to opposing half-spaces. If we add the constraint that S_1 and S_2 are not both contained in H, then S_1 and S_2 are **properly separated**. If $S_3, S_4 \in R^n$ are convex sets, it can be shown that the necessary and sufficient condition for the existence of a hyperplane separating S_3 and S_4 properly is that they have no common points. See (Rockafellar 1970) for proof. Therefore, from (1) we can make the observation that if the minimum distance between S_3 and S_4 is not 0, then a hyperplane exists that properly separates S_3 and S_4. Since one of the convex sets can be contained in H, this implies that S_3 and S_4 can be properly separated by H, where H is a support hyperplane of one of the sets as defined in (4).

Basic 3D modeling primitives such as spheres, boxes, cylinders, cones, etc., can all be approximated by simple convex polyhedra. These basic primitives can be combined to create more complex objects. A polyhedron PH consists of a set of vertices $V \subset R^3$ and a set of simple planar polygons (faces) F. The planes of the faces divide R^3 into two disjoint sets: the polyhedron interior and its exterior. Each vertex is represented by an xyz cartesian coordinate. Each face is represented by a directed graph $G(V, E)$, where V is the set of vertices defined above and E is a set of edges tracing out the face. Each edge E of a polyhedron is a member of exactly two faces. It is convex if its interior is a convex set. It is simple if no pair of non-adjacent faces shares a vertex and no two faces have exactly the same vertex set. In all further references to polyhedra it will be assumed that they are simple and convex.

◇ **Problem** ◇

Given a pair of polyhedra PH_1 and PH_2 with m_1 and m_2 vertices and transformation matrices $\mathbf{M}_1$ and $\mathbf{M}_2$, respectively, detect if PH_1 and PH_2 collide as $\mathbf{M}_1$ and $\mathbf{M}_2$ vary over time.

The goal of a collision detection algorithm is to quickly determine if two polyhedra intersect. If they do intersect it is not necessary to compute the intersection. All we need is a yes or no answer to the intersection question. This question must be answered repeatedly as $\mathbf{M}_1$ and $\mathbf{M}_2$ vary over time. Therefore, we want to exploit spatial coherence when we can to solve a series of collision detection problems efficiently. It is important to incorporate these concepts into the design of the collision detection algorithm.

◇ **Main Algorithm** ◇

If PH_1 and PH_2 are a pair of polyhedra in R^3, we know that if they have no points in common then a plane exists that separates them properly. Therefore, we can answer the question of whether PH_1 and PH_2 intersect by determining if there exists a plane that separates PH_1 and PH_2 properly. If such a plane exists, PH_1 and PH_2 are disjoint; otherwise they intersect.

Now that we know how to answer the intersection question at time t_i, we want to use information from this solution to speed up the computation at time t_{i+1}. The way we do this is by caching witnesses from one time step to another (Baraff 1990). In this Gem the witness is the plane H, which properly separates PH_1 and PH_2 at time t_i.

Suppose at time t_i PH_1 and PH_2 are properly separated by the plane H. Let H also be a supporting plane of the polyhedron with the maximum number of vertices, say PH_1. Then we can say H is a witness to PH_1 and PH_2 being properly separated at time t_i. In most animations the spatial relationship between a pair of polyhedra remains relatively the same during a time step. Using this fact we can cache the separation witness from time t_i and use it as a prospective separation witness at time t_{i+1}. Since H is a supporting plane of the polyhedron with the maximum number of vertices, the test to check if it is a proper separating plane at time t_{i+1} can be performed with at most $\min(m_1, m_2)$ inner products, where m_1 and m_2 are the number of vertices in PH_1 and PH_2, respectively. When a cached witness fails to be a proper separating plane, an attempt is made to compute another proper separating plane, if one exists. The first step in computing a new proper separating plane is to find the two nearest points Q_1 and Q_2 on the boundaries of the two polyhedra. An efficient algorithm to do this is given in the next section. Once Q_1 and Q_2 have been computed the separating plane is then constructed by defining the plane normal as the difference $Q_2 - Q_1$. Then, let Q_1 be a point on the plane. It should be noted that this separating plane construction is different from the one described in (Baraff 1990). The main collision detection algorithm is now defined.

> Input : A pair of polyhedra PH_1 and PH_2 with m_1 and m_2 vertices,
> respectively $(m_1 \geq m_2)$, and a prospective proper separating
> plane H that is also a support plane of PH_1.
> Output : Whether or not the pair of polyhedra intersect.

begin
    for $i = 0$ to $m_2 - 1$ **do**
        $d = \langle Q_i, \mathbf{A} \rangle$ where $Q_i \subset PH_2$ and $\mathbf{A}$ is normal to H.
        if $d \leq 0$
            test for new proper separating plane
            if no proper separating plane exists

        return intersection = TRUE
      else
        return intersection = FALSE
      endelse
    endif
  endfor
  return intersection = FALSE
end;

◇ Determining a Proper Separating Plane ◇

The problem of finding a proper separating plane between two convex polyhedra PH_1 and PH_2 is equivalent to the problem of finding two points W and Q, $W \subset \text{conv}(PH_1)$, $Q \subset \text{conv}(PH_2)$, that satisfy Equation (1), i.e., the two points in $\text{conv}(PH_1)$ and $\text{conv}(PH_2)$ nearest each other. An iterative algorithm due to (Gilbert *et al.* 1988) that solves Equation (1) for convex sets and terminates after a finite number of steps if the sets are polytopes (convex hulls of the polyhedra) will be presented.

Equation (1) requires the computation of the minimum norm of a set difference. We can avoid dealing directly with this set difference by defining the polytopes in terms of their support properties by using Equations (8) and (9). The problem of solving Equation (1) for two polytopes P_1 and P_2 can now be reduced to the problem of finding the minimum norm of a single polytope $P = P_1 - P_2$. This is done by generating a sequence of elementary polytopes contained in P that converge to the polytype containing the point in P closest to the origin and is denoted by

$$V(P) \in P, \quad \|V(P)\| = \min\{\|U\| : U \in P\} \tag{10}$$

When the algorithm terminates, the solution is expressed as

$$V(P) = \sum_{i=1}^{r} \lambda_i U_i = W - Q, \quad \lambda_i \geq 0, \quad \sum_{i=1}^{r} \lambda_i = 1, \quad U_i \in P \tag{11}$$

where

$$W = \sum_{i=1}^{r} \lambda_i W_i, \quad W_i \in P_1, \quad Q = \sum_{i=1}^{r} \lambda_i Q_i, \quad Q_i \in P_2 \tag{12}$$

The points W and Q in (12) represent the near points in P_1 and P_2.

◇ Distance Algorithm ◇

The distance algorithm is based on the following theorem:

Theorem 1 *Let $S \subset R^n$ be compact and convex and define $G_S : R^n \mapsto R$ by*

$$G_S(\mathbf{A}) = \|\mathbf{A}\|^2 + H_S(-\mathbf{A}) \tag{13}$$

Suppose $\mathbf{A} \in S$. Then (1) if $G_S(\mathbf{A}) > 0$ there is a point U in the line segment conv
$\{\mathbf{A}, C_S(-\mathbf{A})\}$ *satisfying $\|U\| < \|\mathbf{A}\|$;* (2) $\mathbf{A} = V(S)$ *if and only if $G_S(\mathbf{A}) = 0$;* (3)
$\|\mathbf{A} - V(S)\|^2 \leq G_S(\mathbf{A})$.

PROOF: See (Gilbert *et al.* 1988). □

Input :   A polytope P in R^n, and an initial set of points $\{Q_1, \ldots, Q_m\} \subset P$,
          where $1 \leq m \leq n + 1$.
Output : $V(P)$, such that $V(P)$ is the point in P closest to the origin.

begin
    set $P_0 = \{Q_1, \ldots, Q_m\}$, and $k = 0$ /* first elementary polytope */
    loop forever
        $V_k = V(P_k) = $ sub-distance(P_k)
        compute $H_p(-V_k)$ /* support function w.r.t. $-V_k$ */
        compute $C_p(-V_k)$ /* contact function w.r.t. $-V_k$ */
        $G_p(V_k) = \|V_k\|^2 + H_P(-V_k)$ /* Eq. (13) */
        if $G_p(V_k) = 0$
            return $V(P) = V_k$
        else
            set $P_{k+1} = \overline{P}_k \cup \{C_P(-V_k)\}$ /* next elementary polytope */
        endif
    continue
end;

The above algorithm is guaranteed to converge to a solution in a finite number of steps. The algorithm generates a sequence of elementary polytopes P_k, until $V(P_k) = V(P)$. For each elementary polytope the function sub-distance computes $V(P_k)$, the point in P_k of minimum norm. sub-distance computes $V(P_k)$ explicitly and is designed to be computationally efficient for lower dimension polytopes.

It is a simple process to generalize the distance algorithm to solve Equation (1) when the sets are polytopes. It has already been shown how to compute the support and contact functions of a set difference using Equations (8) and (9). The only issue that remains is the choice of the initial points $\{Q_1, \ldots, Q_m\} \subset P$ as input. In practice any single point initialization scheme works. One method would be to choose randomly a vertex from each polytope and use the vector difference. In (Gilbert *et al.* 1988) it is suggested to use $C_P(U_2 - U_1)$, where U_1 and U_2 are the centroids of the input polytopes.

For problems which require the distance algorithm to be computed repeatedly for a pair of moving polytopes over time (i.e., collision detection) we can use spatial coherence to converge to a solution quickly. In most cases the convergence occurs in one iteration of the distance algorithm. For example, if we computed the U_i's of (11) at time t_i, we can use these U_i's to initialize the algorithm at time t_{i+1}. In most animations the time step is small and the vertices of the polytopes will remain relatively unchanged. In this case the distance algorithm will only need to compute a new set of λ's for (11) regardless of the size of the polytopes' vertex sets.

Upon termination of the distance algorithm the proper separating plane can be constructed using the points from (12). Choose one of them to be a point on the plane, and form the plane normal vector by subtracting one point from the other.

◇ **Sub-Distance Algorithm** ◇

The sub-distance algorithm originated by (Johnson 1987) finds the point in a polytope P closest to the origin where $P = \{W_1, \ldots, W_m\}$, $W_i \in R^n$, $1 < m \le n+1$. It computes V_k in each iteration of the distance algorithm previously given. It is specifically designed to be efficient when the number of points in P is small and when the solution set is affinely independent. When the algorithm terminates, the solution is expressed as

$$V(P) = \sum_{i \in I_S} \lambda_i W_i \tag{14}$$

where

$$\lambda_i > 0, \quad \sum_{i \in I_S} \lambda_i = 1, \quad i \in I_S \subset \{1, \ldots, m\}$$

and the set $P_S = \{W_i : i \in I_S\} \subset P$ is affinely independent.

S represents a particular member from the collection of all non-empty subsets of P. Since m is small the algorithm examines each of these subsets until a solution to (14) is found.

Let us first consider solving the problem $V(\text{aff}(P_S))$, where $P_S \subset P$. Let $\{Q_1, \ldots, Q_r\}$ be any ordering of P_S. Also, assume $r \ne 1$, since this would be a trivial solution. Then $V(\text{aff}(P_S)) = \lambda_1 Q_1 + \cdots + \lambda_r Q_r$. The λ_i result from the minimization of $f(\lambda_1, \ldots, \lambda_r) = \|\lambda_1 Q_1 + \cdots + \lambda_r Q_r\|^2$ with the constraint that $\lambda_1 + \cdots + \lambda_r - 1 = 0$. This type of minimization can be solved by applying the method of Lagrange multipliers, which yields the linear system of equations $\mathbf{A}\lambda = \mathbf{B}$, where

$$\mathbf{A} = \begin{pmatrix} 1 & \cdots & 1 \\ (Q_2 - Q_1)^T Q_1 & \cdots & (Q_2 - Q_1)^T Q_r \\ \vdots & & \vdots \\ (Q_r - Q_1)^T Q_1 & \cdots & (Q_r - Q_1)^T Q_r \end{pmatrix}, \quad \mathbf{B} = \begin{pmatrix} 1 \\ 0 \\ \vdots \\ 0 \end{pmatrix} \tag{15}$$

We can solve such a system using Cramer's method. Let us define the cofactors of $\mathbf{A}_{0,}$. Denote the cofactor of $\mathbf{A}_{0,j}$ by $\Delta_i(P_S)$, $i \in I_S$, where j satisfies $Q_j = W_j$. Since $\mathbf{A}_0$, contains all 1's, the determinant of $\mathbf{A}$ is defined by

$$\Delta(P_S) = \sum_{i \in I_S} \Delta_i(P_S) \tag{16}$$

If $\Delta(P_S) > 0$, then the solution to $V(\mathrm{aff}(P_S))$ is

$$V(\mathrm{aff}(P_S)) = \sum_{i \in I_S} [\Delta_i(P_S)/\Delta(P_S)]W_i \tag{17}$$

A solution exists whenever P_S is affinely independent.

Suppose we want to compute $V(\mathrm{aff}(P_S))$ for each non-empty subset $P_S \in P$. We could compute the $\Delta_i(P_S)$ and $\Delta(P_S)$ for each P_S; however, there is a more efficient technique. Suppose we recursively compute $\Delta_i(P_S)$ in order of increasing cardinality of S. The idea is to append a row and column to $\mathbf{A}$ using W_j, where $j \in I_S^C$, and I_S^C is the complement of I_S. Then

$$\Delta_j(P_S \cup \{W_j\}) = \sum_{i \in I_S} \Delta_i(P_S)W_i^T(W_k - W_j), \quad j \in I_S^C, \quad k = \min\{i \in I_S\} \tag{18}$$

$$\Delta_i(\{W_i\}) = 1, \quad i \in \{1, \dots, m\}$$

We can now define the sub-distance algorithm, which is based on the following theorem.

Theorem 2 *Given P and a non-empty subset $P_S \in P$, $V(\mathrm{conv}(P))$ can be expressed as in (14) if and only if (1) $\Delta(P_S) > 0$, (2) $\Delta_i(P_S) > 0$, for each $i \in I_S$, and (3) $\Delta_j(P_S \cup \{W_j\}) \leq 0$ for each $j \in I_S^C$. Furthermore, the λ_i in (14) are given by $\lambda_i = \Delta_i(P_S)/\Delta(P_S)$.*

PROOF: See (Johnson 1987). □

Input :   A polytope $P = \{W_1, \dots, W_m\} \in R^n$
          where $1 < m \leq n + 1$.
Output : $V(P)$, such that $V(P)$ is the point in P closest to the origin.

begin
    choose an ordering P_S, $s = 1, \dots, \sigma$ of all subsets of P.
    for $s = 1$ to σ **do**
        if all conditions in Theorem 2 are met
            return $V(\mathrm{conv}(P))$ as computed in (14).
    endloop
end;

On rare occasions the sub-distance algorithm will not find a P_S that satisfies the three conditions in Theorem 2. This is due to numerical roundoff error. In (Gilbert *et al.* 1988) a back-up method is described which solves (14) when this situation occurs by choosing the numerically best P_S. This method has been implemented in the source code.

◇ C Code ◇

```c
#include <math.h>

typedef long            Boolean;

#define FUZZ            (0.00001)
#define TRUE            (1)
#define FALSE           (0)
#define MAX_VERTS       (1026)

#define ABS(x)          ( (x) > 0 ? (x) : -(x) )
#define EQZ(x)          ( ABS((x)) < FUZZ ? TRUE : FALSE )

#define DOT3(u,v)       ( u[0]*v[0] + u[1]*v[1] + u[2]*v[2])
#define VECADD3(r,u,v)  { r[0]=u[0]+v[0]; r[1]=u[1]+v[1]; r[2]=u[2]+v[2]; }
#define VECADDS3(r,a,u,v){r[0]=a*u[0]+v[0]; r[1]=a*u[1]+v[1]; r[2]=a*u[2]+v[2];}
#define VECSMULT3(a,u)  { u[0]= a * u[0]; u[1]= a * u[1]; u[2]= a * u[2]; }
#define VECSUB3(r,u,v)  { r[0]=u[0]-v[0]; r[1]=u[1]-v[1]; r[2]=u[2]-v[2]; }
#define CPVECTOR3(u,v)  { u[0]=v[0];      u[1]=v[1];      u[2]=v[2]; }
#define VECNEGATE3(u)   { u[0]=(-u[0]);   u[1]=(-u[1]);   u[2]=(-u[2]); }

#define GET(u,i,j,s) (*(u+i*s+j))
#define GET3(u,i,j,k,s) (*(u+i*(s*2)+(j*2)+k))

/*************************************************************************
 *
 * The structure polyhedron is used to store the geometry of the primitives
 * used in this collision detection example.  Since the collision detection
 * algorithm only needs to operate on the vertex set of a polyhedron, and
 * no rendering is done in this example, the faces and edges of a
 * polyhedron are not stored.  Adding faces and edges to the structure for
 * rendering purposes should be straightforward and will have no effect on
 * the collision detection computations.
 *
 *************************************************************************/

typedef struct polyhedron {
    double   verts[MAX_VERTS][3]; /* 3D vertices of polyhedron. */
    int      m;                   /* number of 3D vertices.  */
    double   trn[3];              /* translational position in world coords. */
    double   itrn[3];             /* inverse of translational position. */
} *Polyhedron;
```

```
/**************************************************************************
 *
 * The structure couple is used to store the information required to
 * repeatedly test a pair of polyhedra for collision.  This information
 * includes a reference to each polyhedron,  a flag indicating if there
 * is a cached prospective proper separating plane, two points for
 * constructing the proper separating plane, and possibly a cached set
 * of points from each polyhedron for speeding up the distance algorithm.
 *
 **************************************************************************/

typedef struct couple {
    Polyhedron   polyhdrn1;        /* First polyhedron of collision test. */
    Polyhedron   polyhdrn2;        /* Second polyhedron of collision test. */
    Boolean      plane_exists;     /* prospective separating plane flag. */
    double       pln_pnt1[3];      /* 1st point used to form separating plane. */
    double       pln_pnt2[3];      /* 2nd point used to form separating plane. */
    int          vert_indx[4][2];  /* cached points for distance algorithm. */
    int          n;                /* number of cached points, if any. */
} *Couple;


/*** Arrays for vertex sets of three primitives ***/

double box[24];
double cyl[108];
double sphere[1026];

/*** RJR 08/20/93 *********************************************************
 *
 *     Function to create vertex set of a polyhedron used to represent a
 *     box primitive.
 *
 *     On Entry:
 *         box_verts - an empty array of type double of size 24 or more.
 *
 *     On Exit:
 *         box_verts  - vertices of a polyhedron representing a box with
 *                      dimensions length = 5.0, width = 5.0, and height = 5.0.
 *
 *     Function Return : none.
 *
 **************************************************************************/

void mak_box(box_verts)
double          box_verts[];
{
    int             i;
    static  double verts[24] =
            {-5.0,  5.0,  5.0,  -5.0,  5.0, -5.0,  5.0,  5.0, -5.0,
             5.0,  5.0, 5.0,  -5.0, -5.0, 5.0,  -5.0, -5.0, -5.0,
             5.0, -5.0, -5.0,  5.0, -5.0, 5.0};
```

```
  for (i = 0; i < 24; i++)
     box_verts[i] = verts[i];
}



/*** RJR 08/20/93 ***********************************************************
 *
 *    Function to create vertex set of a polyhedron used to approximate
 *    a cylinder primitive.
 *
 *    On Entry:
 *        cyl_verts - an empty array of type double of size 108 or more.
 *
 *    On Exit:
 *        cyl_verts  - vertices of a polyhedron approximating a cylinder with
 *                     a base radius = 5.0, and height = 5.0.
 *    Function Return : none.
 *
 ************************************************************************/

void mak_cyl(cyl_verts)
double        cyl_verts[];
{
    int        i;
    double     *pD_1, *pD_2, rads, stp, radius;

    pD_1 = cyl_verts;       pD_2 = cyl_verts + 54;
    stp = 0.34906585;       rads = 0.0;                 radius = 5.0;

    for (i = 0; i < 18; i++) {
        pD_1[0] = pD_2[0] = radius * cos(rads);     /* X for top and bot. */
        pD_1[1] = 5.0;                              /* Y for top */
        pD_2[1] = 0.0;                              /* Y for bot. */
        pD_1[2] = pD_2[2] = -(radius * sin(rads));  /* Z for top and bot. */
        rads += stp;   pD_1 += 3;   pD_2 += 3;
    }
}



/*** RJR 08/20/93 ***********************************************************
 *
 *    Function to create vertex set of a polyhedron used to approximate
 *    a sphere primitive.
 *
 *    On Entry:
 *        sph_verts - an empty array of type double of size 1026 or more.
 *
 *    On Exit:
 *        sph_verts  - vertices of a polyhedron approximating a sphere with
 *                     a radius = 5.25.
 *    Function Return : none.
 *
 ************************************************************************/
```

```
void mak_sph(sph_verts)
double      sph_verts[];
{
   int      i, j;
   double   rads_1, rads_2, stp_1, stp_2, *pD_1, *pD_2, radius;

   rads_1 = 1.570796327;   stp_1  = 0.174532935;
   rads_2 = 0.0;           stp_2  = 0.34906585;
   pD_1   = sph_verts;     radius = 5.25;

   for (i = 0; i < 19; i++) {
      pD_1[0] = radius * cos(rads_1);      pD_1[1] = radius * sin(rads_1);
      pD_1[2] = 0.0;
      if (EQZ(pD_1[0]))
         pD_1[0] = 0.01;
      rads_2 = 0.0;      stp_2 = 0.34906585;

      for (j = 0; j < 18; j++) {
         pD_2 = pD_1 + j * 3;
         pD_2[0] =   pD_1[0] * cos(rads_2) - pD_1[2] * sin(rads_2);  /* X */
         pD_2[1] =   pD_1[1];                                        /* Y */
         pD_2[2] = -(pD_1[0] * sin(rads_2) + pD_1[2] * cos(rads_2)); /* Z */
         rads_2 += stp_2;
      }
      pD_1 += 54;   rads_1 -= stp_1;
   }
}


/*** RJR 05/26/93 *************************************************************
 *
 *    Function to evaluate the support and contact functions at A for a given
 *    polytope. See Equations (6) & (7).
 *
 *    On Entry:
 *        P    - table of 3-element points containing polytope vertices.
 *        r    - number of points in table.
 *        A    - vector at which support and contact functions will be evaluated.
 *        Cp   - empty 3-element array.
 *        P_i  - pointer to an int.
 *
 *    On Exit:
 *        Cp   - contact point of P w.r.t. A.
 *        P_i  - index into P of contact point.
 *
 *    Function Return :
 *        the result of the evaluation of Eq. (6) for P and A.
 *
 *****************************************************************************/

double Hp(P, r, A, Cp, P_i)
double          P[][3], A[], Cp[];
```

```
int              r, *P_i;
{
   int           i;
   double        max_val, val;

   max_val = DOT3(P[0], A);        *P_i = 0;

   for (i = 1; i < r; i++) {
      val = DOT3(P[i], A);
      if (val > max_val) {
         *P_i = i;
         max_val = val;
      }
   }
   CPVECTOR3(Cp, P[*P_i]);

   return max_val;
}


/*** RJR 05/26/93 *********************************************************
 *
 *    Function to evaluate the support and contact functions at A for the
 *    set difference of two polytopes. See Equations (8) & (9).
 *
 *    On Entry:
 *        P1   - table of 3-element points containing first polytope's vertices.
 *        m1   - number of points in P1.
 *        P2   - table of 3-element points containing second polytope's vertices.
 *        m2   - number of points in P2.
 *        A    - vector at which to evaluate support and contact functions.
 *        Cs   - an empty array of size 3.
 *        P1_i - a pointer to an int.
 *        P2_i - a pointer to an int.
 *
 *    On Exit:
 *        Cs   - solution to Equation (9).
 *        P1_i - index into P1 for solution to Equation (9).
 *        P2_i - index into P2 for solution to Equation (9).
 *
 *    Function Return :
 *        the result of the evaluation of Eq. (8) for P1 and P2 at A.
 *
 *************************************************************************/

double Hs(P1, m1, P2, m2, A, Cs, P1_i, P2_i)
double     P1[][3], P2[][3], A[], Cs[];
int        m1, m2, *P1_i, *P2_i;
{
   double   Cp_1[3], Cp_2[3], neg_A[3], Hp_1, Hp_2;

   Hp_1 = Hp(P1, m1, A, Cp_1, P1_i);
```

```
    CPVECTOR3(neg_A, A);
    VECNEGATE3(neg_A);
    Hp_2 = Hp(P2, m2, neg_A, Cp_2, P2_i);

    VECSUB3(Cs ,Cp_1, Cp_2);

    return (Hp_1 + Hp_2);
}

/*** RJR 05/26/93 ****************************************************
 *
 *   Alternate function to compute the point in a polytope closest to the
 *   origin in 3-space. The polytope size m is restricted to 1 < m <= 4.
 *   This function is called only when comp_sub_dist fails.
 *
 *   On Entry:
 *       stop_index - number of sets to test.
 *       D_P        - array of determinants for each set.
 *       Di_P       - cofactors for each set.
 *       Is         - indices for each set.
 *       c2         - row size offset.
 *
 *   On Exit:
 *
 *   Function Return :
 *       the index of the set that is numerically closest to Eq. (14).
 *
 ****************************************************************************/

int sub_dist_back(P, stop_index, D_P, Di_P, Is, c2)
double          P[][3], Di_P[][4], *D_P;
int             stop_index, *Is, c2;
{
    Boolean     first, pass;
    int         i, k, s, is, best_s;
    float       sum, v_aff, best_v_aff;

    first = TRUE; best_s = -1;
    for (s = 0; s < stop_index; s++) {
        pass = TRUE;
        if (D_P[s] > 0.0) {
            for (i = 1; i <= GET(Is,s,0,c2); i++) {
                is = GET(Is,s,i,c2);
                if (Di_P[s][is] <= 0.0)
                    pass = FALSE;
            }
        }
        else
            pass = FALSE;

        if (pass) {

            /*** Compute Equation (33) in Gilbert ***/
```

```
            k = GET(Is,s,1,c2);
            sum = 0;
            for (i = 1; i <= GET(Is, s, 0, c2); i++) {
                is = GET(Is,s,i,c2);
                sum += Di_P[s][is] * DOT3(P[is],P[k]);
            }
            v_aff = sqrt(sum / D_P[s]);
            if (first) {
                best_s = s;
                best_v_aff = v_aff;
                first = FALSE;
            }
            else {
                if (v_aff < best_v_aff) {
                    best_s = s;
                    best_v_aff = v_aff;
                }
            }
        }
    }
    if (best_s == -1) {
        printf("backup failed\n");
        exit(0);
    }
    return best_s;
}


/*** RJR 05/26/93 ******************************************************
 *
 *    Function to compute the point in a polytope closest to the origin in
 *    3-space. The polytope size m is restricted to 1 < m <= 4.
 *
 *    On Entry:
 *           P  - table of 3-element points containing polytope's vertices.
 *           m  - number of points in P.
 *          jo  - table of indices for storing Dj_P cofactors in Di_P.
 *          Is  - indices into P for all sets of subsets of P.
 *          IsC - indices into P for complement sets of Is.
 *     near_pnt - an empty array of size 3.
 *    near_indx - an empty array of size 4.
 *       lambda - an empty array of size 4.
 *
 *    On Exit:
 *     near_pnt - the point in P closest to the origin.
 *    near_indx - indices for a subset of P which is affinely independent.
 *                See Eq. (14).
 *       lambda - the lambda as in Eq. (14).
 *
 *    Function Return :
 *        the number of entries in near_indx and lambda.
 *
 ********************************************************************/
```

```
int comp_sub_dist(P, m, jo, Is, IsC, near_pnt, near_indx, lambda)
double              P[][3], near_pnt[], lambda[];
int                 m, *jo, *Is, *IsC, near_indx[];
{
   Boolean          pass, fail;
   int              i, j, k, isp, is, s, row, col, stop_index, c1, c2;
   double           D_P[15], x[3], Dj_P, Di_P[15][4];
   static int       combinations[5] = {0,0,3,7,15};

   stop_index = combinations[m];    /** how many subsets in P **/
   c1 = m;   c2 = m + 1;            /** row offsets for IsC and Is **/

   /** Initialize Di_P for singletons **/

   Di_P[0][0] = Di_P[1][1] = Di_P[2][2] = Di_P[3][3] = 1.0;
   s = 0;    pass = FALSE;

   while ((s < stop_index) && (!pass)) {        /* loop through each subset */
      D_P[s] = 0.0;   fail = FALSE;
      for (i = 1; i <= GET(Is,s,0,c2); i++) {   /** loop through all Is **/
         is = GET(Is,s,i,c2);
         if (Di_P[s][is] > 0.0)                 /** Condition 2, Theorem 2 **/
            D_P[s] += Di_P[s][is];              /** sum from Eq. (16)      **/
         else
            fail = TRUE;
      }

      for (j = 1; j <= GET(IsC,s,0,c1); j++) {  /** loop through all IsC **/
         Dj_P = 0;   k = GET(Is,s,1,c2);
         isp = GET(IsC,s,j,c1);

         for (i = 1; i <= GET(Is,s,0,c2); i++) {
            is = GET(Is,s,i,c2);
            VECSUB3(x, P[k], P[isp]);                /** Wk - Wj Eq. (18) **/
            Dj_P += Di_P[s][is] * DOT3(P[is], x); /** sum from Eq. (18) **/
         }
         row = GET3(jo,s,isp,0,c1);
         col = GET3(jo,s,isp,1,c1);
         Di_P[row][col] = Dj_P;                   /** add new cofactors  **/

         if (Dj_P > 0.00001)                      /** Condition 3, Theorem 2 **/
            fail = TRUE;
      }
      if ((!fail) && (D_P[s] > 0.0))   /** Conditions 2 && 3 && 1, Theorem 2  **/
         pass = TRUE;
      else
         s++;
   }
   if (!pass) {
      printf("*** using backup procedure in sub_dist\n");
      s = sub_dist_back(P, stop_index, D_P, Di_P, Is, c2);
   }
```

```
    near_pnt[0] = near_pnt[1] = near_pnt[2] = 0.0;
    j = 0;
    for (i = 1; i <= GET(Is,s,0,c2); i++) {          /** loop through all Is **/
       is = GET(Is,s,i,c2);
       near_indx[j] = is;
       lambda[j] = Di_P[s][is] / D_P[s];                    /** Eq. (17)  **/
       VECADDS3(near_pnt, lambda[j], P[is], near_pnt);  /** Eq. (17)  **/
       j++;
    }

    return (j-1);
}


/*** RJR 05/26/93 **********************************************************
 *
 *   Function to compute the point in a polytope closest to the origin in
 *   3-space.  The polytope size m is restricted to 1 < m <= 4.
 *
 *   On Entry:
 *          P  - table of 3-element points containing polytope's vertices.
 *          m  - number of points in P.
 *   near_pnt - an empty array of size 3.
 *  near_indx - an empty array of size 4.
 *     lambda - an empty array of size 4.
 *
 *   On Exit:
 *   near_pnt - the point in P closest to the origin.
 *  near_indx - indices for a subset of P which is affinely independent.
 *              See Eq. (14).
 *     lambda - the lambda as in Eq. (14).
 *
 *   Function Return :
 *      the number of entries in near_indx and lambda.
 *
 ***************************************************************************/

int sub_dist(P, m, near_pnt, near_indx, lambda)
double        P[][3], near_pnt[], lambda[];
int           near_indx[], m;
{
   int        size;

/*
 *
 *  Tables to index the Di_P cofactor table in comp_sub_dist.  The s,i
 *  entry indicates where to store the cofactors computed with Is_C.
 *
 */

   static int     jo_2[2][2][2]  = { {{0,0}, {2,1}},
                                     {{2,0}, {0,0}}};
```

```
static int      jo_3[6][3][2]  = { {{0,0}, {3,1}, {4,2}},
                                    {{3,0}, {0,0}, {5,2}},
                                    {{4,0}, {5,1}, {0,0}},
                                    {{0,0}, {0,0}, {6,2}},
                                    {{0,0}, {6,1}, {0,0}},
                                    {{6,0}, {0,0}, {0,0}}};

static int      jo_4[14][4][2] = { { {0,0}, {4,1}, {5,2}, {6,3}},
                                   { {4,0}, {0,0}, {7,2}, {8,3}},
                                   { {5,0}, {7,1}, {0,0}, {9,3}},
                                   { {6,0}, {8,1}, {9,2}, {0,0}},
                                   { {0,0}, {0,0},{10,2},{11,3}},
                                   { {0,0},{10,1}, {0,0},{12,3}},
                                   { {0,0},{11,1},{12,2}, {0,0}},
                                   {{10,0}, {0,0}, {0,0},{13,3}},
                                   {{11,0}, {0,0},{13,2}, {0,0}},
                                   {{12,0},{13,1}, {0,0}, {0,0}},
                                   { {0,0}, {0,0}, {0,0},{14,3}},
                                   { {0,0}, {0,0},{14,2}, {0,0}},
                                   { {0,0},{14,1}, {0,0}, {0,0}},
                                   {{14,0}, {0,0}, {0,0}, {0,0}}};

/*
 *  These tables represent each Is.  The first column of each row indicates
 *  the size of the set.
 *
 */
static int      Is_2[3][3] = { {1,0,0}, {1,1,0}, {2,0,1}};

static int      Is_3[7][4] = { {1,0,0,0}, {1,1,0,0}, {1,2,0,0}, {2,0,1,0},
                               {2,0,2,0}, {2,1,2,0}, {3,0,1,2}};

static int      Is_4[15][5] = { {1,0,0,0,0}, {1,1,0,0,0}, {1,2,0,0,0},
                                {1,3,0,0,0}, {2,0,1,0,0}, {2,0,2,0,0},
                                {2,0,3,0,0}, {2,1,2,0,0}, {2,1,3,0,0},
                                {2,2,3,0,0}, {3,0,1,2,0}, {3,0,1,3,0},
                                {3,0,2,3,0}, {3,1,2,3,0}, {4,0,1,2,3}};

/*
 *  These tables represent each Is complement. The first column of each row
 *  indicates the size of the set.
 *
 */
static int      IsC_2[3][2] = { {1,1}, {1,0}, {0,0}};

static int      IsC_3[7][3] = { {2,1,2}, {2,0,2}, {2,0,1}, {1,2,0}, {1,1,0},
                                {1,0,0}, {0,0,0}};

static int      IsC_4[15][4] = { {3,1,2,3}, {3,0,2,3}, {3,0,1,3}, {3,0,1,2},
                                 {2,2,3,0}, {2,1,3,0}, {2,1,2,0}, {2,0,3,0},
                                 {2,0,2,0}, {2,0,1,0}, {1,3,0,0}, {1,2,0,0},
                                 {1,1,0,0}, {1,0,0,0}, {0,0,0,0}};
```

```
   /** Call comp_sub_dist with appropriate tables according to size of P **/

   switch (m) {
      case 2:
         size = comp_sub_dist(P, m, jo_2, Is_2, IsC_2, near_pnt,
                                                   near_indx, lambda);
      break;
      case 3:
         size = comp_sub_dist(P, m, jo_3, Is_3, IsC_3, near_pnt,
                                                   near_indx, lambda);
      break;
      case 4:
         size = comp_sub_dist(P, m, jo_4, Is_4, IsC_4, near_pnt,
                                                    near_indx, lambda);
      break;
   }

   return size;
}


/*** RJR 05/26/93 ********************************************************
 *
 *   Function to compute the minimum distance between two convex polytopes in
 *   3-space.
 *
 *   On Entry:
 *         P1 - table of 3-element points containing first polytope's vertices.
 *         m1 - number of points in P1.
 *         P2 - table of 3-element points containing second polytope's vertices.
 *         m2 - number of points in P2.
 *         VP - an empty array of size 3.
 *   near_indx - a 4x2 matrix possibly containing indices of initialization
 *               points. The first column contains indices into P1, and the second
 *               column contains indices into P2.
 *     lambda - an empty array of size 4.
 *         m3 - a pointer to an int, which indicates how many initial points
 *               to extract from near_indx. If 0, near_indx is ignored.
 *
 *   On Exit:
 *         Vp   - vector difference of the two near points in P1 and P2.
 *               The length of this vector is the minimum distance between P1
 *               and P2.
 *   near_indx - updated indices into P1 and P2 which indicate the affinely
 *               independent point sets from each polytope which can be used
 *               to compute along with lambda the near points in P1 and P2
 *               as in Eq. (12). These indices can be used to re-initialize
 *               dist3d in the next iteration.
 *     lambda - the lambda as in Eqs. (11) & (12).
 *         m3 - the updated number of indices for P1 and P2 in near_indx.
 *
```

```
*    Function Return : none.
*
***************************************************************************/

void dist3d(P1, m1, P2, m2, VP, near_indx, lambda, m3)
double          P1[][3], P2[][3], VP[], lambda[];
int             m1, m2, near_indx[][2], *m3;
{
    Boolean         pass;
    int             set_size, I[4], i, j, i_tab[4], j_tab[4], P1_i, P2_i, k;
    double          Hs(), Pk[4][3], Pk_subset[4][3], Vk[3], neg_Vk[3], Cp[3],
                    Gp;

    if ((*m3) == 0) {           /** if *m3 == 0 use single-point initialization **/
        set_size = 1;
        VECSUB3(Pk[0], P1[0], P2[0]);       /** first elementary polytope **/
        i_tab[0] = j_tab[0] = 0;
    }
    else {                              /** else use indices from near_indx **/
        for (k = 0; k < (*m3); k++) {
            i = i_tab[k] = near_indx[k][0];
            j = j_tab[k] = near_indx[k][1];
            VECSUB3(Pk[k], P1[i], P2[j]);   /** first elementary polytope **/
        }
        set_size = *m3;
    }

    pass = FALSE;
    while (!pass) {

        /** compute Vk **/

        if (set_size == 1) {
            CPVECTOR3(Vk, Pk[0]);
            I[0] = 0;
        }
        else
            set_size = sub_dist(Pk, set_size, Vk, I, lambda);

        /** eq. (13) **/

        CPVECTOR3(neg_Vk, Vk);      VECNEGATE3(neg_Vk);
        Gp = DOT3(Vk, Vk) + Hs(P1, m1, P2, m2, neg_Vk, Cp, &P1_i, &P2_i);

        /** keep track of indices for P1 and P2 **/

        for (i = 0; i < set_size; i++) {
            j = I[i];
            i_tab[i] = i_tab[j];    /** j is value from member of some Is **/
            j_tab[i] = j_tab[j];    /** j is value from member of some Is **/
        }

        if (EQZ(Gp))                    /** Do we have a solution set? **/
```

```
            pass = TRUE;
         else {
            for (i = 0; i < set_size; i++) {
               j = I[i];
               CPVECTOR3(Pk_subset[i], Pk[j]);   /** extract affine subset of Pk **/
            }
            for (i = 0; i < set_size; i++)
               CPVECTOR3(Pk[i], Pk_subset[i]);   /** load into Pk+1 **/

            CPVECTOR3(Pk[i], Cp);                /** Union of Pk+1 with Cp **/
            i_tab[i] = P1_i;  j_tab[i] = P2_i;
            set_size++;
         }
      }

      CPVECTOR3(VP, Vk);                         /** load VP **/
      *m3 = set_size;
      for(i = 0; i < set_size; i++) {
         near_indx[i][0] = i_tab[i];             /** set indices of near pnt. in P1 **/
         near_indx[i][1] = j_tab[i];             /** set indices of near pnt. in P2 **/
      }
   }
}


/*** RJR 05/26/93 ************************************************************
 *
 *    Function to compute a proper separating plane between a pair of
 *    polytopes.  The plane will be a support plane for polytope 1.
 *
 *    On Entry:
 *       couple - couple structure for a pair of polytopes.
 *
 *    On Exit:
 *       couple - containing new proper separating plane, if one was
 *                found.
 *
 *    Function Return :
 *       result of whether or not a separating plane exists.
 *
 *************************************************************************/

Boolean get_new_plane(couple)
Couple          couple;
{
   Polyhedron     polyhedron1, polyhedron2;
   Boolean        plane_exists;
   double         pnts1[MAX_VERTS][3], pnts2[MAX_VERTS][3], dist,
                  u[3], v[3], lambda[4], VP[3];
   int            i, k, m1, m2;

   plane_exists = FALSE;

   polyhedron1 = couple->polyhdrn1;    polyhedron2 = couple->polyhdrn2;
```

```
    /** Apply M1 to vertices of polytope 1 **/

    m1 = polyhedron1->m;
    for (i = 0; i < m1; i++) {
       CPVECTOR3(pnts1[i], polyhedron1->verts[i]);
       VECADD3(pnts1[i], pnts1[i], polyhedron1->trn);
    }

    /** Apply M2 to vertices of polytope 1 **/

    m2 = polyhedron2->m;
    for (i = 0; i < m2; i++) {
       CPVECTOR3(pnts2[i], polyhedron2->verts[i]);
       VECADD3(pnts2[i], pnts2[i], polyhedron2->trn);
    }

    /** solve Eq. (1) for two polytopes **/

    dist3d(pnts1, m1, pnts2, m2, VP, couple->vert_indx, lambda, &couple->n);

    dist = sqrt(DOT3(VP,VP));   /** distance between polytopes **/

    if (!EQZ(dist)) {            /** Does a separating plane exist? **/
       plane_exists = TRUE;
       u[0] = u[1] = u[2] = v[0] = v[1] = v[2] = 0.0;
       for (i = 0; i < couple->n; i++) {
          k = couple->vert_indx[i][0];
          VECADDS3(u, lambda[i], pnts1[k], u);  /** point in P1 **/
          k = couple->vert_indx[i][1];
          VECADDS3(v, lambda[i], pnts2[k], v);  /** point in P2 **/
       }

       /** Store separating plane in P1's local coordinates **/

       VECADD3(u, u, polyhedron1->itrn);
       VECADD3(v, v, polyhedron1->itrn);

       /** Place separating plane in couple data structure **/

       CPVECTOR3(couple->pln_pnt1, u);
       CPVECTOR3(couple->pln_pnt2, v);
    }
    return plane_exists;
}


/*** RJR 05/26/93 ******************************************************
 *
 *    Function to detect if two polyhedra are intersecting.
 *
 *    On Entry:
 *       couple - couple structure for a pair of polytopes.
 *
 *    On Exit:
```

```
 *
 *    Function Return :
 *        result of whether polyhedra are intersecting or not.
 *
 *****************************************************************************/

Boolean Collision(couple)
Couple            couple;
{
    Polyhedron     polyhedron1, polyhedron2;
    Boolean        collide, loop;
    double         u[3], v[3], norm[3], d;
    int            i, m;

    polyhedron1 = couple->polyhdrn1;    polyhedron2 = couple->polyhdrn2;
    collide = FALSE;

    if (couple->plane_exists) {

        /** Transform proper separating plane to P2 local coordinates.   **/
        /** This avoids the computational cost of applying the           **/
        /** transformation matrix to all the vertices of P2.             **/

        CPVECTOR3(u, couple->pln_pnt1);   CPVECTOR3(v, couple->pln_pnt2);
        VECADD3(u, u, polyhedron1->trn);  VECADD3(v, v, polyhedron1->trn);
        VECADD3(u, u, polyhedron2->itrn); VECADD3(v, v, polyhedron2->itrn);
        VECSUB3(norm, v, u);

        m = polyhedron2->m;   i = 0; loop = TRUE;
        while ((i < m) && (loop)) {

            /** Evaluate plane equation **/

            VECSUB3(v, polyhedron2->verts[i], u);
            d = DOT3(v, norm);

            if (d <= 0.0) {               /** is P2 in opposite half-space **/
                loop = FALSE;
                if (!get_new_plane(couple)) {
                    collide = TRUE;        /** Collision **/
                    couple->plane_exists = FALSE;
                }
            }
            i++;
        }
    }
    else
        if (get_new_plane(couple)) {
            couple->plane_exists = TRUE;    /** No collision **/
        }
        else
            collide = TRUE;                 /** Collision **/
```

```
        return collide;
}


/*** RJR 05/26/93 **********************************************************
 *
 *    Function to initialize a polyhedron.
 *
 *    On Entry:
 *    polyhedron - pointer to a polyhedron structure.
 *         verts - verts to load.
 *             m - number of verts.
 *            tx - x translation.
 *            ty - y translation.
 *            tz - z translation.
 *
 *    On Exit:
 *        polyhedron - an initialized polyhedron.
 *
 *    Function Return : none.
 *
 ***********************************************************************/

void init_polyhedron(polyhedron, verts, m, tx, ty, tz)
Polyhedron     polyhedron;
double         *verts, tx, ty, tz;
int            m;
{
    int        i;
    double     *p;

    polyhedron->trn[0]  =  tx;  polyhedron->trn[1]  =  ty;
    polyhedron->trn[2]  =  tz;

    polyhedron->itrn[0] = -tx;  polyhedron->itrn[1] = -ty;
    polyhedron->itrn[2] = -tz;

    polyhedron->m = m;

    p = verts;
    for (i = 0; i < m; i++) {
       CPVECTOR3(polyhedron->verts[i], p);
       p += 3;
    }
}


/*** RJR 05/26/93 **********************************************************
 *
 *    Function to move a polyhedron.
 *
 *    On Entry:
 *    polyhedron - pointer to a polyhedron.
 *            tx - x translation.
 *
```

```
*              ty - y translation.
*              tz - z translation.
*
*    On Exit:
*       polyhedron - an updated polyhedron.
*
*    Function Return : none.
*
********************************************************************************/

void move_polyhedron(polyhedron, tx, ty, tz)
Polyhedron    polyhedron;
double        tx, ty, tz;
{
   polyhedron->trn[0]  += tx;  polyhedron->trn[1]  +=  ty;
   polyhedron->trn[2]  += tz;

   polyhedron->itrn[0] -= tx;  polyhedron->itrn[1] -=  ty;
   polyhedron->itrn[2] -= tz;
}


/*** RJR 05/26/93 ************************************************************
*
*    This is the Main Program for the Collision Detection example. This test
*    program creates the vertices of three polyhedra: a sphere, a box, and a
*    cylinder. The three polyhedra oscillate back and forth along the x-axis.
*    A collision test is done after each movement on each pair of polyhedra.
*    This test program was run on an SGI Onyx/4 and an SGI 4D/80.  A total of
*    30,000 collision detection tests was performed.  There were 3,160
*    collisions detected. The dist3d function was called in 14% of the
*    collision tests.  The average number of iterations in dist3d was 1.7.
*    The above functions are designed to compute accurate solutions when
*    the polyhedra are simple and convex.  The functions will work on
*    concave polyhedra, but the solutions are computed using the convex hulls
*    of the concave polyhedra.  In this case when the algorithm returns a
*    disjoint result, it is exact, but when it returns an intersection result
*    it is approximate.
*
********************************************************************************/
main()
{
   Polyhedron       Polyhedron1, Polyhedron2, Polyhedron3;
   Couple           Couple1, Couple2, Couple3;
   double           xstp1, xstp2, xstp3;
   int              i, steps;
   long             hits = 0;

   /*** Initialize the 3-test polyhedra ***/

   mak_box(box);
   mak_cyl(cyl);
   mak_sph(sphere);
```

```
Polyhedron1 = (Polyhedron)malloc(sizeof(struct polyhedron));
init_polyhedron(Polyhedron1, sphere, 342,  0.0, 0.0, 0.0);

Polyhedron2 = (Polyhedron)malloc(sizeof(struct polyhedron));
init_polyhedron(Polyhedron2, box, 8, 50.0, 0.0, 0.0);

Polyhedron3 = (Polyhedron)malloc(sizeof(struct polyhedron));
init_polyhedron(Polyhedron3, cyl, 36, -50.0, 0.0, 0.0);

Couple1 = (Couple)malloc(sizeof(struct couple));
Couple1->polyhdrn1 = Polyhedron1;   Couple1->polyhdrn2 = Polyhedron2;
Couple1->n = 0;
Couple1->plane_exists = FALSE;

Couple2 = (Couple)malloc(sizeof(struct couple));
Couple2->polyhdrn1 = Polyhedron1;   Couple2->polyhdrn2 = Polyhedron3;
Couple2->n = 0;
Couple2->plane_exists = FALSE;

Couple3 = (Couple)malloc(sizeof(struct couple));
Couple3->polyhdrn1 = Polyhedron3;   Couple3->polyhdrn2 = Polyhedron2;
Couple3->n = 0;
Couple3->plane_exists = FALSE;

/** Perform Collision Tests **/

xstp1 = 1.0;  xstp2 = 5.0; xstp3 = 10.0;  steps = 10000;

for (i = 0; i < steps; i++) {
   move_polyhedron(Polyhedron1, xstp1, 0.0, 0.0);
   move_polyhedron(Polyhedron2, xstp2, 0.0, 0.0);
   move_polyhedron(Polyhedron3, xstp3, 0.0, 0.0);

   if (Collision(Couple1))
      hits++;
   if (Collision(Couple2))
      hits++;
   if (Collision(Couple3))
      hits++;

   if (ABS(Polyhedron1->trn[0]) > 100.0)
      xstp1 = -xstp1;
   if (ABS(Polyhedron2->trn[0]) > 100.0)
      xstp2 = -xstp2;
   if (ABS(Polyhedron3->trn[0]) > 100.0)
      xstp3 = -xstp3;
}
printf("number of tests = %d\n",(steps * 3));
printf("number of hits = %ld\n", hits);
}
```

◇ **Bibliography** ◇

(Baraff 1990) David Baraff. Curved surfaces and coherence for non-penetrating rigid body simulation. *Computer Graphics*, 24(4):19–28, 1990.

(Gilbert *et al.* 1988) E. G. Gilbert, D. W. Johnson, and S. S. Keerthi. A fast procedure for computing the distance between complex object in three-dimensional space. *IEEE Journal of Robotics and Automation*, 4(2):193–203, 1988.

(Johnson 1987) Daniel Johnson. The Optimization of Robot Motion in the Presence of Obstacles. University of Michigan, Ph. D. Dissertation, 1987.

(Rockafellar 1970) R. T. Rockafellar. *Convex Analysis*. Princeton University Press, 1970.

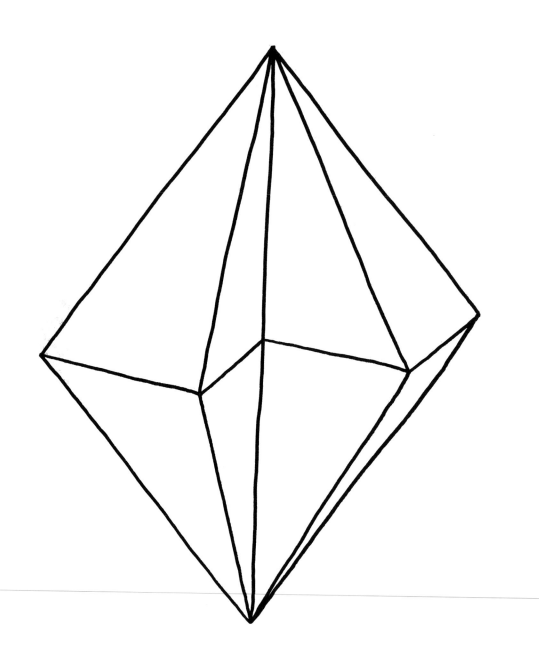

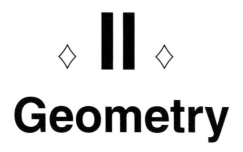

Geometry

This part of the book contains a mix of formulas, optimized algorithms, and tutorial information on the geometry of 2D, 3D, and n-D space.

II.1. Distance to an Ellipsoid, *by John C. Hart.*
Gives the formulas necessary to find the distance from a point to an ellipsoid, or from a point to an ellipse. These formulas can be useful for geometric modeling or for ray tracing. Page 113.

II.2. Fast Linear Approximations of Euclidean Distance in Higher Dimensions, *by Yoshikazu Ohashi.*
Provides optimized formulas for approximating Euclidean distance in two or more dimensions without square roots. Page 120.

II.3. Direct Outcode Calculation for Faster Clip Testing, *by Walt Donovan and Tim Van Hook.*
A very clever optimization of clip testing that exploits the properties of IEEE floating point format. Techniques are described to compute the "outcodes" needed for line clipping using only integer arithmetic. Page 125.

II.4. Computing the Area of a Spherical Polygon, *by Robert D. Miller.*
Gives the formulas needed to find the area of a polygon on a sphere that is bounded by great circle arcs. This is useful in cartography. Page 132.

II.5. The Pleasures of "Perp Dot" Products, *by F. S. Hill, Jr.*
A tutorial on the "perp dot product," which is the dot product, in 2D, of one vector and the vector perpendicular to another. Page 138.

II.6. Geometry for *N*-Dimensional Graphics, *by Andrew J. Hanson.*
A tutorial on n-dimensional geometry. Hanson generalizes a number of familiar concepts, such as plane equations, clipping, volume, and rotation, to n-D. Page 149.

II.1

Distance to an Ellipsoid

John C. Hart

School of Electrical Engineering and Computer Science
Washington State University
Pullman, WA 99164-2752
hart@eecs.wsu.edu

◇ Introduction ◇

The following Gem derives a formula for the distance from a point to an ellipsoid. The problem came to the author's attention when developing a method for rendering surfaces implicitly defined by functions that return the distance to the surface (Hart 1993).

Without loss of generality, the ellipsoid E is centered at the origin with principal axes parallel to the coordinate axes. This canonical state is within an isometry of any particular case. The distance $d(\mathbf{x}_0, E)$ is the length of the shortest line segment connecting $\mathbf{x}_0$ to any point $\mathbf{x}$ on the ellipsoid. This segment will be normal to the ellipsoid at $\mathbf{x}$, as are all such points $\mathbf{x}$ that satisfy the equation

$$\mathbf{x}_0 - \mathbf{x} = \alpha \mathbf{n}(\mathbf{x}) \tag{1}$$

where $\mathbf{n}(\mathbf{x})$ is the (not necessarily unit length) surface normal at $\mathbf{x}$ pointing outside the ellipsoid. The distance to an ellipsoid is hence given by the formula

$$d(\mathbf{x}_0, E) = \alpha_{\max} ||\mathbf{n}|| \tag{2}$$

where $\alpha_{\max}$ is the greatest solution to (1) and $\mathbf{n}$ is the normal of the closest point on the ellipsoid.

◇ Implicit Form ◇

The function

$$f(\mathbf{x}) = \frac{x^2}{a^2} + \frac{y^2}{b^2} + \frac{z^2}{c^2} - 1 \tag{3}$$

implicitly defines an ellipsoid with principal axes of radius $a, b,$ and c. The normal to an implicit surface at $\mathbf{x}$ is defined by the gradient

$$\mathbf{n}(\mathbf{x}) = \nabla f(\mathbf{x}) = \left(\frac{\partial f}{\partial x}, \frac{\partial f}{\partial y}, \frac{\partial f}{\partial z} \right) = 2 \left(\frac{x}{a^2}, \frac{y}{b^2}, \frac{z}{c^2} \right) \tag{4}$$

Since we are only interested in the normal direction, we will drop the factor of two in the following derivations.

Substituting (4) into (1) produces the system of equations

$$x_0 - x = \alpha \frac{x}{a^2}$$

$$y_0 - y = \alpha \frac{y}{b^2}$$

$$z_0 - z = \alpha \frac{z}{c^2}$$

which yields an expression for **x** given α as

$$x = \frac{a^2 x_0}{\alpha + a^2}$$

$$y = \frac{b^2 y_0}{\alpha + b^2}$$

$$z = \frac{c^2 z_0}{\alpha + c^2}$$

Plugging this expression into (3) constrains **x** to the ellipsoid, producing

$$\frac{a^2 x_0^2}{(\alpha + a^2)^2} + \frac{b^2 y_0^2}{(\alpha + b^2)^2} + \frac{c^2 z_0^2}{(\alpha + c^2)^2} = 1$$

which has the same solutions as

$$a^2(\alpha + b^2)^2(\alpha + c^2)^2 x_0^2 + (\alpha + a^2)^2 b^2(\alpha + c^2)^2 y_0^2 + (\alpha + a^2)^2(\alpha + b^2)^2 c^2 z_0^2$$
$$= (\alpha + a^2)^2(\alpha + b^2)^2(\alpha + c^2)^2 \tag{5}$$

◇ Parametric Form ◇

The same formula results from the parametric derivation. A parametric function for an ellipsoid is

$$\mathbf{x}(u, v) = (a C_v C_u, b C_v S_u, c S_v)$$

where $C_v = \cos v$, $S_v = \sin v$, and likewise for u. Then, by the normal transformation rule (Barr 1984), we have

$$\mathbf{n}(u, v) = \left(\frac{1}{a} C_v C_u, \frac{1}{b} C_v S_u, \frac{1}{c} S_v \right) \tag{6}$$

Expanding (1) parametrically produces the system of equations

$$x_0 - aC_vC_u = \frac{\alpha}{a}C_vC_u \tag{7}$$

$$y_0 - bC_vS_u = \frac{\alpha}{b}C_vS_u \tag{8}$$

$$z_0 - cS_v = \frac{\alpha}{c}S_v \tag{9}$$

The substitution $S_v = \sqrt{1 - C_v^2}$ gives the following solution for C_v from (9),

$$C_v = \sqrt{1 - \left(\frac{z_0}{c + \frac{\alpha}{c}}\right)^2} \tag{10}$$

Similarly, (7) and (8) give the competing expressions for C_u,

$$C_u = \frac{x_0}{(a + \frac{\alpha}{a})C_v} \tag{11}$$

$$C_u = \sqrt{1 - \left(\frac{y_0}{(b + \frac{\alpha}{b})C_v}\right)^2} \tag{12}$$

respectively. Setting (11) and (12) equal to each other (squaring both) yields

$$\frac{x_0^2}{(a + \frac{\alpha}{a})^2} = C_v^2 - \frac{y_0^2}{(b - \frac{\alpha}{b})^2} \tag{13}$$

and substituting C_v from (10) produces the first pleasing equation in this derivation:

$$\frac{x_0^2}{(a + \frac{\alpha}{a})^2} + \frac{y_0^2}{(b + \frac{\alpha}{b})^2} + \frac{z_0^2}{(c + \frac{\alpha}{c})^2} = 1 \tag{14}$$

As pleasing as it is, (14) doesn't handle the case where $\mathbf{x}_0$ is the origin. Removing the denominators returns

$$\left(b + \frac{\alpha}{b}\right)^2\left(c + \frac{\alpha}{c}\right)^2 x_0^2 + \left(a + \frac{\alpha}{a}\right)^2\left(c + \frac{\alpha}{c}\right)^2 y_0^2 + \left(a + \frac{\alpha}{a}\right)^2\left(b + \frac{\alpha}{b}\right)^2 z_0^2$$

$$= \left(a + \frac{\alpha}{a}\right)^2\left(b + \frac{\alpha}{b}\right)^2\left(c + \frac{\alpha}{c}\right)^2$$

which can easily be manipulated to yield (5) again.

◇   **Observations**   ◇

Solving (1) requires finding the roots of the sixth-degree polynomial[1] (5). Many numerical methods exist for finding the roots of such polynomials (Press *et al.* 1988). However, a few observations suggest a simple solution.

The first observation explains the six roots. For x_0 outside the ellipsoid, there is only one point on the ellipsoid whose normal points toward x_0. However, there can be as many as five other points whose surface normals point directly away from x_0. This is most easily demonstrated by reducing the problem to two dimensions, setting $c = a$ and $z_0 = 0$.

Consider the parameters $a = 1, b = 2$, and the point $x_0 = (5/4, 1/4)$. Figure 1 illustrates the resulting ellipse and some of its surface normals. The four surface normals intersecting x_0 are highlighted. The shaded region in the center indicates all points intersecting four ellipse normals. Its boundary, called the *evolute* of the ellipse because it is tangent everywhere to an ellipse normal (Millman and Parker 1977), indicates points intersecting three ellipse normals. Points outside the evolute intersect two ellipse normals.

For an ellipse, the evolute is the pinched superellipse

$$|ax|^{2/3} + |by|^{2/3} = |a^2 - b^2|^{2/3}$$

in implicit form, or

$$\left(\frac{a^2 - b^2}{a} \cos^3 \theta, \frac{b^2 - a^2}{b} \sin^3 \theta \right)$$

in parametric form (Spain 1957, p. 44). For an ellipsoid, the six intersecting surface normals lie on a quadric cone (Spain 1960, §40), and its evolute is most likely a pinched superellipsoid (Barr 1981).

The second observation simplifies the numerical solution. Figure 2 plots (5) as a function of α. As this figure demonstrates, the solution graph is strictly decreasing with decreasing slope beyond the largest root. Hence, Newton's method, given a sufficiently large initial point, will converge to the desired solution and swiftly compute the distance to the ellipsoid.

The third observation finds an appropriate initial point for Newton's method. Overestimating the distance and surface normal magnitude produces a value greater than the maximum root. If x_0 is on or inside the ellipsoid, then the maximum root will be zero or negative and an initial value of $\alpha_0 = 0$ suffices.

---

[1]One might assume that the gradient at x_0 points directly away from the closest point on the implicit surface, which yields a quadratic solution (Lorensen 1993). While this is true for the sphere and other natural quadrics, it does not generalize to their stretched versions. In particular, it is not true for ellipsoids.

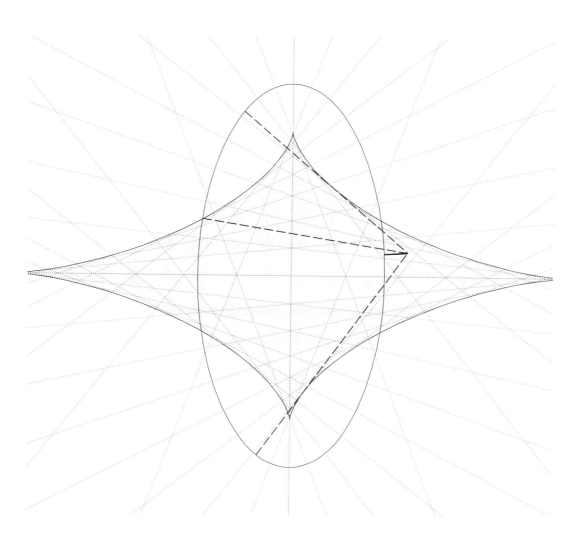

Figure 1. Ellipse and evolute. Dotted lines indicate extended normals to the ellipsoid, enveloping the shaded evolute interior. The solid line segment indicates the only positive solution to (5), whereas the dashed line segments indicate three negative solutions.

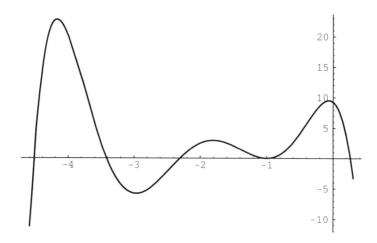

Figure 2. The function in (5) as a function of α. The rightmost root is the root of interest. There is a double root at −1.

Otherwise $\mathbf{x}_0$ is outside the ellipsoid and the initial point needs to satisfy

$$\alpha_0 \geq \frac{d(\mathbf{x}_0, E)}{||\mathbf{n}||}$$

Certainly $||\mathbf{x}_0||$, the distance to the origin, overestimates the distance to the ellipsoid. Since the equation for the distance to an ellipsoid (5) is the same for both implicit and parametric representations, consider the parametric surface normal (6). That function for the normal is the same as the parametric function for an ellipsoid with principal axes of radius $1/a, 1/b$, and $1/c$! Therefore, $||\mathbf{n}|| \geq \min\{1/a, 1/b, 1/c\}$, and a starting value of

$$\alpha_0 = ||\mathbf{x}_0|| \max\{a, b, c\}$$

suffices.

This Gem originated with 10 sheets of hotel stationery from a conversation with Al Barr and Jim Kajiya at SIGGRAPH '92. As editor, Paul Heckbert originated Figure 1, which forced the author to learn more analytic and differential geometry than he had originally intended.

◇ **Bibliography** ◇

(Barr 1981) Alan H. Barr. Superquadrics and angle-preserving transformations. *IEEE Computer Graphics and Applications*, 1(1):11–23, 1981.

(Barr 1984) Alan H. Barr. Global and local deformations of solid primitives. *Computer Graphics*, 18(3):21–30, July 1984.

(Hart 1993) John C. Hart. Sphere tracing: Simple robust antialiased rendering of distance-based implicit surfaces. Technical Report EECS-93-015, School of EECS, Washington State University, Jan. 1993. Appears in Jules Bloomenthal and Brian Wyvill, Eds., SIGGRAPH '93 Course Notes #25, "Modeling, Visualizing and Animating Implicit Surfaces."

(Lorensen 1993) William E. Lorensen. Geometric clipping using boolean textures. In *Proceedings of Visualization '93*, pages 268–274. IEEE Computer Society Press, Los Alamitos, CA, 1993.

(Millman and Parker 1977) Richard S. Millman and George D. Parker. *Elements of Differential Geometry*. Prentice Hall, Englewood Cliffs, NJ, 1977.

(Press *et al.* 1988) William H. Press, Brian P. Flannery, Saul A. Teukolsky, and William T. Vetterling. *Numerical Recipes in C*. Cambridge University Press, New York, 1988.

(Spain 1957) Barry Spain. *Analytical Conics*. Pergamon Press, New York, 1957.

(Spain 1960) Barry Spain. *Analytical Quadrics*. Pergamon Press, New York, 1960.

II.2

Fast Linear Approximations of Euclidean Distance in Higher Dimensions

Yoshikazu Ohashi[1]

Cognex
Needham, MA
yoshi@cognex.com

$\diamond$ **Distance Measures** $\diamond$

In the n-dimensional Euclidean space, the general distance metric L_m between two points $p = \{x_{1p}, x_{2p}, \ldots, x_{np}\}$ and $q = \{x_{1q}, x_{2q}, \ldots, x_{nq}\}$ is defined by

$$L_m = \left(\sum_i^n |x_{ip} - x_{iq}|^m \right)^{1/m}$$

The two most frequently used metrics are the *city block* or *Manhattan distance* (for $m = 1$), and the *Euclidean distance* ($m = 2$), which is given by

$$L_2 = \sqrt{\sum_i^n \Delta x_i^2} \quad \text{where} \quad \Delta x_i = |x_{ip} - x_{iq}|$$

In many cases in computer graphics and machine vision applications, this distance measure has to be evaluated repetitively and, moreover, accuracy is not required. Because the square root function takes a double type argument, a further speedup is possible by avoiding a type conversion in the case of an integer argument such as pixel (or voxel) positions.

In a previous article, Ritter discussed a fast linear approximation for 3D cases (Ritter 1990). This Gem is its extension to higher dimensions to find optimum coefficients, $c_i (i = 1, 2, \ldots, n)$, of the following linear approximation to the Euclidean distance,

$$L_{\text{approx}} = c_1 \cdot \Delta x_1 + c_2 \cdot \Delta x_2 + \cdots + c_n \cdot \Delta x_n = \sum_i^n c_i \cdot \Delta x_i$$

[1]Formerly at ARCO Research Center, Plano, Texas, where a part of this work was conducted.

where the variables are sorted in descending order such that

$$\Delta x_1 \geq \Delta x_2 \geq \cdots \Delta x_n \geq 0$$

Without ordering, the error of the approximation is much larger. Sorting is $O(n \log n)$, and this approach is useful for a small n. The relative error of this approximation is given by

$$e = \left| \frac{\sum\limits_{i}^{n} c_i \cdot \Delta x_i}{\sqrt{\sum\limits_{i}^{n} \Delta x_i^2}} - 1 \right| = \left| \sum\limits_{i}^{n} c_i \cdot u_i - 1 \right|$$

where $u_i = \Delta x_i / \sqrt{\sum_i^n \Delta x_i^2}$ is the ith axis component of a unit vector parallel to Δx.

◇ **Optimum Approximations** ◇

Our goal is to find a set of coefficients $c_i (i = 1, 2, \ldots, n)$ such that

$$\min_{c_i} \left[\max_{u_i} \left\{ \left| \sum\limits_{i}^{n} c_i \cdot u_i - 1 \right| \right\} \right]$$

under the conditions

$$1 \geq u_1 \geq u_2 \geq \cdots \geq u_n \geq 0$$

The summation $\sum_i^n c_i \cdot u_i$, which is a dot product of two vectors $\mathbf{c} = \{c_1, c_2, \ldots, c_n\}$ and $\mathbf{u} = \{u_1, u_2, \ldots, u_n\}$, is maximized when the two vectors are parallel and the maximum value is the length of the vector $|c| = \sqrt{\sum_i^n c_i^2}$. (Note that the antiparallel case will not occur because L and L_{approx} are non-negative.) The maximum can also occur at the boundaries of the region bounded by $1 \geq u_1 \geq u_2 \geq \cdots \geq u_n \geq 0$, i.e.,

$$
\begin{array}{lll}
u_1 = 1 & \text{and} & u_2 = u_3 = u_4 = \cdots = u_n = 0 \\
u_1 = u_2 = 1/\sqrt{2} & \text{and} & u_3 = u_4 = \cdots = u_n = 0 \\
u_1 = u_2 = u_3 = 1/\sqrt{3} & \text{and} & u_4 = \cdots = u_n = 0 \\
\quad \vdots & & \quad \vdots \\
u_1 = u_2 = \cdots = u_{n-1} = 1/\sqrt{n-1} & \text{and} & u_n = 0 \\
u_1 = u_2 = \cdots = u_{n-1} = u_n = 1/\sqrt{n} & &
\end{array}
$$

Considering these $(n+1)$ cases—one from the function maximum and n from boundary conditions—we can explicitly express the relative error as

$$e(c_1, c_2, \ldots, c_n) = \max\{|e_0|, |e_1|, \ldots, |e_n|\}$$

Table 1. Optimum coefficients in linear approximation for Euclidean distance

Dimensions	2	3	4	5	6	7	8
$\max(e)$	3.9%	6.0%	7.4%	8.4%	9.2%	9.8%	10.4%
c_1	0.9604	0.9398	0.9262	0.9161	0.9081	0.9016	0.8961
c_2	0.3978	0.3893	0.3836	0.3794	0.3762	0.3734	0.3712
c_3		0.2987	0.2943	0.2912	0.2887	0.2866	0.2848
c_4			0.2482	0.2455	0.2433	0.2416	0.2401
c_5				0.2162	0.2144	0.2128	0.2115
c_6					0.1938	0.1924	0.1912
c_7						0.1769	0.1759
c_8							0.1637

where

$$e_0 = \sqrt{\sum_i^n c_i^2} - 1$$

$$e_1 = c_1 - 1$$

$$e_2 = \left(\sum_{i=1}^2 c_i / \sqrt{2} \right) - 1$$

$$\vdots$$

$$e_n = \left(\sum_i^n c_i / \sqrt{n} \right) - 1$$

Note that an error can be negative or positive and that there are $(n+1)$ error equations for the n-dimensional cases. For example, in 2D and 3D these errors are

$$
\begin{array}{ll}
2D & 3D \\
e_0 = \sqrt{c_1^2 + c_2^2} - 1 & e_0 = \sqrt{c_1^2 + c_2^2 + c_3^2} - 1 \\
e_1 = c_1 - 1 & e_1 = c_1 - 1 \\
e_2 = (c_1 + c_2)/\sqrt{2} - 1 & e_2 = (c_1 + c_2)/\sqrt{2} - 1 \\
 & e_3 = (c_1 + c_2 + c_2)/\sqrt{3} - 1
\end{array}
$$

The optimum set of coefficients can be found as solutions for n simultaneous equations $|e_0| = |e_1| = |e_2| = \cdots = |e_n|$. (There are only n relationships among $n + 1$ error equations.) The error surface for 2D is shown in Figure 1. The optimum solutions through the eighth dimension are listed in Table 1.

◇ **Computing Speed Enhancement** ◇

In the original form of this linear approximation, floating point multiplication operations are still required. Especially when variables are integers, the performance can be further

Table 2. Comparison of 3D linear approximations for Euclidean distances

Constraints	c_1	c_2	c_3	$\max(e)$
1. None	0.9398	0.3893	0.2987	6.0%
2. $c_1 = 1$	1	0.2968	0.2914	8.3%
3. $c_1 = 1$, $c_2 = c_3$	1	0.2941	0.2941	8.3%
4. $c_2 = c_3$	0.9264	0.3872	0.3872	7.3%
5. fraction	15/16	3/8	9/32	7.2%
6. fraction, $c_2 = c_3$	15/16	3/8	3/8	7.7%
7.[2] fraction, $c_1 = 1$	1	11/32	1/4	8.7%
8.[2] fraction, $c_1 = 1$	1	5/16	1/4	9.8%
9. fraction, $c_1 = 1$, $c_2 = c_3$	1	9/32	9/32	9.8%
10.[2] unit fraction, $c_1 = 1$, $c_2 = c_3$	1	1/4	1/4	13.4%

[2]Coefficients suggested by Ritter (1990).

improved by finding appropriate bit-shift operations. Even if variables are floating point numbers, the following discussion can be applied with pre- and post-operations—i.e., making them integers after scaling up and changing back to floating point numbers after scaling down (see Ritter's pseudocode, p. 433). For the simplest 2D case, the optimum solutions can be approximated by

$$c_1 = 0.1111011_2 = 0.9609 \sim 0.9604$$
$$c_2 = 0.0110011_2 = 0.3984 \sim 0.3978$$

Furthermore, c_1 is two's complement of 0.0000101_2:

$$c_1 \cdot x_1 = (1.0 - 0.0000101_2) \cdot x_1 = \text{x1-(x1>>5)-(x1>>7)}$$
$$c_2 \cdot x_2 = 0.0110011_2 \cdot x_2 = \text{(x2>>2)+(x2>>3)+(x2>>6)+(x2>>7)}$$
$$\text{or } c_2 \cdot x_2 = \text{(t>>2)+(t>>6)} \text{ where t = x2+(x2>>1)}$$

With these coefficient approximations, the maximum relative error remains as low as 4.0% with a mean error of 2.4%.

Another way to improve computational speed is to make some coefficients equal at the sacrifice of the approximation accuracy. By doing so, sorting of parameter x's will be faster, and a cross term c*x can be combined as c*(x+x') for a further savings in the number of multiplication or bit-shift operations. Also, the largest coefficient can be set to unity to avoid multiplication or bit shifts for that term. Considering those factors, typical 3D cases are summarized in Table 2.

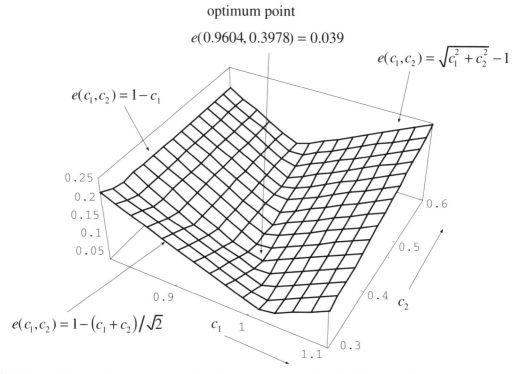

Figure 1. The maximum error is defined by three surfaces for the 2D case. The optimum (minimum relative error) point is (0.9604, 0.3978), at which the relative error is 3.9%.

◇ **Bibliography** ◇

(Ritter 1990) Jack Ritter. A fast approximation to 3D Euclidean distance. In A. Glassner, editor, *Graphics Gems*, pages 432–433. Academic Press, Boston, 1990.

◇ II.3

Direct Outcode Calculation for Faster Clip Testing

Walt Donovan

Sun Microsystems, Mail Stop 17-10
1505 Salado Avenue
Mountain View, CA 94043
donovan@eng.sun.com

Tim Van Hook

Silicon Graphics
2011 N. Shoreline Blvd.
Mountain View, CA 94043-1389
tvh@sgi.com

◇ Introduction ◇

This gem describes a method for calculating clip region outcodes directly from the IEEE-standard floating point representation of the 2D or 4D vertex. This method uses integer and logical operations and no conditional branches, and can be used as an alternative to the obvious method when optimizing a software implementation of the graphics pipeline.

The basic idea is to treat an IEEE floating point value as a two's complement integer. Since the IEEE representation is a sign-magnitude one, an absolute value is calculated by zeroing the sign bit, and a condition code is calculated by subtracting the magnitudes. Multiple condition codes are then assembled into an outcode.

This direct method performs more operations than the obvious method. However, the overall performance of a software implementation of a graphics pipeline on superscalar RISC processors is improved using the direct method. The lack of branches permits more code to be correctly prefetched, and the integer-only nature of the direct method permits the floating point unit to be used for other calculations. On one superscalar RISC processor, for example, the time it takes to transform, clip check, and project a 4D vertex is reduced from about 80 clocks to about 50 clocks.

◇ IEEE Floating Point Review ◇

An IEEE floating point number (ANS 1985) consists of three fields: the sign bit s, the exponent e, and the fraction f. Single-precision numbers use 8 bits to store e and 23 bits to store f; double-precision numbers use 11 and 52 bits, respectively. The sign bit s is stored in the most significant bit, then the next most significant bit is the high-order bit of e, and then the least significant bits store f, high order to low order. This is illustrated in the following figure.

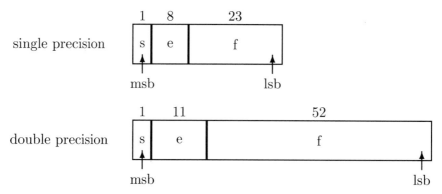

Figure 1. IEEE single- and double-precision floating point formats. msb means most significant bit; lsb least significant bit.

A single-precision number has a value determined by the following rules:

1. If $e = 255$ and $f \neq 0$, then the value is NaN (not a number) regardless of s.
2. If $e = 255$ and $f = 0$, then the value is $(-1)^s \infty$.
3. If $0 < e < 255$, then the value is $(-1)^s 2^{e-127}(1.f)$.
4. If $e = 0$ and $f \neq 0$, then the value is $(-1)^s 2^{-126}(0.f)$.
5. If $e = 0$ and $f = 0$, then the value is $(-1)^s 0$ (zero).

For double precision, the rules are:

1. If $e = 2047$ and $f \neq 0$, then the value is NaN (not a number) regardless of s.
2. If $e = 2047$ and $f = 0$, then the value is $(-1)^s \infty$.
3. If $0 < e < 2047$, then the value is $(-1)^s 2^{e-1023}(1.f)$.
4. If $e = 0$ and $f \neq 0$, then the value is $(-1)^s 2^{-1022}(0.f)$.
5. If $e = 0$ and $f = 0$, then the value is $(-1)^s 0$ (zero).

Let $a(x)$ be the number formed by concatenating the e and f fields of the non-NaN floating point number x; e.g., $a(x) = 2^{23}e + f$ for single precision. Let $v(x)$ be the integral value of the floating point number x; e.g., $v(x) = 2^{31}s + 2^{23}e + f$ for single precision. Let $s(i)$ be the sign bit of some integral value i; e.g., $s(-1) = 1$ and $s(1) = 0$.

First, if $x < 0$, then $s(v(x)) = 1$, and if $x \geq 0$, $s(v(x)) = 0$, by definition. It is easy to see by induction that $|x| \leq |y|$ if and only if $a(x) \leq a(y)$, with equality implying equality. Thus, $\text{sign}(x - y) = \text{sign}(a(x) - a(y))$ for $x, y \geq 0$. The other cases are of less interest to us; e.g., $\text{sign}(x - y) = -1$ for $x < 0, y \geq 0$ as long as $a(x) + a(y)$ doesn't overflow into the sign bit. (The problem is that detecting the overflow case takes more code than is worth doing.)

In the C language code that follows, we assume that single-precision floating point (`float`) is used on 32-bit processors, where $\text{sizeof(long)} = \text{sizeof(float)} = 4$ 8-bit bytes. We also assume that double-precision floating point is used on 64-bit processors, and that $\mathtt{sizeof(long)} = \mathtt{sizeof(double)} = 8$ bytes there. Then the C code for direct outcode calculation will work properly on either 32 and 64 bit processors.

◇ 2D Outcode Calculation ◇

The standard outcode calculation in C for the 2D vertex (x, y) against the clip window with corners at $(xmin, ymin)$ and $(xmax, ymax)$ is (Foley *et al.* 1990, p. 116, function CompOutCode)

```
outcode = 0;
if (x < xmin) outcode |= 1;
if (x > xmax) outcode |= 2;
if (y < ymin) outcode |= 4;
if (y > ymax) outcode |= 8;
```

where we use explicit constants to make the following clearer. We assume that $0 \leq xmin \leq xmax$ and $0 \leq ymin \leq ymax$, since negative clip windows are atypical of 2D graphics pipelines. Let us rewrite the first **if** test above

```
if (x < xmin)
```

as

```
if ( (x < 0 && x < xmin) || (x >= 0 && x < xmin) )
```

which is clearly equivalent. Now, since $xmin \geq 0$, we can simplify the above test to

```
if ( (x < 0) || (x >= 0 && x < xmin))
```

because $x < 0$ implies that $x < xmin$. Finally, we introduce the absolute value and simplify further to

```
if ( (x < 0) || (abs(x) < xmin) )
```

A similar sequence of steps for the $x > xmax$ expression gives

```
if ( (x >= 0) && (abs(x) > xmax) )
```

as an equivalent calculation. We substitute y for x to get the equivalent expressions for the *ymin* and *ymax* **if** tests. The outcode calculation then becomes

```
outcode = 0;
if ( (x < 0)  || (abs(x) < xmin) ) outcode |= 1;
if ( (x >= 0) && (abs(x) > xmax) ) outcode |= 2;
if ( (y < 0)  || (abs(y) < ymin) ) outcode |= 4;
if ( (y >= 0) && (abs(y) > ymax) ) outcode |= 8;
```

We are now ready to translate the above to sign bit form. $x < 0$ is equivalent to $s(v(x))$. $x \geq 0$ is equivalent to $s(\neg v(x))$, where $\neg$ is the Boolean negation operator. $abs(x) < xmin$ is equivalent to $s(a(x) - v(xmin))$. $abs(x) > xmax$ is equivalent to $s(v(xmax) - a(x))$. Putting that all together, we get the following direct outcode calculation. All variables except x and y are assumed declared as **long**.

◇ **Code** ◇

Direct Calculation of 2D Outcodes

```
/* number of bits in a word */
#define NUMBITS     sizeof(long)*8

/* get the integral form of a floating point number */
#define v(x)        *(long *) &(x)

/* get the sign bit of an integer as a value 0 or 1 */
#define s(x)        (((unsigned long)(x)) >> (NUMBITS-1))

/* get the absolute value of a floating point number in integral form */
#define a(x)        ((x) & ~(1 << (NUMBITS-1)))

        /* these values typically would be calculated once and cached */
        ixmin = v(xmin);
        ixmax = v(xmax);
        iymin = v(ymin);
        iymax = v(ymax);

        /* get the bits and absolute value */
        ix = v(x); ax = a(ix);
        /* put the sign bit in bit 0 */
        outcode = s(ix | (ax - ixmin));

        /* put the sign bit in bit 1 */
        outcode |= s(~ix & (ixmax - ax)) << 1;

        /* do the same for y */
        iy = v(y);
        ay = a(iy);
        outcode |= s(iy | (ay - iymin))  << 2;
        outcode |= s(~iy & (iymax - ay)) << 3;
```

In a software 2D pipeline implementation, one would overlap the direct outcode calculation with transforming the next 2D vertex.

◇ **4D (Homogeneous) Outcode Calculation** ◇

In the most general form of homogeneous clipping, we accept points with negative as well as positive w (see (Foley *et al.* 1990, pp. 271–278), which only discusses a 6-bit outcode, but the extension to 7 bits is obvious). Other times, we accept points with positive w only. The following algorithm uses a 7-bit outcode for the homogeneous vertex (x, y, z, w) to implement both cases.

First, we show the computation of the 7-bit outcode.

```
outcode = 0;
if (w < 0)          outcode = 1;
if (abs(x) > abs(w))
    if (x < 0)  outcode |= 2;
    else            outcode |= 4;
if (abs(y) > abs(w))
    if (y < 0)  outcode |= 8;
    else            outcode |= 16;
if (abs(z) > abs(w))
    if (z < 0)  outcode |= 32;
    else            outcode |= 64;
```

This computation assumes that the perspective view volume is completely symmetrical and defined by $-1 \leq x/w, y/w, z/w \leq 1$, which saves some steps in the calculation. Non-symmetric view volumes, e.g., $0 \leq z'/w \leq 1$, can usually be made symmetric with a simple scale and translate concatenated to the view transform. In the example, $z = 2z' - 1$.

Given the 7-bit outcodes for each vertex, we digress a bit to show how to clip test multiple vertices, e.g., a line or a triangle (in (Foley *et al.* 1990, pp. 113–114), trivial reject occurs if the *and_code* is non-zero, and trivial accept occurs if the *or_code* is zero).

The following C pseudocode outlines the steps involved.

```
/* initialize */
and_code         = -1;
or_code          = 0;
...

/* for each vertex in the object ... */
{
    /* calculate outcode for vertex */
    ...

    /* accumulate clip status */
    and_code      &= outcode;
    or_code       |= outcode;
}

/* analyze the clip status for the entire object */

if (reject_negative_w) {
    /* accept positive w only */
    if (and_code)
        trivial reject;
} else {
    /* allow negative w */
    if (and_code & 0x7E)
        trivial reject;
}
if (or_code == and_code)
        trivial accept;
/* else object needs clipping */
```

The last test, for trivial accept, deserves an explanation. For the *reject_negative_w* case, an *or_code* of zero implies trivial accept, and the *and_code* will be zero at that point (a non-zero code would have caused a trivial reject earlier). For the general case, trivial accept can occur only if all vertices have the same w sign; thus either *or_code* is zero (for positive w), which falls into the previous case, or *or_code* is 1 and *and_code* is 1 when all points have negative w. In all cases, the test for trivial accept is seen to be equivalent to *or_code = and_code*.

We return to the outcode calculation now. Since it is already in absolute value form, our work is simplified. In sign bit form, $abs(x) > abs(w)$ is equivalent to $s(a(w) - a(x))$, and $x < 0$ is equivalent to $s(v(x))$. The outcode calculation now has to generate one of three values: 0, 1, or 2. This can be calculated by $s(a(w) - a(x)) << s(v(x))$, where $<<$ is the C binary left shift operator. If the first term is zero, the outcode is zero; otherwise, the outcode is 1 if the second term is 0, or 2 otherwise.

The direct calculation of the 4D outcode is shown below. All variables except x, y, z, and w are assumed declared as **long**.

◇ **Code** ◇

Direct Calculation of 4D Outcodes

```
/* number of bits in a word */
#define NUMBITS     sizeof(long)*8

/* get the integral form of a floating point number */
#define v(x)        *(long *) &(x)

/* get the sign bit of an integer as a value 0 or 1 */
#define s(x)        (((unsigned long)(x)) >> (NUMBITS-1))

/* get the absolute value of a floating point number in integral form */
#define a(x)        ((x) & ~(1 << (NUMBITS-1)))

        iw = v(w);
        abs_w = a(iw);
        outcode = s(iw);         /* 0 or 1 per w's sign */

        ix = v(x);
        diff = s(abs_w - a(ix));
        t = s(ix) + 1;
        outcode |= diff << t;    /* 0, 2, or 4 or'd with outcode */

        iy = v(y);
        diff = s(abs_w - a(iy));
        t = s(iy) + 3;
        outcode |= diff << t;    /* 0, 8, or 16 or'd with outcode */
```

```
iz = v(z);
diff = s(abs_w - a(iz));
t = s(iz) + 5;
outcode |= diff << t;      /* 0, 32, or 64 or'd with outcode */
```

In a software implementation of a 3D pipeline, one would interleave the preceding outcode calculation with the transformation from projective coordinates to device coordinates.

Note that the direct calculation above accepts the invalid homogeneous point $(0, 0, 0, 0)$. One can avoid generating that value by disallowing degenerate projection matrices. Alternatively, one could trap for an invalid operation exception in the device coordinates transformation step and correct the outcode.

◇ **Bibliography** ◇

(ANS 1985) IEEE standard for binary floating-point arithmetic. ANSI/IEEE Standard 754-1985, IEEE, New York, 1985.

(Foley *et al.* 1990) James D. Foley, Andries van Dam, Steven K. Feiner, and John F. Hughes. *Computer Graphics Principles and Practice*, second edition. Addison-Wesley, Reading, MA, 1990.

◊ II.4

Computing the Area of a Spherical Polygon

Robert D. Miller
1837 Burrwood Circle
E. Lansing, MI 48823

◊ Problem ◊

Given a spherical polygon described by its vertices, find its area. Each side of a spherical polygon is a great circle arc on a sphere. Finding the area of a spherical polygon has applications in cartography. The idea used in finding areas of planar triangles by summing the signed areas of component triangles can be extended to apply to spherical polygons. The method described here works for convex as well as concave spherical polygons.

◊ Definitions ◊

Spherical polygons are defined by great circle arcs connecting points on the sphere. On the Earth, these points are specified by latitude and longitude. Latitude is the angle, in degrees, measured northward from the equator, the poles being at latitudes $\pm 90°$. Longitudes are measured in the east–west direction from a central meridian and have values from $0°$ to $360°$.

Areas on a canonical sphere (not just the Earth) are often measured in units of *spherical degree*. Distances on this sphere are measured in degrees along the great circle arc. One spherical degree is the area of a spherical triangle that has two sides that are $90°$ arcs and the third side is a $1°$ arc. The area of a hemisphere is then 360 spherical degrees and the area of a sphere is 720 spherical degrees.

Spherical excess, in spherical degrees, is defined as the sum of the angles of a spherical triangle minus $180°$.

For a spherical polygon of n sides, the spherical excess, E, is generalized to:

$$E = \sum \text{interior angles} - ((n - 2) \times 180°)$$

The area of a spherical polygon in spherical degrees is the spherical excess, E. (McCormack 1931) has a simple proof. In more standard units of area, a spherical polygon with spherical excess E on a sphere of radius r has an area of $\pi r^2 E / 180$.

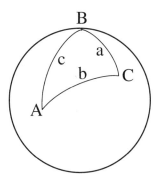

Figure 1.   Spherical triangle.

A spherical triangle with sides of a 90° arc and angles of 90° has a spherical excess and an area of 90 spherical degrees. Eight such triangles cover a sphere: 8×90 spherical degrees $= 720$ spherical degrees.

◇   Method   ◇

For a spherical polygon, we will find its area, given the positions of each of its vertices. These points are known by longitude, λ, and latitude, ϕ. Alternatively, we may know these vertex positions from Cartesian coordinates. For a sphere of radius, r, centered at the origin, longitudes and latitudes are related to Cartesian coordinates by:

$$x = r \cos \phi \cos \lambda; \qquad y = r \cos \phi \sin \lambda; \qquad z = r \sin \phi$$
$$r = \sqrt{x^2 + y^2 + z^2}; \qquad \lambda = \tan^{-1}(y/x); \qquad \phi = \sin^{-1}(z/r)$$

Using spherical triangles allows us to solve for the unknown quantities needed to use the spherical excess to provide the spherical polygon's area. Consider the spherical triangle ABC as shown in Figure 1. Points and the vertex angles are denoted by upper-case letters and the triangle's edge lengths by lower case. For example, $\cos B$ is the cosine of the angle formed by the two adjacent sides, a and c. B is chosen as a vertex at the Earth's pole, so that the angle at B is simply the difference in longitudes of points A and C. Two sides are known from the complements of the latitudes of their vertices, i.e. $a = 90° -$ latitude(C) and $c = 90° -$ latitude(A). The spherical cosine equation (Van de Kamp 1967) yields the third side, given two sides and the included angle:

$$\cos b = \cos a \cos c + \sin a \sin c \cos B$$

The *haversine* function is defined as $\operatorname{hav} x = (1 - \cos x)/2$. The use of haversines avoids computing arc cosines of values near ± 1. Rewriting the cosine formula in terms of haversines is useful for improved numerical accuracy when computing a side of a spherical triangle whose length is very small relative to the other two sides. These situations arise frequently in distance calculations.

Using the haversine, we substitute $1 - 2\operatorname{hav}x$ for $\cos x$ in the cosine equation:

$$\begin{aligned} 1 - 2\operatorname{hav}b &= \cos a \cos c + \sin a \sin c (1 - 2\operatorname{hav}B) \\ &= \cos a \cos c + \sin a \sin c - 2\sin a \sin c \operatorname{hav}B \end{aligned}$$

Applying the trigonometric identity $\cos(x \pm y) = \cos x \cos y \mp \sin x \sin y$, we get:

$$\begin{aligned} 1 - 2\operatorname{hav}b &= \cos(a - c) - 2\sin a \sin c \operatorname{hav}B \quad \text{so,} \\ \operatorname{hav}b &= \operatorname{hav}(a - c) + \sin a \sin c \operatorname{hav}B \end{aligned}$$

To get the inverse haversine, we can use the arc sine since

$$\begin{aligned} 1 - 2\operatorname{hav}b &= \cos b = 1 - 2\sin^2\left(\frac{b}{2}\right) \\ \operatorname{hav}b &= \sin^2\left(\frac{b}{2}\right), \quad \text{therefore} \\ b &= 2\sin^{-1}\sqrt{\operatorname{hav}(a - c) + \sin a \sin c \operatorname{hav}B} \end{aligned}$$

Having all three sides of the spherical triangle, we can use a formula from (Burington 1973) to obtain its spherical excess:

$$E = 4\tan^{-1}\sqrt{\tan\left(\frac{s}{2}\right)\tan\left(\frac{s-a}{2}\right)\tan\left(\frac{s-b}{2}\right)\tan\left(\frac{s-c}{2}\right)}$$

where $s = \frac{1}{2}(a + b + c)$.

To find the area of a spherical polygon, use successive vertices, in pairs, to form spherical triangles as shown in Figure 2. The shaded area is the spherical polygon $ABCD$ and the arcs show the four spherical triangles: APB, BPC, CPD, DPA. Each spherical triangle will have the pole as one vertex to make the calculations convenient, since vertices are given in terms of longitudes and latitudes. The polar angle is the difference in longitudes of the other two vertices, and the two adjacent sides are the complements of the latitudes of those vertices. The haversine formula applied to each spherical triangle solves for the unknown side, which is one arc of the spherical polygon. The spherical excess formula, above, provides the area for each spherical triangle.

In the case of plane polygons, the total area is the absolute value of the sum of the signed areas of the component triangles. The spherical triangle formulas do not yield signed areas, but when calculating the areas of the individual triangles, we will adopt a convention: the sign of the spherical triangle will be the same as the sign of the difference

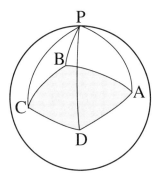

Figure 2.   Spherical polygon.

of the longitudes of a pair of adjacent vertices. The area of the spherical polygon is the absolute value of the sum of spherical excesses of each of the spherical triangles. The area of a spherical polygon with many vertices may be found using this method. There is one provision: in forming the spherical triangles, one must enumerate the vertex points by traversing the polygon in a consistent direction, e.g., counterclockwise.

◇   **Geographic Particulars**   ◇

If the sphere of interest is the Earth, we can use the mean radius $r \approx 3956.5466$ miles, $r^2 = 15{,}654{,}261$ miles^2, and the spherical excess, E, so the area $S = E \times 273{,}218.4$ square miles, or $S = E \times 707{,}632.4$ square kilometers.

When finding the area of a relatively small spherical polygon on the Earth, we should take its slightly oblate shape into account. A better value for the Earth's radius near the latitudes of interest is the radius of the ellipsoid, r, at latitude ϕ:

$$r(\phi) = \frac{a}{\sqrt{1 - e^2 \sin^2 \phi}}$$

where a is the Earth's equatorial radius, ≈ 3963.1905 miles, and e is the eccentricity of the Earth's ellipsoid. For Clarke's Ellipsoid of 1866, $e^2 \approx 0.006768658$. See (Snyder 1987).

◇   **C Code**   ◇

```
#include <math.h>
static const double
    HalfPi= 1.5707963267948966192313,
    Degree= 57.295779513082320876798;   /* degrees per radian */
```

```c
double Hav(double X)
/*  Haversine function: hav(x)= (1-cos(x))/2.  */
{
    return (1.0 -cos(X))/2.0;
}


double SphericalPolyArea(double *Lat, double *Lon, int N)
/*  Returns the area of a spherical polygon in spherical degrees,
      given the latitudes and longitudes in Lat and Lon, respectively.
      The N data points have indices which range from 0 to N-1. */
{
int  J, K;
double
    Lam1, Lam2, Beta1, Beta2,
    CosB1, CosB2, HavA,
    T, A, B, C, S, Sum, Excess;

    Sum= 0;
    for (J= 0; J <= N; J++)
    {
        K= J+1;
        if (J == 0)
        {
            Lam1= Lon[J];       Beta1= Lat[J];
            Lam2= Lon[J+1];     Beta2= Lat[J+1];
            CosB1= cos(Beta1);  CosB2= cos(Beta2);
        }
        else
        {
            K= (J+1) % (N+1);
            Lam1= Lam2;         Beta1= Beta2;
            Lam2= Lon[K];       Beta2= Lat[K];
            CosB1= CosB2;       CosB2= cos(Beta2);
        }

        if (Lam1 != Lam2)
        {
            HavA= Hav(Beta2-Beta1) +CosB1*CosB2*Hav(Lam2-Lam1);
            A= 2*asin(sqrt(HavA));
            B= HalfPi -Beta2;
            C= HalfPi -Beta1;
            S= 0.5*(A+B+C);
            T= tan(S/2)  * tan((S-A)/2) * tan((S-B)/2) * tan((S-C)/2);

            Excess= fabs(4*atan(sqrt(fabs(T))))*Degree;
            if (Lam2 < Lam1) Excess= -Excess;

            Sum= Sum + Excess;
        }
    }
    return fabs(Sum);
}  /*  SphericalPolyArea. */
```

◇ **Bibliography** ◇

(Burington 1973) Richard Stevens Burington. *Handbook of Mathematical Formulas and Tables.* McGraw-Hill, New York, NY, 1973.

(McCormack 1931) Joseph P. McCormack. *Solid Geometry.* D. Appleton-Century, New York, NY, 1931.

(Snyder 1987) John P. Snyder. *Map Projections, A Working Manual.* U.S. Geological Survey, Washington, D.C., 1987.

(Van de Kamp 1967) Peter Van de Kamp. *Principles of Astrometry.* W. H. Freeman, San Francisco, 1967.

II.5

The Pleasures of "Perp Dot" Products

F. S. Hill, Jr.
Dept. of Electrical and Computer Engineering
University of Massachusetts
Amherst, MA 01003
hill@ecs.umass.edu

◇ **Introduction** ◇

While developing code to perform certain geometric tasks in computer graphics, we do a lot of pencil-and-paper calculations to work out the relationships among the various quantities involved. This often requires intricate manipulations involving individual components of points and vectors, which can be both confusing and error-prone. It's a boon, therefore, when a concise and expressive notational device is developed to "expose" key geometric quantities lurking beneath the surface of many problems. This Gem presents two such geometric objects and develops some algebraic tools for working with them. It then applies them to obtain compact explicit formulas for finding incircles, excircles, corner rounding, and other well-known, messy problems.

We work in 2D and make explicit a notation for a vector that lies perpendicular to a given vector. Figure 1 shows vector $\mathbf{a} = (a_x, a_y)$. There are two vectors that have the same length as $\mathbf{a}$ and are perpendicular to it; we give the name $\mathbf{a}^\perp$ (read as *a perp*) to the one that is rotated 90° counterclockwise (ccw). It is easy to see that its coordinates are

$$\mathbf{a}^\perp = \mathbf{a} \begin{pmatrix} 0 & 1 \\ -1 & 0 \end{pmatrix} = (-a_x, a_y) \tag{1}$$

formed by interchanging the components of $\mathbf{a}$ and negating the first. The "perp" symbol $\perp$ may be viewed as the "rotate 90° ccw" operator applied to any vector $\mathbf{a}$, whereupon

Figure 1. Vector **a** and its "perp."

it enjoys the following easily proved properties:

Some Properties of $a^\perp$

- Linearity: $(\mathbf{a} + \mathbf{b})^\perp = \mathbf{a}^\perp + \mathbf{b}^\perp$ and $(A\mathbf{a})^\perp = A\mathbf{a}^\perp$ for any scalar A
- Length of $\mathbf{a}^\perp$: $|\mathbf{a}| = |\mathbf{a}^\perp|$
- Applying $\perp$ twice: $\mathbf{a}^{\perp\perp} = (\mathbf{a}^\perp)^\perp = -\mathbf{a}$

(If we view a vector as a point in the complex plane, the perp operator is equivalent to multiplying by $i = \sqrt{-1}$, which makes these algebraic properties immediately apparent.)

As a simple example, we find the **perpendicular bisector** of the segment between points A and B, which arises in such studies as fractal curves and finding the circle through three points. The perpendicular bisector is the line that passes through the midpoint between A and B (given by $(A + B)/2$) and is perpendicular to the vector $B - A$. So using parameter t gives the compact parametric representation:

$$p(t) = \frac{1}{2}(A + B) + (B - A)^\perp t \tag{2}$$

By itself the perp notation is merely congenial. Its power emerges when we use it in conjunction with a second vector. Given 2D vectors $\mathbf{a}$ and $\mathbf{b}$, what is the nature of the dot product between $\mathbf{a}^\perp$ and $\mathbf{b}$? Just work out the usual component form to obtain

$$\mathbf{a}^\perp \cdot \mathbf{b} = a_x b_y - a_y b_x = \begin{vmatrix} a_x & a_y \\ b_x & b_y \end{vmatrix} \tag{3}$$

which shows that it is the determinant of the matrix with first row $\mathbf{a}$ and second row $\mathbf{b}$. We call $\mathbf{a}^\perp \cdot \mathbf{b}$ the *perp-dot* product of vectors $\mathbf{a}$ and $\mathbf{b}$. Some of its evident properties are

$$\mathbf{a}^\perp \cdot \mathbf{b} = -\mathbf{b}^\perp \cdot \mathbf{a}, \ \mathbf{a}^\perp \cdot \mathbf{b}^\perp = \mathbf{a} \cdot \mathbf{b}, \ \mathbf{a}^\perp \cdot \mathbf{a} = 0, \text{ and } \mathbf{a}^\perp \cdot \mathbf{a}^\perp = |\mathbf{a}^\perp|^2 = |\mathbf{a}|^2$$

(Aside: Pursuing the analogy with complex numbers, $\mathbf{a} \cdot \mathbf{b}$ corresponds to the real part of a^*b where a^* is the complex conjugate of a, and $\mathbf{a}^\perp \cdot \mathbf{b}$ corresponds to the imaginary part of a^*b. These correspondences also make the above properties readily apparent.)

From well-known properties of the dot product we see in Figure 2a that $\mathbf{a}^\perp \cdot \mathbf{b}$ has the value $|\mathbf{a}^\perp||\mathbf{b}| \cos(\phi)$, where ϕ is the angle between $\mathbf{a}^\perp$ and $\mathbf{b}$. Calling θ the angle from $\mathbf{a}$ to $\mathbf{b}$ (measured positive ccw), then $\cos(\phi)$ equals $\sin(\theta)$, so:

$$\mathbf{a}^\perp \cdot \mathbf{b} = |\mathbf{a}||\mathbf{b}| \sin(\theta) \tag{4}$$

This dot product is positive if $\mathbf{a}^\perp$ is less than 90° away from $\mathbf{b}$ (that is, if there is a left turn from $\mathbf{a}$ to $\mathbf{b}$), and is negative otherwise, as seen in Figure 2b. Thus it gives the *sense* of the turn from the direction of $\mathbf{a}$ to that of $\mathbf{b}$, which is a key ingredient in many geometric algorithms. If $\mathbf{a}^\perp \cdot \mathbf{b} = 0$, there is no turn, and $\mathbf{a}$ is parallel to $\mathbf{b}$.

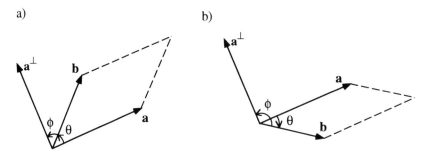

Figure 2. On the geometric nature of $\mathbf{a}^\perp \cdot \mathbf{b}$.

To summarize:

- $\mathbf{a}^\perp \cdot \mathbf{b} > 0$ if $\mathbf{b}$ is ccw from $\mathbf{a}$
- $\mathbf{a}^\perp \cdot \mathbf{b} < 0$ if $\mathbf{b}$ is cw from $\mathbf{a}$
- $\mathbf{a}^\perp \cdot \mathbf{b} = 0$ if $\mathbf{a}$ and $\mathbf{b}$ are parallel or antiparallel (linearly dependent)

The parallelogram determined by $\mathbf{a}$ and $\mathbf{b}$ has base $|\mathbf{a}|$ and altitude $|\mathbf{b}||\sin(\theta)|$, so its area is $|\mathbf{a}||\mathbf{b}||\sin(\theta)|$. Thus, using Equation 4,

$$|\mathbf{a}^\perp \cdot \mathbf{b}| = \text{area of parallelogram determined by } \mathbf{a} \text{ and } \mathbf{b} \qquad (5)$$

which is twice the area of the triangle with vertices $(0,0)$, $\mathbf{a}$, and $\mathbf{b}$. Thus $\mathbf{a}^\perp \cdot \mathbf{b}$ is the familiar **signed area** determined by $\mathbf{a}$ and $\mathbf{b}$. It is the 2D analog of the *vector cross product* $\mathbf{a} \times \mathbf{b}$ that could be applied if $\mathbf{a}$ and $\mathbf{b}$ were 3D vectors. (More precisely, its value is seen from Equation 3 to be $\mathbf{a} \times \mathbf{b} \cdot \mathbf{k}$, where $\mathbf{k} = (0,0,1)$.) The power of the notation $\mathbf{a}^\perp \cdot \mathbf{b}$ in the 2D case is that it shows precisely how a signed area is "decomposed" into a *dot product* of readily recognizable geometric objects in the problem at hand. We see this power in action in the examples below.

Summary of Properties of $\mathbf{a}^\perp \cdot \mathbf{b}$

We list the principal properties of the perp-dot product $\mathbf{a}^\perp \cdot \mathbf{b}$. When the perp-dot product differs from the "regular" dot product $\mathbf{a} \cdot \mathbf{b}$ in an interesting way, we contrast them.

- $\mathbf{a}^\perp \cdot \mathbf{b}$ is linear in $\mathbf{a}$ and in $\mathbf{b}$ individually
- $\mathbf{a}^\perp \cdot \mathbf{b} = -\mathbf{b}^\perp \cdot \mathbf{a}$ versus $\mathbf{a} \cdot \mathbf{b} = \mathbf{b} \cdot \mathbf{a}$
- $\mathbf{a}^\perp \cdot \mathbf{b}^\perp = \mathbf{a} \cdot \mathbf{b}$, so $\mathbf{a}^\perp \cdot \mathbf{a}^\perp = |\mathbf{a}|^2$
- $\mathbf{a}^\perp \cdot \mathbf{a} = 0$ versus $\mathbf{a} \cdot \mathbf{a} = |\mathbf{a}|^2$

- $\mathbf{a}^{\perp} \cdot \mathbf{b} = |\mathbf{a}||\mathbf{b}|\sin(\theta)$ versus $\mathbf{a} \cdot \mathbf{b} = |\mathbf{a}||\mathbf{b}|\cos(\theta)$
- $(\mathbf{a}^{\perp} \cdot \mathbf{b})^2 + (\mathbf{a} \cdot \mathbf{b})^2 = |\mathbf{a}|^2|\mathbf{b}|^2$
- $|\mathbf{a}^{\perp} \cdot \mathbf{b}|$ is the area of the parallelogram defined by $\mathbf{a}$ and $\mathbf{b}$
- $\mathbf{a}^{\perp} \cdot \mathbf{b}$ is positive if and only if there is a ccw turn from $\mathbf{a}$ to $\mathbf{b}$

◇ Example Applications of the Perp-Dot Product ◇

The first example reiterates some classic uses of signed area and just casts them in terms of perp-dot products. For the subsequent examples, however, the perp-dot product appears in more surprising ways and leads to compact, explicit expressions for a number of geometric results. We present brief derivations of some of the formulas in order to show how the perp-dot product can be manipulated and its properties exploited.

Example 1: Convexity and area of polygons

Consider the simple polygon P with vertices P_i and edge vectors $\mathbf{v}_i = P_{i+1} - P_i$, for $i = 1, \ldots, N$ (where P_{N+1} is understood to equal P_1). This polygon is convex if and only if all turns from one edge vector to the next have the same sense. This rule is easily stated in terms of the perp-dot product as:

P is convex iff all $\mathbf{v_i}^{\perp} \cdot \mathbf{v_{i+1}} \geq 0$, or all $\mathbf{v_i}^{\perp} \cdot \mathbf{v_{i+1}} \leq 0$

(Note: A more efficient convexity test is known that doesn't require a priori knowledge that P is simple; see e.g. (Moret and Shapiro 1991). It is also based on signed areas.)

Further, it is well known (e.g. (Goldman 1991, Hill 1990)) that to find the area of P just add up the N signed areas of its "component triangles" (with vertices (0,0), P_{i+1}, and P_i) and take the magnitude. In terms of perp-dot products:

$$\text{area} = \frac{1}{2}\left|\sum_{i=1}^{N} P_{i+1}^{\perp} \cdot P_i\right| \qquad \text{(area of polygon P)} \qquad (6)$$

(Note that points appear in this expression where really only vectors should reside. Consider P_i as shorthand for the vector from $(0,0)$ to P_i, and similarly for $P_{i+1}^{\perp}$.)

Example 2: Find the intersection of two lines

The task of finding the intersection of two lines arises often in clipping and hidden line removal algorithms. Let the first line have parametric representation $A + \mathbf{a}t$, so that it passes through point A with direction $\mathbf{a}$. Similarly, the second line passes through

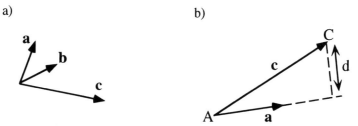

a)   b)

Figure 3.   Finding the perpendicular projection of **c** onto **a**.

point B in direction **b**, and so has parametric representation $B + \mathbf{b}u$. We seek values of the parameters t and u that make these points coincide: $A + \mathbf{a}t = B + \mathbf{b}u$. Calling $B - A = \mathbf{c}$, we must solve

$$\mathbf{a}t = \mathbf{c} + \mathbf{b}u \tag{7}$$

which gives a set of two equations in the two unknowns t and u. At this point one usually writes out the two equations in terms of components such as b_x and a_y, and invokes Cramer's rule. But the perp-dot product provides a much more direct route. Just form the dot product of both sides of the equation with $\mathbf{b}^{\perp}$. Since $\mathbf{b}^{\perp} \cdot \mathbf{b} = 0$, this eliminates the $\mathbf{b}u$ term and yields $(\mathbf{b}^{\perp} \cdot \mathbf{a})t = \mathbf{b}^{\perp} \cdot \mathbf{c}$, whereupon

$$t = \frac{\mathbf{b}^{\perp} \cdot \mathbf{c}}{\mathbf{b}^{\perp} \cdot \mathbf{a}} \tag{8}$$

as long as $\mathbf{b}^{\perp} \cdot \mathbf{a} \neq 0$; i.e., as long as **b** and **a** are not parallel. Hence the point of intersection is given explicitly by

$$A + \frac{\mathbf{b}^{\perp} \cdot \mathbf{c}}{\mathbf{b}^{\perp} \cdot \mathbf{a}}\mathbf{a} \qquad \text{(point of intersection)} \tag{9}$$

(Note: For lines in 3D space the explicit expression for t is more complex (Goldman 1990a): $t = (\mathbf{c} \times \mathbf{b}) \cdot (\mathbf{a} \times \mathbf{b})/|\mathbf{a} \times \mathbf{b}|^2$.)

Example 3: Resolving a vector and orthogonal projections

The previous example is actually a special case of a more general problem: that of resolving a vector into the proper linear combination of two other vectors. (For instance, find "weights" R and S such that $(12, 9) = R(4, -6) + S(2, 7)$.) In general, given three 2D vectors **a**, **b**, and **c** as shown in Figure 3a, where **a** and **b** are not parallel ($\mathbf{a}^{\perp} \cdot \mathbf{b} \neq 0$), we seek R and S that solve $\mathbf{c} = R\mathbf{a} + S\mathbf{b}$.

First take dot products of both sides with $\mathbf{b}^{\perp}$ to obtain R, and then with $\mathbf{a}^{\perp}$ to obtain S.

$$\mathbf{c} = \frac{\mathbf{b}^{\perp} \cdot \mathbf{c}}{\mathbf{b}^{\perp} \cdot \mathbf{a}}\mathbf{a} + \frac{\mathbf{a}^{\perp} \cdot \mathbf{c}}{\mathbf{a}^{\perp} \cdot \mathbf{b}}\mathbf{b} \qquad (\mathbf{c} \text{ resolved into } \mathbf{a} \text{ and } \mathbf{b}) \tag{10}$$

This resolves $\mathbf{c}$ explicitly into the required portion "along" $\mathbf{a}$ and the required portion "along" $\mathbf{b}$. It's just Cramer's rule, of course, but written in a form that avoids dealing with individual components of the vectors involved. Note that it can be written in the symmetrical form:

$$(\mathbf{a}^{\perp} \cdot \mathbf{b})\mathbf{c} + (\mathbf{b}^{\perp} \cdot \mathbf{c})\mathbf{a} + (\mathbf{c}^{\perp} \cdot \mathbf{a})\mathbf{b} = \mathbf{0} \qquad (\text{relation between any three 2D vectors}) \tag{11}$$

which is true for *any* three 2D vectors $\mathbf{a}$, $\mathbf{b}$, and $\mathbf{c}$, even when some are parallel or even $\mathbf{0}$. This form is easily memorized, since each term involves $\mathbf{a}$, $\mathbf{b}$, and $\mathbf{c}$ in cyclic order, $\cdots \mathbf{b} \to \mathbf{c} \to \mathbf{a} \to \mathbf{b} \cdots$, and the three combinations appear once each. The truth of Equation 11 is obvious by dotting it with your choice of $\mathbf{a}^{\perp}$, $\mathbf{b}^{\perp}$, or $\mathbf{c}^{\perp}$.

As a special case of resolving one vector into two others, we often want the **orthogonal projection** of a vector $\mathbf{c}$ onto a given vector $\mathbf{a}$, as pictured in Figure 3b. But this is equivalent to resolving $\mathbf{c}$ into a portion along $\mathbf{a}$ and a portion perpendicular to $\mathbf{a}$, so just set $\mathbf{b} = \mathbf{a}^{\perp}$ in Equation 10, and use some of the properties summarized above to obtain

$$\mathbf{c} = \frac{\mathbf{a} \cdot \mathbf{c}}{|\mathbf{a}|^2}\mathbf{a} + \frac{\mathbf{a}^{\perp} \cdot \mathbf{c}}{|\mathbf{a}|^2}\mathbf{a}^{\perp} \qquad (\mathbf{c} \text{ resolved into } \mathbf{a} \text{ and } \mathbf{a}^{\perp}) \tag{12}$$

The first term is the desired projection, and the second term gives the *error term* explicitly and compactly. This also immediately yields a formula for the distance from a point to a line. In Figure 3b the relevant point is C, and the line is $A + \mathbf{a}t$. The distance d is just the length of the second term in Equation 12:

$$d = \left| \frac{\mathbf{a}^{\perp} \cdot (C - A)}{|\mathbf{a}|^2}\mathbf{a}^{\perp} \right| = \left| \left(\frac{\mathbf{a}^{\perp}}{|\mathbf{a}|} \right) \cdot (C - A) \right| \quad (\text{distance from } C \text{ to the line } A + \mathbf{a}t) \tag{13}$$

which has an appealing simplicity in terms of the unit vector in the direction of $\mathbf{a}^{\perp}$.

Example 4: Finding the excircle (and nine-point circle)

It is often of interest to locate the center S of the unique circle (called the *excircle* or *circumcircle*) that passes through three given points. Previous Gems (Goldman 1990b, Lopez-Lopez 1992) have offered closed forms for S. We derive a very simple one below, making ample use of the perp-dot product.

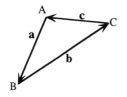
a) positive orientation

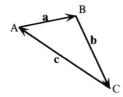
b) negative orientation

Figure 4. Orientation of triangles.

This and subsequent problems are based on a triangle, so we establish some notation for a triangle's ingredients. Figure 4 shows two triangles having vertices A, B, and C. The edges are labeled as vectors: side $\mathbf{a}$ emanates from A toward B, $\mathbf{b}$ from B toward C, etc., cyclically. In Figure 4a there is a ccw turn from each vector to the next (e.g., $\mathbf{a}^\perp \cdot \mathbf{b} > 0$, etc.) so the triangle has positive orientation and its signed area $\mathbf{a}^\perp \cdot \mathbf{b}/2$ is positive. The triangle in Figure 4b has negative orientation, since there is a cw turn from $\mathbf{a}$ to $\mathbf{b}$ ($\mathbf{a}^\perp \cdot \mathbf{b} < 0$), and its signed area $\mathbf{a}^\perp \cdot \mathbf{b}/2$ is negative. It is important that the formulas we develop below be correct for either orientation of the triangle involved, since a designer interacting with a CAD tool might specify its edges in different orders and directions at different moments.

Using either triangle of Figure 4, S must lie on the perpendicular bisector of each edge of triangle ABC. As stated above, the perpendicular bisector of AB is given parametrically by $(A + B)/2 + \mathbf{a}^\perp t$, and that of AC by $(A + C)/2 + \mathbf{c}^\perp u$. Point S lies where these meet, at the solution of: $\mathbf{a}^\perp t = \mathbf{b}/2 + \mathbf{c}^\perp u$. Again take the dot product of both sides, this time with $\mathbf{c}$, to obtain $t = 1/2(\mathbf{b} \cdot \mathbf{c})/(\mathbf{a}^\perp \cdot \mathbf{c})$ so the center S is given by the simple explicit form:

$$S = A + \frac{1}{2}\left(\mathbf{a} + \frac{\mathbf{b} \cdot \mathbf{c}}{\mathbf{a}^\perp \cdot \mathbf{c}}\mathbf{a}^\perp\right) \tag{14}$$

The radius of the excircle follows as the length of $S - A$:

$$\text{radius} = \frac{|\mathbf{a}|}{2}\sqrt{\left(\frac{\mathbf{b} \cdot \mathbf{c}}{\mathbf{a}^\perp \cdot \mathbf{c}}\right)^2 + 1} \tag{15}$$

A similar version of S may be obtained based on edges AB and BC, and a third version can be based on AC and BC. It's a good exercise to obtain a form for S that is symmetrical in the points A, B, and C by averaging the three versions.

The exquisite **nine-point (Feuerbach) circle** contained in any triangle T passes through nine key points: the midpoints of the sides, the feet of the three altitudes, and the midpoints of the lines joining each vertex to the intersection of the altitudes

(Coxeter 1969). So it's just the excircle of the midpoint triangle M defined by the three midpoints of T. To find its center N apply Equation 14 with appropriate substitutions. The sides of M are parallel to those of T itself, so the result is very similar to Equation 14. It's a useful exercise to show that the center lies at

$$N = \frac{1}{2}(B + C) - \frac{1}{4}\left(\mathbf{a} + \frac{\mathbf{b} \cdot \mathbf{c}}{\mathbf{a}^\perp \cdot \mathbf{c}}\mathbf{a}^\perp\right) \tag{16}$$

and that its radius is one half of the value cited in Equation 15.

Example 5: Finding the incircle

For completeness we mention a similar task: locating the center of the *incircle* (or *inscribed* circle) of a triangle. The incircle just touches each of the three sides, so it also locates the circle tangent to three given lines. Its center I lies where the three angle bisectors of the triangle meet. The angle bisector at vertex A of either triangle in Figure 4 has direction $\mathbf{m} = \hat{\mathbf{a}} - \hat{\mathbf{c}}$, where the ˆ symbol denotes that the vector has been normalized to unit length; i.e. $\hat{\mathbf{a}} = \mathbf{a}/|\mathbf{a}|$. Similarly, the angle bisector at B has direction $\mathbf{n} = \hat{\mathbf{b}} - \hat{\mathbf{a}}$. Finding the intersection as before, we obtain

$$I = A + \frac{\mathbf{n}^\perp \cdot \mathbf{a}}{\mathbf{n}^\perp \cdot \mathbf{m}}\mathbf{m} \tag{17}$$

Its radius is found as the distance from I to any of the three sides. This is easy to find explicitly, using Equation 13.

$$\text{radius} = \left|\frac{(\mathbf{n}^\perp \cdot \mathbf{a})(\mathbf{a}^\perp \cdot \mathbf{m})}{(\mathbf{n}^\perp \cdot \mathbf{m})\mathbf{a}}\right| \tag{18}$$

Example 6: Drawing rounded corners

A more challenging geometric problem is the following: given three points A, B, and C, and a distance r, draw the rounded curve shown in Figure 5a. It consists of a straight line from A toward B that blends smoothly into a circular arc of radius r, finally blending into a straight line to C. (It is implemented as the *arcto* operator in PostScript.)

The hard part is finding the center E of the circle (see Figure 5b) and the precise points D and F where the line blends with the arc. (The figure shows the case where there is a right turn from $\mathbf{a}$ to $\mathbf{b}$.) This becomes considerably easier when the perp-dot product is used. As before, the angle bisector at B is given parametrically by $B + \mathbf{n}u$ where $\mathbf{n} = \hat{\mathbf{b}} - \hat{\mathbf{a}}$ for unit vectors $\hat{\mathbf{b}}$ and $\hat{\mathbf{a}}$. E lies on the angle bisector at a distance

a)

b)

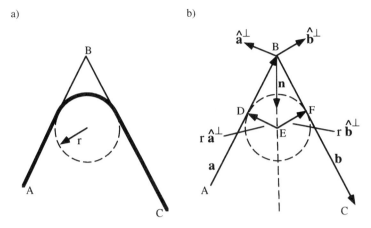

Figure 5. Drawing rounded corners.

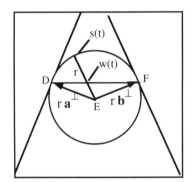

Figure 6. Finding points along the arc.

r from the line AB. Using appropriate ingredients in Equation 13 and simplifying the resulting expression, u must equal $u = r/|\mathbf{n} \cdot \hat{\mathbf{a}}^\perp| = r/|\hat{\mathbf{b}} \cdot \hat{\mathbf{a}}^\perp|$ so E is given explicitly by:

$$E = B + \frac{(\hat{\mathbf{b}} - \hat{\mathbf{a}})r}{\hat{\mathbf{b}} \cdot \hat{\mathbf{a}}^\perp} \tag{19}$$

When there is a right turn from $\mathbf{a}$ to $\mathbf{b}$ (so $\mathbf{b}^\perp \cdot \mathbf{a} > 0$ as in the figure), D and F are given by $D = E + r\hat{\mathbf{a}}^\perp$, and $F = E + r\hat{\mathbf{b}}^\perp$. Otherwise $\hat{\mathbf{a}}^\perp$ and $\hat{\mathbf{b}}^\perp$ point in the opposite directions. We capture both cases with the expression $D = E + \text{sgn}(\mathbf{b}^\perp \cdot \mathbf{a})\hat{\mathbf{a}}^\perp r$ and $F = E + \text{sgn}(\mathbf{b}^\perp \cdot \mathbf{a})\hat{\mathbf{b}}^\perp r$, where sgn(.) means the sign of its argument, +1 or −1.

To find points along the arc without recourse to awkward trigonometric functions, consider the point $w(t)$ that lies a fraction t of the way from D to F (see Figure 6), given by $w(t) = D(1 - t) + Ft$. The corresponding point $s(t)$ on the arc is at distance r along the line from E to $w(t)$, and so is given by $s(t) = E + r(w(t) - E)/|w(t) - E|$.

Suitable manipulations simplify this to:

$$s(t) = E + \text{sgn}(\mathbf{b}^\perp \cdot \mathbf{a}) \frac{\hat{\mathbf{a}}^\perp + (\hat{\mathbf{b}}^\perp - \hat{\mathbf{a}}^\perp)t}{|\hat{\mathbf{a}}^\perp + (\hat{\mathbf{b}}^\perp - \hat{\mathbf{a}}^\perp)t|} r \tag{20}$$

The arc is drawn by making small increments dt in t, and drawing a line between successive values of $s(t)$, as suggested by the pseudocode:

```
moveto(A);
for(t = 0; t <= 1; t += dt) lineto(s(t));
lineto(C);
```

Although equal increments dt in t do not produce arc fragments of equal length, a smooth arc is drawn if dt is small.

◇ Conclusion ◇

We use vectors all the time in pencil-and-paper calculations while developing algorithms for computer graphics. They allow compact manipulations of geometric quantities, often without resort to coordinates. For some problems one can further delay the use of coordinates by giving a name $\mathbf{a}^\perp$ to one of the vectors perpendicular to a given vector $\mathbf{a}$. When such a vector is used in a dot product, the result has useful algebraic and geometric properties equivalent to the signed area of a triangle. Seeing signed area exposed as a dot product between readily interpreted vectors makes otherwise messy formulas more intelligible. In addition, Cramer's rule for solving vector equations arises simply by taking the dot product of both sides of the equation with the proper vector.

◇ Bibliography ◇

(Coxeter 1969) H. M. S. Coxeter. *Introduction to Geometry*. J. Wiley, New York, 1969.

(Goldman 1990a) Ronald Goldman. Intersection of two lines in three-space. In A. Glassner, editor, *Graphics Gems I*, page 304. Academic Press, Boston, 1990.

(Goldman 1990b) Ronald Goldman. Triangles. In A. Glassner, editor, *Graphics Gems I*, pages 20–23. Academic Press, Boston, 1990.

(Goldman 1991) Ronald Goldman. Area of planar polygons and volume of polyhedra. In James Arvo, editor, *Graphics Gems II*, pages 170–171. Academic Press, Boston, 1991.

(Hill 1990) Francis S. Hill, Jr. *Computer Graphics*. Macmillan Publishing Co., New York, 1990.

(Lopez-Lopez 1992) F. J. Lopez-Lopez. Triangles revisited. In D. Kirk, editor, *Graphics Gems III*, pages 215–218. Academic Press, Boston, 1992.

(Moret and Shapiro 1991) B. Moret and H. Shapiro. *Algorithms from P to NP*. Benjamin Cummings, Reading, MA, 1991.

II.6

Geometry for *N*-Dimensional Graphics

Andrew J. Hanson
Department of Computer Science
Indiana University
Bloomington, IN 47405
hanson@cs.indiana.edu

◇   **Introduction**   ◇

Textbook graphics treatments commonly use special notations for the geometry of two and three dimensions that are not obviously generalizable to higher dimensions. Here we collect a family of geometric formulas frequently used in graphics that are easily extensible to N dimensions as well as being helpful alternatives to standard 2D and 3D notations.

What use are such formulas? In mathematical visualization, which commonly must deal with higher dimensions—four real dimensions, two complex dimensions, and so forth—the utility is self-evident (see, e.g., (Banchoff 1990, Francis 1987, Hanson and Heng 1992b, and Phillips *et al.* 1993)). The visualization of statistical data also frequently utilizes techniques of N-dimensional display (see, e.g., (Noll 1967, Feiner and Beshers 1990a, Feiner and Beshers 1990b, Brun *et al.* 1989, and Hanson and Heng 1992a)). We hope that publicizing some of the basic techniques will encourage further exploitation of N-dimensional graphics in scientific visualization problems.

We classify the formulas we present into the following categories: basic notation and the N-simplex; rotation formulas; imaging in N dimensions; N-dimensional hyperplanes and volumes; N-dimensional cross-products and normals; clipping formulas; the point-hyperplane distance; barycentric coordinates and parametric hyperplanes; and N-dimensional ray-tracing methods. An appendix collects a set of obscure Levi-Civita symbol techniques for computing with determinants. For additional details and insights, we refer the reader to classic sources such as (Sommerville 1958, Coxeter 1991, Hocking and Young 1961, Banchoff and Werner 1983, and Efimov and Rozendorn 1975).

◇   **Definitions — What Is a Simplex, Anyway?**   ◇

In a nutshell, an N-simplex is a set of $(N+1)$ points that together specify the simplest non-vanishing N-dimensional volume element (e.g., two points delimit a line segment in

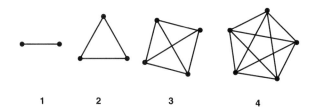

Figure 1. 2D projections of simplexes with dimensions 1–4. An *N*-simplex is defined by (*N* + 1) linearly independent points and generalizes the concept of a line segment or a triangular surface patch.

1D, 3 points a triangle in 2D, 4 points a tetrahedron in 3D, etc.). From a mathematical point of view, there are lots of different *N*-dimensional spaces: here we will restrict ourselves to ordinary flat, real Euclidean spaces of *N* dimensions with global orthogonal coordinates that we can write as

$$\vec{x} = (x, y, z, \ldots, w)$$

or more pedantically as

$$\vec{x} = (x^{(1)}, x^{(2)}, x^{(3)}, \ldots, x^{(N)})$$

We will use the first, less cumbersome, notation whenever it seems clearer.

Our first type of object in *N* dimensions, the 0-dimensional *point* $\vec{x}$, may be thought of as a vector from the origin to the designated set of coordinate values. The next type of object is the 1-dimensional *line*, which is determined by giving two points $(\vec{x}_0, \vec{x}_1)$; the line segment from $\vec{x}_0$ to $\vec{x}_1$ is called a 1-*simplex*. If we now take three noncollinear points $(\vec{x}_0, \vec{x}_1, \vec{x}_2)$, these uniquely specify a *plane*; the triangular area delineated by these points is a 2-*simplex*. A 3-simplex is a solid tetrahedron formed by a set of four noncoplanar points, and so on. In Figure 1, we show schematic diagrams of the first few simplexes projected to 2D.

Starting with the $(N + 1)$ points $(\vec{x}_0, \vec{x}_1, \vec{x}_2, \ldots, \vec{x}_N)$ defining a simplex, one then connects all possible pairs of points to form edges, all possible triples to form faces, and so on, resulting in the structure of component "parts" given in Table 1. The next higher object uses its predecessor as a building block: a triangular face is built from three edges, a tetrahedron is built from four triangular faces, a 4-simplex is built from five tetrahedra.

The general idea should now be clear: $(N + 1)$ linearly independent points define a *hyperplane* of dimension *N* and specify the boundaries of an *N*-dimensional coordinate patch comprising an *N-simplex* (Hocking and Young 1961). Just as the surfaces modeling a 3D object may be broken up (or *tessellated*) into triangular patches, *N*-dimensional objects may be tessellated into $(N - 1)$-dimensional simplexes that define their geometry.

Table 1. Numbers of component structures making up an *N*-simplex. For example, in 2D, the basic simplex is the triangle with three points, three edges, and one 2D face

Type of Simplex	Dimension of Space					
	$N=1$	$N=2$	$N=3$	$N=4$	$\ldots$	N
Points (0D)	2	3	4	5	$\ldots$	$\binom{N+1}{1} = N+1$
Edges (1D simplex)	1	3	6	10	$\ldots$	$\binom{N+1}{2}$
Faces (2D simplex)	0	1	4	10	$\ldots$	$\binom{N+1}{3}$
Volumes (3D simplex)		0	1	5	$\ldots$	$\binom{N+1}{4}$
$\vdots$	$\vdots$	$\vdots$	$\vdots$	$\vdots$	$\ddots$	$\vdots$
$(N-2)$D simplex					$\ldots$	$\binom{N+1}{N-1}$
$(N-1)$D simplex					$\ldots$	$\binom{N+1}{N} = N+1$
ND simplex				1	$\ldots$	$\binom{N+1}{N+1} = 1$

◇ **Rotations** ◇

In N Euclidean dimensions, there are $\binom{N}{2} = N(N-1)/2$ degrees of rotational freedom corresponding to the free parameters of the group $SO(N)$. In 2D, that means we only have one rotational degree of freedom given by the angle used to mix the x and y coordinates. In 3D, there are three parameters, which can be thought of as corresponding either to three Euler angles or to the three independent quaternion coordinates that remain when we represent rotations in terms of unit quaternions. In 4D, there are six degrees of freedom, and the familiar 3D picture of "rotating about an axis" is no longer valid; each rotation leaves an entire plane fixed, not just one axis.

General rotations in N dimensions may be viewed as a sequence of elementary rotations. Each elementary rotation acts in the plane of a particular pair, say (i, j), of coordinates, leaving an $(N-2)$-dimensional subspace unchanged; we may write any such rotation in the form

$$
\begin{aligned}
x'^{(i)} &= x^{(i)} \cos\theta \pm x^{(j)} \sin\theta \\
x'^{(j)} &= \mp x^{(i)} \sin\theta + x^{(j)} \cos\theta \\
x'^{(k)} &= x^{(k)} \quad (k \neq i, j)
\end{aligned}
$$

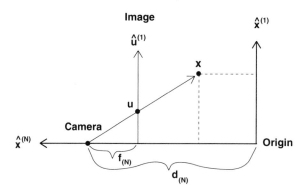

Figure 2.   Schematic view of the projection process for an *N*-dimensional pinhole camera.

It is important to remember that *order matters* when doing a sequence of nested rotations; for example, two sequences of small 3D rotations, one consisting of a $(2,3)$-plane rotation followed by a $(3,1)$-plane rotation, and the other with the order reversed, will differ by a rotation in the $(1,2)$-plane. (See any standard reference such as (Edmonds 1957).)

We then have a number of options for controlling rotations in N-dimensional Euclidean space. Among these are the following:

- (i,j)-**space pairs.** A brute-force choice would be just to pick a sequence of (i,j) planes in which to rotate using a series of matrix multiplications.

- (i,j,k)-**space triples.** A more interesting choice for an interactive system is to provide the user with a family of (i,j,k) triples having a 2D controller like a mouse coupled to two of the degrees of freedom, and having the third degree of freedom accessible in some other way—with a different button, from context using the "virtual sphere" algorithm of (Chen *et al.* 1988), or implicitly using a context-free method like the "rolling-ball" algorithm (Hanson 1992). The simplest example is $(1,2,3)$ in 3D, with the mouse coupled to rotations about the $\hat{\mathbf{x}}$-axis $(2,3)$ and the $\hat{\mathbf{y}}$-axis $(3,1)$, giving $\hat{\mathbf{z}}$-axis $(1,2)$ rotations as a side effect. In 4D, one would have four copies of such a controller, $(1,2,3)$, $(2,3,4)$, $(3,1,4)$, and $(1,2,4)$, or two copies exploiting the decomposition of $SO(4)$ infinitesimal rotations into two independent copies of ordinary 3D rotations. In N dimensions, $\binom{N}{3}$ sets of these controllers (far too many when N is large!) could in principle be used.

◇   *N*-Dimensional Imaging   ◇

The general concept of an "image" is a projection of a point $\vec{x} = (x^{(1)}, x^{(2)}, \ldots, x^{(N)})$ from dimension N to a point $\vec{u}$ of dimension $(N-1)$ along a line. That is, the image of

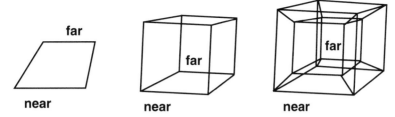

Figure 3. Qualitative results of perspective projection of a wire-frame square, a cube, and a hypercube in 2D, 3D, and 4D, respectively.

a 2D world is a projection to 1D film, 3D worlds project to 2D film, 4D worlds project to 3D film, and so on. Since we can rotate our coordinate system as we please, we lose no generality if we assume this projection is along the Nth coordinate axis. An orthographic or parallel projection results if we simply throw out the Nth coordinate $x^{(N)}$ of each point. A pinhole camera perspective projection (see Figure 2) results when, in addition, we scale the first $(N-1)$ coordinates by dividing by $(d_N - x^{(N)})/f_N$, where d_N is the distance along the positive Nth axis to the camera focal point and f_N is the focal length. One may need to project this first image to successively lower dimensions to make it displayable on a 2D graphics screen; thus a hierarchy of up to $(N-2)$ parameter sets $\{(f_N, d_N), \ldots, (f_3, d_3)\}$ may be introduced if desired.

In the familiar 3D case, we replace a vertex (x, y, z) of an object by the 2D coordinates $(xf/(d-z), yf/(d-z))$, so that more distant objects (in the negative z direction) are shrunk in the 2D image. In 4D, entire solid objects are shrunk, thus giving rise to the familiar wire-frame hypercube shown in Figure 3 that has the more distant cubic hyperfaces actually lying *inside* the projection of the nearest cube.

As we will see later when we discuss normals and cross products, the usual shading approaches allow only $(N-1)$-manifolds to interact uniquely with a light ray. That is, the generalization of a viewable "object" to N dimensions is a manifold of dimension $(N-1)$ that bounds an N-dimensional volume; only this boundary is visible in the projected image if the object is opaque. For example, curves in 2D reflect light toward the focal point to form images on a "film line"; surface patches in 3D form area images on a 2D film plane; volume patches in 4D form volume images in the 3D film volume, and so on. The image of this $(N-1)$-dimensional patch may be ray traced or scan converted. Objects are typically represented as tessellations that consist of a collection of $(N-1)$-dimensional simplexes; for example, triangular surface patches form models of the visible parts of 3D objects, while tetrahedral volumes form models of the visible parts of 4D objects. (An interesting side issue is how to display meaningful illuminated images of lower-dimensional manifolds—lines in 3D, surfaces and lines in 4D, for example; see (Hanson and Heng 1992b) for further discussion.)

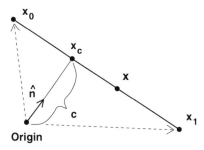

Figure 4. The line from $\vec{x}_0$ to $\vec{x}_1$ whose points obey the equation $\hat{\mathbf{n}} \cdot (\vec{x} - \vec{x}_0) = 0$. The constant c is just $\hat{\mathbf{n}} \cdot \vec{x}_0$.

◇ Hyperplanes and Volume Formulas ◇

Implicit Equation of a Hyperplane. In 2D, a special role is played by the single linear equation defining a line; in 3D, the analogous single linear equation defines a plane. In N-dimensions, the following implicit linear equation describes a set of points belonging to an $(N - 1)$-dimensional hyperplane:

$$\hat{\mathbf{n}} \cdot (\vec{x} - \vec{x}_0) = 0 \tag{1}$$

Here $\vec{x}_0$ is any point on the hyperplane, and conventionally $\hat{\mathbf{n}} \cdot \hat{\mathbf{n}} = 1$. The geometric interpretation of this equation in 2D is the 1D line shown in Figure 4. In general, $\hat{\mathbf{n}}$ is a normalized unit vector that is perpendicular to the hyperplane, and $\hat{\mathbf{n}} \cdot \vec{x}_0 = c$ is simply the (signed) distance from the origin to the hyperplane. The point $\vec{x}_c = c\hat{\mathbf{n}}$ is the point on the hyperplane closest to the origin; the point closest to some other point $\vec{P}$ is $\vec{x}_c = \vec{P} + \hat{\mathbf{n}}\{\hat{\mathbf{n}} \cdot (\vec{x}_0 - \vec{P})\}$.

Simplex Volumes and Subvolumes. The volume (by which we always mean the N-dimensional hypervolume) of an N-simplex is determined in a natural way by a determinant of its $(N + 1)$ defining points (Sommerville 1958):

$$V_N = \frac{1}{N!} \det \begin{bmatrix} x_1 & x_2 & \cdots & x_N & x_0 \\ y_1 & y_2 & \cdots & y_N & y_0 \\ \vdots & \vdots & \ddots & \vdots & \vdots \\ w_1 & w_2 & \cdots & w_N & w_0 \\ 1 & 1 & \cdots & 1 & 1 \end{bmatrix} \tag{2}$$

The bottom row of 1's in Equation (2) corresponds to the familiar homogeneous coordinate used with 4×4 projection matrices in 3D graphics. We will attempt to convince the reader in a moment that disastrous sign inconsistencies result unless the global origin $\vec{x}_0$ of the N-simplex's coordinate system is in the last column as shown.

The expression for the volume in Equation (2) is *signed*, which means that it implicitly defines the N-dimensional generalization of the *right-hand rule* typically adopted to determine triangle orientation in 3D geometry. For example, we observe that if $\vec{x}_0 = (0, 0, \ldots, 0)$ is the origin and we choose $\vec{x}_1 = (1, 0, \ldots, 0)$, $\vec{x}_2 = (0, 1, 0, \ldots, 0)$, and so on, the value of the determinant is $+1$. If we had put $\vec{x}_0$ in the first row in Equation (2), the sign would alternate from dimension to dimension! We will exploit this signed determinant shortly to define N-dimensional normal vectors, and again later to formulate N-dimensional clipping.

First, we use the standard column-subtraction identity for determinants to reduce the dimension of the determinant in Equation (2) by one, expressing it in a form that is manifestly *translation-invariant*:

$$
\begin{aligned}
V_N &= \frac{1}{N!} \det \begin{bmatrix} (x_1 - x_0) & (x_2 - x_0) & \cdots & (x_N - x_0) & x_0 \\ (y_1 - y_0) & (y_2 - y_0) & \cdots & (y_N - y_0) & y_0 \\ \vdots & \vdots & \ddots & \vdots & \vdots \\ (w_1 - w_0) & (w_2 - w_0) & \cdots & (w_N - w_0) & w_0 \\ 0 & 0 & \cdots & 0 & 1 \end{bmatrix} \\[2em]
&= \frac{1}{N!} \det \begin{bmatrix} (x_1 - x_0) & (x_2 - x_0) & \cdots & (x_N - x_0) \\ (y_1 - y_0) & (y_2 - y_0) & \cdots & (y_N - y_0) \\ \vdots & \vdots & \ddots & \vdots \\ (w_1 - w_0) & (w_2 - w_0) & \cdots & (w_N - w_0) \end{bmatrix}
\end{aligned} \tag{3}
$$

These formulas for V_N can be intuitively understood as generalizations of the familiar 3D triple scalar product

$$
[(\vec{x}_1 - \vec{x}_0) \times (\vec{x}_2 - \vec{x}_0)] \cdot (\vec{x}_3 - \vec{x}_0)
$$

which gives the volume of the parallelepiped with sides $((\vec{x}_1 - \vec{x}_0), (\vec{x}_2 - \vec{x}_0), (\vec{x}_3 - \vec{x}_0))$. The corresponding tetrahedron with vertices at the points $(\vec{x}_0, \vec{x}_1, \vec{x}_2, \vec{x}_3)$ has one-sixth the volume of the parallelepiped. The analogous observation in N dimensions is that the factor of $1/N!$ in Equation (3) is the proportionality factor between the volume of the N-simplex and the volume of the parallelepiped whose edges are given by the matrix columns.

Invariance. The volume determinant is invariant under rotations. To see this explicitly, let $|X|$ be the matrix in Equation (3) and let $|R|$ be any orthonormal rotation matrix (i.e., one whose columns are of unit length and are mutually perpendicular, with unit determinant); then, letting $|X'| = |R| \cdot |X|$, we find

$$
\det |X'| = \det(|R| \cdot |X|) = \det |R| \det |X| = \det |X| = N! V_N
$$

since the determinant of a product is the product of the determinants.

A manifestly translation *and* rotation invariant form for the square of the volume element is

$$(V_N)^2 = \left(\frac{1}{N!}\right)^2 \det |X^t \cdot X|$$

$$= \left(\frac{1}{N!}\right)^2 \det \begin{bmatrix} v(1,1) & v(1,2) & \cdots & v(1,N) \\ v(2,1) & v(2,2) & \cdots & v(2,N) \\ \vdots & \vdots & \ddots & \vdots \\ v(N,1) & v(N,2) & \cdots & v(N,N) \end{bmatrix} \tag{4}$$

where $v(i,j) = (\vec{x}_i - \vec{x}_0) \cdot (\vec{x}_j - \vec{x}_0)$.

This invariant form is not presented as an idle observation; we now exploit it to show how to construct volume forms for *subspaces* of N-dimensional spaces, for which the defining vertices of the desired simplex cannot form square matrices!

The trick here is to note that while V_K, for $K < N$, is not expressible in terms of a square matrix of coordinate differences the way V_N is, we may write V_K as the determinant of a square matrix in one particular coordinate frame, and multiply this matrix by its transpose to get a form such as Equation (4), which does not depend on the frame. Since the form is invariant, we can transform back to an arbitrary frame to find the following expression for V_K in terms of its K basis vectors $(\vec{x}_k - \vec{x}_0)$ of dimension N:

$$(V_K)^2 = \left(\frac{1}{K!}\right)^2 \det \begin{bmatrix} \vec{x}_1 - \vec{x}_0 \\ \vec{x}_2 - \vec{x}_0 \\ \vdots \\ \vec{x}_K - \vec{x}_0 \end{bmatrix} \cdot \begin{bmatrix} \vec{x}_1 - \vec{x}_0 & \vec{x}_2 - \vec{x}_0 & \cdots & \vec{x}_K - \vec{x}_0 \end{bmatrix}$$

$$= \left(\frac{1}{K!}\right)^2 \det \begin{bmatrix} v(1,1) & v(1,2) & \cdots & v(1,K) \\ v(2,1) & v(2,2) & \cdots & v(2,K) \\ \vdots & \vdots & \ddots & \vdots \\ v(K,1) & v(K,2) & \cdots & v(K,K) \end{bmatrix} \tag{5}$$

That is, to compute a volume of dimension K in N dimensions, find the K independent basis vectors spanning the subspace, and form a square $K \times K$ matrix of dot products related to V_K^2 by multiplying the $N \times K$ matrix of column vectors by its transpose on the left. When $K = 1$, we see that we have simply the squared Euclidean distance in N dimensions, $v(1,1) = (\vec{x}_1 - \vec{x}_0) \cdot (\vec{x}_1 - \vec{x}_0)$.

◇   **Normals and the Cross Product**   ◇

A frequently asked question in N-dimensional geometry concerns how to define a normal vector as a cross product of edges for use in geometry and shading calculations. To begin with, you must have an $(N-1)$-manifold (a line in 2D, a surface in 3D, a volume in 4D) in order to have a well-defined normal *vector*; otherwise, you may have a normal *space* (a plane, a volume, etc.). Suppose you have an ordered set of $(N-1)$ edge vectors $(\vec{x}_k - \vec{x}_0)$ tangent to this $(N-1)$-manifold at a point $\vec{x}_0$; typically these vectors are the edges of one of the $(N-1)$-simplexes in the tessellation. Then the normal $\vec{N}$ at the point is a *generalized cross product* whose components are cofactors of the last column in the following (notationally abusive!) determinant:

$$
\begin{aligned}
\vec{N} &= N_x\hat{\mathbf{x}} + N_y\hat{\mathbf{y}} + N_z\hat{\mathbf{z}} + \cdots + N_w\hat{\mathbf{w}} \\
&= \det\begin{bmatrix}
(x_1 - x_0) & (x_2 - x_0) & \cdots & (x_{N-1} - x_0) & \hat{\mathbf{x}} \\
(y_1 - y_0) & (y_2 - y_0) & \cdots & (y_{N-1} - y_0) & \hat{\mathbf{y}} \\
(z_1 - z_0) & (z_2 - z_0) & \cdots & (z_{N-1} - z_0) & \hat{\mathbf{z}} \\
\vdots & \vdots & \ddots & \vdots & \vdots \\
(w_1 - w_0) & (w_2 - w_0) & \cdots & (w_{N-1} - w_0) & \hat{\mathbf{w}}
\end{bmatrix}
\end{aligned}
\tag{6}
$$

As usual, we can normalize using $\|\vec{N}\|$, the square root of the sum of the squares of the cofactors, to form the normalized normal $\hat{\mathbf{n}} = \vec{N}/\|\vec{N}\|$. A quick check shows that if the vectors $(\vec{x}_k - \vec{x}_0)$ are assigned to the first $(N-1)$ coordinate axes in order, this normal vector points in the direction of the positive Nth axis. For example, in 2D, we want the normal to the vector $(x_1 - x_0, y_1 - y_0)$ to be $\vec{N} = (-(y_1 - y_0), (x_1 - x_0))$ so that a vector purely in the x direction has a normal in the positive y direction; placing the column of unit vectors $(\hat{\mathbf{x}}, \hat{\mathbf{y}}, \hat{\mathbf{z}}, \ldots, \hat{\mathbf{w}})$ in the *first* column fails this test. The 3D case can be done either way because an even number of columns are crossed! It is tempting to move the column of unit vectors to the first column instead of the last, but one must resist: the choice given here is the one to use for consistent behavior across different dimensions!

The qualitative interpretation of Equation (6) can now be summarized as follows:

- **2D:** Given two points $(\vec{x}_0, \vec{x}_1)$ determining a line in 2D, the cross product of a *single vector* is the normal to the line.
- **3D:** Given three points defining a plane in 3D, the cross product of the two 3D vectors outlining the resulting triangle is the familiar formula $(\vec{x}_1 - \vec{x}_0) \times (\vec{x}_2 - \vec{x}_0)$ for the normal $\vec{N}$ to the plane.
- **4D:** In four dimensions, we use four points to construct the three vectors $(\vec{x}_1 - \vec{x}_0), (\vec{x}_2 - \vec{x}_0), (\vec{x}_3 - \vec{x}_0)$; the cross product of these vectors is a *four-vector* that is perpendicular to each vector and thus is interpretable as the normal to the tetrahedron specified by the original four points.

From this point on, the relationship to standard graphics computations should be evident: If, in N-dimensional space, the $(N-1)$-manifold to be rendered is tessellated into $(N-1)$-simplexes, use Equation (6) to compute the normal of each simplex for flat shading. For interpolated shading, compute the normal at each vertex (e.g., by averaging the normals of all neighboring simplexes and normalizing, or by computing the gradient of an implicit function specifying the vertex). Compute the intensity at a point for which you know the normal by taking the dot product of the appropriate illumination vector with the normal (e.g., by plugging it into the last column of Equation (6)). If appropriate, set the dot product to zero if it is negative (pointing away from the light). Back face culling, to avoid rendering simplexes pointing away from the camera, is accomplished in exactly the same way: plug the camera view vector into the last column of Equation (6) and discard the simplex if the result is negative.

Dot Products of Cross Products. We conclude this section with the remark that sometimes computing the dot product between a normal and a simple vector is not enough; if we need to know the relative orientation of two face normals (e.g., to determine whether a finer tessellation is required), we must compute the dot products of normals. In principle, this can be done by brute force directly from Equation (6). Here we note an alternative formulation that is the N-dimensional generalization of the 3D formula for the decomposition of the dot product of two cross products; in the 3D case, if one normal is given by the cross product $\vec{X} = \vec{A} \times \vec{B}$ and the other by $\vec{Y} = \vec{C} \times \vec{D}$, we can write

$$\vec{X} \cdot \vec{Y} = (\vec{A} \times \vec{B}) \cdot (\vec{C} \times \vec{D}) = (\vec{A} \cdot \vec{C})(\vec{B} \cdot \vec{D}) - (\vec{A} \cdot \vec{D})(\vec{B} \cdot \vec{C}) \qquad (7)$$

We note that the degenerate case for the square of a cross product is

$$(\vec{A} \times \vec{B}) \cdot (\vec{A} \times \vec{B}) = (\vec{A} \cdot \vec{A})(\vec{B} \cdot \vec{B}) - (\vec{A} \cdot \vec{B})^2$$

which, if θ is the angle between $\vec{A}$ and $\vec{B}$, reduces to the identity $\|\vec{A}\|^2 \|\vec{B}\|^2 \sin^2 \theta = \|\vec{A}\|^2 \|\vec{B}\|^2 - \|\vec{A}\|^2 \|\vec{B}\|^2 \cos^2 \theta$.

The generalization of this expression to N dimensions can be derived from the product of two Levi-Civita symbols (see the Appendix). If $\vec{X}$ and $\vec{Y}$ are two cross products formed from the sets of vectors $\vec{x}_1, \vec{x}_2, \ldots, \vec{x}_{N-1}$ and $\vec{y}_1, \vec{y}_2, \ldots, \vec{y}_{N-1}$, then

$$\vec{X} \cdot \vec{Y} = \sum_{\text{all indices}} x_1^{(i_1)} x_2^{(i_2)} \ldots x_{N-1}^{(i_{N-1})} y_1^{(j_1)} y_2^{(j_2)} \ldots y_{N-1}^{(j_{N-1})}$$

$$\det \begin{bmatrix} \delta_{i_1 j_1} & \delta_{i_1 j_2} & \cdots & \delta_{i_1 j_{N-1}} \\ \delta_{i_2 j_1} & \delta_{i_2 j_2} & \cdots & \delta_{i_2 j_{N-1}} \\ \vdots & \vdots & \ddots & \vdots \\ \delta_{i_{N-1} j_1} & \delta_{i_{N-1} j_2} & \cdots & \delta_{i_{N-1} j_{N-1}} \end{bmatrix} \qquad (8)$$

where the Kronecker delta, δ_{ij}, is defined as

$$\begin{aligned} \delta_{ij} &= 1 & i = j \\ &= 0 & i \neq j \end{aligned}$$

It is easy to verify that for $N = 3$ this reduces to Equation (7).

More remarkable, however, is the fact that this formula shows that the square magnitude of the normal $\vec{N}$ of a hyperplane given in Equation (6) is the *subvolume* of the corresponding parallelepiped specified by Equation (5). That is, not only does the *direction* of Equation (6) have an important geometric meaning with respect to the $(N - 1)$-simplex specifying the hyperplane, but so does its *magnitude*! We find

$$\vec{N} \cdot \vec{N} = \det \begin{bmatrix} v(1,1) & v(1,2) & \cdots & v(1, N-1) \\ v(2,1) & v(2,2) & \cdots & v(2, N-1) \\ \vdots & \vdots & \ddots & \vdots \\ v(N-1,1) & v(N-1,2) & \cdots & v(N-1, N-1) \end{bmatrix} = ((N-1)! \, V_{N-1})^2$$

◇ Clipping Tests in *N* Dimensions ◇

Now we can exploit the properties of the volume formula to define clipping ("which side") tests in any dimension. If we replace $(\vec{x}_N - \vec{x}_0)$ by $(\vec{x} - \vec{x}_0)$, Equation (3) becomes a *function* $V_N(\vec{x})$. Furthermore, this function has the remarkable property that it is an alternative form for the hyperplane equation, Equation (1), when $V_N(\vec{x}) = 0$.

We can furthermore determine *on which side* of the $(N - 1)$-dimensional hyperplane determined by $(\vec{x}_0, \vec{x}_1, \ldots, \vec{x}_{N-1})$ an arbitrary point $\vec{x}$ lies simply by checking the sign of $V_N(\vec{x})$. That is,

- $V_N(\vec{x}) = 0 \Rightarrow$ the point $\vec{x}$ lies on a hyperplane and solves an equation of the form Equation (1).

- $V_N(\vec{x}) > 0 \Rightarrow$ the point $\vec{x}$ lies above the hyperplane.

- $V_N(\vec{x}) < 0 \Rightarrow$ the point $\vec{x}$ lies below the hyperplane.

Note: The special case $V_N = 0$ is of course just the general criterion for discovering *linear dependence* among a set of $(N + 1)$ vector variables. This has the following elegant geometric interpretation: in 2D, we use the formula to compute the area of the triangle formed by three points $(\vec{x}_0, \vec{x}_1, \vec{x})$; if the area vanishes, the three points lie on a single line. In 3D, if the volume of the tetrahedron formed by four points $(\vec{x}_0, \vec{x}_1, \vec{x}_2, \vec{x})$ vanishes, all four points are coplanar, and so on. Vanishing N-volume means the points lie in a hyperplane of dimension no greater than $(N - 1)$.

These relationships between the sign of $V_N(\vec{x})$ and the relative position of $\vec{x}$ are precisely those we are accustomed to examining when we *clip* vectors (e.g., edges of a triangle) to lie on one side of a plane in a viewing frustum or within a projected viewing rectangle. For example, a 2D clipping line defined by the vector $\vec{x}_1 - \vec{x}_0 = (x_1 - x_0, \, y_1 - y_0)$ has a right-handed (unnormalized) normal $\vec{N} = (-(y_1 - y_0), \, (x_1 - x_0))$.

Writing the 2D volume as the area A, Equation (3) becomes

$$A(\vec{x}) = \frac{1}{2} \det \begin{bmatrix} (x_1 - x_0) & (x - x_0) \\ (y_1 - y_0) & (y - y_0) \end{bmatrix} = \frac{1}{2} \left[\vec{N} \cdot (\vec{x} - \vec{x}_0) \right]$$

for some arbitrary point $\vec{x}$, and so we recover the form of Equation (1) as

$$\hat{\mathbf{n}} \cdot (\vec{x} - \vec{x}_0) = \frac{2A}{\|\vec{x}_1 - \vec{x}_0\|}$$

where $\hat{\mathbf{n}} = \vec{N}/\|\vec{N}\|$; the relationship of $\vec{x}$ to the clipping line is determined by the sign.

In 3D, when clipping a line against a plane, everything reduces to the traditional form, namely the dot product between a 3D cross product and a vector from a point $\vec{x}_0$ in the clipping plane to the point $\vec{x}$ being clipped. The normal to the plane through $(\vec{x}_0, \vec{x}_1, \vec{x}_2)$ is

$$\begin{aligned} \vec{N} &= (\vec{x}_1 - \vec{x}_0) \times (\vec{x}_2 - \vec{x}_0) \\ &= \left(+ \det \begin{bmatrix} (y_1 - y_0) & (y_2 - y_0) \\ (z_1 - z_0) & (z_2 - z_0) \end{bmatrix}, \right. \\ &\quad \left. - \det \begin{bmatrix} (x_1 - x_0) & (x_2 - x_0) \\ (z_1 - z_0) & (z_2 - z_0) \end{bmatrix}, + \det \begin{bmatrix} (x_1 - x_0) & (x_2 - x_0) \\ (y_1 - y_0) & (y_2 - y_0) \end{bmatrix} \right) \end{aligned} \quad (9)$$

and we again find the same general form

$$\hat{\mathbf{n}} \cdot (\vec{x} - \vec{x}_0) = \frac{6V}{\|\vec{N}\|}$$

whose sign determines where $\vec{x}$ falls. Figure 5 summarizes the relationship of the signed volume to the clipping task in 2D and 3D.

Hyperplanes for clipping applications in any dimension are therefore easily defined and checked by choosing $\vec{x}_N$ to be the test point $\vec{x}$ and checking the sign of Equation (3). If $\vec{N}$ and a point $\vec{x}_0$ are easy to determine directly, then the procedure reduces to checking the sign of the left hand side of Equation (1).

The final step is to find the desired point on the truncated, clipped line. Since the clipped form of a triangle, tetrahedron, etc., can be determined from the clipped forms of the component lines, we need only consider the point at which a line straddling the clipping hyperplane intersects this hyperplane. If the line to be clipped is given parametrically as $\vec{x}(t) = \vec{x}_a + t(\vec{x}_b - \vec{x}_a)$, where $\vec{x}_a$ and $\vec{x}_b$ are on opposite sides of the clipping hyperplane so $0 \le t \le 1$, then we simply plug $\vec{x}(t)$ into $V(\vec{x}) = 0$ and solve for t:

$$t = \frac{\det \begin{bmatrix} \vec{x}_1 - \vec{x}_0 & \vec{x}_2 - \vec{x}_0 & \cdots & \vec{x}_a - \vec{x}_0 \end{bmatrix}}{\det \begin{bmatrix} \vec{x}_1 - \vec{x}_0 & \vec{x}_2 - \vec{x}_0 & \cdots & \vec{x}_a - \vec{x}_b \end{bmatrix}} = \frac{\hat{\mathbf{n}} \cdot (\vec{x}_a - \vec{x}_0)}{\hat{\mathbf{n}} \cdot (\vec{x}_a - \vec{x}_b)} \quad (10)$$

Here $\hat{\mathbf{n}}$ is of course just the normal to the clipping hyperplane, discussed in detail above.

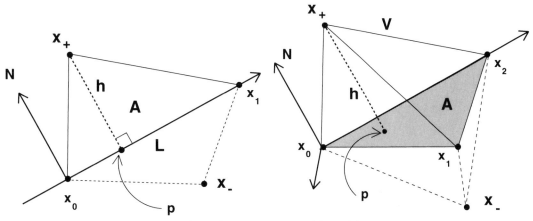

Figure 5. In 2D, the line through $\vec{x}_0$ to $\vec{x}_1$ defined by $\hat{\mathbf{n}} \cdot (\vec{x} - \vec{x}_0) = 0$ partitions the plane into two regions, one where this expression is positive (e.g., for $\vec{x}_+$) and another where it is negative (e.g., for $\vec{x}_-$). In 3D, the analogous procedure uses the plane defined by $(\vec{x}_0, \vec{x}_1, \vec{x}_2)$ to divide 3-space into two half spaces. The same pictures serve to show how the distance h from a point to a hyperplane is computable from the ratio of the simplex volume to the lower-dimensional volume of its base, i.e., $2A/L$ or $3V/A$.

◇   **Point-Hyperplane Distance**   ◇

The general formula for the volume of a parallelepiped is the product of the base and the height, $W = Bh$. In N dimensions, if we take $W_N = N! V_N$ to be the volume of the parallelepiped with edges $(\vec{x}_1 - \vec{x}_0), (\vec{x}_2 - \vec{x}_0), \ldots, (\vec{x}_{N-1} - \vec{x}_0), (\vec{x} - \vec{x}_0)$, this generalizes to

$$W_N = h W_{N-1} \ ,$$

where h is the perpendicular distance from the point $\vec{x}$ to the $(N-1)$-dimensional parallelepiped with volume $W_{N-1} = (N-1)! V_{N-1}$ and edges $(\vec{x}_1 - \vec{x}_0), (\vec{x}_2 - \vec{x}_0), \ldots, (\vec{x}_{N-1} - \vec{x}_0)$. We may thus immediately compute the distance h from a point to a hyperplane as

$$h = \frac{W_N}{W_{N-1}} = \frac{N! V_N}{(N-1)! V_{N-1}} = \frac{N V_N}{V_{N-1}} \tag{11}$$

Note! Here one must use the trick of Equation (4) to express W_{N-1} in terms of the square root of a square determinant given by the product of two non-square matrices.

Thus in 2D, the area of a triangle $(\vec{x}_0, \vec{x}_1, \vec{x})$ is

$$A = V_2 = \frac{1}{2} W_2 = \frac{1}{2} \det \begin{bmatrix} (x_1 - x_0) & (x - x_0) \\ (y_1 - y_0) & (y - y_0) \end{bmatrix}$$

and the length-squared of the base is $L^2 = (\vec{x}_1 - \vec{x}_0) \cdot (\vec{x}_1 - \vec{x}_0)$ so, with $A = (1/2)hL$, the height becomes $h = 2A/L = W_2/L = W_2/W_1$. In 3D, the volume of the tetrahedron

$(\vec{x}_0, \vec{x}_1, \vec{x}_2, \vec{x})$ is $V = V_3 = (1/6)W_3$ and the area $A = (1/2)W_2$ of the triangular base may be written

$$(2A)^2 = (W_2)^2 = \det \begin{bmatrix} (\vec{x}_1 - \vec{x}_0) \cdot (\vec{x}_1 - \vec{x}_0) & (\vec{x}_1 - \vec{x}_0) \cdot (\vec{x}_2 - \vec{x}_0) \\ (\vec{x}_2 - \vec{x}_0) \cdot (\vec{x}_1 - \vec{x}_0) & (\vec{x}_2 - \vec{x}_0) \cdot (\vec{x}_2 - \vec{x}_0) \end{bmatrix}$$

We know $V = (1/3)hA$, and so $h = 3V/A = 6V/2A = W_3/W_2$. (See Figure 5.) We note for reference that, as we showed earlier, the base $(N-1)$-volume is related to its normal by $\vec{N} \cdot \vec{N} = W_{N-1}^2$.

Here we also typically need to answer one last question, namely *where* is the point $\vec{p}$ on the base hyperplane closest to the point $\vec{x}$ whose distance h we just computed? This can be found by parameterizing the line from $\vec{x}$ to the base hyperplane along the normal $\hat{\mathbf{n}}$ to the hyperplane as $\vec{x}(t) = \vec{x} + t\hat{\mathbf{n}}$, writing the implicit equation for the hyperplane as $\hat{\mathbf{n}} \cdot (\vec{x}(t) - \vec{x}_0) = 0$, and solving for the mutual solution $t_p = \hat{\mathbf{n}} \cdot (\vec{x}_0 - \vec{x}) = -h$. Thus

$$\begin{aligned} \vec{p} &= \vec{x} + \hat{\mathbf{n}}(\hat{\mathbf{n}} \cdot (\vec{x}_0 - \vec{x})) \\ &= \vec{x} - h\hat{\mathbf{n}} \end{aligned}$$

◇ **Barycentric Coordinates** ◇

Barycentric coordinates (see, e.g., (Hocking and Young 1961, chapter 5)) are a practical way to parameterize lines, surfaces, etc., for applications that must compute where various geometric objects intersect. In practice, the barycentric coordinate method reduces to specifying two points $(\vec{x}_0, \vec{x}_1)$ on a line, three points $(\vec{x}_0, \vec{x}_1, \vec{x}_2)$ on a plane, four points $(\vec{x}_0, \vec{x}_1, \vec{x}_2, \vec{x}_3)$ in a volume, and so on, and parameterizing the line segment, the enclosed triangular area, the enclosed tetrahedral volume, and so forth, respectively, by

$$\begin{aligned} \vec{x}(t) &= \vec{x}_0 + t(\vec{x}_1 - \vec{x}_0) & (12) \\ \vec{x}(t_1, t_2) &= \vec{x}_0 + t_1(\vec{x}_1 - \vec{x}_0) + t_2(\vec{x}_2 - \vec{x}_0) & (13) \\ \vec{x}(t_1, t_2, t_3) &= \vec{x}_0 + t_1(\vec{x}_1 - \vec{x}_0) + t_2(\vec{x}_2 - \vec{x}_0) + t_3(\vec{x}_3 - \vec{x}_0) & (14) \end{aligned}$$
$$\cdots$$

The line and plane geometries are shown in Figure 6. The interpolated point then lies within the N-simplex defined by the specified points provided that the t's obey

$$0 \leq t \leq 1$$
$$0 \leq t_1 \leq 1, \ 0 \leq t_2 \leq 1, \ 0 \leq (1 - t_1 - t_2) \leq 1$$
$$0 \leq t_1 \leq 1, \ 0 \leq t_2 \leq 1, \ 0 \leq t_3 \leq 1, \ 0 \leq (1 - t_1 - t_2 - t_3) \leq 1$$
$$\cdots$$

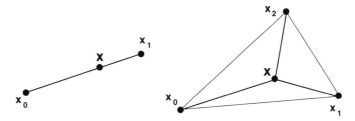

Figure 6.   Barycentric coordinates in *N* dimensions.

Center of What?   However, this is really only half the story of barycentric coordinates. For the other half, we seek a geometric interpretation of the parameters t_i when we are *given* the value of $\vec{x}$.

First let us look at the simple case when $\vec{x}$ lies on the line segment between $\vec{x}_0$ and $\vec{x}_1$. Solving Equation (12) for t directly gives

$$t = \frac{(\vec{x} - \vec{x}_0) \cdot (\vec{x}_1 - \vec{x}_0)}{(\vec{x}_1 - \vec{x}_0) \cdot (\vec{x}_1 - \vec{x}_0)}$$

That is, t is the fraction of the distance that $\vec{x}$ has traveled along the line, the *ratio* between the length from $\vec{x}_0$ to $\vec{x}$ and the total length. But, since $\vec{x}_1 - \vec{x}_0 = \vec{x}_1 - \vec{x} + \vec{x} - \vec{x}_0$, we easily see that an alternative parameterization would be to take $t_1 = t$ and

$$t_0 = \frac{(\vec{x}_1 - \vec{x}) \cdot (\vec{x}_1 - \vec{x}_0)}{(\vec{x}_1 - \vec{x}_0) \cdot (\vec{x}_1 - \vec{x}_0)}$$

so that $1 = t_0 + t_1$ and Equation (12) for $\vec{x}$ becomes

$$\vec{x}(t_0, t_1) = t_0 \vec{x}_0 + t_1 \vec{x}_1$$

If $t_0 = 1$, then the entire fraction of the distance from $\vec{x}_1$ to $\vec{x}$ is assigned to t_0 and $\vec{x} = \vec{x}_0$. If $t_1 = 1$, then the entire fraction of the distance from $\vec{x}_0$ to $\vec{x}$ is assigned to t_1 and $\vec{x} = \vec{x}_1$.

Next, suppose we know $\vec{x}$ in a plane and wish to compute its barycentric coordinates by solving Equation (13) for (t_1, t_2). Once we realize that $(\vec{x}_1 - \vec{x}_0)$ and $(\vec{x}_2 - \vec{x}_0)$ form the basis for an affine coordinate system for the plane specified by $(\vec{x}_0, \vec{x}_1, \vec{x}_2)$ in *any* dimension, we see that we may measure the relative barycentric coordinates by taking the dot product with each basis vector:

$$\begin{aligned}
(\vec{x} - \vec{x}_0) \cdot (\vec{x}_1 - \vec{x}_0) &= t_1 \|\vec{x}_1 - \vec{x}_0\|^2 + t_2 (\vec{x}_2 - \vec{x}_0) \cdot (\vec{x}_1 - \vec{x}_0) \\
(\vec{x} - \vec{x}_0) \cdot (\vec{x}_2 - \vec{x}_0) &= t_1 (\vec{x}_1 - \vec{x}_0) \cdot (\vec{x}_2 - \vec{x}_0) + t_2 \|\vec{x}_2 - \vec{x}_0\|^2
\end{aligned}$$

Extending the previously introduced abbreviation to the form $v(x, j) = (\vec{x} - \vec{x}_0) \cdot (\vec{x}_j - \vec{x}_0)$ and solving this pair of equations by Cramer's rule, we get

$$t_1 = \frac{\det \begin{bmatrix} v(x, 1) & v(1, 2) \\ v(x, 2) & v(2, 2) \end{bmatrix}}{\det \begin{bmatrix} v(1, 1) & v(1, 2) \\ v(2, 1) & v(2, 2) \end{bmatrix}}$$

$$t_2 = \frac{\det \begin{bmatrix} v(1, 1) & v(x, 1) \\ v(1, 2) & v(x, 2) \end{bmatrix}}{\det \begin{bmatrix} v(1, 1) & v(1, 2) \\ v(2, 1) & v(2, 2) \end{bmatrix}}$$

The denominator is clearly proportional to the *square* of the area of the triangle $(\vec{x}_0, \vec{x}_1, \vec{x}_2)$, and the numerators have the form of squared areas as well. In N dimensions, the numerators reduce to determinants of products of non-square matrices and so may *not* be expressed as two separate determinants! However, if we transform to a coordinate system that contains the triangle within the plane of two coordinate axes, or if $N = 2$, an effectively square matrix is recovered; one factor of area in the denominator then cancels out, giving the intuitively expected result that the barycentric coordinates are ratios of two areas: $t_1 = A(\vec{x}, \vec{x}_0, \vec{x}_1)/A(\vec{x}_0, \vec{x}_1, \vec{x}_2)$, $t_2 = A(\vec{x}, \vec{x}_2, \vec{x}_0)/A(\vec{x}_0, \vec{x}_1, \vec{x}_2)$. This leads us to introduce the generalized version of t_0 for the line, namely,

$$t_0 = 1 - t_1 - t_2 = \frac{A(\vec{x}_1, \vec{x}_2, \vec{x})}{A(\vec{x}_0, \vec{x}_1, \vec{x}_2)}$$

$$= \frac{\det \begin{bmatrix} (\vec{x}_1 - \vec{x}_0) \cdot (\vec{x}_1 - \vec{x}) & (\vec{x}_1 - \vec{x}_0) \cdot (\vec{x}_2 - \vec{x}) \\ (\vec{x}_2 - \vec{x}_0) \cdot (\vec{x}_1 - \vec{x}) & (\vec{x}_2 - \vec{x}_0) \cdot (\vec{x}_2 - \vec{x}) \end{bmatrix}}{\det \begin{bmatrix} v(1, 1) & v(1, 2) \\ v(2, 2) & v(2, 2) \end{bmatrix}}$$

Here we used the squaring argument given above to extend t_0 from its special-coordinate-system interpretation as the fraction of the area contributed by the triangle $(\vec{x}, \vec{x}_1, \vec{x}_2)$ to the invariant form. This form obviously has the desired property that $t_0 = 1$ when $\vec{x} = \vec{x}_0$, and we finally have the sought equation (with $1 = t_0 + t_1 + t_2$)

$$\vec{x}(t_0, t_1, t_2) = t_0 \vec{x}_0 + t_1 \vec{x}_1 + t_2 \vec{x}_2 \,.$$

It is amusing to note that the determinant identity $1 = t_0 + t_1 + t_2$ and its higher analogs, which are nontrivial to derive, generalize the simple identity $\vec{x}_1 - \vec{x}_0 = \vec{x}_1 - \vec{x} + \vec{x} - \vec{x}_0$ that we used in the 1D case.

Thus we can construct barycentric coordinates in any dimension which intuitively correspond to *fractions of hypervolumes*; each barycentric coordinate is the hypervolume

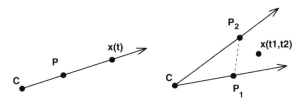

Figure 7. Schematic diagram comparing an ordinary camera ray and a planar "thick ray" used in *N*-dimensional ray-tracing methods.

of an N-simplex defined by the point $\vec{x}$ and all but one of the other simplex-defining points divided by the volume of the whole simplex. The actual computation, however, is best done using the squared-volume form because only that form is independent of the chosen coordinate system.

   Note: The volumes are *signed*; even if $\vec{x}$ lies outside the N-simplex volume, the ratios remain correct due to the cancellation between the larger volumes and the negative volumes. We also remark that the generalized formulas for t_i in any dimension, with $1 = \sum_{i=0}^{N} t_i$, give an elegant geometric interpretation of Cramer's rule as ratios of simplex volumes.

◇ Ray Tracing ◇

It is often useful to compute the intersection of a ray passing through two points (typically the camera focal point $\vec{C}$ and an image point $\vec{P}$) with a geometrical object. In N dimensions, this object will typically be an $(N-1)$-simplex defining an oriented visible "face" with a normal vector computable as described above. We need to do several things: compute the intersection of the ray with the hyperplane containing the "face," check to see whether the point lies within the simplex's boundaries (observe that this is a clipping problem), and see whether the normal vector points in the direction of the ray (making it visible).

   We formulate this procedure by first writing

$$\vec{X}(t) = \vec{C} + t(\vec{P} - \vec{C})$$

for the position of a point on the camera ray, as illustrated in Figure 7. Then we consider a single $(N-1)$-simplex of the tessellation to be described either by a known normal or by using the set of N points giving its vertices to define its normal via Equation (6); in either case, we can write the equation of any *other* point $\vec{x}$ lying within the simplex as

$$\hat{\mathbf{n}} \cdot (\vec{x} - \vec{x}_0) = 0$$

Plugging in the parametric ray equation, we solve for the point $\vec{X}(t)$ in the simplex that lies on the ray:

$$t = \frac{\hat{\mathbf{n}} \cdot \left(\vec{x}_0 - \vec{C}\right)}{\hat{\mathbf{n}} \cdot \left(\vec{P} - \vec{C}\right)}$$

A useful generalization of ray tracing to N dimensions follows from the observation that a "thick ray" is cast into space by an open-ended simplex that is essentially a barycentric coordinate form with the restriction $0 \leq (1 - t_1 - t_2 - \ldots) \leq 1$ relaxed (see, e.g., (Hanson and Cross 1993)). A planar ray such as that shown in Figure 7 then has two parameters,

$$\vec{X}(t_1, t_2) = \vec{C} + t_1(\vec{P}_1 - \vec{C}) + t_2(\vec{P}_2 - \vec{C})$$

with obvious generalizations to M-parameter ray-like M-volumes. Intersecting such a planar ray with an $(N-2)$-dimensional manifold (describable using $(N-2)$ barycentric parameters) results in N equations with N unknown parameters, and thus a unique *point* is determined as the mutual solution. In 3D a plane intersects a line in one point, while in 4D two planes intersect in a single point, and in 5D a plane intersects a volume in a point. Other generalizations, including rays that intersect particular geometries in lines and surfaces, can easily be constructed. For example, the intersection of a planar ray with the single hyperplane equation for a 3-manifold in 4D leaves one undetermined parameter, and is therefore a line.

◇ Conclusion ◇

Geometry is an essential tool employed in the creation of computer graphics images of everyday objects. Statistical data analysis, mathematics, and science, on the other hand, provide many problems where N-dimensional generalizations of the familiar 2D and 3D formulas are required. The N-dimensional formulas and insights into the nature of geometry that we have presented here provide a practical guide for extending computer graphics into these higher-dimensional domains.

◇ Appendix: Determinants and the Levi-Civita Symbol ◇

One of the unifying features that has permitted us throughout this treatment to extend formulas to arbitrary dimensions has been the use of *determinants*. But what if you encounter an expression involving determinants that has not been given here and you wish to work out its algebraic properties for yourself? In this appendix, we outline a useful mathematical tool for treating determinants: the Levi-Civita symbol. References for this are hard to locate; the author learned these techniques by apprenticeship while studying general relativity, but even classic texts like Møller (Møller 1972) contain only passing mention of the methods; somewhat more detail is given in hard-to-find sources such as (Efimov and Rozendorn 1975).

First we define two basic objects, the Kronecker delta, δ_{ij},

$$
\begin{aligned}
\delta_{ij} &= 1 & i = j \\
&= 0 & i \neq j
\end{aligned}
$$

and the Levi-Civita symbol, $\epsilon_{ijk\ldots}$, which is the totally antisymmetric pseudotensor with the properties

$$
\begin{aligned}
\epsilon_{ijk\ldots} &= 1 & & i,j,k,\ldots, \text{ in an even permutation of cyclic order} \\
&= -1 & & i,j,k,\ldots, \text{ in an odd permutation of cyclic order} \\
&= 0 & & \text{when any two indices are equal}
\end{aligned}
$$

All indices are assumed to range from 1 to N, e.g., $i = \{1, 2, \ldots, (N-1), N\}$, so that, for example, (1234,1342,4132,4321) are even permutations and (1324,2134,1243,4312) are odd permutations.

We can use the Kronecker delta to write the dot product between two N-dimensional vectors as a matrix product with the Kronecker delta representing the unit matrix,

$$
\vec{A} \cdot \vec{B} = \sum_{i=1}^{N} \sum_{j=1}^{N} A_i \delta_{ij} B_j = \sum_{i=1}^{N} A_i \left(\sum_{j=1}^{N} \delta_{ij} B_j \right) = \sum_{i=1}^{N} A_i B_i \tag{15}
$$

and the Levi-Civita symbol to write the determinant of a matrix $|M|$ as

$$
\det[M] = \sum_{\text{all } i_k \text{ indices}} \epsilon_{i_1 i_2 \ldots i_N} M_{1,i_1} M_{2,i_2} \cdots M_{N,i_N}
$$

The fundamental formula for the product of two Levi-Civita symbols is:

$$
\epsilon_{i_1 i_2 \ldots i_N} \epsilon_{j_1 j_2 \ldots j_N} = \det \begin{bmatrix} \delta_{i_1 j_1} & \delta_{i_1 j_2} & \cdots & \delta_{i_1 j_N} \\ \delta_{i_2 j_1} & \delta_{i_2 j_2} & \cdots & \delta_{i_2 j_N} \\ \vdots & \vdots & \ddots & \vdots \\ \delta_{i_N j_1} & \delta_{i_N j_2} & \cdots & \delta_{i_N j_N} \end{bmatrix}
$$

(Note that if we set $\{j_1 j_2 \ldots j_N\} = \{1, 2, \ldots, N\}$; the second Levi-Civita symbol reduces to $+1$, and the resulting determinant is an explicit realization of the antisymmetry of the Levi-Civita symbol itself as a determinant of Kronecker deltas!)

With this notation, the generalized cross product $\vec{N}$ of Equation (6), simplified by setting $\vec{x}_0 = 0$, can be written

$$
\vec{N} = \sum_{\text{all indices}} \epsilon_{i_1 i_2 \ldots i_{N-1} i_N} x_1^{(i_1)} x_2^{(i_2)} \cdots x_{N-1}^{(i_{N-1})} \hat{\mathbf{x}}^{(i_N)}
$$

where $\hat{\mathbf{x}}^{(i_N)}$ are the unit vectors $(\hat{\mathbf{x}}, \hat{\mathbf{y}}, \ldots, \hat{\mathbf{w}})$ of the coordinate system. The dot product between the normal and another vector simply becomes

$$\vec{N} \cdot \vec{L} = \sum_{\text{all indices}} \epsilon_{i_1 i_2 i_3 \ldots i_{N-1} i_N} x_1^{(i_1)} x_2^{(i_2)} x_3^{(i_3)} \cdots x_{N-1}^{(i_{N-1})} L^{(i_N)}$$

The reader can verify that, in 2D, $N_k = \sum_{i=1}^{2} x^{(i)} \epsilon_{ik} = (-y, +x)$, and so on. We conclude with two examples of applications.

Rotations of Normals. Is the normal $\vec{N}$ a vector? *Almost.* To check this, we must rotate each column vector in the cross product formula using $x'^{(i)} = \sum_{j=1}^{N} R_{ij} x^{(j)}$ and compute the behavior of $\vec{N}$. Using the identity (Efimov and Rozendorn 1975, p. 203),

$$\epsilon_{i_1 i_2 \ldots i_{N-1} i_N} \det[R] = \sum_{\text{all } j_k \text{ indices}} \epsilon_{j_1 j_2 \ldots j_{N-1} j_N} R_{j_1 i_1} R_{j_2 i_2} \cdots R_{j_{N-1} i_{N-1}} R_{j_N i_N}$$

we find

$$\begin{aligned}
N'^{(i)} &= \sum_{\substack{\text{all indices} \\ \text{except } i}} \epsilon_{i_1 i_2 \ldots i_{N-1} i} R_{i_1 j_1} x_1^{(j_1)} R_{i_2 j_2} x_2^{(j_2)} \cdots R_{i_{N-1} j_{N-1}} x_{N-1}^{(j_{N-1})} \\
&= \sum_{j=1}^{N} R_{ij} N^{(j)} \det[R]
\end{aligned}$$

Therefore $\vec{N}$ is a *pseudotensor* and behaves as a vector for ordinary rotations (which have $\det[R] = 1$), but changes sign if $[R]$ contains an odd number of reflections.

Contraction Formula. The contraction of two partial determinants of $(N - K)$ N-dimensional vectors can be expanded in terms of products of Kronecker deltas as follows:

$$\sum_{i_{N-K+1} \ldots i_N} \epsilon_{i_1 i_2 \ldots i_{N-K} i_{N-K+1} \ldots i_N} \epsilon_{j_1 j_2 \ldots j_{N-K} i_{N-K+1} \ldots i_N} =$$

$$K! \det \begin{bmatrix}
\delta_{i_1 j_1} & \delta_{i_1 j_2} & \cdots & \delta_{i_1 j_{N-K}} \\
\delta_{i_2 j_1} & \delta_{i_2 j_2} & \cdots & \delta_{i_2 j_{N-K}} \\
\vdots & \vdots & \ddots & \vdots \\
\delta_{i_{N-K} j_1} & \delta_{i_{N-K} j_2} & \cdots & \delta_{i_{N-K} j_{N-K}}
\end{bmatrix}$$

The expression in Equation (8) for the dot product of two normals is a special case of this formula.

◇ **Acknowledgment** ◇

This work was supported in part by NSF grant IRI-91-06389.

◇ **Bibliography** ◇

(Banchoff and Werner 1983) T. Banchoff and J. Werner. *Linear Algebra through Geometry.* Springer-Verlag, New York, 1983.

(Banchoff 1990) Thomas F. Banchoff. *Beyond the Third Dimension: Geometry, Computer Graphics, and Higher Dimensions.* Scientific American Library, New York, NY, 1990.

(Brun *et al.* 1989) R. Brun, O. Couet, C. Vandoni, and P. Zanarini. *PAW – Physics Analysis Workstation, The Complete Reference.* CERN, Geneva, Switzerland, October 1989. Version 1.07.

(Chen *et al.* 1988) Michael Chen, S. Joy Mountford, and Abigail Sellen. A study in interactive 3-d rotation using 2-d control devices. In *Proceedings of SIGGRAPH '88, Computer Graphics*, 22(4):121–130, 1988.

(Coxeter 1991) H. S. M. Coxeter. *Regular Complex Polytopes*, second edition. Cambridge University Press, Cambridge, 1991.

(Edmonds 1957) A. R. Edmonds. *Angular Momentum in Quantum Mechanics.* Princeton University Press, Princeton, NJ, 1957.

(Efimov and Rozendorn 1975) N. V. Efimov and E. R. Rozendorn. *Linear Algebra and Multi-Dimensional Geometry.* Mir Publishers, Moscow, 1975.

(Feiner and Beshers 1990a) S. Feiner and C. Beshers. Visualizing n-dimensional virtual worlds with n-vision. *Computer Graphics*, 24(2):37–38, March 1990.

(Feiner and Beshers 1990b) S. Feiner and C. Beshers. Worlds within worlds: Metaphors for exploring n-dimensional virtual worlds. In *Proceedings of UIST '90, Snowbird, Utah*, pages 76–83, October 1990.

(Francis 1987) G. K. Francis. *A Topological Picturebook.* Springer-Verlag, New York, 1987.

(Hanson 1992) Andrew J. Hanson. The rolling ball. In David Kirk, editor, *Graphics Gems III*, pages 51–60. Academic Press, San Diego, CA, 1992.

(Hanson and Cross 1993) A. J. Hanson and R. A. Cross. Interactive visualization methods for four dimensions. In *Proceedings of IEEE Visualization '93*, pages 196–203. IEEE Computer Society Press, Los Alamitos, CA, 1993.

(Hanson and Heng 1992a) Andrew J. Hanson and Pheng A. Heng. Four-dimensional views of 3-D scalar fields. In *Proceedings of Visualization '92*, pages 84–91. IEEE Computer Society Press, Los Alamitos, CA, October 1992.

(Hanson and Heng 1992b) Andrew J. Hanson and Pheng A. Heng. Illuminating the fourth dimension. *IEEE Computer Graphics and Applications*, 12(4):54–62, July 1992.

(Hocking and Young 1961) John G. Hocking and Gail S. Young. *Topology*. Addison-Wesley, Reading, MA, 1961.

(Møller 1972) C. Møller. *The Theory of Relativity*. Oxford University Press, London, 1972.

(Noll 1967) Michael A. Noll. A computer technique for displaying n-dimensional hyperobjects. *Communications of the ACM*, 10(8):469–473, August 1967.

(Phillips *et al.* 1993) Mark Phillips, Silvio Levy, and Tamara Munzner. Geomview: An interactive geometry viewer. In the Computers and Mathematics column of the *Notices of the Amer. Math. Soc.*, 40(8):985–988 (October 1993).

(Sommerville 1958) D. M. Y. Sommerville. *An Introduction to the Geometry of N Dimensions*. Reprinted by Dover Press, 1958.

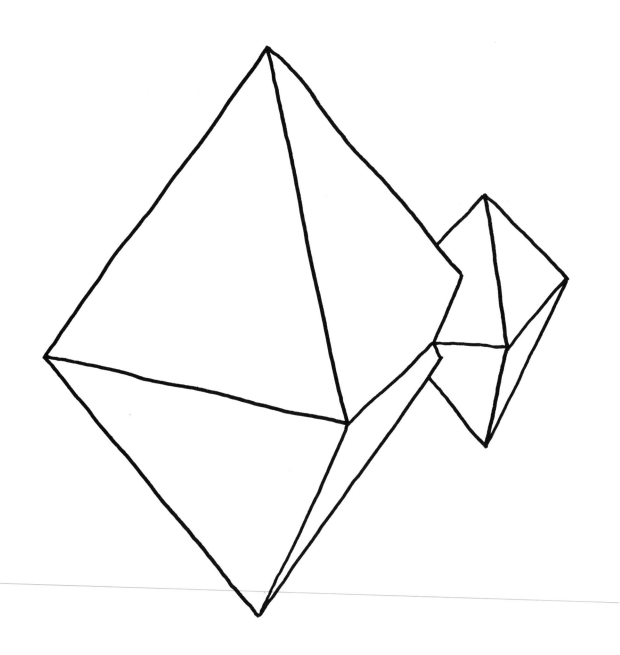

Transformations

This part of the book contains six Gems on the subject of 3D transformations. The title of this part is "Transformations," but it could also be "Shoemake *et al.*," since most of them were written by Ken Shoemake!

III.1. Arcball Rotation Control, *by Ken Shoemake.*
Asks the question: how does one control the three degrees of freedom of rotation in 3D, using a 2D input device such as a mouse? Shoemake's answer: use a pair of points to designate a relative rotation, and use quaternions to make the rotation axis specification intuitive and consistent. Page 175.

III.2. Efficient Eigenvalues for Visualization, *by Robert L. Cromwell.*
Answers the question: if I have a set of points in 3D, from what direction should I view them to get the best view (minimizing bunching in the projection)? Solving this involves the eigenvalues of a 3×3 matrix. Optimized formulas are given for computing the eigenvalues. Page 193.

III.3. Fast Inversion of Length- and Angle-Preserving Matrices, *by Kevin Wu.*
Presents optimized formulas and code to compute the inverse of a 4×4 matrix that is known to be length- and angle-preserving (consisting of only rotation, translation, and uniform scaling). Page 199.

III.4. Polar Matrix Decomposition, *by Ken Shoemake.*
Describes a method for decomposing an affine 3D transformation into translation, scaling, and rotation transformations in a physically meaningful way. This can be useful for keyframe animation. Page 207.

III.5. Euler Angle Conversion, *by Ken Shoemake.*
Gives code to convert a rotation expressed by one triple of axes into another triple. Rotations in 3D are often described in terms of Euler angles: rotations about x, y, and z in some order. The order of rotations is significant, but not standardized. These routines are useful for doing such conversions. Page 222.

III.6. Fiber Bundle Twist Reduction, *by Ken Shoemake.*
Applies some advanced concepts from topology to the problem of minimizing twist (rotation about the z axis of screen space) in animation. Page 230.

III.1

Arcball Rotation Control

Ken Shoemake
University of Pennsylvania
Philadelphia, PA
shoemake@graphics.cis.upenn.edu

◇ Introduction ◇

Previous Gems have explained how to manipulate rotations in 3D with a virtual track-ball (Hultquist 1990), and in both 3D and 4D with a rolling ball (Hanson 1992). Both methods are essentially the virtual sphere of a recent survey (Chen *et al.* 1988), and simulate some physical action. In so doing, however, they exhibit *hysteresis*, or path dependence. That is, when you drag the mouse from point A to point B, the end result will change depending on the path you follow. Hanson uses this effect as a way to rotate around the axis perpendicular to the screen (which I will call z), but usually it is just a counterintuitive nuisance. This Gem presents C code for the Arcball rotation controller (Shoemake 1992), which is path independent. It is cheaper to implement than the other methods, but better behaved and more versatile. One special feature of Arcball is its ability to handle with equal ease both free rotation and constrained rotation about any axis. The simplest implementation uses quaternions (Shoemake 1985).

◇ Arcs to Rotations ◇

Recall that a unit quaternion $q = [(x, y, z), w] = [\hat{\mathbf{v}} \sin \theta, \cos \theta]$ represents a rotation by 2θ around the axis given by the unit vector $\hat{\mathbf{v}}$, and that the quaternion product qp represents the rotation p followed by q. Now suppose we have two points on a unit sphere in 3-space, $\hat{\mathbf{v}}_0$ and $\hat{\mathbf{v}}_1$, considered as unit quaternions $[\hat{\mathbf{v}}_0, 0]$ and $[\hat{\mathbf{v}}_1, 0]$. Their "ratio" $\hat{\mathbf{v}}_1 \hat{\mathbf{v}}_0^{-1}$ converts the arc between them to a rotation.[1] What rotation do we get? Because the points give us pure vector quaternions, we have $\hat{\mathbf{v}}_1 \hat{\mathbf{v}}_0^{-1} = [\hat{\mathbf{v}}_0 \times \hat{\mathbf{v}}_1, \hat{\mathbf{v}}_0 \cdot \hat{\mathbf{v}}_1]$. Thus the axis of rotation is perpendicular to the plane containing the two vectors, and the angle of rotation is twice the angle between them.

The Arcball controller displays this sphere on the screen (cheaply, as the circle of its silhouette), and uses the mouse down and drag positions on the sphere as the end points of an arc generating a rotation. The user clicks down at $\hat{\mathbf{v}}_0$ and drags to $\hat{\mathbf{v}}_1$. As the

---

[1] Be careful not to confuse the unit quaternion hypersphere, where a single point represents a rotation, with this ordinary sphere, where a pair of points is required.

mouse is dragged, $\hat{\mathbf{v}}_1$ changes continuously, and so does the rotation. While dragging, we draw the changing arc and also the turning object.

Broken down into elementary steps, we do the following. Call the screen coordinates of the cursor at mouse down $\mathbf{s}_0 = (x_0, y_0, 0)$, the screen coordinates of the center of the Arcball $\mathbf{c}$, and its screen radius r. Compute $\mathbf{v}_0 = (\mathbf{s}_0 - \mathbf{c})/r$, and $z = \sqrt{1 - \|\mathbf{v}_0\|^2}$. Then $\hat{\mathbf{v}}_0 = \mathbf{v}_0 + (0, 0, z)$ is our first point on the unit sphere. Do the same thing with the current cursor coordinates to get $\hat{\mathbf{v}}_1$, and with these two points compute the unit quaternion $q_{\text{drag}} = [\hat{\mathbf{v}}_0 \times \hat{\mathbf{v}}_1, \hat{\mathbf{v}}_0 \cdot \hat{\mathbf{v}}_1]$. We use the Arcball to manipulate an object's orientation, which at mouse down we save as a quaternion, q_{down}. While dragging, we compute the object's current orientation as $q_{\text{now}} = q_{\text{drag}} q_{\text{down}}$. So long as the mouse button is held we use the same $\hat{\mathbf{v}}_0$ and q_{down}; upon release we permanently update the object's orientation to q_{now}.

◇ Arcball Properties ◇

Arcball's most important properties are hard to convey in print: it has a good "feel" and can be mastered in minutes. This is partly because the object motion mimics the mouse motion. If you drag across the center of the sphere, the object rotates in the direction the mouse moves. If you drag around the edge of the sphere, the object rotates around z in the same direction. But there is more to Arcball. With a single mouse stroke it is possible to rotate 360° around any axis. In fact, opposite points on the edge give the same rotation, so it is possible to wrap around and keep turning. And strokes add like vectors, which is truly remarkable since rotations do not commute.

This last property is the source of Arcball's path independence and requires a brief explanation. Consider two consecutive strokes, as in Figure 1.

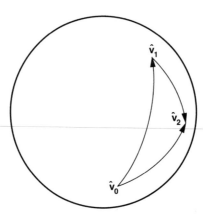

Figure 1.   Arc addition.

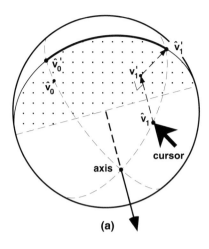
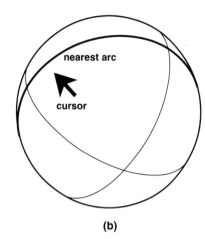

(a)   **(b)**

Figure 2.   (a) Constraint implementation. (b) Constraint selection.

A stroke from $\hat{\mathbf{v}}_0$ to $\hat{\mathbf{v}}_1$ followed by a stroke from $\hat{\mathbf{v}}_1$ to $\hat{\mathbf{v}}_2$ gives the same effect as a direct stroke from $\hat{\mathbf{v}}_0$ to $\hat{\mathbf{v}}_2$. That's because the composite quaternion is $(\hat{\mathbf{v}}_2\hat{\mathbf{v}}_1^{-1})(\hat{\mathbf{v}}_1\hat{\mathbf{v}}_0^{-1}) = \hat{\mathbf{v}}_2\hat{\mathbf{v}}_0^{-1}$. The benefit is a more forgiving interface with a solid feel. Once you start dragging, where the mouse is positioned matters, but not how you got there. There is no permanent penalty for losing a mouse sample, which is often hard to avoid; the behavior is like lossless incremental accumulation. Path independence also makes displaying an arc meaningful, since it really does show you the cumulative effect of your drag.

Like Hanson, we can also use a pair of controllers to turn objects in 4D. The complexity of rotations grows with the square of the dimension, giving in 4D 6 degrees of freedom. We can use an arbitrary quaternion, p, to describe a point, and a pair of unit quaternions, u and v, to describe a rotation. In 3D, we use the formula upu^{-1}; a 4D version is $uvpu^{-1}$. Adjust u with one Arcball, and v with the other.

◇ Adding Constraints ◇

We can now rotate with full freedom, but sometimes we want less. Fortunately, Arcball can easily be augmented with axis constraints.[2] (See Figure 2a.) To implement this, take your original Arcball points, subtract their components parallel to your chosen axis, and renormalize onto the sphere. Call the unit axis vector $\hat{\mathbf{a}}$; then compute $\mathbf{v}_0' = \hat{\mathbf{v}}_0-(\hat{\mathbf{v}}_0\cdot\hat{\mathbf{a}})\hat{\mathbf{a}}$, and $\hat{\mathbf{v}}_0' = \mathbf{v}_0'/\|\mathbf{v}_0'\|$. Do the same for $\mathbf{v}_1$. If either $\mathbf{v}_0'$ or $\mathbf{v}_1'$ ends up with negative z, negate

---

[2]Where you get an axis is up to you. It could be a coordinate axis, a surface normal, a body principal axis of inertia, a light reflection direction, or whatever.

that vector to its opposite on the front hemisphere. Using these new points instead of the originals to compute q_{drag}, your rotation is now constrained.

Here's an easy way to pick one axis from a small set of choices. Signal constraint mode by holding down, say, the [SHIFT] key. Have the controller pop up arcs superimposed on the Arcball, one for each of your axes. As you move the mouse around before clicking, the closest arc should be highlighted. (See Figure 2b.) When you click down with the mouse, you are constrained to the axis for the closest arc, and the other arcs disappear. There is both a visual clue (seeing pop-up arcs) and a kinesthetic clue (holding down the [SHIFT] key) that you are in constraint mode. When you release only the mouse button, you stay in constraint mode and are again shown all the arc choices. When you release the [SHIFT] key, you return to free mode, signaled by having the constraint arcs disappear. If you have different axis sets (object axes, camera axes, et cetera), you can hold down different keys to signal constraint mode.

◇ **Code** ◇

```
/***** BallMath.h - Essential routines for Arcball.  *****/
#ifndef _H_BallMath
#define _H_BallMath
#include "BallAux.h"

HVect MouseOnSphere(HVect mouse, HVect ballCenter, double ballRadius);
HVect ConstrainToAxis(HVect loose, HVect axis);
int NearestConstraintAxis(HVect loose, HVect *axes, int nAxes);
Quat Qt_FromBallPoints(HVect from, HVect to);
void Qt_ToBallPoints(Quat q, HVect *arcFrom, HVect *arcTo);
#endif
/***** EOF *****/
/***** BallAux.h - Vector and quaternion routines for Arcball. *****/
#ifndef _H_BallAux
#define _H_BallAux

typedef int Bool;
typedef struct {float x, y, z, w;} Quat;
enum QuatPart {X, Y, Z, W, QuatLen};
typedef Quat HVect;
typedef float HMatrix[QuatLen][QuatLen];

extern Quat qOne;
HMatrix *Qt_ToMatrix(Quat q, HMatrix out);
Quat Qt_Conj(Quat q);
Quat Qt_Mul(Quat qL, Quat qR);
HVect V3_(float x, float y, float z);
float V3_Norm(HVect v);
HVect V3_Unit(HVect v);
HVect V3_Scale(HVect v, float s);
HVect V3_Negate(HVect v);
```

```
HVect V3_Sub(HVect v1, HVect v2);
float V3_Dot(HVect v1, HVect v2);
HVect V3_Cross(HVect v1, HVect v2);
HVect V3_Bisect(HVect v0, HVect v1);
#endif
/***** EOF *****/
/***** Ball.h *****/
#ifndef _H_Ball
#define _H_Ball
#include "BallAux.h"

typedef enum AxisSet{NoAxes, CameraAxes, BodyAxes, OtherAxes, NSets} AxisSet;
typedef float *ConstraintSet;
typedef struct {
    HVect center;
    double radius;
    Quat qNow, qDown, qDrag;
    HVect vNow, vDown, vFrom, vTo, vrFrom, vrTo;
    HMatrix mNow, mDown;
    Bool showResult, dragging;
    ConstraintSet sets[NSets];
    int setSizes[NSets];
    AxisSet axisSet;
    int axisIndex;
} BallData;

/* Public routines */
void Ball_Init(BallData *ball);
void Ball_Place(BallData *ball, HVect center, double radius);
void Ball_Mouse(BallData *ball, HVect vNow);
void Ball_UseSet(BallData *ball, AxisSet axisSet);
void Ball_ShowResult(BallData *ball);
void Ball_HideResult(BallData *ball);
void Ball_Update(BallData *ball);
void Ball_Value(BallData *ball, HMatrix mNow);
void Ball_BeginDrag(BallData *ball);
void Ball_EndDrag(BallData *ball);
void Ball_Draw(BallData *ball);
/* Private routines */
void DrawAnyArc(HVect vFrom, HVect vTo);
void DrawHalfArc(HVect n);
void Ball_DrawConstraints(BallData *ball);
void Ball_DrawDragArc(BallData *ball);
void Ball_DrawResultArc(BallData *ball);
#endif
/***** EOF *****/
/**** Body.h ****/
#ifndef _H_Body
#define _H_Body
#include <gl/gl.h>
void drawbody(Matrix Rot);
#endif
/***** EOF *****/
```

```
/**** BallMath.c - Essential routines for ArcBall.  ****/
#include <math.h>
#include "BallMath.h"
#include "BallAux.h"

/* Convert window coordinates to sphere coordinates. */
HVect MouseOnSphere(HVect mouse, HVect ballCenter, double ballRadius)
{
    HVect ballMouse;
    register double mag;
    ballMouse.x = (mouse.x - ballCenter.x) / ballRadius;
    ballMouse.y = (mouse.y - ballCenter.y) / ballRadius;
    mag = ballMouse.x*ballMouse.x + ballMouse.y*ballMouse.y;
    if (mag > 1.0) {
        register double scale = 1.0/sqrt(mag);
        ballMouse.x *= scale; ballMouse.y *= scale;
        ballMouse.z = 0.0;
    } else {
        ballMouse.z = sqrt(1 - mag);
    }
    ballMouse.w = 0.0;
    return (ballMouse);
}

/* Construct a unit quaternion from two points on unit sphere */
Quat Qt_FromBallPoints(HVect from, HVect to)
{
    Quat qu;
    qu.x = from.y*to.z - from.z*to.y;
    qu.y = from.z*to.x - from.x*to.z;
    qu.z = from.x*to.y - from.y*to.x;
    qu.w = from.x*to.x + from.y*to.y + from.z*to.z;
    return (qu);
}

/* Convert a unit quaternion to two points on unit sphere */
void Qt_ToBallPoints(Quat q, HVect *arcFrom, HVect *arcTo)
{
    double s;
    s = sqrt(q.x*q.x + q.y*q.y);
    if (s == 0.0) {
        *arcFrom = V3_(0.0, 1.0, 0.0);
    } else {
        *arcFrom = V3_(-q.y/s, q.x/s, 0.0);
    }
    arcTo->x = q.w*arcFrom->x - q.z*arcFrom->y;
    arcTo->y = q.w*arcFrom->y + q.z*arcFrom->x;
    arcTo->z = q.x*arcFrom->y - q.y*arcFrom->x;
    if (q.w < 0.0) *arcFrom = V3_(-arcFrom->x, -arcFrom->y, 0.0);
}
```

```c
/* Force sphere point to be perpendicular to axis. */
HVect ConstrainToAxis(HVect loose, HVect axis)
{
    HVect onPlane;
    register float norm;
    onPlane = V3_Sub(loose, V3_Scale(axis, V3_Dot(axis, loose)));
    norm = V3_Norm(onPlane);
    if (norm > 0.0) {
        if (onPlane.z < 0.0) onPlane = V3_Negate(onPlane);
        return ( V3_Scale(onPlane, 1/sqrt(norm)) );
    } /* else drop through */
    if (axis.z == 1) {
        onPlane = V3_(1.0, 0.0, 0.0);
    } else {
        onPlane = V3_Unit(V3_(-axis.y, axis.x, 0.0));
    }
    return (onPlane);
}


/* Find the index of nearest arc of axis set. */
int NearestConstraintAxis(HVect loose, HVect *axes, int nAxes)
{
    HVect onPlane;
    register float max, dot;
    register int i, nearest;
    max = -1; nearest = 0;
    for (i=0; i<nAxes; i++) {
        onPlane = ConstrainToAxis(loose, axes[i]);
        dot = V3_Dot(onPlane, loose);
        if (dot>max) {
            max = dot; nearest = i;
        }
    }
    return (nearest);
}
/***** EOF *****/
/***** BallAux.c *****/
#include <math.h>
#include "BallAux.h"
Quat qOne = {0, 0, 0, 1};

/* Return quaternion product qL * qR.  Note: order is important!
 * To combine rotations, use the product Mul(qSecond, qFirst),
 * which gives the effect of rotating by qFirst then qSecond. */
Quat Qt_Mul(Quat qL, Quat qR)
{
    Quat qq;
    qq.w = qL.w*qR.w - qL.x*qR.x - qL.y*qR.y - qL.z*qR.z;
    qq.x = qL.w*qR.x + qL.x*qR.w + qL.y*qR.z - qL.z*qR.y;
    qq.y = qL.w*qR.y + qL.y*qR.w + qL.z*qR.x - qL.x*qR.z;
    qq.z = qL.w*qR.z + qL.z*qR.w + qL.x*qR.y - qL.y*qR.x;
    return (qq);
}
```

```
/* Construct rotation matrix from (possibly non-unit) quaternion.
 * Assumes matrix is used to multiply column vector on the left:
 * vnew = mat vold.  Works correctly for right-handed coordinate system
 * and right-handed rotations. */
HMatrix *Qt_ToMatrix(Quat q, HMatrix out)
{
    double Nq = q.x*q.x + q.y*q.y + q.z*q.z + q.w*q.w;
    double s = (Nq > 0.0) ? (2.0 / Nq) : 0.0;
    double xs = q.x*s,        ys = q.y*s,        zs = q.z*s;
    double wx = q.w*xs,       wy = q.w*ys,       wz = q.w*zs;
    double xx = q.x*xs,       xy = q.x*ys,       xz = q.x*zs;
    double yy = q.y*ys,       yz = q.y*zs,       zz = q.z*zs;
    out[X][X] = 1.0 - (yy + zz); out[Y][X] = xy + wz; out[Z][X] = xz - wy;
    out[X][Y] = xy - wz; out[Y][Y] = 1.0 - (xx + zz); out[Z][Y] = yz + wx;
    out[X][Z] = xz + wy; out[Y][Z] = yz - wx; out[Z][Z] = 1.0 - (xx + yy);
    out[X][W] = out[Y][W] = out[Z][W] = out[W][X] = out[W][Y] = out[W][Z] = 0.0;
    out[W][W] = 1.0;
    return ((HMatrix *)&out);
}


/* Return conjugate of quaternion. */
Quat Qt_Conj(Quat q)
{
    Quat qq;
    qq.x = -q.x; qq.y = -q.y; qq.z = -q.z; qq.w = q.w;
    return (qq);
}


/* Return vector formed from components */
HVect V3_(float x, float y, float z)
{
    HVect v;
    v.x = x; v.y = y; v.z = z; v.w = 0;
    return (v);
}


/* Return norm of v, defined as sum of squares of components */
float V3_Norm(HVect v)
{
    return ( v.x*v.x + v.y*v.y + v.z*v.z );
}


/* Return unit magnitude vector in direction of v */
HVect V3_Unit(HVect v)
{
    static HVect u = {0, 0, 0, 0};
    float vlen = sqrt(V3_Norm(v));
    if (vlen != 0.0) {
        u.x = v.x/vlen; u.y = v.y/vlen; u.z = v.z/vlen;
    }
    return (u);
}
```

```
/* Return version of v scaled by s */
HVect V3_Scale(HVect v, float s)
{
    HVect u;
    u.x = s*v.x; u.y = s*v.y; u.z = s*v.z; u.w = v.w;
    return (u);
}

/* Return negative of v */
HVect V3_Negate(HVect v)
{
    static HVect u = {0, 0, 0, 0};
    u.x = -v.x; u.y = -v.y; u.z = -v.z;
    return (u);
}

/* Return sum of v1 and v2 */
HVect V3_Add(HVect v1, HVect v2)
{
    static HVect v = {0, 0, 0, 0};
    v.x = v1.x+v2.x; v.y = v1.y+v2.y; v.z = v1.z+v2.z;
    return (v);
}

/* Return difference of v1 minus v2 */
HVect V3_Sub(HVect v1, HVect v2)
{
    static HVect v = {0, 0, 0, 0};
    v.x = v1.x-v2.x; v.y = v1.y-v2.y; v.z = v1.z-v2.z;
    return (v);
}

/* Halve arc between unit vectors v0 and v1. */
HVect V3_Bisect(HVect v0, HVect v1)
{
    HVect v = {0, 0, 0, 0};
    float Nv;
    v = V3_Add(v0, v1);
    Nv = V3_Norm(v);
    if (Nv < 1.0e-5) {
        v = V3_(0, 0, 1);
    } else {
        v = V3_Scale(v, 1/sqrt(Nv));
    }
    return (v);
}

/* Return dot product of v1 and v2 */
float V3_Dot(HVect v1, HVect v2)
{
    return (v1.x*v2.x + v1.y*v2.y + v1.z*v2.z);
}
```

```c
/* Return cross product, v1 x v2 */
HVect V3_Cross(HVect v1, HVect v2)
{
    static HVect v = {0, 0, 0, 0};
    v.x = v1.y*v2.z-v1.z*v2.y;
    v.y = v1.z*v2.x-v1.x*v2.z;
    v.z = v1.x*v2.y-v1.y*v2.x;
    return (v);
}
/***** EOF *****/
/***** Ball.c *****/
/* Ken Shoemake, 1993 */
#include <gl/gl.h>
#include "Ball.h"
#include "BallMath.h"

#define LG_NSEGS 4
#define NSEGS (1<<LG_NSEGS)
#define RIMCOLOR()    RGBcolor(255, 255, 255)
#define FARCOLOR()    RGBcolor(195, 127, 31)
#define NEARCOLOR()   RGBcolor(255, 255, 63)
#define DRAGCOLOR()   RGBcolor(127, 255, 255)
#define RESCOLOR()    RGBcolor(195, 31, 31)

HMatrix mId = {{1,0,0,0},{0,1,0,0},{0,0,1,0},{0,0,0,1}};
float otherAxis[][4] = {{-0.48, 0.80, 0.36, 1}};

/* Establish reasonable initial values for controller. */
void Ball_Init(BallData *ball)
{
    int i;
    ball->center = qOne;
    ball->radius = 1.0;
    ball->vDown = ball->vNow = qOne;
    ball->qDown = ball->qNow = qOne;
    for (i=15; i>=0; i--)
        ((float *)ball->mNow)[i] = ((float *)ball->mDown)[i] = ((float *)mId)[i];
    ball->showResult = ball->dragging = FALSE;
    ball->axisSet = NoAxes;
    ball->sets[CameraAxes] = mId[X]; ball->setSizes[CameraAxes] = 3;
    ball->sets[BodyAxes] = ball->mDown[X]; ball->setSizes[BodyAxes] = 3;
    ball->sets[OtherAxes] = otherAxis[X]; ball->setSizes[OtherAxes] = 1;
}

/* Set the center and size of the controller. */
void Ball_Place(BallData *ball, HVect center, double radius)
{
    ball->center = center;
    ball->radius = radius;
}
```

```
/* Incorporate new mouse position. */
void Ball_Mouse(BallData *ball, HVect vNow)
{
    ball->vNow = vNow;
}


/* Choose a constraint set, or none. */
void Ball_UseSet(BallData *ball, AxisSet axisSet)
{
    if (!ball->dragging) ball->axisSet = axisSet;
}


/* Begin drawing arc for all drags combined. */
void Ball_ShowResult(BallData *ball)
{
    ball->showResult = TRUE;
}


/* Stop drawing arc for all drags combined. */
void Ball_HideResult(BallData *ball)
{
    ball->showResult = FALSE;
}


/* Using vDown, vNow, dragging, and axisSet, compute rotation etc. */
void Ball_Update(BallData *ball)
{
    int i, setSize = ball->setSizes[ball->axisSet];
    HVect *set = (HVect *)(ball->sets[ball->axisSet]);
    ball->vFrom = MouseOnSphere(ball->vDown, ball->center, ball->radius);
    ball->vTo = MouseOnSphere(ball->vNow, ball->center, ball->radius);
    if (ball->dragging) {
        if (ball->axisSet!=NoAxes) {
            ball->vFrom = ConstrainToAxis(ball->vFrom, set[ball->axisIndex]);
            ball->vTo = ConstrainToAxis(ball->vTo, set[ball->axisIndex]);
        }
        ball->qDrag = Qt_FromBallPoints(ball->vFrom, ball->vTo);
        ball->qNow = Qt_Mul(ball->qDrag, ball->qDown);
    } else {
        if (ball->axisSet!=NoAxes) {
            ball->axisIndex = NearestConstraintAxis(ball->vTo, set, setSize);
        }
    }
    Qt_ToBallPoints(ball->qDown, &ball->vrFrom, &ball->vrTo);
    Qt_ToMatrix(Qt_Conj(ball->qNow), ball->mNow); /* Gives transpose for GL. */
}

/* Return rotation matrix defined by controller use. */
void Ball_Value(BallData *ball, HMatrix mNow)
{
    int i;
    for (i=15; i>=0; i--) ((float *)mNow)[i] = ((float *)ball->mNow)[i];
}
```

```
/* Begin drag sequence. */
void Ball_BeginDrag(BallData *ball)
{
    ball->dragging = TRUE;
    ball->vDown = ball->vNow;
}

/* Stop drag sequence. */
void Ball_EndDrag(BallData *ball)
{
    int i;
    ball->dragging = FALSE;
    ball->qDown = ball->qNow;
    for (i=15; i>=0; i--)
        ((float *)ball->mDown)[i] = ((float *)ball->mNow)[i];
}

/* Draw the controller with all its arcs. */
void Ball_Draw(BallData *ball)
{
    float r = ball->radius;
    pushmatrix();
    loadmatrix(mId);
    ortho2(-1.0, 1.0, -1.0, 1.0);
    RIMCOLOR();
    scale(r, r, r);
    circ(0.0, 0.0, 1.0);
    Ball_DrawResultArc(ball);
    Ball_DrawConstraints(ball);
    Ball_DrawDragArc(ball);
    popmatrix();
}

/* Draw an arc defined by its ends. */
void DrawAnyArc(HVect vFrom, HVect vTo)
{
    int i;
    HVect pts[NSEGS+1];
    double dot;
    pts[0] = vFrom;
    pts[1] = pts[NSEGS] = vTo;
    for (i=0; i<LG_NSEGS; i++) pts[1] = V3_Bisect(pts[0], pts[1]);
    dot = 2.0*V3_Dot(pts[0], pts[1]);
    for (i=2; i<NSEGS; i++) {
        pts[i] = V3_Sub(V3_Scale(pts[i-1], dot), pts[i-2]);
    }
    bgnline();
    for (i=0; i<=NSEGS; i++)
        v3f((float *)&pts[i]);
    endline();
}
```

```
/* Draw the arc of a semicircle defined by its axis. */
void DrawHalfArc(HVect n)
{
    HVect p, m;
    p.z = 0;
    if (n.z != 1.0) {
        p.x = n.y; p.y = -n.x;
        p = V3_Unit(p);
    } else {
        p.x = 0; p.y = 1;
    }
    m = V3_Cross(p, n);
    DrawAnyArc(p, m);
    DrawAnyArc(m, V3_Negate(p));
}

/* Draw all constraint arcs. */
void Ball_DrawConstraints(BallData *ball)
{
    ConstraintSet set;
    HVect axis;
    int j, axisI, setSize = ball->setSizes[ball->axisSet];
    if (ball->axisSet==NoAxes) return;
    set = ball->sets[ball->axisSet];
    for (axisI=0; axisI<setSize; axisI++) {
        if (ball->axisIndex!=axisI) {
            if (ball->dragging) continue;
            FARCOLOR();
        } else NEARCOLOR();
        axis = *(HVect *)&set[4*axisI];
        if (axis.z==1.0) {
            circ(0.0, 0.0, 1.0);
        } else {
            DrawHalfArc(axis);
        }
    }
}

/* Draw "rubber band" arc during dragging. */
void Ball_DrawDragArc(BallData *ball)
{
    DRAGCOLOR();
    if (ball->dragging) DrawAnyArc(ball->vFrom, ball->vTo);
}

/* Draw arc for result of all drags. */
void Ball_DrawResultArc(BallData *ball)
{
    RESCOLOR();
    if (ball->showResult) DrawAnyArc(ball->vrFrom, ball->vrTo);
}
/***** EOF *****/
```

```
/***** Body.c *****/
#include <gl/gl.h>
#include "Body.h"

enum QuatPart {X, Y, Z, W};
int bodyNPoints = 8;
int bodyNFaces = 7;

float theBodyRadius = 3.0;
float thePoints[][4] = {
    { 3.0,      0.0,      0.0,      1},
    {-1.0,      1.0,      0.0,      1},
    {-1.0,     -1.0,      0.0,      1},
    {-0.75,     0.0,     -0.25,     1},
    { 1.0,      0.0,      0.0,      1},
    {-0.75,     0.0,      0.75,     1},
    {-0.5,     -0.125,    0.0,      1},
    {-0.5,      0.125,    0.0,      1}
};
int theFaceVertices[][4] = {
    {3,   0,  1,  2},
    {3,   4,  5,  6},
    {3,   4,  7,  5},
    {3,   5,  7,  6},
    {3,   0,  2,  3},
    {3,   0,  3,  1},
    {3,   1,  3,  2},
};
float theFaceNormals[][4] = {
    {0., 0., 1., 0},
    {0.08152896377979659767, -0.978347565357559172, 0.1902342488195253946, 0},
    {0.08152896377979659767, 0.978347565357559172, 0.1902342488195253946, 0},
    {-0.9486832980505137996, 0., -0.3162277660168379332, 0},
    {0.06428243465332250222, -0.2571297386132900089, -0.9642365197998375334, 0},
    {0.06428243465332250222, 0.2571297386132900089, -0.9642365197998375334, 0},
    {-0.7071067811865475244, 0., -0.7071067811865475244, 0},
};
short theFaceColors[][3] = {
    {102, 204, 255},
    {  0, 153, 204},
    {  0, 153, 204},
    {204,  51, 157},
    { 51, 102, 157},
    { 51, 102, 157},
    {102, 102, 172},
};
```

```
/* Transform body normals, draw front */
void drawbody(Matrix Rot)
{
    double bodyScale = 1.0/theBodyRadius;
    register int i, j, k, n;

    pushmatrix();
    scale(bodyScale, bodyScale, bodyScale);
    for (j=0; j<bodyNFaces; j++) {
        double dot = Rot[X][Z]*theFaceNormals[j][X]
                    +Rot[Y][Z]*theFaceNormals[j][Y]
                    +Rot[Z][Z]*theFaceNormals[j][Z];
        if (dot>0.0) {      /* Front-facing polygon, so draw it */
            short shadedColor[3];
            dot += 0.4; if (dot>1.0) dot = 1.0;
            shadedColor[0] = dot*theFaceColors[j][0];
            shadedColor[1] = dot*theFaceColors[j][1];
            shadedColor[2] = dot*theFaceColors[j][2];
            n = theFaceVertices[j][0];
            RGBcolor(shadedColor[0], shadedColor[1], shadedColor[2]);
            bgnpolygon();
            for (k=1; k<=n; k++) {
                i = theFaceVertices[j][k];
                v4f(thePoints[i]);
            }
            endpolygon();
        }
    }
    popmatrix();
}
/***** EOF *****/
/***** Demo.c *****/
/* Ken Shoemake, 1993 */
#include <gl/gl.h>
#include <gl/device.h>
#include "BallAux.h"
#include "Body.h"
#include "Ball.h"

typedef struct {long x, y;} Place;

#define RADIUS    (0.75)
#define CNTRLDN   1
#define SHIFTDN   2

void main(void)
{
    int gid;
    short active;      /* TRUE if window is attached */
    Device dev;
    short val;
    Place winsize, winorig;
    Place mouseNow, mouseDown;
```

```
int keysDown;
HVect vNow;
BallData ball;

keepaspect(1, 1);
prefposition(50, 950, 50, 950);
gid = winopen("Arcball Demo");
doublebuffer();
RGBmode();
gconfig();
qdevice(MOUSEX); qdevice(MOUSEY); qdevice(LEFTMOUSE);
qdevice(LEFTCTRLKEY); qdevice(RIGHTCTRLKEY);
qdevice(LEFTSHIFTKEY); qdevice(RIGHTSHIFTKEY);
qdevice(CAPSLOCKKEY); qdevice(WINSHUT);
/* perspective(400, 1.0, 0.001, 100000.0); */
ortho(-1.0, 1.0, -1.0, 1.0, 0.001, 100000.0);
translate(0.0, 0.0, -3.0);
active = 0;

getsize(&winsize.x, &winsize.y);
getorigin(&winorig.x, &winorig.y);
keysDown = 0;
Ball_Init(&ball);
Ball_Place(&ball, qOne, RADIUS);

while (TRUE) {
    while (qtest()) {          /* process queued events */
        dev = qread(&val);
        switch (dev) {
            case WINSHUT:     /* exit program */
                gexit();
                exit(0);
                break;
            case INPUTCHANGE:
                active = val;
                break;
            case REDRAW:
                reshapeviewport();
                getsize(&winsize.x, &winsize.y);
                getorigin(&winorig.x, &winorig.y);
                break;
            case MOUSEX:
                mouseNow.x = val;
                vNow.x = 2.0*(mouseNow.x - winorig.x)/winsize.x - 1.0;
                break;
            case MOUSEY:
                mouseNow.y = val;
                vNow.y = 2.0*(mouseNow.y - winorig.y)/winsize.y - 1.0;
                break;
            case LEFTMOUSE:
                if (val) Ball_BeginDrag(&ball);
                else     Ball_EndDrag(&ball);
                break;
```

```
                 case LEFTCTRLKEY: case RIGHTCTRLKEY:
                     keysDown = (keysDown&~CNTRLDN)|(val? CNTRLDN : 0);
                     break;
                 case LEFTSHIFTKEY: case RIGHTSHIFTKEY:
                     keysDown = (keysDown&~SHIFTDN)|(val? SHIFTDN : 0);
                     break;
                 case CAPSLOCKKEY:
                     if (val) Ball_ShowResult(&ball);
                     else     Ball_HideResult(&ball);
                     break;
                 default:
                     break;
             }                     /* end of switch */
             Ball_Mouse(&ball, vNow);
             switch (keysDown) {
                 case CNTRLDN+SHIFTDN: Ball_UseSet(&ball, OtherAxes);  break;
                 case CNTRLDN:         Ball_UseSet(&ball, BodyAxes);   break;
                 case         SHIFTDN: Ball_UseSet(&ball, CameraAxes); break;
                 default:              Ball_UseSet(&ball, NoAxes);     break;
             }
         }                         /* end of while on qtest */
         Ball_Update(&ball);
         scene_Draw(&ball);        /* draw into the back buffer */
         swapbuffers();            /* and show it in the front buffer */
     }
     /* NOT REACHED */
}

/* Draw whole window, including controller. */
void scene_Draw(BallData *ball)
{
    RGBcolor(0, 0, 0);
    clear();
    body_Draw(ball);
    Ball_Draw(ball);
}

/* Draw the object being controlled. */
void body_Draw(BallData *ball)
{
    HMatrix mNow;
    Ball_Value(ball, mNow);
    pushmatrix();
    multmatrix(mNow);
    scale(RADIUS, RADIUS, RADIUS);
    drawbody(mNow);
    popmatrix();
}
/***** EOF *****/
```

◇ **Bibliography** ◇

(Chen *et al.* 1988) Michael Chen, Joy S. Mountford, and Abigail Sellen. A study in interactive 3-d rotation using 2-d control devices. *Computer Graphics*, 22(4):121–129, August 1988. Proceedings of SIGGRAPH '88.

(Hanson 1992) Andrew J. Hanson. The rolling ball. In David Kirk, editor, *Graphics Gems III*, pages 51–60. Academic Press, Boston, 1992.

(Hultquist 1990) Jeff Hultquist. A virtual trackball. In Andrew Glassner, editor, *Graphics Gems*, page 462. Academic Press, Boston, 1990.

(Shoemake 1985) Ken Shoemake. Animating rotation with quaternion curves. *Computer Graphics*, 19(3):245–254, July 1985. Proceedings of SIGGRAPH '85.

(Shoemake 1992) Ken Shoemake. Arcball: A user interface for specifying three-dimensional orientation using a mouse. In *Proceedings of Graphics Interface '92*, pages 151–156, 1992.

III.2

Efficient Eigenvalues for Visualization

Robert L. Cromwell

School of Electrical Engineering
1285 Electrical Engineering Building
Purdue University
West Lafayette, IN 47907-1285
cromwell@ecn.purdue.edu

There are many applications for the efficient visualization of a cloud of independently moving points or small objects flowing through 3D space in a fashion similar to a virtual swarm of bees or school of fish. For instance, in gas or particle dynamics it is important that the user clearly see the overall motions of such a cloud. In biochemistry or molecular biology, the viewer of a simulated reaction or biological process wants to clearly see complex interactions within a constantly flowing cloud of molecules. As a general rule of thumb, the "best" viewpoint is one from which the swarm of points is most spread out—a viewpoint from which the distribution is of minimal thickness. What's more, the alignment of the individual objects or swarm with respect to a world coordinate system is generally of no concern. In other words, there is no "up" at the scale of molecular biology. For these reasons, the most effective visualization tool might be one in which the viewpoint automatically changes from frame to frame, constantly tracking a path of optimal viewpoints.

Treating the swarm of objects as a 3D distribution of points, this optimal view direction is defined by an eigenvector of the matrix of central moments; specifically, the eigenvector associated with the eigenvalue of smallest magnitude. One might informally say that the direction of that eigenvector is the direction along which the distribution exhibits minimal thickness, and so a desirable viewpoint lies along a line parallel to that eigenvector and passing through the distribution's centroid. Therefore, it is crucial to update the eigenvalues, and thus the eigenvectors, of the distribution with each frame. It follows that eigensystem analysis of a 3×3 matrix must be done efficiently. Once the eigenvalues have been found, it is a simple matter to find the eigenvectors through Gaussian elimination. The difficulty lies in efficiently determining the eigenvalues.

Figure 1 shows a 2D view of two interacting clusters of methane molecules. In the interest of simplicity, let's assume that a visualization system must select a viewpoint within this 2D plane, so that it can produce a useful 1D projection of the 2D distribution. This allows us to present an unambiguous example on the written page, and the

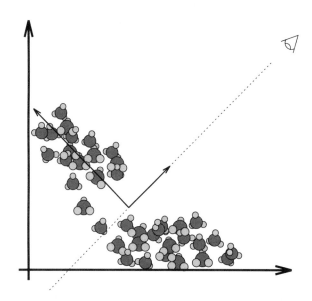

Figure 1. A distribution of particles with eigenvectors and a selected viewpoint.

extension to producing a 2D view of a 3D distribution is a simple one. The eigenvectors of the distribution are shown as solid arrows, and the line along which the selected viewpoint should lie is shown as a dotted line.

The standard approaches use an iterative approach; e.g., the algorithms described in *Numerical Recipes in C* (Press *et al.* 1988). However, if the problem is constrained as in the application described here, such that one knows that the eigenvalues will be real, then it is possible to use a bit of algebra and trigonometry to express the eigenvalues as explicit functions of the terms of the matrix of central moments, allowing the direct computation of the eigenvalues. Recall that $\mathbf{A}$, the matrix of central moments for a collection of n 3D points $[x_i, y_i, z_i]^T$, with centroid $[\bar{x}, \bar{y}, \bar{z}]^T$, is defined as:

$$\mathbf{A} = \begin{bmatrix} a_{11} & a_{12} & a_{13} \\ a_{21} & a_{22} & a_{23} \\ a_{31} & a_{32} & a_{33} \end{bmatrix} \tag{1}$$

$$= \begin{bmatrix} \sum_{i=1}^{n}(x_i - \bar{x})(x_i - \bar{x}) & \sum_{i=1}^{n}(x_i - \bar{x})(y_i - \bar{y}) & \sum_{i=1}^{n}(x_i - \bar{x})(z_i - \bar{z}) \\ \sum_{i=1}^{n}(y_i - \bar{y})(x_i - \bar{x}) & \sum_{i=1}^{n}(y_i - \bar{y})(y_i - \bar{y}) & \sum_{i=1}^{n}(y_i - \bar{y})(z_i - \bar{z}) \\ \sum_{i=1}^{n}(z_i - \bar{z})(x_i - \bar{x}) & \sum_{i=1}^{n}(z_i - \bar{z})(y_i - \bar{y}) & \sum_{i=1}^{n}(z_i - \bar{z})(z_i - \bar{z}) \end{bmatrix} \tag{2}$$

$$= \sum_{i=1}^{n} \begin{bmatrix} (x_i - \bar{x}) \\ (y_i - \bar{y}) \\ (z_i - \bar{z}) \end{bmatrix} [(x_i - \bar{x}), (y_i - \bar{y}), (z_i - \bar{z})] \tag{3}$$

In short, our method explicitly computes the eigenvalues of the 3×3 matrix $\mathbf{A}$ directly from the terms of that matrix. It offers a 5:1 increase in computational speed over the usual approach, and it is much simpler to implement. To find the eigenvalues of 100,000 3×3 matrices and then calculate the eigenvectors by Gaussian elimination, our method required 10.2 CPU seconds on a Sun 4/50MX-16; iterative algorithms (Press *et al.* 1988) required 51.3 CPU seconds. For those uninterested in the mathematical details, we suggest skipping to the final paragraph, which summarizes the equations to be implemented. For those interested in the details, we derive our method in the following paragraphs.

The eigenvalues of a square matrix $\mathbf{A}$ are the roots of the equation $det(\lambda \mathbf{I} - \mathbf{A}) = 0$. The first step in our direct computation method is to evaluate the explicit form of the determinant. This yields a cubic equation, which can be solved by a simple trigonometric method. The final result is a set of trigonometric expressions directly yielding the eigenvalues of a 3×3 matrix. In the method described here, we point out some simplifications that can be made in the computation of the terms of the determinant expansion and in the trigonometric analysis, yielding increased computational efficiency.

The first step is the expansion of the determinant:

$$det(\lambda \mathbf{I} - \mathbf{A}) = \begin{vmatrix} \lambda - a_{11} & -a_{12} & -a_{13} \\ -a_{21} & \lambda - a_{22} & -a_{23} \\ -a_{31} & -a_{32} & \lambda - a_{33} \end{vmatrix} \tag{4}$$

Multiplying through, and gathering terms of the same degree of λ, we find that:

$$\begin{aligned} det(\lambda \mathbf{I} - \mathbf{A}) = & \ \lambda^3 + [-a_{11} - a_{22} - a_{33}] \lambda^2 \\ & + [a_{11}a_{22} + a_{11}a_{33} + a_{22}a_{33} - a_{23}a_{32} - a_{12}a_{21} - a_{13}a_{31}] \lambda \\ & + [-a_{11}a_{22}a_{33} + a_{11}a_{23}a_{32} + a_{12}a_{21}a_{33} - a_{12}a_{23}a_{31} \\ & \qquad\qquad\qquad\qquad - a_{13}a_{21}a_{32} + a_{13}a_{22}a_{31}] \end{aligned} \tag{5}$$

$$= \ \lambda^3 + p\lambda^2 + q\lambda + r \tag{6}$$

To make the calculations of the terms p, q, and r more efficient, one should first note that $\mathbf{A}$, the matrix of central moments, is symmetric, and so the three matrix terms a_{21}, a_{31}, and a_{32} need not be calculated. Second, note that q and r share some products. In the actual implementation, one would first calculate the following intermediate terms: .

$$c = a_{11}a_{22} \tag{7}$$

$$d = a_{23}a_{32} \tag{8}$$

$$e = a_{12}a_{21} \tag{9}$$

$$f = a_{13}a_{31} \tag{10}$$

Now q and r may be calculated much more efficiently:

$$p = -a_{11} - a_{22} - a_{33} \tag{11}$$

$$q = c + (a_{11} + a_{22})a_{33} - d - e - f \tag{12}$$

$$r = (e - c)a_{33} + da_{11} - 2(a_{12}a_{23}a_{31}) + fa_{22} \tag{13}$$

Explicit calculation of the three terms p, q, and r, as in Equation 5, would have required 18 multiplications and 12 additions. The method of Equations 7–13 requires only 11 multiplications and 11 additions.

Given p, q, and r, we must simply solve a cubic equation in λ. As described in (Beyer 1978), we first reduce the cubic equation to:

$$x^3 + ax + b = 0 \tag{14}$$

by the substitutions

$$x = \lambda + p/3 \tag{15}$$

$$a = q - p^2/3 \tag{16}$$

$$b = 2p^3/27 - pq/3 + r \tag{17}$$

To solve for the roots by the trigonometric method, we calculate θ as

$$\theta = \frac{1}{3} \cos^{-1}\left(\frac{3b}{am}\right) \tag{18}$$

where

$$m = 2\sqrt{-a/3} \tag{19}$$

Note that $|3b/am| \le 1$ and $a \le 0$ because **A** is a matrix of central moments. We could solve for the three roots x_i as:

$$x_1 = m \cos(\theta) \tag{20}$$

$$x_2 = m \cos(\theta + 2\pi/3) \tag{21}$$

$$x_3 = m \cos(\theta + 4\pi/3) \tag{22}$$

Resubstituting the values found in Equations 20–22 into Equation 15 would then yield the desired eigenvalues.

$$\lambda_1 = m \cos(\theta) - p/3 \tag{23}$$

$$\lambda_2 = m \cos(\theta + 2\pi/3) - p/3 \tag{24}$$

$$\lambda_3 = m \cos(\theta + 4\pi/3) - p/3 \tag{25}$$

As it is formulated here, in a form equivalent to that in (Schwarze 1990), the calculation of the three eigenvalues requires the calculation of one square root, in Equation 19, and the calculation of four trigonometric functions, in Equations 18, 23, 24, and 25. However, this can be made more computationally efficient. We know that

$$\cos(\alpha + \beta) = \cos(\alpha)\cos(\beta) - \sin(\alpha)\sin(\beta) \tag{26}$$

The β terms in Equations 24 and 25 are known constants, $2\pi/3$ and $4\pi/3$, so their trigonometric functions are themselves constants which can be pre-computed. An optimized algorithm would first calculate c_θ and s_θ:

$$c_\theta = \cos(\theta) \tag{27}$$

$$s_\theta = \sin(\theta) \tag{28}$$

We can now reformulate the eigenvalues more efficiently as:

$$\lambda_1 = mc_\theta - \frac{p}{3} \tag{29}$$

$$\lambda_2 = m\left[\frac{c_\theta + \sqrt{3}s_\theta}{2}\right] - \frac{p}{3} \tag{30}$$

$$\lambda_3 = m\left[\frac{c_\theta - \sqrt{3}s_\theta}{2}\right] - \frac{p}{3} \tag{31}$$

Assuming that the $\sqrt{3}$ terms in Equations 30 and 31 are pre-computed and stored as constants, we now must calculate only one square root, in Equation 19, and three trigonometric functions, in Equations 18, 27, and 28. If one uses the C function `sincos()` to simultaneously calculate both c_θ and s_θ, then only two trigonometric function calls are needed.

To summarize our method for explicit eigenvalue computation, Equations 7–13 are used to calculate efficiently the terms p, q, and r. Those values are then used to find a, b, and m, and thus θ, c_θ, and s_θ, as in Equations 16–19, 27, and 28. Then, the eigenvalues λ_i are directly computed from m, c_θ, s_θ, and p as in Equations 29–31. Given the eigenvalues, the desired eigenvector is then easily found by Gaussian elimination.

◇   **Bibliography**   ◇

(Beyer 1978) William H. Beyer. *CRC Standard Mathematical Tables.* CRC Press, West Palm Beach, FL, 1978.

(Press *et al.* 1988) William H. Press, Brian P. Flannery, Saul A. Teukolsky, and William T. Vetterling. *Numerical Recipes in C, The Art of Scientific Computing.* Cambridge University Press, Cambridge, England, 1988.

(Schwarze 1990) Jochen Schwarze. Cubic and quartic roots. In Andrew S. Glassner, editor, *Graphics Gems*, pages 404–407. Academic Press, Boston, 1990.

III.3

Fast Inversion of Length- and Angle-Preserving Matrices

Kevin Wu

SunSoft
2550 Garcia Avenue
Mail Stop UMTV10-115
Mountain View, CA 94043-1100
kevin.wu@eng.sun.com

This Gem describes methods for quickly inverting 4×4 matrices that preserve lengths and angles. Matrices of these types frequently arise in 3D computer graphics. The distance between two points is invariant after transformation by a length-preserving matrix; likewise for the angle between two vectors and an angle-preserving matrix. Programmers can use these methods within the fast matrix inversion framework described in a previous Gem (Wu 1991), or simply in situations where a program handles matrices without perspective and anisotropic scaling.

◇ Properties and Matrix Forms ◇

Methods for quickly inverting length- and angle-preserving matrices are immediately apparent once their forms are explicitly known. Unlike the previous Gem (Wu 1991), we adopt the convention of representing points with column vectors to conform with a well-known graphics textbook (Foley *et al.* 1990). The two conventions are related by matrix transposition.

The Length-Preserving Matrix Group $\mathcal{P}_l$

Theorem 1 A 4×4 homogeneous matrix $\mathbf{M}$ preserves lengths if and only if it has the block matrix form

$$\mathbf{M} = \left[\begin{array}{cc} \mathbf{A} & \mathbf{C} \\ \mathbf{0} & 1 \end{array} \right]$$

where $\mathbf{A}$ is the 3×3 upper left submatrix, $\mathbf{C}$ is the 3×1 upper right submatrix, $\mathbf{0}$ is the 1×3 lower left submatrix of zeros, and $\mathbf{A}$ is orthogonal: $\mathbf{A}^{-1} = \mathbf{A}^T$.

Proof 1 Let $\mathbf{p}_1$ and $\mathbf{p}_2$ be two points

$$\mathbf{p}_1 = \begin{bmatrix} x_1 \\ y_1 \\ z_1 \end{bmatrix} \qquad \mathbf{p}_2 = \begin{bmatrix} x_2 \\ y_2 \\ z_2 \end{bmatrix}$$

The square of the distance between the two points is given by the inner product of the difference with itself.

$$r^2 = (\mathbf{p}_2 - \mathbf{p}_1)^T (\mathbf{p}_2 - \mathbf{p}_1) \tag{1}$$

A matrix with perspective does not preserve lengths in general. Consider a general 4×4 homogeneous matrix

$$\mathbf{M} = \begin{bmatrix} \mathbf{A} & \mathbf{C} \\ \mathbf{B} & D \end{bmatrix}$$

where $\mathbf{B}$ is the 1×3 lower left submatrix and D is the 1×1 lower right submatrix, which is a scalar. After transforming $\mathbf{p}_1$ and $\mathbf{p}_2$ by this matrix and dividing by the homogeneous coordinate, the length-preserving condition requires that

$$r^2 = \left(\frac{\mathbf{A}\mathbf{p}_2 + \mathbf{C}}{\mathbf{B}\mathbf{p}_2 + D} - \frac{\mathbf{A}\mathbf{p}_1 + \mathbf{C}}{\mathbf{B}\mathbf{p}_1 + D} \right)^T \left(\frac{\mathbf{A}\mathbf{p}_2 + \mathbf{C}}{\mathbf{B}\mathbf{p}_2 + D} - \frac{\mathbf{A}\mathbf{p}_1 + \mathbf{C}}{\mathbf{B}\mathbf{p}_1 + D} \right)$$

which is the square of the distance between the two transformed points. In general, this condition cannot be satisfied by two arbitrary points $\mathbf{p}_1$ and $\mathbf{p}_2$ when $\mathbf{B} \neq \mathbf{0}$; hence, the length-preserving condition requires that $\mathbf{B} = \mathbf{0}$. D is a nonzero scaling factor because all points are transformed to infinity if $D = 0$. We can simply divide the matrix by D without changing the effective geometric mapping because D scales the w component of transformed points, and we eventually divide the other components by that component. This means that D can always be set to 1. Therefore $\mathbf{M}$ is affine, and it can be written

$$\mathbf{M} = \begin{bmatrix} \mathbf{A} & \mathbf{C} \\ \mathbf{0} & 1 \end{bmatrix}$$

Given that $\mathbf{M}$ preserves lengths, we must show that $\mathbf{A}$ is orthogonal. $\mathbf{M}$ preserves lengths so the distance between the points after transformation is the same as before.

$$\begin{aligned} r^2 &= ((\mathbf{A}\mathbf{p}_2 + \mathbf{C}) - (\mathbf{A}\mathbf{p}_1 + \mathbf{C}))^T ((\mathbf{A}\mathbf{p}_2 + \mathbf{C}) - (\mathbf{A}\mathbf{p}_1 + \mathbf{C})) &(2) \\ &= (\mathbf{A}(\mathbf{p}_2 - \mathbf{p}_1))^T (\mathbf{A}(\mathbf{p}_2 - \mathbf{p}_1)) &(3) \\ &= (\mathbf{p}_2 - \mathbf{p}_1)^T \mathbf{A}^T \mathbf{A} (\mathbf{p}_2 - \mathbf{p}_1) &(4) \end{aligned}$$

Given that $\mathbf{M}$ preserves lengths, Equations 1 and 4 are equal for all $\mathbf{p}_1$ and $\mathbf{p}_2$. This condition can be satisfied only when $\mathbf{A}^T \mathbf{A} = \mathbf{I}$ or $\mathbf{A}^{-1} = \mathbf{A}^T$.

The converse (given a matrix with the form shown above implies that the matrix preserves lengths) is straightforward to prove, so this part of the proof is not included here for brevity.

The basic matrices that are members of the length-preserving matrix group include translations, rotations, and reflections. We can write this as follows:

$$\{\mathbf{T}(t_x, t_y, t_z), \mathbf{R}, \mathbf{S}(\pm 1, \pm 1, \pm 1)\} \subset \mathcal{P}_l$$

where $\mathbf{T}(t_x, t_y, t_z)$ is a translation matrix, $\mathbf{R}$ is a rotation matrix in (x, y, z) coordinate space, and $\mathbf{S}(s_x, s_y, s_z)$ is a scale matrix. Any matrix composed of the concatenation of any combination of only these matrices for translations, rotations, and reflections preserves lengths.

A program can identify length-preserving matrices in a number of ways, including the following examples:

- A priori: A program knows in advance that a particular matrix is the concatenation of only translation, rotation, and reflection matrices.
- Groups: A program keeps track of each matrix by maintaining an associated record of memberships to matrix groups (Wu 1991).
- Form: A program checks that a particular matrix has the form stated in Theorem 1. The matrix must be affine, which can be confirmed by checking the last row. Then the program calculates the product $\mathbf{A}^T \mathbf{A}$ and checks that it is the identity matrix $\mathbf{I}$. In practice, provision should be made for roundoff errors arising from floating-point calculations.
- Eigenvalues: A program checks the eigenvalues of $\mathbf{A}$ after confirming that the matrix is affine. $\mathbf{A}$ is an orthogonal matrix, or more generally, a unitary matrix. A property of unitary matrices is that the modulus of every eigenvalue λ is one: $|\lambda| = 1$; in other words, all eigenvalues lie on the unit circle in the complex plane (Strang 1988). For example, the eigenvalues of a 2D rotation matrix are $e^{i\theta}$ and $e^{-i\theta}$, where $i = \sqrt{-1}$ and θ is the angle of rotation in radians. In practice, this method of identification is likely to be slower than any of the examples above. Calculation of the eigenvalues of $\mathbf{A}$ requires the solution to the cubic characteristic equation, which involves square and cubic roots (Spiegel 1968). In general, one eigenvalue is 1 or -1 and the other two are either complex conjugates or both 1 or -1.

The Angle-Preserving Matrix Group $\mathcal{P}_a$

Theorem 2 A 4×4 homogeneous matrix $\mathbf{M}$ preserves angles if and only if it has the block matrix form

$$\mathbf{M} = \begin{bmatrix} \mathbf{A} & \mathbf{C} \\ \mathbf{0} & 1 \end{bmatrix}$$

where $\mathbf{A}$ is the 3×3 upper left submatrix, $\mathbf{C}$ is the 3×1 upper right submatrix, $\mathbf{0}$ is the 1×3 lower left submatrix of zeros, $\mathbf{A} = s\mathbf{Q}$, $s \neq 0$ is a scalar, and $\mathbf{Q}$ is orthogonal: $\mathbf{Q}^{-1} = \mathbf{Q}^T$.

Proof 2 Let $\mathbf{v}_1$ and $\mathbf{v}_2$ be two nonzero direction vectors

$$\mathbf{v}_1 = \begin{bmatrix} x_1 & y_1 & z_1 \end{bmatrix} \qquad \mathbf{v}_2 = \begin{bmatrix} x_2 & y_2 & z_2 \end{bmatrix}$$

The cosine of the angle between the two vectors is given by the inner product of the normalized vectors.

$$\cos\theta = \frac{\mathbf{v}_1 \, \mathbf{v}_2^T}{\|\mathbf{v}_1\| \, \|\mathbf{v}_2\|} \tag{5}$$

$$= \frac{\mathbf{v}_1 \mathbf{v}_2^T}{\sqrt{(\mathbf{v}_1\mathbf{v}_1^T)(\mathbf{v}_2\mathbf{v}_2^T)}} \tag{6}$$

It is intuitive and straightforward to prove that a matrix with perspective does not preserve angles in general. (This part of the proof is slightly more involved than the length-preserving case, but it is similar so it is not included here for brevity.) Therefore $\mathbf{M}$ is affine, and it can be written

$$\mathbf{M} = \begin{bmatrix} \mathbf{A} & \mathbf{C} \\ \mathbf{0} & 1 \end{bmatrix}$$

Since $\mathbf{v}_1$ and $\mathbf{v}_2$ are direction vectors, only the submatrix $\mathbf{A}$ applies to them for transformation (Turkowski 1990).

Given that $\mathbf{M}$ preserves angles, we must show that $\mathbf{A} = s\mathbf{Q}$ where s is a nonzero scalar and $\mathbf{Q}$ is orthogonal. $\mathbf{M}$ preserves angles so the angle between the vectors after transformation is the same as before.

$$\cos\theta = \frac{(\mathbf{v}_1\mathbf{A}) \, (\mathbf{v}_2\mathbf{A})^T}{\|\mathbf{v}_1\mathbf{A}\| \, \|\mathbf{v}_2\mathbf{A}\|} \tag{7}$$

$$= \frac{\mathbf{v}_1\mathbf{A}\mathbf{A}^T\mathbf{v}_2^T}{\sqrt{(\mathbf{v}_1\mathbf{A}\mathbf{A}^T\mathbf{v}_1^T)(\mathbf{v}_2\mathbf{A}\mathbf{A}^T\mathbf{v}_2^T)}} \tag{8}$$

Given that $\mathbf{M}$ preserves angles, Equations 6 and 8 are equal for all $\mathbf{v}_1$ and $\mathbf{v}_2$. This condition can be satisfied when $\mathbf{A}\mathbf{A}^T = \mathbf{I}$ or $\mathbf{A}^{-1} = \mathbf{A}^T$. However, this restriction is more confining than necessary because a nonzero scalar can be introduced without affecting equality since the constant cancels in the numerator and denominator of Equation 8. So we take as our restriction $\mathbf{A} = s\mathbf{Q}$ where s is a nonzero scalar and $\mathbf{Q}^{-1} = \mathbf{Q}^T$.

The converse (given a matrix with the form shown above implies that the matrix preserves angles) is straightforward to prove, so this part of the proof is not included here for brevity.

The basic matrices that are members of the angle-preserving matrix group include translations, rotations, and isotropic scalings (possibly with reflections). We can write this as follows:

$$\{\mathbf{T}(t_x, t_y, t_z), \mathbf{R}, \mathbf{S}(\pm s, \pm s, \pm s) | s \neq 0\} \subset \mathcal{P}_a$$

Any matrix composed of the concatenation of any combination of only matrices for translations, rotations, and isotropic scalings preserves angles. The length-preserving matrix group with scale factor $s = 1$ is a subgroup of the angle-preserving matrix group; a matrix that preserves lengths also preserves angles.

Methods of identifying angle-preserving matrices are similar to those for length-preserving matrices.

- A priori: A program knows in advance that a particular matrix is the concatenation of only translation, rotation, and isotropic scale matrices.
- Groups: A program keeps track of each matrix by maintaining an associated record of memberships to matrix groups.
- Form: A program checks that a particular matrix is affine and the product of $\mathbf{A}$ with its transpose is a scalar times the identity matrix: $\mathbf{A}\mathbf{A}^T = s^2\mathbf{I}$.
- Eigenvalues: A program checks that a particular matrix is affine and that the moduli of all eigenvalues of $\mathbf{A}$ equal the same constant: $|\lambda| = s$.

◇ **Fast Inversion Techniques** ◇

The block matrix forms for length- and angle-preserving matrices are important for deriving fast inversion techniques. Inverses of block matrices often arise in the theory of linear systems (Kailath 1980). The following form is applicable to 3D affine matrices:

$$\mathbf{M}^{-1} = \begin{bmatrix} \mathbf{A} & \mathbf{C} \\ \mathbf{0} & \mathbf{B} \end{bmatrix}^{-1} = \begin{bmatrix} \mathbf{A}^{-1} & -\mathbf{A}^{-1}\mathbf{C}\mathbf{B}^{-1} \\ \mathbf{0} & \mathbf{B}^{-1} \end{bmatrix}$$

This holds for any square submatrices $\mathbf{A}$ and $\mathbf{B}$ as long as their inverses exist. For our affine matrices, we let $\mathbf{A}$ be the 3×3 upper left submatrix of $\mathbf{M}$ and $\mathbf{B}$ be 1. Then this result simplifies to

$$\mathbf{M}^{-1} = \begin{bmatrix} \mathbf{A} & \mathbf{C} \\ \mathbf{0} & 1 \end{bmatrix}^{-1} = \begin{bmatrix} \mathbf{A}^{-1} & -\mathbf{A}^{-1}\mathbf{C} \\ \mathbf{0} & 1 \end{bmatrix}$$

For an angle-preserving matrix, $\mathbf{A}$ is the product of a nonzero scalar with an orthogonal matrix: $\mathbf{A} = s\mathbf{Q}$. The inverse of $\mathbf{A}$ can be written as

$$\mathbf{A}^{-1} = (s\mathbf{Q})^{-1} = s^{-1}\mathbf{Q}^{-1} = s^{-1}\mathbf{Q}^T = s^{-2}(s\mathbf{Q})^T = s^{-2}\mathbf{A}^T$$

The inverse of an angle-preserving matrix is given by

$$\mathbf{M}^{-1} = \begin{bmatrix} s^{-2}\mathbf{A}^T & -s^{-2}\mathbf{A}^T\mathbf{C} \\ \mathbf{0} & 1 \end{bmatrix}$$

The isotropic scale factor of $\mathbf{A}$ is s. Within the framework of the previous Gem for fast matrix inversion (Wu 1991), a program can keep track of the isotropic scale factor, which changes only when the program concatenates an isotropic scale matrix or when it inverts the matrix. Alternatively, if $\mathbf{M}$ is known to preserve angles, the isotropic scale factor can be calculated as the length of any row or column of $\mathbf{A}$ since the length of any row or column of an orthogonal matrix is 1.

A length-preserving matrix also preserves angles, and the isotropic scale factor is always $s = 1$. Therefore, the inverse of a length-preserving matrix is given by

$$\mathbf{M}^{-1} = \left[\begin{array}{cc} \mathbf{A}^T & -\mathbf{A}^T\mathbf{C} \\ \mathbf{0} & 1 \end{array} \right]$$

The fast inversion method for 4×4 affine matrices (Wu 1991) requires 48 multiplications and 2 divisions; it is applicable to affine matrices with anisotropic scaling. The method for angle-preserving matrices can be performed with 19 multiplications and 1 division provided that the isotropic scale factor is known; otherwise, an additional 2 multiplications are needed. The method for length-preserving matrices takes 9 multiplications.

If the purpose of inverting a 4×4 matrix belonging to the affine, angle-preserving, or length-preserving matrix groups is to transform normal or direction vectors, then a program only needs to compute the inverse of the 3×3 upper left submatrix $\mathbf{A}$. This requires nine fewer multiplications in each of the operation counts stated above.

◇ C Code ◇

```
#include "GraphicsGems.h"
#include <stdio.h>
/****
 *
 * angle_preserving_matrix4_inverse
 *
 * Computes the inverse of a 3D angle-preserving matrix.
 *
 * This procedure treats the 4 by 4 angle-preserving matrix as a block
 * matrix and calculates the inverse of one submatrix for a significant
 * performance improvement over a general procedure that can invert any
 * nonsingular matrix:
 *
 *                  --          --                --                  --
 *                  |          | -1              |   -2 T        -2   T  |
 *            ------+ A      C |           |    s  A      - s  A  C |
 *        -1        |          |                 |                    |
 *        M    =    |          |       =         |                    |
 *                  | 0     1  |                 |   0            1    |
 *                  |          |                 |                    |
 *                  |          |                 |                    |
 *                  --          --                --                  --
 * where      M is a 4 by 4 angle-preserving matrix,
 *            A is the 3 by 3 upper left submatrix of M,
 *            C is the 3 by 1 upper right submatrix of M.
```

```
 *
 * Input:
 *    in   - 3D angle-preserving matrix
 *
 * Output:
 *    out  - inverse of 3D angle-preserving matrix
 *
 * Returned value:
 *    TRUE   if input matrix is nonsingular
 *    FALSE  otherwise
 *
 ***/

boolean
angle_preserving_matrix4_inverse (Matrix4 *in, Matrix4 *out)
{
    double  scale;

    /* Calculate the square of the isotropic scale factor */
    scale = in->element[0][0] * in->element[0][0] +
            in->element[0][1] * in->element[0][1] +
            in->element[0][2] * in->element[0][2];

    /* Is the submatrix A singular? */
    if (scale == 0.0) {

        /* Matrix M has no inverse */
        fprintf (stderr, "angle_preserving_matrix4_inverse: singular matrix\n");
        return FALSE;
    }

    /* Calculate the inverse of the square of the isotropic scale factor */
    scale = 1.0 / scale;

    /* Transpose and scale the 3 by 3 upper left submatrix */
    out->element[0][0] = scale * in->element[0][0];
    out->element[1][0] = scale * in->element[0][1];
    out->element[2][0] = scale * in->element[0][2];
    out->element[0][1] = scale * in->element[1][0];
    out->element[1][1] = scale * in->element[1][1];
    out->element[2][1] = scale * in->element[1][2];
    out->element[0][2] = scale * in->element[2][0];
    out->element[1][2] = scale * in->element[2][1];
    out->element[2][2] = scale * in->element[2][2];

    /* Calculate -(transpose(A) / s*s) C */
    out->element[0][3] = - ( out->element[0][0] * in->element[0][3] +
                             out->element[0][1] * in->element[1][3] +
                             out->element[0][2] * in->element[2][3] );
    out->element[1][3] = - ( out->element[1][0] * in->element[0][3] +
                             out->element[1][1] * in->element[1][3] +
                             out->element[1][2] * in->element[2][3] );
    out->element[2][3] = - ( out->element[2][0] * in->element[0][3] +
```

```
                              out->element[2][1] * in->element[1][3] +
                              out->element[2][2] * in->element[2][3] );

    /* Fill in last row */
    out->element[3][0] = out->element[3][1] = out->element[3][2] = 0.0;
    out->element[3][3] = 1.0;

    return TRUE;
}
```

◇ **Bibliography** ◇

(Foley *et al.* 1990) James D. Foley, Andries van Dam, Steven K. Feiner, and John F. Hughes. *Computer Graphics: Principles and Practice*, second edition. Addison-Wesley, Reading, MA, 1990.

(Kailath 1980) Thomas Kailath. *Linear Systems*. Prentice Hall, Englewood Cliffs, NJ, 1980.

(Spiegel 1968) Murray R. Spiegel. *Mathematical Handbook of Formulas and Tables.* Schaum's Outline Series in Mathematics. McGraw-Hill, New York, NY, 1968.

(Strang 1988) Gilbert Strang. *Linear Algebra and Its Applications*, third edition. Harcourt Brace Jovanovich, San Diego, CA, 1988.

(Turkowski 1990) Ken Turkowski. Properties of surface-normal transformations. In Andrew S. Glassner, editor, *Graphics Gems*, pages 539–547. Academic Press, Boston, MA, 1990.

(Wu 1991) Kevin Wu. Fast matrix inversion. In James Arvo, editor, *Graphics Gems II*, pages 342–350. Academic Press, Boston, MA, 1991.

III.4

Polar Matrix Decomposition

Ken Shoemake

University of Pennsylvania
Philadelphia, PA
shoemake@graphics.cis.upenn.edu

◇ Introduction ◇

Extracting meaning from matrices is a compelling challenge, judging by the number of previous Gems on the subject. Affine matrices are especially awkward to dissect (Thomas 1991, Goldman 1992). A combination of rotating, scaling, shearing, and translating will generate any affine transform. Yet while a rotation, say, has a simple geometric meaning by itself, the rotation chosen by these previous Gems generally does not—as a factor. Since it is entirely dependent on the basis chosen to express the transformation as a matrix, the *decomposition* forfeits any claim of being geometrically meaningful. There is, however, an alternative: a physical, intuitive way to decompose an affine matrix. It is based on the linear algebra *polar decomposition*. The text of this Gem sketches the theory and benefits of polar decomposition,[1] and the code gives a sample implementation.

Why does it matter if a decomposition is geometric, and what does it mean? It may not matter if, for example, you simply need to recreate the effect of a given matrix using a graphics library with a limited choice of primitives. But if a human being is going to try to interpret the results, or if an animation program is going to try to interpolate the results, it matters a great deal. A good decomposition will give interpretations and interpolations that correspond to our perceptually based intuitions. Physics and psychology suggest two important criteria: coordinate independence and rigidity preservation. The first of these is the minimum needed for decomposition to have true geometric meaning.

Coordinate independence is an elaborate name for a simple observation. So far as we can tell, the universe has no built-in coordinate system. There is no special direction to call x or y, no self-evident unit of distance, no designated origin. The implication for matrix decomposition is that the results should not depend on the particular coordinate basis used, so long as the axes are perpendicular and scaled the same in all directions. In mathematical terms this has the following consequence. Suppose $\mathbf{M}$ is a linear transformation in one such basis, and $\mathbf{M}'$ is the same transformation expressed in another,

---

[1]See (Shoemake and Duff 1992) for a longer discussion.

so that $\mathbf{M'} = \mathbf{BMB}^{-1}$. Now suppose $\mathbf{M}$ and $\mathbf{M'}$ decompose as, say, $\mathbf{M} = \mathbf{QS}$ and $\mathbf{M'} = \mathbf{Q'S'}$. Then we should find that $\mathbf{Q'} = \mathbf{BQB}^{-1}$ and $\mathbf{S'} = \mathbf{BSB}^{-1}$. The Thomas and Goldman decompositions fail this test.

The second test, rigidity preservation, is more subtle and less certain, but important nevertheless. A variety of experiments in psychology give compelling evidence that the human visual system will interpret motion as rigid motion if possible. All rigid motion consists of rotations and translations, so this is a stringent demand, and not always possible. We can only say that, to the extent we can decompose a transform rigidly, we should do so. The Thomas and Goldman decompositions also fail this test.

◇ Polar Decomposition ◇

The polar form of a non-zero complex number $z = re^{i\theta}$ consists of two factors: a positive scaling r, and a rotation $e^{i\theta}$. The polar decomposition of a non-singular matrix $\mathbf{M} = \mathbf{QS}$ also consists of a positive scaling $\mathbf{S}$, and a rotation $\mathbf{Q}$, with two quibbles. The first quibble is that the $\mathbf{S}$ factor is a little more general than the usual scale matrix, since it need not be diagonal. Formally, it is a symmetric positive semi-definite matrix, which means it is only diagonal in *some* orthonormal basis, and has positive (or zero if $\mathbf{M}$ is singular) scale factors that can differ from each other. There is no standard computer graphics name for such a matrix, but I call it a *stretch* matrix, since it reminds me of cartoon animation's squash and stretch. The second quibble is that the $\mathbf{Q}$ factor is not necessarily a rotation. It is a more general *orthogonal* matrix (which can reflect as well as rotate), having a determinant of the same sign as $\mathbf{M}$. Quibbles aside, the motivation for the name should be clear.

Polar decomposition is ideally suited for our purposes, for three reasons. First, it is coordinate independent, so it tells us about the transformation in physically meaningful terms. Second, any non-singular matrix $\mathbf{M}$ has a unique polar decomposition, and $\mathbf{Q}$ is as close to $\mathbf{M}$ as possible,[2] equaling $\mathbf{M}$ if $\mathbf{M}$ is orthogonal. Thus, to the extent possible, rigidity is preserved. Third, it is simple to calculate. The $\mathbf{Q}$ factor can be obtained by setting $\mathbf{Q}_0 = \mathbf{M}$, then iterating $\mathbf{Q}_{i+1} = (\mathbf{Q}_i + (\mathbf{Q}_i^{-1})^{\mathrm{T}})/2$ until there is negligible change. An earlier Gem (Raible 1990) gives another application and a fast approximate calculation method, though polar decomposition is not explicitly mentioned.

◇ Decomposing an Affine Transformation ◇

We know that any 3D affine transformation can be factored as a 3D linear transformation followed by a translation. To find the translation, transform the zero vector. Assuming the transformation is given as a homogeneous matrix that acts on column

---

[2]Closeness can be measured using the sum of the squares of the element differences.

vectors, this step is trivial: strip off the last column of the matrix. This is the factorization $\mathbf{A} = \mathbf{TM}$. Then find the polar decomposition of $\mathbf{M}$, so we have $\mathbf{A} = \mathbf{TQS}$.

We could stop here, but more often we will want to further decompose the $\mathbf{Q}$ and $\mathbf{S}$ factors. If $\mathbf{Q}$ is not a rotation, it must be the negative of one (since 3 is an odd number of dimensions). Thus we can factor $\mathbf{Q} = \mathbf{FR}$, where $\mathbf{R}$ is a rotation and $\mathbf{F}$ (for flip) is $\pm\mathbf{I}$. If $\mathbf{Q}$ is a rotation, $\det(\mathbf{Q}) = +1$, otherwise $\det(\mathbf{Q}) = -1$, so this factorization is easy to compute. Since a rotation matrix can easily be described with a quaternion or an axis and angle, we will not decompose it further.

As noted above, the $\mathbf{S}$ factor is symmetric positive semi-definite. Thus it has a *spectral decomposition* $\mathbf{S} = \mathbf{UKU}^\mathrm{T}$, where $\mathbf{U}$ is a rotation and $\mathbf{K}$ (for scale) is diagonal with positive or zero entries. The scaling is usually non-uniform, i.e., different along each coordinate axis.[3] For human comprehension and simpler primitives, it will be helpful to include this extra step.

Be aware, however, that the spectral decomposition is not unique. Although $\mathbf{S}$ as a whole has geometric significance, its $\mathbf{U}$ and $\mathbf{K}$ factors are more ambiguous. Changing the labels and reversing the directions of the axes along which $\mathbf{S}$ is diagonalized[4] changes $\mathbf{U}$ and $\mathbf{K}$, but not the product $\mathbf{UKU}^\mathrm{T}$. I suggest picking the $\mathbf{U}$ with the smallest rotation angle; but consult (Shoemake and Duff 1992) for a more extended discussion of polar and spectral decomposition in the context of animation.

We now have a complete decomposition, $\mathbf{M} = \mathbf{TQS} = \mathbf{TFRUKU}^\mathrm{T}$. As a reality check, let's count degrees of freedom. The original matrix, $\mathbf{A}$, has 12 freely chosen entries, and so 12 degrees of freedom. The flip $\mathbf{F}$ is only a sign choice, so it contributes no degrees of freedom. The rotations $\mathbf{R}$ and $\mathbf{U}$ each have three degrees of freedom, as do the scaling $\mathbf{K}$ and the translation $\mathbf{T}$. (We count $\mathbf{U}$ only once, though it's used twice.) Thus we exactly match the needed degrees of freedom.

◇ **Implementation** ◇

Complete $\mathbf{TFRUKU}^\mathrm{T}$ factoring requires computing polar and spectral decompositions. If you already have a singular value decomposition routine, you can use its results to do both. The SVD of $\mathbf{M}$ has the form $\mathbf{VKU}^\mathrm{T}$, directly giving $\mathbf{U}$ and $\mathbf{K}$, and indirectly giving $\mathbf{Q} = \mathbf{VU}^\mathrm{T}$. (It may be necessary to negate $\mathbf{U}$ and $\mathbf{V}$ to ensure that $\mathbf{U}$ is a rotation.) Though SVD routines are complicated, they are also reliable.

But you don't need SVD code. If you have a symmetric eigenvalue routine (another name for spectral decomposition), you can use it instead. Decompose $\mathbf{M}^\mathrm{T}\mathbf{M}$ as $\mathbf{UDU}^\mathrm{T}$, where $\mathbf{D}$ is diagonal, and compute $\mathbf{K}$ from $\mathbf{D}$ by taking the positive square root of each entry. Then if $\mathbf{M}$ is non-singular, $\mathbf{Q}$ can be computed as $\mathbf{MUK}^{-1}\mathbf{U}^\mathrm{T}$. This approach

---

[3]The scale factors are the eigenvalues of $\mathbf{S}$ and the singular values of $\mathbf{M}$.

[4]The axis directions are the eigenvectors of $\mathbf{S}$.

should be used with caution, for $\mathbf{K}$ has no inverse if $\mathbf{M}$ is singular, and some accuracy will always be lost.

As mentioned earlier, however, the simplest approach is to set $\mathbf{Q}_0 = \mathbf{M}$, then iteratively compute $\mathbf{Q}_{i+1} = (\mathbf{Q}_i + (\mathbf{Q}_i^{-1})^{\mathrm{T}})/2$ until the difference between the entries of $\mathbf{Q}_i$ and $\mathbf{Q}_{i+1}$ is nearly zero. (By definition an orthogonal matrix satisfies $\mathbf{Q}^{\mathrm{T}}\mathbf{Q} = \mathbf{I}$, so $\mathbf{Q} = (\mathbf{Q}^{-1})^{\mathrm{T}}$.) When $\mathbf{M}$ is already nearly orthogonal, this iteration will converge quadratically, but the code given below includes a trick (Higham and Schreiber 1988) to accelerate convergence when there are large scale factors.

A singular $\mathbf{M}$ need only be a nuisance for this code, not an impenetrable barrier; but a spectral decomposition will still be needed after computing $\mathbf{S} = \mathbf{Q}^{\mathrm{T}}\mathbf{M}$. Since $\mathbf{S}$ has a characteristic polynomial which is only cubic, its roots (the diagonal of $\mathbf{K}$) can be found in closed form. But accuracy requires care, and $\mathbf{U}$ must still be found; so instead, try the method of Jacobi. A series of plane rotations $\mathbf{U}_i$ will force $\mathbf{S}$ to converge to diagonal form: $\mathbf{U}_n^{\mathrm{T}} \cdots \mathbf{U}_2^{\mathrm{T}}\mathbf{U}_1^{\mathrm{T}}\mathbf{S}\mathbf{U}_1\mathbf{U}_2 \cdots \mathbf{U}_n = \mathbf{K}$; then $\mathbf{U} = \mathbf{U}_1\mathbf{U}_2 \cdots \mathbf{U}_n$.

◇ **Decomposing the Inverse** ◇

If $\mathbf{A}$ has been factored as $\mathbf{TFRUKU}^{\mathrm{T}}$, it is cheap to compute its inverse. The derivation begins by distributing inversion to each of the factors:

$$(\mathbf{TFRUKU}^{\mathrm{T}})^{-1} = (\mathbf{U}^{\mathrm{T}})^{-1}\mathbf{K}^{-1}\mathbf{U}^{-1}\mathbf{R}^{-1}\mathbf{F}^{-1}\mathbf{T}^{-1}.$$

Since $\mathbf{U}$ and $\mathbf{R}$ are orthogonal and $\mathbf{F}$ is its own inverse, this simplifies to

$$\mathbf{U}\mathbf{K}^{-1}\mathbf{U}^{\mathrm{T}}\mathbf{R}^{\mathrm{T}}\mathbf{F}\mathbf{T}^{-1}.$$

These matrices are easy. The inverse of $\mathbf{K} = \mathrm{Scale}(k_x, k_y, k_z)$ is $\mathrm{Scale}(k_x^{-1}, k_y^{-1}, k_z^{-1})$. The inverse of $\mathbf{T} = \mathrm{Translate}(t_x, t_y, t_z)$ is $\mathrm{Translate}(-t_x, -t_y, -t_z)$. In the event we have stored the rotations as quaternions, we simply conjugate them.

If we only need the inverse as a matrix, we multiply everything and quit. But if we want it in the form $\mathbf{A}^{-1} = \mathbf{T}'\mathbf{F}'\mathbf{R}'\mathbf{U}'\mathbf{K}'(\mathbf{U}')^{\mathrm{T}}$, we must manipulate our terms into the correct order. First, premultiply by $\mathbf{R}^{\mathrm{T}}\mathbf{R}$, which is the identity, and regroup to obtain

$$\mathbf{R}^{\mathrm{T}}(\mathbf{RU})\mathbf{K}^{-1}(\mathbf{RU})^{\mathrm{T}}\mathbf{F}\mathbf{T}^{-1}.$$

Now $\mathbf{F}$ commutes with everything, so we can move it to the front and identify the terms $\mathbf{F}' = \mathbf{F}$, $\mathbf{R}' = \mathbf{R}^{\mathrm{T}}$, $\mathbf{U}' = \mathbf{RU}$, and $\mathbf{K}' = \mathbf{K}^{-1}$.

This gives us the form $\mathbf{M}'\mathbf{T}^{-1}$, but what we really want is $\mathbf{T}'\mathbf{M}'$. To order the translation correctly, we take $\mathbf{T}' = \mathrm{Translate}(-\mathbf{M}'T)$, where $\mathbf{T} = \mathrm{Translate}(T)$.

◇ **Code** ◇

```
/**** Decompose.h - Basic declarations ****/
#ifndef _H_Decompose
#define _H_Decompose
typedef struct {float x, y, z, w;} Quat; /* Quaternion */
enum QuatPart {X, Y, Z, W};
typedef Quat HVect; /* Homogeneous 3D vector */
typedef float HMatrix[4][4]; /* Right-handed, for column vectors */
typedef struct {
    HVect t;    /* Translation components */
    Quat  q;    /* Essential rotation     */
    Quat  u;    /* Stretch rotation       */
    HVect k;    /* Stretch factors        */
    float f;    /* Sign of determinant    */
} AffineParts;
float polar_decomp(HMatrix M, HMatrix Q, HMatrix S);
HVect spect_decomp(HMatrix S, HMatrix U);
Quat snuggle(Quat q, HVect *k);
void decomp_affine(HMatrix A, AffineParts *parts);
void invert_affine(AffineParts *parts, AffineParts *inverse);
#endif
/**** EOF ****/


/**** Decompose.c ****/
/* Ken Shoemake, 1993 */
#include <math.h>
#include "Decompose.h"


/******* Matrix Preliminaries *******/

/** Fill out 3x3 matrix to 4x4 **/
#define mat_pad(A)  (A[W][X]=A[X][W]=A[W][Y]=A[Y][W]=A[W][Z]=A[Z][W]=0,A[W][W]=1)

/** Copy nxn matrix A to C using "gets" for assignment **/
#define mat_copy(C,gets,A,n) {int i,j; for(i=0;i<n;i++) for(j=0;j<n;j++)\
    C[i][j] gets (A[i][j]);}

/** Copy transpose of nxn matrix A to C using "gets" for assignment **/
#define mat_tpose(AT,gets,A,n) {int i,j; for(i=0;i<n;i++) for(j=0;j<n;j++)\
    AT[i][j] gets (A[j][i]);}

/** Assign nxn matrix C the element-wise combination of A and B using "op" **/
#define mat_binop(C,gets,A,op,B,n) {int i,j; for(i=0;i<n;i++) for(j=0;j<n;j++)\
    C[i][j] gets (A[i][j]) op (B[i][j]);}

/** Multiply the upper left 3x3 parts of A and B to get AB **/
void mat_mult(HMatrix A, HMatrix B, HMatrix AB)
{
    int i, j;
    for (i=0; i<3; i++) for (j=0; j<3; j++)
        AB[i][j] = A[i][0]*B[0][j] + A[i][1]*B[1][j] + A[i][2]*B[2][j];
}
```

```
/** Return dot product of length 3 vectors va and vb **/
float vdot(float *va, float *vb)
{
    return (va[0]*vb[0] + va[1]*vb[1] + va[2]*vb[2]);
}


/** Set v to cross product of length 3 vectors va and vb **/
void vcross(float *va, float *vb, float *v)
{
    v[0] = va[1]*vb[2] - va[2]*vb[1];
    v[1] = va[2]*vb[0] - va[0]*vb[2];
    v[2] = va[0]*vb[1] - va[1]*vb[0];
}


/** Set MadjT to transpose of inverse of M times determinant of M **/
void adjoint_transpose(HMatrix M, HMatrix MadjT)
{
    vcross(M[1], M[2], MadjT[0]);
    vcross(M[2], M[0], MadjT[1]);
    vcross(M[0], M[1], MadjT[2]);
}


/******* Quaternion Preliminaries *******/

/* Construct a (possibly non-unit) quaternion from real components */
Quat Qt_(float x, float y, float z, float w)
{
    Quat qq;
    qq.x = x; qq.y = y; qq.z = z; qq.w = w;
    return (qq);
}


/* Return conjugate of quaternion */
Quat Qt_Conj(Quat q)
{
    Quat qq;
    qq.x = -q.x; qq.y = -q.y; qq.z = -q.z; qq.w = q.w;
    return (qq);
}


/* Return quaternion product qL * qR.  Note: order is important!
 * To combine rotations, use the product Mul(qSecond, qFirst),
 * which gives the effect of rotating by qFirst then qSecond. */
Quat Qt_Mul(Quat qL, Quat qR)
{
    Quat qq;
    qq.w = qL.w*qR.w - qL.x*qR.x - qL.y*qR.y - qL.z*qR.z;
    qq.x = qL.w*qR.x + qL.x*qR.w + qL.y*qR.z - qL.z*qR.y;
    qq.y = qL.w*qR.y + qL.y*qR.w + qL.z*qR.x - qL.x*qR.z;
    qq.z = qL.w*qR.z + qL.z*qR.w + qL.x*qR.y - qL.y*qR.x;
    return (qq);
}
```

```
/* Return product of quaternion q by scalar w */
Quat Qt_Scale(Quat q, float w)
{
    Quat qq;
    qq.w = q.w*w; qq.x = q.x*w; qq.y = q.y*w; qq.z = q.z*w;
    return (qq);
}


/* Construct a unit quaternion from rotation matrix.  Assumes matrix is
 * used to multiply column vector on the left: vnew = mat vold.  Works
 * correctly for right-handed coordinate system and right-handed rotations.
 * Translation and perspective components ignored. */
Quat Qt_FromMatrix(HMatrix mat)
{
    /* This algorithm avoids near-zero divides by looking for a large component
     * -- first w, then x, y, or z.  When the trace is greater than zero,
     * |w| is greater than 1/2, which is as small as a largest component can be.
     * Otherwise, the largest diagonal entry corresponds to the largest of |x|,
     * |y|, or |z|, one of which must be larger than |w|, and at least 1/2. */
    Quat qu;
    register double tr, s;

    tr = mat[X][X] + mat[Y][Y]+ mat[Z][Z];
    if (tr >= 0.0) {
            s = sqrt(tr + mat[W][W]);
            qu.w = s*0.5;
            s = 0.5 / s;
            qu.x = (mat[Z][Y] - mat[Y][Z]) * s;
            qu.y = (mat[X][Z] - mat[Z][X]) * s;
            qu.z = (mat[Y][X] - mat[X][Y]) * s;
        } else {
            int h = X;
            if (mat[Y][Y] > mat[X][X]) h = Y;
            if (mat[Z][Z] > mat[h][h]) h = Z;
            switch (h) {
#define caseMacro(i,j,k,I,J,K) \
            case I:\
                s = sqrt( (mat[I][I] - (mat[J][J]+mat[K][K])) + mat[W][W] );\
                qu.i = s*0.5;\
                s = 0.5 / s;\
                qu.j = (mat[I][J] + mat[J][I]) * s;\
                qu.k = (mat[K][I] + mat[I][K]) * s;\
                qu.w = (mat[K][J] - mat[J][K]) * s;\
                break
            caseMacro(x,y,z,X,Y,Z);
            caseMacro(y,z,x,Y,Z,X);
            caseMacro(z,x,y,Z,X,Y);
            }
        }
    if (mat[W][W] != 1.0) qu = Qt_Scale(qu, 1/sqrt(mat[W][W]));
    return (qu);
}
```

```
/******* Decomp Auxiliaries *******/

static HMatrix mat_id = {{1,0,0,0},{0,1,0,0},{0,0,1,0},{0,0,0,1}};

/** Compute either the 1 or the infinity norm of M, depending on tpose **/
float mat_norm(HMatrix M, int tpose)
{
    int i;
    float sum, max;
    max = 0.0;
    for (i=0; i<3; i++) {
        if (tpose) sum = fabs(M[0][i])+fabs(M[1][i])+fabs(M[2][i]);
        else       sum = fabs(M[i][0])+fabs(M[i][1])+fabs(M[i][2]);
        if (max<sum) max = sum;
    }
    return max;
}

float norm_inf(HMatrix M) {mat_norm(M, 0);}
float norm_one(HMatrix M) {mat_norm(M, 1);}

/** Return index of column of M containing maximum abs entry, or -1 if M=0 **/
int find_max_col(HMatrix M)
{
    float abs, max;
    int i, j, col;
    max = 0.0; col = -1;
    for (i=0; i<3; i++) for (j=0; j<3; j++) {
        abs = M[i][j]; if (abs<0.0) abs = -abs;
        if (abs>max) {max = abs; col = j;}
    }
    return col;
}

/** Make u for Householder reflection to zero all v components but first **/
void make_reflector(float *v, float *u)
{
    float s = sqrt(vdot(v, v));
    u[0] = v[0]; u[1] = v[1];
    u[2] = v[2] + ((v[2]<0.0) ? -s : s);
    s = sqrt(2.0/vdot(u, u));
    u[0] = u[0]*s; u[1] = u[1]*s; u[2] = u[2]*s;
}

/** Apply Householder reflection represented by u to column vectors of M **/
void reflect_cols(HMatrix M, float *u)
{
    int i, j;
    for (i=0; i<3; i++) {
        float s = u[0]*M[0][i] + u[1]*M[1][i] + u[2]*M[2][i];
        for (j=0; j<3; j++) M[j][i] -= u[j]*s;
    }
}
```

```
/** Apply Householder reflection represented by u to row vectors of M **/
void reflect_rows(HMatrix M, float *u)
{
    int i, j;
    for (i=0; i<3; i++) {
        float s = vdot(u, M[i]);
        for (j=0; j<3; j++) M[i][j] -= u[j]*s;
    }
}


/** Find orthogonal factor Q of rank 1 (or less) M **/
void do_rank1(HMatrix M, HMatrix Q)
{
    float v1[3], v2[3], s;
    int col;
    mat_copy(Q,=,mat_id,4);
    /* If rank(M) is 1, we should find a non-zero column in M */
    col = find_max_col(M);
    if (col<0) return; /* Rank is 0 */
    v1[0] = M[0][col]; v1[1] = M[1][col]; v1[2] = M[2][col];
    make_reflector(v1, v1); reflect_cols(M, v1);
    v2[0] = M[2][0]; v2[1] = M[2][1]; v2[2] = M[2][2];
    make_reflector(v2, v2); reflect_rows(M, v2);
    s = M[2][2];
    if (s<0.0) Q[2][2] = -1.0;
    reflect_cols(Q, v1); reflect_rows(Q, v2);
}


/** Find orthogonal factor Q of rank 2 (or less) M using adjoint transpose **/
void do_rank2(HMatrix M, HMatrix MadjT, HMatrix Q)
{
    float v1[3], v2[3];
    float w, x, y, z, c, s, d;
    int i, j, col;
    /* If rank(M) is 2, we should find a non-zero column in MadjT */
    col = find_max_col(MadjT);
    if (col<0) {do_rank1(M, Q); return;} /* Rank<2 */
    v1[0] = MadjT[0][col]; v1[1] = MadjT[1][col]; v1[2] = MadjT[2][col];
    make_reflector(v1, v1); reflect_cols(M, v1);
    vcross(M[0], M[1], v2);
    make_reflector(v2, v2); reflect_rows(M, v2);
    w = M[0][0]; x = M[0][1]; y = M[1][0]; z = M[1][1];
    if (w*z>x*y) {
        c = z+w; s = y-x; d = sqrt(c*c+s*s); c = c/d; s = s/d;
        Q[0][0] = Q[1][1] = c; Q[0][1] = -(Q[1][0] = s);
    } else {
        c = z-w; s = y+x; d = sqrt(c*c+s*s); c = c/d; s = s/d;
        Q[0][0] = -(Q[1][1] = c); Q[0][1] = Q[1][0] = s;
    }
    Q[0][2] = Q[2][0] = Q[1][2] = Q[2][1] = 0.0; Q[2][2] = 1.0;
    reflect_cols(Q, v1); reflect_rows(Q, v2);
}
```

```
/******* Polar Decomposition *******/

/* Polar Decomposition of 3x3 matrix in 4x4,
 * M = QS.  See Nicholas Higham and Robert S. Schreiber,
 * Fast Polar Decomposition of an Arbitrary Matrix,
 * Technical Report 88-942, October 1988,
 * Department of Computer Science, Cornell University.
 */
float polar_decomp(HMatrix M, HMatrix Q, HMatrix S)
{
#define TOL 1.0e-6
    HMatrix Mk, MadjTk, Ek;
    float det, M_one, M_inf, MadjT_one, MadjT_inf, E_one, gamma, t1, t2, g1, g2;
    int i, j;
    mat_tpose(Mk,=,M,3);
    M_one = norm_one(Mk);  M_inf = norm_inf(Mk);
    do {
        adjoint_transpose(Mk, MadjTk);
        det = vdot(Mk[0], MadjTk[0]);
        if (det==0.0) {do_rank2(Mk, MadjTk, Mk); break;}
        MadjT_one = norm_one(MadjTk); MadjT_inf = norm_inf(MadjTk);
        gamma = sqrt(sqrt((MadjT_one*MadjT_inf)/(M_one*M_inf))/fabs(det));
        g1 = gamma*0.5;
        g2 = 0.5/(gamma*det);
        mat_copy(Ek,=,Mk,3);
        mat_binop(Mk,=,g1*Mk,+,g2*MadjTk,3);
        mat_copy(Ek,-=,Mk,3);
        E_one = norm_one(Ek);
        M_one = norm_one(Mk);  M_inf = norm_inf(Mk);
    } while (E_one>(M_one*TOL));
    mat_tpose(Q,=,Mk,3); mat_pad(Q);
    mat_mult(Mk, M, S);  mat_pad(S);
    for (i=0; i<3; i++) for (j=i; j<3; j++)
        S[i][j] = S[j][i] = 0.5*(S[i][j]+S[j][i]);
    return (det);
}
```

```
/******* Spectral Decomposition *******/

/* Compute the spectral decomposition of symmetric positive semi-definite S.
 * Returns rotation in U and scale factors in result, so that if K is a diagonal
 * matrix of the scale factors, then S = U K (U transpose). Uses Jacobi method.
 * See Gene H. Golub and Charles F. Van Loan, Matrix Computations, Hopkins 1983.
 */
HVect spect_decomp(HMatrix S, HMatrix U)
{
    HVect kv;
    double Diag[3],OffD[3]; /* OffD is off-diag (by omitted index) */
    double g,h,fabsh,fabsOffDi,t,theta,c,s,tau,ta,OffDq,a,b;
    static char nxt[] = {Y,Z,X};
    int sweep, i, j;
    mat_copy(U,=,mat_id,4);
    Diag[X] = S[X][X]; Diag[Y] = S[Y][Y]; Diag[Z] = S[Z][Z];
    OffD[X] = S[Y][Z]; OffD[Y] = S[Z][X]; OffD[Z] = S[X][Y];
    for (sweep=20; sweep>0; sweep--) {
        float sm = fabs(OffD[X])+fabs(OffD[Y])+fabs(OffD[Z]);
        if (sm==0.0) break;
        for (i=Z; i>=X; i--) {
            int p = nxt[i]; int q = nxt[p];
            fabsOffDi = fabs(OffD[i]);
            g = 100.0*fabsOffDi;
            if (fabsOffDi>0.0) {
                h = Diag[q] - Diag[p];
                fabsh = fabs(h);
                if (fabsh+g==fabsh) {
                    t = OffD[i]/h;
                } else {
                    theta = 0.5*h/OffD[i];
                    t = 1.0/(fabs(theta)+sqrt(theta*theta+1.0));
                    if (theta<0.0) t = -t;
                }
                c = 1.0/sqrt(t*t+1.0); s = t*c;
                tau = s/(c+1.0);
                ta = t*OffD[i]; OffD[i] = 0.0;
                Diag[p] -= ta; Diag[q] += ta;
                OffDq = OffD[q];
                OffD[q] -= s*(OffD[p] + tau*OffD[q]);
                OffD[p] += s*(OffDq  - tau*OffD[p]);
                for (j=Z; j>=X; j--) {
                    a = U[j][p]; b = U[j][q];
                    U[j][p] -= s*(b + tau*a);
                    U[j][q] += s*(a - tau*b);
                }
            }
        }
    }
    kv.x = Diag[X]; kv.y = Diag[Y]; kv.z = Diag[Z]; kv.w = 1.0;
    return (kv);
}
```

```
/******* Spectral Axis Adjustment *******/

/* Given a unit quaternion, q, and a scale vector, k, find a unit quaternion, p,
 * which permutes the axes and turns freely in the plane of duplicate scale
 * factors, such that q p has the largest possible w component, i.e., the
 * smallest possible angle. Permutes k's components to go with q p instead of q.
 * See Ken Shoemake and Tom Duff, Matrix Animation and Polar Decomposition,
 * Proceedings of Graphics Interface 1992. Details on pp. 262-263.
 */
Quat snuggle(Quat q, HVect *k)
{
#define SQRTHALF (0.7071067811865475244)
#define sgn(n,v)   ((n)?-(v):(v))
#define swap(a,i,j) {a[3]=a[i]; a[i]=a[j]; a[j]=a[3];}
#define cycle(a,p)  if (p) {a[3]=a[0]; a[0]=a[1]; a[1]=a[2]; a[2]=a[3];}\
                    else   {a[3]=a[2]; a[2]=a[1]; a[1]=a[0]; a[0]=a[3];}
    Quat p;
    float ka[4];
    int i, turn = -1;
    ka[X] = k->x; ka[Y] = k->y; ka[Z] = k->z;
    if (ka[X]==ka[Y]) {if (ka[X]==ka[Z]) turn = W; else turn = Z;}
    else {if (ka[X]==ka[Z]) turn = Y; else if (ka[Y]==ka[Z]) turn = X;}
    if (turn>=0) {
        Quat qtoz, qp;
        unsigned neg[3], win;
        double mag[3], c, s, t;
        static Quat qxtoz = {0,SQRTHALF,0,SQRTHALF};
        static Quat qytoz = {SQRTHALF,0,0,SQRTHALF};
        static Quat qppmm = { 0.5,  0.5,-0.5,-0.5};
        static Quat qpppp = { 0.5,  0.5, 0.5, 0.5};
        static Quat qmpmm = {-0.5,  0.5,-0.5,-0.5};
        static Quat qpppm = { 0.5,  0.5, 0.5,-0.5};
        static Quat q0001 = { 0.0,  0.0, 0.0, 1.0};
        static Quat q1000 = { 1.0,  0.0, 0.0, 0.0};
        switch (turn) {
        default: return (Qt_Conj(q));
        case X: q = Qt_Mul(q, qtoz = qxtoz); swap(ka,X,Z) break;
        case Y: q = Qt_Mul(q, qtoz = qytoz); swap(ka,Y,Z) break;
        case Z: qtoz = q0001; break;
        }
        q = Qt_Conj(q);
        mag[0] = (double)q.z*q.z+(double)q.w*q.w-0.5;
        mag[1] = (double)q.x*q.z-(double)q.y*q.w;
        mag[2] = (double)q.y*q.z+(double)q.x*q.w;
        for (i=0; i<3; i++) if (neg[i] = (mag[i]<0.0)) mag[i] = -mag[i];
        if (mag[0]>mag[1]) {if (mag[0]>mag[2]) win = 0; else win = 2;}
        else               {if (mag[1]>mag[2]) win = 1; else win = 2;}
        switch (win) {
        case 0: if (neg[0]) p = q1000; else p = q0001; break;
        case 1: if (neg[1]) p = qppmm; else p = qpppp; cycle(ka,0) break;
        case 2: if (neg[2]) p = qmpmm; else p = qpppm; cycle(ka,1) break;
        }
```

```
        qp = Qt_Mul(q, p);
        t = sqrt(mag[win]+0.5);
        p = Qt_Mul(p, Qt_(0.0,0.0,-qp.z/t,qp.w/t));
        p = Qt_Mul(qtoz, Qt_Conj(p));
    } else {
        float qa[4], pa[4];
        unsigned lo, hi, neg[4], par = 0;
        double all, big, two;
        qa[0] = q.x; qa[1] = q.y; qa[2] = q.z; qa[3] = q.w;
        for (i=0; i<4; i++) {
            pa[i] = 0.0;
            if (neg[i] = (qa[i]<0.0)) qa[i] = -qa[i];
            par ^= neg[i];
        }
        /* Find two largest components, indices in hi and lo */
        if (qa[0]>qa[1]) lo = 0; else lo = 1;
        if (qa[2]>qa[3]) hi = 2; else hi = 3;
        if (qa[lo]>qa[hi]) {
            if (qa[lo^1]>qa[hi]) {hi = lo; lo ^= 1;}
            else {hi ^= lo; lo ^= hi; hi ^= lo;}
        } else {if (qa[hi^1]>qa[lo]) lo = hi^1;}
        all = (qa[0]+qa[1]+qa[2]+qa[3])*0.5;
        two = (qa[hi]+qa[lo])*SQRTHALF;
        big = qa[hi];
        if (all>two) {
            if (all>big) {/*all*/
                {int i; for (i=0; i<4; i++) pa[i] = sgn(neg[i], 0.5);}
                cycle(ka,par)
            } else {/*big*/ pa[hi] = sgn(neg[hi],1.0);}
        } else {
            if (two>big) {/*two*/
                pa[hi] = sgn(neg[hi],SQRTHALF); pa[lo] = sgn(neg[lo], SQRTHALF);
                if (lo>hi) {hi ^= lo; lo ^= hi; hi ^= lo;}
                if (hi==W) {hi = "\001\002\000"[lo]; lo = 3-hi-lo;}
                swap(ka,hi,lo)
            } else {/*big*/ pa[hi] = sgn(neg[hi],1.0);}
        }
        p.x = -pa[0]; p.y = -pa[1]; p.z = -pa[2]; p.w = pa[3];
    }
    k->x = ka[X]; k->y = ka[Y]; k->z = ka[Z];
    return (p);
}
```

```
/******* Decompose Affine Matrix *******/

/* Decompose 4x4 affine matrix A as TFRUK(U transpose), where t contains the
 * translation components, q contains the rotation R, u contains U, k contains
 * scale factors, and f contains the sign of the determinant.
 * Assumes A transforms column vectors in right-handed coordinates.
 * See Ken Shoemake and Tom Duff, Matrix Animation and Polar Decomposition,
 * Proceedings of Graphics Interface 1992.
 */
void decomp_affine(HMatrix A, AffineParts *parts)
{
    HMatrix Q, S, U;
    Quat p;
    float det;
    parts->t = Qt_(A[X][W], A[Y][W], A[Z][W], 0);
    det = polar_decomp(A, Q, S);
    if (det<0.0) {
        mat_copy(Q,=,-Q,3);
        parts->f = -1;
    } else parts->f = 1;
    parts->q = Qt_FromMatrix(Q);
    parts->k = spect_decomp(S, U);
    parts->u = Qt_FromMatrix(U);
    p = snuggle(parts->u, &parts->k);
    parts->u = Qt_Mul(parts->u, p);
}

/******* Invert Affine Decomposition *******/

/* Compute inverse of affine decomposition.
 */
void invert_affine(AffineParts *parts, AffineParts *inverse)
{
    Quat t, p;
    inverse->f = parts->f;
    inverse->q = Qt_Conj(parts->q);
    inverse->u = Qt_Mul(parts->q, parts->u);
    inverse->k.x = (parts->k.x==0.0) ? 0.0 : 1.0/parts->k.x;
    inverse->k.y = (parts->k.y==0.0) ? 0.0 : 1.0/parts->k.y;
    inverse->k.z = (parts->k.z==0.0) ? 0.0 : 1.0/parts->k.z;
    inverse->k.w = parts->k.w;
    t = Qt_(-parts->t.x, -parts->t.y, -parts->t.z, 0);
    t = Qt_Mul(Qt_Conj(inverse->u), Qt_Mul(t, inverse->u));
    t = Qt_(inverse->k.x*t.x, inverse->k.y*t.y, inverse->k.z*t.z, 0);
    p = Qt_Mul(inverse->q, inverse->u);
    t = Qt_Mul(p, Qt_Mul(t, Qt_Conj(p)));
    inverse->t = (inverse->f>0.0) ? t : Qt_(-t.x, -t.y, -t.z, 0);
}
/**** EOF ****/
```

◇ **Bibliography** ◇

(Goldman 1992) Ronald N. Goldman. Decomposing linear and affine transformations. In David Kirk, editor, *Graphics Gems III*, pages 108–116. Academic Press, Boston, 1992.

(Golub and Van Loan 1989) Gene H. Golub and Charles F. Van Loan. *Matrix Computations*, second edition. Johns Hopkins University Press, Baltimore, 1989.

(Higham and Schreiber 1988) Nicholas Higham and Robert S. Schreiber. Fast polar decomposition of an arbitrary matrix. Technical Report 88–942, Department of Computer Science, Cornell University, October 1988.

(Raible 1990) Eric Raible. Decomposing a matrix into simple transformations. In Andrew Glassner, editor, *Graphics Gems*, page 464. Academic Press, Boston, 1990.

(Shoemake and Duff 1992) Ken Shoemake and Tom Duff. Matrix animation and polar decomposition. In *Proceedings of Graphics Interface '92*, pages 258–264, 1992.

(Thomas 1991) Spencer W. Thomas. Decomposing a matrix into simple transformations. In James Arvo, editor, *Graphics Gems II*, pages 320–323. Academic Press, Boston, 1991.

III.5

Euler Angle Conversion

Ken Shoemake
University of Pennsylvania
Philadelphia, PA
shoemake@graphics.cis.upenn.edu

◇ Introduction ◇

All modern computer graphics systems use homogeneous matrices internally, and most use quaternions (Foley *et al.* 1990). Many, however, retain a text-based interface using Euler angles and need to convert to and from their internal representations. But to exchange data with other systems, an interface may need to handle all of the 24 different ways of specifying rotations with a triple of angles (Craig 1989, Appendix B). The purpose of this Gem is to show how a few lines of code can convert any of these varieties of Euler angles to and from matrices and quaternions, with the choice of variety given as a parameter.

Recall that a triple of Euler angles $[\theta_1, \theta_2, \theta_3]$ describes how a coordinate frame r rotates with respect to a static frame s. The triple is interpreted as a rotation by θ_1 around an axis $\mathbf{A}_1$, then a rotation by θ_2 around an axis $\mathbf{A}_2$, and finally a rotation by θ_3 around an axis $\mathbf{A}_3$, with $\mathbf{A}_2$ different from both $\mathbf{A}_1$ and $\mathbf{A}_3$. The axes are restricted to the coordinate axes, X, Y, and Z, giving 12 possibilities: XYZ, XYX, YZX, YZY, ZXY, ZXZ, XZY, XZX, YXZ, YXY, ZYX, ZYZ. The jump to 24 comes from the choice of using axes from either the static frame s or the rotating frame r. Equivalently, the rotations can be listed right to left or left to right.[1]

◇ Combinatorial Collapse ◇

It will be helpful to designate a convention with a 4-tuple: inner axis, parity, repetition, and frame. The inner axis will be the axis of the first standard matrix to multiply a vector. Since we are assuming column vectors, the inner axis is the axis of the rightmost matrix. Parity is even if the inner axis X is followed by the middle axis Y, or Y is followed by Z, or Z is followed by X; otherwise parity is odd. Repetition means whether the first and last axes are the same or different. Frame refers to the choice of either the static or the rotating frame, and applies to all three axes. With static frame axes the

---

[1]See (Craig 1989, Section 2.8) for a more leisurely discussion.

inner axis is the first axis, while with rotating frame axes the inner axis is the last axis.

Define the standard rotation matrices $\mathbf{R}_x(\theta)$, $\mathbf{R}_y(\theta)$, and $\mathbf{R}_z(\theta)$ as

$$
\begin{bmatrix} 1 & 0 & 0 \\ 0 & \cos\theta & \sin-\theta \\ 0 & \sin\theta & \cos\theta \end{bmatrix}
\quad
\begin{bmatrix} \cos\theta & 0 & \sin\theta \\ 0 & 1 & 0 \\ \sin-\theta & 0 & \cos\theta \end{bmatrix}
\quad
\begin{bmatrix} \cos\theta & \sin-\theta & 0 \\ \sin\theta & \cos\theta & 0 \\ 0 & 0 & 1 \end{bmatrix}
$$

Then $\mathbf{R}_x(\theta_3)\mathbf{R}_y(\theta_2)\mathbf{R}_x(\theta_1)$ is [X,Even,Same,S-frame], which we can abbreviate as XESS, while $\mathbf{R}_z(\theta_1)\mathbf{R}_x(\theta_2)\mathbf{R}_y(\theta_3)$ is [Y,Odd,Diff,R-frame], which we can abbreviate as YODR. Since each of the last three choices in the tuple can be encoded in a single bit, the whole tuple compactly encodes as an integer between 0 and 23. From a human factors perspective, the tuple notation makes it impossible to refer to nonsense conventions like XYY, and the integer values can be given meaningful names (see the code).

From a programming perspective, the tuple helps us collapse 24 cases to 2. Suppose we have code to convert a rotation matrix to XEDS angles, $\mathbf{R} = \mathbf{R}_z(\theta_3)\mathbf{R}_y(\theta_2)\mathbf{R}_x(\theta_1)$. If we are asked to extract XED<u>R</u> angles, $\mathbf{R} = \mathbf{R}_z(\theta_1)\mathbf{R}_y(\theta_2)\mathbf{R}_x(\theta_3)$, we use our code as is, and simply swap θ_1 and θ_3 afterwards.

We can also accomodate <u>Y</u>EDS angles, $\mathbf{R} = \mathbf{R}_x(\theta_3)\mathbf{R}_z(\theta_2)\mathbf{R}_y(\theta_1)$, by first changing the basis of $\mathbf{R}$ by a permutation matrix $\mathbf{P}$ which converts (Y, Z, X) to (X, Y, Z). Now applying our old XEDS code to $\mathbf{PRP}^{\mathrm{T}}$ extracts the YEDS angles we want from $\mathbf{R}$. In fact, we can extract any permutation we like by a suitable choice of $\mathbf{P}$, with one caveat. When the permutation is odd (X<u>O</u>DS), we are switching to a left-handed coordinate frame, and the sense of rotation is reversed. The fix is simple: negate the angles.

No permutation, however, can turn (X, Y, Z) into (X, Y, X); we need new code for XE<u>S</u>S angles. But the XEDS and XESS archetypes, coupled with permuting, negating, and swapping, are all we need. For efficiency, we can permute as we access the matrix entries during extraction. And while the discussion so far has focused on matrix-to-angle extraction, angle-to-matrix conversion permits the same economies. A little more thought shows quaternion conversions can also be collapsed.

◇ **Archetypes** ◇

Now we need archetypes for the conversions. The XEDS and XESS choices list fixed axis rotations in the order they are applied, and yield the matrices

$$
\mathbf{R}_{xyz} = \begin{bmatrix} c_2 c_3 & s_2 s_1 c_3 - c_1 s_3 & s_2 c_1 c_3 + s_1 s_3 \\ c_2 s_3 & s_2 s_1 s_3 + c_1 c_3 & s_2 c_1 s_3 - s_1 c_3 \\ -s_2 & c_2 s_1 & c_2 c_1 \end{bmatrix}
$$

and

$$
\mathbf{R}_{xyx} = \begin{bmatrix} c_2 & s_2 s_1 & s_2 c_1 \\ s_2 s_3 & -c_2 s_1 s_3 + c_1 c_3 & -c_2 c_1 s_3 - s_1 c_3 \\ -s_2 c_3 & c_2 s_1 c_3 + c_1 s_3 & c_2 c_1 c_3 - s_1 s_3 \end{bmatrix}
$$

where c_2 is $\cos\theta_2$, s_1 is $\sin\theta_1$, and so on. The corresponding quaternions are

$$q_{xyz} = [c_2 s_1 c_3 - s_2 c_1 s_3, \; c_2 s_1 s_3 + s_2 c_1 c_3, \; c_2 c_1 s_3 - s_2 s_1 c_3, \; c_2 c_1 c_3 + s_2 s_1 s_3]$$

and

$$q_{xyx} = [c_2(c_1 s_3 + s_1 c_3), \; s_2(c_1 c_3 + s_1 s_3), \; s_2(c_1 s_3 - s_1 c_3), \; c_2(c_1 c_3 - s_1 s_3)]$$

Note that the quaternion w component is given last, not first.

Conversion from Euler angles to quaternions or matrices can take advantage of common subexpressions, but is otherwise obvious. Converting a quaternion to Euler angles is easiest if we first convert to a matrix. Matrix conversion extracts sine and cosine of θ_2, then divides by the results to obtain sine and cosine of θ_1 and θ_3. When $\sin\theta_2 = 0$ (XESS) or $\cos\theta_2 = 0$ (XEDS), an alternate strategy must be used to avoid dividing by zero. In any scheme of Euler angles there are many triples that can describe the same matrix, which is a particularly bad problem when the alternate strategy is needed. The conversion routine cannot avoid this problem, but makes a conservative choice. In either situation atan2 is used to compute each angle from its sine and cosine to obtain quadrant information and good accuracy.

The HMatrix data type in the code represents 4-by-4 homogeneous transforms for right-handed rotations in right-handed coordinates applied to column vectors. If you are using row transforms (such as the Silicon Graphics GL library's Matrix type), you will need to transpose the matrix accesses. Free storage management is much easier if common data types are (multiples of) the same size, so I have chosen to use the Quat data type to hold Euler angles as well. A variety of construction and extraction macros are defined, but most users will only need the constants encoding order, such as EulOrdXYZs. For example, the following program reads ϕ, θ, and ψ and converts them to a matrix using the quantum mechanics convention $\mathbf{R}_x(\phi)\mathbf{R}_y(\theta)\mathbf{R}_x(\psi)$ (Goldstein 1980, Appendix B). It then converts the matrix to roll, pitch, and yaw angles, and prints them.

```
/* EulerSample.c - Read angles as quantum mechanics, write as aerospace */
#include <stdio.h>
#include "EulerAngles.h"
void main(void)
{
    EulerAngles outAngs, inAngs = {0,0,0,EulOrdXYXr};
    HMatrix R;
    printf("Phi Theta Psi (radians): ");
    scanf("%f %f %f",&inAngs.x,&inAngs.y,&inAngs.z);
    Eul_ToHMatrix(inAngs, R);
    outAngs = Eul_FromHMatrix(R, EulOrdXYZs);
    printf(" Roll   Pitch  Yaw    (radians)\n");
    printf("%6.3f %6.3f %6.3f\n", outAngs.x, outAngs.y, outAngs.z);
}
```

◇ **Code** ◇

Headers

```
/**** QuatTypes.h - Basic type declarations ****/
#ifndef _H_QuatTypes
#define _H_QuatTypes
/*** Definitions ***/
typedef struct {float x, y, z, w;} Quat; /* Quaternion */
enum QuatPart {X, Y, Z, W};
typedef float HMatrix[4][4]; /* Right-handed, for column vectors */
typedef Quat EulerAngles;    /* (x,y,z)=ang 1,2,3, w=order code  */
#endif
/**** EOF ****/


/**** EulerAngles.h - Support for 24 angle schemes ****/
/* Ken Shoemake, 1993 */
#ifndef _H_EulerAngles
#define _H_EulerAngles
#include "QuatTypes.h"
/*** Order type constants, constructors, extractors ***/
    /* There are 24 possible conventions, designated by:    */
    /*     o EulAxI = axis used initially                   */
    /*     o EulPar = parity of axis permutation            */
    /*     o EulRep = repetition of initial axis as last    */
    /*     o EulFrm = frame from which axes are taken        */
    /* Axes I,J,K will be a permutation of X,Y,Z.           */
    /* Axis H will be either I or K, depending on EulRep.    */
    /* Frame S takes axes from initial static frame.        */
    /* If ord = (AxI=X, Par=Even, Rep=No, Frm=S), then      */
    /* {a,b,c,ord} means Rz(c)Ry(b)Rx(a), where Rz(c)v      */
    /* rotates v around Z by c radians.                     */
#define EulFrmS        0
#define EulFrmR        1
#define EulFrm(ord)    ((unsigned)(ord)&1)
#define EulRepNo       0
#define EulRepYes      1
#define EulRep(ord)    (((unsigned)(ord)>>1)&1)
#define EulParEven     0
#define EulParOdd      1
#define EulPar(ord)    (((unsigned)(ord)>>2)&1)
#define EulSafe        "\000\001\002\000"
#define EulNext        "\001\002\000\001"
#define EulAxI(ord)    ((int)(EulSafe[(((unsigned)(ord)>>3)&3)]))
#define EulAxJ(ord)    ((int)(EulNext[EulAxI(ord)+(EulPar(ord)==EulParOdd)]))
#define EulAxK(ord)    ((int)(EulNext[EulAxI(ord)+(EulPar(ord)!=EulParOdd)]))
#define EulAxH(ord)    ((EulRep(ord)==EulRepNo)?EulAxK(ord):EulAxI(ord))
    /* EulGetOrd unpacks all useful information about order simultaneously. */
#define EulGetOrd(ord,i,j,k,h,n,s,f) {unsigned o=ord;f=o&1;o>>=1;s=o&1;o>>=1;\
    n=o&1;o>>=1;i=EulSafe[o&3];j=EulNext[i+n];k=EulNext[i+1-n];h=s?k:i;}
    /* EulOrd creates an order value between 0 and 23 from 4-tuple choices. */
#define EulOrd(i,p,r,f)    (((((((i)<<1)+(p))<<1)+(r))<<1)+(f))
```

```
    /* Static axes */
#define EulOrdXYZs     EulOrd(X,EulParEven,EulRepNo,EulFrmS)
#define EulOrdXYXs     EulOrd(X,EulParEven,EulRepYes,EulFrmS)
#define EulOrdXZYs     EulOrd(X,EulParOdd,EulRepNo,EulFrmS)
#define EulOrdXZXs     EulOrd(X,EulParOdd,EulRepYes,EulFrmS)
#define EulOrdYZXs     EulOrd(Y,EulParEven,EulRepNo,EulFrmS)
#define EulOrdYZYs     EulOrd(Y,EulParEven,EulRepYes,EulFrmS)
#define EulOrdYXZs     EulOrd(Y,EulParOdd,EulRepNo,EulFrmS)
#define EulOrdYXYs     EulOrd(Y,EulParOdd,EulRepYes,EulFrmS)
#define EulOrdZXYs     EulOrd(Z,EulParEven,EulRepNo,EulFrmS)
#define EulOrdZXZs     EulOrd(Z,EulParEven,EulRepYes,EulFrmS)
#define EulOrdZYXs     EulOrd(Z,EulParOdd,EulRepNo,EulFrmS)
#define EulOrdZYZs     EulOrd(Z,EulParOdd,EulRepYes,EulFrmS)
    /* Rotating axes */
#define EulOrdZYXr     EulOrd(X,EulParEven,EulRepNo,EulFrmR)
#define EulOrdXYXr     EulOrd(X,EulParEven,EulRepYes,EulFrmR)
#define EulOrdYZXr     EulOrd(X,EulParOdd,EulRepNo,EulFrmR)
#define EulOrdXZXr     EulOrd(X,EulParOdd,EulRepYes,EulFrmR)
#define EulOrdXZYr     EulOrd(Y,EulParEven,EulRepNo,EulFrmR)
#define EulOrdYZYr     EulOrd(Y,EulParEven,EulRepYes,EulFrmR)
#define EulOrdZXYr     EulOrd(Y,EulParOdd,EulRepNo,EulFrmR)
#define EulOrdYXYr     EulOrd(Y,EulParOdd,EulRepYes,EulFrmR)
#define EulOrdYXZr     EulOrd(Z,EulParEven,EulRepNo,EulFrmR)
#define EulOrdZXZr     EulOrd(Z,EulParEven,EulRepYes,EulFrmR)
#define EulOrdXYZr     EulOrd(Z,EulParOdd,EulRepNo,EulFrmR)
#define EulOrdZYZr     EulOrd(Z,EulParOdd,EulRepYes,EulFrmR)

EulerAngles Eul_(float ai, float aj, float ah, int order);
Quat Eul_ToQuat(EulerAngles ea);
void Eul_ToHMatrix(EulerAngles ea, HMatrix M);
EulerAngles Eul_FromHMatrix(HMatrix M, int order);
EulerAngles Eul_FromQuat(Quat q, int order);
#endif
/**** EOF ****/
```

Routines

```
/**** EulerAngles.c - Convert Euler angles to/from matrix or quat ****/
/* Ken Shoemake, 1993 */
#include <math.h>
#include <float.h>
#include "EulerAngles.h"

EulerAngles Eul_(float ai, float aj, float ah, int order)
{
    EulerAngles ea;
    ea.x = ai; ea.y = aj; ea.z = ah;
    ea.w = order;
    return (ea);
}
```

```
/* Construct quaternion from Euler angles (in radians). */
Quat Eul_ToQuat(EulerAngles ea)
{
    Quat qu;
    double a[3], ti, tj, th, ci, cj, ch, si, sj, sh, cc, cs, sc, ss;
    int i,j,k,h,n,s,f;
    EulGetOrd(ea.w,i,j,k,h,n,s,f);
    if (f==EulFrmR) {float t = ea.x; ea.x = ea.z; ea.z = t;}
    if (n==EulParOdd) ea.y = -ea.y;
    ti = ea.x*0.5; tj = ea.y*0.5; th = ea.z*0.5;
    ci = cos(ti);  cj = cos(tj);  ch = cos(th);
    si = sin(ti);  sj = sin(tj);  sh = sin(th);
    cc = ci*ch; cs = ci*sh; sc = si*ch; ss = si*sh;
    if (s==EulRepYes) {
        a[i] = cj*(cs + sc);    /* Could speed up with */
        a[j] = sj*(cc + ss);    /* trig identities. */
        a[k] = sj*(cs - sc);
        qu.w = cj*(cc - ss);
    } else {
        a[i] = cj*sc - sj*cs;
        a[j] = cj*ss + sj*cc;
        a[k] = cj*cs - sj*sc;
        qu.w = cj*cc + sj*ss;
    }
    if (n==EulParOdd) a[j] = -a[j];
    qu.x = a[X]; qu.y = a[Y]; qu.z = a[Z];
    return (qu);
}


/* Construct matrix from Euler angles (in radians). */
void Eul_ToHMatrix(EulerAngles ea, HMatrix M)
{
    double ti, tj, th, ci, cj, ch, si, sj, sh, cc, cs, sc, ss;
    int i,j,k,h,n,s,f;
    EulGetOrd(ea.w,i,j,k,h,n,s,f);
    if (f==EulFrmR) {float t = ea.x; ea.x = ea.z; ea.z = t;}
    if (n==EulParOdd) {ea.x = -ea.x; ea.y = -ea.y; ea.z = -ea.z;}
    ti = ea.x;    tj = ea.y;    th = ea.z;
    ci = cos(ti); cj = cos(tj); ch = cos(th);
    si = sin(ti); sj = sin(tj); sh = sin(th);
    cc = ci*ch; cs = ci*sh; sc = si*ch; ss = si*sh;
    if (s==EulRepYes) {
        M[i][i] = cj;     M[i][j] = sj*si;     M[i][k] =  sj*ci;
        M[j][i] = sj*sh;  M[j][j] = -cj*ss+cc; M[j][k] = -cj*cs-sc;
        M[k][i] = -sj*ch; M[k][j] =  cj*sc+cs; M[k][k] =  cj*cc-ss;
    } else {
        M[i][i] = cj*ch; M[i][j] = sj*sc-cs; M[i][k] = sj*cc+ss;
        M[j][i] = cj*sh; M[j][j] = sj*ss+cc; M[j][k] = sj*cs-sc;
        M[k][i] = -sj;   M[k][j] = cj*si;    M[k][k] = cj*ci;
    }
    M[W][X]=M[W][Y]=M[W][Z]=M[X][W]=M[Y][W]=M[Z][W]=0.0; M[W][W]=1.0;
}
```

```
/* Convert matrix to Euler angles (in radians). */
EulerAngles Eul_FromHMatrix(HMatrix M, int order)
{
    EulerAngles ea;
    int i,j,k,h,n,s,f;
    EulGetOrd(order,i,j,k,h,n,s,f);
    if (s==EulRepYes) {
        double sy = sqrt(M[i][j]*M[i][j] + M[i][k]*M[i][k]);
        if (sy > 16*FLT_EPSILON) {
            ea.x = atan2(M[i][j], M[i][k]);
            ea.y = atan2(sy, M[i][i]);
            ea.z = atan2(M[j][i], -M[k][i]);
        } else {
            ea.x = atan2(-M[j][k], M[j][j]);
            ea.y = atan2(sy, M[i][i]);
            ea.z = 0;
        }
    } else {
        double cy = sqrt(M[i][i]*M[i][i] + M[j][i]*M[j][i]);
        if (cy > 16*FLT_EPSILON) {
            ea.x = atan2(M[k][j], M[k][k]);
            ea.y = atan2(-M[k][i], cy);
            ea.z = atan2(M[j][i], M[i][i]);
        } else {
            ea.x = atan2(-M[j][k], M[j][j]);
            ea.y = atan2(-M[k][i], cy);
            ea.z = 0;
        }
    }
    if (n==EulParOdd) {ea.x = -ea.x; ea.y = - ea.y; ea.z = -ea.z;}
    if (f==EulFrmR) {float t = ea.x; ea.x = ea.z; ea.z = t;}
    ea.w = order;
    return (ea);
}

/* Convert quaternion to Euler angles (in radians). */
EulerAngles Eul_FromQuat(Quat q, int order)
{
    HMatrix M;
    double Nq = q.x*q.x+q.y*q.y+q.z*q.z+q.w*q.w;
    double s = (Nq > 0.0) ? (2.0 / Nq) : 0.0;
    double xs = q.x*s,    ys = q.y*s,    zs = q.z*s;
    double wx = q.w*xs,   wy = q.w*ys,   wz = q.w*zs;
    double xx = q.x*xs,   xy = q.x*ys,   xz = q.x*zs;
    double yy = q.y*ys,   yz = q.y*zs,   zz = q.z*zs;
    M[X][X] = 1.0 - (yy + zz); M[X][Y] = xy - wz; M[X][Z] = xz + wy;
    M[Y][X] = xy + wz; M[Y][Y] = 1.0 - (xx + zz); M[Y][Z] = yz - wx;
    M[Z][X] = xz - wy; M[Z][Y] = yz + wx; M[Z][Z] = 1.0 - (xx + yy);
    M[W][X]=M[W][Y]=M[W][Z]=M[X][W]=M[Y][W]=M[Z][W]=0.0; M[W][W]=1.0;
    return (Eul_FromHMatrix(M, order));
}
/**** EOF ****/
```

◇ **Bibliography** ◇

(Craig 1989) John J. Craig. *Introduction to Robotics: Mechanics and Control*, 2nd edition. Addison-Wesley, Reading, MA, 1989.

(Foley *et al.* 1990) James D. Foley, Andries van Dam, Steven K. Feiner, and John F. Hughes. *Computer Graphics: Principles and Practice*, 2nd edition. Addison-Wesley, Reading, MA, 1990.

(Goldstein 1980) Herbert Goldstein. *Classical Mechanics*, 2nd edition. Addison-Wesley, Reading, MA, 1980.

◊ III.6

Fiber Bundle Twist Reduction

Ken Shoemake

University of Pennsylvania
Philadelphia, PA
shoemake@graphics.cis.upenn.edu

◊ Introduction ◊

Mathematicians are clever at recycling. When an old concept proves inadequate for a new situation, often a little fudging makes it fit. Fiber bundles are such a success story. Computer graphics can use a famous bundle, the Hopf fibration of the quaternion unit sphere, for a little fudging of its own: reducing twist in camera tracking. This Gem provides a brief introduction to fiber bundles, explains the Hopf fibration, and shows how to use it to measure and reduce twist. Don't worry if the mathematical details take a while to sink in. The concepts are subtle, but the calculations are simple.

Patrons of a play sit still, viewing action on the stage in front of them. Early cinematographers did the same, using a static, constantly recording camera. Over time, zooming, panning, trucking, and cutting became accepted practice. Yet, even today, there are conventional limits on camera use.[1] Computer graphics ignores many viewer-friendly conventions, but does respect one: cameras rarely tilt. (See Figure 1a.)

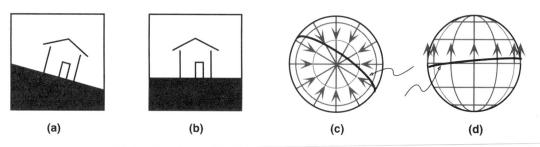

(a)	(b)	(c)	(d)

Figure 1.   (a) Tilted. (b) Untilted. (c) Path with rapid twist, from top. (d) Path with slow twist, from side.

When a camera tracks an object passing directly overhead, or nearly so, avoiding tilt requires a large change in orientation for even a small change in gaze. (See Figure 1c.) This manifests itself as rapid turning, or *twist*, around the gaze direction. Both tilt and

---

[1] You might notice, for example, that a train ride from San Francisco to Chicago is filmed with the train moving from left to right in every scene, to give a sense of progress.

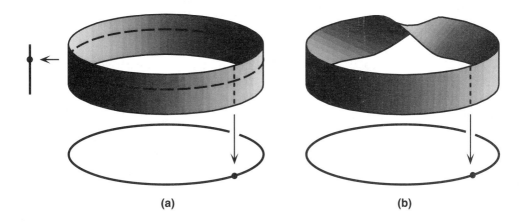

(a)   (b)

Figure 2.   (a) Product. (b) Bundle.

twist are disorienting, so compromise is necessary. Often, animators manually intervene, moving the camera or the object to avoid this situation. Otherwise, some tilt must be accepted to reduce twist. The challenge is to formally define and measure twist, and to add tilt automatically when twist is excessive. That's where fiber bundles come in.

◇   **Fiber Bundles**   ◇

A fiber bundle is a topological space that is "locally" a product. The definition is somewhat like that of manifolds, a patchwork of overlapping neighborhoods that together make up the whole space. In a manifold, each neighborhood looks like n-dimensional Euclidean space; in a fiber bundle, each looks like a product. Figure 2 illustrates the concept by contrasting a cylindrical strip, which is a product (and a trivial bundle), with the famous Möbius strip, which is a bundle but not a product.

The cylindrical strip, like any product space, comes with continuous projection maps, π_1 and π_2, onto each of its factors. In this case the factors are a circle and a line segment. If x is a point on the circle, the points that project to x, $\pi_1^{-1}(x)$, form a line segment. Likewise, the inverse image of a point on the line segment is a circle. Every point of the cylindrical strip can be identified with a unique pair of points, one from the circle and one from the line segment: $p = (p_1, p_2)$.

The Möbius strip also projects continuously onto the circle, again with a line segment for the inverse image of each circle point. It is not possible, however, to project continuously onto a line segment, because of the twist. (Notice, for example, that the Möbius strip has only a single edge.) Nevertheless, if we restrict our attention to a small interval around any point on the circle, we find that the inverse image of that neighborhood is a product of the neighborhood with a line segment. *Segments* of the Möbius strip look just like segments of the cylindrical strip.

Every fiber bundle shares these features of the Möbius strip (Steenrod 1951). There is a *total space*, here the strip, which is a bundle over the *base space*, here a circle. There is a continuous projection, π, from the total space to the base space. The inverse image, $\pi^{-1}(x)$, of a point x in the base space is called the *fiber* over x, and each fiber is topologically the same as (homeomorphic to) the *fiber space*, here a line segment. Every point of the base space has some open neighborhood whose inverse image is (homeomorphic to) the product of that neighborhood with the fiber space. Notice that for a product space both factor spaces have equal status, while for a fiber bundle the single projection introduces an asymmetry between the base space and the fiber space.

Here are a few examples to give the definitions more meaning. Every differentiable n-dimensional manifold M comes with a $2n$-dimensional bundle which is also a manifold: the tangent bundle, TM. (It also has a cotangent bundle, T^*M.) The fiber over a point of M is the space of tangent vectors there. For example, at each point of a sphere there is a tangent plane, which we take as a fiber. The bundle of all these tangent planes, however, is certainly not the product of a sphere and a plane. If it were, we could easily define a smooth non-vanishing field of tangent vectors, which the famous "hairy ball" theorem says is impossible (Milnor 1965). We can throw away the lengths of the tangent vectors to get the contact bundle, CM (Burke 1985). In the next section we will see that unit quaternions and 3D rotations are also bundles over a sphere. We can view a sphere itself as a bundle over 2D projective space; fibers are antipodal points.

◇   Hopf Fibration   ◇

Heinz Hopf discovered the unexpected fiber bundle we are going to use. He showed that S^3, the unit sphere in 4D space, was a fiber bundle over S^2, the unit sphere in 3D space, with fiber space S^1, the unit sphere in 2D space. (The exponent gives the dimension of the sphere, which is one less than the space it is embedded in. So S^1 is a circle, S^2 is an ordinary sphere, and S^3 is a hypersphere.) This dissection is known as the Hopf fibration. It is not terribly complicated, and it is just what we need to limit twist. See the visualization in color plate III.6.1.

Unit quaternions (Shoemake 1985) will serve as our points on S^3. Remember that a quaternion q acts as a rotation R_q on a 3D point p via the formula $R_q(p) = qpq^{-1}$, and that $R_q(R_r(p)) = R_{qr}(p)$. A unit quaternion $q = [(x, y, z), w] = [\hat{\mathbf{v}}\sin\theta, \cos\theta]$ acts as a rotation by 2θ around the axis $\hat{\mathbf{v}}$. Let $\hat{\mathbf{z}} = [(0, 0, 1), 0]$ be a unit vector in the z direction. We choose the projection $\pi(q)$ of a unit quaternion q to be $R_q(\hat{\mathbf{z}})$. Since rotating a unit vector gives a unit vector, this formula clearly produces a point on S^2 (at the tip of the vector). As q varies we will get different points, so $\pi(q)$ really does map points on S^3 (the unit quaternions, q) to points on S^2 (the position of the rotated $\hat{\mathbf{z}}$ tip). From our knowledge of quaternions and their relationship to rotations we can verify that this map is a well-defined and continuous projection.

So far we have S^3, S^2, and a projection map π from one to the other; now we need to find fibers that look like S^1, i.e., circles. The fiber over a point p of S^2 is supposed to be all the quaternions q that project to p. Suppose q is $[(0,0,0),1]$, so that R_q is no rotation at all and $\hat{\mathbf{z}}$ stays where it is. This q is one point that projects to $p = \hat{\mathbf{z}}$; what others are there? That is, what other rotations leave $\hat{\mathbf{z}}$ where it is? The answer is simply any rotation around the z axis. These are given by quaternions r of the form $r = [(0,0,\sin\theta),\cos\theta]$. We could hardly hope for a more obvious circle! A little thought shows the fiber over any point p is a circle, since if $\pi(q) = p$, then also $\pi(qr) = p$ for all r of the form just given. Finally, the product-in-a-neighborhood property can also be verified, so S^3 is indeed a fiber bundle over S^2 with fiber space S^1.

We are going to use an obvious[2] consequence of the discussion so far: The rotations in 3D (collectively called $SO(3)$) also form a fiber bundle over S^2, with fiber space the rotations in 2D (called $SO(2)$). After all, the projection we just described only depended on the behavior of unit quaternions acting as rotations.[3]

◇ **Measuring Twist** ◇

By a lucky coincidence, the projection just described maps a rotation (or a quaternion) to the direction it points a camera. For a given base point—now thought of as a gaze direction—the fiber gives all the possible tilts for that direction.

Animation uses a sequence of frames, each of which aims and tilts the camera. Looking through the lens, the horizontal camera axis is $\hat{\mathbf{x}}_c$, the vertical axis is $\hat{\mathbf{y}}_c$, and the perpendicular to the screen is $\hat{\mathbf{z}}_c$. At each frame i, the camera axes are rotated with respect to the world axes by quaternion q_i. Let's assume the vertical direction in the world is called $\hat{\mathbf{y}}_w$. If the camera is untilted, then $\hat{\mathbf{x}}_c \cdot \hat{\mathbf{y}}_w = 0$. With a static gaze, the twist from one frame to the next is just the difference in tilt; but this trivial case is not what motivates us. Remember, cameras rarely tilt.

Usually the gaze follows some path along the sphere of possible directions, as in Figure 1, so the gaze direction is constantly changing. Measuring the twist between frames with different gaze directions is challenging because the fibers are different. Each fiber is a circle, but how do the points in one match up with the points in the other? For a product space, matching fiber points is easy: Two points match if they map to the same point using the *other* projection. (If $p = (p_1, p_2)$ and $p' = (p'_1, p'_2)$, then p matches p' when $p_2 = p'_2$.) But since we only have a bundle, we don't have that other projection. What to do?

---

[2]Well, maybe not.
[3]In fact, for any positive dimension n, $SO(n+1)$ is a bundle over S^n with fiber space $SO(n)$.

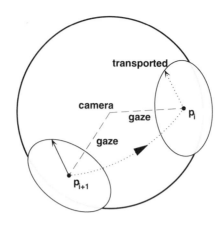

Figure 3. Parallel transport from p_{i+1} to p_i.

As you have probably guessed, we are going to exploit local product structures. In fact, we will "lift" a gaze path on S^2 to a quaternion path on S^3, or to a full rotation path (gaze plus tilt) on $SO(3)$. Begin with q_i on S^3 and $p_i = \pi(q_i)$ on S^2. Now if p_{i+1} on S^2 is close enough to p_i, any product structure around p_i's fiber selects a point in p_{i+1}'s fiber "next to" q_i. We can even match directions around the circles (so we don't go clockwise around one and counterclockwise around the other). Thus we can align fibers over a base path, which is enough to let us measure the twists we want. But we must choose *which* product structure is used at each point. Every point is overlapped by many product neighborhoods, and different product choices give different twist amounts.

There is one choice that is both natural and easy to compute. To understand it, we rephrase our problem as follows. The tilt at a gaze direction can be given by choosing a camera y vector perpendicular to that direction—in effect, a tangent to that point of S^2. This reinterprets our problem in terms of the tangent bundle of S^2. The natural choice will *parallel transport* (Burke 1985) a unit tangent vector of S^2 from p_{i+1} directly to p_i. To do that, we rotate a copy of the sphere and its tangent planes as little as possible to bring p_{i+1} to p_i. (See Figure 3.)

We would prefer to sample gaze direction rather coarsely by topology standards—at frame intervals. Fortunately, the local product structures of the Hopf fibration extend over large neighborhoods. In fact, unless the gaze direction actually reverses from one frame to the next, we will have no problem with parallel transport. (If gaze direction does reverse, twist hardly matters!)

◊   **Twist Calculations**   ◊

All this mathematics cooks down to a few simple calculations. Remember that the gaze direction (from the Hopf projection) is

$$\pi(q) = q\hat{\mathbf{z}}q^{-1}$$

Let

$$p_i = \pi(q_i)$$

and let Δ_i be the quaternion that turns p_i to p_{i+1} around their common perpendicular. Treating p_i and p_{i+1} as quaternions, we can compute Δ_i as

$$\Delta_i = \sqrt{p_{i+1}p_i^{-1}}$$

The Arcball Gem in this volume (Shoemake 1994) may help explain the part inside the square root. The square root itself is used to correct the amount of rotation. Let $p = p_{i+1}p_i^{-1}$ have components $p = [(x, y, z), w]$. Then to find the square root of p, take $p' = [(x, y, z), w + 1]$, and compute

$$\Delta_i = \frac{p'}{\|p'\|}$$

We use Δ_i for parallel transport, computing

$$r = q_i^{-1}\,\Delta_i^{-1}\,q_{i+1}$$

Then the twist angle is

$$\theta = 2\tan^{-1}\frac{r_z}{r_w}$$

◊   **Limiting Twist**   ◊

Now that we can measure the twist from one animation frame to the next, we can decide if the change is too great, and if so, correct it. There are a number of possible strategies. A goal of any strategy is to alter as few twists as possible, to introduce as little tilt as possible.

One simple but effective strategy can be termed "react slowly." When excessive twist is detected between q_i and q_{i+1}, reduce the twist to the maximum we will tolerate by altering q_{i+1}. Note that this may propagate effects forward, since a previously small change can now be larger. For example, suppose the twist is 80° between frames 1 and 2, 5° between 2 and 3, and that we will accept twists of no more than 15°. Then changing frame 2 to limit the first twist will probably increase the second twist. Thus frame 3, which was fine before, may now need adjustment.

To change the twist of q_{i+1} with respect to q_i by $\Delta\theta$, we construct a quaternion

$$r' = [(0, 0, \sin\frac{\Delta\theta}{2}), \cos\frac{\Delta\theta}{2}]$$

and then set

$$q'_{i+1} = q_{i+1}r'$$

A second strategy is "prepare slowly." This is just the react strategy with time reversed. That is, scan the frames from last to first, instead of first to last. Even better, use a dual strategy that is a mix of these two. First scan backward with a loose tolerance, then scan forward with the desired tight tolerance.

These simple strategies can cause sudden accelerations (second-derivative discontinuities) in the twist, so it may be desirable to limit the *change* in twist rate as well. Though other strategies are possible, these are easy to implement and they limit the twist tampering to as few frames as possible.

Notice that none of these calculations refers to tilt. The twist angles are an intrinsic property of the rotation sequence and can be used in situations that have nothing to do with untilted cameras. For example, when a cross section is swept along a curve to give a surface, it must rotate to follow the shape of the curve while remaining perpendicular to it. The preceding twist calculations make sense for these rotations, too.

<h2 style="text-align:center">◇   Bibliography   ◇</h2>

(Burke 1985) William L. Burke. *Applied Differential Geometry.* Cambridge University Press, Cambridge, U.K., 1985.

(Milnor 1965) John W. Milnor. *Topology from the Differentiable Viewpoint.* The University Press of Virginia, Charlottesville, 1965. 6th printing, page 30.

(Shoemake 1985) Ken Shoemake. Animating rotation with quaternion curves. *Computer Graphics*, 19(3):245–254, July 1985. Proceedings of SIGGRAPH '85.

(Shoemake 1994) Ken Shoemake. Arcball rotation control. In Paul Heckbert, editor, *Graphics Gems IV*, 175–192. Academic Press, Boston, 1994.

(Steenrod 1951) Norman Steenrod. *The Topology of Fibre Bundles.* Princeton University Press, Princeton, NJ, 1951.

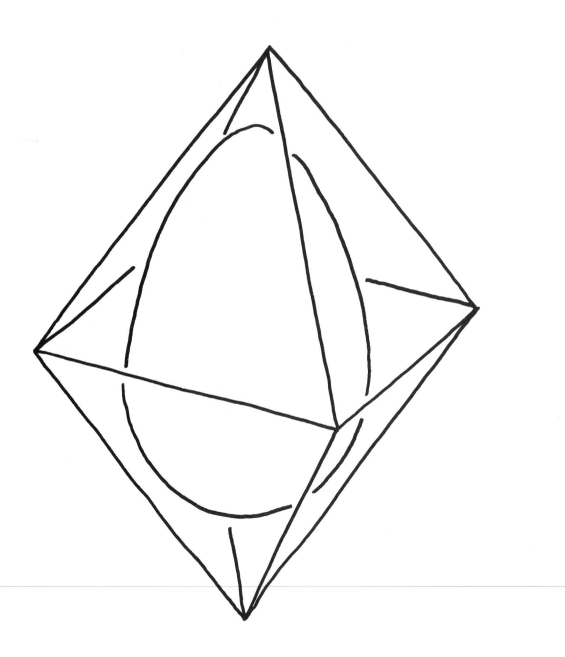

◇ **IV** ◇

Curves and Surfaces

This part of the book contains four Gems on curves and four Gems on surfaces. Most of these deal with parametric curves and surfaces, but the last two discuss implicit surfaces (those of the form $F(x, y, z) = 0$).

IV.6. Tessellation of NURB Surfaces, *by John W. Peterson.*

Gives code for polygonizing a very general class of parametric surfaces: NURBs. Polygonization of parametric surfaces is useful both for rendering and for modeling. Page 286.

IV.7. Equations of Cylinders and Cones, *by Ching-Kuang Shene.*

Derives the implicit equations of cylinders and cones. Page 321.

IV.8. An Implicit Surface Polygonizer, *by Jules Bloomenthal.*

Gives code to polygonize an arbitrary implicit surface. Polygonization is a common approach to implicit surface rendering and volume rendering. If the trilinear interpolation code of Gem X.2 is combined with that given here, a program for polygonizing volume data can easily be constructed. The resulting polygonizations will be superior to those generated by the "Marching Cubes" algorithm, in many cases. Page 324.

 **IV.1**

Smoothing and Interpolation with Finite Differences

Paul H. C. Eilers

DCMR Milieudienst Rijnmond
's-Gravelandseweg 565
3119 XT Schiedam, The Netherlands
paul@dcmr.nl

◇ **Smoothness and Differences** ◇

Splines are very popular these days for constructing smooth curves. But did you know that in 1923 E. T. Whittaker published an algorithm, based on finite differences, that is very well suited to discrete smoothing and interpolation (Whittaker 1923)? He was concerned with the "graduation" of life-tables, but we can take advantage of his method for present-day computer graphics.

Let a series of m points y_i be sampled at equal intervals. We wish to construct a smooth series z that is not too different from the series y. The fit of the two series can be expressed by the following sum of squares of differences:

$$S_1 = \sum_{i=1}^{m}(y_i - z_i)^2$$

The smoothness of z can be expressed in terms of the first differences $\Delta z_i = z_i - z_{i-1}$:

$$S_2 = \sum_{i=2}^{m}(\Delta z_i)^2$$

A combined measure of fit and smoothness is

$$S = \sum_{i=1}^{m}(y_i - z_i)^2 + \lambda \sum_{i=2}^{m}(\Delta z_i)^2$$

where λ is a parameter by which we can trade smoothness of z against fit to the data y.

Some of the datapoints y_i may be missing, therefore we introduce weights w_i. Normally $w_i = 1$, but when y_i is missing, the corresponding $w_i = 0$ and we can give any value we like to y_i. The expression for S is changed as follows:

$$S = \sum_{i=1}^{m} w_i(y_i - z_i)^2 + \lambda \sum_{i=2}^{m}(\Delta z_i)^2$$

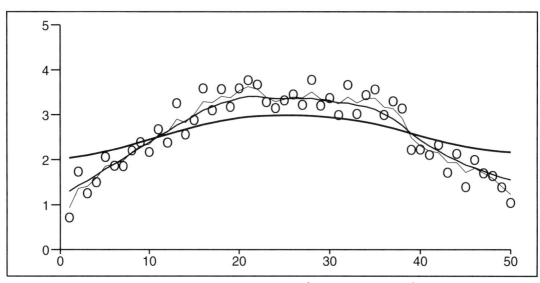

Figure 1. An example of smoothing with first differences: $\lambda = 1$ (thinnest line), $\lambda = 10$ (medium line) and $\lambda = 100$ (thickest line).

To minimize S, we set the partial derivatives $\partial S/\partial z_i$ equal to zero and arrive at the following system of equations:

$$(w_1 + \lambda)z_1 - \lambda z_2 = w_1 y_1 \tag{1}$$
$$-\lambda z_{i-1} + (w_i + 2\lambda)z_i - \lambda z_{i+1} = w_i z_i, \quad i = 2, \ldots, m-1 \tag{2}$$
$$-\lambda z_{m-1} + (w_m + \lambda)z_m = w_m y_m \tag{3}$$

The number of equations is m. It might seem that for long series we have to solve a large system of equations. However, the structure of the equations is very simple. They have a tridiagonal form, which means that the work to solve them is proportional to m. We store the diagonal and one subdiagonal of the matrix of coefficients in two linear arrays; see the C implementation. A simple adaptation of the Cholesky decomposition (Golub and Van Loan 1989) gives a fast and compact algorithm.

Figure 1 shows an application. The data are simulated as a parabolic curve with added noise. Several values of λ are used. Note that a very high value of λ would give a horizontal line, because the second term of S is then dominant. The smoothest z possible has $\Delta z_i = z_i - z_{i-1} = 0$ for all $i > 1$. But this means that all z_i are equal. In fact they have to be equal to the average of the series y, to minimize the first term of S.

In Figure 1 we see that increasing λ increases the smoothness of z, but there remains some wiggliness for moderate λ. We also see, especially at the ends of the interval, that

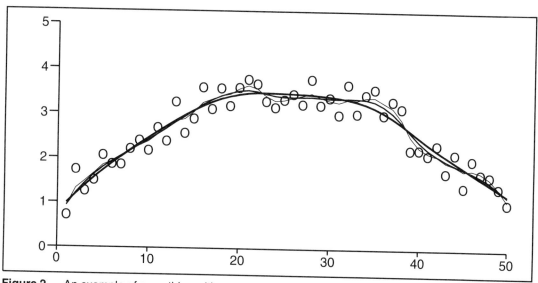

Figure 2. An example of smoothing with second differences: $\lambda = 1$ (thinnest line), $\lambda = 10$ (medium line) and $\lambda = 100$ (thickest line).

the smooth curve tends to move toward the average of the data points. We can improve results by using second, instead of first, differences to express the smoothness:

$$S = \sum_{i=1}^{m} w_i (y_i - z_i)^2 + \lambda \sum_{i=3}^{m} (\Delta^2 z_i)^2$$

where $\Delta^2 z_i = \Delta(\Delta z_i) = z_i - 2z_{i-1} + z_{i-2}$. The resulting equations are

$$
\begin{aligned}
(w_1 + \lambda)z_1 - 2\lambda z_2 + \lambda z_3 &= w_1 y_1 & (4) \\
-2\lambda z_1 + (w_2 + 5\lambda)z_2 - 4\lambda z_3 + \lambda z_4 &= w_2 y_2 & (5) \\
\lambda z_{i-2} - 4\lambda z_{i-1} + (w_i + 6\lambda)z_i - 4\lambda z_{i+1} + \lambda z_{i+2} &= w_i y_i, \quad i = 3, \ldots, m-2 & (6) \\
\lambda z_{m-3} - 4\lambda z_{m-2} + (w_{m-1} + 5\lambda)z_{m-1} - 2\lambda z_m &= w_{m-1} y_{m-1} & (7) \\
\lambda z_{m-2} - 2\lambda z_{m-1} + (w_m + \lambda)z_m &= w_m y_m & (8)
\end{aligned}
$$

Again we have a banded structure, but now five adjacent elements of z are involved in each equation. The strategy for storing the coefficients and solving the equations remains the same. We need three linear arrays for working storage; see program 2. The amount of computation is again proportional to m.

Figure 2 shows results for the same data as in Figure 1. We see that smoother results are obtained. For high values of λ, the linear regression line is approached; this follows from the fact that second differences of a linear sequence are zero.

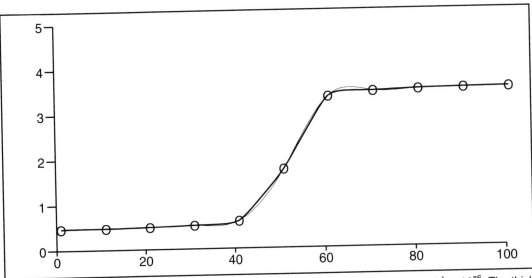

Figure 3.   Example of interpolation: the thin line is based on second differences and $\lambda = 10^{-6}$. The thick line is based on a combination of first and second differences with $\lambda = 10^{-6}$ and $\gamma = 1$.

We can go on and introduce third or higher order differences as a measure of smoothness. The resulting equations become more complex — though they maintain their banded structure — and more care is needed to program their solution explicitly. A more elegant approach is to write a program to construct and solve the system of equations automatically. This is done in Program 3. The user can specify any order of the differences from 0 to 5. As a general purpose tool this program is preferable. In special situations, where only first or second differences will be used, and where memory is at a premium, the other programs might be preferred.

◇   Interpolation   ◇

The weights w_i were introduced to allow for missing values. But they also come in handy when we want to interpolate on a discrete grid. We deliberately introduce the points to be interpolated as missing data. An example is shown by the thin line in Figure 3.

We have data at every tenth index: $y_1, y_{11}, \ldots, y_{101}$ are given. All w_i are zero, except $w_1, w_{11}, \ldots, w_{101}$, which are 1. We choose λ very small (10^{-6}), solve the equations (with second differences) and obtain interpolated values automatically. Because λ is small, z_i is very near to y_i at the given points. But we can combine smoothing and interpolation by using a higher λ. It can be shown that the interpolating series are piecewise third-degree polynomials, when second order differences are used. The result is equivalent to the use of smoothing splines (Reinsch 1967). With first order differences we get piecewise linear interpolation.

In some cases the interpolated curve might be too flexible, for instance when monotonicity is wanted. The thin line in Figure 3 is an example: it shows some under- and overshoot near the jump in the data. We can stiffen the interpolated curve by using a weighted combination of first and second differences (Eilers 1987):

$$S = \sum_{i=1}^{m} w_i(y_i - z_i)^2 + \lambda \sum_{i=3}^{m} (\Delta^2 z_i + \gamma \Delta z_i)^2$$

With $\gamma = 1$, we get the thicker line in Figure 3.

◇ General Difference Equations ◇

From the last problem we can see that in general we combine a measure of fit, the first term of S, with the weighted square of a linear difference equation of order n in z:

$$S = \sum_{i=1}^{m} w_i(y_i - z_i)^2 + \lambda \sum_{i=n+1}^{m} \left(\sum_{j=0}^{n} a_j z_{i-j}\right)^2$$

The function `asmooth` in Program 3 is designed this way. It accepts a vector `A` with the coefficients a_j. With first differences we have $A_1 =$ `[1 -1]`, with second differences $A_2 =$ `[1 -2 1]`, with third differences $A_3 =$ `[1 -3 3 -1]`, and so on. Note that the elements of A_j come from row $j+1$ of Pascal's triangle, but that they have alternating signs. The function `pascalrow` in Program 3 constructs A_n for a given order n of the differences. When first and second differences are combined, as in the last example, we work with a vector $A = A_2 + \gamma A_1$.

A note on the precision of the calculations: when working with first and second differences, single precision is sufficient; with higher orders and strong smoothing, it is advisable to use double precision.

◇ A Comparison with Other Smoothers ◇

It is instructive to compare the finite difference smoother to other methods. Of course this is not the place for an in-depth treatment: only the most characteristic differences will be noted.

The finite difference penalty suggests connections with methods for processing discrete signals. The recursive filter is similar. In its first order form this filter computes a smooth series z from data y by the formula

$$z_i = a z_{i-1} + (1 - a)y_i, \quad \text{with} \quad 0 < a < 1$$

As a starting value (z_0), y_1 or 0 might be used. This type of filter is known as exponential smoother (Thomopoulos 1980), because z can be written as a sum of exponentially weighted values of y:

$$z_i = (1 - a)(y_i + ay_{i-1} + a^2 y_{i-2} + a^3 y_{i-3} + \ldots).$$

This filter is extremely easy to implement. But is has many drawbacks: the series z lags behind y, the more so when strong smoothing (high a) is applied; missing data are not handled easily; and you cannot use the filter for interpolation.

Another type of smoother uses (weighted) running means or regression lines. The weighting function generally has a bell shape and is known as the "kernel," hence the name kernel smoother (Härdle 1990). You can use this smoother for interpolation and it can handle missing data and irregularly spaced data, if the "holes" are not too large. For strong smoothing, the kernel has to have a broad span. Then the computations become proportional to the square of the number of data points. Also, strong boundary effects can occur: at the ends of the interval the smoothed curve is drawn toward zero.

It was already mentioned that there is a strong resemblance between the finite difference smoother and smoothing splines (Reinsch 1967). The latter have many good properties: they can handle missing data and interpolation, there is no boundary effect, and they can be computed efficiently. For discrete smoothing problems there is some overkill, as you compute a continuous (piecewise cubic) function. Smoothing splines of higher degree than three (corresponding to second order differences) are seldom used. As far as I know, there exist no mechanical procedures for working with smoothing splines of arbitrary degree.

Finally we have regression splines (Eubank 1988) and B-splines (Dierckx 1993) where pieces of a smooth curve connect at a relatively small number of joining points, the knots. This type of smoother can handle missing data and interpolation, and no boundary effects occur. Computation is efficient: a regression problem of small size has to be solved. The main problem is the choice of the number and positions of the knots, as these determine the amount of smoothing.

A very detailed and not too technical account of a number of smoothing methods is given in (Buja *et al.* 1989).

It seems fair to conclude that the finite difference smoother compares well to other methods. It is easily implemented and should have a place in your graphics toolbox. Whittaker's pioneering work deserves to live on.

◇ **Programs** ◇

The first program fragment presents the function for smoothing with first differences.

```
/* Program 1. Smoothing and interpolation with first differences. */
```

```
#define MMAX 101          /* choose the right length for your application */

typedef float vec[MMAX+1];

void smooth1(vec w, vec y, vec z, float lambda, int m)
/* Smoothing and interpolation with first differences.
   Input:  weights (w), data (y): vector from 1 to m.
   Input:  smoothing parameter (lambda), length (m).
   Output: smoothed vector (z): vector from 1 to m. */
{
  int i, i1;
  vec c, d;
  d[1] = w[1] + lambda;
  c[1] = -lambda / d[1];
  z[1] = w[1] * y[1];
  for (i = 2; i < m; i++) {
    i1 = i - 1;
    d[i]= w[i] + 2 * lambda - c[i1] * c[i1] * d[i1];
    c[i] = -lambda / d[i];
    z[i] = w[i] * y[i] - c[i1] * z[i1];
  }
  d[m] = w[m] + lambda - c[m - 1] * c[m - 1] * d[m - 1];
  z[m] = (w[m] * y[m] - c[m - 1] * z[m - 1]) / d[m];
  for (i = m - 1; 1 <= i; i--) z[i] = z[i] / d[i] - c[i] * z[i + 1];
}
```

The second program fragment presents the function for smoothing with second differences.

```
/* Program 2. Smoothing and interpolation with second differences. */

#define MMAX 101  /* choose the right length for your application */

typedef float vec[MMAX+1];

void smooth2(vec w, vec y, vec z, float lambda, int m)
/* Smoothing and interpolation with second differences.
   Input:  weights (w), data (y): vector from 1 to m.
   Input:  smoothing parameter (lambda), length (m).
   Output: smoothed vector (z): vector from 1 to m. */
{
  int i, i1, i2;
  vec c, d, e;
  d[1] = w[1] + lambda;
  c[1] = -2 * lambda / d[1];
  e[1] = lambda /d[1];
  z[1] = w[1] * y[1];
  d[2] = w[2] + 5 * lambda - d[1] * c[1] *  c[1];
  c[2] = (-4 * lambda - d[1] * c[1] * e[1]) / d[2];
  e[2] = lambda / d[2];
  z[2] = w[2] * y[2] - c[1] * z[1];
```

```
for (i = 3; i < m-1; i++) {
  i1 = i - 1; i2 = i - 2;
  d[i]= w[i] + 6 * lambda - c[i1] * c[i1] * d[i1] - e[i2] * e[i2] * d[i2];
  c[i] = (-4 * lambda -d[i1] * c[i1] * e[i1])/ d[i];
  e[i] = lambda / d[i];
  z[i] = w[i] * y[i] - c[i1] * z[i1] - e[i2] * z[i2];
};
i1 = m - 2; i2= m - 3;
d[m - 1] = w[m - 1] + 5 * lambda -c[i1] * c[i1] * d[i1] - e[i2] * e[i2] * d[i2];
c[m - 1] = (-2 * lambda - d[i1] * c[i1] * e[i1]) / d[m - 1];
z[m - 1] = w[m - 1] * y[m - 1] - c[i1] * z[i1] - e[i2] * z[i2];
i1 = m - 1; i2 = m - 2;
d[m]  = w[m] + lambda -c[i1] * c[i1] * d[i1] - e[i2] * e[i2] * d[i2];
z[m]  = (w[m] * y[m] - c[i1] * z[i1] - e[i2] * z[i2]) / d[m];
z[m-1] = z[m-1] / d[m-1] - c[m-1] * z[m];
for (i = m - 2; 1<= i; i--)
   z[i] = z[i] / d[i] - c[i] * z[i + 1] - e[i] * z[i + 2];
};
```

A function for smoothing with any order of the differences, up to 5, is presented in program 3.

```
/* Program 3. Smoothing and interpolation with any difference equation. */

#define MMAX 101   /* choose the right length for your application */

typedef float vec[MMAX + 1];
typedef float vecn[6];

void asmooth(vec w, vec y, vec  z, vecn a, float lambda, int m, int n)
/* Smoothing and interpolation with any difference equation of order <=5.
   Input:  weights (w), data (y): vector from 1 to m.
   Input:  smoothing parameter (lambda), length (m).
   Input:  coefficients (a) and order of difference equation (n).
   Output: smoothed vector (z): vector from 1 to m. */
{
  static float b[MMAX + 1][6];
  static int v[MMAX + 1];
  int i, j, j1, j2, k, k1;
  float s;
  for (i = 1; i <= m + n; i++) {
    v[i] = 1; if ((i <= n) || (i > m)) v[i] = 0;
  };
  /*  construct band matrix */
  for (i = 1; i <= m; i++) {
    j2 = m - i; if (j2 > n) j2 = n;
    for (j = 0; j <= j2; j++) {
      s = 0.0; if (j == 0) s = w[i] / lambda;
      for (k = j; k <= n; k++) s = s + v[i + k] * a[k] * a[k - j];
      b[i][j] = s;
    };
  };
```

```
/*  compute Cholesky decomposition  */
for (i = 1; i <= m; i++) {
  s = b[i][0];
  j1 = i - n; if (j1 < 1) j1 = 1;
  for (j = j1; j <= i - 1; j++) s = s - b[j][0] * b[j][i - j] * b[j][i - j];
  b[i][0] = (s);
  j2 = i + n; if (j2 > m) j2 = m;
  for (j = i + 1; j <= j2; j++) {
    s = b[i][j - i];
    k1 = j - n; if (k1 < 1) k1 = 1;
    for (k = k1; k <= i - 1; k++) s = s - b[k][0] * b[k][i - k] * b[k][j - k];
    b[i][j - i] = s / b[i][0];
  };
};
/*  solve triangular systems  */
for (i = 1; i <= m; i++) {
  s = w[i] * y[i] / lambda;
  j1 = i - n; if (j1 < 1) j1 = 1;
  for (j = j1; j <= i - 1; j++) s = s - z[j] * b[j][i - j];
  z[i] = s;
};
for (i = m; i >= 1; i--) {
  s = z[i] / b[i][0];
  j2 = i + n; if (j2 > m) j2 = m;
  for (j = i + 1; j <= j2; j++) s = s - z[j] * b[i][j - i];
  z[i] = s;
};
};

void  pascalrow(vecn a, int n)
/* Construct row n of Pascal's triangle in a */
{
  int i, j;
  for (j = 0; j <= n; j++) a[j] = 0;
  a[0] = 1;
  for (j = 1; j <= n; j++) for (i = n; i >= 1; i--) a[i] = a[i] - a[i - 1];
};

void gensmooth(vec w, vec y, vec z, float lambda, int m, int n)
/* Smoothing and interpolation with differences of order <=5.
   Input:  weights (w), data (y): vector from 1 to m.
   Input:  smoothing parameter (lambda), length (m).
   Input:  order of differences (n).
   Output: smoothed vector (z): vector from 1 to m. */
{
  vecn a;
  int i;
  pascalrow(a, n);
  asmooth(y, w, z, a, lambda, m, n);
};
```

◇ **Bibliography** ◇

(Buja *et al.* 1989) A. Buja, T. Hastie, and R. Tibishirani. Linear smoothers and additive models (with discussion). *Ann. Statist.*, 80:453–555, 1989.

(Dierckx 1993) P. Dierckx. *Curve and Surface Fitting with Splines.* The Clarendon Press, Oxford, U.K., 1993.

(Eilers 1987) P. H. C. Eilers. A uniform algorithm for discrete smoothing and interpolation (in Dutch). *Kwantitatieve Methoden*, 24:115–126, 1987.

(Eubank 1988) R. L. Eubank. *Spline Smoothing and Nonparametric Regression.* Marcel Dekker, New York, 1988.

(Golub and Van Loan 1989) G. H. Golub and C. F. Van Loan. *Matrix Computations.* The Johns Hopkins University Press, Baltimore, MD, 1989.

(Härdle 1990) W. Härdle. *Applied Nonparametric Regression.* Cambridge University Press, Cambridge, U.K., 1990.

(Reinsch 1967) C. Reinsch. Smoothing by spline functions. *Numerische Mathematik*, 10:177–183, 1967.

(Thomopoulos 1980) N. T. Thomopoulos. *Applied Forecasting Methods.* Prentice Hall, Englewood Cliffs, NJ, 1980.

(Whittaker 1923) E. T. Whittaker. On a new method of graduation. *Proceedings of the Edinburgh Mathematical Society*, 41:63–75, 1923.

◇ IV.2

Knot Insertion Using Forward Differences

Phillip Barry

Computer Science Department
University of Minnesota
4-192 EE/CSci Bldg.
200 Union St. SE
Minneapolis, MN 55455
barry@cs.umn.edu

Ron Goldman

Rice University
Houston, TX
rng@cs.rice.edu

Forward differencing is a well-known and commonly used technique for evaluating polynomial curves. This technique is popular because, after an initial start-up step, points on the curve can be found using no multiplications and only a small number of additions. The purpose of this note is to observe that a similar technique applies to inserting knots into B-spline curves.

Let's first recall the key observations about evaluation using forward differences. The forward differences of a sequence $\{c_i\}$ are given by

$$
\begin{aligned}
\Delta^0 c_i &:= c_i \\
\Delta^r c_i &:= \Delta^{r-1} c_{i+1} - \Delta^{r-1} c_i, \qquad r > 0
\end{aligned}
\tag{1}
$$

Suppose we wish to evaluate a degree n polynomial f at domain values $0, h, 2h, \ldots$. For any i, once we have $\Delta^0 f(ih), \ldots, \Delta^n f(ih)$ we can find $\Delta^0 f((i+1)h), \ldots, \Delta^n f((i+1)h)$ by using the fact that the nth forward difference is a constant independent of i, and thus

$$
\Delta^n f((i+1)h) = \Delta^n f(ih)
\tag{2}
$$

and by rearranging Equation (1) to get

$$
\Delta^{r-1} f((i+1)h) = \Delta^r f(ih) + \Delta^{r-1} f(ih), \qquad r = 1, \ldots, n
\tag{3}
$$

In particular, this yields $\Delta^0((i+1)h)$, which is $f((i+1)h)$. So once we find the starting values $\Delta^0 f(0), \ldots, \Delta^n f(0)$ we can repeatedly use these observations to find $f(h), f(2h), \ldots$.

For a cubic polynomial written in the form $f(t) = a_3 t^3 + a_2 t^2 + a_1 t + a_0$, the starting values are given by

$$
\begin{aligned}
\Delta^0 f(0) &= a_0 \\
\Delta^1 f(0) &= a_3 h^3 + a_2 h^2 + a_1 h \\
\Delta^2 f(0) &= 6 a_3 h^3 + 2 a_2 h^2 \\
\Delta^3 f(0) &= 6 a_3 h^3
\end{aligned}
$$

See, e.g., (Wallis 1990, Foley et al. 1990, Bartels *et al.* 1987, and de Boor 1978) for further details.

A similar technique holds for knot insertion of B-spline curves. That is, if we insert enough equally spaced knots into any interval of the curve, then most of the new control points can be found, after a start-up step, using only additions.

Admittedly, this situation will occur less often than evaluation, but it still is interesting because knot insertion is such a powerful operation for B-spline curves.

Let f be a degree n (order $n+1$) B-spline curve with original knots $\{t_i\}$ and control points $\{V_i\}$. Suppose we insert p equally spaced knots into the interval $[t_q, t_{q+1}]$. Denote the refined knot vector (i.e., the knot vector after insertion of the new knots) by $\{u_i\}$. Then the new knots and old knots are related by

$$
u_i = \begin{cases}
t_i & i \le q \\
t_q + (i - q)h & q < i \le q + p \\
t_{i-p} & q + p < i
\end{cases}
\tag{4}
$$

Note $u_{i+1} - u_i = h$ for $q \le i \le q + p$. The knot insertion process finds new control points $\{W_i\}$ expressing f over $\{u_i\}$.

Evaluation using forward differences works with points on the curve; knot insertion works with control points, so we will consider forward differences of the control point sequence $\{W_i\}$. We need the control points and differences involved to depend only on the equally spaced knots $u_q, \ldots, u_{p+q+1}$; thus we consider the control points $W_{q-1}, \ldots, W_{q+p-n+1}$ and the differences $\Delta^0 W_i, \ldots, \Delta^n W_i$ for $i = q-1, \ldots, q+p-2n+1$, and $\Delta^0 W_i, \ldots, \Delta^{q+p-n+1-i} W_i$ for $i = q+p-2n+2, \ldots, q+p-n+1$. Two observations similar to those for evaluation using forward differences apply to these differences. First, $\Delta^n W_i$ is a constant independent of i for $i = q - 1, \ldots, q + p - 2n + 1$, so

$$
\Delta^n W_{i+1} = \Delta^n W_i, \qquad i = q - 1, \ldots, q + p - 2n
\tag{5}
$$

Second,

$$
\Delta^{r-1} W_{i+1} = \Delta^r W_i + \Delta^{r-1} W_i
\tag{6}
$$

for $r = 1, \ldots, n$, when $q - 1 \le i \le q + p - 2n + 1$, and for $r = 1, \ldots, q + p - n + 1 - i$, when $q + p - 2n + 2 \le i \le q + p - n$. Therefore once we know the values $\Delta^0 W_i, \ldots, \Delta^n W_i$ for any

i such that $q - 1 \leq i \leq q + p - 2n$ then we can find the values $\Delta^0 W_{i+1}, \ldots, \Delta^n W_{i+1}$. Or once we know $\Delta^0 W_i, \ldots, \Delta^{q+p-n+1-i} W_i$ for any i such that $q + p - 2n + 1 \leq i \leq q + p - n$, then we can find the values $\Delta^0 W_{i+1}, \ldots, \Delta^{q+p-n-i} W_{i+1}$. By repeatedly using these observations, we can start with $\Delta^0 W_{q-1}, \ldots, \Delta^n W_{q-1}$, and use only additions to find $W_q, \ldots, W_{q+p-n+1}$.

When $i > q + p - 2n$, Equations (5) and (6) no longer hold for all differences. This is because we are approaching the right endpoint of the curve segment over $[t_q, t_{q+1}]$. If we were applying evaluation using forward differences to a segment of a piecewise polynomial curve, a similar situation would occur. To avoid checking if we are computing invalid differences, we can simply use Equations (5) and (6) for all $r = 1, \ldots, n$ and $i = q - 1, \ldots, q + p - n$. This will not affect the output of the algorithm since the invalid values are not used in the computation of the control points $W_q, \ldots, W_{q+p-n+1}$ anyway. Of course, one should not use the invalid values in subsequent computations.

So while the indices make knot insertion using forward differences appear more complicated than in the evaluation case, the process is essentially the same: obtain the starting values, and then apply Equations (5) and (6) repeatedly.

We still need to find the starting values. Moreover, since the procedure above applies only to the new control points $W_{q-1}, \ldots, W_{p+q-n+1}$, we also need to find the other new control points. We have $W_i = V_i$ for $i \leq q - n$, and $W_i = V_{i-p}$ for $i \geq q + p$ since these points are not affected by the new knots. The points $W_{q-n+1}, \ldots, W_{q-2}$ and $W_{q+p-n+2}, \ldots, W_{q+p-1}$ are affected by both new knots and old knots. These point are found by the following procedure, which also finds $\Delta^0 W_{q-1} = W_{q-1}$.

1. For $i = 0, \ldots, n$ set $P_i^0 = V_{q-n+i}$.
2. For $j = 1, \ldots, n - 1$, for $i = 0, \ldots, n - 1 - j$, set

$$P_i^j = \frac{(t_q + jh - t_{q-n+i+j})P_{i+1}^{j-1} + (t_{q+1+i} - t_q - jh)P_i^{j-1}}{t_{q+1+i} - t_{q-n+i+j}}.$$

Then $W_{q-n+j} = P_0^j$ for $j = 1, \ldots, n - 1$.
3. For $j = 1, \ldots, n - 2$, for $i = 2, \ldots, n - j$, set

$$P_i^j = \frac{(t_{q+1} - jh - t_{q-n+i+j})P_{i+1}^{j-1} + (t_{q+1+i} - t_{q+1} + jh)P_i^{j-1}}{t_{q+1+i} - t_{q-n+i+j}}.$$

Then $W_{q+p-n+j} = P_j^{n-j}$ for $j = 2, \ldots, n - 1$.

Then the remainder of the start-up differences are found by starting with the values P_i^0 from Step 1 of the procedure above, and then performing the following steps:

4. For $j = 1, \ldots, n$, for $i = 0, \ldots, n - j$, set

$$P_i^j = \frac{P_{i+1}^{j-1} - P_i^{j-1}}{t_{q+1+i} - t_{q-n+i+j}}$$

5. For $i = 1, \ldots, n$ set

$$Q_i^0 = P_0^i.$$

6. For $j = 1, \ldots, n-1$, for $i = 1, \ldots, n-j$, set

$$Q_i^j = (t_q + (n-j)h - t_{q-n+i+j})Q_{i+1}^{j-1} + Q_i^{j-1}.$$

Then $\Delta^j W_{q-1} = n \cdots (n-j+1)h^j Q_j^{n-j}$ for $j = 1, \ldots, n$.

Note that for the cubic case these steps simplify considerably.

If additional knots are to be inserted into the B-spline curve, one then proceeds using the new knot vector $\{u_i\}$ and the new control points $\{W_i\}$.

There are a number of perspectives on why this algorithm works. For example, one can show that the new control points W_{q+i} for $i = -1, 0, \ldots, p-n+1$ can be expressed as a degree n polynomial in i, and therefore applying evaluation using forward differences to this polynomial yields these control points.

The value p must be large enough that the number of points computed by this technique outweighs the startup cost. At the same time, evaluation by forward differencing is known to have problems with error propagation, and knot insertion using forward differences may share some of this behavior so caution should be exercised (see, e.g., (Bartels *et al.* 1987) for a discussion of evaluation using forward differencing and error propagation).

Some other observations about evaluation using forward differences will also apply to knot insertion using forward differences. In particular, integer implementations or special hardware for evaluation using forward differencing may well be applicable to knot insertion as well.

Knot insertion using forward differences is a specialization of a knot insertion technique which has been called "factored knot insertion" or "high speed refinement," and studied in (Barry and Goldman 1993a, Barry and Goldman 1993b, Silbermann *et al.* 1991). The first and third of these works discuss this more general technique in detail. The second work is a survey which explores the relation among a number of knot insertion techniques, one of which is factored knot insertion.

◇   Bibliography   ◇

(Barry and Goldman 1993a) P. J. Barry and R. N. Goldman. Factored knot insertion. In Ronald N. Goldman and Tom Lyche, editors, *Knot Insertion and Deletion Algorithms for B-spline Curves and Surfaces*, pages 65–88. SIAM, Philadelphia, 1993.

(Barry and Goldman 1993b) P. J. Barry and R. N. Goldman. Knot insertion algorithms. In Ronald N. Goldman and Tom Lyche, editors, *Knot Insertion and*

Deletion Algorithms for B-spline Curves and Surfaces, pages 89–133. SIAM, Philadelphia, 1993.

(Bartels *et al.* 1987) R. H. Bartels, J. C. Beatty, and B. A. Barsky. *An Introduction to Splines for Use in Computer Graphics and Geometric Modeling.* Morgan Kaufmann Publishers, Palo Alto, California, 1987.

(de Boor 1978) C. de Boor. *A Practical Guide to Splines.* Springer-Verlag, New York, 1978.

(Foley *et al.* 1990) J. D. Foley, A. van Dam, S. K. Feiner, and J. F. Hughes. *Computer Graphics: Principles and Practices.* Addison-Wesley, Reading, Massachusetts, 1990.

(Silbermann *et al.* 1991) M. J. Silbermann, S. Y. Wang, and L. A Ferrari. Efficient computation of multiple knot nonuniform spline functions. In P. J. Laurent, A. Le Méhauté, and L. L. Schumaker, editors, *Curves and Surfaces*, pages 449–452. Academic Press, Boston, 1991.

(Wallis 1990) Bob Wallis. Tutorial on forward differencing. In Andrew Glassner, editor, *Graphics Gems*, pages 594–603. Academic Press, Boston, 1990.

◊ IV.3

Converting a Rational Curve to a Standard Rational Bernstein-Bézier Representation

Chandrajit Bajaj

Department of Computer Science
1398 Computer Science Bldg
Purdue University
West Lafayette, IN 47907-1398
bajaj@cs.purdue.edu

Guoliang Xu

Department of Computer Science
Purdue University
West Lafayette, IN 47907-1398
xuguo@cs.purdue.edu

◊   Introduction   ◊

Quite often geometric designers and engineers using an RBB (Rational Bernstein-Bézier) curve like to have it in a standard form, where the denominator polynomial has only positive coefficients (Tiller 1983). This assumption is quite strong, but rids the curve of real poles (roots of the denominator polynomial) and gives the RBB curve its convex hull property. In this gem, we show how to convert a smooth rational curve with no poles in the interval $[a, b]$ into a finite number of C^∞ standard RBB curve segments. We also show that for a degree n smooth rational curve, the number of converted RBB curve segments is bounded above by $\frac{n(n-1)}{2}$. We use this conversion algorithm as a final step in our NURBS approximation of algebraic plane and space curves (Bajaj and Xu 1992), (Bajaj and Xu 1994).

◊   Standard RBB Representation   ◊

Without loss of generality, we assume that the given rational curve has no poles in the interval [a,b], since it is straightforward to break the curve first at the poles. An essential step is to transform the rational curve into Bernstein-Bézier (BB) form. Let

$$R(s) = [x(s), \ y(s), \ z(s)]^T / w(s)$$

be a space rational curve on the interval $[a, b]$, where $x(s), y(s), z(s)$ and $w(s)$ are polynomials of degree n. Since

$$t^i = \sum_{j=i}^{n} \frac{C_i^j}{C_i^n} B_j^n(t)$$

256

where
$$t = \frac{s-a}{b-a} \in [0,1], \quad B_j^n(t) = C_i^n t^j (1-t)^{n-j}, \quad C_i^n = \frac{n!}{i!(n-i)!}$$

we have, for any polynomial $P(s)$ of degree n,

$$P(s) = \sum_{i=0}^{n} c_i t^i = \sum_{i=0}^{n} (\sum_{j=0}^{i} \frac{C_j^i}{C_j^n} c_j) B_i^n(t) = \sum_{i=0}^{n} b_i' B_i^n(t)$$

where $b_i' = \sum_{j=0}^{i} \frac{C_j^i}{C_j^n} c_j$. Therefore $R(s)$ can be expressed as an RBB curve over [a,b]

$$R(s) = \sum_{i=0}^{n} w_i b_i B_i^n(t) / \sum_{i=0}^{n} w_i B_i^n(t)$$

where $w_i \in \mathbb{R}$, $b_i \in \mathbb{R}^3$ are Bézier weights and points, respectively.

The remaining step now is to transform the RBB curve into the standard RBB representation, where the denominator polynomial, say $P(t)$, has only positive coefficients.

We now show how the denominator polynomial $P(t) = \sum_{i=0}^{n} w_i B_i^n(t), \quad t \in [0,1]$ is divided over subintervals, say, $0 = t_0 < t_1 < \ldots < t_{l+1} = 1$, such that the BB form of $P(t)$ on each of the subintervals $P(t)|_{[t_i t_{i+1}]} = P_i(t) = P_i(t_i + (t_{i+1} - t_i)s) = \tilde{P}_i(s) = \sum w_j^i B_i^n(s)$ has positive coefficients. We assume $P(t) > 0$ over [0,1] since the RBB has no poles in [0,1]. Compute the first breakpoint $t_1 = c$ as explained below. The remaining breakpoints can be computed in a similar fashion. By the subdivision formula, $B_i^n(ct) = \sum_{j=0}^{n} B_i^j(c) B_j^n(t)$. We have in [0,c], $(s = ct; \ t \in [0,1])$

$$\begin{aligned}
P(s) = P(ct) &= \sum_{i=0}^{n} w_i B_i^n(ct) \\
&= \sum_{i=0}^{n} w_i \sum_{j=0}^{n} B_i^j(c) B_j^n(t) \\
&= \sum_{j=0}^{n} q_j(c) B_j^n(t)
\end{aligned}$$

where $q_j(c) = \sum_{i=0}^{j} w_i B_i^j(c)$ is a degree j polynomial in BB form.

Note that the $\lim_{c \to 0} q_j(c) = w_0$, since $B_0^j(0) = 1$, $B_i^j(0) = 0$, $i > 0$. But $P(0) = w_0$, and since $P(t) > 0$ for $t \in [0,1]$ we know that $w_0 > 0$. Take $c < \min\{$all roots of $q_j(c)$ in $[0,1]\}$ and $c > 0$. This c will guarantee that **all** $q_j(c)$ are positive.

Example 1.0.1 *Figure 1 shows an example of this conversion for the denominator polynomial* $(1-x)^5 - x(1-x)^4 + 2x^2(1-x)^3 + x^3(1-x)^2 - x^4(1-x) + 0.5x^5$.

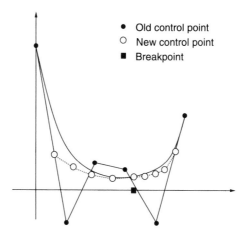

Figure 1. Denominator polynomial with positive Bézier coefficients.

The initial quintic Bézier coefficients over $[0,1]$ are

$$bb[0] = 1.000000 \quad bb[1] = -0.200000 \quad bb[2] = 0.200000$$
$$bb[3] = 0.100000 \quad bb[4] = -0.200000 \quad bb[5] = 0.500000$$

of which two coefficients are negative. The control points are plotted in Figure 1 with dark colored dots. The above conversion yields two pieces in standard BB form over $[0,1]$ with 0.640072 as the breakpoint. The new coefficients of the two quintic BB pieces are

$$bb[0] = 1.000000 \quad bb[1] = 0.231913 \quad bb[2] = 0.119335$$
$$bb[3] = 0.111575 \quad bb[4] = 0.060781 \quad bb[5] = 0.060781$$

and

$$bb[0] = 0.060781 \quad bb[1] = 0.060781 \quad bb[2] = 0.076842$$
$$bb[3] = 0.125649 \quad bb[4] = 0.248051 \quad bb[5] = 0.500000$$

The new control points are plotted in Figure 1 with circles. The curve itself is, of course, the same.

◇ **Upper Bound** ◇

We give an upper bound for the total number of RBB pieces required for a degree n rational curve.

Theorem. *Let* $p(x) = \sum_{i=0}^{n} w_i B_i^n(x), \deg(p) = n$, *and* $p(x) > 0$ *on* $[0,1]$. *Then there exists*

$$0 = x_0 < x_1 < x_1 < \dots x_\ell < x_{\ell+1} = 1 \tag{1}$$

with

$$\ell \le \frac{n(n-1)}{2} \tag{2}$$

such that the BB form of $p(x)$ *on* $[x_i, x_{i+1}]$ *has positive and monotonic coefficients.*

Proof. Let $Z = \bigcup_{i=1}^{n-1} \{x : p^{(j)}(x) = 0\}$. Then the cardinality of $Z \le \frac{n(n-1)}{2}$. Take distinct x_i in $Z \bigcap (0,1)$ and arrange them in increasing order, to obtain (1) and (2). Next subdivide the interval [0,1] into subintervals (x_i, x_{i+1}) for $(i = 0, 1, \dots, \ell)$, such that $p^{(j)}(x)$ has no zero in (x_i, x_{i+1}) for $j = 0, 1, \dots, n-1$. Let $q_i(t) := p(x_i(1-t) + x_{i+1}t)$. Then $\frac{d^j q_i(t)}{dt^j} = \frac{d^j p(x)}{dx^j}(x_{i+1} - x_i)^j$. Hence $q_i^{(j)}(t)$ has no zero in (0,1) for $j = 0, 1, \dots, n-1$. Further, $q_i^{(0)}(t)$ has no zero on [0,1] by the earlier assumption.

Now we prove that the BB form $q_i(t) = \sum_{j=0}^{n} w_j^{(i)} B_j^n(t), i = 0, 1, \dots, \ell$ has positive and monotonic coefficients. In fact we prove a more general conclusion.

Lemma. *If* $q(t)$ *is a polynomial of degree* n, *and* $q^{(j)}(t)$ *has no zero in the open interval (0,1) for* $j = 0, 1, \dots, n$, *then the coefficients of the BB form representation* $q^{(j)}(t) = \sum_{i=0}^{n-j} w_i^{(j)} B_i^{n-j}(t)$ *are monotonic and have the same sign for any fixed* j.

Proof. We prove this fact by induction. For $j = n$, $q^{(j)}(t)$ is a nonzero constant and the required conclusion is obviously true. In general, suppose the lemma is true for $j + 1$, then for j we have since $q^{(j)}(t) = \sum_{i=0}^{n-j} w_i^{(j)} B_i^{n-j}(t)$

$$\begin{aligned} q^{(j+1)}(t) &= \sum_{i=0}^{n-j-1} w_i^{(j+1)} B_i^{n-j-1}(t) \\ &= \sum_{i=0}^{n-j-1} \Delta w_i^{(j)} B_i^{n-j-1}(t) \end{aligned}$$

where $\Delta w_i^{(j)} = w_{i+1}^{(j)} - w_i^{(j)}$, i.e., $w_{i+1}^{(j)} - w_i^{(j)} = w_i^{(j+1)}$. Since $w_i^{(j+1)}$ does not change sign, hence $w_i^{(j)}$ is monotonic. But $w_0^{(j)} = q^{(j)}(0)$ and $w_{n-j}^{(j)} = q^{(j)}(1)$ have the same sign. Hence $w_i^{(j)}$ has the same sign and the induction is complete.

Back to the proof of the theorem. We know from the above lemma that the coefficients $w_j^{(i)}$ of $q_i(t)$ are monotonic for fixed i. Hence they are positive since $w_0^{(i)}$ and $w_n^{(i)}$ are positive.

It should be noted that the partition given in the theorem guarantees not only positivity but also monotonicity of coefficients. This is often important because this stronger condition on the coefficients prevents the standard RBB representation from having very small positive denominator coefficients.

◇ **Pseudocode of the Algorithm** ◇

The algorithm in pseudocode for converting a polynomial into positive coefficients BB form is as follows:

$k \longleftarrow 0, \quad t_0 \longleftarrow 0,$

Transform $P(s)$ to BB form $\sum w_i^{(k)} B_i^n$ on $[0,1]$

while $(t_k < 1)$

begin

    if $(\text{all } w_i^{(k)} > 0)$

        begin

            $t_{k+1} \longleftarrow 1,$

            $l \longleftarrow k,$

            $k \longleftarrow k + 1,$

        end

    else

        begin

            compute the first breakpoint c of $\sum w_i^{(k)} B_i^n$, that is, take

            $0 < c < \min\{ \text{ all roots of } \sum_{i=0}^{j} w_i^{(k)} B_i^n \text{ in } [0,1] \}.$

            $t_{k+1} \longleftarrow t_k + (1 - t_k)c,$

            Transform $\sum w_i^{(0)} B_i^n$ on $[t_{k+1}, 1]$ to BB form $\sum w_i^{(k+1)} B_i^n$ on $[0,1]$

            $k \longleftarrow k + 1,$

        endelse

    endif

endwhile

return$(l, t_0, ..., t_{l+1})$

◇ **Bibliography** ◇

(Bajaj and Xu 1992) C. Bajaj and G. L. Xu. Piecewise rational approximation of real algebraic curves. Technical Report CAPO 92-19, Computer Science Department, Purdue University, 1992.

(Bajaj and Xu 1994) C. Bajaj and G. L. Xu. Nurbs approximation of surface/surface intersection curves. *Advances in Computational Mathematics*, 2(1):1–21, 1994.

(Tiller 1983) W. Tiller. Rational b-splines for curve and surface representation. *IEEE Computer Graphics and Applications*, 3(6):61–69, 1983.

IV.4

Intersecting Parametric Cubic Curves by Midpoint Subdivision

R. Victor Klassen
Xerox Webster Research Center
Webster, NY
klassen.wbst128@xerox.com

◇ **Background** ◇

This Gem describes a C++ implementation of the methods for intersecting Bézier curves embodied in the theorems of (Lane and Riesenfeld 1980) and (Wang 1984). It also clarifies some of the subtleties involved in manipulating Bézier curves. Because cubics are in such common use, and fixing the degree allows for some efficiency, only cubics are used in this Gem. The theorems in the original papers are not restricted in this way.

There are several competing methods for intersecting splines. They differ in the root finding approach: how the parameter values corresonding to intersections are found. The preferred approach depends on the application. The two dominant classes are implicitization and subdivision. For applications requiring eight decimal digits of precision (typical of CAD), implicitization has been recommended as fastest for degree up to four (Sederberg and Parry 1986). This has been extended to as high as ten without loss of accuracy; however, the running time grows much faster with degree than for subdivision (Manocha and Demmel 1992). The running time of implicitization is relatively insensitive to the degree of accuracy required and to the number of intersections. For many graphics applications, typical curves are short, relative to the degree of accuracy required: eight to twelve bits (not digits) of accuracy is sufficient for root finding. And the most common case is zero intersections. Where curves are short, and relatively unlikely to intersect and with only moderate precision required if they do, subdivision is as fast as implicitization. Recursive subdivision is also conceptually simple.

The process is summarized as follows: find the roots (parameter values at intersection points), sort them, and subdivide the curves at the roots. Root finding is done by recursive subdivision, conceptually the simplest method. Accuracy and consistency are guaranteed in the sense that where a root is detected the separation of the curves is less than ϵ, and at ambiguous points near tangency, either zero or two roots are found.

There are a number of acceleration schemes that could be applied using the code in this Gem as a base. Which are worthwhile would depend on the expected average depth

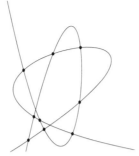

Figure 1. Two parametric cubic curves can intersect at nine points. Self-intersections are not counted.

and breadth of subdivision (depth corresponding to precision, breadth corresponding to number of intersections). One might use tighter bounding regions, to reduce the depth of subdivision, at the expense of greater work at each level (Sederberg *et al.* 1989). Depending on the expected distribution of curves, it might be worthwhile subdividing curves into monotonic segments. This tightens the bounding box used in subsequent intersection tests (Koparkar and Mudur 1983). Bézier clipping (Sederberg and Nishita 1990) is probably the best acceleration scheme, in that it exhibits quadratic convergence. It operates by clipping away parts of the curve known to be outside the range of possible intersections. For many curves, it leaves a much smaller piece for further examination after two clips than the quarter of a curve that will remain after two midpoint subdivisions. Lastly, the root finding could be replaced by an implicitization version.

◇ Class Bézier ◇

A Bézier cubic is represented by the class Bezier. As a cubic parametric curve, it has four control points. When intersected with another parametric cubic curve there can be at most nine intersections (Figure 1), with ten subsegments resulting for each original curve. One of class Bezier's methods allows it to intersect itself with another Bezier, returning two arrays of Bezier, corresponding to the two original segments. For root finding, a Bezier needs to be able to split itself at its midpoint, returning two Bezier subcurves. Because midpoint subdivision has a more efficient implementation than general subdivision, we supply a special method for it. Subdividing the curves at the roots is done by iteratively splitting off the left piece, retaining the right, and building lists of the pieces thus obtained.

```
class Bezier
    {
    public:
    point *p0, *p1, *p2, *p3;
    Bezier() { } // So we can make arrays of these things
    Bezier( point *_p0, point *_p1, point *_p2, point *_p3 );
```

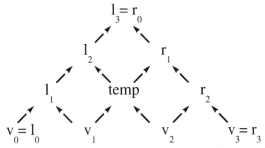

Figure 2. Bézier subdivision. The bottom row contains input control points. The left subcurve's control points can be read off the left edge of the pyramid (l_0, l_1, l_2, l_3); the right subcurve's control points can be read off the right edge (r_0, r_1, r_2, r_3). Arrows are directed from points to be averaged to their averages. Thus, for example, $l_1 = (v_0 + v_1)/2$.

```
Bezier * Split( );
void ParameterSplitLeft( double t, Bezier &result );
Bezier **Intersect( Bezier B ) const;
~Bezier();
}
```

◇   **Subdivision and Reparametrization**   ◇

To subdivide a `Bezier` at its parametric midpoint, we build a pyramid, with the control points at the bottom. To form a new row of the pyramid, average adjacent points in the previous row. The resulting control points can be read off of the sides of the pyramid, as in Figure 2. (I learned this way of describing subdivision from Ron Goldman. I don't know where he learned it, or where it first appears.) Splitting off the left piece is similar, so it is not shown here. The principal difference comes from taking weighted averages. With a little care, one can avoid the temporary variable, re-using `right.p1`.

```
#define left r[0]
#define right r[1]
Bezier *Bezier::Split() const
    {
    Bezier *r = new Bezier[2];
    (left.p0 = p0)->refcount++;
    (right.p3 = p3)->refcount++;
    left.p1 = new point( p0, p1, 1);
    right.p2 = new point( p2, p3, 1);
    right.p1 = new point( p1, p2, 1); // temporary holding spot
    left.p2 = new point ( left.p1, right.p1, 1);
    *right.p1 = mid( right.p1, right.p2 ); // Real value this time
    left.p3 = right.p0 = new point( left.p2, right.p1, 2 );
    return r;
    }
```

(Supplying a third argument to point::point explicitly sets the reference count: points have reference counts to help keep C++ from overzealous garbage collection.)

The remaining method from Bezier is Intersect. When a curve is split, it is implicitly reparametrized — t runs from 0 to 1 in the original, and for each subsegment t' runs from 0 to 1. The calculated roots are in the original parametrization, so as each curve is processed from left to right, the parameters at which to split (after the first) are given by $t_{split} = (t_i - t_{i-1})/(1.0 - t_{i-1})$.

```
Bezier **Bezier::Intersect( Bezier B )
    {
    Bezier **rvalue;
    ...
    double **t = FindIntersections( *this, B );
    if( t[0][0] > -0.5 )
        {
        ParameterSplitLeft( t[0][0], rvalue[0][0] );
        B.ParameterSplitLeft( t[1][0], rvalue[1][0] );
        index++;
        while( t[0][index] > -0.5 )
            {
            double
            splitT = (t[0][index]-t[0][index-1])/(1.0-t[0][index-1]);
            ParameterSplitLeft( splitT, rvalue[0][index] );
            splitT = (t[1][index]-t[1][index-1])/(1.0-t[1][index-1]);
            B.ParameterSplitLeft( splitT, rvalue[1][index] );
            index++;
            }
        }
    rvalue[0][index] = *this;
    rvalue[1][index] = B;
    return rvalue;
    }
```

◇   **Finding Intersections**   ◇

What remains is to find the roots. If the bounding boxes do not overlap, the curves cannot intersect. Otherwise the process is by recursive subdivision. Maximum subdivision depth is computed from an *a priori* bound. If we compute three vectors from the differences of adjacent control points, and then take differences of adjacent vectors, the resulting two vectors are proportional to the curvature vectors at the start and end of the segment. Let l_0 be the magnitude of the largest component of the two vectors thus computed. If the curve is approximated by subdividing to depth $r = \lceil \log_4(3\sqrt{2}l_0/(4\epsilon)) \rceil$, and the ends of the subsegments are joined by straight lines, the approximation will always be within ϵ of the curve (Wang 1984).

```
double ** FindIntersections( Bezier a, Bezier b )
    {
    double **parameters = new double *[2];
    parameters[0] = new double[10];
    parameters[1] = new double[10];
    int index = 0;
    if( IntersectBB( a, b ) )
        {
        // Compute ra and rb, the recursive intersection depths
        // for the two curves
        ...
        RecursivelyIntersect( a, 0, 1, ra, b, 0, 1, rb,
                              parameters, index );
        }
    if( index < 9 ) // Flag the last entry
        {
        parameters[0][index] = parameters[1][index] = -1.0;
        }
    Sort( parameters[0], index );
    Sort( parameters[1], index );
    return parameters;
    }
```

`RecursivelyIntersect` takes as arguments two (sub)curves, the global parameters corresponding to their starts and ends, their respective remaining subdivision depths, an array into which to put solution points, and the index of the next available slot in the array. If it finds a root, it stores it in the array and increments the index. If either or both of the curves has subdivisions left to be applied, it is subdivided, and each resulting pair of (sub)curves is tested for overlap, and possibly intersected recursively. Recursion stops when either the bounding boxes are distinct, or both curves are fully subdivided, in which case the lines connecting their end control points are intersected as far as finding the parameter corresponding to the intersection point. Line intersection follows the method described by Bowyer and Woodwark (Bowyer and Woodwark 1983).

```
void
RecursivelyIntersect( Bezier a, double t0, double t1, int deptha,
                      Bezier b, double u0, double u1, int depthb,
                      double **parameters, int &index )
    {
    if( deptha > 0 )
        {
        Bezier *A = a.Split();
        double tmid = (t0+t1)*0.5;
        deptha--;
        if( depthb > 0 )
            {
            Bezier *B = b.Split();
            double umid = (u0+u1)*0.5;
            depthb--;
            if( IntersectBB( A[0], B[0] )
```

```
                    RecursivelyIntersect( A[0], t0, tmid, deptha,
                                          B[0], u0, umid, depthb,
                                          parameters, index );
            // ... test and possibly intersect
            //     the other three combinations...
            }
        else // depthb == 0
            {
            // ... handle the two remaining cases
            }
        }
    else // deptha == 0
        {
        if( depthb > 0 )
            {
                // ....
            }
        else // Both are fully subdivided; now do line segments
            {
            // ... compute xnm, ylk, etc
            //     from differences of endpoints ...
            double det = xnm * ylk - ynm * xlk;
            if( 1.0 + det == 1.0 )
                return;
            else
                {
                double detinv = 1.0 / det;
                double s = ( xnm * ymk - ynm *xmk ) * detinv;
                double t = ( xlk * ymk - ylk * xmk ) * detinv;
                if( ( s < 0.0 ) || ( s > 1.0 )
                  || ( t < 0.0 ) || ( t > 1.0 ) )
                    return;
                parameters[0][index] = t0 + s * ( t1 - t0 );
                parameters[1][index] = u0 + t * ( u1 - u0 );
                index++;
                }
            }
        }
    }
```

The full implementation is listed below.

◇   **vector.h**   ◇

```
// Floating point vector library
#ifndef VECTORS_INCLUDED__
#include <math.h>
class point
    {
    private:
    int refcount;
```

```
    public:
    double x, y;
    point()
        {
        refcount = 0;
        }
    point( const double _x, const double _y )
        {
        x = _x, y = _y;
        refcount = 1;
        }
    point( const point &p )
        {
        x = p.x, y = p.y; refcount = 1;
        }
    point( const point &p, const int count )
        {
        x = p.x, y = p.y; refcount = count;
        }
    point( const point *a, const point *b, const int count ) // midpoint
        {
        x = ( a->x + b->x ) * 0.5;
        y = ( a->y + b->y ) * 0.5;
        refcount = count;
        }
    friend class Bezier;
    };

class vector
    {
    public:
    double x, y;
    vector()
        {
        ;
        }
    vector( const vector &v )
        {
        x = v.x, y = v.y;
        }
    vector( const double _x, const double _y )
        {
        x = _x, y = _y;
        }
    }
;

inline vector operator-(const point a, const point b ) // p - p = v
    {
    return vector( a.x - b.x, a.y - b.y );
    }

inline vector operator-(const vector a, const vector b ) // v - v = v
```

```
        {
        return vector( a.x - b.x, a.y - b.y );
        }

inline point operator+(const point *a, const vector b ) // p + v = p
        {
        return point ( a->x + b.x, a->y + b.y );
        }

inline point operator+(const point a, const vector b ) // p + v = p
        {
        return point ( a.x + b.x, a.y + b.y );
        }

inline vector operator+(const vector a, const vector b ) // v + v = v
        {
        return vector( a.x + b.x, a.y + b.y );
        }

inline vector operator*(const double s, const vector v ) // sv = v
        {
        return vector( s * v.x, s * v.y );
        }

inline vector operator*(const vector v, const double s) // v s = v
        {
        return vector( s * v.x, s * v.y );
        }

inline double operator*(const vector a, const vector b) // v * v = s (dot product)
        {
        return a.x * b.x + a.y * b.y;
        }

inline point mid( const point *a, const point *b )
        {
        return point ( ( a->x + b->x ) * 0.5, ( a->y + b->y ) * 0.5 );
        }

inline vector vabs( const vector a )
        {
        return vector( fabs( a.x ), fabs( a.y ) );
        }
;
#define VECTORS_INCLUDED__
#endif
```

◇ **Bézier.h** ◇

```
#include "vector.h"
#ifndef _BEZIER_INCLUDED_
```

```
class Bezier
    {
    public:
    point *p0, *p1, *p2, *p3;
    Bezier()
        {
        p0 = 0; p1 = 0; p2 = 0; p3 = 0;
        }
    Bezier( point *_p0, point *_p1, point *_p2, point *_p3 )
        {
        p0 = _p0; p1 = _p1; p2 = _p2; p3 = _p3;
        }
    Bezier * Split( );
    void ParameterSplitLeft( double t, Bezier &result );

    // Intersect with another curve.  Return two 10-elt arrays. Array 0
    // contains fragments of self. Array 1 contains fragments of other curve.
    // Fragments continue until one with nil pointers pointing at point data.
    Bezier **Intersect( Bezier B );
    ~Bezier()
        {
        if( --p0->refcount <= 0 ) delete p0;
        if( --p1->refcount <= 0 ) delete p1;
        if( --p2->refcount <= 0 ) delete p2;
        if( --p3->refcount <= 0 ) delete p3;
        }
    }
;
#define _BEZIER_INCLUDED_
#endif
```

◇　**Bézier.cc**　◇

```
#include <sys/stdtypes.h> // for size_t
#include "vector.h"
#include "Bezier.h"
#include <math.h>
#define INV_EPS (1L<<14) // close enough for most applications

extern "C" void
qsort( char *base, int nel, size_t width, int (*compar)(void *, void *));

int compare_doubles( void *a, void *b )
    {
    register double *A = (double *)a, *B = (double *)b;
    return( *A > *B )?1:(*A < *B ? -1 : 0 );
    }

void Sort( double *array, int length )
    {
    qsort( (char *)array, length, sizeof( double ), compare_doubles );
```

```
        }

/*
 * Split the curve at the midpoint, returning an array with the two parts.
 * Temporary storage is minimized by using part of the storage for the result
 * to hold an intermediate value until it is no longer needed.
 */
#define left r[0]
#define right r[1]
Bezier *Bezier::Split()
    {
    Bezier *r = new Bezier[2];
    (left.p0 = p0)->refcount++;
    (right.p3 = p3)->refcount++;
    left.p1 = new point(  p0, p1, 1);
    right.p2 = new point( p2, p3, 1);
    right.p1 = new point( p1, p2, 1); // temporary holding spot
    left.p2 = new point ( left.p1, right.p1, 1);
    *right.p1 = mid( right.p1, right.p2 ); // Real value this time
    left.p3 = right.p0 = new point( left.p2, right.p1, 2 );
    return r;
    }
#undef left
#undef right


/*
 * Test the bounding boxes of two Bezier curves for interference.
 * Several observations:
 *      First, it is cheaper to compute the bounding box of the second curve
 *      and test its bounding box for interference than to use a more direct
 *      approach of comparing all control points of the second curve with
 *      the various edges of the bounding box of the first curve to test
 *      for interference.
 *      Second, after a few subdivisions it is highly probable that two corners
 *      of the bounding box of a given Bezier curve are the first and last
 *      control points.  Once this happens once, it happens for all subsequent
 *      subcurves.  It might be worth putting in a test and then short-circuit
 *      code for further subdivision levels.
 *      Third, in the final comparison (the interference test) the comparisons
 *      should both permit equality.  We want to find intersections even if they
 *      occur at the ends of segments.
 *      Finally, there are tighter bounding boxes that can be derived. It isn't
 *      clear whether the higher probability of rejection (and hence fewer
 *      subdivisions and tests) is worth the extra work.
 */
int IntersectBB( Bezier a, Bezier b )
    { // Compute bounding box for a
    double minax, maxax, minay, maxay;
    if( a.p0->x > a.p3->x )       // These are the most likely to be extremal
        minax = a.p3->x, maxax = a.p0->x;
    else
```

```
        minax = a.p0->x, maxax = a.p3->x;
if( a.p2->x < minax )
    minax = a.p2->x;
else if( a.p2->x > maxax )
    maxax = a.p2->x;
if( a.p1->x < minax )
    minax = a.p1->x;
else if( a.p1->x > maxax )
    maxax = a.p1->x;
if( a.p0->y > a.p3->y )
    minay = a.p3->y, maxay = a.p0->y;
else
    minay = a.p0->y, maxay = a.p3->y;
if( a.p2->y < minay )
    minay = a.p2->y;
else if( a.p2->y > maxay )
    maxay = a.p2->y;
if( a.p1->y < minay )
    minay = a.p1->y;
else if( a.p1->y > maxay )
    maxay = a.p1->y;
// Compute bounding box for b
double minbx, maxbx, minby, maxby;
if( b.p0->x > b.p3->x )
    minbx = b.p3->x, maxbx = b.p0->x;
else
    minbx = b.p0->x, maxbx = b.p3->x;
if( b.p2->x < minbx )
    minbx = b.p2->x;
else if( b.p2->x > maxbx )
    maxbx = b.p2->x;
if( b.p1->x < minbx )
    minbx = b.p1->x;
else if( b.p1->x > maxbx )
    maxbx = b.p1->x;
if( b.p0->y > b.p3->y )
    minby = b.p3->y, maxby = b.p0->y;
else
    minby = b.p0->y, maxby = b.p3->y;
if( b.p2->y < minby )
    minby = b.p2->y;
else if( b.p2->y > maxby )
    maxby = b.p2->y;
if( b.p1->y < minby )
    minby = b.p1->y;
else if( b.p1->y > maxby )
    maxby = b.p1->y;
// Test bounding box of b against bounding box of a
if( ( minax > maxbx ) || ( minay > maxby )  // Not >= : need boundary case
    || ( minbx > maxax ) || ( minby > maxay ) )
    return 0; // they don't intersect
else
    return 1; // they intersect
```

```
    }

/*
 * Recursively intersect two curves keeping track of their real parameters
 * and depths of intersection.
 * The results are returned in a 2D array of doubles indicating the parameters
 * for which intersections are found.  The parameters are in the order the
 * intersections were found, which is probably not in sorted order.
 * When an intersection is found, the parameter value for each of the two
 * is stored in the index elements array, and the index is incremented.
 *
 * If either of the curves has subdivisions left before it is straight
 *       (depth > 0)
 * that curve (possibly both) is (are) subdivided at its (their) midpoint(s).
 * The depth(s) is (are) decremented, and the parameter value(s) corresponding
 * to the midpoint(s) is (are) computed.
 * Then each of the subcurves of one curve is intersected with each of the
 * subcurves of the other curve, first by testing the bounding boxes for
 * interference.  If there is any bounding box interference, the corresponding
 * subcurves are recursively intersected.
 *
 * If neither curve has subdivisions left, the line segments from the first
 * to last control point of each segment are intersected.  (Actually
 * only the parameter value corresponding to the intersection point is found.)
 *
 * The a priori flatness test is probably more efficient than testing at each
 * level of recursion, although a test after three or four levels would
 * probably be worthwhile, since many curves become flat faster than their
 * asymptotic rate for the first few levels of recursion.
 *
 * The bounding box test fails much more frequently than it succeeds, providing
 * substantial pruning of the search space.
 *
 * Each (sub)curve is subdivided only once, hence it is not possible that for
 * one final line intersection test the subdivision was at one level, while
 * for another final line intersection test the subdivision (of the same curve)
 * was at another.  Since the line segments share endpoints, the intersection
 * is robust: a near-tangential intersection will yield zero or two
 * intersections.
 */
void RecursivelyIntersect( Bezier a, double t0, double t1, int deptha,
                           Bezier b, double u0, double u1, int depthb,
                           double **parameters, int &index )
    {
    if( deptha > 0 )
        {
        Bezier *A = a.Split();
        double tmid = (t0+t1)*0.5;
        deptha--;
        if( depthb > 0 )
            {
            Bezier *B = b.Split();
            double umid = (u0+u1)*0.5;
```

```
            depthb--;
            if( IntersectBB( A[0], B[0] ) )
                RecursivelyIntersect( A[0], t0, tmid, deptha,
                                      B[0], u0, umid, depthb,
                                      parameters, index );
            if( IntersectBB( A[1], B[0] ) )
                RecursivelyIntersect( A[1], tmid, t1, deptha,
                                      B[0], u0, umid, depthb,
                                      parameters, index );
            if( IntersectBB( A[0], B[1] ) )
                RecursivelyIntersect( A[0], t0, tmid, deptha,
                                      B[1], umid, u1, depthb,
                                      parameters, index );
            if( IntersectBB( A[1], B[1] ) )
                RecursivelyIntersect( A[1], tmid, t1, deptha,
                                      B[1], umid, u1, depthb,
                                      parameters, index );
            }
        else
            {
            if( IntersectBB( A[0], b ) )
                RecursivelyIntersect( A[0], t0, tmid, deptha,
                                      b, u0, u1, depthb,
                                      parameters, index );
            if( IntersectBB( A[1], b ) )
                RecursivelyIntersect( A[1], tmid, t1, deptha,
                                      b, u0, u1, depthb,
                                      parameters, index );
            }
        }
else
    if( depthb > 0 )
        {
        Bezier *B = b.Split();
        double umid = (u0 + u1)*0.5;
        depthb--;
        if( IntersectBB( a, B[0] ) )
            RecursivelyIntersect( a, t0, t1, deptha,
                                  B[0], u0, umid, depthb,
                                  parameters, index );
        if( IntersectBB( a, B[1] ) )
            RecursivelyIntersect( a, t0, t1, deptha,
                                  B[0], umid, u1, depthb,
                                  parameters, index );
        }
    else // Both segments are fully subdivided; now do line segments
        {
        double xlk = a.p3->x - a.p0->x;
        double ylk = a.p3->y - a.p0->y;
        double xnm = b.p3->x - b.p0->x;
        double ynm = b.p3->y - b.p0->y;
        double xmk = b.p0->x - a.p0->x;
        double ymk = b.p0->y - a.p0->y;
```

```
              double det = xnm * ylk - ynm * xlk;
              if( 1.0 + det == 1.0 )
                  return;
              else
                  {
                  double detinv = 1.0 / det;
                  double s = ( xnm * ymk - ynm *xmk ) * detinv;
                  double t = ( xlk * ymk - ylk * xmk ) * detinv;
                  if( ( s < 0.0 ) || ( s > 1.0 ) || ( t < 0.0 ) || ( t > 1.0 ) )
                      return;
                  parameters[0][index] = t0 + s * ( t1 - t0 );
                  parameters[1][index] = u0 + t * ( u1 - u0 );
                  index++;
                  }
          }
      }

inline double log4( double x ) { return 0.5 * log2( x ); }

/*
 * Wang's theorem is used to estimate the level of subdivision required,
 * but only if the bounding boxes interfere at the top level.
 * Assuming there is a possible intersection, RecursivelyIntersect is
 * used to find all the parameters corresponding to intersection points.
 * These are then sorted and returned in an array.
 */

double ** FindIntersections( Bezier a, Bezier b )
    {
    double **parameters = new double *[2];
    parameters[0] = new double[9];
    parameters[1] = new double[9];
    int index = 0;
    if( IntersectBB( a, b ) )
        {
        vector la1 = vabs( ( *(a.p2) - *(a.p1) ) - ( *(a.p1) - *(a.p0) ) );
        vector la2 = vabs( ( *(a.p3) - *(a.p2) ) - ( *(a.p2) - *(a.p1) ) );
        vector la;
        if( la1.x > la2.x ) la.x = la1.x; else la.x = la2.x;
        if( la1.y > la2.y ) la.y = la1.y; else la.y = la2.y;
        vector lb1 = vabs( ( *(b.p2) - *(b.p1) ) - ( *(b.p1) - *(b.p0) ) );
        vector lb2 = vabs( ( *(b.p3) - *(b.p2) ) - ( *(b.p2) - *(b.p1) ) );
        vector lb;
        if( lb1.x > lb2.x ) lb.x = lb1.x; else lb.x = lb2.x;
        if( lb1.y > lb2.y ) lb.y = lb1.y; else lb.y = lb2.y;
        double l0;
        if( la.x > la.y )
            l0 = la.x;
        else
            l0 = la.y;
        int ra;
        if( l0 * 0.75 * M_SQRT2 + 1.0 == 1.0 )
            ra = 0;
```

```
            else
                ra = (int)ceil( log4( M_SQRT2 * 6.0 / 8.0 * INV_EPS * 10 ) );
            if( lb.x > lb.y )
                l0 = lb.x;
            else
                l0 = lb.y;
            int rb;
            if( l0 * 0.75 * M_SQRT2 + 1.0 == 1.0 )
                rb = 0;
            else
                rb = (int)ceil(log4( M_SQRT2 * 6.0 / 8.0 * INV_EPS * 10 ) );
            RecursivelyIntersect( a, 0., 1., ra, b, 0., 1., rb, parameters, index );
            }
        if( index < 9 )
            parameters[0][index] = parameters[1][index] = -1.0;
        Sort( parameters[0], index );
        Sort( parameters[1], index );
        return parameters;
        }

void
Bezier::ParameterSplitLeft( double t, Bezier &left )
    {
    left.p0 = p0;
    left.p1 = new point( *p0 + t * ( *p1 - *p0 ) );
    left.p2 = new point( *p1 + t * ( *p2 - *p1 ) ); // temporary holding spot
    p2->refcount--;
    p2 = new point( *p2 + t * ( *p3 - *p2 ) );
    p1->refcount--;
    p1 = new point( *(left.p2) + t * ( *p2 - *(left.p2) ) );
    *(left.p2) = ( *(left.p1) + t * ( *(left.p2) - *(left.p1) ) );
    (left.p3 = p0 = new point(*(left.p2) + t * (*(p1)-*(left.p2))))->refcount++;
    left.p0->refcount++; left.p1->refcount++;
    left.p2->refcount++; left.p3->refcount++;
    }


/*
 * Intersect two curves, returning an array of two arrays of curves.
 * The first array of curves corresponds to `this' curve, the second
 * corresponds to curve B, passed in.
 * The intersection parameter values are computed by FindIntersections,
 * and they come back in the range 0..1, using the original parametrization.
 * Once one segment has been removed, i.e., the curve is split at splitT, the
 * parametrization of the second half is from 0..1, so the parameter for
 * the next split point, if any, must be adjusted.
 * If we split at t[i], the split point at t[i+1] is
 * ( t[i+1] - t[i] ) / ( 1 - t[i] ) of the way to the end from the new
 * start point.
 */


Bezier **Bezier::Intersect( Bezier B )
    {
    // The return from FindIntersections will decrement all refcounts.
```

```
// (a c++-ism)
B.p0->refcount++; B.p1->refcount++; B.p2->refcount++; B.p3->refcount++;
Bezier **rvalue = new Bezier *[2];
rvalue[0] = new Bezier[9];
rvalue[1] = new Bezier[9];
double **t;
t = FindIntersections( *this, B );
int index = 0;
if( t[0][0] > -0.5 )
    {
    ParameterSplitLeft( t[0][0], rvalue[0][0] );
    B.ParameterSplitLeft( t[1][0], rvalue[1][0] );
    index++;
    while( t[0][index] > -0.5 && index < 9 )
        {
        double splitT = (t[0][index] - t[0][index-1])/(1.0 - t[0][index-1]);
        ParameterSplitLeft( splitT, rvalue[0][index] );
        splitT = (t[1][index] - t[1][index-1])/(1.0 - t[1][index-1]);
        B.ParameterSplitLeft( splitT, rvalue[1][index] );
        index++;
        }
    }
rvalue[0][index] = *this;
rvalue[1][index] = B;
return rvalue;
}
```

◇ **Bibliography** ◇

(Bowyer and Woodwark 1983) A. Bowyer and J. R. Woodwark. *A Programmer's Geometry.* Butterworths, London, 1983.

(Koparkar and Mudur 1983) P. A. Koparkar and S. P. Mudur. A new class of algorithms for the processing of parametric curves. *Computer-Aided Design,* 15(1):41–45, 1983.

(Lane and Riesenfeld 1980) J. Lane and R. Riesenfeld. A theoretical development for the computer generation and display of piecewise polynomial surfaces. *IEEE Transactions on Pattern Analysis and Machine Intelligence,* PAMI-2(1):35–46, January 1980.

(Manocha and Demmel 1992) D. Manocha and J. Demmel. Algorithms for intersecting parametric and algebraic curves. In *Proc. Graphics Interface 92,* pages 232–241, 1992.

(Sederberg and Nishita 1990) T. Sederberg and T. Nishita. Curve intersection using Bézier clipping. *Computer-Aided Design,* 22(9):538–549, November 1990.

(Sederberg and Parry 1986) T. W. Sederberg and S. R. Parry. A comparison of three curve intersection algorithms. *Computer-Aided Design*, 18(1):58–63, 1986.

(Sederberg *et al.* 1989) T. W. Sederberg, S. White, and A. Zundel. Fat arcs: A bounding region with cubic convergence. *Computer Aided Geometric Design*, 6:205–218, 1989.

(Wang 1984) G. Wang. The subdivision method for finding the intersection between two Bézier curves or surfaces. *Zhejiang University Journal, special issue on Computational Geometry (in Chinese)*, 1984.

IV.5

Converting Rectangular Patches into Bézier Triangles

Dani Lischinski

580 ETC Building
Cornell University
Ithaca, NY 14853
danix@graphics.cornell.edu

◇ Introduction ◇

In the third volume of *Graphics Gems* I described a method of converting Bézier triangles into rectangular Bézier patches (Lischinski 1992). This Gem addresses the "inverse" problem of representing a rectangular Bézier patch with Bézier triangles.

I will describe how to convert a biquadratic patch into two quartic triangles. The same technique can be used to derive a conversion for patches of higher order. For completeness I will briefly repeat the definitions for rectangular and triangular Bézier patches; Farin's excellent book (Farin 1990) is recommended as a more comprehensive reference.

◇ Bézier Rectangles and Triangles ◇

A rectangular Bézier patch is a mapping $R(s, t)$ from a unit square $[0, 1] \times [0, 1]$ into E^3, defined by a set of control points $\mathbf{p}_{ij} \in E^3$ as

$$R(s, t) = \sum_{i=0}^{m} \sum_{j=0}^{n} \mathbf{p}_{ij} \frac{m!n!}{i!j!(m-i)!(n-j)!} s^i t^j (1-s)^{m-i} (1-t)^{n-j} \qquad (1)$$

where m and n are the degrees of the patch in s and t, respectively. In the biquadratic case, for example, this simplifies to

$$
\begin{aligned}
R(s, t) \;=\; & \left(\mathbf{p}_{00}(1-s)^2 + 2\mathbf{p}_{01}s(1-s) + \mathbf{p}_{02}s^2 \right)(1-t)^2 \\
& + \left(\mathbf{p}_{10}(1-s)^2 + 2\mathbf{p}_{11}s(1-s) + \mathbf{p}_{12}s^2 \right) 2t(1-t) \\
& + \left(\mathbf{p}_{20}(1-s)^2 + 2\mathbf{p}_{21}s(1-s) + \mathbf{p}_{22}s^2 \right) t^2
\end{aligned}
\qquad (2)
$$

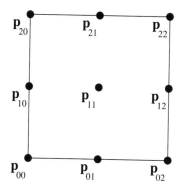

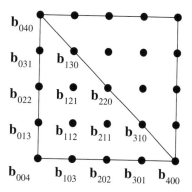

Figure 1. Control points defining a biquadratic Bézier patch (left) and two quartic Bézier triangles (right).

A Bézier triangle of degree n is essentially a mapping $T(u, v)$ from a unit triangle $((0,0),(1,0),(0,1))$ into E^3. It is defined by a set of control points $\mathbf{b}_{ijk} \in E^3$ as

$$T(u, v) = \sum \mathbf{b}_{ijk} \frac{n!}{i!j!k!} u^i v^j w^k \qquad (3)$$

where $w = 1 - u - v$, and the summation is over all $i, j, k \geq 0$ such that $i + j + k = n$. In the quartic case, for example, this simplifies to

$$
\begin{aligned}
T(u, v) \quad = \quad & \mathbf{b}_{004}w^4 + 4\mathbf{b}_{103}uw^3 + 6\mathbf{b}_{202}u^2w^2 + 4\mathbf{b}_{301}u^3w \\
& + \mathbf{b}_{400}u^4 + 4\mathbf{b}_{013}vw^3 + 12\mathbf{b}_{112}uvw^2 + 12\mathbf{b}_{211}u^2vw \\
& + 4\mathbf{b}_{310}u^3v + 6\mathbf{b}_{022}v^2w^2 + 12\mathbf{b}_{121}uv^2w + 6\mathbf{b}_{220}u^2v^2 \\
& + 4\mathbf{b}_{031}v^3w + 4\mathbf{b}_{130}uv^3 + \mathbf{b}_{040}v^4
\end{aligned}
\qquad (4)
$$

As can be seen from Equation (1), each of the control points $\mathbf{p}_{ij}$ of a Bézier rectangle is weighted by a basis function that is a bivariate polynomial of total degree $m + n$. Thus, Bézier triangles of order $m + n$ are required in order to represent exactly the same surface. For example, a bilinear patch can be converted to quadratic triangles, a biquadratic patch to quartic triangles, and a bicubic patch to sixth degree triangles. We need two triangles to tile a square; hence, two Bézier triangles are needed to represent a single rectangular patch.

◇ Converting Biquadratic Patches ◇

Given the nine control points $\mathbf{p}_{ij}$ that define the biquadratic patch $R(s, t)$, we need to find fifteen control points for each of the two quartic triangles (see Figure 1). In this section we derive the values of the control points for the lower left triangle. The points for the upper right triangle are defined symmetrically.

The three boundary control points $\mathbf{p}_{00}, \mathbf{p}_{01}, \mathbf{p}_{02}$, are simply the Bézier control points that define a quadratic boundary curve. We need to find five Bézier control points that would define the same curve. This can be done by using the degree elevation algorithm (Farin 1990):

$$
\begin{aligned}
\mathbf{b}_{004} &\leftarrow \mathbf{p}_{00} \\
\mathbf{b}_{103} &\leftarrow (\mathbf{p}_{00} + \mathbf{p}_{01})/2 \\
\mathbf{b}_{202} &\leftarrow (\mathbf{p}_{00} + 4\mathbf{p}_{01} + \mathbf{p}_{02})/6 \\
\mathbf{b}_{301} &\leftarrow (\mathbf{p}_{01} + \mathbf{p}_{02})/2 \\
\mathbf{b}_{400} &\leftarrow \mathbf{p}_{02}
\end{aligned}
$$

Similarly,

$$
\begin{aligned}
\mathbf{b}_{013} &\leftarrow (\mathbf{p}_{00} + \mathbf{p}_{10})/2 \\
\mathbf{b}_{022} &\leftarrow (\mathbf{p}_{00} + 4\mathbf{p}_{10} + \mathbf{p}_{20})/6 \\
\mathbf{b}_{031} &\leftarrow (\mathbf{p}_{10} + \mathbf{p}_{20})/2 \\
\mathbf{b}_{040} &\leftarrow \mathbf{p}_{20}
\end{aligned}
$$

Now we turn our attention to the points on the boundary between the two triangles. These control points should define the curve corresponding to the line $s = 1 - t$ in the parameter space of the biquadratic patch. Substituting $1 - t$ for s in Equation (2) and rewriting in terms of the quartic Bernstein-Bézier basis we get

$$
\begin{aligned}
R(1 - t, t) =\ & \mathbf{p}_{00}t^2(1 - t)^2 + 2\mathbf{p}_{01}t(1 - t)^3 + \mathbf{p}_{02}(1 - t)^4 + 2\mathbf{p}_{10}t^3(1 - t) + \\
& 4\mathbf{p}_{11}t^2(1 - t)^2 + 2\mathbf{p}_{12}t(1 - t)^3 + \mathbf{p}_{20}t^4 + 2\mathbf{p}_{21}t^3(1 - t) + \mathbf{p}_{22}t^2(1 - t)^2 \\
=\ & \mathbf{p}_{02}(1 - t)^4 + (\mathbf{p}_{01} + \mathbf{p}_{12})\, 2t(1 - t)^3 + (\mathbf{p}_{00} + 4\mathbf{p}_{11} + \mathbf{p}_{22})\, t^2(1 - t)^2 + \\
& (\mathbf{p}_{10} + \mathbf{p}_{21})\, 2t^3(1 - t) + \mathbf{p}_{20}t^4
\end{aligned}
$$

It follows that

$$
\begin{aligned}
\mathbf{b}_{310} &\leftarrow (\mathbf{p}_{01} + \mathbf{p}_{12})/2 \\
\mathbf{b}_{220} &\leftarrow (\mathbf{p}_{00} + 4\mathbf{p}_{11} + \mathbf{p}_{22})/6 \\
\mathbf{b}_{130} &\leftarrow (\mathbf{p}_{10} + \mathbf{p}_{21})/2
\end{aligned}
$$

We are now left with the three interior control points $\mathbf{b}_{112}, \mathbf{b}_{121}, \mathbf{b}_{211}$. Their values can be obtained by solving the three simultaneous linear equations

$$
\begin{aligned}
T(\tfrac{1}{4}, \tfrac{1}{4}) &= R(\tfrac{1}{4}, \tfrac{1}{4}) \\
T(\tfrac{1}{2}, \tfrac{1}{4}) &= R(\tfrac{1}{2}, \tfrac{1}{4}) \\
T(\tfrac{1}{4}, \tfrac{1}{2}) &= R(\tfrac{1}{4}, \tfrac{1}{2})
\end{aligned}
$$

which yields the solution

$$\mathbf{b}_{112} \leftarrow (2\mathbf{p}_{00} + \mathbf{p}_{01} + \mathbf{p}_{10} + 2\mathbf{p}_{11})/6$$
$$\mathbf{b}_{121} \leftarrow (\mathbf{p}_{00} + 2\mathbf{p}_{10} + 2\mathbf{p}_{11} + \mathbf{p}_{21})/6$$
$$\mathbf{b}_{211} \leftarrow (\mathbf{p}_{00} + 2\mathbf{p}_{01} + 2\mathbf{p}_{11} + \mathbf{p}_{12})/6$$

◇   C++ Code   ◇

Given here are skeletal class definitions for the control point (`ControlPoint`) class, definitions and code for quadratic and quartic Bézier triangle classes (`BezierTri2` and `BezierTri4`, respectively), and for the bilinear and biquadratic Bézier rectangular patch classes (`BezierRect1` and `BezierRect2`.) The conversion described in the Gem takes place in the `Convert` member functions of the `BezierRect1` and `BezierRect2` classes, which each take references to two Bézier triangles (of appropriate degree) as an argument.

Note that control points do not have to be (x, y, z) triplets. For instance, they can be scalars, RGB triplets, etc., as long as the operators `+`, `*`, `/`, and `=` (assignment) are provided. If you have a class that you wish to use instead of the one given in the code, all you have to do is to remove the definitions of the `ControlPoint` class and its operators, and insert instead something like:

```
#include <my_class.h>
typedef MyClass ControlPoint;
```

```
/************* Control Point Class ****************************************/

class ControlPoint {
public:
    ControlPoint operator+(const ControlPoint&);
    friend ControlPoint operator*(float, const ControlPoint&);
    friend ControlPoint operator/(const ControlPoint&, float);
private:
    float x, y, z;
};
```

```
/************* Quadratic Bezier Triangle Class ***************************/

class BezierTri2 {
private:
    ControlPoint cp[6];
public:
    ControlPoint& b(int, int, int);
    ControlPoint operator()(float, float);
};
```

```
ControlPoint& BezierTri2::b(int i, int j, int /* k */)
// Returns the (i,j,k) control point.
{
    static int row_start[3] = {0, 3, 5};
    return cp[row_start[j] + i];
}

ControlPoint BezierTri2::operator()(float u, float v)
// Evaluates the Bezier triangle at (u,v).
{
    float w = 1 - u - v;
    float u2 = u * u;
    float v2 = v * v;
    float w2 = w * w;
    return (w2*b(0,0,2) + (2*u*w)*b(1,0,1) + u2*b(2,0,0) +
            (2*v*w)*b(0,1,1) + (2*u*v)*b(1,1,0) + v2*b(0,2,0));
}


/************* Quartic Bezier Triangle Class ****************************/

class BezierTri4 {
private:
    ControlPoint cp[15];
public:
    ControlPoint& b(int, int, int);
    ControlPoint operator()(float, float);
};

ControlPoint& BezierTri4::b(int i, int j, int /* k */)
// Returns the (i,j,k) control point.
{
    static int row_start[5] = {0, 5, 9, 12, 14};
    return cp[row_start[j] + i];
}

ControlPoint BezierTri4::operator()(float u, float v)
// Evaluates the Bezier triangle at (u,v).
{
    float w = 1 - u - v;
    float u2 = u * u, u3 = u2 * u, u4 = u3 * u;
    float v2 = v * v, v3 = v2 * v, v4 = v3 * v;
    float w2 = w * w, w3 = w2 * w, w4 = w3 * w;
    return (w4*b(0,0,4) + (4*u*w3)*b(1,0,3) + (6*u2*w2)*b(2,0,2) +
            (4*u3*w)*b(3,0,1) + u4*b(4,0,0) + (4*v*w3)*b(0,1,3) +
            (12*u*v*w2)*b(1,1,2) + (12*u2*v*w)*b(2,1,1) + (4*u3*v)*b(3,1,0) +
            (6*v2*w2)*b(0,2,2) + (12*u*v2*w)*b(1,2,1) + (6*u2*v2)*b(2,2,0) +
            (4*v3*w)*b(0,3,1) + (4*u*v3)*b(1,3,0) + v4*b(0,4,0));
}
```

```
/************** Bilinear Bezier Rectangle Class ****************************/


class BezierRect1 {
private:
    ControlPoint cp[2][2];
public:
    ControlPoint& p(int i, int j)        { return cp[i][j]; }
    ControlPoint operator()(float, float);
    void Convert(BezierTri2&, BezierTri2&);
};


ControlPoint BezierRect1::operator()(float s, float t)
// Evaluates the Bezier rectangle at (s,t).
{
    float s1 = 1 - s;

    return ((1-t) * (s1*p(0,0) + s*p(0,1)) +
                t * (s1*p(1,0) + s*p(1,1)));
}


void BezierRect1::Convert(BezierTri2& t1, BezierTri2& t2)
// Converts a bilinear Bezier rectangle into two quadratic Bezier
// triangles t1 and t2, such that the value of the bilinear
// at (s,t) is equal to t1(s,t) if (s + t <= 1), and t2(1-t,1-s)
// otherwise.
{
    // lower left triangle:
    t1.b(0,0,2) = p(0,0);
    t1.b(1,0,1) = 0.5 * (p(0,0) + p(0,1));
    t1.b(2,0,0) = p(0,1);

    t1.b(0,1,1) = 0.5 * (p(0,0) + p(1,0));
    t1.b(1,1,0) = 0.5 * (p(0,0) + p(1,1));

    t1.b(0,2,0) = p(1,0);

    // upper right triangle:
    t2.b(0,0,2) = p(1,1);
    t2.b(1,0,1) = 0.5 * (p(1,1) + p(0,1));
    t2.b(2,0,0) = p(0,1);

    t2.b(0,1,1) = 0.5 * (p(1,1) + p(1,0));
    t2.b(1,1,0) = 0.5 * (p(0,0) + p(1,1));

    t2.b(0,2,0) = p(1,0);
}
```

```
/************* Biquadratic Bezier Rectangle Class *************************/

class BezierRect2 {
private:
    ControlPoint cp[3][3];
public:
    ControlPoint& p(int i, int j)        { return cp[i][j]; }
    ControlPoint operator()(float, float);
    void Convert(BezierTri4&, BezierTri4&);
};

ControlPoint BezierRect2::operator()(float s, float t)
// Evaluates the Bezier rectangle at (s,t).
{
    float s1 = 1 - s, ss1 = 2*s*s1, s2 = s*s, s12 = s1*s1;
    float t1 = 1 - t, tt1 = 2*t*t1, t2 = t*t, t12 = t1*t1;

    return (t12 * (s12*p(0,0) + ss1*p(0,1) + s2*p(0,2)) +
            tt1 * (s12*p(1,0) + ss1*p(1,1) + s2*p(1,2)) +
            t2  * (s12*p(2,0) + ss1*p(2,1) + s2*p(2,2)));
}

void BezierRect2::Convert(BezierTri4& t1, BezierTri4& t2)
// Converts a biquadratic Bezier rectangle into two quartic Bezier
// triangles t1 and t2, such that the value of the biquadratic
// at (s,t) is equal to t1(s,t) if (s + t <= 1), and t2(1-t,1-s)
// otherwise.
{
    // lower left triangle:
    t1.b(0,0,4) = p(0,0);
    t1.b(1,0,3) = 0.5 * (p(0,0) + p(0,1));
    t1.b(2,0,2) = (p(0,0) + 4 * p(0,1) + p(0,2)) / 6;
    t1.b(3,0,1) = 0.5 * (p(0,1) + p(0,2));
    t1.b(4,0,0) = p(0,2);

    t1.b(0,1,3) = 0.5 * (p(0,0) + p(1,0));
    t1.b(1,1,2) = (p(0,0) + p(1,1)) / 3 + (p(0,1) + p(1,0)) / 6;
    t1.b(2,1,1) = (p(0,0) + p(1,2)) / 6 + (p(0,1) + p(1,1)) / 3;
    t1.b(3,1,0) = 0.5 * (p(0,1) + p(1,2));

    t1.b(0,2,2) = (p(0,0) + 4 * p(1,0) + p(2,0)) / 6;
    t1.b(1,2,1) = (p(0,0) + p(2,1)) / 6 + (p(1,0) + p(1,1)) / 3;
    t1.b(2,2,0) = (p(0,0) + 4 * p(1,1) + p(2,2)) / 6;

    t1.b(0,3,1) = 0.5 * (p(1,0) + p(2,0));
    t1.b(1,3,0) = 0.5 * (p(1,0) + p(2,1));

    t1.b(0,4,0) = p(2,0);

    // upper right triangle:
    t2.b(0,0,4) = p(2,2);
    t2.b(1,0,3) = 0.5 * (p(2,2) + p(1,2));
    t2.b(2,0,2) = (p(2,2) + 4 * p(1,2) + p(0,2)) / 6;
```

```
t2.b(3,0,1) = 0.5 * (p(1,2) + p(0,2));
t2.b(4,0,0) = p(0,2);

t2.b(0,1,3) = 0.5 * (p(2,2) + p(2,1));
t2.b(1,1,2) = (p(2,2) + p(1,1)) / 3 + (p(1,2) + p(2,1)) / 6;
t2.b(2,1,1) = (p(2,2) + p(0,1)) / 6 + (p(1,2) + p(1,1)) / 3;
t2.b(3,1,0) = 0.5 * (p(0,1) + p(1,2));

t2.b(0,2,2) = (p(2,2) + 4 * p(2,1) + p(2,0)) / 6;
t2.b(1,2,1) = (p(2,2) + p(1,0)) / 6 + (p(2,1) + p(1,1)) / 3;
t2.b(2,2,0) = (p(2,2) + 4 * p(1,1) + p(0,0)) / 6;

t2.b(0,3,1) = 0.5 * (p(2,1) + p(2,0));
t2.b(1,3,0) = 0.5 * (p(1,0) + p(2,1));

t2.b(0,4,0) = p(2,0);
}
```

◇ **Bibliography** ◇

(Farin 1990) Gerald E. Farin. *Curves and Surfaces for Computer Aided Geometric Design: A Practical Guide*, 2nd edition. Academic Press, Boston, 1990.

(Lischinski 1992) Dani Lischinski. Converting Bézier triangles into rectangular patches. In David Kirk, editor, *Graphics Gems III*, pages 256–261. Academic Press, Boston, 1992.

IV.6

Tessellation of NURB Surfaces

John W. Peterson
Taligent, Inc.
10201 N. DeAnza Blvd.
Cupertino, CA 95014-2233
jp@taligent.com

◇ Introduction ◇

NURB (Non-uniform rational B-spline) surfaces are commonly used to represent curved or smooth objects in computer graphics. Despite their popularity, many people experimenting with 3D graphics don't support NURBs (or curved surfaces) because of their perceived complexity. However, with a few basic techniques, like those provided here, it's straightforward to add curved surfaces to your 3D rendering package. Doing so greatly increases the variety of objects you can model and render.

The goal of this Gem is to provide a worked example of how to triangulate a NURB surface. It is relatively light on the underlying derivation of the mathematics, as this is covered in detail in the textbooks on the subject. (See the bibliography at the end.)

Rendering NURB surfaces directly from the spline representation is generally prohibitive. It requires evaluating the surface in the inner pixel rendering loop (which is very slow) and root-finding or other awkward methods to find silhouette edges. In order to render surfaces quickly, a better method is to convert the surface into much simpler primitives (like triangles) that existing rendering code handles easily. Tessellation refers to the process of breaking a curved surface into flat pieces approximating the surface well enough that artifacts (shading problems, faceted edges) aren't visible.

This Gem presents two techniques for tessellation: a simple surface evaluation scheme and a more elaborate adaptive subdivision method. These operatate on NURB surfaces of arbitrary order (> 2) using any valid knot sequence. The implementation for these is provided in portable C code, listed at the end.

◇ Surface Evaluation ◇

The formula for a point $\mathbf{Q}(u, v)$ on a NURB surface is:

$$\mathbf{Q}(u, v) = \frac{\sum_{i=0}^{m_u} \sum_{j=0}^{m_v} B_{i,k_u}(u) B_{j,k_v}(v) \mathbf{V}_{i,j}}{\sum_{i=0}^{m_u} \sum_{j=0}^{m_v} B_{i,k_u}(u) B_{j,k_v}(v) \mathbf{w}_{i,j}}$$

where:

u, v are the parameters of the surface,
$B_{i,k}(u)$ are the B-Spline basis functions,
k_u, k_v are the orders in the u and v directions, respectively,
$\mathbf{V}_{i,j}$ is a mesh of control points, of size $i = 0 \ldots m_u, j = 0 \ldots m_v$,
$\mathbf{w}_{i,j}$ is the "rational" component of the control points,
        (the weights). They should be > 0.

A surface also has two *knot vectors*, $\{u_i\}_{i=0}^{m_u+k_u}$ and $\{v_i\}_{i=0}^{m_v+k_v}$, used by the basis functions for controlling the continuity of the surface. The basis functions are for general B-splines, defined by:

$$B_{i,1}(u) \quad = \quad \begin{cases} 1 & u_i \leq u < u_{i+1} \\ 0 & \text{otherwise} \end{cases}$$

$$B_{i,r}(u) \quad = \quad \frac{u - u_i}{u_{i+r-1} - u_i} B_{i,r-1}(u) + \frac{u_{i+r} - u}{u_{i+r} - u_{i+1}} B_{i+1,r-1}(u) \Big|_{r=2,3,\ldots k}$$

The tangents of the surface in the u and v directions at $\mathbf{Q}(u, v)$ are determined by taking two partial derivatives,

$$\frac{\partial}{\partial u} \mathbf{Q}(u, v) \quad \text{and} \quad \frac{\partial}{\partial v} \mathbf{Q}(u, v)$$

to find the tangents to the surface in the u and v directions. Note that performing these derivatives requires the quotient rule to handle the rational denominator properly. Taking the cross product of these two tangent vectors produces the normal to the surface.

With a routine for evaluating the surface at a particular u, v, a simple tessellation scheme is simply to step across in u and down in v, generating a grid of points. These are easily broken into triangles for use with a polygon rendering package.

◇ Adaptive Subdivision ◇

A second technique for tessellation is "adaptive subdivision." This method is more complex to implement, but has a number of nice properties — it reduces the number of triangles, it avoids cracks between them, and the hierarchical nature of subdivision is useful for some rendering methods, like generating hierarchical bounding volumes for ray tracing. It also makes use of the object size and surface curvature to determine how many triangles to generate; if a surface is relatively flat, subdivision generates few triangles. If an object is scaled up to appear larger on the screen, the subdivision code can automatically generate more triangles to prevent facets from appearing (see Figure 1).

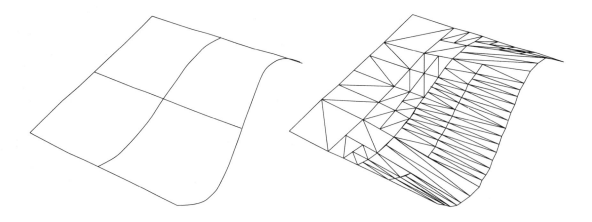

Figure 1. A surface tessellated with adaptive subdivision.

The subdivision process works according to the following recursive algorithm:

```
Subdiv( surf )
        if IsFlat( surf ) then
                EmitTriangles( surf )
        else
                SplitSurf( surf , leftSurf, rightSurf )
                Subdiv( leftSurf )
                Subdiv( rightSurf )
```

Let's look at each of the components of this algorithm.

Flatness Testing

To see if the control mesh for the surface (or more often, a subdivided piece of a surface) is flat enough to triangulate, the flatness testing checks the mesh of control points in the following ways:

- Are the edges straight?
- Is each row straight?
- Is each column straight?
- Do all four corners of the surface lie in the same plane (i.e., not twisted)?

These tests are not exact, but employ a tolerance to determine when the approximation is acceptable. To test if an edge, row, or column of control points is straight, the following algorithm is used:

```
/* Test if points V_i for i = 1 to n are collinear within Tolerance */
StraightnessTest( V, n, Tolerance )
            if the row has only two control points (i.e., linear), then
                    return TRUE;
            Select a point V_0
            for i = n to 1 step −1
                    while ||V_i − V_0|| < ε, next i
            if i < 0 then
                    return TRUE /* row is degenerate to a point */
            T ← V_i − V_0
            for i = n to 1 step −1
                    if ||(V_i − V_0) × T|| > Tolerance then
                            return FALSE
            return TRUE
```

This algorithm finds a line between two of the points that are greater than ϵ apart and then tests the distance between each remaining point and the line to see if it's greater than the specified tolerance for the subdivision.

To see if the surface is twisted, we take the cross product of two adjacent edges and use this to form a plane equation $Ax + By + Cz + D = 0$. The opposing corner is tested with this equation to see if it is more than the acceptable distance from the plane.

An important optimization for flatness testing is to propagate the known flatnesses from the parent surface to its children. If we find that a surface is flat in a particular direction, then its children are also. For example, consider a cylinder. Since it's flat along its length, the test only needs to be done once. All subsequent tests and subdivisions only occur about its circumference. Six flags are used to cache the flatness tests: one for the row direction, another for the column direction, and four more for each edge. The edge flags are also used for crack prevention (discussed below).

If the surface isn't flat in either direction, the subdivision code alternates the direction (in u or in v) the surface is split. If the surface is flat in only one direction, the subdivision is performed only in the other direction.

Splitting the Surface

To split the surface, adaptive subdivision uses *refinement*, a process that adds additional control points to a surface without changing its shape. This process is implemented with the Oslo algorithm (Bartels *et al.* 1987). The Oslo algorithm takes a new knot vector with additional knots, and adds control points corresponding to the new knots. For splitting a curve or surface, subdivision uses the following property of refinement: If we insert a number of knots at the same parametric value, where the number added is equal to the order of the curve (e.g., cubic = 4), then two new curves are generated with the same shape as the original unrefined curve. The two new curves together have

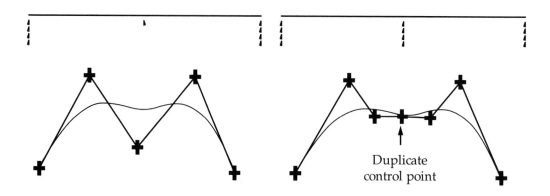

Figure 2.   Splitting a curve.

exactly the same shape as the old curve, and they each have a control point on the curve where they join, as shown in Figure 2.

For surfaces, splitting the control mesh looks something like Figure 3.

Once the surface is split, the four corners of the parent surface are copied to the respective corners of the children. New normals are computed for the four new corners between the children.

The next step is to propagate the cache of "straightness" flags mentioned above. The two flags for all rows and all columns straight are passed directly (e.g., the cylinder example mentioned above). All of the edge straightness flags are passed from the parent to the children except for the new edges created along the seam between the two halves. These must be re-tested. Once the two child surfaces are complete, the storage for the parent is deleted.

The Corners

Each surface contains four corner data structures. The corners contain a copy of the control point at the corner, and the surface normal. The normals are computed from the control mesh. This is trivial for Bézier surfaces, by taking cross products of vectors formed from the corners of the control mesh.[1] For example, in the mesh shown in Figure 4, the frontmost normal is computed as shown.

The corner structure must also store its own copy of the control point at the corner of the mesh (e.g., $C_{0,0}$). This is used for crack prevention, explained below.

---

[1] In effect, the subdivision process breaks the original B-spline surface into a series of piecewise Bézier patches.

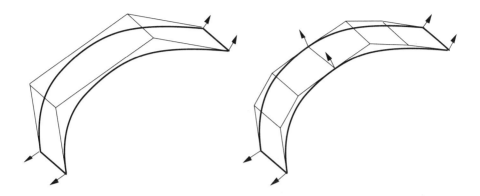

Figure 3. Splitting a surface.

$$\mathbf{N} = (\mathbf{C}_{0,1} - \mathbf{C}_{0,0}) \times (\mathbf{C}_{1,0} - \mathbf{C}_{0,0})$$

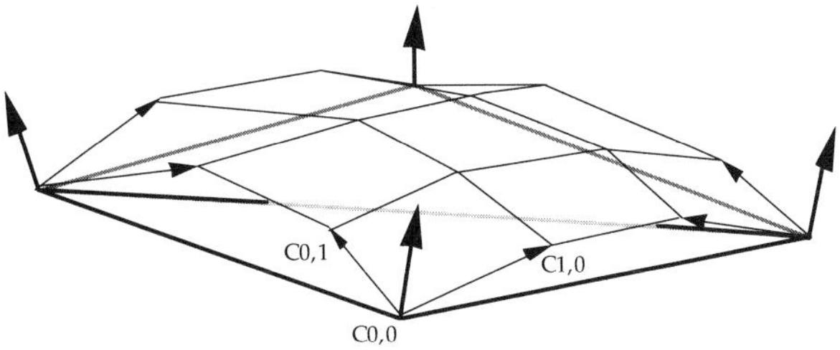

Figure 4. Finding the normal.

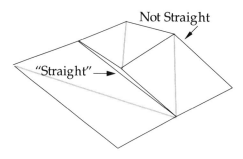

Figure 5. "Crack" in the triangulation.

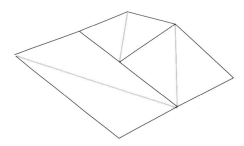

Figure 6. Fixed crack.

Crack Prevention

Each time the surface is split, checks must be made to avoid cracks. Cracks occur when one subsurface receives more subdivision than an adjacent one. Consider the example shown in Figure 5.

In this example, when the right half of the original surface is created, the flatness test finds its left edge "straight" (to within the tolerance specified) but its right edge is still curved, so it is split. The left half of the original is found to be flat, so it is turned directly into triangles. Because the right half is subdivided more than the left if the subdivision is done naively, a crack forms between the two. However, because the splitting procedure knows that the left edge of the right half was a straight line, it can project the points stored in the corners onto the line, eliminating the crack, as shown in Figure 6.

It's important that the points stored in the corner structure are moved to prevent the crack, not points stored in the control mesh of the surface. If the surface control points are moved, then subsequent normal computations give erroneous results.

Emitting the Triangles

If a surface passes all of the straightness tests, the final step is to emit the triangles. The vertices of the triangles (and their normals) are simply taken from the corner data structures. Some care needs to be taken with the normals before they are emitted — in some cases they may be degenerate, causing shading errors. To help avoid this problem, check the length of each normal. If it's collapsed to near zero, a reasonable approach is to take the value of a neighboring normal. If all the triangle's normals are degenerate, then the plane equation of the triangle should be used.

◇ **Further Reading** ◇

There are a large number of books and papers on curves and surfaces. Two of the most popular are (Bartels *et al.* 1987) and (Farin 1988). Bartels *et al.* provides a detailed mathematical background along with several useful algorithms for rendering and evaluating splines (the implementation of the basis functions and the Oslo algorithm presented here are based on this book). Farin's book provides a more geometric treatment of curves and surfaces, and provides an overview of how rational curves and surfaces work. (Rogers and Adams 1990) and (Foley et al. 1990) also cover NURB surfaces.

◇ **Implementation** ◇

The implementation consists of six files:

nurbs.h	Basic structure and constant definitions
drawing.h	External routines called by the tessellation package
NurbEval.c	Evaluation and simple tessellation scheme
NurbUtils.c	Allocating, deleting, and copying surfaces
NurbRefine.c	Refine a surface using the Oslo algorithm
NurbSubdiv.c	Subdivision implementation
Main.c	Simple test program using the above routines

The code employs some types and routines defined in GraphicsGems.h and GGVecLib.c, which were published in previous Gems volumes.

To use the package, you need to create a **NurbSurface** structure with the data for your surface. Calling **DrawEvaluation** tessellates it into a grid of triangles. The size of the grid is determined by the value **Granularity** in **DrawEvaluation**.

For tessellating with subdivision, call `DrawSubdivision`. This calls the routine `ScreenProject` to convert a point from 4D world space (x, y, z, w) to 3D screen space (x, y, z). The subdivision code uses the global `SubdivTolerance` to determine how far to subdivide the surface. This value must be in the same units as the points returned from `ScreenProject`. As discussed above in the section on flatness testing, `SubdivTolerance` specifies the allowed distance from the ideal curve. In practice this is usually kept to the size of a few pixels, to avoid facets from appearing on the edges of the curved surface.

Both routines generate triangles as output. The vertices are defined by the `SurfSample` struct, and contain the point on the surface, the normal, and the values of u and v (for texture mapping). To render a triangle, the tessellation package calls the function pointed to by `DrawTriangle`. This should be a function taking three `SurfSample` pointers as arguments (like the prototypes for `FastTriangle` and `SlowTriangle` given in `drawing.h`). Paul Heckbert's generic polygon scan converter in Graphics Gems I is an excellent source for a triangle renderer to use with this tessellation package (Heckbert 1990).

Some of the routines used internally by the tessellation package may be useful in other applications besides tessellation, for example `CalcPoint`, which returns a point and two tangents on a surface at a given u and v; and `RefineSurface`, which adds control points to a surface using the Oslo algorithm.

◇ nurbs.h ◇

```
/*
 * Nurbs.h Nurb surface processing code.
 *
 * John Peterson
 */

#include "GraphicsGems.h"

#ifndef THINK_C
typedef unsigned char Boolean;
#endif

/* Rational (homogeneous) point */

typedef struct Point4Struct {
    double x, y, z, w;
    } Point4;
typedef Point4 Vector4;

/*
 * Sampled point on a surface.  This contains the point, normal and
 * surface coordinates (u,v).  This structure is passed to the rendering
```

```
 * code for shading, etc.
 */
typedef struct SurfSample {
    Point3 point, normal;   /* Point on surface, normal at that point */
    double normLen;         /* Used for normalizing normals */
    double u, v;            /* Parameters, e.g., used for texture mapping. */
    /* Note the parameter's range is determined by the surface's knot vector,
     * i.e., u goes from kvU[orderU-1] to kvU[numU], and likewise for v */
} SurfSample;

#define MAXORDER 20         /* Maximum order allowed (for local array sizes) */

typedef struct NurbSurface {
    /* Number of Points in the U and V directions, respectivly */
    long numU, numV;
    /* Order of the surface in U and V (must be >= 2, < MAXORDER) */
    long orderU, orderV;
    /* Knot vectors, indexed as [0..numU+orderU-1] and [0..numV+orderV-1] */
    double * kvU, * kvV;
    /* Control points, indexed as points[0..numV-1][0..numU-1] */
    /* Note the w values are *premultiplied* with the x, y and z values */
    Point4 ** points;

    /* These fields are added to support subdivision */
    Boolean strV0, strVn,   /* Edge straightness flags for subdivision */
            strU0, strUn;
    Boolean flatV, flatU;   /* Surface flatness flags for subdivision */
    SurfSample c00, c0n,
               cn0, cnn;    /* Corner data structures for subdivision */
} NurbSurface;

extern double SubdivTolerance;  /* Screen space tolerance for subdivision */

#define CHECK( n ) \
    { if (!(n)) { fprintf( stderr, "Ran out of memory\n" ); exit(-1); } }

#define DIVW( rpt, pt ) \
    { (pt)->x = (rpt)->x / (rpt)->w; \
      (pt)->y = (rpt)->y / (rpt)->w; \
      (pt)->z = (rpt)->z / (rpt)->w; }

/* Function prototypes */

extern void DrawSubdivision( NurbSurface * );
extern void DrawEvaluation( NurbSurface * );

extern long FindBreakPoint( double u, double * kv, long m, long k );
extern void AllocNurb( NurbSurface *, double *, double * );
extern void CloneNurb( NurbSurface *, NurbSurface * );
extern void FreeNurb( NurbSurface * );
extern void RefineSurface( NurbSurface *, NurbSurface *, Boolean );

extern void CalcPoint( double, double, NurbSurface *, Point3 *, Point3 *, Point3 * );
```

◇ **drawing.h** ◇

```
/*
 * These routines need to be provided by your rendering package.
 */

extern void FastTriangle( SurfSample *, SurfSample *, SurfSample * );
extern void SlowTriangle( SurfSample *, SurfSample *, SurfSample * );

extern void (*DrawTriangle)( SurfSample *, SurfSample *, SurfSample * );

extern void ScreenProject( Point4 *, Point3 * );
```

◇ **NurbEval.c** ◇

```
/*
 * NurbEval.c - Code for evaluating NURB surfaces.
 *
 * John Peterson
 */

#include <stdlib.h>
#include <stdio.h>
#include <math.h>

#include "nurbs.h"
#include "drawing.h"


/*
 * Return the current knot the parameter u is less than or equal to.
 * Find this "breakpoint" allows the evaluation routines to concentrate on
 * only those control points actually affecting the curve around u.
 *
 *      m    is the number of points on the curve (or surface direction)
 *      k    is the order of the curve (or surface direction)
 *      kv   is the knot vector ([0..m+k-1]) to find the break point in
 */

long
FindBreakPoint( double u, double * kv, long m, long k )
{
    long i;

    if (u == kv[m+1])    /* Special case for closed interval */
        return m;

    i = m + k;
    while ((u < kv[i]) && (i > 0))
        i--;
    return( i );
```

```
}
    .
/*
 * Compute Bi,k(u), for i = 0..k.
 *  u           is the parameter of the spline to find the basis functions for
 *  brkPoint    is the start of the knot interval ("segment")
 *  kv          is the knot vector
 *  k           is the order of the curve
 *  bvals       is the array of returned basis values
 *
 * (From Bartels, Beatty & Barsky, p. 387)
 */

static void
BasisFunctions( double u, long brkPoint, double * kv, long k, double * bvals )
{
    register long r, s, i;
    register double omega;

    bvals[0] = 1.0;
    for (r = 2; r <= k; r++)
    {
        i = brkPoint - r + 1;
        bvals[r - 1] = 0.0;
        for (s = r-2; s >= 0; s--)
        {
            i++;
            if (i < 0)
                omega = 0;
            else
                omega = (u - kv[i]) / (kv[i + r - 1] - kv[i]);
            bvals[s + 1] = bvals[s + 1] + (1 - omega) * bvals[s];
            bvals[s] = omega * bvals[s];
        }
    }
}


/*
 * Compute derivatives of the basis functions Bi,k(u)'
 */
static void
BasisDerivatives( double u, long brkPoint, double * kv, long k, double * dvals )
{
    register long s, i;
    register double omega, knotScale;

    BasisFunctions( u, brkPoint, kv, k - 1, dvals );

    dvals[k-1] = 0.0;           /* BasisFunctions misses this */

    knotScale = kv[brkPoint + 1L] - kv[brkPoint];

    i = brkPoint - k + 1L;
```

```
    for (s = k - 2L; s >= 0L; s--)
    {
        i++;
        omega = knotScale * ((double)(k-1L)) / (kv[i+k-1L] - kv[i]);
        dvals[s + 1L] += -omega * dvals[s];
        dvals[s] *= omega;
    }
}


/*
 * Calculate a point p on NurbSurface n at a specific u, v using the tensor product.
 * If utan and vtan are not nil, compute the u and v tangents as well.
 *
 * Note the valid parameter range for u and v is
 * (kvU[orderU] <= u < kvU[numU]), (kvV[orderV] <= v < kvV[numV])
 */

void
CalcPoint(double u, double v, NurbSurface * n,
          Point3 * p, Point3 * utan, Point3 * vtan)
{
    register long i, j, ri, rj;
    register Point4 * cp;
    register double tmp;
    register double wsqrdiv;
    long ubrkPoint, ufirst;
    double bu[MAXORDER], buprime[MAXORDER];
    long vbrkPoint, vfirst;
    double bv[MAXORDER], bvprime[MAXORDER];
    Point4 r, rutan, rvtan;

    r.x = 0.0;
    r.y = 0.0;
    r.z = 0.0;
    r.w = 0.0;

    rutan = r;
    rvtan = r;

    /* Evaluate non-uniform basis functions (and derivatives) */

    ubrkPoint = FindBreakPoint( u, n->kvU, n->numU-1, n->orderU );
    ufirst = ubrkPoint - n->orderU + 1;
    BasisFunctions( u, ubrkPoint, n->kvU, n->orderU, bu );
    if (utan)
        BasisDerivatives( u, ubrkPoint, n->kvU, n->orderU, buprime );

    vbrkPoint = FindBreakPoint( v, n->kvV, n->numV-1, n->orderV );
    vfirst = vbrkPoint - n->orderV + 1;
    BasisFunctions( v, vbrkPoint, n->kvV, n->orderV, bv );
    if (vtan)
        BasisDerivatives( v, vbrkPoint, n->kvV, n->orderV, bvprime );
```

```
/* Weigh control points against the basis functions */

for (i = 0; i < n->orderV; i++)
    for (j = 0; j < n->orderU; j++)
    {
        ri = n->orderV - 1L - i;
        rj = n->orderU - 1L - j;

        tmp = bu[rj] * bv[ri];
        cp = &( n->points[i+vfirst][j+ufirst] );
        r.x += cp->x * tmp;
        r.y += cp->y * tmp;
        r.z += cp->z * tmp;
        r.w += cp->w * tmp;

        if (utan)
        {
            tmp = buprime[rj] * bv[ri];
            rutan.x += cp->x * tmp;
            rutan.y += cp->y * tmp;
            rutan.z += cp->z * tmp;
            rutan.w += cp->w * tmp;
        }
        if (vtan)
        {
            tmp = bu[rj] * bvprime[ri];
            rvtan.x += cp->x * tmp;
            rvtan.y += cp->y * tmp;
            rvtan.z += cp->z * tmp;
            rvtan.w += cp->w * tmp;
        }
    }

/* Project tangents, using the quotient rule for differentiation */

wsqrdiv = 1.0 / (r.w * r.w);
if (utan)
{
    utan->x = (r.w * rutan.x - rutan.w * r.x) * wsqrdiv;
    utan->y = (r.w * rutan.y - rutan.w * r.y) * wsqrdiv;
    utan->z = (r.w * rutan.z - rutan.w * r.z) * wsqrdiv;
}
if (vtan)
{
    vtan->x = (r.w * rvtan.x - rvtan.w * r.x) * wsqrdiv;
    vtan->y = (r.w * rvtan.y - rvtan.w * r.y) * wsqrdiv;
    vtan->z = (r.w * rvtan.z - rvtan.w * r.z) * wsqrdiv;
}

p->x = r.x / r.w;
p->y = r.y / r.w;
p->z = r.z / r.w;
}
```

```
/*
 * Draw a mesh of points by evaluating the surface at evenly spaced
 * points.
 */
void
DrawEvaluation( NurbSurface * n )
{
    Point3 p, utan, vtan;
    register long i, j;
    register double u, v, d;
    SurfSample ** pts, *sptr;

    long Granularity = 10;   /* Controls the number of steps in u and v */

    /* Allocate storage for the grid of points generated */

    CHECK( pts = (SurfSample**) malloc( (Granularity+1L) * sizeof( SurfSample* )));
    CHECK( pts[0] = (SurfSample*) malloc( (Granularity+1L)*(Granularity+1L)
                  * sizeof( SurfSample )));
    for (i = 1; i <= Granularity; i++)
        pts[i] = &(pts[0][(Granularity+1L) * i]);
    sptr = pts[0];

    /* Compute points on curve */

    for (i = 0; i <= Granularity; i++)
    {
        v = ((double) i / (double) Granularity)
            * (n->kvV[n->numV] - n->kvV[n->orderV-1])
            + n->kvV[n->orderV-1];

        for (j = 0; j <= Granularity; j++)
        {
            u = ((double) j / (double) Granularity)
                * (n->kvU[n->numU] - n->kvU[n->orderU-1])
                + n->kvU[n->orderU-1];

            CalcPoint( u, v, n, &(pts[i][j].point), &utan, &vtan );
            (void) V3Cross( &utan, &vtan, &p );
            d = V3Length( &p );
            if (d != 0.0)
            {
                p.x /= d;
                p.y /= d;
                p.z /= d;
            }
            else
            {
                p.x = 0;
                p.y = 0;
                p.z = 0;
            }
```

```
                pts[i][j].normLen = d;
                pts[i][j].normal = p;
                pts[i][j].u = u;
                pts[i][j].v = v;
            }
    }

    /* Draw the grid */

    for (i = 0; i < Granularity; i++)
        for (j = 0; j < Granularity; j++)
        {
            (*DrawTriangle)( &pts[i][j], &pts[i+1][j+1], &pts[i+1][j] );
            (*DrawTriangle)( &pts[i][j], &pts[i][j+1],   &pts[i+1][j+1] );
        }

    free( pts[0] );
    free( pts );
}
```

◇ **NurbUtils.c** ◇

```
/*
 * NurbUtils.c - Code for Allocating, freeing, and copying NURB surfaces.
 *
 * John Peterson
 */

#include <stdlib.h>
#include <stdio.h>
#include <math.h>

#include "nurbs.h"

/*
 * Allocate memory for a NURB (assumes numU, numV, orderU
 * and orderV have been set).  If ukv or vkv are not NIL, they
 * are assumed to be pointers to valid knot vectors.
 */

void
AllocNurb( NurbSurface * n, double * ukv, double * vkv )
{
    long i;

    if (! ukv)
        CHECK( n->kvU = (double *) malloc( (n->numU + n->orderU) * sizeof( double ) ) )
    else
        n->kvU = ukv;
    if (! vkv)
```

```
        CHECK( n->kvV = (double *) malloc( (n->numV + n->orderV) * sizeof( double ) ) )
    else
        n->kvV = vkv;

    CHECK( n->points = (Point4 **) malloc( (long) n->numV
                                    * (long) sizeof( Point4 * ) ) );
    for (i = 0; i < n->numV; i++)
        CHECK( n->points[i] = (Point4 *) malloc( (long) n->numU
                                    * (long) sizeof( Point4 )) );
}


/*
 * Release storage for a patch
 */

void
FreeNurb( NurbSurface * n )
{
    long i;

    if (n->kvU) free( n->kvU );
    n->kvU = NULL;
    if (n->kvV) free( n->kvV );
    n->kvV = NULL;
    for (i = 0; i < n->numV; i++)
        free( n->points[i] );
    free( n->points );
}


/*
 * Clone a nurb (deep copy)
 */

void
CloneNurb( NurbSurface * src, NurbSurface * dst )
{
    long i, j;
    double * srcp, *dstp;

    *dst = *src;            /* Copy fields that don't change */
    dst->kvU = NULL;
    dst->kvV = NULL;        /* So they get allocated */
    dst->points = NULL;

    AllocNurb( dst, NULL, NULL );

    /* Copy kv's */
    srcp = src->kvU;
    dstp = dst->kvU;
    for (i = 0; i < src->numU + src->orderU; i++)
        *dstp++ = *srcp++;

    srcp = src->kvV;
```

```
        dstp = dst->kvV;
        for (i = 0; i < src->numV + src->orderV; i++)
            *dstp++ = *srcp++;

        /* Copy control points */
        for (i = 0; i < src->numV; i++)
            for (j = 0; j < src->numU; j++)
                dst->points[i][j] = src->points[i][j];
}
```


◇   NurbRefine.c   ◇

```
/*
 * NurbRefine.c - Given a refined knot vector, add control points to a surface.
 *
 * John Peterson
 */

#include <stdlib.h>
#include <stdio.h>
#include <math.h>

#include "nurbs.h"

/*
 * Given the original knot vector ukv, and a new knot vector vkv, compute
 * the "alpha matrix" used to generate the corresponding new control points.
 * This routines allocates the alpha matrix if it isn't allocated already.
 *
 * This is from Bartels, Beatty & Barsky, p. 407
 */
static void
CalcAlpha( double * ukv, double * wkv, long m, long n, long k, double *** alpha )
{
    register long i, j;
    long brkPoint, r, rm1, last, s;
    double omega;
    double aval[MAXORDER];

    if (! *alpha)           /* Must allocate alpha */
    {
        CHECK( *alpha = (double **) malloc( (long) ((k+1) * sizeof( double * ))) );
        for (i = 0; i <= k; i++)
            CHECK( (*alpha)[i] = (double *) malloc( (long) ((m + n + 1)
                                                   * sizeof( double ))) );
    }

    for (j = 0; j <= m + n; j++)
    {
        brkPoint = FindBreakPoint( wkv[j], ukv, m, k );
        aval[0] = 1.0;
```

```
        for (r = 2; r <= k; r++)
        {
            rm1 = r - 1;
            last = MIN( rm1, brkPoint );
            i = brkPoint - last;
            if (last < rm1)
                aval[last] = aval[last] * (wkv[j + r - 1] - ukv[i])
                                / (ukv[i + r - 1] - ukv[i]);
            else
                aval[last] = 0.0;

            for (s = last - 1; s >= 0; s-- )
            {
                i++;
                omega = (wkv[j + r - 1] - ukv[i]) / (ukv[i + r - 1] - ukv[i]);
                aval[s + 1] = aval[s+1] + (1 - omega) * aval[s];
                aval[s] = omega * aval[s];
            }
        }
        last = MIN( k - 1, brkPoint );
        for (i = 0; i <= k; i++)
            (*alpha)[i][j] = 0.0;
        for (s = 0; s <= last; s++)
            (*alpha)[last - s][j] = aval[s];
    }
}


/*
 * Apply the alpha matrix computed above to the rows (or columns)
 * of the surface.  If dirflag is true do the U's (row), else do V's (col).
 */
void
RefineSurface( NurbSurface * src, NurbSurface * dest, Boolean dirflag )
{
    register long i, j, out;
    register Point4 * dp, * sp;
    long i1, brkPoint, maxj, maxout;
    register double tmp;
    double ** alpha = NULL;

    /* Compute the alpha matrix and indexing variables for the requested direction */

    if (dirflag)
    {
        CalcAlpha( src->kvU, dest->kvU, src->numU - 1, dest->numU - src->numU,
                src->orderU, &alpha );
        maxj = dest->numU;
        maxout = src->numV;
    }
    else
    {
        CalcAlpha( src->kvV, dest->kvV, src->numV - 1, dest->numV - src->numV,
                src->orderV, &alpha );
```

```
        maxj = dest->numV;
        maxout = dest->numU;
    }

    /* Apply the alpha matrix to the original control points, generating new ones */

    for (out = 0; out < maxout; out++)
        for (j = 0; j < maxj; j++)
        {
            if (dirflag)
            {
                dp = &(dest->points[out][j]);
                brkPoint = FindBreakPoint( dest->kvU[j], src->kvU,
                                           src->numU-1, src->orderU );
                i1 = MAX( brkPoint - src->orderU + 1, 0 );
                sp = &(src->points[out][i1]);
            } else {
                dp = &(dest->points[j][out]);
                brkPoint = FindBreakPoint( dest->kvV[j], src->kvV,
                                           src->numV-1, src->orderV );
                i1 = MAX( brkPoint - src->orderV + 1, 0 );
                sp = &(src->points[i1][out]);
            }
            dp->x = 0.0;
            dp->y = 0.0;
            dp->z = 0.0;
            dp->w = 0.0;
            for (i = i1; i <= brkPoint; i++)
            {
                tmp = alpha[i - i1][j];
                sp = (dirflag ? &(src->points[out][i]) : &(src->points[i][out]) );
                dp->x += tmp * sp->x;
                dp->y += tmp * sp->y;
                dp->z += tmp * sp->z;
                dp->w += tmp * sp->w;
            }
        }

    /* Free up the alpha matrix */
    for (i = 0; i <= (dirflag ? src->orderU : src->orderV); i++)
        free( alpha[i] );
    free( alpha );
}
```

◇   **NurbSubdiv.c**   ◇

```
/*
 * NurbSubdiv.c - Perform adaptive subdivision on a NURB surface.
 *
 * John Peterson
 *
```

```
     */

#include <stdlib.h>
#include <stdio.h>
#include <math.h>

#include "nurbs.h"
#include "drawing.h"

#define EPSILON 0.0000001    /* Used to determine when things are too small. */
#define DIVPT( p, dn ) { ((p).x) /= (dn); ((p).y) /= (dn); ((p).z) /= (dn); }

double SubdivTolerance;       /* Size, in pixels of facets produced */

#define maxV(surf) ((surf)->numV-1L)
#define maxU(surf) ((surf)->numU-1L)

/*
 * Split a knot vector at the center, by adding multiplicity k knots near
 * the middle of the parameter range.  Tries to start with an existing knot,
 * but will add a new knot value if there's nothing in "the middle" (e.g.,
 * a Bezier curve).
 */
static long
SplitKV( double * srckv,
         double ** destkv,
         long * splitPt,    /* Where the knot interval is split */
         long m, long k )
{
    long i, last;
    long middex, extra, same;   /* "middex" ==> "middle index" */
    double midVal;

    extra = 0L;
    last = (m + k);

    middex = last / 2;
    midVal = srckv[middex];

    /* Search forward and backward to see if multiple knot is already there */

    i = middex+1L;
    same = 1L;
    while ((i < last) && (srckv[i] == midVal)) {
        i++;
        same++;
    }

    i = middex-1L;
    while ((i > 0L) && (srckv[i] == midVal)) {
        i--;
        middex--;              /* middex is start of multiple knot */
        same++;
```

```
    }

    if (i <= 0L)              /* No knot in middle, must create it */
    {
        midVal = (srckv[0L] + srckv[last]) / 2.0;
        middex = last / 2L;
        while (srckv[middex + 1L] < midVal)
            middex++;
        same = 0L;
    }

    extra = k - same;
    CHECK( *destkv = (double *) malloc( (long) (sizeof( double )
                                    * (m+k+extra+1L) ) ) );

    if (same < k)             /* Must add knots */
    {
        for (i = 0L; i <= middex; i++)
            (*destkv)[i] = srckv[i];

        for (i = middex+1L; i <= middex+extra; i++)
            (*destkv)[i] = midVal;

        for (i = middex + k - same + 1L; i <= m + k + extra; i++)
            (*destkv)[i] = srckv[i - extra];
    }
    else
    {
        for (i = 0L; i <= m + k; i++)
        (*destkv)[i] = srckv[i];
    }

    *splitPt = (extra < k) ? middex - 1L : middex;
    return( extra );
}

/*
 * Given a line defined by firstPt and lastPt, project midPt onto
 * that line.  Used for fixing "cracks".
 */
static void
ProjectToLine( Point3 * firstPt, Point3 * lastPt, Point3 * midPt )
{
    Point3 base, v0, vm;
    double fraction, denom;

    base = *firstPt;

    (void) V3Sub( lastPt, &base, &v0 );
    (void) V3Sub( midPt, &base, &vm );

    denom = V3SquaredLength( &v0 );
    fraction = (denom == 0.0) ? 0.0 : (V3Dot( &v0, &vm ) / denom);
```

```
        midPt->x = base.x + fraction * v0.x;
        midPt->y = base.y + fraction * v0.y;
        midPt->z = base.z + fraction * v0.z;
}


/*
 * If a normal has collapsed to zero (normLen == 0.0) then try
 * and fix it by looking at its neighbors.  If all the neighbors
 * are sick, then re-compute them from the plane they form.
 * If that fails too, then we give up...
 */
static void
FixNormals( SurfSample * s0, SurfSample * s1, SurfSample * s2 )
{
    Boolean goodnorm;
    long i, j, ok;
    double dist;
    SurfSample * V[3];
    Point3 norm;

    V[0] = s0; V[1] = s1; V[2] = s2;

    /* Find a reasonable normal */
    for (ok = 0, goodnorm = FALSE;
        (ok < 3L) && !(goodnorm = (V[ok]->normLen > 0.0)); ok++);

    if (! goodnorm)      /* All provided normals are zilch, try and invent one */
    {
        norm.x = 0.0; norm.y = 0.0; norm.z = 0.0;

        for (i = 0; i < 3L; i++)
        {
            j = (i + 1L) % 3L;
            norm.x += (V[i]->point.y - V[j]->point.y) * (V[i]->point.z + V[j]->point.z);
            norm.y += (V[i]->point.z - V[j]->point.z) * (V[i]->point.x + V[j]->point.x);
            norm.z += (V[i]->point.x - V[j]->point.x) * (V[i]->point.y + V[j]->point.y);
        }
        dist = V3Length( &norm );
        if (dist == 0.0)
            return;                 /* This sucker's hopeless... */

        DIVPT( norm, dist );

        for (i = 0; i < 3; i++)
        {
            V[i]->normal = norm;
            V[i]->normLen = dist;
        }
    }
    else            /* Replace a sick normal with a healthy one nearby */
    {
        for (i = 0; i < 3; i++)
```

```
                    if ((i != ok) && (V[i]->normLen == 0.0))
                        V[i]->normal = V[ok]->normal;
        }
        return;
    }


    /*
     * Normalize the normal in a sample.  If it's degenerate,
     * flag it as such by setting the normLen to 0.0
     */
    static void
    AdjustNormal( SurfSample * samp )
    {
        /* If it's not degenerate, do the normalization now */
        samp->normLen = V3Length( &(samp->normal) );

        if (samp->normLen < EPSILON)
            samp->normLen = 0.0;
        else
            DIVPT( (samp->normal), samp->normLen );
    }


    /*
     * Compute the normal of a corner point of a mesh.  The
     * base is the value of the point at the corner, indU and indV
     * are the mesh indices of that point (either 0 or numU|numV).
     */
    static void
    GetNormal( NurbSurface * n, long indV, long indU )
    {
        Point3 tmpL, tmpR;   /* "Left" and "Right" of the base point */
        SurfSample * crnr;

        if ( (indU && indV) || ((! indU) && (!indV)) )
        {
            if (indU)
                crnr = &(n->cnn);
            else
                crnr = &(n->c00);
            DIVW( &(n->points[indV][(indU ? (indU-1L) : 1L)]), &tmpL );
            DIVW( &(n->points[(indV ? (indV-1L) : 1L)][indU]), &tmpR );
        }
        else
        {
            if (indU)
                crnr = &(n->c0n);
            else
                crnr = &(n->cn0);
            DIVW( &(n->points[indV][(indU ? (indU-1L) : 1L)]), &tmpR );
            DIVW( &(n->points[(indV ? (indV-1L) : 1L)][indU]), &tmpL );
        }

        (void) V3Sub( &tmpL, &(crnr->point), &tmpL );
```

```
        (void) V3Sub( &tmpR, &(crnr->point), &tmpR );
        (void) V3Cross( &tmpL, &tmpR, &(crnr->normal) );
    AdjustNormal( crnr );
}


/*
 * Build the new corners in the two new surfaces, computing both
 * point on the surface along with the normal.  Prevent cracks that may occur.
 */
static void
MakeNewCorners( NurbSurface * parent,
                NurbSurface * kid0,
                NurbSurface * kid1,
                Boolean dirflag )
{
    DIVW( &(kid0->points[maxV(kid0)][maxU(kid0)]), &(kid0->cnn.point) );
    GetNormal( kid0, maxV(kid0), maxU(kid0) );

    if (dirflag)
    {
        kid0->strUn = FALSE;      /* Must re-test new edge straightness */

        DIVW( &(kid0->points[0L][maxU(kid0)]), &(kid0->c0n.point) );
        GetNormal( kid0, 0L, maxU(kid0) );
        /*
         * Normals must be re-calculated for kid1 in case the surface
         * was split at a c1 (or c0!) discontinuity
         */
        kid1->c00.point = kid0->c0n.point;
        GetNormal( kid1, 0L, 0L );
        kid1->cn0.point = kid0->cnn.point;
        GetNormal( kid1, maxV(kid1), 0L );

        /*
         * Prevent cracks from forming by forcing the points on the seam to
         * lie along any straight edges.  (Must do this BEFORE finding normals)
         */
        if (parent->strV0)
           ProjectToLine( &(parent->c00.point),
                          &(parent->c0n.point),
                          &(kid0->c0n.point) );
        if (parent->strVn)
           ProjectToLine( &(parent->cn0.point),
                          &(parent->cnn.point),
                          &(kid0->cnn.point) );

        kid1->c00.point = kid0->c0n.point;
        kid1->cn0.point = kid0->cnn.point;
        kid1->strU0 = FALSE;
    }
    else
    {
        kid0->strVn = FALSE;
```

```
            DIVW( &(kid0->points[maxV(kid0)][0]), &(kid0->cn0.point) );
            GetNormal( kid0, maxV(kid0), 0L );
            kid1->c00.point = kid0->cn0.point;
            GetNormal( kid1, 0L, 0L );
            kid1->c0n.point = kid0->cnn.point;
            GetNormal( kid1, 0L, maxU(kid1) );

            if (parent->strU0)
                ProjectToLine( &(parent->c00.point),
                               &(parent->cn0.point),
                               &(kid0->cn0.point) );
            if (parent->strUn)
                ProjectToLine( &(parent->c0n.point),
                               &(parent->cnn.point),
                               &(kid0->cnn.point) );

            kid1->c00.point = kid0->cn0.point;
            kid1->c0n.point = kid0->cnn.point;
            kid1->strV0 = FALSE;
        }
}


/*
 * Split a surface into two halves.  First inserts multiplicity k knots
 * in the center of the parametric range.  After refinement, the two
 * resulting surfaces are copied into separate data structures.  If the
 * parent surface had straight edges, the points of the children are
 * projected onto those edges.
 */
static void
SplitSurface( NurbSurface * parent,
              NurbSurface * kid0, NurbSurface * kid1,
              Boolean dirflag )      /* If true subdivided in U, else in V */
{
    NurbSurface tmp;
    double * newkv;
    long i, j, splitPt;

    /*
     * Add a multiplicty k knot to the knot vector in the direction
     * specified by dirflag, and refine the surface.  This creates two
     * adjacent surfaces with c0 discontinuity at the seam.
     */

    tmp = *parent;      /* Copy order, # of points, etc. */
    if (dirflag)
    {
        tmp.numU = parent->numU + SplitKV( parent->kvU,
                                           &newkv,
                                           &splitPt,
                                           maxU(parent),
                                           parent->orderU );
```

```
        AllocNurb( &tmp, newkv, NULL );
        for (i = 0L; i < tmp.numV + tmp.orderV; i++)
            tmp.kvV[i] = parent->kvV[i];
    }
    else
    {
        tmp.numV = parent->numV + SplitKV( parent->kvV,
                                           &newkv,
                                           &splitPt,
                                           maxV(parent),
                                           parent->orderV );
        AllocNurb( &tmp, NULL, newkv );
        for (i = 0L; i < tmp.numU + tmp.orderU; i++)
            tmp.kvU[i] = parent->kvU[i];
    }
    RefineSurface( parent, &tmp, dirflag );

    /*
     * Build the two child surfaces, and copy the data from the refined
     * version of the parent (tmp) into the two children
     */

    /* First half */

    *kid0 = *parent;    /* copy various edge flags and orders */

    kid0->numU = dirflag ? splitPt+1L : parent->numU;
    kid0->numV = dirflag ? parent->numV : splitPt+1L;
    kid0->kvU = kid0->kvV = NULL;
    kid0->points = NULL;
    AllocNurb( kid0, NULL, NULL );

    for (i = 0L; i < kid0->numV; i++)    /* Copy the point and kv data */
        for (j = 0L; j < kid0->numU; j++)
            kid0->points[i][j] = tmp.points[i][j];
    for (i = 0L; i < kid0->orderU + kid0->numU; i++)
        kid0->kvU[i] = tmp.kvU[i];
    for (i = 0L; i < kid0->orderV + kid0->numV; i++)
        kid0->kvV[i] = tmp.kvV[i];

    /* Second half */

    splitPt++;
    *kid1 = *parent;

    kid1->numU = dirflag ? tmp.numU - splitPt : parent->numU;
    kid1->numV = dirflag ? parent->numV : tmp.numV - splitPt;
    kid1->kvU = kid1->kvV = NULL;
    kid1->points = NULL;
    AllocNurb( kid1, NULL, NULL );

    for (i = 0L; i < kid1->numV; i++)    /* Copy the point and kv data */
        for (j = 0L; j < kid1->numU; j++)
```

```
                kid1->points[i][j]
                    = tmp.points[dirflag ? i: (i + splitPt) ][dirflag ? (j + splitPt) : j];
        for (i = 0L; i < kid1->orderU + kid1->numU; i++)
            kid1->kvU[i] = tmp.kvU[dirflag ? (i + splitPt) : i];
        for (i = 0L; i < kid1->orderV + kid1->numV; i++)
            kid1->kvV[i] = tmp.kvV[dirflag ? i : (i + splitPt)];

        /* Construct new corners on the boundary between the two kids */
        MakeNewCorners( parent, kid0, kid1, dirflag );

        FreeNurb( &tmp );        /* Get rid of refined parent */
}


/*
 * Test if a particular row or column of control points in a mesh
 * is "straight" with respect to a particular tolerance.  Returns true
 * if it is.
 */

#define GETPT( i )  (( dirflag ? &(n->points[crvInd][i]) : &(n->points[i][crvInd]) ))

static Boolean
IsCurveStraight( NurbSurface * n,
                 double tolerance,
                 long crvInd,
                 Boolean dirflag )  /* If true, test in U direction, else test in V */
{
    Point3 p, vec, prod;
    Point3 cp, e0;
    long i, last;
    double linelen, dist;

    /* Special case: lines are automatically straight. */
    if ((dirflag ? n->numU : n->numV) == 2L)
        return( TRUE );

    last = (dirflag ? n->numU : n->numV) - 1L;
    ScreenProject( GETPT( 0L ), &e0 );

    /* Form an initial line to test the other points against (skipping degen lines) */

    linelen = 0.0;
    for (i = last; (i > 0L) && (linelen < EPSILON); i--)
    {
        ScreenProject( GETPT( i ), &cp );
        (void) V3Sub( &cp, &e0, &vec );

        linelen = sqrt( V3SquaredLength( &vec ) );
    }

    DIVPT( vec, linelen );

    if (linelen > EPSILON)       /* If no non-degenerate lines found, it's all degen */
```

```
        for (i = 1L; i <= last; i++)
        {
            /* The cross product of the vector defining the
             * initial line with the vector of the current point
             * gives the distance to the line. */
            ScreenProject( GETPT( i ), &cp );
            (void) V3Sub( &cp,&e0,&p );

            (void) V3Cross( &p, &vec, &prod );
            dist = V3Length( &prod );

            if (dist > tolerance)
                return( FALSE );
        }

    return( TRUE );
}


/*
 * Check to see if a surface is flat.  Tests are only performed on edges and
 * directions that aren't already straight.  If an edge is flagged as straight
 * (from the parent surface) it is assumed it will stay that way.
 */
static Boolean
TestFlat( NurbSurface * n, double tolerance )
{
    long i;
    Boolean straight;
    Point3 cp00, cp0n, cpn0, cpnn, planeEqn;
    double dist,d ;

    /* Check edge straightness */

    if (! n->strU0)
        n->strU0 = IsCurveStraight( n, tolerance, 0L, FALSE );
    if (! n->strUn)
        n->strUn = IsCurveStraight( n, tolerance, maxU(n), FALSE );
    if (! n->strV0)
        n->strV0 = IsCurveStraight( n, tolerance, 0L, TRUE );
    if (! n->strVn)
        n->strVn = IsCurveStraight( n, tolerance, maxV(n), TRUE );

    /* Test to make sure control points are straight in U and V */

    straight = TRUE;
    if ( (! n->flatU) && (n->strV0) && (n->strVn) )
        for (i = 1L;
             (i < maxV(n)) && (straight = IsCurveStraight( n, tolerance, i, TRUE ));
             i++);

    if (straight && n->strV0 && n->strVn)
        n->flatU = TRUE;
```

```
        straight = TRUE;
        if ( (! n->flatV) && (n->strU0) && (n->strUn) )
            for (i = 1L;
                    (i < maxU(n)) && (straight = IsCurveStraight( n, tolerance, i, FALSE ));
                    i++);

        if (straight && n->strU0 && n->strUn)
            n->flatV = TRUE;

        if ( (! n->flatV) || (! n->flatU) )
            return( FALSE );

        /* The surface can pass the above tests but still be twisted. */

        ScreenProject( &(n->points[0L][0L]),              &cp00 );
        ScreenProject( &(n->points[0L][maxU(n)]),         &cp0n );
        ScreenProject( &(n->points[maxV(n)][0L]),         &cpn0 );
        ScreenProject( &(n->points[maxV(n)][maxU(n)]),   &cpnn );

        (void) V3Sub( &cp0n, &cp00, &cp0n );     /* Make edges into vectors */

        (void) V3Sub( &cpn0, &cp00, &cpn0 );

        /*
         * Compute the plane equation from two adjacent sides, and
         * measure the distance from the far point to the plane.  If it's
         * larger than tolerance, the surface is twisted.
         */

        (void) V3Cross( &cpn0, &cp0n, &planeEqn );

        (void) V3Normalize( &planeEqn );     /* Normalize to keep adds in sync w/ mults */

        d = V3Dot( &planeEqn, &cp00 );
        dist = fabs( V3Dot( &planeEqn, &cpnn ) - d );

        if ( dist > tolerance ) /* Surface is twisted */
            return( FALSE );
        else
            return( TRUE );
}


/*
 * Turn a sufficiently flat surface into triangles.
 */
static void
EmitTriangles( NurbSurface * n )
{
    Point3 vecnn, vec0n;            /* Diagonal vectors */
    double len2nn, len20n;         /* Diagonal lengths squared */
    double u0, un, v0, vn;         /* Texture coords; */

    /*
```

```
             * Measure the distance along the two diagonals to decide the best
             * way to cut the rectangle into triangles.
             */

            (void) V3Sub( &n->c00.point, &n->cnn.point, &vecnn );
            (void) V3Sub( &n->c0n.point, &n->cn0.point, &vec0n );

            len2nn = V3SquaredLength( &vecnn ); /* Use these to reject triangles */
            len20n = V3SquaredLength( &vec0n ); /* that are too small to render */

            if (MAX(len2nn, len20n) < EPSILON)
                return;                         /* Triangles are too small to render */

            /*
             * Assign the texture coordinates
             */
            u0 = n->kvU[n->orderU-1L];
            un = n->kvU[n->numU];
            v0 = n->kvV[n->orderV-1L];
            vn = n->kvV[n->numV];
            n->c00.u = u0; n->c00.v = v0;
            n->c0n.u = un; n->c0n.v = v0;
            n->cn0.u = u0; n->cn0.v = vn;
            n->cnn.u = un; n->cnn.v = vn;

            /*
             * If any normals are sick, fix them now.
             */
            if ((n->c00.normLen == 0.0) || (n->cnn.normLen == 0.0) || (n->cn0.normLen == 0.0))
                FixNormals( &(n->c00), &(n->cnn), &(n->cn0) );
            if (n->c0n.normLen == 0.0)
                FixNormals( &(n->c00), &(n->c0n), &(n->cnn) );

            if ( len2nn < len20n )
            {
                (*DrawTriangle)( &n->c00, &n->cnn, &n->cn0 );
                (*DrawTriangle)( &n->c00, &n->c0n, &n->cnn );
            }
            else
            {
                (*DrawTriangle)( &n->c0n, &n->cnn, &n->cn0 );
                (*DrawTriangle)( &n->c0n, &n->cn0, &n->c00 );
            }
}


/*
 * The recursive subdivision algorithm.  Test if the surface is flat.
 * If so, split it into triangles.  Otherwise, split it into two halves,
 * and invoke the procedure on each half.
 */
static void
DoSubdivision( NurbSurface * n, double tolerance, Boolean dirflag, long level )
{
```

```
        NurbSurface left, right;    /* ...or top or bottom. Whatever spins your wheels. */

    if (TestFlat( n, tolerance ))
    {
        EmitTriangles( n );
    }
    else
    {
        if ( ((! n->flatV) && (! n->flatU)) || ((n->flatV) && (n->flatU)) )
            dirflag = ! dirflag;    /* If twisted or curved in both directions, */
        else                        /* then alternate subdivision direction */
        {
            if (n->flatU)           /* Only split in directions that aren't flat */
                dirflag = FALSE;
            else
                dirflag = TRUE;
        }
        SplitSurface( n, &left, &right, dirflag );
        DoSubdivision( &left, tolerance, dirflag, level + 1L );
        DoSubdivision( &right, tolerance, dirflag, level + 1L );
        FreeNurb( &left );
        FreeNurb( &right );         /* Deallocate surfaces made by SplitSurface */
    }
}


/*
 * Main entry point for subdivision */
void
DrawSubdivision( NurbSurface * surf )
{
    surf->flatV = FALSE;
    surf->flatU = FALSE;
    surf->strU0 = FALSE;
    surf->strUn = FALSE;
    surf->strV0 = FALSE;
    surf->strVn = FALSE;

    /*
     * Initialize the projected corners of the surface
     * and the normals.
     */
    DIVW( &(surf->points[0L][0L]),                      &surf->c00.point );
    DIVW( &(surf->points[0L][surf->numU-1L]),           &surf->c0n.point );
    DIVW( &(surf->points[surf->numV-1L][0L]),           &surf->cn0.point );
    DIVW( &(surf->points[surf->numV-1L][surf->numU-1L]), &surf->cnn.point );

    GetNormal( surf, 0L, 0L );
    GetNormal( surf, 0L, maxU(surf) );
    GetNormal( surf, maxV(surf), 0L );
    GetNormal( surf, maxV(surf), maxU(surf) );

    DoSubdivision( surf, SubdivTolerance, TRUE, 0L );
    /* Note surf is deallocated by the subdivision process */
}
```

◇ **Main.c** ◇

```c
#include <stdio.h>
#include <stdlib.h>
#include <math.h>

#include "nurbs.h"
#include "drawing.h"

extern void MakeWindow( void );        /* External system routine to create a window */

void (*DrawTriangle)();                /* Pointer to triangle drawing function */

/* This generates the NURB surface for a torus, centered about the origin */

static NurbSurface *
generateTorus(double majorRadius, double minorRadius)
{
    /* These define the shape of a unit torus centered about the origin. */
    double xvalues[] = { 0.0, -1.0, -1.0, -1.0, 0.0, 1.0, 1.0, 1.0, 0.0 };
    double yvalues[] = { 1.0, 1.0, 0.0, -1.0, -1.0, -1.0, 0.0, 1.0, 1.0 };
    double zvalues[] = { 0.0, 1.0, 1.0, 1.0, 0.0, -1.0, -1.0, -1.0, 0.0 };
    double offsets[] = { -1.0, -1.0, 0.0, 1.0, 1.0, 1.0, 0.0, -1.0, -1.0 };

    /* Piecewise Bezier knot vector for a quadratic curve with four segments */
    long knots[] = { 0, 0, 0, 1, 1, 2, 2, 3, 3, 4, 4, 4 };

    long i, j;

    double r2over2 = sqrt( 2.0 ) / 2.0;
    double weight;

    NurbSurface * torus = (NurbSurface *) malloc( sizeof(NurbSurface) );
    CHECK( torus );

    /* Set up the dimension and orders of the surface */

    torus->numU = 9;        /* A circle is formed from nine points */
    torus->numV = 9;
    torus->orderU = 3;      /* Quadratic in both directions */
    torus->orderV = 3;

    /* After the dimension and orders are set, AllocNurb creates the dynamic
     * storage for the control points and the knot vectors */

    AllocNurb( torus, NULL, NULL );

    for (i = 0; i < 9; i++)
    {
        for (j = 0; j < 9; j++)
        {
            weight = ((j & 1) ? r2over2 : 1.0) * ((i & 1) ? r2over2 : 1.0);
            /* Notice how the weights are pre-multiplied with the x, y and z values */
            torus->points[i][j].x = xvalues[j]
```

```
                                     * (majorRadius + offsets[i] * minorRadius) * weight;
            torus->points[i][j].y = yvalues[j]
                                     * (majorRadius + offsets[i] * minorRadius) * weight;
            torus->points[i][j].z = (zvalues[i] * minorRadius) * weight;
            torus->points[i][j].w = weight;
        }
    }

    /* The knot vectors define piecewise Bezier segments (the same in both U and V). */

    for (i = 0; i < torus->numU + torus->orderU; i++)
        torus->kvU[i] = torus->kvV[i] = (double) knots[i];

    return torus;
}

/* These drawing routines assume a window of around 400x400 pixels */

void
ScreenProject( Point4 * worldPt, Point3 * screenPt )
{
    screenPt->x = worldPt->x / worldPt->w * 100 + 200;
    screenPt->y = worldPt->y / worldPt->w * 100 + 200;
    screenPt->z = worldPt->z / worldPt->w * 100 + 200;
}

static void
LineTriangle( SurfSample * v0, SurfSample * v1, SurfSample * v2 )
{
    MoveTo( (short) (v0->point.x * 100 + 200), (short) (v0->point.y * 100 + 200) );
    LineTo( (short) (v1->point.x * 100 + 200), (short) (v1->point.y * 100 + 200) );
    LineTo( (short) (v2->point.x * 100 + 200), (short) (v2->point.y * 100 + 200) );
    LineTo( (short) (v0->point.x * 100 + 200), (short) (v0->point.y * 100 + 200) );
}

main()
{
    NurbSurface * torus;

    MakeWindow();            /* Create a window on the screen */

    /* Set up the subdivision tolerance (facets span about two pixels) */
    SubdivTolerance = 2.0;

    DrawTriangle = LineTriangle;

    torus = generateTorus( 1.3, 0.3 );

    DrawSubdivision( torus );
/*  DrawEvaluation( torus );   */   /* Alternate drawing method */
}
```

◇ **Bibliography** ◇

(Bartels *et al.* 1987) Richard Bartels, John Beatty, and Brian Barsky. *An Introduction to Splines for Use in Computer Graphics and Geometric Modeling.* Morgan Kaufmann, Los Altos, CA, 1987.

(Farin 1988) Gerald Farin. *Curves and Surfaces for Computer Aided Geometric Design.* Academic Press, Boston, MA, 1988.

(Foley et al. 1990) James Foley, Andries van Dam, Steve Feiner, and John Hughes. *Computer Graphics: Principles and Practice*, 2nd ed. Addison-Wesley, Reading, MA, 1990.

(Heckbert 1990) Paul Heckbert. Generic convex polygon scan conversion and clipping. In Andrew Glassner, editor, *Graphics Gems*, pages 84–86, 667–680. Academic Press, Boston, MA, 1990.

(Rogers and Adams 1990) David F. Rogers and J. Alan Adams. *Mathematical Elements for Computer Graphics*, 2nd ed. McGraw-Hill, New York, 1990.

◇ IV.7

Equations of Cylinders and Cones

Ching-Kuang Shene
Department of Mathematics and Computer Science
Northern Michigan University
Marquette, MI 49855-5340
facs@nmumus.bitnet

Although spheres, cylinders and cones are frequently represented with vector notation, in some cases, we may want to use their equations. Since these are quadric surfaces, their equations share a common form, $\mathbf{x}^T\mathbf{Q}\mathbf{x} = 0$, where $\mathbf{Q}$ is a 4×4 symmetric matrix and $\mathbf{x}^T = [x_1, x_2, x_3, 1]$ (Dresden 1967, Spain 1960). In this Gem, we shall compute $\mathbf{Q}$ for spheres, cylinders, and cones. Since $\mathbf{Q}$ is symmetric, only its upper triangular part will be shown.

Consider a sphere with center $\vec{O} = [o_1, o_2, o_3]^T$ and radius r. Since its equation is $(x_1 - o_1)^2 + (x_2 - o_2)^2 + (x_3 - o_3)^2 - r^2 = 0$, we have

$$\mathbf{Q} = \begin{bmatrix} 1 & 0 & 0 & -o_1 \\ & 1 & 0 & -o_2 \\ & & 1 & -o_3 \\ & & & |\vec{O}|^2 - r^2 \end{bmatrix}$$

Now consider the cylinder case. Let $\vec{X}$ be any point on the cylinder with axis $\vec{A} + t\vec{u}$ and radius r, where $\vec{A} = [a_1, a_2, a_3]^T$, $\vec{u} = [u_1, u_2, u_3]^T$, and $|\vec{u}| = 1$. Since the distance from $\vec{X}$ to the axis of the cylinder is r, we have

$$|\vec{X} - \vec{A}|^2 - [(\vec{X} - \vec{A}) \cdot \vec{u}]^2 = r^2 \tag{1}$$

The first term $|\vec{X} - \vec{A}|^2$ has the following form

$$\begin{bmatrix} 1 & 0 & 0 & -a_1 \\ & 1 & 0 & -a_2 \\ & & 1 & -a_3 \\ & & & |\vec{A}|^2 \end{bmatrix}$$

while the symmetric matrix of the second term, $[(\vec{X} - \vec{A}) \cdot \vec{u}]^2$, is the following:

$$\begin{bmatrix} u_1^2 & u_1u_2 & u_1u_3 & -(\vec{A} \cdot \vec{u})u_1 \\ & u_2^2 & u_2u_3 & -(\vec{A} \cdot \vec{u})u_2 \\ & & u_3^2 & -(\vec{A} \cdot \vec{u})u_3 \\ & & & (\vec{A} \cdot \vec{u})^2 \end{bmatrix}$$

Combining these two matrices and the constant term, we have our final result:

$$\mathbf{Q} = \begin{bmatrix} 1 - u_1^2 & -u_1u_2 & -u_1u_3 & -a_1 + (\vec{A} \cdot \vec{u})u_1 \\ & 1 - u_2^2 & -u_2u_3 & -a_2 + (\vec{A} \cdot \vec{u})u_2 \\ & & 1 - u_3^2 & -a_3 + (\vec{A} \cdot \vec{u})u_3 \\ & & & |\vec{A}|^2 - (\vec{A} \cdot \vec{u})^2 - r^2 \end{bmatrix}$$

Finally, consider a cone with vertex $\vec{V} = [v_1, v_2, v_3]^T$, axis direction $\vec{u} = [u_1, u_2, u_3]^T$, $|\vec{u}| = 1$, and cone angle α. For any point $\vec{X}$ on the cone that is not the vertex, the vector $\vec{X} - \vec{V}$ and the axis direction $\vec{u}$ make an angle of α or $\pi - \alpha$. Therefore, we have

$$\frac{\vec{X} - \vec{V}}{|\vec{X} - \vec{V}|} \cdot \vec{u} = \pm \cos \alpha \tag{2}$$

Squaring and rearranging gives

$$(\vec{X} \cdot \vec{u} - \vec{V} \cdot \vec{u})^2 - \cos^2\alpha(\vec{X} - \vec{V}) \cdot (\vec{X} - \vec{V}) = 0$$

The same technique as above delivers the following matrix:

$$\mathbf{Q} = \begin{bmatrix} u_1^2 - \cos^2\alpha & u_1u_2 & u_1u_3 & v_1\cos^2\alpha - (\vec{u} \cdot \vec{V})u_1 \\ & u_2^2 - \cos^2\alpha & u_2u_3 & v_2\cos^2\alpha - (\vec{u} \cdot \vec{V})u_2 \\ & & u_3^2 - \cos^2\alpha & v_3\cos^2\alpha - (\vec{u} \cdot \vec{V})u_3 \\ & & & (\vec{u} \cdot \vec{V})^2 - |\vec{V}|^2\cos^2\alpha \end{bmatrix}$$

Equations (1) and (2) give us a simple way to perform point classification (i.e., determine if a point lies inside, on, or outside a surface). For a cylinder, if $|\vec{X} - \vec{A}|^2 - [(\vec{X} - \vec{A}) \cdot \vec{u}]^2$ is greater than (*resp.*, equal to or less than) r^2, point $\vec{X}$ lies outside (*resp.*, on, or inside) the cylinder. For a cone, if $\vec{X} - \vec{V}$ and $\vec{u}$ make an angle that is smaller than α or greater than $\pi - \alpha$, then $\vec{X}$ lies inside the cone. Hence, if $\left(\frac{\vec{X} - \vec{V}}{|\vec{X} - \vec{V}|} \cdot \vec{u}\right)^2$ is greater than (*resp.*, equal to or less than) $\cos^2\alpha$, then $\vec{X}$ lies inside (*resp.*, on or outside) the cone.

◇   **Bibliography**   ◇

(Dresden 1967) Arnold Dresden. *Solid Analytical Geometry and Determinants*. Dover, New York, 1967.

(Spain 1960) Barry Spain. *Analytical Quadrics*. Pergamon Press, New York, 1960.

◇ IV.8

An Implicit Surface Polygonizer

Jules Bloomenthal
Visual Information Technologies
George Mason University
Fairfax, VA 22030-4444
jbloom@beauty.gmu.edu

This Gem describes an algorithm for the polygonization of implicit surfaces, and provides an implementation in C. The discussion reviews implicit surface polygonization and compares various methods.

◇ Introduction ◇

Some shapes are more readily defined by implicit, rather than parametric, techniques. For example, consider a sphere centered at C with radius r. It can be described parametrically as $\{P\}$, where:

$$(P_x, P_y, P_z) = (C_x, C_y, C_z) + (r\cos\beta\cos\alpha, r\cos\beta\sin\alpha, r\sin\beta),$$
$$\alpha \in [0, 2\pi), \ \beta \in [-\pi/2, \pi/2]$$

The implicit definition for the same sphere is more compact:

$$(P_x - C_x)^2 + (P_y - C_y)^2 + (P_z - C_z)^2 - r^2 = 0$$

Because an implicit representation does not produce points by substitution, root-finding must be employed to render its surface. One such method is ray tracing, which can generate excellent images of implicit surfaces. Alternatively, an image of the function (not surface) can be created with volume rendering.

Polygonization is a method whereby a polygonal (i.e., parametric) approximation to the implicit surface is created from the implicit surface function. This allows the surface to be rendered with conventional polygon renderers; it also permits non-imaging operations, such as positioning an object on the surface. Polygonization consists of two principal steps. First, space is partitioned into adjacent cells at whose corners the implicit surface function is evaluated; negative values are considered inside the surface, positive values outside. Second, within each cell, the intersections of cell edges with the implicit surface are connected to form one or more polygons.

In this Gem we present software that performs spatial partitioning and polygonal approximation. We hope this software, which includes a simple test application, will encourage experimentation with implicit surface modeling.

The implementation is relatively simple (less than 400 lines, ignoring comments, the test application, and the cubical polygonization option). Some of this simplicity derives from the use of the cube as the *partitioning cell*; its symmetries provide a simple means to compute and index corner locations. We do not employ automatic techniques (such as interval analysis) to set polygonization parameters (such as cell size); these are set by the user, who also must judge the success of the polygonization. This not only simplifies the implementation, but permits the implicit surface function to be treated as a "black box." The function, for example, can be procedural or, even, discontinuous (although discontinuous functions may produce undesirable results). The use of a fixed resolution (i.e., unchanging cell size) also simplifies the implementation, which explains the popularity of fixed resolution over adaptive resolution methods.[1] This makes the choice of cell size important: too small a size produces too many polygons; too large a size obscures detail.

Before listing the code, we'll describe its operation and features. These include:

- fixed resolution partitioning by continuation,
- automatic surface detection,
- root-finding by binary subdivision,
- unambiguous triangulated output in points-polygon format, and
- function evaluation caching.

◇ **Overview** ◇

The spatial partitioning implemented here is based on the continuation scheme presented by (Wyvill *et al.* 1986), in which an initial cube is centered on a surface point (the starting point). Continuation consists of generating new cubes across any face that contains corners of opposite polarity (of the implicit surface function); this process continues until the entire surface is contained by the collection of cubes. The surface within each cube is then approximated by one or more polygons. Unfortunately, some polarity combinations are ambiguous; the "marching cubes" method produces errant holes in the surface because it treats these ambiguities inconsistently.

The implementation presented here treats all cube cases consistently, in one of two user-selectable ways. Either the cube is directly polygonized according to an algorithm given in (Bloomenthal 1988), or it is decomposed into tetrahedra that are then

---

[1](Bloomenthal 1988) and (Moore 1992) provide descriptions of adaptive polygonization.

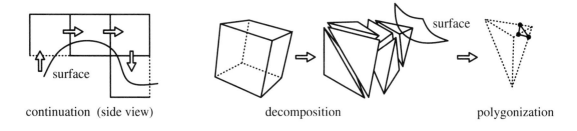

continuation (side view)   decomposition   polygonization

Figure 1. Overview of the polygonizer.

polygonized, as suggested by (Payne and Toga 1990). Thus, either a cube or a tetrahedron serves as the *polygonizing cell.* Each edge of the polygonizing cell that connects corners of differing polarity is intersected with the surface; we call these surface/edge intersections *surface vertices.* When connected together, they form polygons.

The continuation, decomposition, and polygonization steps are illustrated in Figure 1.

◇ Continuation versus Exhaustive Search ◇

Continuation methods require $O(n^2)$ function evaluations, where n is some measure of the size of the object (thus, n^2 corresponds to the object's surface area). Methods that employ exhaustive search through a given volume require $O(n^3)$ function evaluations. We know of only one other published polygonization implementation, which is given in (Watt and Watt 1993); it employs a marching cubes exhaustive search.

One benefit of exhaustive search is its detection of all pieces of a set of disjoint surfaces. This is not guaranteed with continuation methods, which require a starting point for each disjoint surface. With the implementation provided here, a surface is automatically detected by random search; thus, only a single object is detected and polygonized. If, however, the client provides a starting point for the partitioning, random search is not performed and disjoint objects may be polygonized by repeated calls to the polygonizer, each with a different starting point.

◇ Root-Finding ◇

Most exhaustive search methods were designed to process three-dimensional arrays (i.e., discrete samples such as produced by *CAT* or *MRI* scans); the present polygonizer, however, was designed for objects defined by a continuous, real-valued function. Such

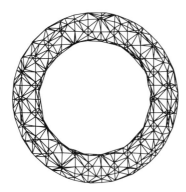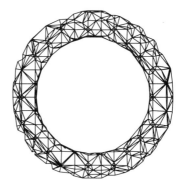

Figure 2. Surface vertex computation: accurate (left) and interpolated (right).

functions allow the location of a surface vertex to be computed accurately, rather than approximated by linear interpolation as is commonly employed with discrete arrays. The effects of interpolation can be seen in Figure 2.

Binary subdivision is a reliable and simple method to compute accurately the surface vertex location; given one point inside the surface and one outside, the subdivision converges to a point on the surface. Binary subdivision can, at times, be more efficient than other convergence methods, such as *regula falsi*. In our implementation, the number of iterations is fixed (at 10); the client can modify this constant or pass it to the program as a variable.

In our implementation, the number of function evaluations is held to a minimum. The location of a surface vertex is computed only once; it is cached and subsequently indexed according to the coordinates of its edge endpoints, using a hashing technique reported in (Wyvill *et al.* 1986). Function values at cube corners are cached similarly. The overhead in storing function values may exceed the cost of additional evaluations for very simple functions; for complex functions, however, the elimination of redundant evaluation is a significant advantage.

Although designed for continuous functions, the polygonizer can process three-dimensional arrays if the cube size is set to the sampling resolution of the array and the real-valued coordinates are converted to indices into the array. In this case, binary subdivision isn't possible, and linear interpolation must be used to estimate the surface vertex locations. Alternatively, the implicit surface function can provide a tri-linear interpolation of the discrete samples in the neighborhood of the query point (i.e., the argument to the function). This will work well for functions that are locally linear. The following pseudocode produces an interpolated value given a three-dimensional array of evenly spaced values and a query point P within the range *Min, Max* of the array. The array resolution in three dimensions is given by *Res*.

```
ValueFromDiscreteArray (values, P, Min, Max, Res)
  if P not in (Min..Max)
    then error(OutOfRange)
  else begin
```

x: **real** $\leftarrow$ $(P_x - Min_x) * (Res_x - 1) / (Max_x - Min_x)$;

y: **real** $\leftarrow$ $(P_x - Min_y) * (Res_y - 1) / (Max_y - Min_y)$;

z: **real** $\leftarrow$ $(P_z - Min_z) * (Res_z - 1) / (Max_z - Min_z)$;

$v000$: **real** $\leftarrow$ values$[\lfloor x \rfloor][\lfloor y \rfloor][\lfloor z \rfloor]$; *(first of eight corner values)*

$v001$: **real** $\leftarrow$ values$[\lfloor x \rfloor][\lfloor y \rfloor][\lfloor z \rfloor + 1]$;

$v010$: **real** $\leftarrow$ values$[\lfloor x \rfloor][\lfloor y \rfloor + 1][\lfloor z \rfloor]$;

$v011$: **real** $\leftarrow$ values$[\lfloor x \rfloor][\lfloor y \rfloor + 1][\lfloor z \rfloor + 1]$;

$v100$: **real** $\leftarrow$ values$[\lfloor x \rfloor + 1][\lfloor y \rfloor][\lfloor z \rfloor]$;

$v101$: **real** $\leftarrow$ values$[\lfloor x \rfloor + 1][\lfloor y \rfloor][\lfloor z \rfloor + 1]$;

$v110$: **real** $\leftarrow$ values$[\lfloor x \rfloor + 1][\lfloor y \rfloor + 1][\lfloor z \rfloor]$;

$v111$: **real** $\leftarrow$ values$[\lfloor x \rfloor + 1][\lfloor y \rfloor + 1][\lfloor z \rfloor + 1]$; *(last of 8 values)*

$v00$: **real** $\leftarrow$ $v000 + \text{frac}(z) * (v001\text{-}v000)$; *(interpolate along $x0y0$ edge)*

$v01$: **real** $\leftarrow$ $v010 + \text{frac}(z) * (v011\text{-}v010)$; *(interpolate along $x0y1$ edge)*

$v10$: **real** $\leftarrow$ $v100 + \text{frac}(z) * (v101\text{-}v100)$; *(interpolate along $x1y0$ edge)*

$v11$: **real** $\leftarrow$ $v110 + \text{frac}(z) * (v111\text{-}v110)$; *(interpolate along $x1y1$ edge)*

$v0$: **real** $\leftarrow$ $v00 + \text{frac}(y) * (v01\text{-}v00)$; *(interpolate along $x0$ face)*

$v1$: **real** $\leftarrow$ $v10 + \text{frac}(y) * (v11\text{-}v10)$; *(interpolate along $x1$ face)*

return$[v0 + \text{frac}(x) * (v1\text{-}v0)]$; *(tri-linearly interpolated value)*

```
  end;
```

◇ Polygonization ◇

Polygonization of an individual cell is performed using a table that contains one entry for each of the possible configurations of the cell vertex polarities. For the tetrahedron, this is a 16-entry table; for the cube, it is a 256-entry table.

The tetrahedral configurations are shown in Figure 3; each configuration produces either nothing, a triangle, or a quadrilateral (i.e., two triangles). In the figure, the elements of the set (denoted by braces) represent the edges of the tetrahedron that contain a surface vertex.

Although the tetrahedral table may be generated by inspection, the greater number of configurations for the cube motivates an algorithmic generation, which is illustrated in Figure 4. For each of the possible 256 polarity configurations, a surface vertex is presumed to exist on those edges connecting differently signed vertices. The surface vertices are ordered by proceeding from one surface vertex to the next, around a face in clockwise order; upon arriving at a new vertex, the face across the vertex's edge from the current face becomes the new current face.

Because the tetrahedral edges include the diagonals of the cube faces, the tetrahedral decomposition yields a greater number of surface vertices per surface area than does

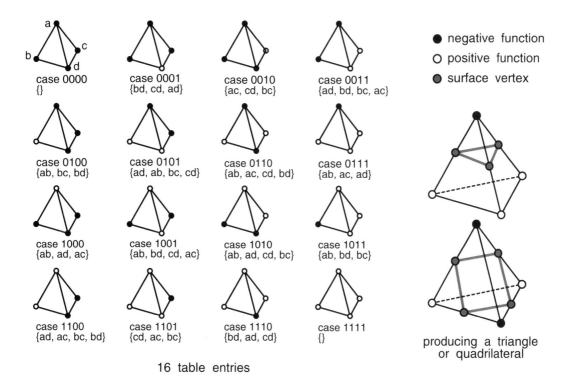

negative function
positive function
surface vertex

case 0000
{}

case 0001
{bd, cd, ad}

case 0010
{ac, cd, bc}

case 0011
{ad, bd, bc, ac}

case 0100
{ab, bc, bd}

case 0101
{ad, ab, bc, cd}

case 0110
{ab, ac, cd, bd}

case 0111
{ab, ac, ad}

case 1000
{ab, ad, ac}

case 1001
{ab, bd, cd, ac}

case 1010
{ab, ad, cd, bc}

case 1011
{ab, bd, bc}

case 1100
{ad, ac, bc, bd}

case 1101
{cd, ac, bc}

case 1110
{bd, ad, cd}

case 1111
{}

16 table entries

producing a triangle
or quadrilateral

Figure 3. Tetrahedral polygonization.

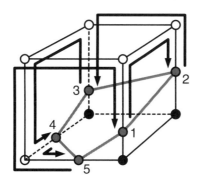

Figure 4. Cubical polygonization. (Appeared in CAGD, '88. Reprinted by permission.)

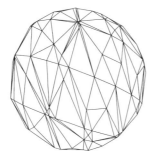 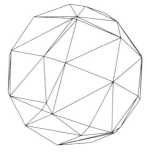

Figure 5. Polygonization with tetrahedral decomposition (left) and without (right).

cubical polygonization, as shown in Figure 4. Cubical polygonization requires less computation than does tetrahedral decomposition and polygonization, but requires a more complex implementation.

Some implementations produce surface vertices on a per polygon basis, duplicating a vertex every time it appears in an adjoining polygon. A more efficient format, known as "points/polygons," is to list the vertices separately and to define each polygon as a set of indices into the vertex list. This format often is more convenient for polygon renderers. Our implementation supports this format, producing polygons first, then vertices.

◇ Client Use ◇

The client of this software calls the procedure `polygonize()`, passing an arbitrary implicit surface function (in the test application provided, the function `torus()` is used); `polygonize()` will produce a set of triangles that approximates the implicit surface. In our test application, a `triangleProc` updates a pointer to the (ever-growing) array of vertices, and copies the indices for the triangle onto an (ever-growing) array of triangles. The `triangleProc` can also be used to indicate a user-specified abort and to provide a graphical display of the polygonization progress. The polygonizer computes the normal at each surface vertex as an approximation to the function gradient. Presently, each vertex is a structure containing the position and normal of the vertex; the client may wish to add other fields, such as color.

The client may wish to experiment with reversing the normal direction and/or the triangle orientation, in order to suit a particular modeling or rendering environment. As presently implemented, triangles are produced (in a left-handed coordinate system) with vertices in counterclockwise order when viewed from the out (positive) side of the object; surface normals will point outwards. Inverting the sign of the implicit surface function will reverse the normals and triangle orientation. If these are incorrect with respect to the rendering system, then algorithms that rely on back-facing polygon tests

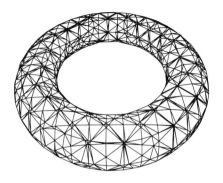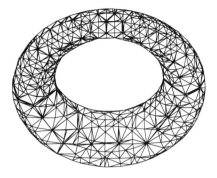

Figure 6.   Correctly and incorrectly oriented polygons.

will fail. For example, reversing the polygon orientation for the torus shown on the left in Figure 6 causes the inside polygons to be displayed, resulting in the improbable looking torus on the right.

◇   **Function Considerations**   ◇

Many implicitly defined objects, such as the tori in Figure 7, are bounded. The tori are both of the form $(x^2 + y^2 + z^2 + R^2 - r^2)^2 - 4R^2(x^2 + y^2)$, where R and r are the major and minor radii (in this example, $r = R/4$). To achieve a rotation and offset, the lower torus is defined by $(x^2 + (y + R)^2 + z^2 + R^2 - r^2)^2 - 4R^2((y + R)^2 + z^2)$. The right side of the figure depicts an equi-potential surface, i.e., those points for which the torus functions are equal. This surface is not bounded and demonstrates the need to limit the polygonizer during propagation. In our implementation, the client sets the parameter *bounds*, which restricts the propagation in all six (left, right, above, below, near, and far) directions from the starting cube. For the equi-potential surface below, *bounds* is seven.

There is no limit to the complexity of the implicit surface function. For example, the object in Figure 8, which resembles a piece used in the game of jacks, is defined by:

$$(1/(x^2/9 + 4y^2 + 4z^2)^4 + 1/(y^2/9 + 4x^2 + 4z^2)^4 + 1/(z^2/9 + 4y^2 + 4x^2)^4$$
$$+1/((4x/3 - 4)^2 + 16y^2/9 + 16z^2/9)^4 + 1/((4x/3 + 4)^2 + 16y^2/9 + 16z^2/9)^4$$
$$+1/((4y/3 - 4)^2 + 16x^2/9 + 16z^2/9)^4 + 1/((4y/3 + 4)^2 + 16x^2/9 + 16z^2/9)^4)^{-1/4} - 1$$

Although its complexity is unrestricted, the implicit surface function should be C^1 continuous; otherwise the object that results may be incomplete, have truncated edges, or contain small jutting pieces. This latter artifact is demonstrated by the "wiffle cube,"

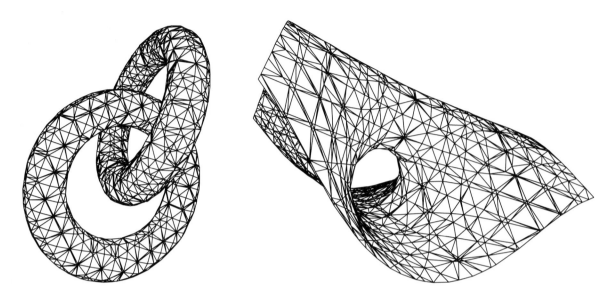

Figure 7. *Torus r us*: two tori and their equi-potential surface

Figure 8. A jack.

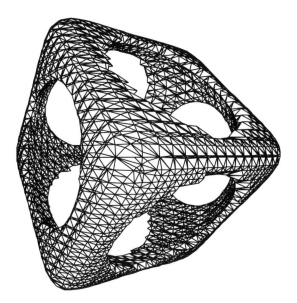

Figure 9. The wiffle cube.

a rounded cube with a sphere removed (see Figure 9); it is defined by: $1 - (a^2x^2 + a^2y^2 + a^2z^2)^{-6} - (b^8x^8 + b^8y^8 + b^8z^8)^6$, with $a = 1/2.3$ and $b = 1/2$. A sharply edged wedge occurs along each circular opening of the cuboid.

Here the disadvantage of a fixed grid resolution is evident; higher resolution is desirable along the sharp edges. The jutting pieces visible along the circular openings are due to the chance occurrence that a polygonizing cell edge intersects the wedge close to its center. A surface vertex calculated for this edge will lie very close to the center of the wedge; it will appear shifted with respect to neighboring vertices, which will lie along a wider part of the wedge.

Despite this difficulty (which is due to the inherently numerical nature of polygonizers), we believe the expanded range of modeling afforded by implicit surfaces holds great promise, and that polygonization is an important tool for implicit design. Happy modeling!

◇ **Acknowledgments** ◇

Many thanks to Paul Haeberli, Paul Heckbert, and Mark Hammel for assistance while at C; to Stewart Dickson for his comments; to Mark Ganter (ganter@u.washington.edu), who provided the jack, equi-potential tori, and wiffle cube functions; and, especially, to the editor, who carefully catalogued numerous facets in need of polishing.

◇ **C Code** ◇

```
/* implicit.c
 *      an implicit surface polygonizer, translated from Mesa
 *      applications should call polygonize()
 *
 * to compile a test program for ASCII output:
 *      cc implicit.c -o implicit -lm
 *
 * to compile a test program for display on an IRIS workstation:
 *      cc -DSGIGFX implicit.c -o implicit -lgl_s -lm
 *
 * Authored by Jules Bloomenthal, Xerox PARC.
 * Copyright (c) Xerox Corporation, 1991.  All rights reserved.
 * Permission is granted to reproduce, use and distribute this code for
 * any and all purposes, provided that this notice appears in all copies. */

#include <math.h>
#include <stdio.h>
#include <sys/types.h>

#define TET       0  /* use tetrahedral decomposition */
#define NOTET     1  /* no tetrahedral decomposition   */

#define RES      10  /* # converge iterations       */

#define L         0  /* left direction:   -x, -i */
#define R         1  /* right direction:  +x, +i */
#define B         2  /* bottom direction: -y, -j */
#define T         3  /* top direction:    +y, +j */
#define N         4  /* near direction:   -z, -k */
#define F         5  /* far direction:    +z, +k */
#define LBN       0  /* left bottom near corner   */
#define LBF       1  /* left bottom far corner    */
#define LTN       2  /* left top near corner      */
#define LTF       3  /* left top far corner       */
#define RBN       4  /* right bottom near corner  */
#define RBF       5  /* right bottom far corner   */
#define RTN       6  /* right top near corner     */
#define RTF       7  /* right top far corner      */

/* the LBN corner of cube (i, j, k), corresponds with location
 * (start.x+(i-.5)*size, start.y+(j-.5)*size, start.z+(k-.5)*size) */

#define RAND()      ((rand()&32767)/32767.)    /* random number between 0 and 1 */
#define HASHBIT     (5)
#define HASHSIZE    (size_t)(1<<(3*HASHBIT))    /* hash table size (32768) */
#define MASK        ((1<<HASHBIT)-1)
#define HASH(i,j,k) ((((((i)&MASK)<<HASHBIT)|((j)&MASK))<<HASHBIT)|((k)&MASK))
#define BIT(i, bit) (((i)>>(bit))&1)
#define FLIP(i,bit) ((i)^1<<(bit)) /* flip the given bit of i */
```

```
typedef struct point {            /* a three-dimensional point */
    double x, y, z;               /* its coordinates */
} POINT;

typedef struct test {             /* test the function for a signed value */
    POINT p;                      /* location of test */
    double value;                 /* function value at p */
    int ok;                       /* if value is of correct sign */
} TEST;

typedef struct vertex {           /* surface vertex */
    POINT position, normal;       /* position and surface normal */
} VERTEX;

typedef struct vertices {         /* list of vertices in polygonization */
    int count, max;               /* # vertices, max # allowed */
    VERTEX *ptr;                  /* dynamically allocated */
} VERTICES;

typedef struct corner {           /* corner of a cube */
    int i, j, k;                  /* (i, j, k) is index within lattice */
    double x, y, z, value;        /* location and function value */
} CORNER;

typedef struct cube {             /* partitioning cell (cube) */
    int i, j, k;                  /* lattice location of cube */
    CORNER *corners[8];           /* eight corners */
} CUBE;

typedef struct cubes {            /* linked list of cubes acting as stack */
    CUBE cube;                    /* a single cube */
    struct cubes *next;           /* remaining elements */
} CUBES;

typedef struct centerlist {       /* list of cube locations */
    int i, j, k;                  /* cube location */
    struct centerlist *next;      /* remaining elements */
} CENTERLIST;

typedef struct cornerlist {       /* list of corners */
    int i, j, k;                  /* corner id */
    double value;                 /* corner value */
    struct cornerlist *next;      /* remaining elements */
} CORNERLIST;

typedef struct edgelist {         /* list of edges */
    int i1, j1, k1, i2, j2, k2;   /* edge corner ids */
    int vid;                      /* vertex id */
    struct edgelist *next;        /* remaining elements */
} EDGELIST;

typedef struct intlist {          /* list of integers */
    int i;                        /* an integer */
    struct intlist *next;         /* remaining elements */
```

```
} INTLIST;

typedef struct intlists {          /* list of list of integers */
    INTLIST *list;                 /* a list of integers */
    struct intlists *next;         /* remaining elements */
} INTLISTS;

typedef struct process {           /* parameters, function, storage */
    double (*function)();          /* implicit surface function */
    int (*triproc)();              /* triangle output function */
    double size, delta;            /* cube size, normal delta */
    int bounds;                    /* cube range within lattice */
    POINT start;                   /* start point on surface */
    CUBES *cubes;                  /* active cubes */
    VERTICES vertices;             /* surface vertices */
    CENTERLIST **centers;          /* cube center hash table */
    CORNERLIST **corners;          /* corner value hash table */
    EDGELIST **edges;              /* edge and vertex id hash table */
} PROCESS;

void *calloc();
char *mycalloc();


/**** A Test Program ****/


/* torus: a torus with major, minor radii = 0.5, 0.1, try size = .05 */

double torus (x, y, z)
double x, y, z;
{
    double x2 = x*x, y2 = y*y, z2 = z*z;
    double a = x2+y2+z2+(0.5*0.5)-(0.1*0.1);
    return a*a-4.0*(0.5*0.5)*(y2+z2);
}


/* sphere: an inverse square function (always positive) */

double sphere (x, y, z)
double x, y, z;
{
    double rsq = x*x+y*y+z*z;
    return 1.0/(rsq < 0.00001? 0.00001 : rsq);
}


/* blob: a three-pole blend function, try size = .1 */

double blob (x, y, z)
double x, y, z;
{
```

```
        return 4.0-sphere(x+1.0,y,z)-sphere(x,y+1.0,z)-sphere(x,y,z+1.0);
}


#ifdef SGIGFX /*************************************************************/

#include "gl.h"

/* triangle: called by polygonize() for each triangle; set IRIS lines */

triangle (i1, i2, i3, vertices)
int i1, i2, i3;
VERTICES vertices;
{
    float v[3];
    int i, ids[3];
    ids[0] = i1;
    ids[1] = i2;
    ids[2] = i3;
    bgnclosedline();
    for (i = 0; i < 3; i++) {
        POINT *p = &vertices.ptr[ids[i]].position;
        v[0] = p->x; v[1] = p->y; v[2] = p->z;
        v3f(v);
    }
    endclosedline();
    return 1;
}


/* main: call polygonize() with torus function
 * display lines on IRIS */

main ()
{
    char *err, *polygonize();

    keepaspect(1, 1);
    winopen("implicit");
    doublebuffer();
    gconfig();
    perspective(450, 1.0/1.0, 0.1, 10.0);
    color(7);
    clear();
    swapbuffers();
    makeobj(1);
    if ((err = polygonize(torus, .05, 20, 0.,0.,0., triangle, TET)) != NULL) {
        fprintf(stderr, "%s\n", err);
        exit(1);
    }
    closeobj();
    translate(0.0, 0.0, -2.0);
    pushmatrix();
```

```
    while(1) { /* spin the object */
        reshapeviewport();
        color(7);
        clear();
        color(0);
        callobj(1);
        rot(0.8, 'x');
        rot(0.3, 'y');
        rot(0.1, 'z');
        swapbuffers();

    }
}

#else /*********************************************************************/

int gntris;          /* global needed by application */
VERTICES gvertices;  /* global needed by application */


/* triangle: called by polygonize() for each triangle; write to stdout */

triangle (i1, i2, i3, vertices)
int i1, i2, i3;
VERTICES vertices;
{
    gvertices = vertices;
    gntris++;
    fprintf(stdout, "%d %d %d\n", i1, i2, i3);
    return 1;
}


/* main: call polygonize() with torus function
 * write points-polygon formatted data to stdout */

main ()
    {
    int i;
    char *err, *polygonize();
    gntris = 0;
    fprintf(stdout, "triangles\n\n");
    if ((err = polygonize(torus, .05, 20, 0.,0.,0., triangle, TET)) != NULL) {
        fprintf(stdout, "%s\n", err);
        exit(1);
        }
    fprintf(stdout, "\n%d triangles, %d vertices\n", gntris, gvertices.count);
    fprintf(stdout, "\nvertices\n\n");
    for (i = 0; i < gvertices.count; i++) {
        VERTEX v;
        v = gvertices.ptr[i];
        fprintf(stdout, "%f  %f  %f\t%f  %f  %f\n",
            v.position.x, v.position.y,  v.position.z,
```

```
                v.normal.x,    v.normal.y,     v.normal.z);
    }
    fprintf(stderr, "%d triangles, %d vertices\n", gntris, gvertices.count);
    exit(0);
}

#endif /**********************************************************************/


/**** An Implicit Surface Polygonizer ****/


/* polygonize: polygonize the implicit surface function
 *    arguments are:
 *        double function (x, y, z)
 *                double x, y, z (an arbitrary 3D point)
 *            the implicit surface function
 *            return negative for inside, positive for outside
 *        double size
 *            width of the partitioning cube
 *        int bounds
 *            max. range of cubes (+/- on the three axes) from first cube
 *        double x, y, z
 *            coordinates of a starting point on or near the surface
 *            may be defaulted to 0., 0., 0.
 *        int triproc (i1, i2, i3, vertices)
 *                int i1, i2, i3 (indices into the vertex array)
 *                VERTICES vertices (the vertex array, indexed from 0)
 *            called for each triangle
 *            the triangle coordinates are (for i = i1, i2, i3):
 *                vertices.ptr[i].position.x, .y, and .z
 *            vertices are ccw when viewed from the out (positive) side
 *                in a left-handed coordinate system
 *            vertex normals point outwards
 *            return 1 to continue, 0 to abort
 *        int mode
 *            TET: decompose cube and polygonize six tetrahedra
 *            NOTET: polygonize cube directly
 *    returns error or NULL
 */

char *polygonize (function, size, bounds, x, y, z, triproc, mode)
double (*function)(), size, x, y, z;
int bounds, (*triproc)(), mode;
{
    PROCESS p;
    int n, noabort;
    CORNER *setcorner();
    TEST in, out, find();

    p.function = function;
    p.triproc = triproc;
    p.size = size;
```

```
p.bounds = bounds;
p.delta = size/(double)(RES*RES);

/* allocate hash tables and build cube polygon table: */
p.centers = (CENTERLIST **) mycalloc(HASHSIZE,sizeof(CENTERLIST *));
p.corners = (CORNERLIST **) mycalloc(HASHSIZE,sizeof(CORNERLIST *));
p.edges =   (EDGELIST   **) mycalloc(2*HASHSIZE,sizeof(EDGELIST *));
makecubetable();

/* find point on surface, beginning search at (x, y, z): */
srand(1);
in = find(1, &p, x, y, z);
out = find(0, &p, x, y, z);
if (!in.ok || !out.ok) return "can't find starting point";
converge(&in.p, &out.p, in.value, p.function, &p.start);

/* push initial cube on stack: */
p.cubes = (CUBES *) mycalloc(1, sizeof(CUBES)); /* list of 1 */
p.cubes->cube.i = p.cubes->cube.j = p.cubes->cube.k = 0;
p.cubes->next = NULL;

/* set corners of initial cube: */
for (n = 0; n < 8; n++)
    p.cubes->cube.corners[n] = setcorner(&p, BIT(n,2), BIT(n,1), BIT(n,0));

p.vertices.count = p.vertices.max = 0; /* no vertices yet */
p.vertices.ptr = NULL;

setcenter(p.centers, 0, 0, 0);

while (p.cubes != NULL) { /* process active cubes till none left */
    CUBE c;
    CUBES *temp = p.cubes;
    c = p.cubes->cube;

    noabort = mode == TET?
            /* either decompose into tetrahedra and polygonize: */
            dotet(&c, LBN, LTN, RBN, LBF, &p) &&
            dotet(&c, RTN, LTN, LBF, RBN, &p) &&
            dotet(&c, RTN, LTN, LTF, LBF, &p) &&
            dotet(&c, RTN, RBN, LBF, RBF, &p) &&
            dotet(&c, RTN, LBF, LTF, RBF, &p) &&
            dotet(&c, RTN, LTF, RTF, RBF, &p)
            :
            /* or polygonize the cube directly: */
            docube(&c, &p);
    if (! noabort) return "aborted";

    /* pop current cube from stack */
    p.cubes = p.cubes->next;
    free((char *) temp);
    /* test six face directions, maybe add to stack: */
    testface(c.i-1, c.j, c.k, &c, L, LBN, LBF, LTN, LTF, &p);
```

```
        testface(c.i+1, c.j, c.k, &c, R, RBN, RBF, RTN, RTF, &p);
        testface(c.i, c.j-1, c.k, &c, B, LBN, LBF, RBN, RBF, &p);
        testface(c.i, c.j+1, c.k, &c, T, LTN, LTF, RTN, RTF, &p);
        testface(c.i, c.j, c.k-1, &c, N, LBN, LTN, RBN, RTN, &p);
        testface(c.i, c.j, c.k+1, &c, F, LBF, LTF, RBF, RTF, &p);
    }
    return NULL;
}


/* testface: given cube at lattice (i, j, k), and four corners of face,
 * if surface crosses face, compute other four corners of adjacent cube
 * and add new cube to cube stack */

testface (i, j, k, old, face, c1, c2, c3, c4, p)
CUBE *old;
PROCESS *p;
int i, j, k, face, c1, c2, c3, c4;
{
    CUBE new;
    CUBES *oldcubes = p->cubes;
    CORNER *setcorner();
    static int facebit[6] = {2, 2, 1, 1, 0, 0};
    int n, pos = old->corners[c1]->value > 0.0 ? 1 : 0, bit = facebit[face];

    /* test if no surface crossing, cube out of bounds, or already visited: */
    if ((old->corners[c2]->value > 0) == pos &&
        (old->corners[c3]->value > 0) == pos &&
        (old->corners[c4]->value > 0) == pos) return;
    if (abs(i) > p->bounds || abs(j) > p->bounds || abs(k) > p->bounds) return;
    if (setcenter(p->centers, i, j, k)) return;

    /* create new cube: */
    new.i = i;
    new.j = j;
    new.k = k;
    for (n = 0; n < 8; n++) new.corners[n] = NULL;
    new.corners[FLIP(c1, bit)] = old->corners[c1];
    new.corners[FLIP(c2, bit)] = old->corners[c2];
    new.corners[FLIP(c3, bit)] = old->corners[c3];
    new.corners[FLIP(c4, bit)] = old->corners[c4];
    for (n = 0; n < 8; n++)
        if (new.corners[n] == NULL)
            new.corners[n] = setcorner(p, i+BIT(n,2), j+BIT(n,1), k+BIT(n,0));

    /*add cube to top of stack: */
    p->cubes = (CUBES *) mycalloc(1, sizeof(CUBES));
    p->cubes->cube = new;
    p->cubes->next = oldcubes;
}
```

```
/* setcorner: return corner with the given lattice location
   set (and cache) its function value */

CORNER *setcorner (p, i, j, k)
int i, j, k;
PROCESS *p;
{
    /* for speed, do corner value caching here */
    CORNER *c = (CORNER *) mycalloc(1, sizeof(CORNER));
    int index = HASH(i, j, k);
    CORNERLIST *l = p->corners[index];
    c->i = i; c->x = p->start.x+((double)i-.5)*p->size;
    c->j = j; c->y = p->start.y+((double)j-.5)*p->size;
    c->k = k; c->z = p->start.z+((double)k-.5)*p->size;
    for (; l != NULL; l = l->next)
        if (l->i == i && l->j == j && l->k == k) {
            c->value = l->value;
            return c;
            }
    l = (CORNERLIST *) mycalloc(1, sizeof(CORNERLIST));
    l->i = i; l->j = j; l->k = k;
    l->value = c->value = p->function(c->x, c->y, c->z);
    l->next = p->corners[index];
    p->corners[index] = l;
    return c;
}



/* find: search for point with value of given sign (0: neg, 1: pos) */

TEST find (sign, p, x, y, z)
int sign;
PROCESS *p;
double x, y, z;
{
    int i;
    TEST test;
    double range = p->size;
    test.ok = 1;
    for (i = 0; i < 10000; i++) {
        test.p.x = x+range*(RAND()-0.5);
        test.p.y = y+range*(RAND()-0.5);
        test.p.z = z+range*(RAND()-0.5);
        test.value = p->function(test.p.x, test.p.y, test.p.z);
        if (sign == (test.value > 0.0)) return test;
        range = range*1.0005; /* slowly expand search outwards */
        }
    test.ok = 0;
    return test;
}
```

```
/**** Tetrahedral Polygonization ****/


/* dotet: triangulate the tetrahedron
 * b, c, d should appear clockwise when viewed from a
 * return 0 if client aborts, 1 otherwise */

int dotet (cube, c1, c2, c3, c4, p)
CUBE *cube;
int c1, c2, c3, c4;
PROCESS *p;
{
    CORNER *a = cube->corners[c1];
    CORNER *b = cube->corners[c2];
    CORNER *c = cube->corners[c3];
    CORNER *d = cube->corners[c4];
    int index = 0, apos, bpos, cpos, dpos, e1, e2, e3, e4, e5, e6;
    if (apos = (a->value > 0.0)) index += 8;
    if (bpos = (b->value > 0.0)) index += 4;
    if (cpos = (c->value > 0.0)) index += 2;
    if (dpos = (d->value > 0.0)) index += 1;
    /* index is now 4-bit number representing one of the 16 possible cases */
    if (apos != bpos) e1 = vertid(a, b, p);
    if (apos != cpos) e2 = vertid(a, c, p);
    if (apos != dpos) e3 = vertid(a, d, p);
    if (bpos != cpos) e4 = vertid(b, c, p);
    if (bpos != dpos) e5 = vertid(b, d, p);
    if (cpos != dpos) e6 = vertid(c, d, p);
    /* 14 productive tetrahedral cases (0000 and 1111 yield no polygons) */
    switch (index) {
        case 1:  return p->triproc(e5, e6, e3, p->vertices);
        case 2:  return p->triproc(e2, e6, e4, p->vertices);
        case 3:  return p->triproc(e3, e5, e4, p->vertices) &&
                        p->triproc(e3, e4, e2, p->vertices);
        case 4:  return p->triproc(e1, e4, e5, p->vertices);
        case 5:  return p->triproc(e3, e1, e4, p->vertices) &&
                        p->triproc(e3, e4, e6, p->vertices);
        case 6:  return p->triproc(e1, e2, e6, p->vertices) &&
                        p->triproc(e1, e6, e5, p->vertices);
        case 7:  return p->triproc(e1, e2, e3, p->vertices);
        case 8:  return p->triproc(e1, e3, e2, p->vertices);
        case 9:  return p->triproc(e1, e5, e6, p->vertices) &&
                        p->triproc(e1, e6, e2, p->vertices);
        case 10: return p->triproc(e1, e3, e6, p->vertices) &&
                        p->triproc(e1, e6, e4, p->vertices);
        case 11: return p->triproc(e1, e5, e4, p->vertices);
        case 12: return p->triproc(e3, e2, e4, p->vertices) &&
                        p->triproc(e3, e4, e5, p->vertices);
        case 13: return p->triproc(e6, e2, e4, p->vertices);
        case 14: return p->triproc(e5, e3, e6, p->vertices);
    }
    return 1;
}
```

```
/**** Cubical Polygonization (optional) ****/


#define LB      0   /* left bottom edge  */
#define LT      1   /* left top edge      */
#define LN      2   /* left near edge     */
#define LF      3   /* left far edge      */
#define RB      4   /* right bottom edge */
#define RT      5   /* right top edge     */
#define RN      6   /* right near edge    */
#define RF      7   /* right far edge     */
#define BN      8   /* bottom near edge   */
#define BF      9   /* bottom far edge    */
#define TN     10   /* top near edge      */
#define TF     11   /* top far edge       */


static INTLISTS *cubetable[256];

/*                      edge: LB, LT, LN, LF, RB, RT, RN, RF, BN, BF, TN, TF */
static int corner1[12]    = {LBN,LTN,LBN,LBF,RBN,RTN,RBN,RBF,LBN,LBF,LTN,LTF};
static int corner2[12]    = {LBF,LTF,LTN,LTF,RBF,RTF,RTN,RTF,RBN,RBF,RTN,RTF};
static int leftface[12]   = {B,  L,  L,  F,  R,  T,  N,  R,  N,  B,  T,  F};
                            /* face on left when going corner1 to corner2 */
static int rightface[12]  = {L,  T,  N,  L,  B,  R,  R,  F,  B,  F,  N,  T};
                            /* face on right when going corner1 to corner2 */



/* docube: triangulate the cube directly, without decomposition */

int docube (cube, p)
CUBE *cube;
PROCESS *p;
{
    INTLISTS *polys;
    int i, index = 0;
    for (i = 0; i < 8; i++) if (cube->corners[i]->value > 0.0) index += (1<<i);
    for (polys = cubetable[index]; polys; polys = polys->next) {
        INTLIST *edges;
        int a = -1, b = -1, count = 0;
        for (edges = polys->list; edges; edges = edges->next) {
            CORNER *c1 = cube->corners[corner1[edges->i]];
            CORNER *c2 = cube->corners[corner2[edges->i]];
            int c = vertid(c1, c2, p);
            if (++count > 2 && ! p->triproc(a, b, c, p->vertices)) return 0;
            if (count < 3) a = b;
            b = c;
        }
    }
    return 1;
}


/* nextcwedge: return next clockwise edge from given edge around given face */
```

```
int nextcwedge (edge, face)
int edge, face;
{
    switch (edge) {
        case LB: return (face == L)? LF : BN;
        case LT: return (face == L)? LN : TF;
        case LN: return (face == L)? LB : TN;
        case LF: return (face == L)? LT : BF;
        case RB: return (face == R)? RN : BF;
        case RT: return (face == R)? RF : TN;
        case RN: return (face == R)? RT : BN;
        case RF: return (face == R)? RB : TF;
        case BN: return (face == B)? RB : LN;
        case BF: return (face == B)? LB : RF;
        case TN: return (face == T)? LT : RN;
        case TF: return (face == T)? RT : LF;
    }
}


/* otherface: return face adjoining edge that is not the given face */

int otherface (edge, face)
int edge, face;
{
    int other = leftface[edge];
    return face == other? rightface[edge] : other;
}


/* makecubetable: create the 256 entry table for cubical polygonization */

makecubetable ()
{
    int i, e, c, done[12], pos[8];
    for (i = 0; i < 256; i++) {
        for (e = 0; e < 12; e++) done[e] = 0;
        for (c = 0; c < 8; c++) pos[c] = BIT(i, c);
        for (e = 0; e < 12; e++)
            if (!done[e] && (pos[corner1[e]] != pos[corner2[e]])) {
                INTLIST *ints = 0;
                INTLISTS *lists = (INTLISTS *) mycalloc(1, sizeof(INTLISTS));
                int start = e, edge = e;
                /* get face that is to right of edge from pos to neg corner: */
                int face = pos[corner1[e]]? rightface[e] : leftface[e];
                while (1) {
                    edge = nextcwedge(edge, face);
                    done[edge] = 1;
                    if (pos[corner1[edge]] != pos[corner2[edge]]) {
                        INTLIST *tmp = ints;
                        ints = (INTLIST *) mycalloc(1, sizeof(INTLIST));
                        ints->i = edge;
```

```
                           ints->next = tmp; /* add edge to head of list */
                           if (edge == start) break;
                           face = otherface(edge, face);
                       }
                   }
                   lists->list = ints; /* add ints to head of table entry */
                   lists->next = cubetable[i];
                   cubetable[i] = lists;
               }
       }
}


/**** Storage ****/


/* mycalloc: return successful calloc or exit program */

char *mycalloc (nitems, nbytes)
int nitems, nbytes;
{
   char *ptr = calloc(nitems, nbytes);
   if (ptr != NULL) return ptr;
   fprintf(stderr, "can't calloc %d bytes\n", nitems*nbytes);
   exit(1);
}


/* setcenter: set (i,j,k) entry of table[]
 * return 1 if already set; otherwise, set and return 0 */

int setcenter(table, i, j, k)
CENTERLIST *table[];
int i, j, k;
{
    int index = HASH(i, j, k);
    CENTERLIST *new, *l, *q = table[index];
    for (l = q; l != NULL; l = l->next)
        if (l->i == i && l->j == j && l->k == k) return 1;
    new = (CENTERLIST *) mycalloc(1, sizeof(CENTERLIST));
    new->i = i; new->j = j; new->k = k; new->next = q;
    table[index] = new;
    return 0;
}


/* setedge: set vertex id for edge */

setedge (table, i1, j1, k1, i2, j2, k2, vid)
EDGELIST *table[];
int i1, j1, k1, i2, j2, k2, vid;
{
    unsigned int index;
```

```
    EDGELIST *new;
    if (i1>i2 || (i1==i2 && (j1>j2 || (j1==j2 && k1>k2)))) {
        int t=i1; i1=i2; i2=t; t=j1; j1=j2; j2=t; t=k1; k1=k2; k2=t;
    }
    index = HASH(i1, j1, k1) + HASH(i2, j2, k2);
    new = (EDGELIST *) mycalloc(1, sizeof(EDGELIST));
    new->i1 = i1; new->j1 = j1; new->k1 = k1;
    new->i2 = i2; new->j2 = j2; new->k2 = k2;
    new->vid = vid;
    new->next = table[index];
    table[index] = new;
}


/* getedge: return vertex id for edge; return -1 if not set */

int getedge (table, i1, j1, k1, i2, j2, k2)
EDGELIST *table[];
int i1, j1, k1, i2, j2, k2;
{
    EDGELIST *q;
    if (i1>i2 || (i1==i2 && (j1>j2 || (j1==j2 && k1>k2)))) {
        int t=i1; i1=i2; i2=t; t=j1; j1=j2; j2=t; t=k1; k1=k2; k2=t;
    };
    q = table[HASH(i1, j1, k1)+HASH(i2, j2, k2)];
    for (; q != NULL; q = q->next)
        if (q->i1 == i1 && q->j1 == j1 && q->k1 == k1 &&
            q->i2 == i2 && q->j2 == j2 && q->k2 == k2)
            return q->vid;
    return -1;
}


/**** Vertices ****/


/* vertid: return index for vertex on edge:
 * c1->value and c2->value are presumed of different sign
 * return saved index if any; else compute vertex and save */

int vertid (c1, c2, p)
CORNER *c1, *c2;
PROCESS *p;
{
    VERTEX v;
    POINT a, b;
    int vid = getedge(p->edges, c1->i, c1->j, c1->k, c2->i, c2->j, c2->k);
    if (vid != -1) return vid;                        /* previously computed */
    a.x = c1->x; a.y = c1->y; a.z = c1->z;
    b.x = c2->x; b.y = c2->y; b.z = c2->z;
    converge(&a, &b, c1->value, p->function, &v.position); /* position */
    vnormal(&v.position, p, &v.normal);                    /* normal */
    addtovertices(&p->vertices, v);                        /* save vertex */
```

```
        vid = p->vertices.count-1;
        setedge(p->edges, c1->i, c1->j, c1->k, c2->i, c2->j, c2->k, vid);
        return vid;
}


/* addtovertices: add v to sequence of vertices */

addtovertices (vertices, v)
VERTICES *vertices;
VERTEX v;
{
    if (vertices->count == vertices->max) {
        int i;
        VERTEX *new;
        vertices->max = vertices->count == 0 ? 10 : 2*vertices->count;
        new = (VERTEX *) mycalloc((unsigned) vertices->max, sizeof(VERTEX));
        for (i = 0; i < vertices->count; i++) new[i] = vertices->ptr[i];
        if (vertices->ptr != NULL) free((char *) vertices->ptr);
        vertices->ptr = new;
    }
    vertices->ptr[vertices->count++] = v;
}


/* vnormal: compute unit length surface normal at point */

vnormal (point, p, v)
POINT *point, *v;
PROCESS *p;
{
    double f = p->function(point->x, point->y, point->z);
    v->x = p->function(point->x+p->delta, point->y, point->z)-f;
    v->y = p->function(point->x, point->y+p->delta, point->z)-f;
    v->z = p->function(point->x, point->y, point->z+p->delta)-f;
    f = sqrt(v->x*v->x + v->y*v->y + v->z*v->z);
    if (f != 0.0) {v->x /= f; v->y /= f; v->z /= f;}
}


/* converge: from two points of differing sign, converge to zero crossing */

converge (p1, p2, v, function, p)
double v;
double (*function)();
POINT *p1, *p2, *p;
{
    int i = 0;
    POINT pos, neg;
    if (v < 0) {
        pos.x = p2->x; pos.y = p2->y; pos.z = p2->z;
        neg.x = p1->x; neg.y = p1->y; neg.z = p1->z;
    }
```

```
else {
    pos.x = p1->x; pos.y = p1->y; pos.z = p1->z;
    neg.x = p2->x; neg.y = p2->y; neg.z = p2->z;
}
while (1) {
    p->x = 0.5*(pos.x + neg.x);
    p->y = 0.5*(pos.y + neg.y);
    p->z = 0.5*(pos.z + neg.z);
    if (i++ == RES) return;
    if ((function(p->x, p->y, p->z)) > 0.0)
        {pos.x = p->x; pos.y = p->y; pos.z = p->z;}
    else {neg.x = p->x; neg.y = p->y; neg.z = p->z;}
}
}
```

◇ **Bibliography** ◇

(Bloomenthal 1988) J. Bloomenthal. Polygonization of implicit surfaces. *Computer Aided Geometric Design*, 5(4):53–60, November 1988.

(Moore 1992) D. Moore. *Simplicial Mesh Generation with Applications*. Ph.D. thesis, Computer Science, Rice University, Houston, TX, 1992.

(Payne and Toga 1990) B. Payne and A. Toga. Surface mapping brain function on 3d models. *IEEE Computer Graphics and Applications*, September 1990.

(Watt and Watt 1993) A. Watt and M. Watt. *Advanced Animation and Rendering Techniques*. Addison-Wesley, Reading, MA, 1993.

(Wyvill *et al.* 1986) G. Wyvill, C. McPheeters, and B. Wyvill. Data structure for soft objects. *The Visual Computer*, 2(4), August 1986.

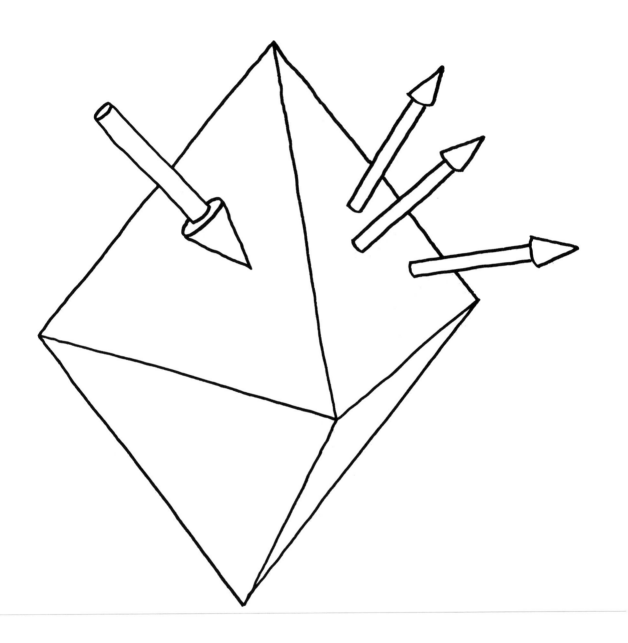

◇ V ◇
Ray Tracing

This part of the book contains five Gems on ray tracing.

◇ V.1

Computing the Intersection of a Line and a Cylinder

Ching-Kuang Shene
Department of Mathematics and Computer Science
Northern Michigan University
Marquette, MI 49855-5340
facs@nmumus.bitnet

Computing the intersection of a line and a surface is a common operation in graphics applications. Traditional methods usually assume that the surface is given by an implicit equation and reduce the intersection problem to solving a single-variable equation. However, in many graphics applications, a cylinder or a cone is represented by some geometric form like the one used in this Gem. Although a geometric form can be transformed to an implicit equation (Shene 1994) so that traditional methods could be applied, a direct geometric method would be more efficient and robust. In this Gem, we shall present a simple geometric technique to compute the intersection of a line and a circular cylinder. The following notations will be used throughout this Gem:

- Upper- (*resp.,* lower-) case vectors are position (*resp.,* direction) vectors. Position vectors are sometimes referred to as points. Therefore, $\vec{P}$ and P are equivalent. All direction vectors are of unit length. $|\vec{U}|$ is the length of vector $\vec{U}$.
- $\overleftrightarrow{PQ}$ and $\overline{PQ}$ are the line and the segment, respectively, determined by points $\vec{P}$ and $\vec{Q}$.
- $\vec{u} \times \vec{v}$ denotes the cross product of vectors $\vec{u}$ and $\vec{v}$.
- $\vec{u} \otimes \vec{v}$ is the normalized $\vec{u} \times \vec{v}$. That is, $\vec{u} \otimes \vec{v} = \vec{u} \times \vec{v}/|\vec{u} \times \vec{v}|$.
- $\ell(\vec{A}, \vec{u})$ is the line defined by base point $\vec{A}$ and direction $\vec{u}$.
- $\mathcal{C}(\vec{A}, \vec{u}, r)$ is the circular cylinder with axis $\ell(\vec{A}, \vec{u})$ and radius r.

Let $\ell(\vec{A}, \vec{u})$ and $\mathcal{C}(\vec{B}, \vec{v}, r)$ be a line and a circular cylinder. If $\vec{u}$ and $\vec{v}$ are parallel, then we have two cases to consider based on the distance from $\vec{B}$ to ℓ. If this distance is not equal to r, ℓ does not intersect $\mathcal{C}$; otherwise, ℓ lies on $\mathcal{C}$.

Suppose ℓ and the axis of $\mathcal{C}$ are not parallel. Let θ be the acute angle between $\vec{u}$ and $\vec{v}$. Thus, $\cos\theta = |\vec{u} \cdot \vec{v}|$. Let $\overleftrightarrow{OP}$ be the common perpendicular of ℓ and the axis of the cylinder, where $\vec{O}$ is on the cylinder's axis and $\vec{P}$ is on ℓ. Let $|d|$ be the length of the segment $\overline{OP}$. Then, the plane containing $\ell(\vec{A}, \vec{u})$ and $\overleftrightarrow{OP}$ cuts $\mathcal{C}$ in an ellipse with

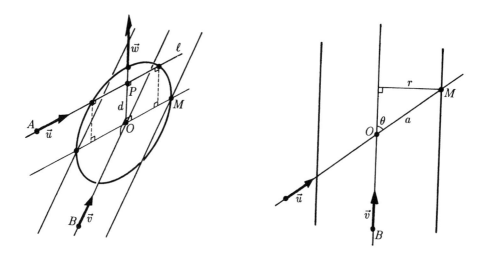

Figure 1. Computing the intersection point of a line and a circular cylinder.

semi-major axis length $a = |\vec{M} - \vec{O}| = r/\sin\theta = r/\sqrt{1 - (\vec{u} \cdot \vec{v})^2}$ and semi-minor axis length r, where M is the intersection point of $\mathcal{C}$ and the line through O and parallel to ℓ (see Figure 1). If $\overleftrightarrow{OM}$ and $\overleftrightarrow{OP}$ are chosen to be the x- and the y-axes, respectively, and O the origin, the intersection ellipse has equation $\frac{x^2}{a^2} + \frac{y^2}{r^2} = 1$. Since $\ell(\vec{A}, \vec{u})$ is parallel to the x-axis at a distance of $|d|$, its intersection points with the ellipse can be determined by computing the x-coordinates corresponding to $y = |d|$. Hence, we have

$$x = \pm\frac{a}{r}\sqrt{r^2 - d^2} = \pm\sqrt{\frac{r^2 - d^2}{1 - (\vec{u} \cdot \vec{v})^2}}$$

If $r < |d|$, ℓ intersects $\mathcal{C}$ at two points,

$$\vec{P} \pm \sqrt{\frac{r^2 - d^2}{1 - (\vec{u} \cdot \vec{v})^2}}\,\vec{u}$$

If $r = |d|$, ℓ is tangent to $\mathcal{C}$ at $\vec{P}$; otherwise, ℓ does not intersect $\mathcal{C}$.

Remark. $\vec{P}$ and $|d|$ are not difficult to compute. Since the common perpendicular of ℓ and the cylinder's axis has direction $\vec{w} = \vec{u} \otimes \vec{v}$, we have

$$\vec{A} + r\vec{u} + d\vec{w} = \vec{B} + s\vec{v} \tag{1}$$

for some appropriate r and s. Since both $\vec{u}$ and $\vec{v}$ are perpendicular to $\vec{w}$, computing the inner product of Equation (1) with $\vec{w}$ gives $d = (\vec{B} - \vec{A}) \cdot \vec{w}$. Computing the cross product of Equation (1) with $\vec{v}$ gives $(\vec{B} - \vec{A} - d\vec{w}) \times \vec{v} = r(\vec{u} \times \vec{v})$. Computing the inner product of this result with $\vec{u} \times \vec{v}$ delivers $r = [(\vec{B} - \vec{A} - d\vec{w}) \times \vec{v}] \cdot (\vec{u} \times \vec{v})/|\vec{u} \times \vec{v}|^2$. Therefore, $\vec{P} = \vec{A} + r\vec{u}$ is determined. □

Using some results from classic theory of conic sections (Drew 1875, Macaulay 1895), we can apply the same technique to compute the intersection of a line and a cone; however, the resulting formulæ are more involved. The interested reader should refer to (Johnston and Shene 1992) for the details.

See also the other article on ray-cylinder intersection in this volume (Cychosz and Waggenspack 1994).

◇ **Bibliography** ◇

(Cychosz and Waggenspack 1994) J. M. Cychosz and W. N. Waggenspack, Jr. Intersecting a ray with a cylinder. In Paul Heckbert, editor, *Graphics Gems IV*, pages 356–365. Academic Press, Boston, 1994.

(Drew 1875) William H. Drew. *A Geometric Treatise on Conic Sections*, fifth edition. Macmillan and Co., London, UK, 1875.

(Johnstone and Shene 1992) John K. Johnstone and Ching-Kuang Shene. Computing the intersection of a plane and a natural quadric. *Computers & Graphics*, 16(2):179–186, 1992.

(Macaulay 1895) Francis S. Macaulay. *Geometric Conics*. Cambridge University Press, Cambridge, UK, 1895.

(Shene 1994) Ching-Kuang Shene. Equations of cylinders and cones. In Paul Heckbert, editor, *Graphics Gems IV*, pages 321–323. Academic Press, Boston, 1994.

◇ V.2

Intersecting a Ray with a Cylinder

Joseph M. Cychosz
Purdue University CADLAB
West Lafayette, IN 47907
3ksnn64@ecn.purdue.edu

Warren N. Waggenspack, Jr.
IMRLAB, Mechanical Engineering
Louisiana State University
Baton Rouge, LA 70803-6413
mewagg@mewnw.dnet.lsu.edu

This Gem presents a geometric algorithm for locating the points of intersection between a ray and a circular cylinder and the means for determining the normal to the surface at the point of intersection. It also presents an algorithm for intersecting a finite cylinder bounded by two planar end-caps of arbitrary orientation.

The cylinder is a common modeling primitive used in a variety of computer graphics and computer-aided design applications (Haines 1989), (Roth 1982). To render an image consisting of cylinders using ray tracing, the intersection points, the corresponding distances along the intersecting ray, and the surface normal required in lighting model computations all must be computed. The authors in a previous Gem (Cychosz and Waggenspack 1992) presented a general solution for intersecting a ray with a general quadric surface; however, much like the well-known solution for intersecting a ray with a sphere (Haines 1989), (Hultquist 1991), a simpler geometric solution exists. Summarized below is an algorithm for locating the circular cylinder intersection points, distances along the ray, and the means for determining the surface normal at the points of intersection.

◇ Intersection of a Ray with a Cylinder ◇

Let the semi-infinite ray be defined by a base point B_R and unit vector (direction cosines) $\mathbf{R}$. The associated infinite cylinder is described by its radius, r, a unit vector A defining its centerline or axis, and a base point B_C located on the cylinder axis. Analogous to the sphere intersection procedure, the first step in computing the intersection between a ray and cylinder is also a quick elimination test. It involves computing the shortest distance, d, between the ray and axis of the cylinder (see Figure 1a). This shortest path between the two lies along a direction, $\mathbf{D}$, perpendicular to both $\mathbf{A}$ and $\mathbf{R}$. Using

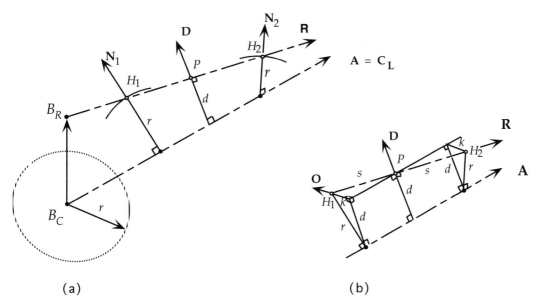

(a)   (b)

Figure 1.   Geometric presentation of the ray-cylinder intersection problem.

a combination of vector and scalar products it can be shown that the direction **D** and the distance d are computed as follows.

$$\mathbf{D} = \frac{\mathbf{R} \times \mathbf{A}}{|\mathbf{R} \times \mathbf{A}|} \quad d = |(B_R - B_C) \cdot \mathbf{D}|$$

If d is greater than r, then the ray misses the cylinder and no further processing is necessary. Otherwise the ray intersects the cylinder in two points, H_1 and H_2, located symmetrically about the point P where the ray passes closest to the axis of the cylinder. The distance t along the ray from the base point to the point P is determined by:

$$t = \frac{\{(B_R - B_C) \times \mathbf{A}\} \cdot \mathbf{D}}{|\mathbf{R} \times \mathbf{A}|} = \frac{\{(B_R - B_C) \times \mathbf{A}\} \cdot \mathbf{R} \times \mathbf{A}}{|\mathbf{R} \times \mathbf{A}|^2}$$

From the symmetry formed about the midpoint P, a set of right triangles can be assembled where $k^2 + d^2 = r^2$ (see Figure 1b). The distance s, along the ray between the intersections and the midpoint P, can now be computed by defining the unit vector orthogonal to both **A** and **D**

$$\mathbf{O} = \frac{\mathbf{D} \times \mathbf{A}}{|\mathbf{D} \times \mathbf{A}|}$$

and noting that

$$s\mathbf{R} \cdot \mathbf{O} = \pm k$$

thus

$$s = \left| \frac{k}{\mathbf{R} \cdot \mathbf{O}} \right| = \left| \frac{\sqrt{r^2 - d^2}}{\mathbf{R} \cdot \mathbf{O}} \right|$$

The intersection distances, t_{in} and t_{out}, and the corresponding points of intersection, H_{in} and H_{out} are then simply:

$$t_{in} = t - s$$
$$t_{out} = t + s$$

with

$$H_{in} = B_R + t_{in}\mathbf{R}$$
$$H_{out} = B_R + t_{out}\mathbf{R}$$

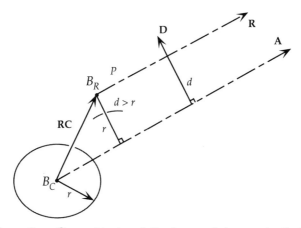

Figure 2.   Geometric description for parallel ray and cylinder.

For the special case where the ray is parallel to the axis of the cylinder (i.e., $\mathbf{R} \times \mathbf{A} = \mathbf{0}$), the distance, d, between the ray base point and the axis of the cylinder dictates if the ray travels inside or outside of the cylinder. The alternate formulation for d is shown below and, again, if d is greater than r, then the ray falls outside the cylinder and no further computation is required. (See Figure 2.)

$$\begin{aligned}
\mathbf{RC} &= B_R - B_C = \mathbf{RC}_{\perp \mathbf{A}} + \mathbf{RC}_{\parallel \mathbf{A}} = d\mathbf{N} + (\mathbf{RC} \cdot \mathbf{A})\mathbf{A} \\
d\mathbf{N} &= \mathbf{RC} - (\mathbf{RC} \cdot \mathbf{A})\mathbf{A} \\
d &= |\mathbf{RC}_{\perp \mathbf{A}}| = |\mathbf{RC} - (\mathbf{RC} \cdot \mathbf{A})\mathbf{A}|
\end{aligned}$$

Should the ray travel inside the cylinder ($d \le r$), the entering and exiting distances, t_{in} and t_{out} are set to negative and positive infinity, respectively. As detailed in a section to follow, these results are used in determining the appropriate bounded cylinder intersections.

A different derivation of the intersection of a ray with an infinite cylinder is contained in another article in this volume (Shene 1994).

◇ **Determining the Surface Normal** ◇

Much like determining the normal on the surface of a sphere, where the normal is defined as the vector originating from the center of the sphere and passing through the point on the surface, a simple geometric solution exists for the cylinder also. The normal, $\mathbf{N}$, at a given location H on the surface of the cylinder is simply the vector perpendicular to the cylinder's axis that passes through H (see Figure 1). It can be formulated in terms of the unit vector parallel to the component of $\mathbf{HB} = \mathbf{H} - \mathbf{B_C}$ that is perpendicular to $\mathbf{A}$.

$$\mathbf{HB} = H - B_C = \mathbf{HB}_{\perp \mathbf{A}} + \mathbf{HB}_{\parallel \mathbf{A}} = r\mathbf{N} + (\mathbf{HB} \cdot \mathbf{A})\mathbf{A}$$
$$r\mathbf{N} = \mathbf{HB} - (\mathbf{HB} \cdot \mathbf{A})\mathbf{A}$$
$$\mathbf{N} = \frac{\mathbf{HB} - (\mathbf{HB} \cdot \mathbf{A})\mathbf{A}}{r}$$

◇ **Intersecting a Ray with a Finite Cylinder** ◇

Rarely are infinite cylinders used as modeling primitives; instead the cylinder is often bounded by two planar end-caps. In addition to testing the infinite cylinder, a comparison must be made with the planar end-caps to determine if the ray does indeed intersect the bounded portion of the cylinder, one of the planar end-caps, or misses the finite surfaces altogether.

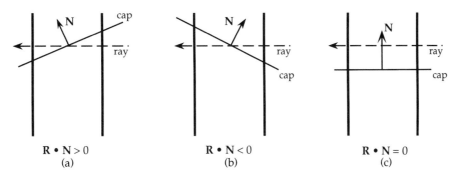

Figure 3. Determination of intersecting surfaces for a cylinder bounded by two end-cap planes.

Each end-cap plane is described with an outward pointing unit normal $\mathbf{N}$, and an offset d defining an oriented, shortest distance from the plane to the origin. A point lies on the plane iff $(\mathbf{P} \cdot \mathbf{N} + d = 0)$. A positive d indicates the origin lies above the plane or on the outside in terms of bounding the cylinder. The distance along the ray to the intersection point on a planar end-cap can be computed as:

$$t = -\frac{B_R \cdot \mathbf{N} + d}{\mathbf{R} \cdot \mathbf{N}}$$

Once computed, the intersection distances to the end-caps are compared with those from the infinite cylinder (t_{in} and t_{out}). If the ray points in the same direction as the corresponding end-plane normal ($\mathbf{R} \cdot \mathbf{N} > 0$), then it potentially exits the finite cylinder volume there. This intersection is thus compared with the exiting distance of the cylinder, t_{out}. The minimum of these two distances dictates which of the two surfaces defines the true intersection (see Figure 3a). Where the ray direction opposes that of the corresponding end-plane normal ($\mathbf{R} \cdot \mathbf{N} > 0$), it may be that it enters the finite cylinder volume there. The resulting intersection distance is therefore compared to t_{in} and the maximum of the two indicates which of the two surface intersections is actually where the ray enters the bounded volume (see Figure 3b). Upon integrating the results from the two end-caps, a quick comparison of the intersection distances will indicate if the ray completely misses the bounded cylinder (i.e., $t_{out} < t_{in}$).

Special attention must be given where the ray is determined to be parallel to an end-cap plane ($\mathbf{R} \cdot \mathbf{N} = 0$). In this instance, the location of the ray base point relative to the cap plane is enough to establish where the ray passes with respect to the bounded volume. If the numerator in the ray-plane intersection computation is positive, ($B_R \cdot \mathbf{N} + d > 0$), then the ray misses the cylinder (see Figure 3c). Otherwise, the current t_{in} and t_{out} remain valid intersection distances.

The object clipping presented here can be used for any object with one pair of intersection points such as the family of quadric surfaces presented in (Cychosz and Waggenspack 1992). An analogous intersection procedure can also be derived for other quadrics such as the cone from the plane-quadric intersection procedures described in (Johnston and Shene 1992). For the simplified case of a right circular cylinder where the end-cap planes are parallel and the normals are aligned with the axis of the cylinder, the computation of the intersection distances to the end-caps is greatly simplified and all that must be determined when the ray is parallel to the end-cap planes is whether the ray lies between the two planes.

◇ **Summary** ◇

A benefit of this geometric approach to the ray-cylinder intersection is that it deals directly in object space coordinates. This avoids the overhead of transforming either the rays and/or the bounded cylinder into a canonical form for testing. This is especially true for instances when the cylinder is in motion (i.e., rendering a cylinder that is changing either size or position with motion blur), which would require re-computation of the transfrom at each instance. For stationary cylinders, the approach presented here basically requires the computation of 3 cross products (each cross product requires 6 multiplies and 3 additions), whereas the approaches that perform a transformation require the computation of 1 cross product and 1 vector-matrix multiplication (a vector-matrix multiplication that ignores perspective requires 12 multiplies and 9 additions). In the context of this problem, there are going to be times where transforming an object in a canonical space may be faster, but one still can't handle the arbitrary end-caps in a "canonical" fashion. It would require non-linear transformations to normalize the end-caps while not distorting the cylinder!

◇ **C Implementation** ◇

The following code calls vector arithmetic routines defined in Chapter X.4.

```
#include        "GraphicsGems.h"
#include        <math.h>

/* ---- intcyl - Intersect a ray with a cylinder. -------------------- */
/*                                                                      */
/*                                                                      */
/*      Description:                                                    */
/*          Intcyl determines the intersection of a ray with a         */
/*          cylinder.                                                   */
/*                                                                      */
/*      On entry:                                                       */
/*          raybase = The base point of the intersecting ray.          */
/*          raycos  = The direction cosines of the above ray. (unit)    */
/*          base    = The base location of the cylinder.                */
/*          axis    = The axis of symmetry for the cylinder.  (unit)    */
/*          radius  = The radius of the cylinder.                       */
/*                                                                      */
/*      On return:                                                      */
/*          in      = The entering distance of the intersection.        */
/*          out     = The leaving  distance of the intersection.        */
/*                                                                      */
/*      Returns:  True if the ray intersects the cylinder.             */
/*                                                                      */
/*      Note:      In and/or out may be negative indicating the         */
/*                 cylinder is located behind the origin of the ray.    */
/*                                                                      */
/* -------------------------------------------------------------------- */

#define HUGE            1.0e21          /* Huge value                 */
```

```
boolean intcyl   (raybase,raycos,base,axis,radius,in,out)

        Point3           *raybase;          /* Base of the intersection ray */
        Vector3          *raycos;           /* Direction cosines of the ray */
        Point3           *base;             /* Base of the cylinder         */
        Vector3          *axis;             /* Axis of the cylinder         */
        double           radius;            /* Radius of the cylinder       */
        double           *in;               /* Entering distance            */
        double           *out;              /* Leaving distance             */

{
        boolean          hit;               /* True if ray intersects cyl   */
        Vector3          RC;                /* Ray base to cylinder base     */
        double           d;                 /* Shortest distance between     */
                                            /*   the ray and the cylinder    */
        double           t, s;              /* Distances along the ray       */
        Vector3          n, D, O;
        double           ln;
const   double           pinf = HUGE;       /* Positive infinity             */


        RC.x = raybase->x - base->x;
        RC.y = raybase->y - base->y;
        RC.z = raybase->z - base->z;
        V3Cross (raycos,axis,&n);

        if  ( (ln = V3Length (&n)) == 0. ) {    /* ray parallel to cyl  */
            d      = V3Dot (&RC,axis);
            D.x    = RC.x - d*axis->x;
            D.y    = RC.y - d*axis->y;
            D.z    = RC.z - d*axis->z;
            d      = V3Length (&D);
            *in    = -pinf;
            *out   = pinf;
            return (d <= radius);                  /* true if ray is in cyl*/
        }

        V3Normalize (&n);
        d      = fabs (V3Dot (&RC,&n));            /* shortest distance    */
        hit    = (d <= radius);

        if  (hit) {                                /* if ray hits cylinder */
            V3Cross (&RC,axis,&O);
            t = - V3Dot (&O,&n) / ln;
            V3Cross (&n,axis,&O);
            V3Normalize (&O);
            s = fabs (sqrt(radius*radius - d*d) / V3Dot (raycos,&O));
            *in  = t - s;                          /* entering distance    */
            *out = t + s;                          /* exiting  distance    */
        }

        return (hit);
}
```

```
/* ---- clipobj - Clip object with plane pair. ----------------------- */
/*                                                                      */
/*                                                                      */
/*      Description:                                                    */
/*          Clipobj clips the supplied infinite object with two         */
/*          (a top and a bottom) bounding planes.                       */
/*                                                                      */
/*      On entry:                                                       */
/*          raybase = The base point of the intersecting ray.           */
/*          raycos  = The direction cosines of the above ray. (unit)    */
/*          bot     = The normal and perpendicular distance of the      */
/*                    bottom plane.                                     */
/*          top     = The normal and perpendicular distance of the      */
/*                    top plane.                                        */
/*          objin   = The entering distance of the intersection with    */
/*                    the object.                                       */
/*          objout  = The exiting  distance of the intersection with    */
/*                    the object.                                       */
/*                                                                      */
/*      On return:                                                      */
/*          objin   = The entering distance of the intersection.        */
/*          objout  = The exiting  distance of the intersection.        */
/*          surfin  = The identifier for the entering surface.          */
/*          surfout = The identifier for the leaving surface.           */
/*                                                                      */
/*      Returns:  True if the ray intersects the bounded object.        */
/*                                                                      */
/* -------------------------------------------------------------------- */

#define      SIDE    0                  /* Object surface           */
#define      BOT     1                  /* Bottom end-cap surface   */
#define      TOP     2                  /* Top end-cap surface      */

typedef struct {                        /* Plane: ax + by + cz + d = 0  */
        double  a ,b ,c, d;
}       Plane;


boolean clipobj         (raybase,raycos,bot,top,objin,objout,surfin,surfout)

        Point3          *raybase;       /* Base of the intersection ray */
        Vector3         *raycos;        /* Direction cosines of the ray */
        Plane           *bot;           /* Bottom end-cap plane     */
        Plane           *top;           /* Top end-cap plane        */
        double          *objin;         /* Entering distance        */
        double          *objout;        /* Exiting  distance        */
        int             *surfin;        /* Entering surface identifier */
        int             *surfout;       /* Exiting  surface identifier */

{
        boolean hit;
        double  dc, dw, t;
        double  in, out;                /* Object  intersection dists.  */
```

```
        *surfin = *surfout = SIDE;
        in  = *objin;
        out = *objout;

/*      Intersect the ray with the bottom end-cap plane.           */

        dc = bot->a*raycos->x  + bot->b*raycos->y  + bot->c*raycos->z;
        dw = bot->a*raybase->x + bot->b*raybase->y + bot->c*raybase->z + bot->d;

        if ( dc == 0.0 ) {                /* If parallel to bottom plane */
            if ( dw >= 0. ) return (FALSE);
        } else {
            t = - dw / dc;
            if ( dc >= 0.0 ) {                       /* If far plane      */
                if ( t > in && t < out ) { out = t; *surfout = BOT; }
                if ( t < in  ) return (FALSE);
            } else {                                 /* If near plane     */
                if ( t > in && t < out ) { in  = t; *surfin  = BOT; }
                if ( t > out ) return (FALSE);
            }
        }

/*      Intersect the ray with the top end-cap plane.              */

        dc = top->a*raycos->x  + top->b*raycos->y  + top->c*raycos->z;
        dw = top->a*raybase->x + top->b*raybase->y + top->c*raybase->z + top->d;

        if ( dc == 0.0 ) {                /* If parallel to top plane     */
            if ( dw >= 0. ) return (FALSE);
        } else {
            t = - dw / dc;
            if ( dc >= 0.0 ) {                       /* If far plane      */
                if ( t > in && t < out ) { out = t; *surfout = TOP; }
                if ( t < in  ) return (FALSE);
            } else {                                 /* If near plane     */
                if ( t > in && t < out ) { in  = t; *surfin  = TOP; }
                if ( t > out ) return (FALSE);
            }
        }

        *objin  = in;
        *objout = out;
        return (in < out);
}
```

◇   **Bibliography**   ◇

(Cychosz and Waggenspack 1992) J. M. Cychosz and W. N. Waggenspack, Jr. Intersecting a ray with a quadric surface. In David Kirk, editor, *Graphics Gems III*, pages 275–283. Academic Press, Boston, 1992.

(Haines 1989) Eric Haines. Essential ray tracing algorithms. In A. Glassner, editor, *An Introduction to Ray Tracing*, pages 33–77. Academic Press, London, 1989.

(Hultquist 1991) Jeff Hultquist. Intersection of a ray with a sphere. In A. Glassner, editor, *Graphics Gems*, pages 275–283. Academic Press, Boston, 1991.

(Johnston and Shene 1992) John K. Johnston and Ching-Kuang Shene. Computing the intersection of a plane and a natural quadric. *Computers and Graphics*, 16(2):179–186, 1992.

(Roth 1982) S. Roth. Ray casting for modeling solids. *Computer Graphics and Image Processing*, 18:109–144, 1982.

(Shene 1994) Ching-Kuang Shene. Computing the intersection of a line and a cylinder. In Paul Heckbert, editor, *Graphics Gems IV*, 353–355. Academic Press, Boston, 1994.

◊ V.3

Voxel Traversal along a 3D Line

Daniel Cohen
Department of Math and Computer Science
Ben Gurion University, Beer-Sheva 84105, Israel
danny@cs.bgu.ac.il

This algorithm generates the sequence of all the voxels visited by a 3D line with end-points on an integer grid. Unlike other algorithms (Amanatides and Woo 1987, Cleary and Wyvill 1988, Fujimoto *et al.* 1986), this algorithm (Cohen and Kaufman 1991) uses only integers and no trigonometric functions for its initialization. In many senses it can be regarded as an extension of the 2D line rasterization algorithms (Bresenham 1965, Aken and Novak 1985) to 3D (Kaufman and Shimony 1986, Cohen and Kaufman 1990), but here the algorithm guarantees to visit exactly **all** the voxels pierced by the 3D continuous line.

Each voxel along the 3D line is face-adjacent to its predecessor. That is, the next voxel can be determined by the face which the continuous line pierces when it leaves the voxels. Three faces are the candidates for the pierced face. Assume the line direction is positive in all three coordinates, then the continuous line departs from a voxel either through a side-face, an upper-face, or a back-face. The three faces, shown in Figure 1(a), share a vertex marked by **O** in Figure 1(b). The three edges emanating from **O** connect adjacent faces. The face from which the continuous line departs can be detected by testing the relation between the three edges L1, L2, L3 (Figure 1(c)) and the continuous line. The midpoint technique (Aken and Novak 1985) is used to accomplish these tests in order to get the pierced face.

The projection of the 3D line on the xy plane introduces a line from (x_0, y_0) to $(x_0 + \Delta x, y_0 + \Delta y)$ with an implicit equation:

$$e_{xy} = y\Delta x - x\Delta y - c_{xy} = 0 \tag{1}$$

Similarly, the projection of the 3D line on the xz plane is a line from (x_0, z_0) to $(x_0 + \Delta x, z_0 + \Delta z)$ with an implicit equation:

$$e_{xz} = z\Delta x - x\Delta z - c_{xz} = 0 \tag{2}$$

and on the zy plane we get

$$e_{zy} = y\Delta z - z\Delta y - c_{zy} = 0 \tag{3}$$

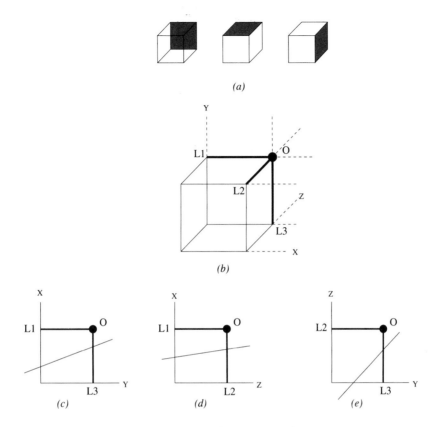

Figure 1. The tripod concept: (a) the three candidate faces, (b) the three edges L1, L2, L3 form a tripod whose apex is marked with O, (c)—(e) the tests of intersection with the tripod legs.

The previous three 2D lines are defined on the three main planes, which are parallel to the z axis, to the y axis, and to the x axis, respectively.

Observe the projected line on the xy-plane. The residual value of e_{xy}, tested at **O**, tests whether the projection of the continuous line that traverses to the next voxel intersects **L1** or **L3**. If the line intersects **L3**, then the continuous line does not depart from the upper-face and may depart either from the side-face or from a back-face. If the line intersects **L1**, then the continuous line may depart either from the upper-face or from the back-face. One more test is needed to isolate the exact face. The traversal algorithm presented below is based on these three tests, shown in Figure 1(c)–(e), structured as a decision tree:

1. If $(e_{xy} < 0)$ the next voxel is not y-adjacent.
2. If $(e_{xz} < 0)$ the next voxel is not z-adjacent.
3. If $(e_{zy} < 0)$ the next voxel is not y-adjacent.

The evaluation of the decision variables is similar to the midpoint mechanism. The midpoint location is at an equidistant point from the two candidates at the corner of the pixel, such that its sign determines whether the line intersects a side-edge or an upper-edge.

◇ The Integer Base Incremental Traversal ◇

```c
/* The following C subroutine visits all voxels along the line
segment from (x, y, z) and (x + dx, y + dy, z + dz) */

Line ( x, y, z, dx, dy, dz )
int x, y, z, dx, dy, dz;
{
    int n, sx, sy, sz, exy, exz, ezy, ax, ay, az, bx, by, bz;

    sx = sgn(dx);   sy = sgn(dy);   sz = sgn(dz);
    ax = abs(dx);   ay = abs(dy);   az = abs(dz);
    bx = 2*ax;      by = 2*ay;      bz = 2*az;
    exy = ay-ax;    exz = az-ax;    ezy = ay-az;
    n = ax+ay+az;
    while ( n-- ) {
        VisitVoxel ( x, y, z );
        if ( exy < 0 ) {
            if ( exz < 0 ) {
                x += sx;
                exy += by; exz += bz;
            }
            else {
                z += sz;
                exz -= bx; ezy += by;
            }
        }
        else {
            if ( ezy < 0 ) {
                z += sz;
                exz -= bx; ezy += by;
            }
            else {
                y += sy;
                exy -= bx; ezy -= bz;
            }
        }
    }
}
```

◇   **Bibliography**   ◇

(Aken and Novak 1985) J. R. Van Aken and M. Novak. Curve-drawing algorithms for raster displays. *ACM Transactions on Graphics*, 4(2):147–169, April 1985.

(Amanatides and Woo 1987) John Amanatides and Andrew Woo. A fast voxel traversal algorithm for ray tracing. In G. Marechal, editor, *Proceedings of EUROGRAPH-ICS'87*, pages 3–9, North-Holland, 1987. Elsevier Science Publishers B.V.

(Bresenham 1965) J. E. Bresenham. Algorithm for computer control of a digital plotter. *IBM Systems Journal*, 4(1):25–30, 1965.

(Cleary and Wyvill 1988) John G. Cleary and Geoff Wyvill. Analysis of an algorithm for fast ray tracing using uniform space subdivision. *The Visual Computer*, 4:65–83, July 1988.

(Cohen and Kaufman 1990) D. Cohen and A. Kaufman. Scan-conversion algorithms for linear and quadratic objects. In A. Kaufman, editor, *Volume Visualization*, pages 280–301. IEEE Computer Society Press, Los Alamitos, CA, 1990.

(Cohen and Kaufman 1991) D. Cohen and A. Kaufman. 3D discrete lines: Voxelization algorithms and connectivity control. *TR 91.05.09, Computer Science, SUNY at Stony Brook*, May 1991. Submitted for publication.

(Fujimoto *et al.* 1986) Akira Fujimoto, Takayu Tanaka, and Kansei Iwata. ARTS: Accelerated ray-tracing system. *IEEE Computer Graphics and Applications*, 6(4):16–26, April 1986.

(Kaufman and Shimony 1986) A. Kaufman and E. Shimony. 3d scan-conversion algorithms for voxel-based graphics. In *Proceedings of the 1986 Workshop on Interactive 3D Graphics*, pages 45–75, Chapel Hill, NC, 1986. ACM, New York.

V.4

Multi-Jittered Sampling

Kenneth Chiu

215 Lindley Hall
Indiana University
Bloomington, IN 47405
chiuk@cs.indiana.edu

Changyaw Wang

Indiana University
Bloomington, IN 47405
wangc@iuvax.cs.indiana.edu

Peter Shirley

Computer Science Department
Lindley Hall
Indiana University
Bloomington, IN 47405
shirley@iuvax.cs.indiana.edu

◇ **Abstract** ◇

Jittered sampling patterns perform better than random sampling patterns because they limit the degree of clumping that can occur. Clumping can still be present in one-dimensional projections of jittered patterns, however. We present a simple method to reduce the clumping of the X-axis and Y-axis projections by imposing an additional N-rooks constraint on the jittered sampling pattern. The resulting sampling pattern can reduce the number of rays necessary for a satisfactory image when ray-tracing.

◇ **Introduction** ◇

Monte-Carlo integration is often used to compute pixel values. For every pixel, a set of sample points is generated. The radiances of each point are then computed and averaged. To avoid aliasing, the sample points must be generated randomly such that every point is equally likely to be selected. However, a sampling pattern that is "too random" can overemphasize some parts of the pixel, resulting in excessive noise unless the number of samples is very large.

This variance can be reduced by selecting a sampling pattern that is well distributed. Intuitively, by "well distributed" we mean uniform and without clumping. Determining exactly what kinds of uniformity are important is difficult, though, especially since some patterns work well on some classes of image functions but not others.

The usual sampling pattern in computer graphics is *jittered* (Figure 1) (Cook *et al.* 1984). The pixel is divided into an $n \times n$ rectangular grid of cells. One sample point is randomly selected from within each cell, yielding $N = n^2$ samples. This method performs well in practice. Some clumping can occur, but the severity is limited.

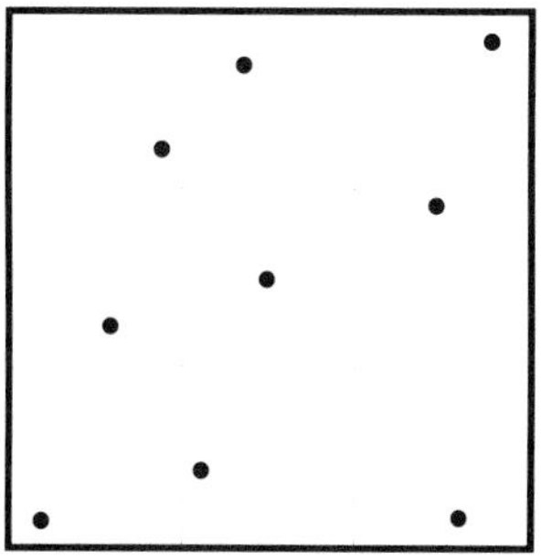

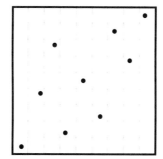

Figure 1.   Jittered sampling for $n = 3$, $N = 9$.

Figure 2. N-rooks sampling for $N = 9$.

The jittered sampling pattern is well distributed in two dimensions. When projected onto the X-axis or Y-axis, however, the clumping can be greatly increased. For an $n \times n$ grid, up to $2n$ sample points may project to essentially the same point on the X-axis. The poor quality of the projection is not important for some images, but for something like a vertical edge, the variance will increase.

To improve the distribution of the projected sampling pattern, Shirley (Shirley 1991) suggested an N-*rooks* pattern (Figure 2). The pixel is divided into an $N \times N$ rectangular grid of cells. N cells are then randomly selected with the constraint that no two selected cells may be in the same row or column. Within each selected cell, a sample point is randomly selected.

This method really amounts to jittering separately in each dimension and is well distributed in one dimension when projected to the X-axis or Y-axis, but not in the two dimensions combined. Consequently, it works better than jittering for horizontal and vertical edges, but for other images it usually performs no better when the number of samples is small, and considerably worse than jittering when the number of samples is large (Mitchell 1992).

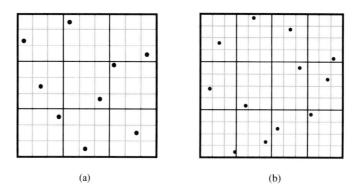

(a)   (b)

Figure 3. (a) Multi-jittered sampling for $n = 3$, $N = 9$. (b) Multi-jittered sampling for $m = 4$, $n = 3$, $N = 12$.

◇ Multi-Jittering ◇

To minimize the two-dimensional variations, yet still preserve the projected distribution, we can combine the two methods (Figure 3a). The new pattern appears jittered when viewed separately in each one-dimensional projection, and also when viewed in two dimensions. For $N = n^2$ samples, an $n \times n$ grid of cells is superimposed over an $N \times N$ subgrid of subcells. So each cell is an $n \times n$ array of subcells. One sample point is then selected from each cell as in jittered sampling, but simultaneously the N-rooks condition is also satisfied on the subgrid. The resulting sampling pattern is a jittered pattern relative to the $n \times n$ grid, and an N-rooks pattern relative to the $N \times N$ subgrid. It is well distributed in the one-dimensional projections and in two dimensions.

If the number of samples per pixel is not a perfect square, this method can still be used, as long as two acceptable factors can be found (Figure 3b). For $N = mn$ samples, an $m \times n$ grid of cells is superimposed over an $N \times N$ subgrid of subcells. So each cell is an $n \times m$ array of subcells. One sample point is again selected from each cell while simultaneously observing the N-rooks condition on the subgrid.

This method has performed better than either jittering or N-rooks on our test images regardless of feature orientation. This is probably because imposing the N-rooks condition on the jittered pattern improves not only the one-dimensional projected distributions, but also the two-dimensional distribution.

◇ C Code ◇

The code below fills a $[0, 1] \times [0, 1]$ square with an $m \times n$ multi-jittered pattern. The points are placed into an array that is passed in as an argument. The "canonical" multi-jittered pattern mentioned in the comment is shown in Figure 4.

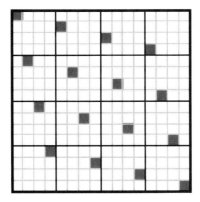

Figure 4.   Canonical multi-jittered pattern. One point is chosen inside each shaded square.

```
#include <math.h>


#define RAN_DOUBLE(l, h)    (((double) random()/0x80000000U)*((h) - (l)) + (l))
#define RAN_INT(l, h)       ((int) (RAN_DOUBLE(0, (h)-(l)+1) + (l)))


typedef struct {
    double x, y;
} Point2;


unsigned long random();     /* expected to return a random int in [0, 2^31-1] */


/*
 * MultiJitter() takes an array of Point2's and the dimension, and fills the
 * the array with the generated sample points.
 *
 *     p[] must have length m*n.
 *     m is the number of columns of cells.
 *     n is the number of rows of cells.
 */
void
MultiJitter(Point2 p[], int m, int n) {

    double subcell_width;
    int i, j;

    subcell_width = 1.0/(m*n);

    /* Initialize points to the "canonical" multi-jittered pattern. */
    for (i = 0; i < m; i++) {
        for (j = 0; j < n; j++) {
```

```
        p[i*n + j].x = i*n*subcell_width + j*subcell_width
          + RAN_DOUBLE(0, subcell_width);
        p[i*n + j].y = j*m*subcell_width + i*subcell_width
          + RAN_DOUBLE(0, subcell_width);
    }
}

/* Shuffle x coordinates within each column of cells. */
for (i = 0; i < m; i++) {
    for (j = 0; j < n; j++) {

        double t;
        int k;

        k = RAN_INT(j, n - 1);
        t = p[i*n + j].x;
        p[i*n + j].x = p[i*n + k].x;
        p[i*n + k].x = t;
    }
}

/* Shuffle y coordinates within each row of cells. */
for (i = 0; i < n; i++) {
    for (j = 0; j < m; j++) {

        double t;
        int k;

        k = RAN_INT(j, m - 1);
        t = p[j*n + i].y;
        p[j*n + i].y = p[k*n + i].y;
        p[k*n + i].y = t;
    }
}
}
```

◇ **Bibliography** ◇

(Cook *et al.* 1984) Robert L. Cook, Thomas Porter, and Loren Carpenter. Distributed ray tracing. *Computer Graphics*, 18(3):137–145, 1984.

(Mitchell 1992) Don Mitchell. Ray tracing and irregularities of distribution. In *Proceedings of Third Eurographics Workshop on Rendering*, pages 61–69, 1992.

(Shirley 1991) Peter Shirley. Discrepancy as a quality measure for sampling distributions. In *Eurographics '91*, pages 183–193, September 1991.

V.5

A Minimal Ray Tracer

Paul S. Heckbert

Computer Science Department
Carnegie Mellon University
5000 Forbes Ave.
Pittsburgh, PA 15213-3891
ph@cs.cmu.edu

In the Spring of 1987 I ran a "minimal ray tracer programming contest" over the Internet on the USENET group *comp.graphics*, challenging people to write the shortest Whitted-style ray tracing program in C. This Gem summarizes the contest and lists an ultra-minimal hybrid of the winning entries. In 21 lines of C code, this program ray traces a scene consisting of spheres, recursing for specular reflected and transmitted rays, and simulating shadows and colored lights.

First, the contest rules are briefly summarized, then the announcement of winners is given, and finally, C code is listed. The text here is a condensed version of the e-mail messages from *comp.graphics*. For full listings, see the Gems IV distribution on floppy or by FTP.

◇   Contest Rules   ◇

The goal: write the shortest Whitted-style ray tracing program in C (Whitted 1980). Countless people have written basic sphere ray tracers and made pictures of glass and chrome balls, so isn't it time we found out just how short such a program can be?

An entry in the contest was considered valid if it met the following conditions:

- it consisted of a single C source file, which compiled into an executable with no warnings,
- it ray traced spheres using Whitted's recursive shading model, simulating shadows and colored lights (more precisely, the pixel values output had to agree within ± 10 with a solution computed using a specified shading formula),
- the scene description was compiled into the program from a header file,
- it used a specified perspective camera model,
- a color picture was output in a specified ascii format.

Not required were: antialiasing, any geometric primitives besides spheres, CSG, Jell-O, any distribution ray tracing effects, lint-free code, or speed.

The winner was the valid entry with the minimum number of tokens after running the source through the C preprocessor. (This is a better measure of program length than number of lines or object code size, since it is machine-independent and more hacker-resistant.) Code to count tokens was provided to the entrants.

The contest was announced on 4 May 1987 and the winners were announced on 20 June 1987.

◇ **Contest Winners** ◇

I received entries from five people. The entries I received all passed my validation tests and they were all quite clever. Joe Cychosz of Purdue won first place with an incredibly short program of just 916 tokens.

PLACE	#TOKENS	AUTHOR	NOTES
		GENUINE ENTRIES	
1	916	Joe Cychosz, Purdue	compiler-dependent
1a	932	Joe Cychosz, Purdue	portable
2	956	Darwyn Peachey, Saskatchewan	portable
3	981	Michel Burgess, Montreal	portable
4	1003	Greg Ward, Berkeley	portable
		HONORABLE MENTIONS	
c1	10	Tony Apodaca, Pixar	cheater
c2	66	Greg Ward, Berkeley	cheater

Interestingly, the entries had nearly identical modularization into six subroutines: main, trace, intersect-sphere, vector-normalize, vector-add, and dot-product. One person, Greg Ward, cleverly exploited a loophole in my rules which allowed arbitrarily long character strings to count as a single token, and submitted a program which writes a source file, compiles it, and runs it! Tony Apodaca used a different cheat: hiding the real program in an unused part of the source file and compiling and running that program with a single call to `system()`. His program is about as minimal as you can get: 10 tokens.

What did we learn from all this? The first thing I learned is that there aren't many real hackers in *comp.graphics*. Various people offered explanations for the sparse turnout:

"The unwashed might think that the task is too difficult and the cognoscenti might think 'I know I could do it, but it's too much trouble just for a contest'. "

"We're all busy with previous hacking commitments."

"If you had a 'Get a job at Pixar Ray Tracer Contest', I might be motivated to enter."[1]

[1] Actually, Darwyn Peachey did get a job at Pixar shortly after this contest, but it's not clear if there was a connection.

Those who entered the contest also learned some repulsive C coding tricks:

- color = point: `struct {float r, g, b;}` ⇒ `struct {float x, y, z;}`
- pass structures (not just pointers to structs) to allow vector expressions
- use global variables for return values
- no optimizations: trace specular and transmitted rays even if coeff=0!
- reuse variables!
- `for (i=0; i<n; i++)` ⇒ `i = n; while (i--)`
- merge x and y loops into one
- assume statics are initialized to 0
- `&sph[i]` ⇒ `sph+i`
- choose just the right set of utility routines
- creative use of commas, e.g.: `if (a) {b;c;}` ⇒ `if (a) b,c;`
- move assignments into expressions: `b = vdot(D, U = vcomb(-1., P, s->cen))`

Cheats (non-portable C):

- eliminate semicolons in struct def: `struct {int a;}` ⇒ `struct {int a}`
- assume right-to-left argument evaluation order

Winner of the most shocking cheat award, a little gem by Joe Cychosz:

- `printf("%f %f %f\n", pt.x, pt.y, pt.z);` ⇒ `printf("%f %f %f\n", pt);`

Since Joe Cychosz said this was only his second C program (!), I asked him how he managed to do so well. He responded:

> "My primary program language is FORTRAN and COMPASS (CDC assembly) for the CYBER 205 and the CYBER 800s. ... This is an interesting way to learn C. I spent the weekend looking through Kernighan & Ritchie trying to determine if what I wanted to do was legal C. Finally, Kirk Smith found 12 tokens while we were sitting in a bar."

But if you were expecting a useful ray tracing program out of this, a warning: as one would expect of any "minimal" program, the winning program is cryptic, inefficient, unmaintainable, and nearly useless except as a source of C coding tricks. If you want a good ray tracer, look elsewhere!

◇ C Code ◇

After the contest, I took some of the tricks from Darwyn Peachey's and Joe Cychosz's programs and combined them with some of my own to create an ultra-minimal hybrid program. Two versions are reproduced below: a compacted version, `minray.card.c` that fits nicely on a business card or on an old-fashioned 24 × 80 terminal screen, and a "readable" version, `minray.c`.

minray.card.c

```
typedef struct{double x,y,z}vec;vec U,black,amb={.02,.02,.02};struct sphere{
vec cen,color;double rad,kd,ks,kt,kl,ir}*s,*best,sph[]={0.,6.,.5,1.,1.,1.,.9,
.05,.2,.85,0.,1.7,-1.,8.,-.5,1.,.5,.2,1.,.7,.3,0.,.05,1.2,1.,8.,-.5,.1,.8,.8,
1.,.3,.7,0.,0.,1.2,3.,-6.,15.,1.,.8,1.,7.,0.,0.,0.,.6,1.5,-3.,-3.,12.,.8,1.,
1.,5.,0.,0.,0.,.5,1.5,};yx;double u,b,tmin,sqrt(),tan();double vdot(A,B)vec A
,B;{return A.x*B.x+A.y*B.y+A.z*B.z;}vec vcomb(a,A,B)double a;vec A,B;{B.x+=a*
A.x;B.y+=a*A.y;B.z+=a*A.z;return B;}vec vunit(A)vec A;{return vcomb(1./sqrt(
vdot(A,A)),A,black);}struct sphere*intersect(P,D)vec P,D;{best=0;tmin=1e30;s=
sph+5;while(s-->sph)b=vdot(D,U=vcomb(-1.,P,s->cen)),u=b*b-vdot(U,U)+s->rad*s
->rad,u=u>0?sqrt(u):1e31,u=b-u>1e-7?b-u:b+u,tmin=u>=1e-7&&u<tmin?best=s,u:
tmin;return best;}vec trace(level,P,D)vec P,D;{double d,eta,e;vec N,color;
struct sphere*s,*l;if(!level--)return black;if(s=intersect(P,D));else return
amb;color=amb;eta=s->ir;d= -vdot(D,N=vunit(vcomb(-1.,P=vcomb(tmin,D,P),s->cen
)));if(d<0)N=vcomb(-1.,N,black),eta=1/eta,d= -d;l=sph+5;while(l-->sph)if((e=l
->kl*vdot(N,U=vunit(vcomb(-1.,P,l->cen))))>0&&intersect(P,U)==l)color=vcomb(e
,l->color,color);U=s->color;color.x*=U.x;color.y*=U.y;color.z*=U.z;e=1-eta*
eta*(1-d*d);return vcomb(s->kt,e>0?trace(level,P,vcomb(eta,D,vcomb(eta*d-sqrt
(e),N,black))):black,vcomb(s->ks,trace(level,P,vcomb(2*d,N,D)),vcomb(s->kd,
color,vcomb(s->kl,U,black))));}main(){printf("%d %d\n",32,32);while(yx<32*32)
U.x=yx%32-32/2,U.z=32/2-yx++/32,U.y=32/2/tan(25/114.5915590261),U=vcomb(255.,
trace(3,black,vunit(U)),black),printf("%.0f %.0f %.0f\n",U);}/*minray!*/
```

ray.h

```
/* ray.h for test1, first test scene */
#define DEPTH 3          /* max ray tree depth */
#define SIZE 32          /* resolution of picture in x and y */
#define AOV 25           /* total angle of view in degrees */
#define NSPHERE 5        /* number of spheres */

AMBIENT = {.02, .02, .02};      /* ambient light color */

/* sphere: x y z  r g b  rad  kd ks kt kl  ir */
SPHERE = {
    0., 6., .5,    1., 1., 1.,    .9,    .05, .2, .85, 0.,    1.7,
   -1., 8., -.5,   1., .5, .2,    1.,    .7, .3, 0., .05,     1.2,
    1., 8., -.5,   .1, .8, .8,    1.,    .3, .7, 0., 0.,      1.2,
    3., -6., 15.,  1., .8, 1.,    7.,    0., 0., 0., .6,      1.5,
   -3., -3., 12.,  .8, 1., 1.,    5.,    0., 0., 0., .5,      1.5,
};
```

minray.c

```
/* minimal ray tracer, hybrid version - 888 tokens
 * Paul Heckbert, Darwyn Peachey, and Joe Cychosz  13 Jun 87 */

#define TOL 1e-7
#define AMBIENT vec U, black, amb
#define SPHERE struct sphere {vec cen, color; double rad, kd, ks, kt, kl, ir} \
    *s, *best, sph[]
typedef struct {double x, y, z} vec;
#include "ray.h"
yx;
double u, b, tmin, sqrt(), tan();

double vdot(A, B)
vec A, B;
{ return A.x*B.x + A.y*B.y + A.z*B.z; }

vec vcomb(a, A, B)        /* aA+B */
double a;
vec A, B;
{
    B.x += a*A.x;
    B.y += a*A.y;
    B.z += a*A.z;
    return B;
}

vec vunit(A)
vec A;
{ return vcomb(1./sqrt(vdot(A, A)), A, black); }

struct sphere *intersect(P, D)
vec P, D;
{
    best = 0;
    tmin = 1e30;
    s = sph+NSPHERE;
    while (s-->sph)
        b = vdot(D, U = vcomb(-1., P, s->cen)),
        u = b*b-vdot(U, U)+s->rad*s->rad,
        u = u>0 ? sqrt(u) : 1e31,
        u = b-u>TOL ? b-u : b+u,
        tmin = u>=TOL && u<tmin ?
            best = s, u : tmin;
    return best;
}

vec trace(level, P, D)
vec P, D;
{
    double d, eta, e;
    vec N, color;
    struct sphere *s, *l;
```

```
        if (!level--) return black;
        if (s = intersect(P, D));
        else return amb;

        color = amb;
        eta = s->ir;
        d = -vdot(D, N = vunit(vcomb(-1., P = vcomb(tmin, D, P), s->cen)));
        if (d<0)
            N = vcomb(-1., N, black),
            eta = 1/eta,
            d = -d;
        l = sph+NSPHERE;
        while (l-->sph)
            if ((e = l->kl*vdot(N, U = vunit(vcomb(-1., P, l->cen)))) > 0 &&
                intersect(P, U)==l)
                    color = vcomb(e, l->color, color);
        U = s->color;
        color.x *= U.x;
        color.y *= U.y;
        color.z *= U.z;
        e = 1-eta*eta*(1-d*d);
        /* the following is non-portable: we assume right to left arg evaluation.
         * (use U before call to trace, which modifies U) */
        return vcomb(s->kt,
            e>0 ? trace(level, P, vcomb(eta, D, vcomb(eta*d-sqrt(e), N, black)))
                : black,
            vcomb(s->ks, trace(level, P, vcomb(2*d, N, D)),
                vcomb(s->kd, color, vcomb(s->kl, U, black))));
}

main()
{
    printf("%d %d\n", SIZE, SIZE);
    while (yx<SIZE*SIZE)
        U.x = yx%SIZE-SIZE/2,
        U.z = SIZE/2-yx++/SIZE,
        U.y = SIZE/2/tan(AOV/114.5915590261),    /* 360/PI~=114 */
        U = vcomb(255., trace(DEPTH, black, vunit(U)), black),
        printf("%.0f %.0f %.0f\n", U);           /* yowsa! non-portable! */
}
```

◇ **Acknowledgments** ◇

I'd like to thank everyone who participated in the contest, especially Darwyn Peachey, who helped me debug the rules, and Paul Haeberli, who hatched the idea for the contest with me. A Postscript version of the minimal ray tracer was written by John Hartman of U.C. Berkeley. It runs on most printers.

◇ **Bibliography** ◇

(Whitted 1980) Turner Whitted. An improved illumination model for shaded display. *CACM*, 23(6):343–349, June 1980.

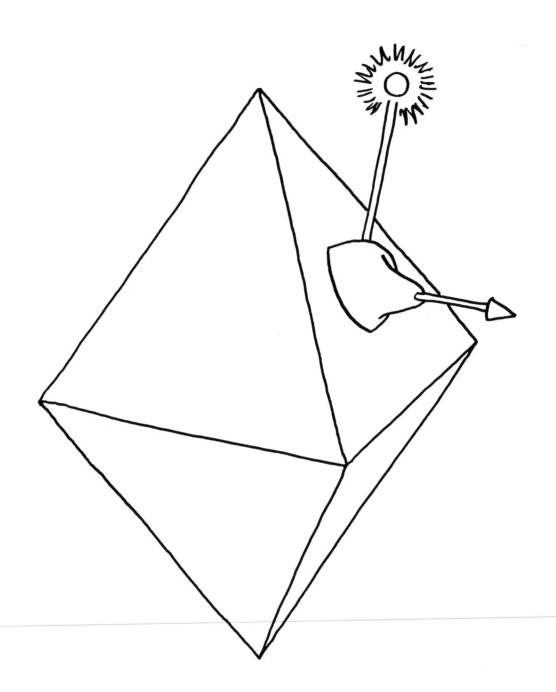

◇ VI ◇
Shading

This part of the book contains four Gems on shading 3D models.

VI.1. A Fast Alternative to Phong's Specular Model, *by Christophe Schlick.*
Describes a simple approximation to Phong's specular reflection formula that does not require exponentiation or table lookup. Page 385.

VI.2. R.E versus N.H Specular Highlights, *by Frederick Fisher and Andrew Woo.*
Compares two common variants of Phong's specular reflection formula and derives a surprising relationship between them. Page 388.

VI.3. Fast Alternatives to Perlin's Bias and Gain Functions, *by Christophe Schlick.*
Gives a simple approximation to some formulas that are commonly used in procedural texture synthesis and volume synthesis. Page 401.

VI.4. Fence Shading, *by Uwe Behrens.*
Proposes an approach halfway between Gouraud shading and Phong shading: shade along the edges of the polygon, but interpolate across the interior. Page 404.

◇ VI.1

A Fast Alternative to Phong's Specular Model

Christophe Schlick
Laboratoire Bordelais de Recherche en Informatique (LaBRI)
351, Cours de la Libération
33400 Talence, France
schlick@labri.u-bordeaux.fr

Despite its known faults (no physical validity, no energy conservation, etc.) Phong's illumination model (Phong 1975) is still the most popular reflectance model in computer graphics. The most time consuming point in that model is the computation of the specular term which involves an exponentiation. A fast, simple formula is proposed here to replace that exponentiation. The original expression of the specular term S_n in the Phong reflectance model is

$$S_n(t) = t^n$$

where $n \in [1, \infty)$ is a parameter that controls the highlight size and t is the cosine of the angle either between the viewing direction V and the reflected light direction R (Phong 1975) or between the normal vector N and the bisector vector H between the light and the viewing direction (Blinn 1977). The left part of Figure 1 shows the shape of $S_n(t)$ for different values of n.

◇ Previous Work ◇

Several solutions have been proposed to reduce the cost of the exponentiation required by the Phong model. The most straightforward techniques for exponentiation, computing $\exp(n \log t)$, or multiplying t by itself $n-1$ times, are often too slow. A first alternative is that when the exponent n is a power of two, t^n can be evaluated by $\log_2 n$ successive squarings. This trick can be generalized to arbitrary integer exponents (Knuth 1981, p. 441). Another solution is to tabulate $S_n(t)$ with a sufficient set of values and interpolate the missing ones (Bishop and Weimer 1986). When using a linear interpolation, the computation cost of such a technique is 1 addition, 1 subtraction, 2 multiplications, 1 integer part extraction and 2 table accesses. But linear interpolation often creates visible Mach banding that can only be eliminated by taking larger tables or higher order interpolations, leading to a memory/speed tradeoff. Moreover,

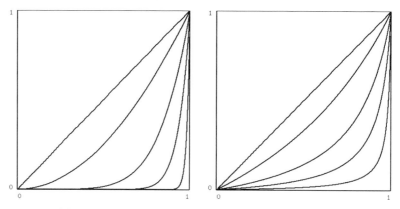

Figure 1. $S_n(t)$ for $n = 1, 2, 6, 16, 64$. Left: Phong model, Right: Alternative model.

a different table is needed for each value of parameter n, therefore the memory cost cannot be neglected for scenes with many different objects.

Another solution is to replace the function by its Taylor or Chebyshev approximation, in order to replace the exponentiation by a polynomial (Poulin and Fournier 1990). Such a technique works well for small values of n, but when n increases, keeping good accuracy rapidly requires high degree polynomials (and thus involves many multiplications).

A last solution has been presented in (Kuijk and Blake 1989) in which $S_n(t)$ is approximated by a piecewise quadratic function. Unfortunately, the quadratic function acts directly on the angle and not on its cosine, therefore a call to `acos` (almost as expensive as an exponentiation) is needed.

◇ **Description** ◇

As previous papers have observed, there is no need for great accuracy when approximating $S_n(t)$, since the Phong model is totally empirical and is not intended for physical rendering: its only purpose is to give a visual impression of specularity by adding highlights on objects. Such highlights usually facilitate the understanding of a three-dimensional scene by giving additional information about the curvature of an object. Therefore, every function that evokes a similar visual impression can be used instead of the exponentiation. We propose here such an alternative to the original formula:

$$S_n(t) = \frac{t}{n - nt + t}$$

In fact, several expressions with equivalent costs (1 addition, 1 subtraction, 1 multiplication and 1 division) can be found. This one has been chosen because the approximation of the Phong model is particularly close in the neighborhood of $t = 1$ — where the values of $S_n(t)$ are high — instead of the neighborhood of $t = 0$ as with classical approximation techniques.

The new formulation compares favorably with previous work. Compared to an implementation using Taylor or Chebyshev approximation, both the memory and the computation costs are lower. According to the architecture, the speed is more or less equivalent to look-up tables with linear interpolations (it depends on the cost of the division compared to the cost of the multiplication for the given architecture). But compared to look-up tables, the new implementation is not prone to Mach banding (all derivatives of the function are continuous) and does not require memory at all (only n has to be stored). Therefore, the formulation is particularly well adapted for hardware implementations.

The right part of Figure 1 shows the shape of $S_n(t)$ for different values of n. Compared to the left part, one can see that the decrease of the function starting from $S_n(1) = 1$ is slower as t decreases. Visually, it means that the main difference between the two models appears that the highlight frontiers are broader with the new model than with the original one.

◇   **Bibliography**   ◇

(Bishop and Weimer 1986) G. F. Bishop and D. M. Weimer. Fast phong shading. *Computer Graphics*, 20(4):103–106, 1986.

(Blinn 1977) J. F. Blinn. Models of light reflection for computer synthesized pictures. *Computer Graphics*, 11(4):192–198, 1977.

(Knuth 1981) D. E. Knuth. *The Art of Computer Programming, vol. 2, Seminumerical Algorithms*, 2nd ed. Addison-Wesley, Reading, MA, 1981.

(Kuijk and Blake 1989) A. A. Kuijk and E. H. Blake. Faster phong shading via angular interpolation. *Computer Graphics Forum*, 8(4):315–324, 1989.

(Phong 1975) B. T. Phong. Illumination for computer generated pictures. *Communications of the ACM*, 18(8):311–317, 1975.

(Poulin and Fournier 1990) P. Poulin and A. Fournier. A model for anisotropic reflection. *Computer Graphics*, 19(3):15–21, 1990.

◇ VI.2

R.E versus N.H Specular Highlights

Frederick Fisher

2630 Walsh Avenue
Kubota Pacific Computer, Inc.
Santa Clara, CA
fred@kpc.com

Andrew Woo

Alias Research, Inc.
110 Richmond Street East
Toronto, Ontario, M5C 1P1, Canada
awoo@alias.com

◇ Abstract ◇

Phong's illumination model is one popular method for calculating the specular contribution from a light source, which involves taking the dot product of the light's reflection vector R and the eye vector E (Phong 1975). Another method involves finding the vector halfway between the eye and the light vector (call this H), and taking the dot product of H and the surface normal vector N (Blinn 1977). In either case, the resulting dot product is raised to an exponent to control the shininess of the specular contribution. This Gem will discuss some commonalities and misconceptions regarding the two models and show that similar highlights result if Blinn's exponent is four times Phong's exponent, that is: $(N \cdot H)^{4r} \approx (R \cdot E)^r$.

◇ Organization and Definitions ◇

This Gem is organized as follows:

- Definitions for each lighting model are presented along with some history about the origins of each model, and some common misconceptions.
- Motivation for using the $N.H$ model and why it is faster in some situations.
- Relationships between the two models are derived for the cases where L, N, and E are coplanar. Associated errors are examined.
- Images relating the two lighting models.
- Pixel errors when N is not coplanar with L and E.
- A general relationship between the two lighting models.
- Characterizing the maximum error and its location.
- Summarizing the pixel errors.
- Summary.

388

For the following, refer to Figure 1. All vectors are normalized and anchored at the point to be lit. For convenience, some vector examples may be specified in their unnormalized form, such as $[-1, 1, 0]$ instead of $[-\sqrt{2}, \sqrt{2}, 0]$. This paper uses a right-handed coordinate system.

$L = $ Vector from point to light
$N = $ Surface normal at the point
$E = $ Vector from point to eye
$R = $ Reflected light vector $= 2(L \cdot N)N - L$
$M = $ Reflected eye vector $= 2(E \cdot N)N - E$
$H = $ Half angle vector $= Normalize(L + E) = (L + E)/\text{sqrt}(2 + 2(L \cdot E))$

Let α be the angle between L and N, which is the same as between N and R

Let β be the angle between L and H, which is the same as between H and E

Let $R.E$ be the name of the lighting model which uses the dot product of R and E to calculate the specular contribution

Let $N.H$ be the name of the lighting model which uses the dot product of H and N to calculate the specular contribution

Let ρ be the angle from R to E (rho for reflection); $\cos \rho = R \cdot E$

Let ν be the angle from N to H (nu for normal); $\cos \nu = N \cdot H$

Let r be the shininess exponent for the $R.E$ model

Let n be the shininess exponent for the $N.H$ model

Let f be the factor required to make the following true: $\cos^r \rho = \cos^{fr} \nu$, $n = fr$

LNR refers to the plane containing the vectors L, N, and R

LHE refers to the plane containing the vectors L, H, and E

$[a, b]$ means the angle between vector a and b

In this Gem, all pixel errors are represented on a scale from -255 to 255. These represent the maximum error in typical images, because the peak pixel value (radiance) of a highlight is usually chosen to be 255 or less for frame buffers with 8 bits per channel.

◇   Some History   ◇

Bui-Tuong Phong was the first to propose a model for specular reflections (Phong 1975). This model basically evaluates the highlight intensity at $(R \cdot E)^r$ (see Figure 1). Blinn later proposed a variation of this highlight evaluation: $(N \cdot H)^n$, where $H = (L + E)/|L + E|$ (Blinn 1977). Both models have often been referred to as Phong's illumination model (not to be confused with Phong shading).

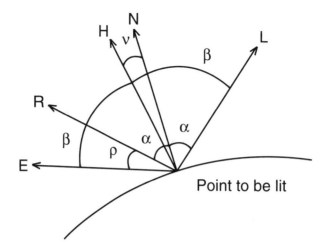

Figure 1. Vectors associated with the *R.E* and *N.H* lighting models in coplanar case.

There are numerous misconceptions about these two models such as the notion that the *R.E* and *N.H* models are actually the same (Hearn and Baker 1986, pp. 281–282) (this was corrected in a later edition of the book). In a later section, it will be shown that $[R, E]$ (ρ) is in certain cases equal to twice $[N, H]$ (ν). Watt and Watt stated this relationship as generally true in their textbook (Watt and Watt 1992, p. 45). However, this is not generally correct since it assumes that all the vectors described in Figure 1 are coplanar.

There are two extreme sets of conditions where ρ is constant and ν can vary over a wide range. Consider: $E = [0, 0, 1]$, $L = [-\epsilon, 0, -1]$, and $N = [x, y, 0]$. Various combinations of x and y will all produce a reflection vector such that ρ is small, yet ν ranges from $0°$ to $90°$. If $N = [-1, 0, 0]$, then ν is also about $0°$. If $N = [-1, 1, 0]$, then ν is about $45°$. If $N = [0, 1, 0]$, then ν is about $90°$. Conditions of this type produce a number of visual artifacts.

A second set of extreme conditions are situations like $E = [0, 0, 1]$, $L = [-1, 0, 0]$, and $N = [x, y, 0]$. In this case R is always in the xy plane and ρ is always $90°$. When $N = [0, 1, 0]$, then $H = [-1, 0, 1]$ and ν is also $90°$. As N is rotated about the z-axis from $[0, 1, 0]$ to $[-1, 0, 0]$, then ν changes from $90°$ to $45°$. Conditions of this type do not produce visual artifacts if the exponent is large. For example, even when n is as small as 10, the maximum pixel error is $255 \cos^{10} 45° = 8$.

Clearly $\rho \neq 2\nu$ for many non-coplanar conditions. Errors associated with this fact will be examined later. However, note that for all cases, the maximum highlight for each model resides at exactly the same location. Proof of this is simple and left to the reader.

Other references on this topic can be found, though lightly discussed, in textbooks (Foley *et al.* 1990, pp. 738–739, 813), (Hall 1989, pp. 76–78, 87). Also, Max mentioned that $\rho \approx 2\nu$ and the use of $n = 4r$ for some limited conditions (Max 1988, p. 39).

◇ **Motivations for Using the *N.H* Model** ◇

It can be argued that the $N.H$ evaluation is computationally faster than $R.E$. If we have a directional light with a constant viewing vector (perhaps an orthographic view or the eye at infinity for lighting), then the H vector is constant for the entire rendered scene. Thus the $N.H$ evaluation only requires finding H when the light vectors change. If H is not constant, then $N \cdot H$ can be evaluated as $(N \cdot L + N \cdot E)/\text{sqrt}(2 + 2(L \cdot E))$. Generally, $N \cdot L$ is already calculated for the diffuse component, while $N \cdot E$ is constant for all lights being considered with N.

When using the $R.E$ model, it's not necessary to compute R for every light. By computing the eye's reflection vector (M), then the value of $R \cdot E$ is equivalent to $L \cdot M$. Therefore, only one reflection calculation is required for each normal. This implies that M is constant for each shading pass (computed only once per shading pass), and can be reused as the mirror reflection ray during ray tracing as well. As a result, it can be seen that for different assumptions, the $R.E$ model is faster than the $N.H$ model.

We also need to consider which of the two models is more physically based. Hall plotted and compared the distribution functions of $R \cdot E$ and $N \cdot H$ (Hall 1989). Hall showed that the $N \cdot H$ distribution matched the more physically based Torrance-Sparrow model much more closely than $R \cdot E$. In addition, renderings were done by the authors that supported the conclusions of these function plots, in which $N \cdot H$ highlights were much more similar in shape to the Torrance-Sparrow model than the $R \cdot E$ highlights.

Understanding the relationship between these two lighting models is helpful in matching software between an Application Programming Interface (API) that uses the $R.E$ model (such as PEX) and ones that use the $N.H$ lighting model (such as Silicon Graphics' GL).

◇ **Coplanar *L, N,* and *E*** ◇

When L, N, and E are coplanar, it can be shown that:

$$\rho = 2\nu, \quad 0° \le \rho < 180° \tag{1}$$

$$\begin{aligned} \rho + 2\alpha &= 2\beta; \text{ and } \beta = \nu + \alpha \\ \rho + 2\alpha &= 2(\nu + \alpha) = 2\nu + 2\alpha \\ \rho &= 2\nu \end{aligned}$$

Although this relationship is valid as long as $N \cdot H > 0$, keep in mind that this is only meaningful for $\rho < 90°$, otherwise the $R.E$ lighting model implies that the specular contribution should be zero while the $N.H$ specular contribution may exist until ρ is almost $180°$. This difference can often be ignored because the specular contribution from the $N.H$ lighting model becomes negligible for typical exponents with $\rho > 90°$.

One way to simulate $R.E$ lighting with the $N.H$ model would be to calculate $N \cdot H$ and convert it to $R \cdot E$ before raising the value to the exponent. Using standard trigonometric identities produces:

$$\cos \rho = \cos 2\nu = 2\cos^2 \nu - 1 \tag{2}$$

So, if $N \cdot H$ is available, it could be converted to $R \cdot E$ with:

$$R \cdot E = 2(N \cdot H)(N \cdot H) - 1 \tag{3}$$

The drawback of this approach is that it requires modifying the internals of whatever is calculating $N \cdot H$ and raising it to the power of r.

Alternatively, what is the value of f that would satisfy the following?

$$(R \cdot E)^r = (N \cdot H)^{fr} \tag{4}$$

In other words, given that the specular contribution will be calculated using $N \cdot H$ raised to some power, how should the exponent for the $R.E$ model be modified such that (4) is true.

To solve for f, start by taking the rth root of both sides of Equation (4):

$$(R \cdot E) = (N \cdot H)^f$$
$$\text{Substitute } (R \cdot E) = 2(N \cdot H)^2 - 1$$
$$2(N \cdot H)^2 - 1 = (N \cdot H)^f$$
$$\text{Take the log of both sides}$$
$$\log(2(N \cdot H)(N \cdot H) - 1) = f \, \log(N \cdot H)$$
$$\text{And solve for } f$$

$$f = \log(2(N \cdot H)(N \cdot H) - 1) \ / \ \log(N \cdot H) \tag{5}$$

Thus, we see that the f is independent of the exponent, depending solely on the $N \cdot H$ result. Table 1 shows some substitutions of $N \cdot H$ into (5).

From this we hypothesize that using a constant f of 4 might provide an acceptable approximation. Comparing the Taylor series expansion of $\cos^r 2\nu$ and $\cos^{4r} \nu$ shows that this is quite accurate for small ρ, and $\rho \approx 2\nu$.

By definition, $\cos(a) = 1 - \frac{a^2}{2} + O(a^4)$ and $(1 + x)^p = 1 + px + O(x^2)$ so for small ν

$$\cos^r 2\nu \approx (1 - 2\nu^2)^r \approx 1 - 2r\nu^2$$
$$\cos^{4r} \nu \approx (1 - \frac{\nu^2}{2})^{4r} \approx 1 - 2r\nu^2$$

thus $\cos^r 2\nu \approx \cos^{4r} \nu$

Table 1. Required f for ρ given any exponent, coplanar *LNE*

ρ (degrees)	5	20.0	40.0	60.0	80.0	85.0	87.00	89.00	89.50	89.90
Required f	4.0038	4.06	4.28	4.82	6.57	8.01	9.19	11.98	13.85	18.37

Given $\rho = 2\nu$, this table shows the value of f required to make the following true: $\cos^r \rho = \cos^{fr} \nu$.

Table 2. Pixel value errors for r from 5 to 45, coplanar *LNE*

	Shininess exponent r								
ρ (deg.)	5.00	10.00	15.00	20.00	25.00	30.00	35.00	40.00	45.00
10.00	0.069	0.128	0.179	0.221	0.255	0.284	0.307	0.325	0.339
20.00	0.906	1.330	1.466	1.435	1.318	1.161	0.995	0.835	0.690
30.00	3.252	3.210	2.376	1.564	0.965	0.571	0.329	0.186	0.103
40.00	6.227	3.437	1.424	0.525	0.181	0.060	0.019	0.006	0.002
50.00	7.668	1.913	0.360	0.060	0.010	0.001	0.000	0.000	0.000
60.00	6.391	0.560	0.038	0.002	0.000	0.000	0.000	0.000	0.000
70.00	3.525	0.082	0.002	0.000	0.000	0.000	0.000	0.000	0.000
80.00	1.195	0.006	0.000	0.000	0.000	0.000	0.000	0.000	0.000
85.00	0.573	0.001	0.000	0.000	0.000	0.000	0.000	0.000	0.000

Given $\rho = 2\nu$, and pixel values that range from 0 to 255, this table shows the error associated with calculating the specular contribution using: $\cos^{4r} \nu$ instead of $\cos^r \rho$.
Specifically, table value $= 255(\cos^{4r} \nu - \cos^r \rho)$.

As ρ increases beyond $90°$, the $R.E$ result would be less than zero, but $N \cdot H$ is still greater than zero because the $N \cdot H$ curve does not fall off as rapidly as $R \cdot E$. This means that for large angles from the eye to the reflection vector, the error increases without bounds. Fortunately, when the value of $(N \cdot H)^{fr}$ is calculated, and combined with the pixel range of $[0, 255]$, the maximum pixel value error is limited. We measure the absolute error using the following definition:

$$\text{pixel error} = 255(\cos^{4r} \nu - \cos^r \rho) \tag{6}$$

For exponents from 5 to 45, Table 2 shows the error in pixel values. Note that using $f = 4$ produces very little error. Although the required f from Table 1 increases with ρ, the final pixel values are smaller, and the overall effect is very little pixel value errors even when using a constant f of 4. For exponents greater than 45 (which are typical values), the error remains less than one pixel value. When the exponent is less than 5 (not typical), and ρ approaches $90°$, the maximum pixel error may be from 10 to greater than 60.

◇ Images Relating the Two Lighting Models ◇

In order to test the notion of using $f = 4$ in the general case, we rendered some spheres under varying conditions. Figure 2 was rendered with the values of $E = [0, 0, 1]$, $L = [Lx, 0, Lz]$, and $N = [Nx, Ny, Nz]$.

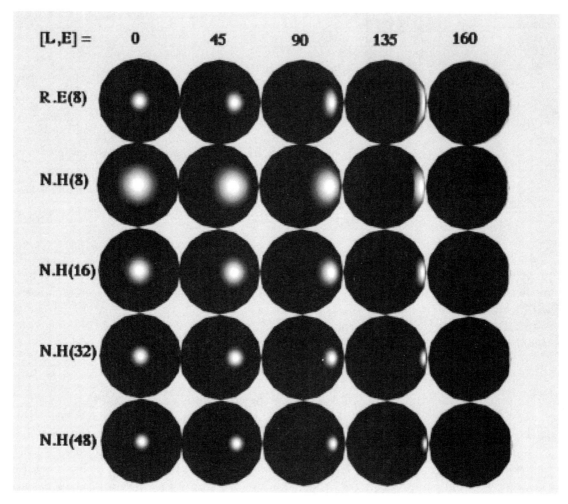

Figure 2. Normalized images comparing *R.E* and *N.H* specular highlights.

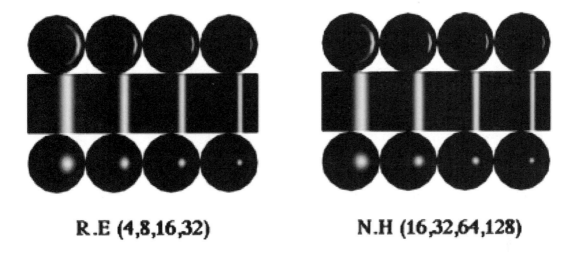

R.E (4,8,16,32)   N.H (16,32,64,128)

Figure 3.   Some quadric surfaces comparing *R.E* and *N.H* specular highlights.

Columns of images from left to right correspond to $[L, E]$ of: $0°$, $45°$, $90°$, $135°$, and $160°$. From top to bottom, each row of spheres was rendered with: $R.E$ model, $N.H$ model with $f = 1, 2, 4$, and 6. Note that for $[L, E] \leq 45°$, the $R.E$ model and $N.H$ model with $f = 4$ exhibit almost identical highlights. However, for $[L, E] > 45°$, their highlights look noticeably different. This is when ρ is small and $[L, E]$ becomes large. Even more interesting are the general shapes of the differing highlights: the $N.H$ model appears to generate more circular highlights regardless of the geometry, whereas the $R.E$ model produces highlights that appear to wrap around the geometry. The $N.H$ highlight effect more closely corresponds to the physically based lighting effects observed in nature.

Figure 3 shows three distinct geometry types (bottle cap, cylinder, sphere) lit by a single directional light source.

Geometries exhibit different patterns of highlight (from different surface normal orientations). The left image was produced with the $R.E$ model, using cosine exponents of 4, 8, 16 and 32. The right image was produced with the $N.H$ model, with the exponent values multiplied by $f = 4$. The highlights look to be very similar, and hardly distinguishable from each other, except for the left-most cylinders in each image.

A final note: it is possible to generate results where both models will exhibit a sharp discontinuity in highlights, as can be seen in Figure 2 when $[N, H]$'s exponent is 8, and $[L, E] = 135°$. This occurs when $N.L < 0$, but the highlight dot products ($R.E$ or $N.H$) are still positive. In most rendering software, the $N \cdot L < 0$ check determines if any diffuse or specular light is received. Thus, this is a common flaw in both models.

◇ **Pixel Errors When *N* Is Not Coplanar with *L* and *E*** ◇

Unfortunately, when E is not coplanar with L and N, the relationship of $\rho = 2\nu$ can only be an approximation. However, the associated errors are minimized by using f equal to four.

In order to visualize the errors, note that L, N, R are always coplanar, and L, H, E are also coplanar. Given any system of L, N, and E, it's possible to transform the original coordinates to a normalized right-handed reference coordinate system such that:

- The eye vector is pointing along the +z axis. $E = [0, 0, 1]$.
- The LHE plane is transformed such that L, H, and E lie in the $-x$ half space, on the xz plane.
- The L vector is in the xz plane where $x \leq 0$. $L = [Lx, 0, Lz]$, $Lx^2 + Lz^2 = 1$.
- The normal can be anywhere in the +z halfspace. This implies that the reflection vector may be anywhere. To characterize the position of the normal, we define the angles ϕ and θ. See Figure 4. ϕ is measured from the $-x$ axis. θ is measured from the +y axis. Both these angles range from 0° to 180°. Definitions for the normal angles were chosen such that plots and tables enumerating information have roughly the same orientation.
  $N = [-\sin\theta\cos\phi, \cos\theta, \sin\theta\sin\phi]$
- All possible normal positions are representable with: $0° \leq \phi \leq 180°$ and $0° \leq \theta \leq 180°$.

This scenario corresponds to looking at the specular highlight on a unit sphere, using directional lights with the eye at infinity (constant angle between L and E). These assumptions leave three degrees of freedom: two for the direction of the normal and one for the angle between the light and eye.

Figure 5 shows the pixel errors for different N vectors, given $[L, E] = 90°$, $f = 4$, and $r = 10$.

◇ **A General Relationship between the Two Lighting Models** ◇

It was possible to derive the following generalization which relates ρ and ν:

$$\cos\rho = \cos 2\nu + 2\sin^2\beta\cos^2\theta \tag{7}$$

The coplanar cases correspond to $\theta = 90°$. Note the error increases as β increases or the normal moves from the coplanar cases. Equation 7 was perceived by a stroke of intuition, preceded by hours of looking at function plots of various sub-terms associated with $N.H$ and $R.E$.

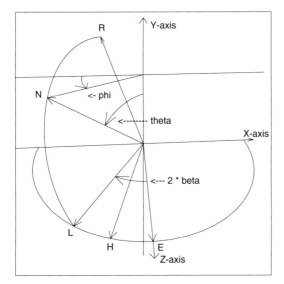

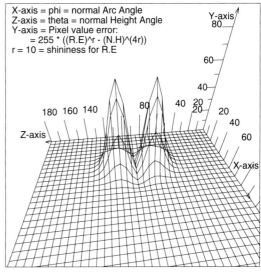

Figure 4. Reference coordinate system for visualizing lighting model parameters.

Figure 5. Pixel errors: $f = 4$, $[L, E] = 90°$, $Y = 255$ $((R \cdot E)^r - (N \cdot H)^{4r})$.

Equation 7 can be completely generalized by noting that:

$$\cos\theta = \frac{L \times H \cdot N}{|L \times H|} = \frac{L \times E \cdot N}{|L \times E|}$$

$$|L \times H| = \sin\beta$$

$$|L \times E| = \sin 2\beta$$

$$1 + L \cdot E = 1 + \cos 2\beta = 2\cos^2\beta$$

Appropriate substitutions into 7 will lead to:

$$\cos\rho = \cos 2\nu + 2(L \times H \cdot N)^2 = \cos 2\nu + \frac{(L \times E \cdot N)^2}{1 + L \cdot E} \tag{8}$$

$$R \cdot E = 2(N \cdot H)(N \cdot H) - 1 + 2(L \times H \cdot N)^2 \tag{9}$$

Equation 9 is not strictly a function of $N.H$ because of the cross product term. Such a function may not exist because of the degrees of freedom associated with α and β. Further substitutions of expressions that only involve L, E, or N will result in:

$$(L \cdot E)^2 + (E \cdot N)^2 + (N \cdot L)^2 - 2(L \cdot E)(E \cdot N)(N \cdot L) - 1 + (L \times E \cdot N)^2 = 0 \tag{10}$$

Although Equations 7 through 9 are more useful when considering the lighting models, the proof of their validity has only been verified by showing that 10 is an identity. Equation 10 is also interesting because it is valid for any three normalized vectors.

Equation 10 may be proved by expanding terms and recombining. A more elegant proof was found by Alan Paeth. For square matrices, the following identity is true:

$$|M^T M| = |M|^2 \tag{11}$$

Let $M = [L|E|N]$, the matrix formed by augmenting column vectors L, E, and N. Substituting M into Equation 11 will lead to Equation 10, which may be done with unnormalized vectors to get a similar identity.

Points along the plane where $L \times E \cdot N = 0$ will generate pixel values with little difference between the two models, even though $R \cdot E$ falls off more rapidly than $N \cdot H$ when moving away from the highlight. This corresponds to the coplanar LNE cases.

As N changes from the case producing the highlight along the plane where $L \times E \times N$ points in the same direction as $L \times E \times H$, then $N \cdot H$ falls off more rapidly than $R \cdot E$. These are the cases which produce the error bumps as depicted in Figure 5. Somewhere in between this case and coplanar LNE there is a contour of points where the error is zero.

Visual differences occur when two conditions are met: ρ is small *and* $[L, E]$ is large, i.e., when looking at points near a highlight caused by a light vector that is nearly opposite the eye vector. See Figure 2.

A more complex interaction is introduced by considering the eye at varying distances from a unit sphere. Again the shape of the error function is similar to the previous examples, but the error increases as the eye is brought closer to the unit sphere. When the eye is farther than about 5 units from the unit sphere, then the error function roughly corresponds to the one with the eye at infinity.

Similar complications occur when the light is not directional, i.e., it is a spot or positional light.

◇ Characterizing the Maximum Error and Its Location ◇

This section is intended to provide a feel for how the bumps in the pixel error plot of Figure 5 change with $[L, E]$ and shininess. Although the error function is quite complex for small shininess values (less than 10), some generalizations can be made for larger exponents.

It's possible to derive closed form error functions for some combinations of f and shininess; however, many conditions produce intractable equations to solve. The following observations were obtained using numerical techniques.

When $f = 4$, the shape of the plots depicting the pixel errors is roughly the same for other values of $[L, E]$, except when $[L, E]$ is very small or very large. As $[L, E]$ becomes

Table 3.   Maximum pixel error given shininess and [*L, E*], with *f* = 4

	\multicolumn{7}{c}{2β = angle between L and E (degrees)}
r	0.00	30.00	60.00	90.00	120.00	150.00	180.00
10.00	-3.63	4.73	25.56	63.75	122.24	198.52	255.00
20.00	-1.77	5.53	26.23	63.75	121.35	197.23	255.00
40.00	-0.87	6.00	26.56	63.75	120.91	196.59	255.00
60.00	-0.58	6.16	26.67	63.75	120.77	196.37	255.00
80.00	-0.44	6.24	26.73	63.75	120.69	196.27	255.00
100.00	-0.35	6.29	26.76	63.75	120.65	196.20	255.00
200.00	-0.18	6.40	26.83	63.75	120.56	196.08	255.00
300.00	-0.12	6.43	26.86	63.76	120.54	196.03	255.00
400.00	-0.09	6.45	26.87	63.76	120.52	196.01	255.00

small, the peaks merge to form a ring around the maximum highlight. At the same time, the maximum pixel value error decreases to less than 4 for a shininess of 10.

As [*L, E*] becomes large, the peaks grow to a maximum of 255 pixel values.

For a given [*L, E*], the location of the maximum error moves toward the point of maximum highlight as the shininess increases.

Curiously, the maximum pixel error is relatively independent of the exponent, depending mostly on the angle [*L, E*]. While this may appear to be a problem with the approximation, closer examination reveals that the volume of the error bumps decreases significantly as the shininess increases. Table 3 shows the maximum pixel error for some values of [*L, E*].

◇   Summarizing the Pixel Errors   ◇

For each error surface like the one depicted in Figure 5, it's possible to characterize the pixel error by calculating the average and standard deviation. A summary of sampled pixel error averages is not presented since the average is always close to zero because of the many samples, only a few are non-zero near the highlight. A summary of the standard deviations would show error values less than 10 for exponents of 40 and [*L, E*] less than 120°, or with exponents of 180 and [*L, E*] less than 140°.

While the volume under the error region decreases as the shininess increases, the peak error values remain nearly the same. This is due to the nature of the equations which produce zero error along a line through the center of the highlight.

◇   Summary   ◇

The *R.E* and *N.H* lighting models are different, although similar highlights result if Blinn's exponent is four times Phong's exponent, that is: $(N \cdot H)^{4r} \approx (R \cdot E)^r$.

Visual differences occur when two conditions are met: ρ is small and $[L, E]$ is large, i.e., when looking at points near a highlight caused by a light vector that is nearly opposite the eye vector.

An identity was derived which relates angles involved in the $R.E$ and $N.H$ lighting models:

$$\cos \rho = \cos 2\nu + \frac{(L \times E \cdot N)^2}{1 + L \cdot E} \tag{12}$$

Demonstrating the validity of Equation 12 resulted in proving an interesting identity that is valid for any three normalized vectors, L, E, and N:

$$(L \cdot E)^2 + (E \cdot N)^2 + (N \cdot L)^2 - 2(L \cdot E)(E \cdot N)(N \cdot L) - 1 + (L \times E \cdot N)^2 = 0 \tag{13}$$

◇ Acknowledgments ◇

Fred would like to thank Mike Toelle for getting him started on this by showing that $\rho = 2\nu$ for coplanar LNE, and Karen Melchior for her support and encouragement during the post inspiration phase of this paper. Both Andrew and Fred would like to thank Paul Heckbert for his insight and suggestions, and Alan Paeth for the elegant proof of the vector identity.

◇ Bibliography ◇

(Blinn 1977) J. Blinn. Models of light reflection for computer synthesized pictures. *Computer Graphics*, 11(2):192–198, July 1977.

(Foley *et al.* 1990) J. Foley, A. Van Dam, S. Feiner, and J. Hughes. *Computer Graphics: Principles and Practice*. Addison-Wesley, Reading, MA, 1990.

(Hall 1989) R. Hall. *Illumination and Color in Computer Generated Imagery*. Springer-Verlag, New York, 1989.

(Hearn and Baker 1986) B. Hearn and M. Baker. *Computer Graphics*. Prentice-Hall, Englewood Cliffs, NJ, 1986.

(Max 1988) N. Max. Shading algorithms, 1988. Tutorial notes on Image Synthesis, ACM SIGGRAPH '88, August 1988, Chapter 7.

(Phong 1975) Bui-Tuong Phong. Illumination for computer generated pictures. *Communications of the ACM*, 18(6):311–317, June 1975.

(Watt and Watt 1992) A. Watt and M. Watt. *Advanced Animation and Rendering Techniques, Theory and Practice*. Addison-Wesley, Reading, MA, 1992.

◇ VI.3

Fast Alternatives to Perlin's Bias and Gain Functions

Christophe Schlick
Laboratoire Bordelais de Recherche en Informatique (LaBRI)
351, Cours de la Libération
33400 Talence, France
schlick@labri.u-bordeaux.fr

In (Perlin and Hoffert 1989), the authors presented two basic functions `bias` and `gain`. Initially proposed to modify density distributions in the so-called hypertexture technique, `bias` and `gain` have become very general tools, almost as famous as the `noise` function from the same author (Perlin 1985). We propose here alternate formulas for the two functions which require less computation time.

Applications for `bias` and `gain` can be found at every step of the rendering pipeline, including geometrical modeling by implicit surfaces, procedural textures, goniometric distributions of light sources, colormap manipulation, and image filtering.

The purpose of `bias` is to alter the result of a given function, in order to favor either its low or its high values.[1] The purpose of `gain` is to increase or decrease the gradient of a function at a given point. The original functions proposed in (Perlin and Hoffert 1989) were the following:

$$\text{Bias}: \quad \forall t \in [0,1] \quad \beta_a(t) = t^{-\frac{\ln a}{\ln 2}}$$

$$\text{Gain}: \quad \forall t \in [0,1] \text{ if } t < \frac{1}{2} \text{ then } \gamma_a(t) = \frac{1}{2}\,\beta_a(2t) \text{ else } \gamma_a(t) = 1 - \frac{1}{2}\,\beta_a(2-2t)$$

where $a \in (0,1)$ is a parameter that defines the strength of the deformation applied to the function — note that $\beta_{\frac{1}{2}}(t) = \gamma_{\frac{1}{2}}(t) = t$. Figure 1 shows `bias` and `gain` with different values for a.

In scenes of medium or high complexity (including many procedural textures, for instance) a heavy use of `bias` and `gain` is usually made (one hundred times per antialiased pixel is common), therefore a fast implementation for the two functions is desirable.

A first possibility is to create look-up tables for them. Such a solution works well when variables are discrete with few different values (like an 8-bit colormap), but it becomes

---

[1] Note that the `bias` function is essentially the same as the "gamma function" that has been used for years for gamma correction of pictures. The contribution of Perlin and Hoffert was mainly to give the function a name and to propose some innovative ways to extend its applicability.

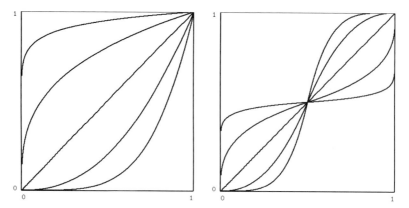

Figure 1. Original `bias` and `gain` functions for $a = 0.05, 0.2, 0.5, 0.8, 0.95$.

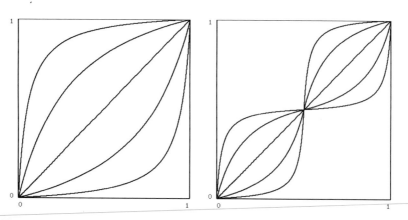

Figure 2. New `bias` and `gain` functions for $a = 0.05, 0.2, 0.5, 0.8, 0.95$.

less efficient when the number of discrete values increases. When continuous variables are considered, it is even less efficient because an interpolation scheme between different look-up values is required (and usually simple linear interpolation is not sufficient due to the visible Mach banding effects it creates). But the main drawback of look-up tables for the implementation of `bias` and `gain` is that a different table is needed for each different value of parameter a. Therefore the memory cost can become troublesome for complex scenes with many procedural textures, for instance.

A second possibility is to use a simpler mathematical function to replace the exponentiation. We propose here such an alternative (see Figure 2):[2]

$$\text{Bias}: \ \beta_a(t) = \frac{t}{(1/a - 2)(1 - t) + 1}$$

$$\text{Gain}: \text{if } t < \frac{1}{2} \text{ then } \gamma_a(t) = \frac{t}{(1/a - 2)(1 - 2t) + 1} \text{ else } \gamma_a(t) = \frac{(1/a - 2)(1 - 2t) - t}{(1/a - 2)(1 - 2t) - 1}$$

In an efficient implementation (by precomputing one or two values), the cost of `bias` can be reduced to 1 addition, 1 multiplication and 1 division, and the cost of `gain` to 1 comparison, 3 additions, 1 multiplication and 1 division. Compared to an implementation using a look-up table with linear interpolations, the computation of the new formulation is almost equivalent, but of course, it is not prone to Mach banding and only requires the storage of one or two precomputed values for each parameter a. Therefore, the formulation is particularly well adapted for hardware implementations.

In addition to speed, this Gem presents two other advantages over the original formulas. First, the curves are symmetric across the second diagonal (that is, $\beta_a(1 - \beta_a(t)) = 1 - t$): it means that low and high values are treated similarly. Second, by replacing a by $1 - a$, symmetric curves across to the first diagonal are obtained (that is, $\beta_{1-a}(\beta_a(t)) = t$): it means that the effect of the functions can be reversed by giving a symmetric value to parameter a.

◇ **Bibliography** ◇

(Perlin 1985) K. Perlin. An image synthesizer. *Computer Graphics*, 19(3):183–190, 1985.

(Perlin and Hoffert 1989) K. Perlin and E. Hoffert. Hypertexture. *Computer Graphics*, 23(3):287–296, 1989.

(Schlick 1994) C. Schlick. Rational fraction approximation: A basic tool for computer graphics. Technical Report, 94/795, LaBRI, 1994.

---

[2]How the formulas have been found is out of the scope of this Gem. The interested reader is invited to refer to (Schlick 1994) or to contact the author for a full explanation of the approximation process.

◇ VI.4

Fence Shading

Uwe Behrens
Am Neuen Markt 21
28199 Bremen, Germany
l11h@zfn.uni-bremen.de

◇ Introduction ◇

A nice and easily implemented way to enhance the quality of Gouraud shading is to use Fence shading instead. Remember: Gouraud shading first calculates the illumination model at the vertices of a convex polygon. Afterwards, it linearly interpolates between these colors along the edges of the polygon and then between edges along each scan line (Gouraud 1971). A method that results in reduced Mach banding and better image quality is Phong shading. Instead of interpolating the colors of the vertices over the entire polygon, Phong interpolated the normals of the surface at the vertices and calculated the illumination model at each pixel, using the interpolated normals (Phong 1975). As a link between these algorithms we propose Fence shading. Here, illumination is computed along polygon edges, but interpolated across scan lines.

◇ Fence Shading ◇

Fence shading is a mixture of Phong and Gouraud shading. In Fence shading, normals are interpolated along the edges of the polygon and then used to calculate the illumination at the end points of each span. These colors are then linearly interpolated along the scan line, resulting in the color for each pixel. Using this method, you get a "fence" of Phong shaded pixels at the boundary of the polygon surrounding a set of Gouraud shaded spans. See Figure 1 for a comparison of the three methods. For Gouraud shading, the number of pixels that have to be illuminated is constant for a given polygon. Doing Phong shading, the number of pixels to be illuminated equals the number of pixels in the polygon, which increases with the square of the polygon's diameter in pixels. For Fence shading, only two pixels per scan line must be illuminated. Consequently, the sum of pixels that have to be illuminated grows linearly with the polygon's diameter. It it is clear that Fence shading drastically reduces the time for illuminating a polygon, compared to Phong shading, when the polygon is large.

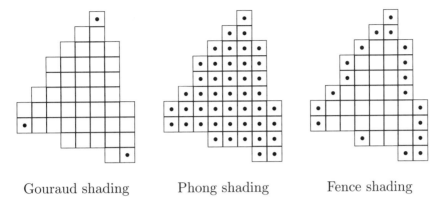

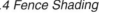

Gouraud shading   Phong shading   Fence shading

Figure 1. Comparison of Gouraud, Phong and Fence shading. Marked pixels are those for which the Illumination Model must be evaluated.

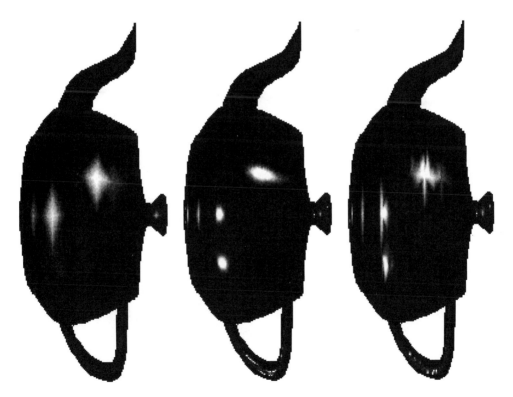

Figure 2. left: Gouraud shading, middle: Phong shading, right: Fence shading. Note: pictures have been rotated $90°$, so scanlines are now vertical.

◇ **Related Work** ◇

Different methods that try to interpolate in some way between Phong and Gouraud shading are InterPhong shading (Magnenat-Thalmann *et al.* 1991) and Highlight shading (Pöpsel and Hornung 1990). Unfortunately, both methods are much more complicated and require additional memory or far greater calculation time. Other methods have been proposed for speeding up Phong shading. Phong and Crow analytically decide whether polygons contain highlights and use Phong shading on those but Gouraud shading on the rest (Phong and Crow 1975). Further methods are interpolation of dot products (van Dam 1988), transformation of normals to polar coordinates and interpolation in this representation (Kuijk and Blake 1989), reformulation of Phong's formula with Taylor series (Bishop and Weimer 1986), and similar optimized methods. A good overview of this subject is (Claussen 1990). All these methods also require far more computation time than Fence shading but usually give better results.

If your model contains only a few, relatively large polygons, Fence shading results are quite similar to Gouraud shading. As the size of the polygons decreases, the illumination becomes more and more Phong-like. This is also true for Gouraud shading while giving a slower convergence than Fence shading. Obviously, Fence shading has no theoretical or empirical background; it is only a "hack."

◇ **Characteristics** ◇

Fence shading has some advantages:

- It catches more specular highlights than Gouraud shading while requiring only a moderate increase in computing resources.
- It is much faster than Phong shading, especially if the model contains only a few large polygons.
- It does not require any additional memory for adaptively created primitives as, for example, Highlight shading.
- The underlying geometrical model (polygons) is not as obviously visible as in Gouraud shading.
- Fence shading is very easily adapted to an existent Gouraud shader. This is not true for most Phong speed-ups mentioned above. Pseudocode for a Fence shader is given below.

Naturally, there are some disadvantages too:

- Specular highlights look smeared and washed out (see Figure 2). This is due to the Gouraud shading along the spans. This effect is also visible in Gouraud shading, but more remarkable in Fence shading.

- For polygon meshes, a different data structure may be appropriate to avoid reshading of already treated edges in the mesh.

- The output of a given polygon depends on its orientation on the screen. This effect is also noticeable in Gouraud shading.

The pseudocode for a Fence shader is given below:

```
for all polygons {
  for all scanlines intersecting the actual polygon {
    for each span {
(*)    calculate span end points, remap to world coordinates
(*)    calculate illumination for span vertices
      for each pixel in the actual span {
        calculate color from linear interpolation of
        span vertex colors
      }
    }
  }
}
```

Lines with (∗) mark code to be adapted/added to a classical Gouraud shader.

◇ **Further Work** ◇

- It would be nice to have a shader that is able to choose from different shading algorithms, only on an abstract specification like "quick results," "high quality," etc. Perhaps Fence shading would nicely integrate as a link between Gouraud and Phong shading.

- Fence shading can work most quickly if an appropriate data structure is used that avoids reshading of formerly treated edges.

- For renderers that are not scanline oriented, there is another improvement: You can scan convert polygons that are relatively wide compared to their height not in y- but in x-direction. That helps to reduce the artifacts introduced by Fence shading. As you can see in the lower part of the "Fence shaded" triangle in Figure 1, shading gaps occur in edges with slope between 1 and −1. That would not occur if the scan conversion was done in x-direction. A decision whether to change the direction of scan conversion could be based on the value of the polygon's bounding box side-length ratio.

◇ **Comparison** ◇

Figure 3 and the table below compare the ability to catch highlights on a polygon for several locations between Gouraud, Phong, and Fence shading.

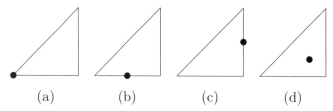

| (a) | (b) | (c) | (d) |

Figure 3. Various locations for highlights on a triangle; see table below for a comparison of Gouraud vs. Phong vs. Fence shading.

Method/Location	(a)	(b)	(c)	(d)
Gouraud	hit	miss	miss	miss
Phong	hit	hit	hit	hit
Fence	hit	hit/miss[1]	hit	miss

◇ **Acknowledgments** ◇

Many thanks go to Ute Claussen for her aid in editing and translating this paper. Stefan Hahn and Thomas Dunkhase made the production of the screenshots possible.

◇ **Bibliography** ◇

(Bishop and Weimer 1986) G. Bishop and D. M. Weimer. Fast phong shading. *Computer Graphics (SIGGRAPH '86 Proceedings)*, 20(4):103–106, August 1986.

(Claussen 1990) Ute Claussen. On reducing the phong shading method. *Computers and Graphics*, 14(1):73–81, 1990.

(Gouraud 1971) H. Gouraud. Continuous shading of curved surfaces. *IEEE Transactions on Computers*, C-20(6):623–629, June 1971.

(Kuijk and Blake 1989) A. A. M. Kuijk and E. H. Blake. Faster phong shading via angular interpolation. *Computer Graphics Forum*, 8(4):315–324, December 1989.

---

[1]If scan conversion was done in x-direction, this highlight will be visible; otherwise, it won't.

(Magnenat-Thalmann *et al.* 1991) Nadia Magnenat-Thalmann, Daniel Thalmann, and Hong Tong Minh. InterPhong shading. In James Arvo, editor, *Graphics Gems II*, pages 232–241. Academic Press, Boston, 1991.

(Phong 1975) Bui-T. Phong. Illumination for computer generated pictures. *Communications of the ACM*, 18(6):311–317, June 1975.

(Phong and Crow 1975) Bui-T. Phong and F. C. Crow. Improved rendition of polygonal models of curved surfaces. In *Proceedings of the 2nd USA-Japan Computer Conference*, 1975.

(Pöpsel and Hornung 1990) J. Pöpsel and Ch. Hornung. Highlight shading: Lighting and shading in a PHIGS+/PEX-environment. *Computers and Graphics*, 14(1):55–64, 1990.

(van Dam 1988) Andries van Dam. PHIGS+ functional description Revision 3.0. *Computer Graphics*, 22(3):125–218, July 1988.

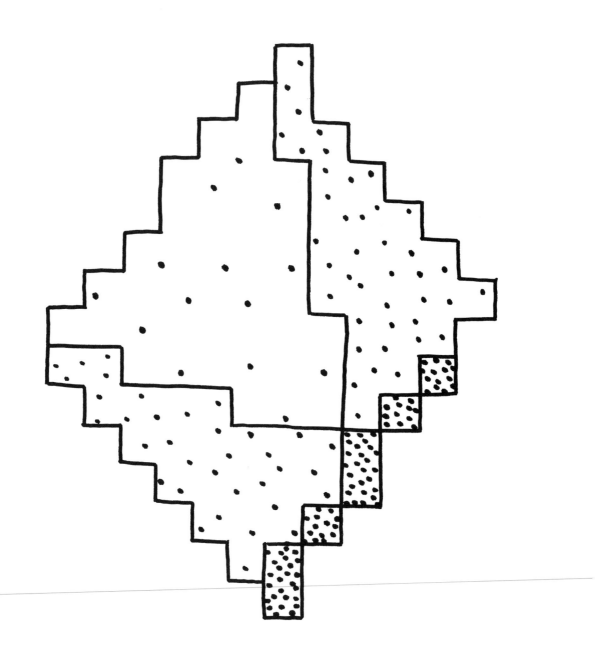

◇ VII ◇
Frame Buffer Techniques

This part of the book contains one Gem on interactive raster graphics and two on high fidelity image display and storage. They apply to both grayscale and color images.

VII.1. XOR-Drawing with Guaranteed Contrast, *by Manfred Kopp and Michael Gervautz.*
Gives simple guidelines for the choice of write mask when drawing cursors and other graphics with exclusive-OR on multi-bit frame buffers. Page 413.

VII.2. A Contrast-Based Scalefactor for Luminance Display, *by Greg Ward.*
Presents a simple technique for displaying pictures that have a dynamic range (ratio of brightest to dimmest pixel) beyond that of the display. Page 415.

VII.3. High Dynamic Range Pixels, *by Christophe Schlick.*
Proposes a pixel encoding technique that allows color images with high dynamic range to be stored using only 24 bits per pixel. Page 422.

◊ VII.1

XOR-Drawing with Guaranteed Contrast

Manfred Kopp

Technical University of Vienna
Vienna, Austria
kopp@eigvs4.una.ac.at

Michael Gervautz

Technical University of Vienna
Vienna, Austria
gervautz@eigvs4.una.ac.at

Cursors, rubber band lines, and other graphics often must be drawn very quickly during interaction. Using an XOR operation to draw such graphics is very fast, since it can be undone with another XOR. Other techniques such as double buffering, or saving and restoring a window around the graphic element, are much slower. Consequently XOR's are the most commonly used technique for fast, reversible graphics. This Gem describes the best XOR masks to use for guaranteed color contrast of graphics with background.

Frame buffers with 8 or fewer bits per pixel are typically used either with a smooth colormap that ramps smoothly from black to white (sometimes linear, sometimes a "gamma" power curve), or otherwise with a less regular colormap. Frame buffers with more than 8 bits per pixel usually have their bits segregated into red bits, green bits, and blue bits by the hardware. Common configurations are 15 bits per pixel and 24 bits per pixel, with 5 and 8 bits per component, respectively. Such frame buffers sometimes have colormaps and sometimes not. When colormaps are available, they are almost always set to a smooth black-to-white ramp. Like in the case of the grayscale, these colormaps typically use either a linear or a gamma power curve.

For the purpose of XOR graphics, there are really only two cases to consider: frame buffers with a smooth colormap (no colormap is like an identity colormap), and frame buffers with a "non-smooth" colormap. When XOR-ing all bits in a frame buffer with a smooth colormap, colors near mid-gray are hardly changed (Figure 1). If the colormap is an identity, then the crossover point is at 50% gray. In frame buffers with a non-smooth colormap, the results are, regardless of the XOR-mask, very colormap-dependent.

Let us examine the color 50% gray. The greatest color difference relative to gray is 50% in each color component red, green, and blue. The appropriate colors are black, white, red, green, blue, yellow, magenta, and cyan. So the minimum over all colors of the maximal color difference for any arbitrary color is 50% in each color component. The only XOR-mask that fulfills this constraint is the color where the most significant bit of each color component is set to 1 and all others set to 0. The effect of such an

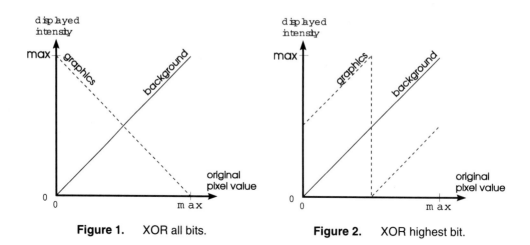

Figure 1.   XOR all bits.   **Figure 2.**   XOR highest bit.

XOR-mask is that the most significant bit of every color component is inverted, causing a color difference of about 50% in every color component (Figure 2). The exact color difference depends on the colormap: In the case of an identity or a linear grayscale from black to white, the color difference is about 50%. In the other case of a gamma power curve, this gamma curve represents the real intensity curve of the monitor, thus the real color difference observed on the screen is again about 50%, even though the color values may suggest a lower or higher difference.

◇   Conclusions   ◇

Inverting all bits of the pixel is not a good solution when using a frame buffer with no colormap, or a smooth colormap, because drawings near mid-gray are hardly recognizable. A better solution is an XOR-mask where only the most significant bit of each color component is inverted, because it gains a good color contrast for every color to its inversion. So appropriate XOR-masks on frame buffers with a smooth or no colormap are, in hexadecimal:

80   on an 8-bit frame buffer with a grayscale colormap,
4210   on a 15-bit frame buffer,
808080   on a 24-bit frame buffer.

Plate VIII.1.1. A marble-like texture embossed using text as bump map.

Plate III.6.1. Hopf fibration. The hypersphere in four-dimensional space can be viewed as a collection of circles. Each circle projects to a single point on the surface of an ordinary sphere. We can make a picture of the hypersphere as a solid ball, just as we can puncture and flatten an ordinary sphere to make a disk. In this image, only a selection of circles is shown, with each circle colored the same as its projection onto the sphere in the bottom corner.

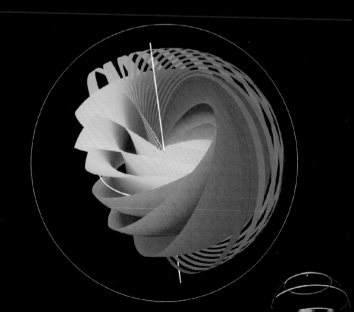

Plate VII.2.1a. Automatic exposure algorithm applied to daylit cabin.

Plate VII.2.1b. Automatic exposure algorithm applied to nighttime scene.

Plate VII.2.2a. Tumblin–Rushmeier brightness mapping applied to daylit cabin.

Plate VII.2.2b. Tumblin–Rushmeier brightness mapping applied to nighttime scene.

Plate VII.2.4a. Contrast-based scalefactor adjusted to local adaptation on window during the day.

Plate VII.2.4b. Contrast-based scalefactor adjusted to local adaptation on window at night.

Plate VII.2.5a. Contrast-based scalefactor applied to lower deck of navy vessel under normal lighting conditions.

Plate VII.2.5b. Contrast-based scalefactor applied to lower deck of navy vessel under emergency lighting conditions.

Plate VIII.2.1. Pamela — source image.

Plate VIII.2.2. Pammouth — bilinear Coons warping with extreme distortion.

Plate VIII.2.3. Pamsiam — bilinear Coons warping with foldover.

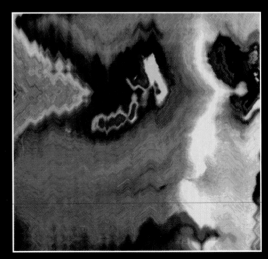

Plate VIII.2.4. Pamwiggle — bilinear Coons warping with wiggly boundary curve.

◊ VII.2

A Contrast-Based Scalefactor for Luminance Display

Greg Ward

Lawrence Berkeley Laboratory
1 Cyclotron Rd., 90-3111
Berkeley, CA 94720
gjward@lbl.gov

Global illumination methods allow us to calculate physical values such as radiance and luminance at each pixel, but they do not tell us how to display these values. If we attempt to fully reproduce the world luminance levels on a computer monitor, slide, or print, the results are usually disappointing, for a couple of reasons. First, contemporary display media fall short of the real world's dynamic range by a few orders of magnitude. It isn't possible to reproduce the luminances in bright and dark regions accurately. Second, the "adaptation luminance," or light level to which the viewer is accustomed, is almost always different under the real-world and computer display viewing conditions, and this affects visual response dramatically.

A common solution to this problem is that of an automatic exposure camera: determine the average luminance value on the image and compute a scalefactor that takes this level to a reasonable value for display, perhaps one half the maximum display brightness (i.e., input = 0.5).[1] This solution has the effect of making visible on the display values that are close to the average world luminance in the image. Values much higher or lower are clipped to the maximum and minimum display values, respectively. Bright areas appear as white and dark areas appear as black. Color plate VII.2.1a shows a simulation of a daylit cabin space. A scalefactor for the display values was computed from a logarithmic average of the image luminance at each pixel. Plate VII.2.1b shows a simulation of the same cabin space at night with electric lighting. Since we are scaling the nighttime image to the same average display value as the daytime scene, the second image does not properly convey that there is in fact less light and decreased visibility under nighttime conditions.

---

[1]In this Gem, we assume that monitor gamma response and other such non-linear effects have been corrected, so we have a linear relationship between input pixel value and output display luminance. We further assume that the minimum display luminance corresponds to an input of 0 and the maximum luminance corresponds to an input of 1.

An early attempt to induce appropriate viewer responses from a CRT display was put forth in (Miller *et al.* 1984). Their method was based on the brightness sensitivity work of (Stevens and Stevens 1963), and its explicit goal was to reproduce equivalent brightness ratios on the CRT as would be present in the real world.[2] Thus, if a given object looks twice as bright as another in the real world, they wanted it to look twice as bright on the display. Although this seems logical, the eye is much more attuned to contrast than it is to brightness, so mapping brightness ratios independent of contrast does little to represent how well a person is actually able to "see" in an environment. The difference between images created with the Miller-Ngai-Miller brightness mapping and those created with the automatic exposure algorithm is slight, and in general we have not found this to be a very useful brightness mapping for judging lighting quality.

Perhaps the best treatment of the display problem to date is that of (Tumblin and Rushmeier 1991, Tumblin and Rushmeier 1993). Using the brightness mapping function they developed, bright scenes will show good visibility (i.e., high contrast), and dark scenes will show poor visibility (i.e., low contrast). Plates VII.2.2a and VII.2.2b show the Tumblin-Rushmeier formula applied to our previous simulation. Notice that the contrast is slightly lower than the average exposure in the nighttime case, and overall it is a little darker. In the daytime image (2a), the Tumblin-Rushmeier mapping works out to:

$$\text{input} = 0.00427 L^{1.04}$$

In the nighttime image (2b), the Tumblin-Rushmeier mapping works out to:

$$\text{input} = 0.221 L^{0.747}$$

The coefficients and exponents in these formulas were determined by the world adaptation luminance taken from the log averages, 29.6 cd/m^2 (candelas/meter^2) for daytime and 0.567 cd/m^2 for nighttime. (A candela is a lumen per steradian, and lumens are related to watts by the photopic sensitivity curve, $v(\lambda)$ (Wyszecki and Stiles 1982).) The original pixel value, L, is expressed in cd/m^2.[3] We must emphasize that the above mapping parameters are peculiar to this scene and these two lighting conditions, and the coefficients and powers shown here would be different under other conditions. In general, darker scenes have lower powers (reducing contrast), and brighter scenes have higher powers (increasing contrast). The reader should refer to the original technical report to learn how these values are derived.

The Tumblin-Rushmeier brightness mapping attacks the adaptation problem with a non-linear formulation based on contrast. Rather than attempt to improve on their

---

[2]Brightness is defined as the psychophysiological response to light stimulus, as opposed to luminance, which is a physical quantity that can be more easily measured.

[3]We separated color information to reduce color shifts, though this is probably not the best approach. Very little conclusive work has been published on color adaptation, and this seems to be a ripe area for new research.

formula by adding terms, we want to derive a simpler, linear function that has some of the same advantages. A linear function also has the potential advantage of representing a darker scene with a darker display, which may be more natural than a display with a similar mean value but reduced contrast.

◇ **Derivation** ◇

Our goal is simple: find a constant of proportionality between display luminance and world luminance that yields a display with roughly the same *contrast visibility* as the actual scene. We base our scalefactor on the subject studies conducted in the early 1970s by Blackwell (CIE 1981). Using a briefly flashed dot on a uniform background, Blackwell established the following relationship between adaptation luminance (L_a) and minimum discernible difference in luminance:

$$\Delta L(L_a) = 0.0594(1.219 + L_a^{0.4})^{2.5}$$

(Luminances in this formula are expressed in SI units of cd/m^2.) This formula tells us what is visible at a given luminance level. That is, $L_a \pm \Delta L$ is discernible on a background of L_a, but $L_a \pm \epsilon$ for $\epsilon < \Delta L$ is not. We can exploit this relationship simply by linking display adaptation and visibility to world adaptation and visibility.

We want a linear formula, so we seek a multiplier m such that:

$$L_d = mL_w$$

where:

$$L_d = \text{display luminance at an image point}$$
$$L_w = \text{world luminance at an image point}$$

Thus, the displayed image will be some factor more or less luminous than the real scene. The contrast visibility can be made the same simply because a darker display has reduced contrast visibility and a brighter display has increased contrast visibility.

Using $\Delta L(L_a)$, we can correlate visible luminance differences on the display to luminance differences in the scene:

$$\Delta L(L_{da}) = m\,\Delta L(L_{wa})$$

where:

$$\Delta L(L_{da}) = \text{minimum discernible luminance change at } L_{da}$$
$$L_{da} = \text{display adaptation luminance}$$
$$L_{wa} = \text{world adaptation luminance}$$

This equation is really the key assumption that allows us to calculate m, so let's try to understand what it means. On the left side, we have $\Delta L(L_{da})$, which is the minimum visible luminance difference at the display adaptation level. On the right side, we have $m \Delta L(L_{wa})$, which is our multiplier, m, times the minimum visible luminance difference at the world adaptation level. That is, when we apply our multiplier to the calculated luminance values and display the result, the differences that are just visible in the real world should be just visible on our display. Solving for m, we arrive at our multiplier:

$$m = \left[\frac{1.219 + L_{da}^{0.4}}{1.219 + L_{wa}^{0.4}} \right]^{2.5}$$

Remember that this multiplier converts from world luminance to display luminance. To get a scalefactor that computes display input in the range 0 to 1, we need to know the maximum display luminance, L_{dmax}.[4] We also need to know the display adaptation luminance of the viewer, L_{da}. Assuming nominal viewing conditions, i.e., the display is in surroundings that are not very much brighter or darker than the display itself, we can relate adaptation luminance to maximum display luminance. We have found that $L_{da} = L_{\mathrm{dmax}}/2$ is close enough for most applications. The final scalefactor to get from world luminance to display input is then:

$$sf = \frac{1}{L_{\mathrm{dmax}}} \left[\frac{1.219 + (L_{\mathrm{dmax}}/2)^{0.4}}{1.219 + L_{wa}^{0.4}} \right]^{2.5}$$

The two unknowns in the equation are the maximum display luminance, L_{dmax}, and the world adaptation luminance, L_{wa}. The maximum display luminance can be measured with a luminance meter. A typical value for a modern color CRT display is 100 cd/m^2. Under good indoor lighting, a photograph has a maximum luminance close to this value at around 120 cd/m^2. The world adaptation level can be determined a couple of ways. One way is to take a log average of the image as was done by Tumblin and Rushmeier, possibly excluding light sources not in direct line of sight. This approach assumes that since we cannot determine the true viewer adaptation, which changes as a function of fixation, a global average is the best guess. Another approach is to assume that an imaginary person in the scene has fixated on a certain point, and use that area of the image to set the adaptation level. We can then interpret the result as telling us how well a person would see in an environment while looking at this point.

◇ **Results** ◇

Plate VII.2.3a shows our daylit scene with a scalefactor of 0.0145 computed from a log average approximation of the world adaptation luminance. Plate VII.2.3b shows

---

[4]For simplicity, we assume that the minimum display luminance is zero. As long as it is small in relation to the maximum value, it has little effect on visible contrast and is therefore a minor consideration.

our nighttime scene with its corresponding scalefactor of 0.147. Since the computed luminances in Plate VII.2.3b were much smaller than under daylight conditions, the final image is darker despite the larger scalefactor.

Because our scalefactors were derived from contrast visibility predictions, we can argue that these two pictures give a reasonable impression of how well a person could see under the two lighting conditions. Furthermore, it is obvious which scene is darker.

Continuing our exploration of contrast visibility, we may produce images using a local viewer adaptation instead of a global adaptation. For example, let's say a person is only looking at the cabin window and is adapted to the luminance of that local area. Under daylight conditions, that would mean an adaptation luminance of about 918 cd/m^2. We calculate a corresponding scalefactor of 0.000765, which produces Plate VII.2.4a. Note that we can now see what is outside the window quite clearly, though our new adaptation means we cannot see the interior as well. However, when we adjust our adaptation in the nighttime scene for looking at the cabin window ($L_{wa} = 0.34$ cd/m^2, $sf = 0.457$), the resulting image (Plate VII.2.4b) shows little local improvement in visibility. This tells us that we cannot see such dark areas at this low light level.

Plate VII.2.5a shows the lower deck of a naval vessel under standard lighting conditions. Plate VII.2.5b shows the same deck under emergency lighting conditions. Scalefactors were computed from a linear average of non-source luminances, which we think is more appropriate for scenes with small light sources. Images like these together with walk-through animations have been used to evaluate alternatives for shipboard lighting. Without some tie to visibility, there would be no basis for such comparisons.

◇ **Conclusion** ◇

We have presented the calculation of a linear scalefactor for display of global illumination results. The calculation is based on contrast sensitivity studies conducted by Blackwell in the early 1970s. The net result is a display that represents visibility under known lighting and viewing conditions, showing bright lighting conditions as a bright display and dark lighting conditions as a dark display. It is easy to dismiss this as too obvious, but the scalefactor is not the same for all scenes; it adjusts to maintain the same visibility level on the display as would be present in the real world. Thus, the subjective reaction of the viewer under real and simulated conditions should be similar, and the display is that much more meaningful. If an object is discernible on the display, then it would be discernible in the actual space. If it is too dark to see on the display, then it would be too dark to see in real life.

We wish to emphasize that our approach is not necessarily better or worse than other approaches. In fact, it uses a much simpler viewer model than that of Tumblin and Rushmeier. The main advantage is the convenience of a global linear scalefactor, which preserves color and image contrast, making dark scenes really appear dark.

◇ **Related Work** ◇

Early investigation of subjective image processing was done by Thomas Stockham (Stockham 1972), who recommended (among other things) a logarithmic pixel encoding to preserve dynamic range.

Interested readers should also look up the recent paper on spatially nonuniform brightness mappings (Chiu *et al.* 1993). Their paper addresses some of the problems in representing images with wide dynamic ranges and offers an interesting solution.

The Radiance Synthetic Imaging System was used to render and process the images presented in this article. This software is available from anonymous ftp at hobbes.lbl.gov (128.3.12.38). This type of image processing almost demands a floating-point image format. Such a format is used in Radiance, and described in (Ward 1991).

◇ **Acknowledgments** ◇

Robert Clear provided much of the background that led to this formulation, which was inspired by some comments from Sam Berman. Thanks also to Jack Tumblin and Holly Rushmeier, who helped us to understand and apply their mapping function. Cindy Larson created the cabin model. Saba Rofchaei developed much of the ship model, which was funded under contract N6153392F0854 by the U.S. Department of Navy, Carderock Division, Naval Surface Warfare Center, to improve energy-efficiency of shipboard lighting. This work was supported by the Assistant Secretary for Conservation and Renewable Energy, Office of Building Technologies, Buildings Equipment Division of the U.S. Department of Energy under Contract No. DE-AC03-76SF00098.

◇ **Bibliography** ◇

(Chiu *et al.* 1993) K. Chiu, M. Herf, P. Shirley, S. Swamy, C. Wang, and K. Zimmerman. Spatially nonuniform scaling functions for high contrast images. In *Proceedings of Graphics Interface '93*, June 1993.

(CIE 1981) An analytic model for describing the influence of lighting parameters upon visual performance, vol 1. Technical foundations. CIE 19/2.1, Technical Committee 3.1, 1981.

(Miller *et al.* 1984) Naomi Johnson Miller, Peter Y. Ngai, and David D. Miller. The application of computer graphics in lighting design. *Journal of the Illuminating Engineering Society*, 14(1), October 1984.

(Stevens and Stevens 1963) S. S. Stevens and J. C. Stevens. Brightness function: Effects of adaptation. *Journal of the Optical Society of America*, 53(3), March 1963.

(Stockham 1972) Thomas G. Stockham, Jr. Image processing in the context of a visual model. *Proceedings of the IEEE*, July 1972.

(Tumblin and Rushmeier 1991) Jack Tumblin and Holly Rushmeier. Tone reproduction for realistic computer generated images. Technical Report GIT-GVU-91-13, Graphics, Visualization & Usability Center, College of Computing, Georgia Institute of Technology, Atlanta, GA 30332-0280, 1991.

(Tumblin and Rushmeier 1993) Jack Tumblin and Holly E. Rushmeier. Tone reproduction for realistic images. *Computer Graphics and Applications*, pages 42–48, Nov. 1993.

(Ward 1991) Greg Ward. Real pixels. In James Arvo, editor, *Graphics Gems II*. Academic Press, Boston, 1991.

(Wyszecki and Stiles 1982) Gunter Wyszecki and W. S. Stiles. *Color Science: Concepts and Methods, Quantitative Data and Formulae*, 2nd ed. Wiley, New York, 1982.

◇ VII.3

High Dynamic Range Pixels

Christophe Schlick

Laboratoire Bordelais de Recherche en Informatique (LaBRI)
351, Cours de la Libération
33400 Talence, France
schlick@labri.u-bordeaux.fr

This Gem presents a picture encoding technique for RGB color images that uses non-linear quantization of pixel values to achieve a much higher dynamic range than the usual 256 values per primary color. The encoding uses only 24 bits per pixel.

◇ Introduction ◇

Global illumination algorithms (radiosity, Monte Carlo ray tracing) usually generate pictures with much higher dynamic ranges than direct illumination ones: a factor of 2000 between the highest and the lowest intensity values is common and a factor of 30,000 is sometimes reached with special illumination cases (Chiu *et al.* 1993). Therefore traditional 24-bit picture representations with a dynamic range of 256 are inadequate. Moreover, when applying gamma correction, even pure 24-bit pictures can create color banding for low values (Hall 1989) showing that a greater dynamic range is needed.

Ward has proposed a technique (Ward 1991) in which pixel values are coded with a floating-point format. Four bytes per pixel are used (one byte for a common exponent and one byte for the mantissa of each primary color), which provides a huge dynamic range of 2^{256}, more than enough for rendering purposes.

Nevertheless, that method has several weak points. First, the memory cost is increased by a third. Second, the coding/decoding routines make heavy use of the math routines `frexp` and `ldexp`, which are typically slow (though more efficient implementations can be found). Third, using a common exponent for R, G, and B favors the dominant color and can lead to color shifts (only the dominant component uses a full 8-bit mantissa, the two others can have several leading zeros in their mantissa in order to compensate for the inadequate common exponent).

Moreover, floating-point pixels only solve half the problem: if they enable storage and manipulation of high dynamic range pictures, mapping these pictures to the 256 values allowed by the typical frame buffer is still unclear.

Logarithmic quantization has been proposed as a remedy to these problems (an overview as well as some implementation issues can be found in (Blinn 1989)). The technique is based on the observation that when quantizing pixel intensities, one should pay more attention when encoding low values than high ones. There are at least two main reasons for doing so. First, the human visual system is much more sensitive to small differences between low values than between high values. Second, if low intensities are not stored with enough precision, gamma correction will create gaps between consecutive values, leading to visible color bandings in dark parts of the picture.

Logarithmic quantization has often been recommended but rarely implemented, certainly because finding a good quantization function for a given picture is not trivial. The present Gem proposes a fast, simple way to convert any dynamic range of pixel intensities into 256-integer values, thus enabling the storage of high dynamic range pictures using only 24 bits per pixel.

◇ **Description** ◇

Let's suppose that we have rendered a picture in which the intensity values range from 0 to 1000 (whatever the units). In order to compute the dynamic range, we have to find the lowest *nonzero* value; let's say that it is 0.25. So the dynamic range of the picture is $1000/0.25 = 4000$, which means that we need at least 4000 quantized values to account correctly for the smallest intensity increment.

A linear quantization of the intensity values to the 256 values accepted by the visualization device will create regular gaps throughout the range (the 256 quantization steps will map to the following intensity values: 0.0, 3.9, 7.8, 11.7, ..., 992.2, 996.1, 1000.0). The idea behind logarithmic quantization is to enlarge gaps for high values in order to reduce them for low values where human vision is uncompromising (this time, the mapping will be: 0.0, 1.0, 3.0, 4.0, 5.1, ..., 980.2, 990.1, 1000.0).

Rather than using a logarithmic function, we propose to transform the values (linearly scaled to [0,1]) with a function similar to the bias function described elsewhere in the present book (see *Fast Alternatives to Perlin's Bias and Gain Functions*, (Schlick 1994b)). The function we use here is identical to one we proposed for shading (see *A Fast Alternative to Phong's Specular Model*, (Schlick 1994a)):

$$\forall t \in [0, 1] \quad f_r(t) = \frac{t}{t - rt + r}$$

where $r \in (0, 1]$ controls the strength of the deformation applied to the incoming range; $r = 1$ yields the identity.

The function has two interesting properties for our quantization scheme. First, its inverse is a function of the same class: (i.e., $f_{1/r}(f_r(t)) = t$), therefore encoding and decoding will be similar processes, simply by changing r into $1/r$. Second, there is an optimal value for parameter r that minimizes round-off errors after an encoding/decoding sequence. That optimal value is simply the ratio between the outcoming and the incoming ranges (in our example $r = 256/4000$ for the encoding and $r = 4000/256$ for the decoding).

◇ **Implementation** ◇

The implementation that we propose here uses one look-up table, two functions and one macro, both for the encoding and the decoding steps.

The function `init_HDP_encode` creates the encoding LUT and it takes three parameters: `LoVal` (the lowest nonzero intensity of the picture), `HiVal` (the highest intensity of the picture), and `NbVal` (the number of entries for the look-up table). As each entry uses one byte, `NbVal` is also the memory size needed for storing the table. When the allocation of the table fails, `init_HDP_encode` returns zero.

The function `init_HDP_decode` creates the decoding LUT, which has 256 entries, each of them being a floating-point value (that is one kilobyte for single precision and two kilobytes for double precision). The function takes three parameters: `LoVal` and `HiVal`, which have the same meaning as in `init_HDP_encode`, and `Bright`, which allows one to alter the brightness during the decoding operation. When `Bright` lies in (-1,0) the picture is darkened, when `Bright` lies in (0,1) the picture is lightened, and when `Bright` is 0, the decoded picture is the same as the initial one (except for round-off errors, of course). It should be noted that even when lightened or darkened, the picture intensities still lie in [0, `HiVal`] — only the ratio of bright versus dark pixels changes.

The macro functions `HDP_ENCODE` and `HDP_DECODE` convert between `RealColor` (an array of three float values in the range [0,`HiVal`]) and `ByteColor` (an array of three char values in the range [0,255]). Finally, `exit_HDP_encode` and `exit_HDP_decode` are called to deallocate the look-up tables.

The encoding/decoding package proposed here can be used in two different ways. A first solution is to use it as a post-processing stage for a rendering program that uses a floating-point coding for picture storage (either with true floating-point variables or with Ward's common exponent technique). The result of that post-processing will be a 24-bit picture which can be directly displayed or converted into standard picture formats for file exchanges.

The package can also be directly included in the rendering program. In that case, there is an additional complication: one has to set `LoVal` and `HiVal` *before* the picture is computed. But a good guess is quite easy to find: `HiVal` is usually the intensity of the brightest light source, and almost every rendering program includes an epsilon value — beneath which intensities are considered as negligible — that gives a perfect `LoVal`.

◇ **Acknowledgments** ◇

I wish to thank Paul Heckbert and Greg Ward for their constructive reviews of an earlier version of this article. Thanks to their comments and suggestions, the two versions are so different that even a mother would not recognize this one as her own child!

◇   **C Code**   ◇

hdp.h

```
/*
** HDP.H : Encoding and Decoding of High Dynamic Range Pixels
*/

/*
** Encoding and Decoding Types
*/
typedef unsigned char byte;
typedef float real; /* change to "double" if you work with double precision */

typedef byte bytecolor[3];
typedef real realcolor[3];

/*
** Encoding and Decoding Tables
*/
extern byte *EncodeLut;
extern real *DecodeLut;
extern real  LutScale;

/*
** Encoding and Decoding Functions
*/
extern int  init_HDP_encode (real,real,int);
extern int  init_HDP_decode (real,real,real);
extern void exit_HDP_encode (void);
extern void exit_HDP_decode (void);

/*
** Encoding and Decoding Macros
*/
#define HDP_ENCODE(RealColor,ByteColor) ( \
    ByteColor[0] = EncodeLut [(int) (RealColor[0] * LutScale + 0.5)], \
    ByteColor[1] = EncodeLut [(int) (RealColor[1] * LutScale + 0.5)], \
    ByteColor[2] = EncodeLut [(int) (RealColor[2] * LutScale + 0.5)])

#define HDP_DECODE(ByteColor,RealColor) ( \
    RealColor[0] = DecodeLut [ByteColor[0]], \
    RealColor[1] = DecodeLut [ByteColor[1]], \
    RealColor[2] = DecodeLut [ByteColor[2]])
```

hdp.c

```c
/*
** HDP.C : Encoding and Decoding of High Dynamic Range Pixels
*/

#include <stdio.h>
void *malloc(unsigned int);
#include "hdp.h"

/*
** Encoding and Decoding Look-Up Tables
*/
byte *EncodeLut;
real *DecodeLut;
real  LutScale;

/*
** Construction of the Encoding Look-Up Table
**
** Input :
**     LoVal = Less significant (i.e., lowest non-zero) value of the incoming range
**     HiVal = Most significant (i.e., highest) value of the incoming range
**     NbVal = Number of elements in the encoding LUT
**
** Output :
**     The function returns 0 if the allocation failed
*/
int init_HDP_encode (real LoVal, real HiVal, int NbVal)
{
    real t, r;
    int  n;

  EncodeLut = (byte *) malloc (NbVal * sizeof (byte));
  if (! EncodeLut) return (NULL);

  NbVal--;

/* Scaling factor = ratio between the encoding LUT and the incoming range */
  LutScale = NbVal / HiVal;

/* Bias factor = ratio between the outcoming and the incoming range */
  r = 256.0 * LoVal / HiVal;

  for (n = 0; n <= NbVal; n++) {
      t = (float) n / NbVal;
      EncodeLut[n] = 255.0 * t / (t-r*t+r) + 0.5;
  }
  return (! NULL);
}
```

```
/*
** Destruction of the Encoding Look-Up Table
*/
void exit_HDP_encode (void)
{
  free (EncodeLut);
}


/*
** Construction of the Decoding Look-Up Table
**
** Input :
**    LoVal  = Less significant (i.e., lowest non-zero) value of the incoming range
**    HiVal  = Most significant (i.e., highest) value of the incoming range
**    Bright = Brightness factor in the range (-1,1)
**            (Bright < 0 : Image is darkened, Bright > 0 : Image is lightened)
**
** Output :
**    The function returns 0 if the allocation failed
*/
int init_HDP_decode (real LoVal, real HiVal, real Bright)
{
    float t, r;
    int n;

  DecodeLut = (real *) malloc (256 * sizeof (real));
  if (! DecodeLut) return (NULL);

/* Change Bright from (-1,1) into a scaling coefficient (0,infinity) */
  Bright = Bright < 0.0 ? Bright+1.0 : 1.0 / (1.0-Bright);

/* Bias factor = ratio of incoming and outcoming range * brightness factor */
  r = Bright * HiVal / LoVal / 256.0;

  for (n = 0; n <= 256; n++) {
    t = (float) n / 255.0;
    DecodeLut[n] = t / (t-t*r+r) * HiVal;
  }
  return (! NULL);
}


/*
** Destruction of the Decoding Look-Up Table
*/
void exit_HDP_decode (void)
{
  free (DecodeLut);
}
```

test_hdp.c

```c
/*
** TEST_HDP.C : Simple testing program for the HDP routines
*/

#include "hdp.h"

void main (void)
{
    realcolor RealColor;
    bytecolor ByteColor;
    real LoVal, HiVal, Bright;
    int  Index, NbTst, NbVal;

/* Dynamic range of 4000 (try also larger or smaller values) */
  LoVal = 0.25;
  HiVal = 1000.0;

/* Memory for encoding LUT = 8 Kbytes */
  NbVal = 8192;

/* Construction of the encoding LUT */
  init_HDP_encode (LoVal, HiVal, NbVal);

/* No brightness modification (try also negative and positive values) */
  Bright = 0.0;

/* Construction of the decoding LUT */
  init_HDP_decode (LoVal, HiVal, Bright);

/*
   Test NbTst sample values (ranging from 0 to HiVal)
   before and after a coding/decoding sequence
*/
  NbTst = HiVal / LoVal;
  for (Index = 0; Index <= NbTst; Index++) {
    RealColor[0] = RealColor[1] = RealColor[2] = Index * HiVal / NbTst;
    printf ("Before = %.2f\t", RealColor[0]);
    HDP_ENCODE (RealColor, ByteColor);
    printf ("Coded value = %d\t", ByteColor[0]);
    HDP_DECODE (ByteColor, RealColor);
    printf ("After = %.2f\n", RealColor[0]);
  }

/* Destruction of the look-up tables */
    exit_HDP_encode ();
    exit_HDP_decode ();
}
```

◇ **Bibliography** ◇

(Blinn 1989) J. F. Blinn. Dirty pixels. *IEEE Computer Graphics and Applications*, 9(3):100–105, 1989.

(Chiu *et al.* 1993) K. Chiu, M. Herf, P. Shirley, S. Swamy, C. Wang, and K. Zimmerman. Spatially nonuniform scaling functions for high contrast images. In *Proceedings of Graphics Interface 93*, pages 182–191, 1993.

(Hall 1989) R. Hall. *Illumination and color in computer generated imagery*. Springer Verlag, New York, 1989.

(Schlick 1994a) C. Schlick. A fast alternative to Phong's specular model. In Paul Heckbert, editor, *Graphics Gems IV*, pages 385–387. Academic Press, Boston, 1994.

(Schlick 1994b) C. Schlick. Fast alternatives to Perlin's bias and gain functions. In Paul Heckbert, editor, *Graphics Gems IV*, pages 401–403. Academic Press, Boston, 1994.

(Ward 1991) G. Ward. Real pixels. In James Arvo, editor, *Graphics Gems II*. Academic Press, Boston, 1991.

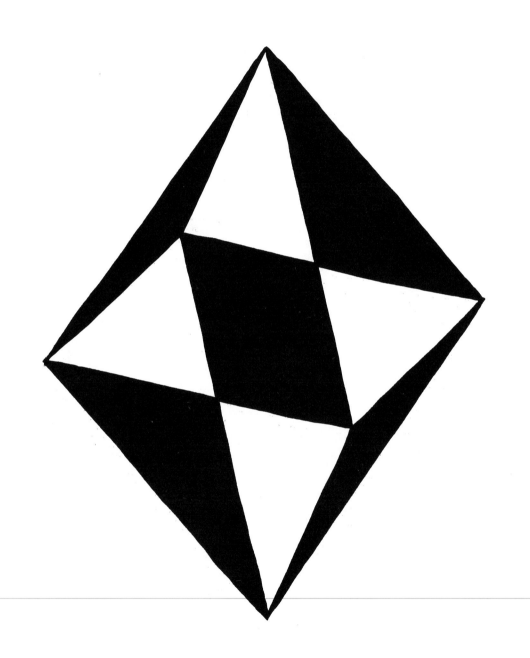

◇ VIII ◇
Image Processing

This part of the book contains six Gems on image processing.

VIII.1. Fast Embossing Effects on Raster Image Data, *by John Schlag.*
Presents a simple, fast technique that interprets an image as a height field or bump map, and then shades it, yielding an embossing effect. Page 433.

VIII.2. Bilinear Coons Patch Image Warping, *by Paul S. Heckbert.*
Presents a fast technique to warp an image according to four boundary curves. This can be used to correct distortions in images, or to introduce them, for special effects purposes. Page 438.

VIII.3. Fast Convolution with Packed Lookup Tables, *by George Wolberg and Henry Massalin.*
Gives optimized code for convolution of discrete signals. This is useful for image resampling and filtering. Page 447.

VIII.4. Efficient Binary Image Thinning Using Neighborhood Maps, *by Joseph M. Cychosz.*
Provides fast code to thin a bitmap image and find its "skeleton." Image thinning is used for pattern recognition. Page 465.

VIII.5. Contrast Limited Adaptive Histogram Equalization, *by Karel Zuiderveld.*
Presents a contrast enhancement technique that overcomes some of the flaws of simple histogram equalization, such as noise amplification and suppression of local contrast. Page 474.

VIII.1

Fast Embossing Effects on Raster Image Data

John Schlag
Computer Graphics Group
Industrial Light and Magic
PO Box 2459
San Rafael, CA 94912

By viewing an image as a 3D surface over a regular grid, one can apply standard 3D shading techniques to it to good effect. This is a useful tool to have in a paint system. The shading can be considerably optimized due to the constrained nature of the surface. This note concentrates on embossing — better known in 3D rendering circles as bump mapping (Blinn 1978) — although once a surface position and normal are available, many of the standard 3D shading techniques can be applied. Input images can be obtained from a variety of sources, including paint work, scanned logos, text (from outline fonts), or even z-buffers.

Consider a bump map image as a 3D surface $p(u, v) = [u \ v \ i(u, v)]$. This interprets black pixels (0) as low, and white (255) as high. With $i_u = \partial i / \partial u$, etc., the surface normal is then

$$N(p) = p_u \times p_v = \begin{vmatrix} 1 & 0 & i_u \\ 0 & 1 & i_v \\ \mathbf{x} & \mathbf{y} & \mathbf{z} \end{vmatrix} = [-i_u \ -i_v \ 1]$$

The partial derivatives i_u and i_v at a point p can be estimated from the image by convolving with the following masks:

$$i_u(p) \approx \begin{bmatrix} -1 & 0 & 1 \\ -1 & 0 & 1 \\ -1 & 0 & 1 \end{bmatrix} \quad i_v(p) \approx \begin{bmatrix} 1 & 1 & 1 \\ 0 & 0 & 0 \\ -1 & -1 & -1 \end{bmatrix}$$

Edge conditions for evaluating these masks are left to the reader. Note that since the masks are 3 by 3 pixels, this will blur the bump map image a bit, lending some antialiasing to sharp edges.

The normal thus obtained must be corrected for the response of the masks. It is also useful to be able to control the "bump height." Both of these aims can be accomplished by scaling $i(u, v)$, or, equivalently, by scaling N_z. The latter is preferable since N_z is a constant. (Note that $[-\alpha i_u \ -\alpha i_v \ 1]$ is the same normal as $[-i_u \ -i_v \ 1/\alpha]$.) If the bump

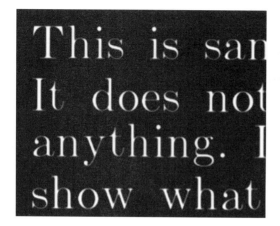

Figure 1. A bump map.

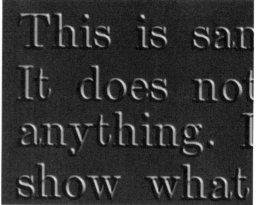

Figure 2. Embossed image lit from above right.

map is obtained from a decal or logo of some sort, as is often the case, the size of the transition region, or "bevel" — and, hence, the apparent depth of the effect — can be modulated by blurring the map image. In this case, a useful control is the edge transition width w that corresponds to a 45° angle for N (i.e., the diameter of the blurring filter). Consider the image function $i(u, v) = au$. The convolution will produce an estimate $i_u = 3(a(u + 2)) - 3au = 6a$. The slope is $a = 255/w$, so we set $N_z = 6 * 255/w$.

By restricting ourselves to a single distant light source, we can get cheap but pleasing results from the Lambertian shading formula $N \cdot L/(|N||L|)$. The multiplications necessary to scale the shading result to a pixel value can be avoided by scaling L to length 256. The calculations can be further optimized by noting that often many of the bump map pixels are black. This results in vertical normals, all of which yield the same pixel value. This value can be computed ahead of time and is simply $[0\,0\,1] \cdot L$ or L_z. In these cases, we can skip the calculation of N (especially the normalization). When the length of N must be computed, there are other optimizations that apply (Ritter 1990). Figure 1 shows a bump map and Figure 2 the result of shading.

The shading result can be used directly as a monochrome pixel value, put through a color map to produce a color value, or multiplied by another texture image. When using a texture image, most of the texture pixels get darkened by a factor of L_z. If this is undesirable, shading results larger than L_z can be used to lighten pixels, and shades less than L_z to darken pixels. Color plate VIII.1.1 shows an embossed, textured image.

One interesting psychophysical note on embossing is that people typically perceive the result of this process as embossing if the light is coming from the top of the image, and as engraving if the light is coming from the lower half.

Although not as heavily optimizable as embossing, other effects such as reflection and refraction can be applied by choosing an eyepoint somewhere above the image. The view vector from the eyepoint to each pixel can then be reflected into an environment map, or refracted into a background texture. For highest quality results, however, some technique for both texture and highlight antialising must be applied, as in 3D (Williams 1983, Crow 1984).

◇ **Source Code** ◇

```
/*
 * Emboss - shade 24-bit pixels using a single distant light source.
 * Normals are obtained by differentiating a monochrome 'bump' image.
 * The unary case ('texture' == NULL) uses the shading result as output.
 * The binary case multiples the optional 'texture' image by the shade.
 * Images are in row major order with interleaved color components (rgbrgb...).
 * E.g., component c of pixel x,y of 'dst' is dst[3*(y*xSize + x) + c].
 */

#include <math.h>
#include <sys/types.h>

void
Emboss(
    double azimuth, double elevation,   /* light source direction */
    u_short width45,                    /* filter width */
    u_char *bump,                       /* monochrome bump image */
    u_char *texture, u_char *dst,       /* texture & output images */
    u_short xSize, u_short ySize        /* image size */
)
{
    long Nx, Ny, Nz, Lx, Ly, Lz, Nz2, NzLz, NdotL;
    register u_char *s1, *s2, *s3, shade, background;
    register u_short x, y;

    #define pixelScale 255.9

    /*
     * compute the light vector from the input parameters.
     * normalize the length to pixelScale for fast shading calculation.
     */
    Lx = cos(azimuth) * cos(elevation) * pixelScale;
    Ly = sin(azimuth) * cos(elevation) * pixelScale;
    Lz = sin(elevation) * pixelScale;

    /*
     * constant z component of image surface normal - this depends on the
     * image slope we wish to associate with an angle of 45 degrees, which
     * depends on the width of the filter used to produce the source image.
     */
```

```
Nz = (6 * 255) / width45;
Nz2 = Nz * Nz;
NzLz = Nz * Lz;

/* optimization for vertical normals: L.[0 0 1] */
background = Lz;

/* mung pixels, avoiding edge pixels */
dst += xSize*3;
if (texture) texture += xSize*3;
for (y = 1; y < ySize-1; y++, bump += xSize, dst += 3)
{
    s1 = bump + 1;
    s2 = s1 + xSize;,
    s3 = s2 + xSize;
    dst += 3;
    if (texture) texture += 3;
    for (x = 1; x < xSize-1; x++, s1++, s2++, s3++)
    {
        /*
         * compute the normal from the bump map. the type of the expression
         * before the cast is compiler dependent. in some cases the sum is
         * unsigned, in others it is signed. ergo, cast to signed.
         */
        Nx = (int)(s1[-1] + s2[-1] + s3[-1] - s1[1] - s2[1] - s3[1]);
        Ny = (int)(s3[-1] + s3[0] + s3[1] - s1[-1] - s1[0] - s1[1]);

        /* shade with distant light source */
        if ( Nx == 0 && Ny == 0 )
            shade = background;
        else if ( (NdotL = Nx*Lx + Ny*Ly + NzLz) < 0 )
            shade = 0;
        else
            shade = NdotL / sqrt(Nx*Nx + Ny*Ny + Nz2);

        /* do something with the shading result */
        if ( texture ) {
            *dst++ = (*texture++ * shade) >> 8;
            *dst++ = (*texture++ * shade) >> 8;
            *dst++ = (*texture++ * shade) >> 8;
        }
        else {
            *dst++ = shade;
            *dst++ = shade;
            *dst++ = shade;
        }
    }
    if (texture) texture += 3;
}
}
```

◇ **Bibliography** ◇

(Blinn 1978) James Blinn. Simulation of wrinkled surfaces. *Computer Graphics*, 12(3), 1978.

(Crow 1984) Franklin C. Crow. Summed-area tables for texture mapping. *Computer Graphics*, 18(3):207–212, 1984.

(Ritter 1990) Jack Ritter. A fast approximation to 3D Euclidean distance. In Andrew S. Glassner, editor, *Graphics Gems*, pages 432–433. Academic Press, Boston, 1990.

(Williams 1983) Lance Williams. Pyramidal parametrics. *Computer Graphics*, 17(3), 1983.

◊ VIII.2

Bilinear Coons Patch Image Warping

Paul S. Heckbert

Computer Science Department
Carnegie Mellon University
5000 Forbes Ave.
Pittsburgh, PA 15213-3891
ph@cs.cmu.edu

This Gem describes how the bilinear Coons patch, a bivariate parametric function, can be used to warp a region of one raster image bounded by four arbitrary curves to a rectangular region in another image. C code is given which performs this warp very quickly using only integer adds, shifts, and table lookups in its inner loop.

◊ Bilinear Coons Patch ◊

In the 1960s, Steve Coons developed a family of parametric surfaces that we today call *Coons patches* (Coons 1967, Forrest 1972, Böhm *et al.* 1984), (Rogers and Adams 1990, pp. 422–425). They are defined by boundary curves around the perimeter of the patch and blending functions that are used to interpolate a surface between the boundary curves. Coons patches are very general; they are a superset of the more widely used tensor product surfaces.

The bilinear Coons patch is the class of Coons patches obtained when there are four boundary curves and the blending functions are linear. Suppose that we want to create a surface $\mathbf{p}(u, v)$ over the unit square that interpolates the four boundary curves $\mathbf{p}_{u0}(u)$, $\mathbf{p}_{u1}(u)$, $\mathbf{p}_{0v}(v)$, and $\mathbf{p}_{1v}(v)$, which correspond to the bottom, top, left, and right of the

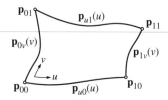

Figure 1. Boundary curve notation.

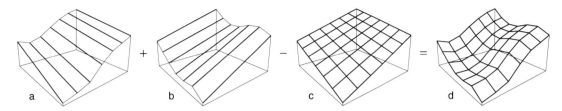

Figure 2. The sum of a surface lofted in the v direction between the bottom and top curves (a), plus a surface lofted in the u direction between the left and right curves (b), minus a bilinear surface through the four corner points (c), yields a bilinear Coons patch (d). This is a plot of x as a function of (u, v); y and z are similar.

square, respectively (Figure 1). That is, we want $\mathbf{p}_{u0}(u) = \mathbf{p}(u, 0)$, $\mathbf{p}_{u1}(u) = \mathbf{p}(u, 1)$, $\mathbf{p}_{0v}(v) = \mathbf{p}(0, v)$, and $\mathbf{p}_{1v}(v) = \mathbf{p}(1, v)$ for all u and v. For surface modeling applications, $\mathbf{p}$ will typically be a 3-vector: $\mathbf{p}(u, v) = (p_x(u, v), p_y(u, v), p_z(u, v))$, but the Coons patch can be generalized to arbitrary dimensions.

We can easily construct a surface that interpolates the bottom and top boundary curves by *lofting*: linear interpolation in v between corresponding points of the two curves yields the surface $(1 - v)\mathbf{p}_{u0}(u) + v\mathbf{p}_{u1}(u)$, shown in Figure 2(a). We can likewise create a surface that interpolates the left and right boundary curves: $(1 - u)\mathbf{p}_{0v}(v) + u\mathbf{p}_{1v}(v)$, seen in Figure 2(b). Can these two be combined to yield a surface that interpolates all four curves? Coons observed that if we add these two surfaces, then subtract a bilinear surface through the four corner points, the resulting surface does just that! The bilinear surface, shown in Figure 2(c), is defined by $(1 - u)(1 - v)\mathbf{p}_{00} + u(1 - v)\mathbf{p}_{10} + (1 - u)v\mathbf{p}_{01} + uv\mathbf{p}_{11}$.

The only condition on the boundary curves to guarantee interpolation is that endpoints of the corner curves are coincident, that is, $\mathbf{p}_{00} = \mathbf{p}_{u0}(0) = \mathbf{p}_{0v}(0)$, $\mathbf{p}_{10} = \mathbf{p}_{u0}(1) = \mathbf{p}_{1v}(0)$, $\mathbf{p}_{01} = \mathbf{p}_{u1}(0) = \mathbf{p}_{0v}(1)$, and $\mathbf{p}_{11} = \mathbf{p}_{u1}(1) = \mathbf{p}_{1v}(1)$. Other than this restriction, the boundary curves can take any shape whatsoever.

If the endpoints of the corner curves are not coincident, then the surface will not interpolate them, in general, but a useful surface can still be constructed by taking the corner points to be the midpoints of the corresponding endpoints: $\mathbf{p}_{00} = (\mathbf{p}_{u0}(0) + \mathbf{p}_{0v}(0))/2$, etc.

The formula for a bilinear Coons patch is thus:

$$
\begin{aligned}
\mathbf{p}(u, v) = \quad & (1 - v)\mathbf{p}_{u0}(u) + v\mathbf{p}_{u1}(u) \\
& + (1 - u)\mathbf{p}_{0v}(v) + u\mathbf{p}_{1v}(v) \\
& - (1 - u)(1 - v)\mathbf{p}_{00} - u(1 - v)\mathbf{p}_{10} - (1 - u)v\mathbf{p}_{01} - uv\mathbf{p}_{11}
\end{aligned} \tag{1}
$$

◇ **Bilinear Coons Image Warp** ◇

In the late 1970s, Lance Williams at the New York Institute of Technology (NYIT) Computer Graphics Lab employed the bilinear Coons patch for image warping. In image warping, we are given a source image and a 2D-to-2D mapping between the source image space and the destination image space, and we wish to compute the destination image. The most straightforward warping algorithm simply loops over each destination pixel, computes the corresponding source pixel, and copies it to the destination image. The mapping between source and destination spaces can be specified by either the forward mapping from source space to destination space or its inverse. The straightforward warping algorithm requires the inverse mapping.

The bilinear Coons patch, as defined above, is a mapping from 2D to an arbitrary number, n, of dimensions. For image warping, we take the special case $n = 2$. Since the bilinear Coons patch defines a mapping that is very difficult to invert, in general, we will use it directly as the inverse mapping from destination space to source space. For that reason, we use coordinates (x, y) for the source image and (u, v) for the destination image.[1]

Williams's idea was to allow a user to draw four boundary curves on the source image with a tablet, mouse, or other input device and use the bilinear Coons patch to warp the region bounded by those curves into a rectangle. If the rectangle has corner $(u0, v0)$, width $nu + 1$, and height $nv + 1$, then the warp is performed by scanning the destination image like so:

```
for iv ← 0 to nv
    for iu ← 0 to nu
        (x, y) ← p(iu/nu, iv/nv)
        dest[u0 + iu, v0 + iv] ← source[x, y]
```

If higher quality results are desired, filtering can be used instead of simply copying the nearest pixel.

The bilinear Coons patch image warp, or *bilinear Coons warp* for short, is a very flexible transformation. The boundary curves are arbitrary; they can be linear or higher degree polynomial; they can be defined by one function or piecewise; they can cross themselves; they can be roughly arc-length parameterized (constant speed) or not; and they can be defined by an array of points. Most transformations that are used for image warping, including piecewise affine, bilinear, biquadratic, or bicubic mappings (Wolberg 1990), are defined by a much smaller number of control points, giving the user less control over the shape of the boundary. On the other hand, the bilinear Coons

---

[1]The opposite convention is common in texture mapping; we use this one here in keeping with standard Coons patch notation.

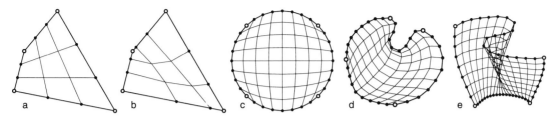

Figure 3. Bilinear Coons patches in source space with u and v isoparametric curves: (a) a bilinear patch, (b) a quadrilateral with non–arc-length-parameterized boundary curves, (c) a circle, (d) a concave region, (e) a wiggly region exhibiting fold-over. The four boundary curves are shown in bold, and corners are shown as white dots.

warp does not allow the user direct control over the interior of the patch, as does a bicubic tensor product patch, for instance.

Figure 3 shows examples of the deformations that are possible with the bilinear Coons warp.

◇ Implementation ◇

In an implementation, the boundary curves are best stored as arrays; this allows arbitrary curves to be accommodated quickly and easily. The bottom and top curves $\mathbf{p}_{u0}$ and $\mathbf{p}_{u1}$ should be resampled to create arrays whose length is the width of the destination image, $nu + 1$, and the left and right curves $\mathbf{p}_{0v}$ and $\mathbf{p}_{1v}$ should be resampled to create arrays whose length is the height, $nv + 1$. The following code implements arc-length-parameterized curve resampling, that is, successive points of the output curve are (approximately) equispaced. Arc-length-parameterized boundary curves yield smoother warps.

```
typedef struct {        /* 2D POINT OR VECTOR */
    float x, y;
} Point2f;

typedef struct {        /* A CURVE DEFINED BY A SEQUENCE OF POINTS */
    int npt;            /* number of points */
    Point2f *pt;        /* array of npt points */
} Curve;

#include <assert.h>
#define ALLOC(ptr, type, n)  assert(ptr = (type *)malloc((n)*sizeof(type)))

static double len(double x, double y) {return sqrt(x*x+y*y);}

/* resample: resample curve a to create curve b, with n points
 * allocates b->pt to have length n */
```

```
static void resample(Curve *a, Curve *b, int n) {
    int i;
    double step, l, d;
    Point2f *ap, *bp;

    assert(a->npt>=2);
    for (step=0., ap=a->pt, i=a->npt-1; i>0; i--, ap++)
        step += len(ap[1].x-ap[0].x, ap[1].y-ap[0].y);
    step /= n-1;                   /* length of each output segment (ideally) */
    ALLOC(b->pt, Point2f, n);
    b->npt = n;
    d = .0001;                     /* = 0 + tolerance for round-off error */
    for (ap=a->pt, bp=b->pt, i=a->npt-1; i>0; i--, ap++) {
        l = len(ap[1].x-ap[0].x, ap[1].y-ap[0].y);
        d += l;
        /* d is the remaining length of the line segment from ap[0] to ap[1]
         * that needs to be subdivided into segments of length step */
        while (d>0.) {
            bp->x = ap[1].x - d/l*(ap[1].x-ap[0].x);
            bp->y = ap[1].y - d/l*(ap[1].y-ap[0].y);
            bp++;
            d -= step;
        }
    }
    assert(bp-b->pt == n);         /* check that we made requested no. of pts. */
}
```

With the boundary curves stored in arrays, the Coons warp, if implemented directly from Equation (1), requires 24 multiplications and 8 table lookups per destination pixel (remember that $\mathbf{p}$ is a 2-vector). These counts do not include the cost of copying or filtering pixels.

These formulas can be optimized substantially, however. We can use forward differencing to incrementalize the terms that are linear in u, pulling six of the eight curve and corner references out of the inner loop into the variable $\mathbf{q}$:

> for $iv \leftarrow 0$ to nv
> $\quad v \leftarrow iv/nv$
> $\quad \mathbf{q} \leftarrow \mathbf{p}_{0v}[iv] - (1-v)\mathbf{p}_{00} - v\mathbf{p}_{01}$
> $\quad \mathbf{dq} \leftarrow \Big(\mathbf{p}_{1v}[iv] - \mathbf{p}_{0v}[iv] - (1-v)(\mathbf{p}_{10} - \mathbf{p}_{00}) - v(\mathbf{p}_{11} - \mathbf{p}_{01})\Big)/nu$
> $\quad$ for $iu \leftarrow 0$ to nu
> $\quad\quad (x, y) \leftarrow \mathbf{p} \leftarrow \mathbf{p}_{u0}[iu] + v(\mathbf{p}_{u1}[iu] - \mathbf{p}_{u0}[iu]) + \mathbf{q}$
> $\quad\quad \text{dest}[u0 + iu, v0 + iv] \leftarrow \text{source}[x, y]$
> $\quad\quad \mathbf{q} \leftarrow \mathbf{q} + \mathbf{dq}$

This leaves 2 multiplications and 4 array references per destination pixel.

Eliminating the last two multiplications (without precomputing everything) seems impossible until we observe that the sum of the first two terms of $\mathbf{p}$, which we denote as

$\mathbf{pu}[iu] = (1-v)\mathbf{p}_{u0}[iu]+v\mathbf{p}_{u1}[iu]$, changes by a constant increment within any column of the destination image. If we precompute the array $\Delta\mathbf{pu}[iu] = (\mathbf{p}_{u1}[iu]-\mathbf{p}_{u0}[iu])/nv$ then $\mathbf{pu}$ can be updated from scan line to scan line by incrementing it by $\Delta\mathbf{pu}$. In addition to these optimizations, we can switch from floating-point to integer arithmetic. The resulting inner loop computes the warp with just six adds, two shifts, and six indirect memory references.

An implementation in C is listed below. This code uses the previous formulas with one change: the comments refer to $\mathbf{p}_{u0}$ as "top" and $\mathbf{p}_{u1}$ as "bottom," since most frame buffers have their y-coordinate pointing down. For maximum portability, the code calls generic routines `pixel_read` and `pixel_write`.

```
#define SHIFT 20        /* number of fractional bits in fixed point coords */
#define SCALE (1<<SHIFT)

typedef struct {        /* INTEGER POINT AND VECTOR */
    int px, py;         /* position */
    int dx, dy;         /* incremental displacement */
} Ipoint;

/*
 * coons_warp: warps the picture in source image into a rectangular
 * destination image according to four boundary curves, using a
 * bilinear Coons patch.
 * bound[0] through bound[3] are the top, right, bottom, and left
 * boundary curves, respectively, clockwise from upper left.
 *    (These comments are written assuming that y points down on your
 *    frame buffer. Otherwise, bound should proceed CCW from lower left.)
 * The lengths of bound[0] and bound[2] are assumed to be the width of
 * the destination rectangle, and the lengths of bound[1] and bound[3]
 * are assumed to be the height of the rectangle.
 * The upper left corner of the destination rectangle is (u0,v0).
 *
 * Paul Heckbert        25 Feb 82, 15 Oct 93
 */

void coons_warp(Pic *source, Pic *dest, Curve *bound, int u0, int v0) {
    register Ipoint *pu;
    register int u, x, y, qx, qy, dqx, dqy;
    int nu, nv, v, count;
    float du, dv, fv;
    Point2f p00, p01, p10, p11, *pu0, *pu1, *p0v, *p1v;
    Ipoint *pua;

    nu = bound[0].npt-1;                        /* nu = dest_width-1 */
    nv = bound[1].npt-1;                        /* nv = dest_height-1 */
    assert(bound[2].npt==nu+1);
    assert(bound[3].npt==nv+1);

    pu0 = &bound[0].pt[0];                      /* top boundary curve */
    p1v = &bound[1].pt[0];                      /* right */
```

```
        pu1 = &bound[2].pt[nu];                      /* bottom */
        p0v = &bound[3].pt[nv];                      /* left */
        /* arrays pu1 and p0v are in the reverse of the desired order,
           running from right to left and bottom to top, resp., so we
           index them with negative subscripts from their ends (yeeeha!) */

        p00.x = (p0v[ 0].x + pu0[  0].x)/2.;         /* upper left patch corner */
        p00.y = (p0v[ 0].y + pu0[  0].y)/2.;
        p10.x = (pu0[nu].x + p1v[  0].x)/2.;         /* upper right */
        p10.y = (pu0[nu].y + p1v[  0].y)/2.;
        p11.x = (p1v[nv].x + pu1[-nu].x)/2.;         /* lower right */
        p11.y = (p1v[nv].y + pu1[-nu].y)/2.;
        p01.x = (pu1[ 0].x + p0v[-nv].x)/2.;         /* lower left */
        p01.y = (pu1[ 0].y + p0v[-nv].y)/2.;

        du = 1./nu;
        dv = 1./nv;

        ALLOC(pua, Ipoint, nu+1);
        for (pu=pua, u=0; u<=nu; u++, pu++) {
            pu->dx = (pu1[-u].x - pu0[u].x)*dv*SCALE + .5;
            pu->dy = (pu1[-u].y - pu0[u].y)*dv*SCALE + .5;
            pu->px = pu0[u].x*SCALE + .5;
            pu->py = pu0[u].y*SCALE + .5;
        }

        count = 0;
        for (fv=0., v=0; v<=nv; v++, fv+=dv) {
            qx = (p0v[-v].x - (1.-fv)*p00.x - fv*p01.x + .5)*SCALE + .5;
            qy = (p0v[-v].y - (1.-fv)*p00.y - fv*p01.y + .5)*SCALE + .5;
            dqx = (p1v[v].x - p0v[-v].x - (1.-fv)*(p10.x-p00.x) - fv*(p11.x-p01.x))
                    *du*SCALE + .5;
            dqy = (p1v[v].y - p0v[-v].y - (1.-fv)*(p10.y-p00.y) - fv*(p11.y-p01.y))
                    *du*SCALE + .5;
            for (pu=pua, u=0; u<=nu; u++, pu++) {
                x = pu->px+qx >> SHIFT;
                y = pu->py+qy >> SHIFT;
                pixel_write(dest, u0+u, v0+v, pixel_read(source, x, y));
                qx += dqx;
                qy += dqy;
                pu->px += pu->dx;
                pu->py += pu->dy;
            }
        }
        free(pua);
}
```

On a Silicon Graphics workstation with a MIPS R4000 processor, the code above warps a 512×486 image in .25 seconds. The speedup relative to the unoptimized algorithm on this machine is a factor of 4; on other machines with relatively slower multipliers or slower floating point, the speedup would be greater.

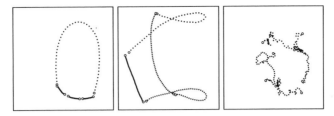

Figure 4.   Boundary curves for color plates VIII.2.2–4. Each warp is controlled by four boundary curves. The region of the source image bounded by the four curves is warped into the rectangular destination image.

This code can be modified to do filtering. As it is written, blockiness (rastering) results where the warp locally scales up the image; this could easily be improved using a bilinear reconstruction filter (Hill 1994). Eliminating aliasing where the warp locally scales down is more difficult.

Color plates VIII.2.1–4 show several examples of images created using the bilinear Coons warp. The boundary curves that generated them are shown in figure 4.

◇   Acknowledgments and History   ◇

This work could not have been done without Lance Williams, who was the first to apply the Coons patch to image warping. Also instrumental in this work was another colleague at the NYIT Computer Graphics Lab, Tom Brigham, who in 1982 bet me a cheeseburger that I couldn't double the speed of our Coons warp program. Before these optimizations, our program took two minutes to warp a 486-line image on a PDP 11/34. Afterward, it took 20 seconds. Settlement was made at the Landmark Diner.

Tom Brigham went on to use the program described here as a building block in his pioneering "morphing" work around 1983. In his approach, two images are decomposed into a mosaic of potentially overlapping regions bounded by closed curves, and a pairwise correspondence is established from regions of one image to regions of the other. The regions and correspondence are specified interactively by the user/animator. To metamorphose a fraction α from one image to the other, Brigham warped the shapes and cross-dissolved the colors of each of the regions by this fraction α, drawing them one by one into a frame buffer. Individual regions were warped by interpolating between Coons patches. The most difficult step in this process is inversion of a Coons warp; Brigham accomplished this with a large two-dimensional lookup table.

In more recent work, Pete Litwinowicz at Apple has employed meshes of Coons patches to animate textured regions as part of a keyframe animation system (Litwinowicz 1991).

◇ **Bibliography** ◇

(Böhm *et al.* 1984) Wolfgang Böhm, Gerald Farin, and Jurgen Kahmann. A survey of curve and surface methods in CAGD. *Computer Aided Geometric Design*, 1:1–60, 1984.

(Coons 1967) Steven A. Coons. Surfaces for computer-aided design of space forms. Technical Report MAC-TR-41, Project MAC, MIT, June 1967.

(Forrest 1972) A. Robin Forrest. On Coons and other methods for the representation of curved surfaces. *Computer Graphics and Image Processing*, 1:341–359, 1972.

(Hill 1994) Steve Hill. Tri-linear interpolation. In Paul Heckbert, editor, *Graphics Gems IV*, pages 521–525. Academic Press, Boston, 1994.

(Litwinowicz 1991) Peter C. Litwinowicz. Inkwell: A 2 1/2-D animation system. *Computer Graphics (SIGGRAPH '91 Proceedings)*, 25(4):113–121, July 1991.

(Rogers and Adams 1990) David F. Rogers and J. Alan Adams. *Mathematical Elements for Computer Graphics, 2nd ed.* McGraw-Hill, New York, 1990.

(Wolberg 1990) George Wolberg. *Digital Image Warping*. IEEE Computer Society Press, Los Alamitos, CA, 1990.

◇ VIII.3

Fast Convolution with Packed Lookup Tables

George Wolberg
Dept. of Computer Science
City College of New York / CUNY
New York, NY 10031
wolcc@cunyvm.cuny.edu

Henry Massalin
Microunity Corporation
Sunnyvale, CA 94089
qua@microunity.com

◇ Abstract ◇

Convolution plays a central role in many image processing applications, including image resizing, blurring, and sharpening. In all such cases, each output sample is computed to be a weighted sum of several input pixels. This is a computationally expensive operation that is subject to optimization. In this Gem, we describe a novel algorithm to accelerate convolution for those applications that require the same set of filter kernel values to be applied throughout the image. The algorithm exploits some nice properties of the convolution summation for this special, but common, case to minimize the number of pixel fetches and multiply/add operations. Computational savings are realized by precomputing and packing all necessary products into lookup table fields that are then subjected to simple integer (fixed-point) shift/add operations.

◇ Introduction ◇

Discrete convolution is expressed as the following convolution summation:

$$f(x) = \sum_{k=0}^{N-1} f(x_k) h(x - x_k)$$

where h is the convolution kernel weighted by N input samples $f(x_k)$. In practice, h is nearly always a symmetric kernel, i.e., $h(-x) = h(x)$. We shall assume this to be true in the discussion that follows.

   The computation of one output point is illustrated in Figure 1, where a convolution kernel is shown centered at x among the input samples. The value of that point is equal to the sum of the values of the discrete input scaled by the corresponding values of the convolution kernel. This example is appropriate for image resizing, where integer output addresses map back into real-valued input locations. For instance, output locations

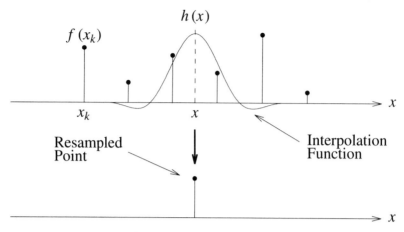

Figure 1. Convolution.

$0, 1, 2, 3, \ldots$, correspond to input locations $0, .5, 1, 1.5, \ldots$, upon two-fold magnification. In other applications, such as blurring, the image dimensions remain the same after convolution, and the convolution kernel is always centered on an input sample.

There are two time-consuming phases in convolution: computing the convolution kernel weights $h(x - x_k)$ to be used, and the actual multiply/add core operations. The first problem is apparent if we consider what happens when the kernel in Figure 1 is moved slightly. A new set of kernel values must now be applied to the input. Several researchers have looked at ways of speeding up this computation. In (Ward and Cok 1989, Wolberg 1990), a technique using coefficient bins is described that places constraints on where the kernel may be centered. By limiting the kernel to be placed at any one of, say, 64 subpixel positions, the kernel weights may be precomputed and stored in a table before the actual multiply/add operations begin. As the kernel makes its way across the input image, it must be recentered to the closest subpixel position. In (Schumacher 1992), a scaling algorithm is given which stores the computed kernel values after processing an input row, and reuses those weights for all subsequent scanlines.

This Gem describes an efficient means for implementing fast convolution using lookup table operations. It assumes one important constraint: the same set of kernel values are applied throughout the image. This is appropriate for low-pass filtering (blurring), for instance, where the kernel is always centered directly on an input sample, and the same set of weights are applied to the neighbors. It is also appropriate for two-fold magnification or minification where, again, only a single set of kernel values is needed (Wolberg and Massalin 1993).

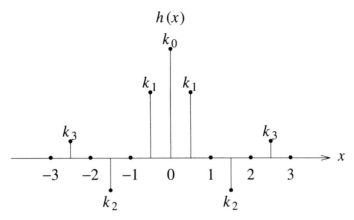

Figure 2. Six-point kernel samples.

◇ **A Fast Convolver for Two-fold Magnification** ◇

In order to place this presentation on firm ground, we will first describe this approach in the context of two-fold image magnification. We will later demonstrate how these results are generalized to fast convolution with filter kernels of arbitrary length. This is relevant to any linear filtering operation, such as image blurring, sharpening, and edge detection. It is important to note that the algorithm is developed for the 1D case, where only rows or columns may be processed. In 2D, the image is processed separably. That is, each input row is filtered to produce an intermediate image I. Image I is then convolved along its columns to produce the final output image. For convenience, our discussion will assume that we are convolving 8-bit data with a 6-point kernel for the purpose of image magnification.

Due to symmetry, a 6-point kernel has only three unique kernel values: k_1, k_2, and k_3 (see Figure 2). The seventh kernel value, k_0, in Figure 2 is unused here since it sits between the input samples. It will be necessary later when we consider general linear filtering.

Since each kernel value k_i can be applied to an integer in the range $[0, 255]$, we may precompute their products and store them in three lookup tables tab_i, for $1 \le i \le 3$. The product of data sample s with weight k_i now reduces to a simple lookup table access, e.g., $tab_i[s]$. This makes it possible to implement a 6-point convolver without multiplication; only lookup table and addition operations are necessary. In order to retain numerical accuracy during partial evaluations, we designate each 256-entry lookup table to be 10-bits wide. This accommodates 8-bit unsigned integers with 2-bit fractions.

The use of lookup tables to eliminate multiplication becomes unfeasible when a large number of distinct kernel values are required in the convolution summation. This is particularly true of general convolution. Fortunately, many filtering applications, including two-fold magnification, require only a few distinct kernel values. The memory demands to support the corresponding lookup tables are very modest, i.e., $256(N/2)$ 10-bit entries for an N-point kernel, where N is even.

Further computational savings are possible by exploiting some nice properties of the convolution summation for our special two-fold rescaling problem. These properties are best understood by considering the output expressions after a 6-point kernel is applied to input samples A through H. The expanded expressions for convolution output CD, DE, and EF are given below. Note that CD refers to the output sample lying halfway between pixels C and D. The same notation applies to DE and EF.

$$
\begin{aligned}
CD &= k_3 A + k_2 B + k_1 C + k_1 D + k_2 E + k_3 F \\
DE &= k_3 B + k_2 C + k_1 D + k_1 E + k_2 F + k_3 G \\
EF &= k_3 C + k_2 D + k_1 E + k_1 F + k_2 G + k_3 H
\end{aligned}
$$

These results demonstrate a pattern: each input sample s is weighted by all k_i values during the course of advancing the kernel across the data. This is apparent for samples C and F in all three expressions. Rather than individually accessing each of the three tables with sample s, all three tables may be packed side by side into one wide table having 30 bits in width. This permits one index to access three packed products at once. The largest number of tables that may be packed together is limited only by the precision with which we store the products and the width of the longest integer, e.g., 32 bits on most computers.

Figure 3 shows table entries for input samples A through H. Three 10-bit fields are used to pack three fixed-point products. Each field is shown to be involved in some convolution summation, as denoted by the arrows, to compute output CD, DE (shown shaded), and EF. The organization of the data in this manner not only reduces the number of table accesses, but it also lends itself to a fast convolution algorithm requiring only shift and add operations. The downward (upward) arrows denote a sequence of right-shift (left-shift) and addition operations, beginning with the table entry for A (D). Let *fwd* and *rev* be two integers that store both sets of results. The first few shift-add operations produce *fwd* and *rev* with the fields shown in Table 1.

Table 1.   10-bit Fields in *fwd* and *rev*

fwd			*rev*		
bits 20-29	bits 10-19	bits 0-9	bits 20-29	bits 10-19	bits 0-9
$k_3 B$	$k_3 A + k_2 B$	$k_2 A + k_1 B$	$k_3 E + k_2 D$	$k_2 E + k_1 D$	$k_1 E$
$k_3 C$	$k_3 B + k_2 C$	$k_3 A + k_2 B + k_1 C$	$k_3 F + k_2 E + k_1 D$	$k_2 F + k_1 E$	$k_1 F$
$k_3 D$	$k_3 C + k_2 D$	$k_3 B + k_2 C + k_1 D$	$k_3 G + k_2 F + k_1 E$	$k_2 G + k_1 F$	$k_1 G$
$k_3 E$	$k_3 D + k_2 E$	$k_3 C + k_2 D + k_1 E$	$k_3 H + k_2 G + k_1 F$	$k_2 H + k_1 G$	$k_1 H$

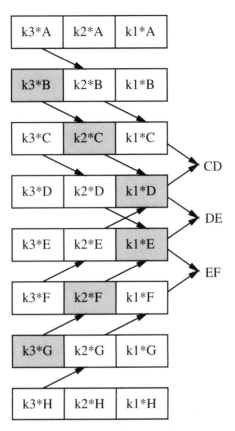

Figure 3.   A fast convolver.

Notice that the low-order 10-bit fields of *fwd* contain half of the convolution summation necessary to compute the output. The other half is contained in the high-order 10-bit fields of *rev*. Simply adding both fields together generates the output values.

This scheme is hampered by one complication: addition may cause one field to spill into the next, thereby corrupting its value. This will happen if a field value exceeds the range $[0, 2^8 - 1]$. Note that although we use 10-bit fields, the integer part is 8 bits wide. We now consider the two range limits on field value $v = k_3A + k_2B + k_1C$.

We may guard against negative values by simply adding a bias to the field of all negative kernel values k_i. After rescaling the bias to a 10-bit quantity, it is simply $1024k_i$. Simultaneously, we must guarantee that the sum of the three kernel values and the biases is less than unity to ensure that the upper limit is satisfied. Note that the bias is removed from the computation when we add the low-order 10-bit field of *fwd* to the high-order 10-bit field of *rev*.

The following fragment of C code demonstrates the initialization of the packed lookup table *lut*, consisting of 256 32-bit integers.

```
#define MASK 0x3FF
#define ROUND 1
#define PACK(A,B,C) (((A)<<20) + ((B)<<10) + (C))
#define INT(A) ((int) ((A)*262144+32768) >> 16)

b1 = b2 = b3 = 0;
if(k1 < 0) b1 = -k1 * 1024;
if(k2 < 0) b2 = -k2 * 1024;
if(k3 < 0) b3 = -k3 * 1024;
bias = 2 * (b1 + b2 + b3);

for(i=0; i<256; i++)
lut[i] = PACK( INT(i*k3)+b3, INT(i*k2)+b2+ROUND, INT(i*k1)+b1 );
```

The *INT* macro converts the real-valued kernel samples into 10-bit fixed-point quantities. Notice that since the macro argument *A* has an 8-bit magnitude, we form an intermediate 26-bit result by multiplying *A* by 1<<18. Round-off is achieved by adding 1<<15 (or .5) before right-shifting by 16 bits to obtain the final 10-bit number. A bias is added to each field to prevent negative numbers and the undesirable sign extension that would corrupt its neighbors. *ROUND* is necessary to avoid round-off error when adding the *fwd* and *rev* terms together to compute the output. Adding *ROUND* directly in *lut* spares us from having to explicitly add it at every output computation.

Once *lut* is initialized, it is used in the following code to realize fast convolution. The variable *len* refers to the number of input samples, and *ip* and *op* are input and output pointers that reference the padded working buffer *buf*. We assume that the input samples have already been copied into the even addresses of *buf* in order to trivially compute half of the two-fold magnification output. Since we are now using a 6-point kernel, the left padding occupies positions 0 and 2, the first input sample lies in position 4, and the first output sample will lie in position 5.

```
/* clamp definition: clamp A into the range [L,H] */
#define CLAMP(A,L,H) ((A)<=(L) ? (L) : (A)<=(H) ? (A) : (H))

/* initialize input and output pointers, ip and op, respectively */
ip = &buf[0];
op = &buf[5];

fwd = (lut[ip[0]] >> 10) + lut[ip[2]];
rev = (lut[ip[6]] << 10) + lut[ip[8]];
ip += 4;

while(len--) {
        fwd = (fwd >> 10) + lut[ip[0]];
```

```
        rev = (rev << 10) + lut[ip[6]];
        val = ((fwd & MASK) + ((rev >> 20) & MASK) - bias) >> 2;
        *op = CLAMP(val, 0, 255);

        /* input and output strides are 2 */
        ip += 2;
        op += 2;
}
```

The bias terms find their way into the low-order and high-order fields of *fwd* and *rev* through the sequence of shift-add operations. Since these two fields are used to compute *val*, we must subtract twice the sum of the bias terms from *val* to restore its proper value. Recall that *bias* was defined in the previous code fragment. We then discard the fractional part of *val* by a two-bit right shift, leaving us with an 8-bit integer. Since *val* may now be negative, it is necessary to clamp it into the range $[0, 255]$.

Operating with symmetric kernels has already been shown to reduce the number of arithmetic operations: $N/2$ multiplies and $N - 1$ for an N-point kernel, where N is even. This algorithm, however, does far better. It requires no multiplication (other than that needed to initialize *lut*), and a total of four adds per output sample, for a 6-point kernel. Furthermore, no distinction is made between 2-, 4-, and 6-point kernels because they are all packed into the same integer. That is, a 4-point kernel is actually implemented as a 6-point kernel with $k_3 = 0$. Since there is no additional penalty for using a 6-point kernel, we are induced to use a superior (6-point) filter at low cost. Larger kernels can be assembled by cascading additional 6-point kernel stages together (see the supplied code).

◇   **General Convolution**   ◇

The C code provided with this Gem demonstrates the use of the fast convolver for general linear filtering. This is essentially the same technique as for the two-fold magnifier shown earlier. There is one important difference though: the N-point kernels are centered on input samples and so N must be odd. The extra kernel value corresponds to the center pixel, that must now be weighted by k_0. Although this can be explicitly added to the weighted sum of the neighboring six pixels, the number of addition operations to compute an output pixel would rise by one. For instance, the following C statement could be used:

```
val = ((fwd & MASK) + ((rev >> 20) & MASK) - bias + lut0[*ip]) >> 2;
```

where *ip* points to the center pixel that is used to index *lut0*, a lookup table storing the product of the pixel with kernel sample k_0. Note that a total of 5 additions are needed to compute a 7-point kernel: 1 each for *fwd* and *rev*, and 3 for *val*. We will refer to this

Table 2. Comparison of Operation Counts

N	Method 1	Method 2
3	5	4
5	5	4
7	5	8
9	9	8
11	9	8
13	9	12
15	13	12

approach as Method 1. In order to reduce one addition, we can embed that weighting directly in the packed lookup tables by halving k_0 and permitting it to be applied on the center pixel in both *fwd* and *rev* for the purpose of adding the contribution of that pixel (Method 2). This, however, reduces the extent of the kernel by one. Table 2 compares the number of additions needed to compute an output value using the two methods for various values of N in an N-point kernel.

It is important to note that multiple instances of *fwd* and *rev* are needed when they are cascaded to realize wider kernels. This explains why the number of additions above rises by increments of four: two to compute a new pair of *fwd* and *rev* terms, and two to add them to *val*. Method 2 is generally more efficient than Method 1, except in instances when the overhead cost of adding an additional *fwd* and *rev* pair sets in. The supplied code implements Method 2.

◇ Summary and Conclusions ◇

In summary, this Gem has focused on optimizing the evaluation of the convolution summation. We achieve large performance gains by packing all weighted instances of an input sample into one 32-bit integer and then using these integers in a series of shift-add operations to compute the output. The algorithm benefits from a technique well known in the folklore of assembler programmers and microcoders: multiple integers can be added in parallel in a single word if their bit fields do not overlap. This alone, however, is not the basis of the algorithm. Rather, the novelty of the algorithm lies in identifying a particularly efficient structure for the fast convolver that can exploit this straightforward technique for parallel addition and apply it to kernels of arbitrary length. An additional feature of the fast convolver is that it requires each pixel to be fetched only once, even though it is used in the computation of several output pixels.

The sequence of shift-add operations essentially mimics a pipelined vector processor on a general 32-bit computer. This approach will likely find increased use with the forthcoming generation of 64-bit computers. The additional bits will permit us to handle wider kernels at finer precision.

◇ **Acknowledgments** ◇

This work was supported in part by the NSF (PYI Award IRI-9157260), PSC-CUNY (RF-664314), and the Xerox Foundation.

◇ **C Code** ◇

The following C code implements the fast convolution algorithm. The program takes three arguments: filenames for the input image, kernel, and output image. Utility functions are provided to read and write 8-bit grayscale images. The image format used is simple: two integers specifying the width and height followed by a stream of 8-bit unsigned pixel data. The kernel is stored in an ASCII file containing one kernel value per row beginning with k_0. For instance, the following kernel file contains a 7-point low-pass filter:

```
.33333333333333333333
.23958333333333333333
.08333333333333333333
.01041666666666666666
```

The program handles up to 17-point kernels. Extending this to handle larger kernels is a simple matter of accommodating additional stages in the *lutS* data structure and *fastconv*() function.

Execution time on a SUN 4/50 (IPX) workstation was measured on the repeated calls to *fastconv*() in function *convolve*(). Convolution of a 256×256 image with a 7-point and 17-point kernel took .75 seconds and .85 seconds, respectively. The same convolution took 1.75 seconds and 3.96 seconds, respectively, when implemented with standard multiply/add operations. Due to the separable implementation, execution time grows linearly with filter width.

```c
/* =======================================================================
 *
 *      Fast Convolution with Packed Lookup Tables
 *
 *          by George Wolberg and Henry Massalin
 *
 *      Compile: cc convolve.c -o convolve
 *      Execute: convolve in.bw kernel out.bw
 * =======================================================================
 */

#include <stdio.h>
#include <stdlib.h>

typedef unsigned char    uchar;
```

```c
typedef struct {                    /* image data structure   */
        int width;                  /* image width  (# cols) */
        int height;                 /* image height (# rows) */
        uchar *image;               /* pointer to image data */
} imageS, *imageP;

typedef struct {                    /* packed lut structure      */
        int lut0[256];              /* stage 0 for  5-pt kernel */
        int lut1[256];              /* stage 1 for 11-pt kernel */
        int lut2[256];              /* stage 2 for 17-pt kernel */
        int bias;                   /* accumulated stage biases */
        int stages;                 /* # of stages used: 1,2,3  */
} lutS, *lutP;

/* definitions */
#define MASK            0x3FF
#define ROUNDD          1
#define PACK(A,B,C)     (((A)<<20) + ((B)<<10) + (C))
#define INT(A)          ((int) ((A)*262144+32768) >> 16)
#define CLAMP(A,L,H)    ((A)<=(L) ? (L) : (A)<=(H) ? (A) : (H))
#define ABS(A)          ((A) >= 0 ? (A) : -(A))

/* declarations for convolution functions */
void    convolve();
void    initPackedLuts();
void    fastconv();

/* declarations for image utility functions */
imageP  allocImage();
imageP  readImage();
int     saveImage();
void    freeImage();

/* ~~~~~~~~~~~~~~~~~~~~~~~~~~~~~~~~~~~~~~~~~~~~~~~~~~~~~~~~~~~~~~~~~~~~~~~~~~~
 * main:
 *
 * Main function to collect input image and kernel values.
 * Pass them to convolve() and save result in output file.
 */
main(argc, argv)
int     argc;
char    **argv;
{
        int     n;
        imageP  I1, I2;
        float   kernel[9];
        char    buf[80];
        FILE    *fp;

        /* make sure the user invokes this program properly */
        if(argc != 4) {
                fprintf(stderr, "Usage: convolve in.bw kernel out.bw\n");
                exit(1);
```

```
        }

        /* read input image */
        if((I1=readImage(argv[1])) == NULL) {
                fprintf(stderr, "Can't read input file %s\n", argv[1]);
                exit(1);
        }

        /* read kernel: n lines in file specify a (2n-1)-point kernel
         * Don't exceed 9 kernel values (17-point symmetric kernel is limit)
         */
        if((fp=fopen(argv[2], "r")) == NULL) {
                fprintf(stderr, "Can't read kernel file %s\n", argv[2]);
                exit(1);
        }
        for(n=0; n<9 && fgets(buf, 80, fp); n++) kernel[n] = atof(buf);

        /* convolve input I1 with fast convolver */
        I2 = allocImage(I1->width, I1->height);
        convolve(I1, kernel, n, I2);

        /* save output to a file */
        if(saveImage(I2, argv[3]) == NULL) {
                fprintf(stderr, "Can't save output file %s\n", argv[3]);
                exit(1);
        }
}



/* ~~~~~~~~~~~~~~~~~~~~~~~~~~~~~~~~~~~~~~~~~~~~~~~~~~~~~~~~~~~~~~~~~~~~~~~~~~~
 * convolve:
 *
 * Convolve input image I1 with kernel, a (2n-1)-point symmetric filter
 * kernel containing n entries: h[i] = kernel[ |i| ] for -n < i < n.
 * Output is stored in I2.
 */
void
convolve(I1, kernel, n, I2)
imageP  I1, I2;
float   *kernel;
int     n;
{
        int     x, y, w, h;
        uchar   *src, *dst;
        imageP  II;
        lutS    luts;

        w = I1->width;                          /* image width          */
        h = I1->height;                         /* image height         */

        II = allocImage(w, h);                  /* reserve tmp image    */
        initPackedLuts(kernel, n, &luts);       /* init packed luts     */
```

```
        for(y=0; y<h; y++) {                          /* process all rows     */
                src = I1->image + y*w;                /* ptr to input  row    */
                dst = II->image + y*w;                /* ptr to output row    */
                fastconv(src, w, 1, &luts, dst);/* w pixels; stride=1    */
        }

        for(x=0; x<w; x++) {                          /* process all columns  */
                src = II->image + x;                  /* ptr to input  column */
                dst = I2->image + x;                  /* ptr to output column */
                fastconv(src, h, w, &luts, dst);/* h pixels; stride=w    */
        }

        freeImage(II);                                /* free temporary image */
}




/* ~~~~~~~~~~~~~~~~~~~~~~~~~~~~~~~~~~~~~~~~~~~~~~~~~~~~~~~~~~~~~~~~~~~~~~~~~~~~
 * initPackedLuts:
 *
 * Initialize scaled and packed lookup tables in lut.
 * Permit up to 3 cascaded stages for the following kernel sizes:
 *      stage 0:  5-point kernel
 *      stage 1: 11-point kernel
 *      stage 2: 17-point kernel
 * lut->lut0 <== packed entries (i*k2, i*k1, .5*i*k0), for i in [0, 255]
 * lut->lut1 <== packed entries (i*k5, i*k4,    i*k3), for i in [0, 255]
 * lut->lut2 <== packed entries (i*k8, i*k7,    i*k6), for i in [0, 255]
 * where k0,...k8 are taken in sequence from kernel[].
 *
 * Note that in lut0, k0 is halved since it corresponds to the center
 * pixel's kernel value and it appears in both fwd0 and rev0 (see text).
 */
static void
initPackedLuts(kernel, n, luts)
float   *kernel;
int     n;
lutP    luts;
{
        int     i, k, s, *lut;
        int     b1, b2, b3;
        float   k1, k2, k3;
        float   sum;

        /* enforce flat-field response constraint: sum of kernel values = 1 */
        sum = kernel[0];
        for(i=1; i<n; i++) sum += 2*kernel[i];  /* account for symmetry */
        if(ABS(sum - 1) > .001)
                fprintf(stderr, "Warning: filter sum != 1 (=%f)\n", sum);

        /* init bias added to fields to avoid negative numbers (underflow) */
        luts->bias = 0;
```

```
        /* set up lut stages, 3 kernel values at a time */
        for(k=s=0; k<n; s++) {                  /* init lut (stage s)   */
                k1 = (k < n) ? kernel[k++] : 0;
                k2 = (k < n) ? kernel[k++] : 0;
                k3 = (k < n) ? kernel[k++] : 0;
                if(k <= 3) k1 *= .5;            /* kernel[0]: halve k0  */

                /* select proper array in lut structure based on stage s */
                switch(s) {
                case 0: lut = luts->lut0;       break;
                case 1: lut = luts->lut1;       break;
                case 2: lut = luts->lut2;       break;
                }

                /* check k1,k2,k3 to avoid overflow in 10-bit fields */
                if(ABS(k1) + ABS(k2) + ABS(k3) > 1) {
                        fprintf(stderr, "|%f|+|%f|+|%f| > 1\n", k1, k2, k3);
                        exit(1);
                }

                /* compute bias for each field to avoid underflow */
                b1 = b2 = b3 = 0;
                if(k1 < 0) b1 = -k1 * 1024;
                if(k2 < 0) b2 = -k2 * 1024;
                if(k3 < 0) b3 = -k3 * 1024;

                /* luts->bias will be subtracted in convolve() after adding
                 * stages; multiply by 2 because of combined effect of fwd
                 * and rev terms
                 */
                luts->bias += 2*(b1 + b2 + b3);

                /* scale and pack kernel values in lut */
                for(i=0; i<256; i++) {
                        /*
                         * INT(A) forms fixed point field:
                         * (A*(1<<18)+(1<<15)) >> 16
                         */
                        lut[i] = PACK(  INT(i*k3) + b3,
                                        INT(i*k2) + b2 + ROUNDD,
                                        INT(i*k1) + b1 );
                }
        }
        luts->stages = s;
}



/* ~~~~~~~~~~~~~~~~~~~~~~~~~~~~~~~~~~~~~~~~~~~~~~~~~~~~~~~~~~~~~~~~~~~~~~~
 * fastconv:
 *
 * Fast 1D convolver.
```

```
 * Convolve len input samples in src with a symmetric kernel packed in luts,
 * a lookup table that is created by initPackedLuts() from kernel values.
 * The output goes into dst.
 */
static void
fastconv(src, len, offst, luts, dst)
int     len, offst;
uchar   *src, *dst;
lutP    luts;
{
        int     x, padlen, val, bias;
        int     fwd0, fwd1, fwd2;
        int     rev0, rev1, rev2;
        int     *lut0, *lut1, *lut2;
        uchar   *p1, *p2, *ip, *op;
        uchar   buf[1024];

        /* copy and pad src into buf with padlen elements on each end */
        padlen = 3*(luts->stages) - 1;
        p1 = src;               /* pointer to row (or column) of input  */
        p2 = buf;               /* pointer to row of padded buffer      */
        for(x=0; x<padlen; x++) /* pad left side: replicate first pixel */
                *p2++ = *p1;
        for(x=0; x<len; x++) {  /* copy input row (or column)           */
                *p2++ = *p1;
                p1   += offst;
        }
        p1 -= offst;            /* point to last valid input pixel      */
        for(x=0; x<padlen; x++) /* pad right side: replicate last pixel */
                *p2++ = *p1;

        /* initialize input and output pointers, ip and op, respectively */
        ip = buf;
        op = dst;

        /* bias was added to lut entries to deal with negative kernel values */
        bias = luts->bias;

        switch(luts->stages) {
        case 1:         /* 5-pt kernel */
                lut0 = luts->lut0;

                ip  += 2;       /* ip[0] is center pixel */
                fwd0 = (lut0[ip[-2]] >> 10) + lut0[ip[-1]];
                rev0 = (lut0[ip[ 0]] << 10) + lut0[ip[ 1]];

                while(len--) {
                        fwd0 = (fwd0 >> 10) + lut0[ip[0]];
                        rev0 = (rev0 << 10) + lut0[ip[2]];
                        val = ((fwd0 & MASK) + ((rev0 >> 20) & MASK) - bias)
                                >> 2;
                        *op = CLAMP(val, 0, 255);
```

```
                ip++;
                op += offst;
        }
        break;
case 2:         /* 11-pt kernel */
        lut0 = luts->lut0;
        lut1 = luts->lut1;

        ip  += 5;       /* ip[0] is center pixel */
        fwd0 = (lut0[ip[-2]] >> 10) + lut0[ip[-1]];
        rev0 = (lut0[ip[ 0]] << 10) + lut0[ip[ 1]];

        fwd1 = (lut1[ip[-5]] >> 10) + lut1[ip[-4]];
        rev1 = (lut1[ip[ 3]] << 10) + lut1[ip[ 4]];

        while(len--) {
                fwd0 = (fwd0 >> 10) + lut0[ip[0]];
                rev0 = (rev0 << 10) + lut0[ip[2]];

                fwd1 = (fwd1 >> 10) + lut1[ip[-3]];
                rev1 = (rev1 << 10) + lut1[ip[ 5]];

                val  = ((fwd0 & MASK) + ((rev0 >> 20) & MASK)
                        +(fwd1 & MASK) + ((rev1 >> 20) & MASK) - bias)
                        >> 2;
                *op = CLAMP(val, 0, 255);

                ip++;
                op += offst;
        }
        break;
case 3:         /* 17-pt kernel */
        lut0 = luts->lut0;
        lut1 = luts->lut1;
        lut2 = luts->lut2;

        ip  += 8;       /* ip[0] is center pixel */
        fwd0 = (lut0[ip[-2]] >> 10) + lut0[ip[-1]];
        rev0 = (lut0[ip[ 0]] << 10) + lut0[ip[ 1]];

        fwd1 = (lut1[ip[-5]] >> 10) + lut1[ip[-4]];
        rev1 = (lut1[ip[ 3]] << 10) + lut1[ip[ 4]];

        fwd2 = (lut2[ip[-8]] >> 10) + lut2[ip[-7]];
        rev2 = (lut2[ip[ 6]] << 10) + lut2[ip[ 7]];

        while(len--) {
                fwd0 = (fwd0 >> 10) + lut0[ip[0]];
                rev0 = (rev0 << 10) + lut0[ip[2]];

                fwd1 = (fwd1 >> 10) + lut1[ip[-3]];
                rev1 = (rev1 << 10) + lut1[ip[ 5]];
```

```
                        fwd2 = (fwd2 >> 10) + lut2[ip[-6]];
                        rev2 = (rev2 << 10) + lut2[ip[ 8]];

                        val  =  ((fwd0 & MASK) + ((rev0 >> 20) & MASK)
                                +(fwd1 & MASK) + ((rev1 >> 20) & MASK)
                                +(fwd2 & MASK) + ((rev2 >> 20) & MASK) - bias)
                                >> 2;
                        *op = CLAMP(val, 0, 255);

                        ip++;
                        op += offst;
                }
                break;
        }
}


/* ~~~~~~~~~~~~~~~~~~~~~~~~~~~~~~~~~~~~~~~~~~~~~~~~~~~~~~~~~~~~~~~~~~~~~~~~
 * readImage:
 *
 * Read an image from file.
 * Format: two integers to specify width and height, followed by uchar data.
 * Return image structure pointer.
 */
imageP
readImage(file)
char    *file;
{
        int     sz[2];
        FILE    *fp;
        imageP  I = NULL;

        /* open file for reading */
        if((fp = fopen(file, "r")) != NULL) {   /* open file for read   */
                fread(sz, sizeof(int), 2, fp);  /* read image dimensions*/
                I = allocImage( sz[0],sz[1]);   /* init image structure */
                fread(I->image, sz[0],sz[1],fp);/* read data into I     */
                fclose(fp);                      /* close image file     */
        }
        return(I);                               /* return image pointer */
}


/* ~~~~~~~~~~~~~~~~~~~~~~~~~~~~~~~~~~~~~~~~~~~~~~~~~~~~~~~~~~~~~~~~~~~~~~~~
 * saveImage:
 *
 * Save image I into file.
 * Return NULL for failure, 1 for success.
 */
int
saveImage(I, file)
```

```
imageP   I;
char     *file;
{
        int      sz[2], status = NULL;
        FILE     *fp;

        if((fp = fopen(file, "w")) != NULL) {   /* open file for save    */
                sz[0] = I->width;
                sz[1] = I->height;
                fwrite(sz, sizeof(int), 2, fp); /* write dimensions      */
                fwrite(I->image,sz[0],sz[1],fp);/* write image data      */
                fclose(fp);                     /* close image file      */
                status = 1;                     /* register success      */
        }
        return(status);
}




/* ~~~~~~~~~~~~~~~~~~~~~~~~~~~~~~~~~~~~~~~~~~~~~~~~~~~~~~~~~~~~~~~~~~~~~~~~~
 * allocImage:
 *
 * Allocate space for an uchar image of width w and height h.
 * Return image structure pointer.
 */
imageP
allocImage(w, h)
int w, h;
{
        imageP   I;

        /* allocate memory for image data structure */
        if((I = (imageP) malloc(sizeof(imageS))) != NULL) {
                I->width  = w;                  /* init width            */
                I->height = h;                  /* init height           */
                I->image  =(uchar*) malloc(w*h);/* init data pointer     */
        }
        return(I);                              /* return image pointer  */
}




/* ~~~~~~~~~~~~~~~~~~~~~~~~~~~~~~~~~~~~~~~~~~~~~~~~~~~~~~~~~~~~~~~~~~~~~~~~~
 * freeImage:
 *
 * Free image memory.
 */
void
freeImage(I)
imageP I;
{
        free((char *) I->image);
        free((char *) I);
}
```

◇ **Bibliography** ◇

(Schumacher 1992) Dale Schumacher. General filtered image rescaling. In David Kirk, editor, *Graphics Gems III*. Academic Press, Boston, 1992.

(Ward and Cok 1989) Joseph Ward and David R. Cok. Resampling algorithms for image resizing and rotation. In *Proc. SPIE Digital Image Processing Applications*, volume 1075, pages 260–269, 1989.

(Wolberg 1990) George Wolberg. *Digital Image Warping*. IEEE Computer Society Press, Los Alamitos, CA, 1990.

(Wolberg and Massalin 1993) George Wolberg and Henry Massalin. A fast algorithm for digital image scaling. In *Proc. Computer Graphics International*, 1993.

VIII.4

Efficient Binary Image Thinning Using Neighborhood Maps

Joseph M. Cychosz
Purdue University CADLAB
West Lafayette, IN 47907
3ksnn64@ecn.purdue.edu

◇ **Introduction** ◇

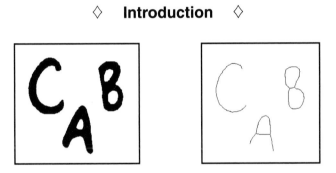

Figure 1.   Image thinning, left: original image, right: thinned image.

Image thinning is a common binary image processing operation and is usually applied to gray scale images that have been thresholded to a binary representation. For example, all pixels within an image that have an intensity value of 50 or less are set to a value of zero. Figure 1 illustrates this processing showing an image with its resulting thinned image to the right. One well-known thinning algorithm is Rosenfeld's parallel thinning algorithm (Rosenfeld 1975) (Rosenfeld and Kak 1982), which makes a number of passes over the image deleting border pixels that are not end points and are 8-simple. An *end point* is a pixel with only one *8-neighbor* (8-neighbor denotes that all 8 neighbors of the pixel are considered, as opposed to 4-neighbor, which only considers the pixels directly to the north, south, east, and west), and an *8-simple* pixel is one that can be deleted without changing the connectedness of the neighboring pixels. To prevent objects from vanishing completely and to produce a skeleton that is as close to the center line as possible, each thinning pass consists of four sub-passes of alternating opposite sides (e.g., a north-south pass, followed by an east-west pass) in which only pixels that are border points in the given direction are considered for deletion.

A summary of Rosenfeld's algorithm follows:

```
pixel_deleted:  boolean := true;
while ( pixel_deleted ) do
    pixel_deleted := false;
    for ( each direction d := N, S, E, W ) do
        for (each pixel i_x,y with neighbor pixel i_d ) do
            if  ( i_x,y = 0 ) loop;
            if  ( i_d  ≠ 0 ) loop;
            if  ( i_x,y is an end point ) loop;
            if  ( i_x,y is not 8-simple ) loop;
            mark pixel i_x,y for deletion;
            pixel_deleted := true;
            endloop
        delete marked pixels;
        endloop
    endloop
```

◇ Thinning Using Neighborhood Maps ◇

The previous algorithm requires a minimum of two accesses to the image, one to examine the pixel being considered and another to examine the neighbor pixel in the given boarder direction to determine if the pixel is a border point in that direction. If the considered pixel passes these two initial tests, the other neighbors must then be examined to determine if the pixel is either an end point or is not 8-simple.

The thinning process can be made more efficient by maintaining a bitmap of the neighborhood (i.e., non-zero neighbors have a bit value of 1, while zero neighbors have a bit value of 0) of each pixel as it is processed. Assuming a top-down, left-right scan of the image, this approach would still essentially require two accesses to the image to maintain the right edge of the neighborhood. One access is to the lower right pixel in the image, and the other is to a scanline buffer containing the neighborhood map codes for the previous scanline. Given the bit assignment and thus the encoding scheme, for the neighborhood shown in Figure 1, the neighborhood for a given pixel (p') is determined by masking, left shifting, and ORing together the previous pixel's neighborhood (p), the neighborhood of the pixel directly above (q), and the condition of the lower right neighbor (i). This process is illustrated in Figure 2 and computed with the equation (constants are in octal):

$$p' = \text{or}\Big\{\text{and}\Big(\text{lshift}(p, 1), 666\Big),\ \text{and}\Big(\text{lshift}(q, 3), 110\Big),\ \text{notequal}\Big(i[x+1, y+1], 0\Big)\Big\}$$

1	0	0	100 011 011 -> 433
0	1	1	not an end point
0	1	1	not 8-simple

a	b	c
d	e	f
g	h	i

0	0	0	000 011 001 -> 031
0	1	1	not an end point
0	0	1	8-simple

neighborhood map = *abc def ghi*

0	1	0	010 011 001 -> 231
0	1	1	not an end point
0	0	1	8-simple

Figure 2. Bit assignments for neighborhood map encoding with example pixel neighborhoods and their corresponding encodings (codes are shown in octal).

$$
q \quad
\begin{matrix}
q_a & q_b & q_c \\
q_d & q_e & q_f \\
q_g & q_h & q_i
\end{matrix}
$$

|
V

$$
\begin{matrix}
p_a & p_b & p_c \\
p_d & p_e & p_f \\
p_g & p_h & p_i \\
 & p &
\end{matrix}
\quad -> \quad
\begin{matrix}
p_a & p_b & q_c \\
p_d & p_e & q_f \\
p_g & p_h & i \\
 & p' &
\end{matrix}
$$

Figure 3. Neighborhood map computation.

Table 1. Performance comparison for the three test images

Image	Image size	No. Thinning Passes	Pixels Deleted	CPU Time (seconds) New Method	Old Method
Cooling tubes	512 x 480	4	40595	2.700	4.270
Large text	512 x 480	5	31303	3.390	4.650
Hallway edges	512 x 480	4	10735	2.700	3.680

Once the neighborhood code has been computed, the border direction can easily be tested by ANDing the neighborhood map with the appropriate direction mask (i.e., north = 200, south = 002, east = 010, and west = 040). A non-zero result means the pixel under consideration has a non-zero neighbor and thus is not a border point in that direction. End point and 8-simple determination is done using a precomputed table indexed by the integer value of the neighborhood map. Since the neighborhood of the previous scanline is maintained in an independent buffer and updated as each pixel is processed, the pixel can be immediately set to zero if it is deleted, thereby eliminating the need of a deletion pass over the image.

All that remains now is the special consideration required for the boundary pixels of the image, the computation of the initial values in the scanline buffer and the initial value of the left edge pixels. The C implementation of the algorithm presented ahead assumes that all out-of-bounds pixels have zero values. However, the algorithm adapts very easily, through the use of indexed tables, for applications that consider the values of off-image pixels to be dependent on the on-image pixels.

◇ Test Results ◇

Figure 4 shows three sample test images and their resulting thinned image. Table 1 compares the performance of the new algorithm versus the original algorithm in which the neighborhood map is computed for non-zero border pixels by examining all eight neighbors. Shown is the CPU time in seconds required to thin each of the images on a Silicon Graphics Iris 4D35, as well as the image size, number of passes required to thin the image, and the total number of pixels deleted.

In the original algorithm the CPU time depends upon the content of the image. An image with few border pixels will thin faster than an image with many border pixels (e.g., Cooling tubes versus Hallway edges). With the new algorithm using neighborhood maps, the CPU time is for the most part independent of the content of the image and executes in constant time for a given resolution and number of passes. This is due to the necessity to maintain the neighborhood map at each pixel regardless of whether the pixel is zero or is a border pixel.

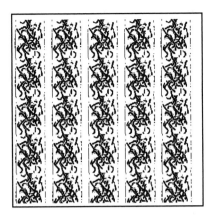

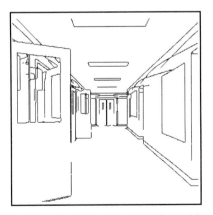

Figure 4. Comparison images, left: original image, right: thinned image; top: 25 replicated images of cooling tubes (courtesy of Bob Cromwell, Purdue Robot Vision Lab), middle: large text, bottom: Sobel edge operator applied to hallway scene (courtesy of Steve Blask, Purdue Robot Vision Lab).

◇   **C Code**   ◇

```c
#include <stdio.h>

typedef unsigned char    Pixel;              /* Pixel data type              */

typedef struct  {                            /* Image control structure      */
        short   Hres;                        /*    Horizontal resolution (x) */
        short   Vres;                        /*    Vertical   resolution (y) */
        int     Size;                        /*    Image size (bytes)        */
        Pixel   *i;                          /*    Image array               */
        Pixel   *p[1];                       /*    Scanline pointer array     */
                                             /*    Pixel (x,y) is given by   */
                                             /*    image->p[y][x]            */
}       Image;


/* ---- ThinImage - Thin binary image. -------------------------------- */
/*                                                                       */
/*      Description:                                                     */
/*          Thins the supplied binary image using Rosenfeld's parallel  */
/*          thinning algorithm.                                         */
/*                                                                       */
/*      On Entry:                                                        */
/*          image = Image to thin.                                       */
/*                                                                       */
/* --------------------------------------------------------------------- */


                              /* Direction masks:                        */
                              /*   N      S      W      E                 */
static  int     masks[]       = { 0200, 0002, 0040, 0010 };

/*      True if pixel neighbor map indicates the pixel is 8-simple and   */
/*      not an end point and thus can be deleted.  The neighborhood      */
/*      map is defined as an integer of bits abcdefghi with a non-zero   */
/*      bit representing a non-zero pixel.  The bit assignment for the   */
/*      neighborhood is:                                                 */
/*                                                                       */
/*                                                                       */
/*                          a b c                                        */
/*                          d e f                                        */
/*                          g h i                                        */

static  unsigned char    delete[512] = {
                0, 0, 0, 0, 0, 0, 0, 0, 0, 0, 0, 0, 0, 0, 0, 0,
                0, 0, 0, 1, 0, 0, 1, 1, 0, 1, 1, 1, 0, 0, 1, 1,
                0, 0, 0, 0, 0, 0, 0, 0, 0, 0, 0, 0, 0, 0, 0, 0,
                0, 0, 1, 1, 1, 0, 1, 1, 0, 0, 1, 1, 0, 0, 1, 1,
                0, 0, 0, 0, 0, 0, 0, 0, 0, 0, 0, 0, 0, 0, 0, 0,
                0, 0, 0, 0, 0, 0, 0, 0, 1, 1, 1, 1, 0, 0, 1, 1,
                0, 0, 0, 0, 0, 0, 0, 0, 0, 0, 0, 0, 0, 0, 0, 0,
                0, 0, 0, 0, 0, 0, 0, 0, 0, 0, 1, 1, 0, 0, 1, 1,
                0, 0, 0, 0, 0, 0, 0, 0, 0, 0, 0, 0, 0, 0, 0, 0,
```

```
              0, 0, 0, 0, 0, 0, 0, 0, 1, 1, 1, 1, 0, 0, 1, 1,
              0, 0, 0, 0, 0, 0, 0, 0, 0, 0, 0, 0, 0, 0, 0, 0,
              1, 0, 1, 1, 1, 0, 1, 1, 1, 1, 1, 1, 1, 1, 1, 1,
              0, 0, 0, 0, 0, 0, 0, 0, 0, 0, 0, 0, 0, 0, 0, 0,
              1, 0, 0, 0, 0, 0, 0, 0, 1, 1, 1, 1, 0, 0, 1, 1,
              0, 0, 0, 0, 0, 0, 0, 0, 0, 0, 0, 0, 0, 0, 0, 0,
              1, 0, 1, 1, 1, 0, 1, 1, 1, 1, 1, 1, 1, 1, 1, 1,
              0, 0, 0, 0, 0, 0, 0, 0, 0, 0, 0, 0, 0, 0, 0, 0,
              0, 0, 0, 0, 0, 0, 0, 0, 0, 0, 0, 0, 0, 0, 0, 0,
              0, 0, 0, 0, 0, 0, 0, 0, 0, 0, 0, 0, 0, 0, 0, 0,
              1, 0, 1, 1, 1, 0, 1, 1, 0, 0, 1, 1, 0, 0, 1, 1,
              0, 0, 0, 0, 0, 0, 0, 0, 0, 0, 0, 0, 0, 0, 0, 0,
              0, 0, 0, 0, 0, 0, 0, 0, 0, 0, 0, 0, 0, 0, 0, 0,
              0, 0, 0, 0, 0, 0, 0, 0, 0, 0, 0, 0, 0, 0, 0, 0,
              0, 0, 0, 0, 0, 0, 0, 0, 0, 0, 1, 1, 0, 0, 1, 1,
              0, 0, 0, 0, 0, 0, 0, 0, 0, 0, 0, 0, 0, 0, 0, 0,
              1, 0, 0, 0, 0, 0, 0, 0, 1, 1, 1, 1, 0, 0, 1, 1,
              0, 0, 0, 0, 0, 0, 0, 0, 0, 0, 0, 0, 0, 0, 0, 0,
              1, 0, 1, 1, 1, 0, 1, 1, 1, 1, 1, 1, 1, 1, 1, 1,
              0, 0, 0, 0, 0, 0, 0, 0, 0, 0, 0, 0, 0, 0, 0, 0,
              1, 0, 0, 0, 0, 0, 0, 0, 1, 1, 1, 1, 0, 0, 1, 1,
              0, 0, 0, 0, 0, 0, 0, 0, 0, 0, 0, 0, 0, 0, 0, 0,
              1, 0, 1, 1, 1, 0, 1, 1, 1, 1, 1, 1, 1, 1, 1, 1};

void    ThinImage       (image)

        Image           *image;         /* Image control structure    */

{

        int             xsize, ysize;   /* Image resolution           */
        int             x, y;           /* Pixel location             */
        int             i;              /* Pass index                 */
        int             pc      = 0;    /* Pass count                 */
        int             count   = 1;    /* Deleted pixel count        */
        int             p, q;           /* Neighborhood maps of adjacent*/
                                        /* cells                      */
        Pixel           *qb;            /* Neighborhood maps of previous*/
                                        /* scanline                   */
        int             m;              /* Deletion direction mask    */

        xsize = image->Hres;
        ysize = image->Vres;
        qb    = (Pixel *) malloc (xsize*sizeof(Pixel));
        qb[xsize-1] = 0;                /* Used for lower right pixel  */

        while ( count ) {               /* Scan image while deletions  */
            pc++;
            count = 0;

            for ( i = 0 ; i < 4 ; i++ ) {

                m = masks[i];
```

```
                /* Build initial previous scan buffer.              */

            p = image->p[0][0] != 0;
            for ( x = 0 ; x < xsize-1 ; x++ )
                qb[x] = p = ((p<<1)&0006) | (image->p[0][x+1] != 0);

                /* Scan image for pixel deletion candidates.         */

            for ( y = 0 ; y < ysize-1 ; y++ ) {

                q = qb[0];
                p = ((q<<3)&0110) | (image->p[y+1][0] != 0);

                for ( x = 0 ; x < xsize-1 ; x++ ) {
                    q = qb[x];
                    p = ((p<<1)&0666) | ((q<<3)&0110) |
                        (image->p[y+1][x+1] != 0);
                    qb[x] = p;
                    if ( ((p&m) == 0) && delete[p] ) {
                        count++;
                        image->p[y][x] = 0;
                    }
                }

                /* Process right edge pixel.                         */

                p = (p<<1)&0666;
                if ( (p&m) == 0 && delete[p] ) {
                    count++;
                    image->p[y][xsize-1] = 0;
                }
            }

                /* Process bottom scan line.                         */

            for ( x = 0 ; x < xsize ; x++ ) {
                q = qb[x];
                p = ((p<<1)&0666) | ((q<<3)&0110);
                if ( (p&m) == 0 && delete[p] ) {
                    count++;
                    image->p[ysize-1][x] = 0;
                }
            }
        }

        printf ("ThinImage: pass %d, %d pixels deleted\n", pc, count);
    }

    free (qb);
}
```

◇ **Bibliography** ◇

(Rosenfeld 1975) A. Rosenfeld. A characterization of parallel thinning algorithms. *Information Control*, 29:286–291, 1975.

(Rosenfeld and Kak 1982) Azriel Rosenfeld and Avinash C. Kak. *Digital Picture Processing, Volume 2*, 2nd edition. Academic Press, Orlando, FL, 1982.

◊ VIII.5

Contrast Limited Adaptive Histogram Equalization

Karel Zuiderveld
Computer Vision Research Group
Utrecht University
Utrecht, The Netherlands
karel@cv.ruu.nl

This Gem describes a contrast enhancement technique called *adaptive histogram equalization*, AHE for short, and an improved version of AHE, named *contrast limited adaptive histogram equalization*, CLAHE, that both overcome the limitations of standard histogram equalization. CLAHE was originally developed for medical imaging and has proven to be successful for enhancement of low-contrast images such as portal films (Rosenman *et al.* 1993).

◊   Introduction   ◊

Probably the most used image processing function is contrast enhancement with a lookup table, a 1-to-1 pixel transform as described in (Jain 1989). When an image has poor contrast, the use of an appropriate mapping function (usually a linear ramp) often results in an improved image.

The mapping function can also be non-linear; a well-known example is gamma correction. Another non-linear technique is *histogram equalization*; it is based on the assumption that a good gray-level assignment scheme should depend on the frequency distribution (histogram) of image gray levels. As the number of pixels in a certain class of gray levels increases, one likes to assign a larger part of the available output gray ranges to the corresponding pixels. This condition is met when cumulative histograms are used as a gray-level transform as is shown in Figure 1.

The histogram of the resulting image is approximately flat, which suggests an optimal distribution of the gray values. However, Figure 1 shows that histogram equalization in its basic form can give a result that is worse than the original image. Large peaks in the histogram can also be caused by uninteresting areas (especially background noise); in this case, histogram equalization mainly leads to an improved visibility of image noise. The technique does also not adapt to local contrast requirements; minor contrast differences can be entirely missed when the number of pixels falling in a particular gray range is small.

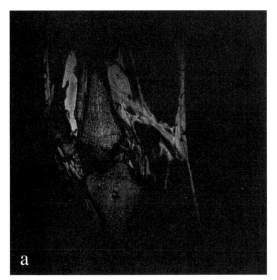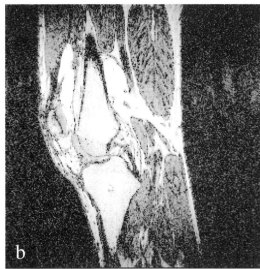

Figure 1. Example of contrast enhancement using histogram equalization. (a) The original image, an image of a human knee obtained with Magnetic Resonance Imaging. (b) Result of histogram equalization.

◇ Adaptive Histogram Equalization (AHE) ◇

Since our eyes adapt to the local context of images to evaluate their contents, it makes sense to optimize local image contrast (Pizer *et al.* 1987). To accomplish this, the image is divided in a grid of rectangular *contextual regions* in which the optimal contrast must be calculated. The optimal number of contextual regions depends on the type of input image, and its determination requires some experimentation. Division of the image into 8×8 contextual regions usually gives good results; this implies 64 contextual regions of size 64×64 when AHE is performed on a 512×512 image.

For each of these contextual regions, the histogram of the contained pixels is calculated. Calculation of the corresponding cumulative histograms results in a gray-level assignment table that optimizes contrast in each of the contextual regions, essentially a histogram equalization based on local image data.

To avoid visibility of region boundaries, a bilinear interpolation scheme is used (see Figure 2).

Applying adaptive histogram equalization on the image in Figure 1a results in the image that can be found in Figure 2b. Although the contrast of the relevant structures in the knee is largely improved, the most striking feature of the image is the background noise that has become visible. Although one can argue that AHE does what it is supposed to do — optimal presentation of information present in the image — noise present in AHE images turns out to be a major drawback of the method.

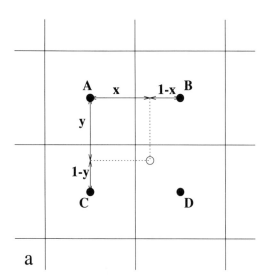 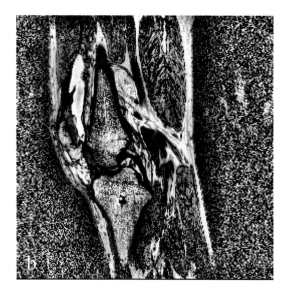

Figure 2. Subdivision and interpolation scheme used with adaptive histogram equalization and a typical result of AHE. (a) The gray-level assignment at the sample position, indicated by a white dot, is derived from the gray-value distributions in the surrounding contextual regions. The points A, B, C, and D form the center of the relevant contextual regions; region-specific gray-level mappings ($g_A(s)$, $g_B(s)$, $g_C(s)$ and $g_D(s)$) are based on the histogram of the pixels contained. Assuming that the original pixel intensity at the sample point is s, its new gray value is calculated by bilinear interpolation of the gray-level mappings that were calculated for each of the surrounding contextual regions: $s' = (1 - y)((1 - x)g_A(s) + xg_B(s)) + y((1 - x)g_C(s) + xg_D(s))$ where x and y are normalized distances with respect to the point A. At edges and corners, a slightly different interpolation scheme is used. (b) Result of AHE using 8×8 contextual regions applied on the image in Figure 1a. Although structures in the knee can be better distinguished, the overall appearance of the image suffers due to noise enhancement.

◇ **Contrast Limited Adaptive Histogram Equalization (CLAHE)** ◇

The noise problem associated with AHE can be reduced by limiting contrast enhancement specifically in homogeneous areas. These areas can be characterized by a high peak in the histogram associated with the contextual regions since many pixels fall inside the same gray range. With CLAHE, the slope associated with the gray-level assignment scheme is limited; this can be accomplished by allowing only a maximum number of pixels in each of the bins associated with local histograms. After clipping the histogram, the pixels that were clipped are equally redistributed over the whole histogram to keep the total histogram count identical (see Figure 3).

The clip limit (or contrast factor) is defined as a multiple of the average histogram contents. With a low factor, the maximum slope of local histograms will be low and

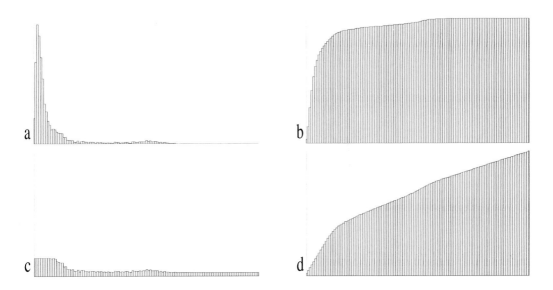

Figure 3. Principle of contrast limiting as used with CLAHE. (a) Histogram of a contextual region containing many background pixels. (b) Calculated cumulative histogram; when used as a gray-level mapping, many bins are wasted for visualization of background noise. (c) Clipped histogram obtained using a clip limit of three. Excess pixels are redistributed through the histogram. (d) Cumulative clipped histogram; its maximum slope (equal to the contrast enhancement obtained) is equal to the clip limit.

therefore result in limited contrast enhancement. A factor of one prohibits contrast enhancement (giving the original image); redistribution of histogram bin values can be avoided by using a very high clip limit (one thousand or higher), which is equivalent to the AHE technique.

Figure 4 shows two examples of contrast enhancement using CLAHE; although the image at the right was CLAHE processed using a high clip limit, image noise is still acceptable.

The main advantages of the CLAHE transform as presented in this Gem are the modest computational requirements, its ease of use (requiring only one parameter: the clip limit), and its excellent results on most images.

CLAHE does have disadvantages. Since the method is aimed at optimizing contrast, there is no 1 to 1 relationship between the gray values of the original image and the CLAHE processed result; consequently, CLAHE images are not suited for quantitative measurements that rely on a physical meaning of image intensity. A more serious problem are artifacts that sometimes occur when high-intensity gradients are present; see (Cromartie and Pizer 1991) for an explanation of these artifacts and a possible (but computationally expensive) solution. A detailed overview of AHE and other histogram equalization methods can be found in (Gauch 1992).

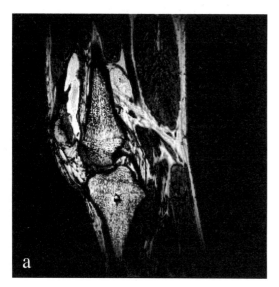 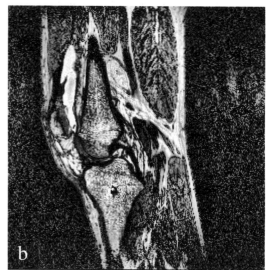

Figure 4. Result of CLAHE applied on the image in Figure 1a. (a) CLAHE with clip limit 3. (b) CLAHE with clip limit 10. Both images were obtained using 8 x 8 contextual regions.

◇ **Implementation** ◇

Since CLAHE has its roots in medical imaging, the earlier CLAHE implementations assumed 16-bit image pixels, since medical scanners often generate 12-bit images. This implementation is a rewrite of a K&R C version written more than five years ago; it is now Ansi-C as well as C++ compliant and can also process 8-bit images.

For a 512×512 image, this implementation of CLAHE requires less than a second on an HP 9000/720 workstation when 8×8 contextual regions are used.

```
/*
 *   These functions implement contrast limited adaptive histogram equalization.
 *   The main routine (CLAHE) expects an input image that is stored contiguously in
 *   memory;  the CLAHE output image overwrites the original input image and has the
 *   same minimum and maximum values (which must be provided by the user).
 *   This implementation assumes that the X- and Y image resolutions are an integer
 *   multiple of the X- and Y sizes of the contextual regions. A check on various other
 *   error conditions is performed.
 *
 *   #define the symbol BYTE_IMAGE to make this implementation suitable for
 *   8-bit images. The maximum number of contextual regions can be redefined
 *   by changing uiMAX_REG_X and/or uiMAX_REG_Y; the use of more than 256
 *   contextual regions is not recommended.
 *
 *   The code is ANSI-C and is also C++ compliant.
 *
 *   Author: Karel Zuiderveld, Computer Vision Research Group,
 *           Utrecht, The Netherlands (karel@cv.ruu.nl)
 */

#ifdef BYTE_IMAGE
typedef unsigned char kz_pixel_t;          /* for 8 bit-per-pixel images */
#define uiNR_OF_GREY (256)
#else
typedef unsigned short kz_pixel_t;         /* for 12 bit-per-pixel images (default) */
# define uiNR_OF_GREY (4096)
#endif

/******** Prototype of CLAHE function. Put this in a separate include file. *****/
int CLAHE(kz_pixel_t* pImage, unsigned int uiXRes, unsigned int uiYRes, kz_pixel_t Min,
          kz_pixel_t Max, unsigned int uiNrX, unsigned int uiNrY,
          unsigned int uiNrBins, float fCliplimit);

/********************** Local prototypes ***********************/
static void ClipHistogram (unsigned long*, unsigned int, unsigned long);
static void MakeHistogram (kz_pixel_t*, unsigned int, unsigned int, unsigned int,
              unsigned long*, unsigned int, kz_pixel_t*);
static void MapHistogram (unsigned long*, kz_pixel_t, kz_pixel_t,
              unsigned int, unsigned long);
static void MakeLut (kz_pixel_t*, kz_pixel_t, kz_pixel_t, unsigned int);
static void Interpolate (kz_pixel_t*, int, unsigned long*, unsigned long*,
        unsigned long*, unsigned long*, unsigned int, unsigned int, kz_pixel_t*);

/************* Start of actual code **************/
#include <stdlib.h>                        /* To get prototypes of malloc() and free() */

const unsigned int uiMAX_REG_X = 16;       /* max. # contextual regions in x-direction */
const unsigned int uiMAX_REG_Y = 16;       /* max. # contextual regions in y-direction */
```

```
/*********************** main function CLAHE ****************/
int CLAHE (kz_pixel_t* pImage, unsigned int uiXRes, unsigned int uiYRes,
          kz_pixel_t Min, kz_pixel_t Max, unsigned int uiNrX, unsigned int uiNrY,
              unsigned int uiNrBins, float fCliplimit)
/*    pImage - Pointer to the input/output image
 *    uiXRes - Image resolution in the X direction
 *    uiYRes - Image resolution in the Y direction
 *    Min - Minimum gray-value of input image (also becomes minimum of output image)
 *    Max - Maximum gray-value of input image (also becomes maximum of output image)
 *    uiNrX - Number of contextial regions in the X direction (min 2, max uiMAX_REG_X)
 *    uiNrY - Number of contextial regions in the Y direction (min 2, max uiMAX_REG_Y)
 *    uiNrBins - Number of gray bins for histogram ("dynamic range")
 *    float fCliplimit - Normalized clip limit (higher values give more contrast)
 * The number of "effective" gray levels in the output image is set by uiNrBins; selecting
 * a small value (eg. 128) speeds up processing and still produce an output image of
 * good quality. The output image will have the same minimum and maximum value as the input
 * image. A clip limit smaller than 1 results in standard (non-contrast-limited) AHE.
 */
{
    unsigned int uiX, uiY;                      /* counters */
    unsigned int uiXSize, uiYSize, uiSubX, uiSubY; /* size of context. reg. and subimages */
    unsigned int uiXL, uiXR, uiYU, uiYB;    /* auxiliary variables interpolation routine */
    unsigned long ulClipLimit, ulNrPixels;/* clip limit and region pixel count */
    kz_pixel_t* pImPointer;                     /* pointer to image */
    kz_pixel_t aLUT[uiNR_OF_GREY];          /* lookup table used for scaling of input image */
    unsigned long* pulHist, *pulMapArray; /* pointer to histogram and mappings*/
    unsigned long* pulLU, *pulLB, *pulRU, *pulRB; /* auxiliary pointers interpolation */

    if (uiNrX > uiMAX_REG_X) return -1;     /* # of regions x-direction too large */
    if (uiNrY > uiMAX_REG_Y) return -2;     /* # of regions y-direction too large */
    if (uiXRes % uiNrX) return -3;          /* x-resolution no multiple of uiNrX */
    if (uiYRes & uiNrY) return -4;          /* y-resolution no multiple of uiNrY */
    if (Max >= uiNR_OF_GREY) return -5;     /* maximum too large */
    if (Min >= Max) return -6;              /* minimum equal or larger than maximum */
    if (uiNrX < 2 || uiNrY < 2) return -7;  /* at least 4 contextual regions required */
    if (fCliplimit == 1.0) return 0;        /* is OK, immediately returns original image. */
    if (uiNrBins == 0) uiNrBins = 128;      /* default value when not specified */

    pulMapArray=(unsigned long *)malloc(sizeof(unsigned long)*uiNrX*uiNrY*uiNrBins);
    if (pulMapArray == 0) return -8;        /* Not enough memory! (try reducing uiNrBins) */

    uiXSize = uiXRes/uiNrX; uiYSize = uiYRes/uiNrY;  /* Actual size of contextual regions */
    ulNrPixels = (unsigned long)uiXSize * (unsigned long)uiYSize;

    if(fCliplimit > 0.0) {                  /* Calculate actual cliplimit */
       ulClipLimit = (unsigned long) (fCliplimit * (uiXSize * uiYSize) / uiNrBins);
       ulClipLimit = (ulClipLimit < 1UL) ? 1UL : ulClipLimit;
    }
    else ulClipLimit = 1UL<<14;             /* Large value, do not clip (AHE) */
```

```
MakeLut(aLUT, Min, Max, uiNrBins);      /* Make lookup table for mapping of gray values */
/* Calculate gray-level mappings for each contextual region */
for (uiY = 0, pImPointer = pImage; uiY < uiNrY; uiY++) {
    for (uiX = 0; uiX < uiNrX; uiX++, pImPointer += uiXSize) {
        pulHist = &pulMapArray[uiNrBins * (uiY * uiNrX + uiX)];
        MakeHistogram(pImPointer,uiXRes,uiXSize,uiYSize,pulHist,uiNrBins,aLUT);
        ClipHistogram(pulHist, uiNrBins, ulClipLimit);
        MapHistogram(pulHist, Min, Max, uiNrBins, ulNrPixels);
    }
    pImPointer += (uiYSize - 1) * uiXRes;                /* skip lines, set pointer */
}


/* Interpolate gray-level mappings to get CLAHE image */
for (pImPointer = pImage, uiY = 0; uiY <= uiNrY; uiY++) {
    if (uiY == 0) {                                     /* special case: top row */
        uiSubY = uiYSize >> 1;  uiYU = 0; uiYB = 0;
    }
    else {
        if (uiY == uiNrY) {                             /* special case: bottom row */
            uiSubY = uiYSize >> 1;  uiYU = uiNrY-1;  uiYB = uiYU;
        }
        else {                                          /* default values */
            uiSubY = uiYSize; uiYU = uiY - 1; uiYB = uiYU + 1;
        }
    }
    for (uiX = 0; uiX <= uiNrX; uiX++) {
        if (uiX == 0) {                                 /* special case: left column */
            uiSubX = uiXSize >> 1; uiXL = 0; uiXR = 0;
        }
        else {
            if (uiX == uiNrX) {                         /* special case: right column */
                uiSubX = uiXSize >> 1;  uiXL = uiNrX - 1; uiXR = uiXL;
            }
            else {                                      /* default values */
                uiSubX = uiXSize; uiXL = uiX - 1; uiXR = uiXL + 1;
            }
        }

        pulLU = &pulMapArray[uiNrBins * (uiYU * uiNrX + uiXL)];
        pulRU = &pulMapArray[uiNrBins * (uiYU * uiNrX + uiXR)];
        pulLB = &pulMapArray[uiNrBins * (uiYB * uiNrX + uiXL)];
        pulRB = &pulMapArray[uiNrBins * (uiYB * uiNrX + uiXR)];
        Interpolate(pImPointer,uiXRes,pulLU,pulRU,pulLB,pulRB,uiSubX,uiSubY,aLUT);
        pImPointer += uiSubX;                           /* set pointer on next matrix */
    }
    pImPointer += (uiSubY - 1) * uiXRes;
}
free(pulMapArray);                                      /* free space for histograms */
return 0;                                               /* return status OK */
}
```

```
void ClipHistogram (unsigned long* pulHistogram, unsigned int
                    uiNrGreylevels, unsigned long ulClipLimit)
/* This function performs clipping of the histogram and redistribution of bins.
 * The histogram is clipped and the number of excess pixels is counted. Afterwards
 * the excess pixels are equally redistributed across the whole histogram (providing
 * the bin count is smaller than the clip limit).
 */
{
    unsigned long* pulBinPointer, *pulEndPointer, *pulHisto;
    unsigned long ulNrExcess, ulUpper, ulBinIncr, ulStepSize, i;
    long lBinExcess;

    ulNrExcess = 0;  pulBinPointer = pulHistogram;
    for (i = 0; i < uiNrGreylevels; i++) { /* calculate total number of excess pixels */
        lBinExcess = (long) pulBinPointer[i] - (long) ulClipLimit;
        if (lBinExcess > 0) ulNrExcess += lBinExcess;        /* excess in current bin */
    };

    /* Second part: clip histogram and redistribute excess pixels in each bin */
    ulBinIncr = ulNrExcess / uiNrGreylevels;                 /* average bin increment */
    ulUpper =  ulClipLimit - ulBinIncr;  /* Bins larger than ulUpper set to clip limit */

    for (i = 0; i < uiNrGreylevels; i++) {
      if (pulHistogram[i] > ulClipLimit) pulHistogram[i] = ulClipLimit; /* clip bin */
      else {
          if (pulHistogram[i] > ulUpper) {                   /* high bin count */
             ulNrExcess -= pulHistogram[i] - ulUpper; pulHistogram[i]=ulClipLimit;
          }
          else {                                             /* low bin count */
             ulNrExcess -= ulBinIncr; pulHistogram[i] += ulBinIncr;
          }
      }
    }

    while (ulNrExcess) {    /* Redistribute remaining excess  */
        pulEndPointer = &pulHistogram[uiNrGreylevels]; pulHisto = pulHistogram;

        while (ulNrExcess && pulHisto < pulEndPointer) {
            ulStepSize = uiNrGreylevels / ulNrExcess;
            if (ulStepSize < 1) ulStepSize = 1;              /* stepsize at least 1 */
            for (pulBinPointer=pulHisto; pulBinPointer < pulEndPointer && ulNrExcess;
                pulBinPointer += ulStepSize) {
                if (*pulBinPointer < ulClipLimit) {
                    (*pulBinPointer)++;  ulNrExcess--;       /* reduce excess */
                }
            }
            pulHisto++;                /* restart redistributing on other bin location */
        }
    }
}
```

```
void MakeHistogram (kz_pixel_t* pImage, unsigned int uiXRes,
                unsigned int uiSizeX, unsigned int uiSizeY,
                unsigned long* pulHistogram,
                unsigned int uiNrGreylevels, kz_pixel_t* pLookupTable)
```
/* *This function classifies the gray-levels present in the array image into*
 * *a grey-level histogram. The pLookupTable specifies the relationship*
 * *between the gray-value of the pixel (typically between 0 and 4095) and*
 * *the corresponding bin in the histogram (usually containing only 128 bins).*
 */
```
{
    kz_pixel_t* pImagePointer;
    unsigned int i;

    for (i = 0; i < uiNrGreylevels; i++) pulHistogram[i] = 0L; /* clear histogram */

    for (i = 0; i < uiSizeY; i++) {
        pImagePointer = &pImage[uiSizeX];
        while (pImage < pImagePointer) pulHistogram[pLookupTable[*pImage++]]++;
        pImagePointer += uiXRes;
        pImage = &pImagePointer[-uiSizeX];
    }
}
```

```
void MapHistogram (unsigned long* pulHistogram, kz_pixel_t Min, kz_pixel_t Max,
                unsigned int uiNrGreylevels, unsigned long ulNrOfPixels)
```
/* *This function calculates the equalized lookup table (mapping) by*
 * *cumulating the input histogram. Note: lookup table is rescaled in range [Min..Max].*
 */
```
{
    unsigned int i;  unsigned long ulSum = 0;
    const float fScale = ((float)(Max - Min)) / ulNrOfPixels;
    const unsigned long ulMin = (unsigned long) Min;

    for (i = 0; i < uiNrGreylevels; i++) {
        ulSum += pulHistogram[i]; pulHistogram[i]=(unsigned long)(ulMin+ulSum*fScale);
        if (pulHistogram[i] > Max) pulHistogram[i] = Max;
    }
}
```

```
void MakeLut (kz_pixel_t * pLUT, kz_pixel_t Min, kz_pixel_t Max, unsigned int uiNrBins)
```
/* *To speed up histogram clipping, the input image [Min,Max] is scaled down to*
 * *[0,uiNrBins-1]. This function calculates the LUT.*
 */
```
{
    int i;
    const kz_pixel_t BinSize = (kz_pixel_t) (1 + (Max - Min) / uiNrBins);

    for (i = Min; i <= Max; i++)  pLUT[i] = (i - Min) / BinSize;
}
```

```
void Interpolate (kz_pixel_t * pImage, int uiXRes, unsigned long * pulMapLU,
      unsigned long * pulMapRU, unsigned long * pulMapLB,  unsigned long * pulMapRB,
      unsigned int uiXSize, unsigned int uiYSize, kz_pixel_t * pLUT)
/* pImage        - pointer to input/output image
 * uiXRes        - resolution of image in x-direction
 * pulMap*       - mappings of gray-levels from histograms
 * uiXSize       - uiXSize of image submatrix
 * uiYSize       - uiYSize of image submatrix
 * pLUT          - lookup table containing mapping gray values to bins
 * This function calculates the new gray-level assignments of pixels within a submatrix
 * of the image with size uiXSize and uiYSize. This is done by a bilinear interpolation
 * between four different mappings in order to eliminate boundary artifacts.
 * It uses a division; since division is often an expensive operation, I added code to
 * perform a logical shift instead when feasible.
 */
{
    const kz_pixel_t Max = (kz_pixel_t) uiNR_OF_GREY - 1;
    const unsigned int uiIncr = uiXRes-uiXSize; /* Pointer increment after processing row */
    kz_pixel_t GreyValue; unsigned int uiNum = uiXSize*uiYSize; /* Normalization factor */

    unsigned int uiXCoef, uiYCoef, uiXInvCoef, uiYInvCoef, uiShift = 0;

    if (uiNum & (uiNum - 1))    /* If uiNum is not a power of two, use division */
    for (uiYCoef = 0, uiYInvCoef = uiYSize; uiYCoef < uiYSize;
         uiYCoef++, uiYInvCoef--,pImage+=uiIncr) {
       for (uiXCoef = 0, uiXInvCoef = uiXSize; uiXCoef < uiXSize;
            uiXCoef++, uiXInvCoef--) {
          GreyValue = pLUT[*pImage];             /* get histogram bin value */
          *pImage++ = (kz_pixel_t ) ((uiYInvCoef * (uiXInvCoef*pulMapLU[GreyValue]
                             + uiXCoef * pulMapRU[GreyValue])
                      + uiYCoef * (uiXInvCoef * pulMapLB[GreyValue]
                          + uiXCoef * pulMapRB[GreyValue])) / uiNum);
       }
    }
    else {                        /* avoid the division and use a right shift instead */
       while (uiNum >>= 1) uiShift++;            /* Calculate 2log of uiNum */
       for (uiYCoef = 0, uiYInvCoef = uiYSize; uiYCoef < uiYSize;
            uiYCoef++, uiYInvCoef--,pImage+=uiIncr) {
          for (uiXCoef = 0, uiXInvCoef = uiXSize; uiXCoef < uiXSize;
             uiXCoef++, uiXInvCoef--) {
             GreyValue = pLUT[*pImage];           /* get histogram bin value */
             *pImage++ = (kz_pixel_t)((uiYInvCoef* (uiXInvCoef * pulMapLU[GreyValue]
                                + uiXCoef * pulMapRU[GreyValue])
                         + uiYCoef * (uiXInvCoef * pulMapLB[GreyValue]
                             + uiXCoef * pulMapRB[GreyValue])) >> uiShift);
          }
       }
    }
}
```

$\diamond$ **Bibliography** $\diamond$

(Cromartie and Pizer 1991) R. Cromartie and S.M. Pizer. Edge-affected context for adaptive contrast enhancement. In A. C. S. Colchester and D. J. Hawkes, editors, *Proceedings of the XIIth International Meeting on Information Processing in Medical Imaging: Lecture Notes in Computer Science*, pages 474–485, Springer-Verlag, Berlin, 1991.

(Gauch 1992) J. M. Gauch. Investigations of image contrast space defined by variations on histogram equalization. *CVGIP: Graphical Models and Image Processing*, 54(4):269–280, July 1992.

(Jain 1989) A. K. Jain. *Fundamentals of digital image processing*. Prentice Hall, Englewood Cliffs, NJ, 1989.

(Pizer *et al.* 1987) S. M. Pizer, E. P. Amburn, J. D. Austin, R. Cromartie, A. Geselowitz, B. ter Haar Romeny, J. B. Zimmerman, and K. Zuiderveld. Adaptive histogram equalization and its variations. *Computer Vision, Graphics, and Image Processing*, 39:355–368, 1987.

(Rosenman *et al.* 1993) J. Rosenman, C. A. Roe, R. Cromartie, K. E. Muller, and S. M. Pizer. Portal film enhancement: Technique and clinical utility. *Int. J. Radiat. Oncol. Biol. Physics*, pages 333–338, 1993.

◇ VIII.6

Ideal Tiles for Shading and Halftoning

Alan W. Paeth

Okanagan University College
Kelowna, British Columbia, Canada
awpaeth@okanagan.bc.ca

The placement of objects on an 8×8 matrix, such as non-attacking queens on a chess board, has an extensive history. This Gem derives useful 4×4 and 8×8 matrices in which half the cells are occupied. Suitable placement criteria reveal solutions having graphical application on bi-level displays. These include the gray shading of objects by stippling (as when indicating their selection) and the halftoning of continuous tone images using a "disorderly" ordered dither.

◇ Background and History ◇

Many bi-level displays, such those based on X windows, support pixel rendering under control of a tile whose $n \times m$ cells serve as a spatial write mask. That is, an active cell indicates that a destination pixel may be drawn or copied to, otherwise it remains unaltered. The tile may be conveniently represented by an integer(s) whose "1" bits indicate activity in a corresponding cell. The tile's contents are replicated as needed to cover the region of potential pixel activity. A common use is in stippling (adding fine spatial texture) to adjust the brightness of an object (Ahuja and Rosenfeld 1981).

An early example is the BitBLT operation originally developed by Daniel Ingalls at Xerox PARC for use on the Alto personal computer. It supported a 4×4 tile called the *mask*, which was defined by a 16-bit machine word. A salient feature of this bit-aligned block transfer[1] is that the pattern remains fixed relative to the display (the so-called "Ingall's shuffle"). This feature persists; it guarantees that the tiling of adjacent regions shows no seams where they abut. RasterOps[2] supporting this model have enjoyed an on-going vogue since they were popularized by the Apple Macintosh.

---

[1] The origin of BitBlt may be traced to BLT: the PDP-10 assembly code mnemonic for block transfer. PARC's first research machine was a PDP-10 build from scratch.

[2] For some, the politically correct term for BitBlt.

(a)   (a')   (b)   (b')

Figure 1.   4 x 4 tiles.

Four sections follow. The requirements for an ideal tile are identified first. Next, a set of candidate tiles are created to satisfy these defining constraints. In the third, the tiles are applied to methods of digital halftoning (Ulichney 1987). The concluding section presents nearly ideal tiles, suggesting methods of extension.

◇ Stipple Problem ◇

Tiles may be used to stipple (pattern with fine dots) display objects, producing a gray appearance. A useful stipple has distinct requirements for two common classes of objects: filled areas and lines. The requirements are partially in conflict. A stippled line must not exhibit Moiré patterns that may arise by interaction with runs of dots created by cyclic repetition of the underlying tile (Roetling 1976). This suggests tiles whose active cells are grouped together. Conversely, stipple dots in a filled area must be distributed so that no visible accretion is built up (this is in contrast to the formation of a halftone dot).

An ideal tile satisfies both requirements simultaneously and may be used universally to stipple display objects. The worst case stipple of 50% gray must consider these requirements equally for regions formed by both the active and inactive cells. The stipple problem can now be stated: find an ideal tile having half its cells (in)active.

As an example, the 1×8 tile represented by the byte 10101010_2 produces a gray pattern of alternating vertical lines that are unresolved by the eye. However, the pattern is useless in stippling vertical lines of single bit extent. Lines rendered under this spatial mask either vanish or are unaffected depending on their placement relative to the stipple. The 2×2 checkerboard tile is a common work-around. Unfortunately, it fails in similar fashion when rendering diagonal lines (having slope ± 1).

◇ Solutions ◇

Square ideal tiles having an even number of cells are now examined. The smallest tile is the 2×2 checkerboard, whose unique solution was rejected. The 4×4 tile is the next candidate. Enumeration of all patterns having half the cells active yields $16!/(8!)^2 = 12,870$ cases. In 90 cases the rows and columns are additionally half occupied. Finally, in

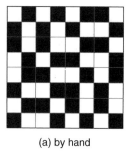
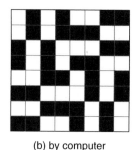

(a) by hand   (b) by computer

Figure 2.   8 x 8 tiles.

eight cases the eight (broken) diagonals are half occupied. Considering patterns identical under bit complementation halves the number of cases. The four model solutions are easily found by hand and are presented in Figure 1.

The two entries forming Figures 1(a,a') and Figures 1(b,b') differ only by spatial shift. The (a) and (b) styles differ only by 90° rotation. Thus, there is only one unique 4×4 solution under mirroring, translation, and transposition. Note that any occupied cell has at most one edge-adjacent neighbor: there is no "blobbiness." Unfortunately, the 4×4 tile likewise fails when stippling lines having slope ± 2 or $\pm\frac{1}{2}$. The segments forming these lines through repetition are best seen in Figures 1(a') and 1(b'). The near-ideal 4×4 tile forms a useful stipple when only area fills or the graying of rectilinear lines are required.

A solution is sought that correctly stipples lines of arbitrary slope. The 8×8 tile is considered over the 6×6 case as the former is easily created using 4×4 subtiles. A solution that is self-similar after translation and complementation is desirable. Arranging the tiles (1a) and (1b) in checkerboard fashion is one solution. That is, the tiles (1a), (1b) are adjoined to form the 4×8 block forming the top half of the master tile, and their transposition (1b), (1a) fills the bottom half. The hand-generated tile appears in Figure 2(a).

The construction of tiles preserves the 50% gray of their subtiles. In addition, careful subtile composition does not introduce any new blobbiness where edges abut. Each subtile protects against false rendering of rectilinear lines. The alternation of the subtiles protects against the false rendering of lines having slope ± 2 or $\pm\frac{1}{2}$, as the "grain" of each "ply" opposes its four edge-connected neighbors. Considered as a whole, the 8×8 hand-generated tile in (2a) contains rows and columns all formed from the cyclic permutation of the pattern 1 1 1 0 1 1 0 0, guaranteeing complete uniformity in the rendering of rectilinear objects. Unfortunately, closer examination reveals one NW/SE path two cells below the main diagonal having all cells active. Its transposition reveals a diagonal of all active cells. Clearly, complications can occur where subcells adjoin. The hand enumeration of representative solutions becomes difficult.

Closer study reveals one valid solution (proved unique by the computer). It is the checkerboard tiling of patterns (1a') and (1b') appearing as (2b). This ideal 8×8 tile is symmetric under central inversion: identical after $180°$ rotation and hence by x and y mirroring, but not by either taken alone. (Instead, each $90°$ turn is equivalent to a bit complementation.) Rows and columns are not similar: some show runs of three, leading to slightly increased blobbiness. No lone cells (those having no edge neighbors) appear. Conceptually, the computer solution is a pattern of interlocking active and inactive L's at all eight possible orientations.

Related Work

The solutions (2a) and (2b) may be considered a tiling of the plane with n-polyominoes (Golomb 1966) where $2 \leq n \leq 4$ and in which regular shapes such as the 2×2 box or 4×1 strip are omitted. Tiles having half the cells of any row or column filled are called *anallagmatic pavements* by (Ball and Coxeter 1974) on pages 107–109. Solution of the related queen's placement problem using matrix determinants appears on pages 166–171. An automated enumeration of tiles is a straightforward programming exercise. Less simple are the definition and identification of local features which may arise through cyclic patterning, as seen above. Candidate tiles may be selected based on the number of active adjacent neighbors of each cell, considered cyclically. This suggests using the cellular automaton rules of Conway's "LIFE" (Gardner 1970) as a density test. Remarkably, an arbitrarily large area patterned by (2b) is stable, save for erosion along the pattern's boundary, a consequence of the repeated interlocking pattern. (The tile itself persists for 302 generations, ending in still life.)

◇ **Digital Halftoning** ◇

Digital halftoning of continuous tone images requires the creation of a weight matrix whose entries are a sequence of integers. These indicate the placement of ink for tones of increasing density. Halftoning for print media employs a sequence forming a contiguous region, building up an ink dot which achieves dot gain (Schreiber 1986). The opposite is true when halftoning for bi-level displays. The sequence of elements is not adjacent, thus introducing dither, a form of local noise (Roberts 1962). Ordered dither matrices (Jarvis *et al.* 1976) based on a recursive tiling of 2×2 blocks are a familiar example. The similar construction methods used for stipple patterns above suggest that they could be helpful for dithering.

When the 4×4 ordered dither is used to halftone an image, a visually distracting (Hamey 1992) grid may appear. The 25% gray tone is pronounced, as a 1-in-4 dot pattern is created (Figure 3(a)). In printing parlance, the screen angle is zero, a condition normally avoided. A set of weights based on the ideal 4×4 or 8×8 tiles allows for

```
1  .  4  .        1  .  7  .          8 184 104 216
.  5  .  8        .  3  .  5        152  40 248  82
3  .  2  .        .  8  .  2        200 120 168  24
.  7  .  6        6  .  4  .         88 232  56 136

(a) orderly      (b) disorderly    (c) weight matrix
```

Figure 3.   4 x 4 dither matrices.

Figure 4.   Halftoning using 4 x 4 dither.

an equally fine-textured gray while introducing less prominent horizontal and vertical regularity. The ordered dither then has additional local disorder.

Numbering the first eight inactive cells of (1a) in a regular fashion produces a matrix which reconstructs the ideal stipple appearing in (1a) when producing a 50% halftone instead of 4 × 4 checkerboard. An experimental sequence appears in (3b) in which no successive elements are edge-adjacent.

The fill sequence chosen is a knight's tour along the first eight active cells, beginning at the upper left. The "L" steps may cross the tile's edge (PacMan's Projective Plane). The same sequence fills the remaining eight vacancies beginning at the lower right under a 180° rotation. Halftone matrices which are self-complementary in this fashion enjoy a number of useful properties (Stucki 1979).

An image halftoned under the ideal 4 × 4 tile appears in Figure 4. The output was produced by reusing the data sets and procedures employed in creation of similar figures for (Foley *et al.* 1990), inviting further comparison. The dither matrices used with the eight-bit (256-level) continuous tone images appear as Figure 3(c); the image files may be found on the Gems file server.

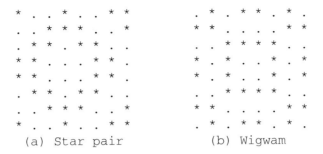

(a) Star pair   (b) Wigwam

Figure 5.   Computer-generated near-ideal tiles.

The regular features of (4a) have been replaced in (4b) with chain mail-like patterns, apparent in regions of constant tone.

◇ **Extensions and Conclusions** ◇

Additional computer search of all 8×8 matrices having 50% row, column, and diagonal coverage, self-similarity under complementation, and little "blobbiness" confirmed the solutions presented above. Removing or reversing the last selection criterion revealed other classes of structure worthy of further study. Two examples (both having possible halftoning application) appear in Figure 5: an annulus with conjugate "star satellite" and a blanket weave.

No tiles larger than 8×8 were studied. It is the author's belief that interactive, automated exploration of this domain might reveal additional tiles that are useful to computer graphics applications and interesting in their own right. Tiles with arbitrary edge lengths, including rectangular tiles, deserve particular attention.

◇ **Bibliography** ◇

(Ahuja and Rosenfeld 1981) N. Ahuja and A. Rosenfeld. Mosaic models for textures. *IEEE Transactions on Pattern Analysis and Machine Intelligence*, PAMI(1):1–11, 1981.

(Ball and Coxeter 1974) W. W. Rouse Ball and H. S. M. Coxeter. *Mathematical Recreations & Essays*. University of Toronto Press, 12th edition, 1974.

(Foley *et al.* 1990) James D. Foley, Andries van Dam, Steven K. Feiner, and John F. Hughes. *Computer Graphics: Principles and Practice*. Addison-Wesley, 2nd edition, Reading, MA, 1990.

(Gardner 1970) Martin Gardner. The game of LIFE. *Scientific American*, October 1970.

(Golomb 1966) Solomon Wolf Golomb. *Polyominoes*. Allen & Unwin, London, 1966.

(Hamey 1992) L. G. C. Hamey. On human perception of regular repetitive textures. Technical Report 92-0094C, School of MPCE, Macquarie University, Australia, 1992.

(Jarvis *et al.* 1976) J. F. Jarvis, N. Judice, and W. H. Ninke. A survey of techniques for the display of continuous tone pictures on bilevel displays. *Computer Graphics and Image Processing*, 5(1):13–40, March 1976.

(Roberts 1962) L. G. Roberts. Picture coding using pseudo-random noise. *IRE Trans. Info. Theory*, BIT-8:145, February 1962.

(Roetling 1976) Paul G. Roetling. Halftone method with edge enhancement and moiré suppression. *Jour. Opt. Soc. Amer.*, 66(10):985–989, October 1976.

(Schreiber 1986) William F. Schreiber. *Fundamentals of Electronic Imaging Systems*. Springer Verlag, Berlin, 1986.

(Stucki 1979) Peter Stucki. Digital screening of continuous tone image data for bilevel display. In Peter Stucki, editor, *Symposium on Advances in Digital Image Processing*, Plenum Press, New York, 1979.

(Ulichney 1987) Robert Ulichney. *Digital Halftoning*. MIT Press, Cambridge, MA, 1987.

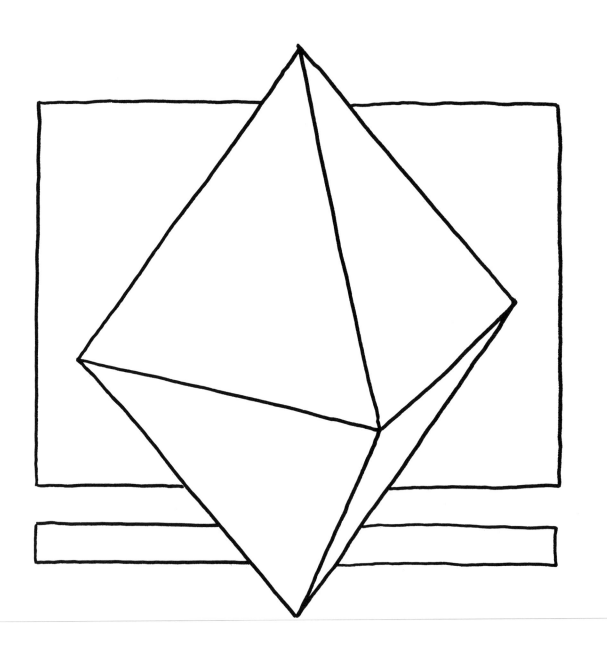

◇ **IX** ◇
Graphic Design

This part of the book contains two Gems on algorithms for graphical layout.

IX.1. Placing Text Labels on Maps and Diagrams, *by Jon Christensen, Joe Marks, and Stuart Shieber.*
Presents an algorithm to arrange text labels in a way that avoids overlap. This is useful in cartography. Page 497.

IX.2. Dynamic Layout Algorithm to Display General Graphs, *by László Szirmay-Kalos.*
Gives code that finds aesthetic arrangements for a graph. This could be used to graphically display data structures. Page 505.

IX.1

Placing Text Labels on Maps and Diagrams

Jon Christensen

Harvard University
Cambridge, MA
christen@das.harvard.edu

Joe Marks

Digital Equipment Corporation
Cambridge Research Lab
Cambridge, MA
marks@das.harvard.edu

Stuart Shieber

Harvard University
Cambridge, MA
shieber@das.harvard.edu

◇ Introduction ◇

Tagging graphical objects with text labels is a fundamental task in the design of many types of informational graphics. This problem is seen in its most essential form in cartography, but it also arises frequently in the production of other informational graphics such as scatterplots. The quality of a labeling is determined essentially by the degree to which labels obscure other labels or features of the underlying graphic. The goal is to choose positions for the labels that do not give rise to label overlaps and that minimize obscuration of features. Construction of a good labeling is thus a combinatorial optimization problem, which has been shown to be NP-hard (Formann and Wagner 1991, Marks and Shieber 1991). In this Gem, we describe a method for heuristically solving this optimization problem using simulated annealing (Kirkpatrick *et al.* 1983, Cerny 1985). Extensive empirical testing has shown that the simulated-annealing approach to the label-placement problem produces higher quality labelings than other previously published algorithms and is competitive with respect to efficiency (Christensen *et al.* 1992).

◇ Iterative Local Improvement ◇

As an example, suppose one is given a set of point features (perhaps a set of city locations on a map or point locations on a scatterplot), each of which may be labeled in one of eight positions, as shown in Figure 1. As a hypothetical baseline algorithm, randomly choosing positions for each label, as in Figure 2, is likely to generate a poor labeling. The apparent poor quality of the labeling can be quantified using a metric

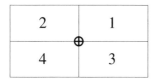 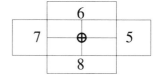

Figure 1.   A set of potential label positions and their relative desirability.

that counts the number of *conflicted* labels, i.e., those that obscure point features or other labels. Using this metric, this labeling has a score of 86.

One might attempt to improve the labeling by an iterative local improvement method, adjusting a label position if it leads to a better overall score. Such a local method is prone to ending up in unacceptable local optima. Repeatedly performing the best local improvements (i.e., the local improvements that give the greatest decrease in the number of conflicted labels at each step) on the example of Figure 2 generates the locally optimal labeling in Figure 3, which, though better than the original random labeling, can still be greatly improved upon.

◇ Simulated Annealing ◇

In order to escape from local optima in the search space, we use simulated annealing (Kirkpatrick *et al.* 1983, Cerny 1985, van Laarhoven and Aarts 1987) to allow occasional label adjustments that make the overall score worse. Of course, such anarchic behavior cannot be tolerated uniformly. Rather, the ability of the algorithm to degrade the solution is controlled by a parameter T, called the *temperature*, that decreases over time according to an *annealing schedule*. At zero temperature, such backwards steps are disallowed completely, so that the algorithm reduces to a local optimization method. At higher temperatures, however, a wider range of the search space can be explored, so that regions surrounding better local optima (and perhaps even the global optimum) may be visited. The following outline describes the essential characteristics of a simulated-annealing algorithm for the label-placement problem:

1. For each point feature, place its label randomly in any of the available potential positions.
2. Initialize the temperature T to T_0.
3. Repeat until the rate of improvement falls below a given threshold:

    (a) Decrease the temperature, T, according to the annealing schedule.
    (b) Pick a label at random and move it to a new position at random.
    (c) Compute ΔE, the change in the score caused by repositioning the label.

(d) If the new labeling is worse, undo the label repositioning with probability $P = 1.0 - e^{-\Delta E/T}$.

A geometric annealing schedule is recommended, where the temperature remains constant for a given number of iterations, and then is decreased by a constant factor. We have used the following particular annealing schedule with success. The initial temperature T_0 is set so that $P = 1/3$ when $\Delta E = 1$. This gives a value for T_0 of about 2.5. The temperature is decreased by 10 percent every $50n$ iterations through loop (3), where n is the number of point features. If more than $10n$ successful configuration changes are made at any temperature, the temperature is immediately decreased. This process is repeated for at most 50 temperature stages. However, if we stay at a particular temperature for the full $50n$ steps without accepting a single label repositioning, and if the cost is the lowest seen so far, then the algorithm stops with the current labeling as the final solution. In limited experimentation we found the particular choice of annealing schedule to have a relatively minor effect on the performance of the algorithm. This schedule was chosen primarily to provide reasonable execution times; longer annealing schedules result in moderately improved solutions.

Figure 4 shows the labeling generated by this algorithm for the same point data used in Figure 2. This labeling was generated in under a second on a DEC 3000 Model 400 AXP workstation.

◇ Augmentations and Comparisons ◇

To make the algorithm practical, care must be taken in the computation of ΔE. Cartographic practice requires that provision be made for a priori preferences among label positions and the ability to delete labels in congested areas (Yoeli 1972). In this section, we discuss these issues and conclude with an informal comparison along several dimensions of the simulated annealing approach and other previously proposed approaches to label placement.

Computation of ΔE

Because simulated annealing is a statistical method that relies on a large number of evaluations for its success, the best scoring functions are those for which ΔE can be computed easily. The most straightforward scoring function simply counts the number of pairwise overlaps. In practice, however, it is often preferable to have a single label with three overplots (four labels conflicted) instead of three distinct pairwise overplots (six labels conflicted). Therefore, the scoring function we choose counts the number of labels obstructed by at least one other label or graphical object.

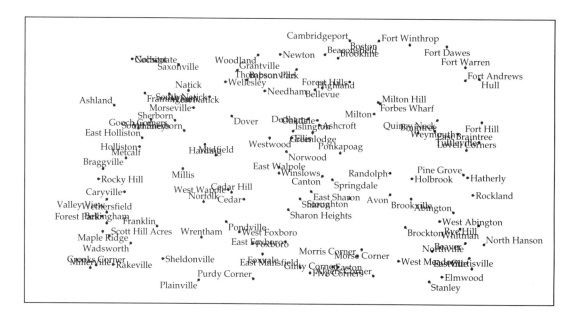

Figure 2. Initial random labeling of a set of 120 points in Massachusetts (86 labels conflicted).

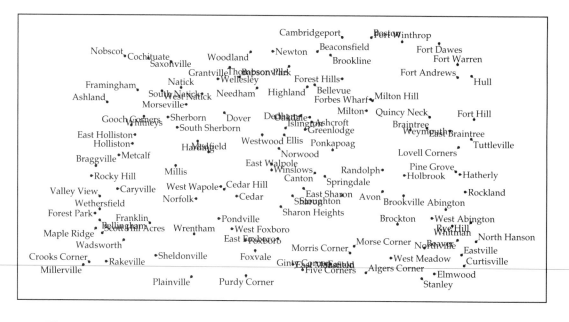

Figure 3. Random labeling improved by iterative local improvement (42 labels conflicted).

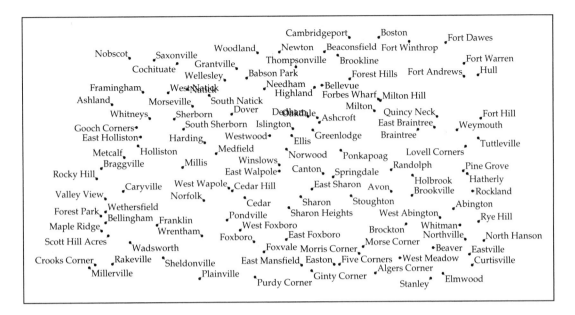

Figure 4. Labeling of the same set of points generated by the simulated-annealing algorithm (4 labels conflicted).

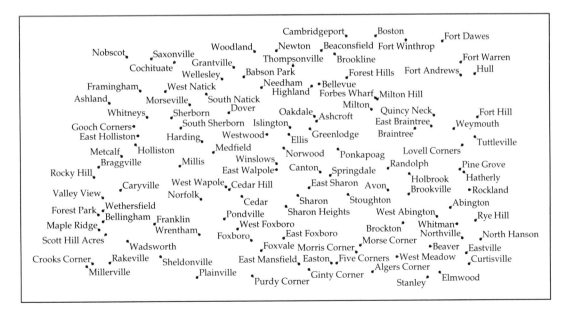

Figure 5. A labeling of the same set of points with point deletion (2 points deleted).

Initialization of the algorithm involves the following five steps:

1. Precompute all intersections between potential label positions, recording for each label position a list of which points and label positions overlap it.
2. Generate an initial random labeling.
3. For each point, store a counter of the number of pairwise overlaps between its current label position and those of the other points.
4. Calculate an initial score, the number of points with non-zero counters.

Calculation of ΔE at each step can now be done with reasonable efficiency. Given a single label repositioning for a source point p, the change in the score is simply the number of newly conflicted labels minus the number of newly cleared labels. To count the number of newly cleared labels, each point q that potentially conflicts with the old label position is examined, using the table set up in step (1). If the current label position of q is in a conflicting position with the old label position of p (as precomputed in step (1)), the conflict counter for q (initialized in step (3)) is decremented. If the conflict counter of q reaches zero, the number of cleared labels is incremented. The calculation of newly created conflicts is analogous: The algorithm examines the list of points that potentially conflict with the new position. If a point switches from zero pairwise conflicts to one or more, then the candidate repositioning has created a new label conflict. Finally, the algorithm notes whether the source point p itself has switched from unconflicted to conflicted, or vice-versa, and adjusts the score accordingly.

Placement Preferences

Typically, not all of the potential label positions for a given point are equally desirable. It is standard in cartography applications, for instance, to give highest preference to the upper right label position, all else being equal (Yoeli 1972). Although this additional consideration makes the labeling problem more difficult, the simulated-annealing algorithm handles preferences easily by adding a penalty to the scoring function for each point feature that reflects the relative undesirability of its label position. Given a ranking of the positions such as that given by the numbers in Figure 1, a penalty of $(r - 1)/N$ is associated with the rth ranked of N positions. In the example, the upper right position is therefore given a penalty of 0, the upper left a penalty of 1/8, and so forth. Placement preferences were incorporated in the runs of the simulated-annealing algorithm that produced Figures 4 and 5.

Deletion of Labels

In many applications, especially automated cartography, an alternative to placing a label in a highly congested area is to delete the label and often its associated point feature. This strategy can be incorporated into the algorithm by modifying the scoring function to be the number of conflicted labels plus the number of deleted labels. This is equivalent to maximizing the number of labels displayed without conflicts and ensures that an optimal map will have no conflicted labels. Optionally, deletion terms may be weighted to discourage deletion of important features, such as capital cities.

Figure 5 shows the result of allowing point deletion for the set of point features used in Figure 2.

Comparison with Other Algorithms

A wide variety of approaches — greedy heuristics (Doerschler and Freeman 1992, Jones 1989), physical models (Hirsch 1982), and reductions to integer programming (Zoraster 1990), among others — have been pursued to solve the label-placement problem. (A more complete bibliography is provided by Christensen et al. (1992).) Empirical testing of a wide variety of algorithms, including essentially all practical published algorithms, has shown that the simulated-annealing method finds better solutions at all label densities (Christensen et al. 1992, 1993). The simulated-annealing algorithm is also competitive with its alternatives in terms of efficiency, falling roughly in the mid-range of running times. In practice, the algorithm requires only a few seconds on a modern workstation for page-sized maps at typical cartographic labeling densities. The simulated-annealing algorithm may be the easiest algorithm to implement beyond random placement or iterative local improvement. Finally, the simulated-annealing approach has the advantage of generality. Although the discussion here has used labeling of point features to exemplify the algorithm, simulated annealing can be used to solve the labeling problem for any features — points, lines, areas — for which alternative label positions can be generated and quality of labeling can be quantified.

◇ **Acknowledgments** ◇

The research reported in this article was supported in part by a contract with U S WEST Advanced Technologies, by grant IRI-9157996 from the National Science Foundation, and by a matching grant from Digital Equipment Corporation.

◇ **Bibliography** ◇

(Cerny 1985) V. Cerny. A thermodynamical approach to the travelling salesman problem: An efficient simulation algorithm. *Journal of Optimization Theory Applications*, 45:41–51, 1985.

(Christensen *et al.* 1992) Jon Christensen, Joe Marks, and Stuart Shieber. Labeling point features on maps and diagrams. Technical Report TR-25-92, Harvard University, November 1992.

(Christensen *et al.* 1993) Jon Christensen, Joe Marks, and Stuart Shieber. Algorithms for cartographic label placement. In *Proceedings of the American Congress on Surveying and Mapping '93, Vol. 1*, pages 75–89, New Orleans, Louisiana, February 15–18, 1993.

(Doerschler and Freeman 1992) Jeffrey S. Doerschler and Herbert Freeman. A rule-based system for dense-map name placement. *Communications of the Association of Computing Machinery*, 35(1):68–79, January 1992.

(Formann and Wagner 1991) Michael Formann and Frank Wagner. A packing problem with applications to lettering of maps. In *Proceedings of the Seventh Annual Symposium on Computational Geometry*, pages 281–288, North Conway, New Hampshire, July 1991. ACM.

(Hirsch 1982) Stephen A. Hirsch. An algorithm for automatic name placement around point data. *The American Cartographer*, 9(1):5–17, 1982.

(Jones 1989) Christopher Jones. Cartographic name placement with Prolog. *IEEE Computer Graphics and Applications*, 9(5):36–47, September 1989.

(Kirkpatrick *et al.* 1983) S. Kirkpatrick, C. D. Gelatt Jr., and M. P. Vecchi. Optimization by simulated annealing. *Science*, 220:671–680, 1983.

(Marks and Shieber 1991) J. Marks and S. Shieber. The computational complexity of cartographic label placement. Technical Report TR-05-91, Harvard University, March 1991.

(van Laarhoven and Aarts 1987) P. J. M. van Laarhoven and E. H. L. Aarts. *Simulated Annealing: Theory and Applications*. D. Reidel, Dordrecht, Holland, 1987.

(Yoeli 1972) P. Yoeli. The logic of automated map lettering. *The Cartographic Journal*, 9(2):99–108, December 1972.

(Zoraster 1990) Steven Zoraster. The solution of large 0–1 integer programming problems encountered in automated cartography. *Operations Research*, 38(5):752–759, September-October 1990.

IX.2

Dynamic Layout Algorithm to Display General Graphs

László Szirmay-Kalos
Department of Process Control
Technical University of Budapest
Budapest, Műegyetem rkp. 11, H-1111, Hungary
szirmay@fsz.bme.hu

This Gem proposes a simple and effective algorithm for the display of graphs. The algorithm is based on physical simulation of an analogous mechanical system and also on heuristics to increase its speed and to introduce useful features not provided by the simulation.

◇ Introduction ◇

Many programs designed for interactive applications, scientific visualization, multimedia etc., should display graphs on the computer screen. The emphasis is usually on the topological relationships, the exact position of the nodes is not important (just for a few of them), but the picture of the graph should be easy to understand by human observers. An easy-to-interpret or "nice looking" graph is expected to:

- be in the center of the screen (or in a given part the world coordinate system if ZOOM/PAN operations are allowed), and expand loosely over the available area.
- contain straight line edges crossing each other as little as possible and nodes having enough room around them to provide some textual information.
- place strongly coupled node groups in a compact manner and put nodes which have large topological distance far away.
- have a "natural" arrangement (similar to those human observers are used to).

These subjective criteria, however, are almost impossible to be formulated by mathematical means that could serve as the basis for the definition of an optimality condition or a computer algorithm for finding it. In these poorly defined problems we can rely on heuristics and also on analogies of systems that behave somehow similarly but allow a more rigorous analysis (Tamassia *et al.* 1988) (Hofman *et al.* 1991).

This Gem is based on a combined effort to deal with this problem:

1. It uses an analogous approach, applying mechanical system theory (X. Pintado 1991) providing solution for the "natural" arrangement problem.
2. It takes advantage of heuristic methods to drive the analogous solution, to add those features that are not reflected by the behavior of mechanical systems, and also to reduce the response time of the algorithm.

◇   **Mechanical Simulation**   ◇

The idea of using a mechanical or physical analogy comes from the fact that the graph is supposed to be arranged "naturally," since this approach makes sure that the layout of the graph will be similar to everyday systems. Since physical systems are driven to their energy minimum, in the analogous approach the energy minimum, or the stable state of the graph model, is to be found.

Let's model the graph as a mechanical system, where the nodes correspond to particles, while edges, or absence of edges, correspond to driving forces among these particles. Let the force be attractive between those pairs of particles which are not very close to each other, and let it be repulsive otherwise. Since objects (or particles in the analogy) are expected to be near if they have an edge between them and far away otherwise, the threshold distance of repulsion is defined differently if the two objects are connected by an edge. For connected edges this threshold distance (or constraint) is set to exceed the required minimum radius around an object to hold space for some text, and to provide a loose picture, where the graph expands uniformly over the screen. For unconnected objects it should be much greater depending on the screen size (or on the size of the world coordinate system) and the number of objects. This binary classification can be further refined for weighted graphs, where the constraint can be proportional to the value of the weight:

If A and B are arbitrary objects:

$$constraint(A, B) = constraint_{\min} + (weight_{\max} - weight(A, B)) \cdot constraint_{\text{scale}}$$

We define the repulsing and attracting forces to be proportional to the difference of the actual distance of the objects and the constraint. The force on A due to B is:

$$\vec{force}(A, B) = (constraint(A, B) - distance(A, B))/distance(A, B) \cdot (\vec{pos}(A) - \vec{pos}(B))$$

where $\vec{pos}(A)$ is the position vector of object A.

In order to keep the objects inside the working area, forces of the walls of the area boundaries are also taken into account. Let's define the force of a wall to be zero if the object is far, proportional to the distance from the wall if it is close (in some margin) but still inside, and proportional with some greater value if it is outside. The direction of this force always points inward and is perpendicular to the wall.

If A is inside the working area, but not in the margin:

$$\vec{force}_{\text{wall}}(A) = 0$$

If A is in the margin:

$$\vec{force}_{\text{wall}}(A) = (margin_{\text{wall}} - distance(A, wall)) \cdot \vec{margin\_drive}_{\text{wall}}$$

If A is outside:

$$\vec{force}_{\text{wall}}(A) = distance(A, wall) \cdot \vec{out\_drive}_{\text{wall}} + margin_{\text{wall}} \cdot \vec{margin\_drive}_{\text{wall}}$$

The particles (or nodes) of the graph can be fixed to some location or can be moveable, in which case they are placed by the algorithm. Responding to the resultant force, each moveable particle will move until the system reaches equilibrium, where the resultant driving force and the speed of all particles are zero. In order to guarantee convergence, friction proportional to speed is introduced.

Since the energy is minimized in the stable state, attracting particles (related objects) can be expected to be placed close to each other and repelling (unrelated) objects placed far away. The total system will be located somewhere in the middle of the working area.

The stable state can be found by discrete time simulation using the following formulas:

Let the resultant driving force of a given particle be $\vec{D}$, the mass m, the coefficient of the friction μ, the current speed $\vec{v}(t)$ and the current position $\vec{r}(t)$ in time t.
The resultant force is

$$\vec{F} = \vec{D} - \vec{v}(t) \cdot \mu$$

Applying Newton's law the approximate speed and position in time $t + dt$ can be calculated:

$$(\vec{v}(t + dt) - \vec{v}(t))/dt = \vec{F}/m$$
$$(\vec{r}(t + dt) - \vec{r}(t))/dt = (\vec{v}(t) + \vec{v}(t + dt))/2$$

Using the previous definitions, $\vec{v}(t + dt)$ and $\vec{r}(t + dt)$ can be expressed:

$$\vec{v}(t + dt) = (1 - f) \cdot \vec{v}(t) + I \cdot \vec{D}$$
$$\vec{r}(t + dt) = \vec{r}(t) + (\vec{v}(t) + \vec{v}(t + dt)) \cdot dt/2$$

where f is the friction parameter:

$$f = \mu/m \cdot dt$$

and I is the inverse inertia describing how quickly a node reacts to forces:

$$I = dt/m$$

If the friction parameter is small and the inverse inertia is large, the system will react to the forces very quickly, which is an advantage in the beginning of the simulation but can result in excessive transients and oscillation around the stability point. To overcome this problem, I and f are also time-dependent allowing quick stabilization without excessive transients and oscillation:

$$
\begin{aligned}
f(t) &= friction_{min} + (friction_{max} - friction_{min}) \cdot t/time_{max} \\
I(t) &= iinertia_{max} - (iinertia_{max} - iinertia_{min}) \cdot t/time_{max}
\end{aligned}
$$

where $time_{max}$ is the maximum response time allowed in an interactive environment.

The simulation keeps going until

1. a stable state has been found ($\vec{D}$ is zero for all the objects)
2. the transient becomes too big ($\vec{D} > \vec{force}_{max}$) (hopefully this never happens)
3. too much time has elapsed without finding a stable state.

◇ **Initial Positions** ◇

The initial arrangement of the simulation is also critical because the simulation does not always converge to the global minimum energy, there are many possible stable states giving better or worse arrangement, and the necessary simulation time also depends on the careful selection of the initial positions.

In order to find appropriate initial positions, a heuristic method is proposed which guarantees that related objects are close while unrelated objects are distant, and also that the initial positions are not too far from mechanical stability. The heuristic algorithm places the fixed objects first, then introduces the moveable objects step by step, calculating the center of gravity of the nodes that have an edge to the new node and the center of gravity of unrelated objects. The new node is placed at the reflection of the center of gravity of unrelated objects about the center of gravity of related objects. Having placed a new object, its position is perturbed randomly to avoid solutions corresponding to locally extremal energy when, for example, all the objects are on a single line. The amplitude of the perturbation decreases as the number of already placed nodes increases. Finally, the node is moved inside the working area if it falls outside, and the mechanical simulation is applied to find a nearly stable state before introducing the next object.

In the sample program the `InitialPlacement` function is responsible for this initial placement of nodes, while the mechanical simulation routine is called `DynamicLayout`.

◇ **Conclusions and Applications** ◇

The implementation of the proposed algorithm was successful in many applications, including modeling of human relationships and information flow in a company, software engineering support for object-oriented development, etc. Although the algorithm does not take any explicit steps to eliminate the edge crossings, it is quite effective in doing so since it minimizes the length of edges and keeps objects far from unrelated parts.

In interactive systems, where the user supplies and deletes nodes and edges, only the `DynamicLayout` algorithm is used to refine the arrangement while sustaining the general outline specified by the user. In other cases when the graph should be built from scratch, the `InitialPlacement` function has to be called.

Concerning possible enhancements to the algorithm, in many applications the edges are also labeled, which makes it necessary to repel other nodes from the midpoints of the edges. This can be achieved if the edge midpoints also have some repulsive force.

Global control of the layout can be introduced by simulating field forces. A simple example of the application of the field force is the display of the hierarchical relationships in an office, where the boss is expected to be on the top of the screen, and the employees are supposed to be located below him according to their level in the hierarchy. In order to generate this kind of picture, the boss should be fixed to the top of the screen, and a global force should be introduced to attract other employees toward the bottom of the screen.

The computational time required by the algorithm depends on many factors, including the number of nodes, edges, and loops in the graph, and the used tolerance of equilibrium. This tolerance has resulted the slight asymmetry in Figure 2. Having made running time experiments with wheel-like graphs of Figure 2, in the range of 10 to 100 nodes, I concluded that the number of total iterations is a sublinear function of the size of the graph, but the probability of finding the global optimum decreases as the number of nodes increases. Since the required computation in a single iteration is proportional to the square of number of nodes, the complexity of the algorithm is between $O(n^2)$ and $O(n^3)$. Since the mechanical simulation algorithm goes from the initial position toward the "optimal" arrangement, even if it is stopped before the stabilization due to the response time constraints, a quasi-optimal picture can be expected. This allows graphs containing more than 50 vertices to be rendered interactively.

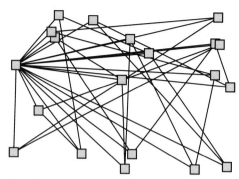

Figure 1. A sample graph arranged randomly (20 nodes).

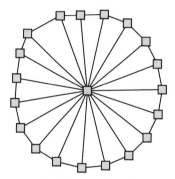

Figure 2. The same graph after running the algorithm (276 iterations).

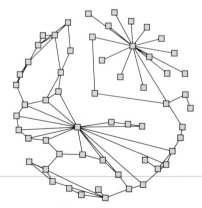

Figure 3. A complex graph containing 60 nodes (1195 iterations).

◇ **C++ Code** ◇

```
/****************************************************************************
/** DYNAMIC LAYOUT ALGORITHM OF GENERAL GRAPHS
/** Author: dr. Szirmay-Kalos Laszlo
/**         szirmay@fsz.bme.hu
/** Date: May 9, 1993, Budapest.
/****************************************************************************/
#include <stdlib.h>

#define OVERWINDOW_X              1000.0           // geometry of the world
#define OVERWINDOW_Y              1000.0
#define WALL_MARGIN               (OVERWINDOW_X / 10.0)
#define MAXRELATION               10.0             // maximal weight of the graph
#define FOUND                     2                // return of the search functions
#define NOT_FOUND                 3
#define ALL_NODE                  -1               // dummy node serial number
enum STAT { STOPPED, UNSTABLE, TOO_LONG };         // return of DynamicLayout
enum TYPE { MOVEABLE_NODE, FIXED_NODE   };         // type of nodes


/****************************************************************************/
class  vector {                   // 2D GEOMETRIC VECTOR TYPE
/****************************************************************************/
    double x, y;                                   // coordinates
public:
    vector()                      { x = 0.0; y = 0.0;                     }
    vector(double x0, double y0)  { x = x0; y = y0;                       }
    void     operator=(vector&  a)  { x = a.x; y = a.y;                   }
    void     operator+=(vector& a)  { x += a.x; y += a.y;                 }
    void     operator/=(double d)   { if (d != 0.0) {x /= d; y /= d;}}
    double   X()                    { return x;                          }
    double   Y()                    { return y;                          }
    double   Size();
    friend vector operator+(vector&, vector&);
    friend vector operator-(vector&, vector&);
    friend vector operator*(double, vector&);
};


/****************************************************************************/
class Node {                      // NODE OF THE GRAPH
/****************************************************************************/
    char     name[MAXNAME + 1];    // node name
    TYPE     type;                 // fixed or movable
    vector   pos;                  // actual position
    vector   speed;                // speed
    vector   force;                // driving force to this node
public:
             Node( pchar, TYPE );
    vector&  Position( void )       { return pos;      }
    vector&  Speed( void )          { return speed;    }
    vector&  Force( void )          { return force;    }
    void     AddForce( vector& f )  { force += f;      }
};
```

```
/****************************************************************************/
class Relation {                    // EDGE OF THE GRAPH
/****************************************************************************/
    char     name[MAXNAME + 1];     // relation name
    double   intensity;             // relation intensity
    Node   * relation_to;           // related node
public:
             Relation( pchar , Node *, double );
    double   GetRelation( void )      { return intensity;     }
    Node   * GetOtherNode( void )     { return relation_to;   }
};


/****************************************************************************/
class RelationElem : public Relation { // EDGE ITEM IN DYNAMIC DATA STRUCT
/****************************************************************************/
    RelationElem * next_relation;   // next on the list
public:
    RelationElem( pchar name, Node * p, double r );
};
/****************************************************************************/
class NodeElem : public Node {      // NODE ITEM IN DYNAMIC DATA STRUCT.
/****************************************************************************/
    int             ser_num;        // serial number in list
    NodeElem      * next_node;      // pointer to next node
    RelationElem  * relation;       // first relation of this node
public:
                    NodeElem(pchar, TYPE);
    void            SetRelation( RelationElem * p ) { relation = p;       }
    void            SetSerNum( int sernum )         { ser_num = sernum;   }
    NodeElem      * GetNext( void )                 { return next_node;   }
    RelationElem  * GetRelation( void )             { return relation;    }
    int             GetSerNum( void )               { return ser_num;     }
};


/****************************************************************************/
class Graph { // GRAPH IS AN ORTHOGONAL LIST OF NODES AND EDGES
/****************************************************************************/
    int             nfixnode;       // number of fixed nodes
    int             nmovnode;       // number of moveable nodes
    NodeElem      * currnode;       // current node
    NodeElem      * relatenode;     // actual relation of curr
    RelationElem  * currelation;    // relation of nodes list
public:
    BOOL    AddNode( pchar, TYPE );  // add new node to the graph (INPUT)
    void    AddRelation( pchar, double ); // add new relation (INPUT)
    BOOL    SearchRelation( void );  // relation currnode and relatenode
    STAT    InitialPlacement( void );// place nodes step-by-step
    void    RandomArrange( void );   // arrange nodes randomly
    STAT    DynamicLayout( int );    // mechanical system analogy
    BOOL    FirstNode( void );       // select first node on the list
    BOOL    FirstMoveNode( void );   // select first moveable node
    BOOL    NextNode( int max = ALL_NODES ); // select next to currnode
};
```

```
/*******************************************************************
 *    CONSTANTS
 *******************************************************************/

const double OVERWINDOW_X   = 1000;     // geometry of the working area
const double OVERWINDOW_Y   = 1000;
const double WALL_MARGIN     = OVERWINDOW_X / 10;
const double TIME_STEP       = 1;        // time step of diff equ
const double MAX_FORCE       = 500;      // force shows instability
const double MIN_FORCE       = 5;        // force cosidered as 0
const double MAX_TIME_SCALE = 100;       // scale of max time of solution
const double MINFRICTION     = 0.6;      // friction boundaries
const double MAXFRICTION     = 0.9;
const double MINIINERTIA     = 0.1;      // inverse inertia boundaries
const double MAXIINERTIA     = 0.4;
const double ZERO_DIST = OVERWINDOW_X / 100;   // distance considered as 0
const double WOUT_DRV        =   80;     // forces of the wall
const double WMARGIN_DRV     =    1;
const double SCALECONSTRAINT = OVERWINDOW_X / 3.5 / MAXRELATION;
const double MINCONSTRAINT   = OVERWINDOW_X / 7; // minimal constraint




/********************************************************************/
/* DYNAMIC LAYOUT based on MECHANICAL SYSTEM ANALOGY                */
/* IN  : The serial number of the maximal moveable node to be considered  */
/* OUT : STOPPED   = All objects stopped                           */
/*       UNSTABLE = Unstable, force goes to infinity               */
/*       TOO_LONG = Too much time elapsed                          */
/********************************************************************/
STAT Graph :: DynamicLayout( int maxsernum )
/*----------------------------------------------------------------*/
{
    double constraint, friction, iinertia, dist;
    vector drive;                        // drive forces
    vector direction;                    // direction of drives
    double MAX_TIME = MAX_TIME_SCALE * (nmovnode + nfixnode + 1);

    if ( !FirstMoveNode() ) return STOPPED; // INIT SPEED OF NODES TO 0
    do   currnode->Speed() = vector(0, 0); while ( NextNode(maxsernum) );

/*
 *   MAIN CYCLE OF TIME IN THE SOLUTION OF DIFF EQUATION
 */
    for ( double t = 0.0 ; t < MAX_TIME ; t += TIME_STEP ) {

        FirstNode();        //           INITIALIZE FORCE IN NODES TO 0
        do currnode->Force() = vector(0, 0); while( NextNode(maxsernum) );
                            //      CALCULATE FRICTION AND RESPONSE VALUES FROM t
        friction = MINFRICTION + (MAXFRICTION - MINFRICTION) * t / MAX_TIME;
        iinertia = MAXIINERTIA - (MAXIINERTIA - MINIINERTIA) * t / MAX_TIME;
```

```
/*
 *    CALCULATE DRIVE FORCE BETWEEN EACH PAIR OF NODES
 */
        FirstNode();
        do {
          relatenode = currnode->GetNext();
          while( relatenode != NULL && relatenode->GetSerNum() <= maxsernum ) {
            direction = currnode->Position() - relatenode->Position();
            dist  = direction.Size();
            if ( dist < ZERO_DIST ) dist = ZERO_DIST;
            switch( SearchRelation() ) {  // CALCULATE FORCE FROM THEIR RELATION
            case NOT_FOUND:
                constraint = MINCONSTRAINT + MAXRELATION * SCALECONSTRAINT;
                break;
            case FOUND:
                constraint = MINCONSTRAINT +
                    (MAXRELATION - correlation->GetRelation()) * SCALECONSTRAINT;
                break;
            }
            drive = (constraint - dist) / dist * direction; // SET FORCE
            drive /= (double)(maxsernum + nfixnode);
            currnode->AddForce(drive);
            relatenode->AddForce(-drive);
            relatenode = relatenode->GetNext();
          }
        } while ( NextNode( maxsernum ) );
/*
 *    ADD FORCES OF THE WALLS AND DETERMINE MAXIMAL FORCE
 */
        double max_force = 0.0;
        FirstMoveNode();
        do {
          dist = currnode->Position().X();
          if (dist < 0) {                          // OUT LEFT
            drive = vector(-dist * WOUT_DRV + WALL_MARGIN * WMARGIN_DRV, 0);
            currnode->AddForce(drive);
          } else if (dist < WALL_MARGIN) {       // IN LEFT MARGIN
            drive = vector((WALL_MARGIN - dist) * WMARGIN_DRV, 0);
            currnode->AddForce(drive);
          }

          dist = currnode->Position().X() - OVERWINDOW_X;
          if (dist > 0) {                          // OUT RIGHT
            drive = vector(-dist * WOUT_DRV + WALL_MARGIN * WMARGIN_DRV, 0);
            currnode->AddForce(drive);
          } else if (-dist < WALL_MARGIN) {      // IN RIGHT MARGIN
            drive = vector((-WALL_MARGIN - dist) * WMARGIN_DRV, 0);
            currnode->AddForce(drive);
          }

          dist = currnode->Position().Y();
          if (dist < 0) {                          // OUT BOTTOM
            drive = vector(0, -dist * WOUT_DRV + WALL_MARGIN * WMARGIN_DRV);
```

```
                  currnode->AddForce(drive);
              } else if (dist < WALL_MARGIN) {     // IN BOTTOM MARGIN
                  drive = vector(0, (WALL_MARGIN - dist) * WMARGIN_DRV);
                  currnode->AddForce(drive);
              }

              dist = currnode->Position().Y() - OVERWINDOW_Y;
              if (dist > 0) {                       // OUT TOP -> FORCE OF TOP WALL
                  drive = vector(0, -dist * WOUT_DRV + WALL_MARGIN * WMARGIN_DRV);
                  currnode->AddForce(drive);
              } else if (-dist < WALL_MARGIN) {    // IN TOP MARGIN
                  drive = vector(0, (-WALL_MARGIN - dist) * WMARGIN_DRV);
                  currnode->AddForce(drive);
              }
/*
 *    NEWTON'S LAW -> STEP TO t + dt
 */
              vector old_speed = currnode->Speed( );
              currnode->Speed() =
                   (1 - friction) * old_speed + iinertia * currnode->Force();
              currnode->Position() +=
                   0.5 * TIME_STEP * (old_speed + currnode->Speed() );

              double abs_force = currnode->Force().Size( ); // CALC. MAX FORCE
              if ( abs_force > max_force) max_force = abs_force;
          } while ( NextNode( maxsernum ) );
/*
 *    STOP CALCULATION IF
 */
          if ( max_force < MIN_FORCE ) return STOPPED;  // All objects stopped
          if ( max_force > MAX_FORCE ) return UNSTABLE; // Too big transient
     }
     return TOO_LONG; // Too much time elapsed
}


/*************************************************************************/
/* INITIAL PLACEMENT ALGORITHM                                         */
/* OUT : STOPPED  = All objects stopped                                */
/*       UNSTABLE = Unstable, force goes to infinity                   */
/*       TOO_LONG = Too much time elapsed                              */
/*************************************************************************/
STAT Graph :: InitialPlacement( )
/*-------------------------------------------------------------------*/
{
    vector     candidate; // candidate position
    vector     relate_cent;           // center of related nodes
    vector     notrel_cent;           // center of not related nodes
    vector     center(OVERWINDOW_X / 2, OVERWINDOW_Y / 2); // center point
    int        nrel;                  // number of related nodes
    int        nnotrel;               // number of not related nodes
    double     perturb_x = OVERWINDOW_X / (double)RAND_MAX ;
    double     perturb_y = OVERWINDOW_Y / (double)RAND_MAX ;
```

```
    if ( !FirstMoveNode() ) return STOPPED;      //  SKIP FIXED NODES
/*
*    MAIN CYCLE OF INTRODUCING MOVEABLE NODES STEP-BY-STEP
*    CALCULATE THE CENTER OF GRAVITY OF ALREADY INTRODUCED NODES
*    relate_cent IS FOR RELATED NODES
*    notrel_cent IS FOR NON_RELATED NODES
*/
    for( int inode = 1; ; inode++ ) {
        relate_cent = notrel_cent = vector(0, 0);
        nrel = nnotrel = 0;                       // displayed nodes
        relatenode = currnode;

        for( FirstNode(); currnode != relatenode; NextNode() ) {
            switch ( SearchRelation() ) {
            case NOT_FOUND: notrel_cent += currnode->Position();
                            nnotrel++;
                            break;
            case FOUND:     relate_cent += currnode->Position();
                            nrel++;
                            break;
            }
        }

        if ( nrel != 0 )    relate_cent /= (double)nrel;
        if ( nnotrel != 0 ) notrel_cent /= (double)nnotrel;
/*
*    IF THIS IS THE FIRST POINT->PUT TO THE MIDDLE
*/
        if (nrel == 0 && nnotrel == 0) candidate = center;
        else
/*
*    IF NO NOT_RELATED NODE -> PUT TO THE CENTER OF GRAVITY OF RELATED NODES
*/
        if ( nnotrel == 0 ) candidate = relate_cent;
        else
/*
*    IF NO RELATED NODE->PUT TO THE MIRROR OF THE nrel_cent ON THE CENTER
*/
        if ( nrel == 0 )  candidate = 2.0 * center - notrel_cent;
        else
/*
*    BOTH TYPE OF NODES EXIST ->
*    CALCULATE THE CANDIDATE POINT AS THE MIRROR OF notrel_cent TO relate_cent
*/
            candidate = 2.0 * relate_cent - notrel_cent;
/*
*    PERTURBATE RANDOMLY
*/
        candidate += vector( perturb_x / (double)(nfixnode + inode + 5) *
                            (double)( rand() - RAND_MAX / 2),
                            perturb_y / (double)(nfixnode + inode + 5) *
                            (double)( rand() - RAND_MAX / 2 ));
```

```
/*
 *    DECIDE IF IT IS OUTSIDE->FIND THE NEAREST INSIDE POINT
 */
        if ( candidate.X() < WALL_MARGIN)
            candidate = vector( 2 * WALL_MARGIN, candidate.Y() );
        if ( candidate.X() > OVERWINDOW_X - WALL_MARGIN)
            candidate = vector(OVERWINDOW_X - 2 * WALL_MARGIN, candidate.Y());
        if ( candidate.Y() < WALL_MARGIN)
            candidate = vector( candidate.X(), 2 * WALL_MARGIN );
        if ( candidate.Y() > OVERWINDOW_Y - WALL_MARGIN)
            candidate = vector(candidate.X(), OVERWINDOW_Y - 2 * WALL_MARGIN );

        relatenode->Position( ) = candidate; // SET POSITION OF THE NEW NODE
/*
 *    ARRANGE ALREADY DEFINED NODES BY DYNAMIC LAYOUT
 */
        NodeElem * oldcurrnode = currnode;
        int ret = DynamicLayout( inode );
        currnode = oldcurrnode;
        if ( ret != STOPPED || !NextNode() ) return ret;
    }
}
```

◇ **Bibliography** ◇

(Hofman *et al.* 1991) M. Hofman, H. Langendoerfer, K. Laue, and E. Luebben. The principle of locality used for hypertext navigation. Technical Report 1991, TU University of Braunschweig, 1991.

(Tamassia *et al.* 1988) Roberto Tamassia, Giuseppe Battista, and Carlo Batini. Automatic graph drawing and readibility of diagrams. *Transactions of Systems, Man, and Cybernetics*, 18(1):61–79, 1988.

(X. Pintado 1991) D. Tsichritzis and X. Pintado. Fuzzy relationships and affinity links. In Dennis Tsichritzis, editor, *Object Composition*, pages 273–285. Université de Genève, Geneva, 1991.

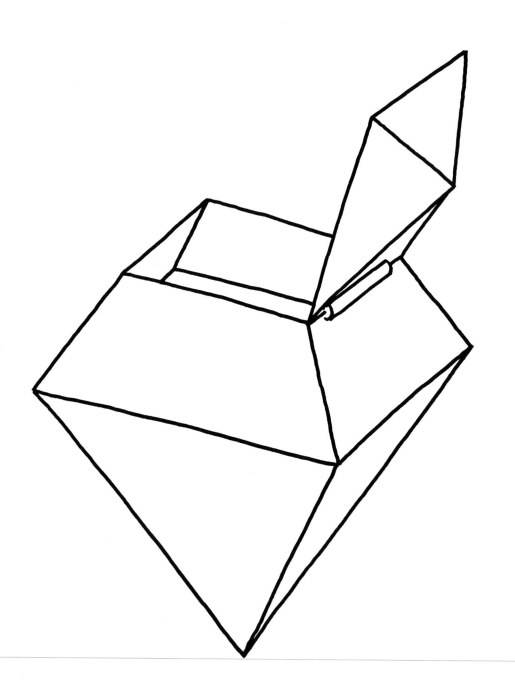

◇ **X** ◇
Utilities

This part of the book contains two Gems on basic interpolation methods, and two Gems providing subroutine libraries for vector and matrix algebra.

X.1. Tri-linear Interpolation, *by Steve Hill.*
Gives optimized code for performing linear interpolation in a 3D grid. Trilinear interpolation is useful for volume rendering, and its 2D variant, bilinear interpolation, is a very common operation in image processing. Page 521.

X.2. Faster Linear Interpolation, *by Steven Eker.*
Gives optimized code for generic linear interpolation. This is most useful for assembler language programming of graphics operations such as Gouraud shading and image scaling. Page 526.

X.3. C++ Vector and Matrix Algebra Routines, *by Jean-François Doué.*
A C++ subroutine library for 2D, 3D, and 4D vector and matrix operations. Page 534.

X.4. C Header File and Vector Library, *by Andrew Glassner and Eric Haines.*
Revised version of the "Graphics Gems" subroutine library, used in several other Gems in this book. Page 558.

◇ X.1

Tri-linear Interpolation

Steve Hill

Computing Laboratory
University of Kent
Canterbury, UK
sah@ukc.ac.uk

When rendering volume data and when magnifying raster images, it is usually necessary to interpolate between data points. According to circumstance we may need to interpolate in one, two, three, or more dimensions. The most common forms of interpolation are linear and cubic. Thus, for image processing purposes we often require bi-linear and bi-cubic interpolation (Andrews and Patterson 1976). For a more detailed account of digital filtering in general; see (Hamming 1989).

In this Gem we describe linear interpolation for one, two, and three dimensions, and provide an implementation of tri-linear interpolation. The code should prove useful as an off-the-shelf routine for anyone implementing a volume renderer.

◇ Linear Interpolation ◇

Interpolating between two data points in one dimension is simple. If we have two sampled values v_0 and v_1, a linear interpolation between these points is:

$$v_x = (1 - f_x)v_0 + f_x v_1$$

where $0 \le f_x \le 1$ and represents the fractional position between the data points. For the purposes of computation it is better to formulate this as:

$$v_x = v_0 + f_x(v_1 - v_0)$$

which saves us one multiplication. See the macro LERP defined in the Graphics Gems header file.

In two dimensions, we interpolate between four data points v_{00}, v_{01}, v_{10}, and v_{11}. The interpolation can be formulated directly thus:

$$
\begin{aligned}
v_{xy} = (1 - f_x)(1 - f_y)v_{00} + \\
(1 - f_x)\quad f_y \quad v_{01} + \\
f_x \quad (1 - f_y)v_{10} + \\
f_x \quad\quad f_y \quad v_{11}
\end{aligned}
$$

This method involves eight multiplications. A more efficient formulation can be achieved by cascading three one-dimensional interpolations. We proceed by interpolating between v_{00} and v_{10} to obtain v_{x0} and can calculate v_{x1} similarly. The interpolation then proceeds between v_{x0} and v_{x1} as for the one-dimensional case.

$$
\begin{aligned}
v_{x0} &= v_{00} + f_x(v_{10} - v_{00}) \\
v_{x1} &= v_{01} + f_x(v_{11} - v_{01})
\end{aligned}
$$

$$
v_{xy} = v_{x0} + f_y(v_{x1} - v_{x0})
$$

This involves just three multiplications, so it is considerably more efficient.

Adopting this approach for three dimensions requires seven interpolations, and hence seven multiplications, thus:

$$
\begin{aligned}
v_{x00} &= v_{000} + f_x(v_{100} - v_{000}) \\
v_{x01} &= v_{001} + f_x(v_{101} - v_{001}) \\
v_{x10} &= v_{010} + f_x(v_{110} - v_{010}) \\
v_{x11} &= v_{011} + f_x(v_{111} - v_{011})
\end{aligned}
$$

$$
\begin{aligned}
v_{xy0} &= v_{x00} + f_y(v_{x10} - v_{x00}) \\
v_{xy1} &= v_{x01} + f_y(v_{x11} - v_{x01})
\end{aligned}
$$

$$
v_{xyz} = v_{xy0} + f_z(v_{xy1} - v_{xy0})
$$

The direct formulation would require twenty-four multiplications. In general, for an n-dimensional interpolation, the direct method would perform $n2^n$ multiplications, whereas the cascaded method requires just $2^n - 1$.

◇ **The Implementation** ◇

The implementation provides a function `trilinear()` which computes the interpolated value of a point within a cube ranging from `(0,0,0)` to `(xsize-1, ysize-1, zsize-1)`. The parameters are as follows:

- `p` — the point of interest — note that it is not required to lie within the cube.
- `d` — a three-dimensional array of density values implemented as a contiguous array of `double`. An element `(ix, iy, iz)` is stored at `&d[ix+xsize*(iy+ysize*iz)]`, that is with the x coordinate varying fastest.
- `xsize, ysize, zsize` — the dimensions of the array.
- `def` — a default density value for points which lie outside the cube.

The implementation is complicated by the need to check for points outside the cube. This is necessary, in part, because data points that lie at the edge of the volume have influence that extends beyond its boundary. We expect that most points of interest will fall within the volume, so test for this eventuality first. For these points, we use pointer arithmetic to speed access to the array. There is some scope for optimization (with loss of clarity) in the case of points that lie outside. The final part of the routine performs the seven interpolations using the LERP macro.

◇ C Code ◇

```c
#include "GraphicsGems.h"

double
trilinear(p, d, xsize, ysize, zsize, def)
Point3   *p;
double   *d;
int      xsize, ysize, zsize;
double   def;
{
#    define DENS(X, Y, Z) d[(X)+xsize*((Y)+ysize*(Z))]

    int        x0, y0, z0,
               x1, y1, z1;
    double     *dp,
               fx, fy, fz,
               d000, d001, d010, d011,
               d100, d101, d110, d111,
               dx00, dx01, dx10, dx11,
               dxy0, dxy1, dxyz;

    x0 = FLOOR(p->x); fx = p->x - x0;
    y0 = FLOOR(p->y); fy = p->y - y0;
    z0 = FLOOR(p->z); fz = p->z - z0;

    x1 = x0 + 1;
    y1 = y0 + 1;
    z1 = z0 + 1;

    if (x0 >= 0 && x1 < xsize &&
        y0 >= 0 && y1 < ysize &&
        z0 >= 0 && z1 < zsize)
    {
        dp = &DENS(x0, y0, z0);
        d000 = dp[0];
        d100 = dp[1];
```

```
        dp += xsize;
        d010 = dp[0];
        d110 = dp[1];
        dp += xsize*ysize;
        d011 = dp[0];
        d111 = dp[1];
        dp -= xsize;
        d001 = dp[0];
        d101 = dp[1];
    }
    else
    {
#       define INRANGE(X, Y, Z) \
                ((X) >= 0 && (X) < xsize && \
                 (Y) >= 0 && (Y) < ysize && \
                 (Z) >= 0 && (Z) < zsize)

        d000 = INRANGE(x0, y0, z0) ? DENS(x0, y0, z0) : def;
        d001 = INRANGE(x0, y0, z1) ? DENS(x0, y0, z1) : def;
        d010 = INRANGE(x0, y1, z0) ? DENS(x0, y1, z0) : def;
        d011 = INRANGE(x0, y1, z1) ? DENS(x0, y1, z1) : def;

        d100 = INRANGE(x1, y0, z0) ? DENS(x1, y0, z0) : def;
        d101 = INRANGE(x1, y0, z1) ? DENS(x1, y0, z1) : def;
        d110 = INRANGE(x1, y1, z0) ? DENS(x1, y1, z0) : def;
        d111 = INRANGE(x1, y1, z1) ? DENS(x1, y1, z1) : def;
    }

    dx00 = LERP(fx, d000, d100);
    dx01 = LERP(fx, d001, d101);
    dx10 = LERP(fx, d010, d110);
    dx11 = LERP(fx, d011, d111);

    dxy0 = LERP(fy, dx00, dx10);
    dxy1 = LERP(fy, dx01, dx11);

    dxyz = LERP(fz, dxy0, dxy1);

    return dxyz;
}
```

◇ **Bibliography** ◇

(Andrews and Patterson 1976) Harry C. Andrews and Claude L. Patterson, III. Digital interpolation of discrete images. *IEEE Transactions on Computers*, 25(2):196–202, February 1976.

(Hamming 1989) R. W. Hamming. *Digital Filters*, 3rd edition. Signal Processing Series. Prentice-Hall, Englewood Cliffs, NJ, 1989.

◇ X.2

Faster Linear Interpolation

Steven Eker
Department of Computer Science
City University
Northampton Square
London EC1V 0HB, UK
steve@cs.city.ac.uk

◇ Introduction ◇

Linear interpolation is one of the fundamental procedures in computer graphics and has many applications including line drawing, computing polygon edges, approximate texture mapping, image scaling, and Gouraud shading. Since linear interpolation is often used at the lowest level in a graphics driver it needs to be done as rapidly as possible and thus it is often implemented in assembler. We examine some coding tricks that can be expressed in a higher level notation but whose advantage is best seen at assembler level. In particular, we give an improved error analysis of the integer digital differential analyzer method and develop an "unrolled" implementation of the decision variable method.

Given integers a, b, c with $a > 0$, $b \geq 0$ the problem is to compute a sequence of $a + 1$ integer values starting at c, ending at $c + b$, and spaced as evenly as possible over the interval. More formally we wish to compute a sequence of values

$$y = c + \left\lfloor \frac{b}{a}x + \frac{1}{2} \right\rfloor \tag{1}$$

for $x = 0, \ldots, a$.

The digital differential analyzer (DDA) approach is shown below.

```
f:real ← b/a;
s:real ← c + 0.5;
for x : integer← 0 to a do
    output(⌊s⌋);
    s ← s + f;
endloop
```

This has the disadvantage of requiring floating-point arithmetic and giving only approximate results due to the accumulation of truncation error. The decision variable approach was developed by Bresenham (Bresenham 1965) in the case where $a \geq b$. A number of improvements have been proposed (Wu and Rokne 1987, Wyvill 1990) which reduce the number of additions and comparisons required to compute each value at the cost of a more complicated algorithm. Decision variable algorithms analogous to Bresenham's can be used for fast image resampling (Braccini and Marino 1980, Weiman 1980). The generalization of the decision variable approach to handle the case $a < b$ as well was given by Field (Field 1985) and is shown in the following pseudocode.

```
i₁:integer← b div a; e₁:integer← 2 * (b mod a);
i₂:integer← i₁ + 1; e₂:integer← e₁ - 2 * a;
t:integer← c; r:integer← e₁ - a;
for x:integer← 0 to a do
    output(t);
    if r < 0 then begin
        t ← t + i₁; r ← r + e₁;
        end
    else begin
        t ← t + i₂; r ← r + e₂;
        end
endloop
```

◇ Digital Differential Analyzer Method   ◇

The two obvious ways to speed up the DDA method are to unroll the loop and to use fixed point arithmetic. Field (Field 1985) gives an analysis of the accumulated error in a fixed point implementation; we will give a different analysis where we determine the range of input values for which a fixed point implementation can be used without error. We consider two cases. In the first case we insist that the last value is correct but allow intermediate values to be off by one. In the second case we insist that all values are correct.

Since c plays no role in the error analysis we assume for clarity that $c = 0$. Suppose we use $k \geq 1$ bits for the fractional part. Then we really calculate

$$y = \left\lfloor Sx + \frac{1}{2} \right\rfloor$$

where S is the fixed point representation of b/a. Since in (1) we are rounding half-values upwards we put

$$S = \frac{1}{2^k} \left\lceil \frac{2^k b}{a} \right\rceil$$

to avoid errors on such values even for small a and large k. Clearly if $(2^k b \bmod a) = 0$ we have $S = b/a$ and no errors occur. Suppose $(2^k b \bmod a) \neq 0$. Then

$$S = \frac{1}{2^k} \left(\left\lfloor \frac{2^k b}{a} \right\rfloor + 1 \right) = \frac{b}{a} + \frac{a - (2^k b \bmod a)}{2^k a}$$

Consider the last value, where $x = a$. We have

$$y = \left\lfloor b + \frac{a - (2^k b \bmod a)}{2^k} + \frac{1}{2} \right\rfloor$$

Now in the worst case $a - (2^k b \bmod a) = a - 1$ (since $(2^k b \bmod a) \neq 0$), and thus as long as $(a - 1)/2^k < 1/2$ or equivalently $a \leq 2^{k-1}$ we will have the last value correctly calculated as $y = b$ and clearly intermediate values will be off by at most one. Typically we might have $k = 16$, in which case we require $a \leq 32768$.

We now consider intermediate values which are computed as

$$y = \left\lfloor \frac{b}{a} x + \frac{1}{2} + \varepsilon \right\rfloor$$

where

$$\varepsilon = \frac{a - (2^k b \bmod a)}{2^k a} x \tag{2}$$

is the accumulated error. The possibility of an off by one error in the value of y occurs when the fractional part of $(b/a)x$ lies between 0 and $1/2$, so that adding ε gives a fractional part greater or equal to $1/2$. The fractional part of $(b/a)x$ can be written as

$$f = \frac{bx}{a} - \left\lfloor \frac{bx}{a} \right\rfloor = \frac{bx \bmod a}{a}$$

If a is even, the worst case occurs when $(bx \bmod a) = a/2 - 1$, giving $f = 1/2 - 1/a$. If a is odd the worst case occurs when $(bx \bmod a) = (a - 1)/2$, giving $f = 1/2 - 1/(2a)$. These worst cases actually occur if a and b are relatively prime. To avoid an error we require that $f + \varepsilon < 1/2$ or equivalently $\varepsilon < 1/(2a)$. Now from (2) we know

$$\varepsilon \leq \frac{(a - 1)^2}{2^k a}$$

so to avoid an error we require

$$\frac{(a - 1)^2}{2^k a} < \frac{1}{2a}$$

or $a < \sqrt{2^{k-1}} + 1$. Again taking $k = 16$ we require $a \leq 182$.

A practical problem with fixed point arithmetic is the need to extract the integer part of the result; making a copy of the fixed point value and doing a right shift is usually too expensive. Some processors allow the top 16 bits of a 32-bit register to be stored/moved separately, so on these processors it is natural to have 16 bits for both integer and fraction parts. On other processors which allow the bottom 16 bits of a 32-bit register to be stored/moved separately but not the top 16 bits, it is possible to store the integer part in the bottom 16 bits and the fractional part in the top 16 bits and use add-with-carry instructions. In this case a register holds the integer part of one value and the fractional part of the next value. Finally, it is possible to keep fractional and integer parts in different registers. This then requires two add instructions per value but with $k = 32$ we only require $a \leq 46341$ for complete accuracy. In all cases we end up with a piece of linear code consisting of register-to-register add instructions together with instructions to use/store the calculated values. We avoid branches; this may be an advantage on heavily pipelined architectures.

◇ **Decision Variable Method** ◇

In the decision variable algorithm given previously, the decision variable r ranges between $2(b \bmod a) - 2a$ and $2(b \bmod a) - 1$. At worst we know that $r \in \{-2a, \ldots, 2a-3\}$. We can reduce the range to $\{-a, \ldots, a - 2\}$ by dividing the decision variable and its increments by two. Although the increments are always even, r may start off as even or odd. Let $p = \lfloor r/2 \rfloor$ be the new decision variable. Clearly

$$r \geq 0 \Leftrightarrow p \geq 0$$

Thus we want to initialize r with $((b \bmod a) - \lceil a/2 \rceil)$. Note that the alternative of putting $p = \lceil r/2 \rceil$ would cause an error at $r = -1$ because $p \geq 0$. This gives us the following algorithm.

i_1:**integer**$\leftarrow b$ div a; e_1:**integer**$\leftarrow b$ mod a;
i_2:**integer**$\leftarrow i_1 + 1$; e_2:**integer**$\leftarrow e_1 - a$;
t:**integer**$\leftarrow c$; p:**integer**$\leftarrow e_1 - (a + 1)$ div 2;
for x:**integer**$\leftarrow 0$ **to** a **do**
    output(t);
    if $p < 0$ **then begin**
        $t \leftarrow t + i_1$; $p \leftarrow p + e_1$;
    end
    else begin
        $t \leftarrow t + i_2$; $p \leftarrow p + e_2$;
    end
endloop

This trick may allow faster 8- or 16-bit arithmetic to be used for the error term on low performance processors. On many processors $e_1 - (a + 1)$ div 2 can be evaluated by a right shift (of a) followed by a subtract-with-carry (from e_1).

    Typically the decision variable method requires a test, a branch, and two add instructions plus the overhead of the loop for each iteration. We now reduce this to a branch and one add together with some fraction of the loop overhead. We first unroll the loop into a pair of loops. Here for conciseness we will calculate two interpolated values within each loop; in practice eight or sixteen would be more realistic. Since $a + 1$ in general will not be a multiple of this number we enter the first loop using a "Duff's device" type construction, which can easily be coded in C or assembler but is not so easy to code in higher level languages.

i_1:**integer**$\leftarrow b$ div a; e_1:**integer**$\leftarrow b$ mod a;
i_2:**integer**$\leftarrow i_1 + 1$; e_2:**integer**$\leftarrow e_1 - a$;
t:**integer**$\leftarrow c$; p:**integer**$\leftarrow e_1 - (a + 1)$ div 2;
x:**integer**$\leftarrow a$;
select a mod 2 **from**
label *neg_loop*:
    case 1:
        output(t);
        if $p \geq 0$ **then goto** *pos1* ;
    label *neg1*:
        $t \leftarrow t + i_1$; $p \leftarrow p + e_1$;
    case 0:
        output(t);
        if $p \geq 0$ **then goto** *pos2* ;
    label *neg2*:
        $t \leftarrow t + i_1$; $p \leftarrow p + e_1$;
        $x \leftarrow x - 2$;
        if $x \geq 0$ **then goto** *neg_loop*
endcase;
return;
label *pos_loop*:
    output(t);
    if $p < 0$ **then goto** *neg1* ;
label *pos1*:
    $t \leftarrow t + i_2$; $p \leftarrow p + e_2$;
    output(t);
    if $p < 0$ **then goto** *neg2* ;
label *pos2*:
    $t \leftarrow t + i_2$; $p \leftarrow p + e_2$;
    $x \leftarrow x - 2$;
    if $x \geq 0$ **then goto** *pos_loop*
return;

Since we compute two values for each iteration the loop overhead is reduced by a factor of two. Also, since we count down rather than up, on most processors an explicit test for $x \geq 0$ is unnecessary. The optimum number of values per iteration for a given processor will depend chiefly on cache size, but will typically be a power of two to make the calculation of the select value cheap. For CISC processors, the span of faster short branch instructions should also be taken into account to avoid the use of slower long branch forms.

The next refinement is to rearrange the order of the computations so that the test on the sign of p takes place immediately after p is incremented. On most architectures this should eliminate the need for an explicit test instruction at assembler level. Also, under the assumption that the target architecture uses (at least) 32-bit twos complement for representing integers and that $c + b$ fits into 16 bits, we can combine t and p into a single value $t + 65536 * p$ and save an addition.

i_1:**integer**$\leftarrow b$ div $a + 65536 * (b \bmod a)$;
i_2:**integer**$\leftarrow i_1 + 1 - 65536 * a$;
t:**integer**$\leftarrow c - i1 - 65536 * ((a + 1)$ div $2)$; x:**integer**$\leftarrow a$;
select $a \bmod 2$ **from**
label *neg_loop*:
    case 1:
        $t \leftarrow t + i_1$;
        if $t \geq 0$ **then goto** *pos1* ;
label *neg1*:
        output(t);
    case 0:
        $t \leftarrow t + i_1$;
        if $t \geq 0$ **then goto** *pos2* ;
label *neg2*:
        output(t);
        $x \leftarrow x - 2$;
        if $x \geq 0$ **then goto** *neg_loop*
endcase;
return;
label *pos_loop*:
    $t \leftarrow t + i_2$;
    if $t < 0$ **then goto** *neg1* ;
label *pos1*:
    output(t);
    $t \leftarrow t + i_2$;
    if $t < 0$ **then goto** *neg2* ;
label *pos2*:
    output(t);
    $x \leftarrow x - 2$;
    if $x \geq 0$ **then goto** *pos_loop*
return;

In our C implementation we test for $a > b$ and avoid the division and modulo computation if so. The division, modulo, and multiplication by powers of 2 is done with shifts and bitwise ands. The interpolated values are stored on the array o. Using the GNU C compiler (with optimization flag) the calculation and storage of each value requires three MC68020 instructions (an add and a branch to compute the value and a move to store it in the array) and four SPARC instructions (an add and a branch to compute the value and a store and an add to store it in the array) together with one quarter of the loop overhead.

◇   **C Implementation of the Unrolled Decision Variable Method**   ◇

```
/*
    Compute o[x] = c + floor(b*x/a + 0.5) for x = 0 to a

    We assume that int is 32 bits, short is 16 bits, and int to short
    conversion produces the least significant 16 bits of the int
    with respect to twos complement representation.
*/

linear(a, b, c, o)
int a, b, c;
short *o;
{
  int t, i1, i2;

  if(a > b){
    t = 0; i1 = b;
  }
  else{
    t = b / a; i1 = b % a;
  }
  i1 = (i1 << 16) + t;
  i2 = i2 - (a << 16) - 1;
  t = c - t - (((a + 1) >> 1) << 16);
  switch(a & 3){
  do{
  case 3:
    if((t += i1) >= 0) goto pos1;
neg1:
    *o++ = t;
  case 2:
    if((t += i1) >= 0) goto pos2;
neg2:
    *o++ = t;
  case 1:
    if((t += i1) >= 0) goto pos3;
neg3:
    *o++ = t;
  case 0:
```

```
      if((t += i1) >= 0) goto pos4;
neg4:
      *o++ = t;
  }while((a -= 4) >= 0);
  }
  return;
  do{
      if((t += i2) < 0) goto neg1;
pos1:
      *o++ = t;
      if((t += i2) < 0) goto neg2;
pos2:
      *o++ = t;
      if((t += i2) < 0) goto neg3;
pos3:
      *o++ = t;
      if((t += i2) < 0) goto neg4;
pos4:
      *o++ = t;
  }while((a -= 4) >= 0);
}
```

◇   **Bibliography**   ◇

(Braccini and Marino 1980) Carlo Braccini and Giuseppe Marino. Fast geometrical manipulations of digital images. *Computer Graphics and Image Processing*, 13:127–141, 1980.

(Bresenham 1965) J. E. Bresenham. Algorithm for the control of a digital plotter. *IBM Systems Journal*, 4(1):106–111, May 1965.

(Field 1985) Dan Field. Incremental linear interpolation. *ACM Transactions on Graphics*, 4(1):1–11, January 1985.

(Weiman 1980) Carl F. R. Weiman. Continuous anti-aliased rotation and zoom of raster images. *Computer Graphics (SIGGRAPH '80 Proceedings)*, 14(3):286–293, July 1980.

(Wu and Rokne 1987) Xiaolin Wu and Jon G. Rokne. Double-step incremental generation of lines and circles. *Computer Vision, Graphics and Image Processing*, 37:331–344, 1987.

(Wyvill 1990) Brian Wyvill. Symmetric double step line algorithm. In A. Glassner, editor, *Graphics Gems*, pages 101–104. Academic Press, Boston, 1990.

◊ X.3

C++ Vector and Matrix Algebra Routines

Jean-François Doué
HEC, Paris, France
h058@frhec1.hec.fr

This gem consists of a collection of C++ routines written to make the programming of computer graphics applications easier. The library takes care of many low-level operations on vectors and matrices, both in 2D and 3D, and also supplies the most basic 2D and 3D transformations, such as rotation around an arbitrary axis or scaling. The library is composed of five different classes:

- three vector classes (2D, 3D, and 4D vectors)
- two matrix classes (3×3 and 4×4)

The library makes code shorter and easier to read. I have used it to rewrite a ray-tracing program and have reduced the number of code lines by at least 30% relative to a traditional C implementation.[1] The library also helps when debugging applications.

Implementation.   The 2D vector class and the 3×3 matrix class work together to provide 2D graphics, while the 3D vector class and 4×4 matrix class do the same for 3D graphics. The 3D vector class together with the 3×3 matrix class are useful for color transforms. The 4D vector class serves a variety of purposes. It is used internally to implement the 4×4 matrix class. It can also be used to store 3D vectors in homogeneous coordinates and is helpful when working with planes or cubic splines.

Casting.   The vector types can be cast back and forth between each other. When one casts a type to a higher dimension, one can either supply the coordinate in the higher dimension, or let the cast function automatically add 1.0 as the coordinate in the new dimension. When one casts a type to a lower dimension, there are two choices as well: either let the routine get rid of the last dimension (in which case the coordinates of the remaining dimensions are divided by the coordinates of the removed dimension); or use a constructor which specifies the dimension to drop (in which case no division is made).

---

[1]The code for this program, which does ray casting (non-recursive ray tracing) of spheres and concave polyhedra, is included in the Gems IV software distribution on floppy disk or by FTP.

◇ **C++ Code** ◇

algebra3.H

```
/******************************************************************
*                                                                *
* C++ Vector and Matrix Algebra routines                         *
* Author: Jean-Francois DOUE                                     *
* Version 3.1 --- October 1993                                   *
*                                                                *
******************************************************************/

#include <stream.h>
#include <stdlib.h>

// this line defines a new type: pointer to a function which returns a
// double and takes as argument a double
typedef double (*V_FCT_PTR)(double);

// min-max macros
#define MIN(A,B) ((A) < (B) ? (A) : (B))
#define MAX(A,B) ((A) > (B) ? (A) : (B))

// error handling macro
#define V_ERROR(E) { cerr << E; exit(1); }

class vec2;
class vec3;
class vec4;
class mat3;
class mat4;

enum {VX, VY, VZ, VW};              // axes
enum {PA, PB, PC, PD};              // planes
enum {RED, GREEN, BLUE};            // colors
enum {KA, KD, KS, ES};              // phong coefficients


/******************************************************************
*                                                                *
*                         2D Vector                              *
*                                                                *
******************************************************************/

class vec2
{
protected:

 double n[2];

public:

// Constructors
```

```
vec2();
vec2(const double x, const double y);
vec2(const double d);
vec2(const vec2& v);                      // copy constructor
vec2(const vec3& v);                      // cast v3 to v2
vec2(const vec3& v, int dropAxis);        // cast v3 to v2

// Assignment operators

vec2& operator  = ( const vec2& v );      // assignment of a vec2
vec2& operator += ( const vec2& v );      // incrementation by a vec2
vec2& operator -= ( const vec2& v );      // decrementation by a vec2
vec2& operator *= ( const double d );     // multiplication by a constant
vec2& operator /= ( const double d );     // division by a constant
double& operator [] ( int i);             // indexing

// Special functions

double length();                          // length of a vec2
double length2();                         // squared length of a vec2
vec2& normalize();                        // normalize a vec2
vec2& apply(V_FCT_PTR fct);               // apply a func. to each component

// Friends

friend vec2 operator - (const vec2& v);                     // -v1
friend vec2 operator + (const vec2& a, const vec2& b);      // v1 + v2
friend vec2 operator - (const vec2& a, const vec2& b);      // v1 - v2
friend vec2 operator * (const vec2& a, const double d);     // v1 * 3.0
friend vec2 operator * (const double d, const vec2& a);     // 3.0 * v1
friend vec2 operator * (const mat3& a, const vec2& v);      // M . v
friend vec2 operator * (const vec2& v, mat3& a);            // v . M
friend double operator * (const vec2& a, const vec2& b);    // dot product
friend vec2 operator / (const vec2& a, const double d);     // v1 / 3.0
friend vec3 operator ^ (const vec2& a, const vec2& b);      // cross product
friend int operator == (const vec2& a, const vec2& b);      // v1 == v2 ?
friend int operator != (const vec2& a, const vec2& b);      // v1 != v2 ?
friend ostream& operator << (ostream& s, vec2& v);          // output to stream
friend istream& operator >> (istream& s, vec2& v);          // input from strm.
friend void swap(vec2& a, vec2& b);                         // swap v1 & v2
friend vec2 min(const vec2& a, const vec2& b);              // min(v1, v2)
friend vec2 max(const vec2& a, const vec2& b);              // max(v1, v2)
friend vec2 prod(const vec2& a, const vec2& b);             // term by term *

// necessary friend declarations

friend class vec3;
};
```

```
/****************************************************************
*                                                              *
*                       3D Vector                              *
*                                                              *
****************************************************************/

class vec3
{
protected:

 double n[3];

public:

// Constructors

vec3();
vec3(const double x, const double y, const double z);
vec3(const double d);
vec3(const vec3& v);                        // copy constructor
vec3(const vec2& v);                        // cast v2 to v3
vec3(const vec2& v, double d);              // cast v2 to v3
vec3(const vec4& v);                        // cast v4 to v3
vec3(const vec4& v, int dropAxis);          // cast v4 to v3

// Assignment operators

vec3& operator  = ( const vec3& v );        // assignment of a vec3
vec3& operator += ( const vec3& v );        // incrementation by a vec3
vec3& operator -= ( const vec3& v );        // decrementation by a vec3
vec3& operator *= ( const double d );       // multiplication by a constant
vec3& operator /= ( const double d );       // division by a constant
double& operator [] ( int i);               // indexing

// Special functions

double length();                            // length of a vec3
double length2();                           // squared length of a vec3
vec3& normalize();                          // normalize a vec3
vec3& apply(V_FCT_PTR fct);                 // apply a func. to each component

// Friends

friend vec3 operator - (const vec3& v);                 // -v1
friend vec3 operator + (const vec3& a, const vec3& b);  // v1 + v2
friend vec3 operator - (const vec3& a, const vec3& b);  // v1 - v2
friend vec3 operator * (const vec3& a, const double d); // v1 * 3.0
friend vec3 operator * (const double d, const vec3& a); // 3.0 * v1
friend vec3 operator * (const mat4& a, const vec3& v);  // M . v
friend vec3 operator * (const vec3& v, mat4& a);        // v . M
friend double operator * (const vec3& a, const vec3& b); // dot product
friend vec3 operator / (const vec3& a, const double d); // v1 / 3.0
friend vec3 operator ^ (const vec3& a, const vec3& b);  // cross product
```

```
friend int operator == (const vec3& a, const vec3& b);        // v1 == v2 ?
friend int operator != (const vec3& a, const vec3& b);        // v1 != v2 ?
friend ostream& operator << (ostream& s, vec3& v);            // output to stream
friend istream& operator >> (istream& s, vec3& v);            // input from strm.
friend void swap(vec3& a, vec3& b);                           // swap v1 & v2
friend vec3 min(const vec3& a, const vec3& b);                // min(v1, v2)
friend vec3 max(const vec3& a, const vec3& b);                // max(v1, v2)
friend vec3 prod(const vec3& a, const vec3& b);               // term by term *

// necessary friend declarations

friend class vec2;
friend class vec4;
friend class mat3;
friend vec2 operator * (const mat3& a, const vec2& v);        // linear transform
friend mat3 operator * (mat3& a, mat3& b);                    // matrix 3 product
};


/****************************************************************
*                                                              *
*                        4D Vector                             *
*                                                              *
****************************************************************/

class vec4
{
protected:

 double n[4];

public:

// Constructors

vec4();
vec4(const double x, const double y, const double z, const double w);
vec4(const double d);
vec4(const vec4& v);                        // copy constructor
vec4(const vec3& v);                        // cast vec3 to vec4
vec4(const vec3& v, const double d);        // cast vec3 to vec4

// Assignment operators

vec4& operator  = ( const vec4& v );        // assignment of a vec4
vec4& operator += ( const vec4& v );        // incrementation by a vec4
vec4& operator -= ( const vec4& v );        // decrementation by a vec4
vec4& operator *= ( const double d );       // multiplication by a constant
vec4& operator /= ( const double d );       // division by a constant
double& operator [] ( int i);               // indexing

// Special functions

double length();                            // length of a vec4
```

```
double length2();                              // squared length of a vec4
vec4& normalize();                             // normalize a vec4
vec4& apply(V_FCT_PTR fct);                    // apply a func. to each component

// Friends

friend vec4 operator - (const vec4& v);                     // -v1
friend vec4 operator + (const vec4& a, const vec4& b);      // v1 + v2
friend vec4 operator - (const vec4& a, const vec4& b);      // v1 - v2
friend vec4 operator * (const vec4& a, const double d);     // v1 * 3.0
friend vec4 operator * (const double d, const vec4& a);     // 3.0 * v1
friend vec4 operator * (const mat4& a, const vec4& v);      // M . v
friend vec4 operator * (const vec4& v, mat4& a);            // v . M
friend double operator * (const vec4& a, const vec4& b);    // dot product
friend vec4 operator / (const vec4& a, const double d);     // v1 / 3.0
friend int operator == (const vec4& a, const vec4& b);      // v1 == v2 ?
friend int operator != (const vec4& a, const vec4& b);      // v1 != v2 ?
friend ostream& operator << (ostream& s, vec4& v);          // output to stream
friend istream& operator >> (istream& s, vec4& v);          // input from strm.
friend void swap(vec4& a, vec4& b);                         // swap v1 & v2
friend vec4 min(const vec4& a, const vec4& b);              // min(v1, v2)
friend vec4 max(const vec4& a, const vec4& b);              // max(v1, v2)
friend vec4 prod(const vec4& a, const vec4& b);             // term by term *

// necessary friend declarations

friend class vec3;
friend class mat4;
friend vec3 operator * (const mat4& a, const vec3& v);      // linear transform
friend mat4 operator * (mat4& a, mat4& b);                  // matrix 4 product
};

/*****************************************************************
*                                                               *
*                       3x3 Matrix                              *
*                                                               *
*****************************************************************/

class mat3
{
protected:

  vec3 v[3];

public:

// Constructors

mat3();
mat3(const vec3& v0, const vec3& v1, const vec3& v2);
mat3(const double d);
mat3(const mat3& m);
```

```
// Assignment operators

mat3& operator  = ( const mat3& m );          // assignment of a mat3
mat3& operator += ( const mat3& m );          // incrementation by a mat3
mat3& operator -= ( const mat3& m );          // decrementation by a mat3
mat3& operator *= ( const double d );         // multiplication by a constant
mat3& operator /= ( const double d );         // division by a constant
vec3& operator [] ( int i );                  // indexing

// Special functions

mat3 transpose();                             // transpose
mat3 inverse();                               // inverse
mat3& apply(V_FCT_PTR fct);                   // apply a func. to each element

// Friends

friend mat3 operator - (const mat3& a);                       // -m1
friend mat3 operator + (const mat3& a, const mat3& b);        // m1 + m2
friend mat3 operator - (const mat3& a, const mat3& b);        // m1 - m2
friend mat3 operator * (mat3& a, mat3& b);                    // m1 * m2
friend mat3 operator * (const mat3& a, const double d);       // m1 * 3.0
friend mat3 operator * (const double d, const mat3& a);       // 3.0 * m1
friend mat3 operator / (const mat3& a, const double d);       // m1 / 3.0
friend int operator == (const mat3& a, const mat3& b);        // m1 == m2 ?
friend int operator != (const mat3& a, const mat3& b);        // m1 != m2 ?
friend ostream& operator << (ostream& s, mat3& m);            // output to stream
friend istream& operator >> (istream& s, mat3& m);            // input from strm.
friend void swap(mat3& a, mat3& b);                           // swap m1 & m2

// necessary friend declarations

friend vec3 operator * (const mat3& a, const vec3& v);        // linear transform
friend vec2 operator * (const mat3& a, const vec2& v);        // linear transform
};

/******************************************************************
*                                                                *
*                        4x4 Matrix                              *
*                                                                *
******************************************************************/

class mat4
{
protected:

 vec4 v[4];

public:

// Constructors

mat4();
```

```
mat4(const vec4& v0, const vec4& v1, const vec4& v2, const vec4& v3);
mat4(const double d);
mat4(const mat4& m);

// Assignment operators

mat4& operator  = ( const mat4& m );        // assignment of a mat4
mat4& operator += ( const mat4& m );        // incrementation by a mat4
mat4& operator -= ( const mat4& m );        // decrementation by a mat4
mat4& operator *= ( const double d );       // multiplication by a constant
mat4& operator /= ( const double d );       // division by a constant
vec4& operator [] ( int i);                 // indexing

// Special functions

mat4 transpose();                           // transpose
mat4 inverse();                             // inverse
mat4& apply(V_FCT_PTR fct);                 // apply a func. to each element

// Friends

friend mat4 operator - (const mat4& a);                     // -m1
friend mat4 operator + (const mat4& a, const mat4& b);      // m1 + m2
friend mat4 operator - (const mat4& a, const mat4& b);      // m1 - m2
friend mat4 operator * (mat4& a, mat4& b);                  // m1 * m2
friend mat4 operator * (const mat4& a, const double d);     // m1 * 4.0
friend mat4 operator * (const double d, const mat4& a);     // 4.0 * m1
friend mat4 operator / (const mat4& a, const double d);     // m1 / 3.0
friend int operator == (const mat4& a, const mat4& b);      // m1 == m2 ?
friend int operator != (const mat4& a, const mat4& b);      // m1 != m2 ?
friend ostream& operator << (ostream& s, mat4& m);          // output to stream
friend istream& operator >> (istream& s, mat4& m);          // input from strm.
friend void swap(mat4& a, mat4& b);                         // swap m1 & m2

// necessary friend declarations

friend vec4 operator * (const mat4& a, const vec4& v);      // linear transform
friend vec3 operator * (const mat4& a, const vec3& v);      // linear transform
};

/****************************************************************
 *                                                              *
 *          2D functions and 3D functions                       *
 *                                                              *
 ****************************************************************/

mat3 identity2D();                                  // identity 2D
mat3 translation2D(vec2& v);                        // translation 2D
mat3 rotation2D(vec2& Center, const double angleDeg);   // rotation 2D
mat3 scaling2D(vec2& scaleVector);                  // scaling 2D
mat4 identity3D();                                  // identity 3D
mat4 translation3D(vec3& v);                        // translation 3D
mat4 rotation3D(vec3& Axis, const double angleDeg); // rotation 3D
```

```
mat4 scaling3D(vec3& scaleVector);                    // scaling 3D
mat4 perspective3D(const double d);                   // perspective 3D
```

algebra3.C

```
#include "algebra3.H"
#include <ctype.h>

/******************************************************************
 *                                                                *
 *                    vec2 member functions                       *
 *                                                                *
 ******************************************************************/

// Constructors

vec2::vec2() {}

vec2::vec2(const double x, const double y)
{ n[VX] = x; n[VY] = y; }

vec2::vec2(const double d)
{ n[VX] = n[VY] = d; }

vec2::vec2(const vec2& v)
{ n[VX] = v.n[VX]; n[VY] = v.n[VY]; }

vec2::vec2(const vec3& v) // it is up to caller to avoid divide-by-zero
{ n[VX] = v.n[VX]/v.n[VZ]; n[VY] = v.n[VY]/v.n[VZ]; };

vec2::vec2(const vec3& v, int dropAxis) {
    switch (dropAxis) {
        case VX: n[VX] = v.n[VY]; n[VY] = v.n[VZ]; break;
        case VY: n[VX] = v.n[VX]; n[VY] = v.n[VZ]; break;
        default: n[VX] = v.n[VX]; n[VY] = v.n[VY]; break;
    }
}


// Assignment operators

vec2& vec2::operator = (const vec2& v)
{ n[VX] = v.n[VX]; n[VY] = v.n[VY]; return *this; }

vec2& vec2::operator += ( const vec2& v )
{ n[VX] += v.n[VX]; n[VY] += v.n[VY]; return *this; }

vec2& vec2::operator -= ( const vec2& v )
{ n[VX] -= v.n[VX]; n[VY] -= v.n[VY]; return *this; }

vec2& vec2::operator *= ( const double d )
{ n[VX] *= d; n[VY] *= d; return *this; }
```

```
vec2& vec2::operator /= ( const double d )
{ double d_inv = 1./d; n[VX] *= d_inv; n[VY] *= d_inv; return *this; }

double& vec2::operator [] ( int i) {
    if (i < VX || i > VY)
        V_ERROR("vec2 [] operator: illegal access; index = " << i << '\n')
    return n[i];
}

// Special functions

double vec2::length()
{ return sqrt(length2()); }

double vec2::length2()
{ return n[VX]*n[VX] + n[VY]*n[VY]; }

vec2& vec2::normalize() // it is up to caller to avoid divide-by-zero
{ *this /= length(); return *this; }

vec2& vec2::apply(V_FCT_PTR fct)
{ n[VX] = (*fct)(n[VX]); n[VY] = (*fct)(n[VY]); return *this; }


// Friends

vec2 operator - (const vec2& a)
{ return vec2(-a.n[VX],-a.n[VY]); }

vec2 operator + (const vec2& a, const vec2& b)
{ return vec2(a.n[VX]+ b.n[VX], a.n[VY] + b.n[VY]); }

vec2 operator - (const vec2& a, const vec2& b)
{ return vec2(a.n[VX]-b.n[VX], a.n[VY]-b.n[VY]); }

vec2 operator * (const vec2& a, const double d)
{ return vec2(d*a.n[VX], d*a.n[VY]); }

vec2 operator * (const double d, const vec2& a)
{ return a*d; }

vec2 operator * (const mat3& a, const vec2& v) {
    vec3 av;

    av.n[VX] = a.v[0].n[VX]*v.n[VX] + a.v[0].n[VY]*v.n[VY] + a.v[0].n[VZ];
    av.n[VY] = a.v[1].n[VX]*v.n[VX] + a.v[1].n[VY]*v.n[VY] + a.v[1].n[VZ];
    av.n[VZ] = a.v[2].n[VX]*v.n[VX] + a.v[2].n[VY]*v.n[VY] + a.v[2].n[VZ];
    return av;
}

vec2 operator * (const vec2& v, mat3& a)
{ return a.transpose() * v; }
```

```
double operator * (const vec2& a, const vec2& b)
{ return (a.n[VX]*b.n[VX] + a.n[VY]*b.n[VY]); }

vec2 operator / (const vec2& a, const double d)
{ double d_inv = 1./d; return vec2(a.n[VX]*d_inv, a.n[VY]*d_inv); }

vec3 operator ^ (const vec2& a, const vec2& b)
{ return vec3(0.0, 0.0, a.n[VX] * b.n[VY] - b.n[VX] * a.n[VY]); }

int operator == (const vec2& a, const vec2& b)
{ return (a.n[VX] == b.n[VX]) && (a.n[VY] == b.n[VY]); }

int operator != (const vec2& a, const vec2& b)
{ return !(a == b); }

ostream& operator << (ostream& s, vec2& v)
{ return s << "| " << v.n[VX] << ' ' << v.n[VY] << " |"; }

istream& operator >> (istream& s, vec2& v) {
    vec2        v_tmp;
    char        c = ' ';

    while (isspace(c))
        s >> c;
    // The vectors can be formatted either as x y or as | x y |
    if (c == '|') {
        s >> v_tmp[VX] >> v_tmp[VY];
        while (s >> c && isspace(c)) ;
        if (c != '|')
            s.set(_bad);
        }
    else {
        s.putback(c);
        s >> v_tmp[VX] >> v_tmp[VY];
        }
    if (s)
        v = v_tmp;
    return s;
}

void swap(vec2& a, vec2& b)
{ vec2 tmp(a); a = b; b = tmp; }

vec2 min(const vec2& a, const vec2& b)
{ return vec2(MIN(a.n[VX], b.n[VX]), MIN(a.n[VY], b.n[VY])); }

vec2 max(const vec2& a, const vec2& b)
{ return vec2(MAX(a.n[VX], b.n[VX]), MAX(a.n[VY], b.n[VY])); }

vec2 prod(const vec2& a, const vec2& b)
{ return vec2(a.n[VX] * b.n[VX], a.n[VY] * b.n[VY]); }
```

```
/******************************************************************
*                                                                *
*                   vec3 member functions                        *
*                                                                *
******************************************************************/

// Constructors

vec3::vec3() {}

vec3::vec3(const double x, const double y, const double z)
{ n[VX] = x; n[VY] = y; n[VZ] = z; }

vec3::vec3(const double d)
{ n[VX] = n[VY] = n[VZ] = d; }

vec3::vec3(const vec3& v)
{ n[VX] = v.n[VX]; n[VY] = v.n[VY]; n[VZ] = v.n[VZ]; }

vec3::vec3(const vec2& v)
{ n[VX] = v.n[VX]; n[VY] = v.n[VY]; n[VZ] = 1.0; }

vec3::vec3(const vec2& v, double d)
{ n[VX] = v.n[VX]; n[VY] = v.n[VY]; n[VZ] = d; }

vec3::vec3(const vec4& v) // it is up to caller to avoid divide-by-zero
{ n[VX] = v.n[VX] / v.n[VW]; n[VY] = v.n[VY] / v.n[VW];
  n[VZ] = v.n[VZ] / v.n[VW]; }

vec3::vec3(const vec4& v, int dropAxis) {
    switch (dropAxis) {
        case VX: n[VX] = v.n[VY]; n[VY] = v.n[VZ]; n[VZ] = v.n[VW]; break;
        case VY: n[VX] = v.n[VX]; n[VY] = v.n[VZ]; n[VZ] = v.n[VW]; break;
        case VZ: n[VX] = v.n[VX]; n[VY] = v.n[VY]; n[VZ] = v.n[VW]; break;
        default: n[VX] = v.n[VX]; n[VY] = v.n[VY]; n[VZ] = v.n[VZ]; break;
    }
}


// Assignment operators

vec3& vec3::operator = (const vec3& v)
{ n[VX] = v.n[VX]; n[VY] = v.n[VY]; n[VZ] = v.n[VZ]; return *this; }

vec3& vec3::operator += ( const vec3& v )
{ n[VX] += v.n[VX]; n[VY] += v.n[VY]; n[VZ] += v.n[VZ]; return *this; }

vec3& vec3::operator -= ( const vec3& v )
{ n[VX] -= v.n[VX]; n[VY] -= v.n[VY]; n[VZ] -= v.n[VZ]; return *this; }

vec3& vec3::operator *= ( const double d )
{ n[VX] *= d; n[VY] *= d; n[VZ] *= d; return *this; }
```

```
vec3& vec3::operator /= ( const double d )
{ double d_inv = 1./d; n[VX] *= d_inv; n[VY] *= d_inv; n[VZ] *= d_inv;
  return *this; }

double& vec3::operator [] ( int i) {
    if (i < VX || i > VZ)
        V_ERROR("vec3 [] operator: illegal access; index = " << i << '\n')
    return n[i];
}


// Special functions

double vec3::length()
{  return sqrt(length2()); }

double vec3::length2()
{  return n[VX]*n[VX] + n[VY]*n[VY] + n[VZ]*n[VZ]; }

vec3& vec3::normalize() // it is up to caller to avoid divide-by-zero
{ *this /= length(); return *this; }

vec3& vec3::apply(V_FCT_PTR fct)
{ n[VX] = (*fct)(n[VX]); n[VY] = (*fct)(n[VY]); n[VZ] = (*fct)(n[VZ]);
return *this; }


// Friends

vec3 operator - (const vec3& a)
{  return vec3(-a.n[VX],-a.n[VY],-a.n[VZ]); }

vec3 operator + (const vec3& a, const vec3& b)
{ return vec3(a.n[VX]+ b.n[VX], a.n[VY] + b.n[VY], a.n[VZ] + b.n[VZ]); }

vec3 operator - (const vec3& a, const vec3& b)
{ return vec3(a.n[VX]-b.n[VX], a.n[VY]-b.n[VY], a.n[VZ]-b.n[VZ]); }

vec3 operator * (const vec3& a, const double d)
{ return vec3(d*a.n[VX], d*a.n[VY], d*a.n[VZ]); }

vec3 operator * (const double d, const vec3& a)
{ return a*d; }

vec3 operator * (const mat4& a, const vec3& v)
{ return a * vec4(v); }

vec3 operator * (const vec3& v, mat4& a)
{ return a.transpose() * v; }

double operator * (const vec3& a, const vec3& b)
{ return (a.n[VX]*b.n[VX] + a.n[VY]*b.n[VY] + a.n[VZ]*b.n[VZ]); }
```

```
vec3 operator / (const vec3& a, const double d)
{ double d_inv = 1./d; return vec3(a.n[VX]*d_inv, a.n[VY]*d_inv,
  a.n[VZ]*d_inv); }

vec3 operator ^ (const vec3& a, const vec3& b) {
    return vec3(a.n[VY]*b.n[VZ] - a.n[VZ]*b.n[VY],
                a.n[VZ]*b.n[VX] - a.n[VX]*b.n[VZ],
                a.n[VX]*b.n[VY] - a.n[VY]*b.n[VX]);
}

int operator == (const vec3& a, const vec3& b)
{ return (a.n[VX] == b.n[VX]) && (a.n[VY] == b.n[VY]) && (a.n[VZ] == b.n[VZ]);
}

int operator != (const vec3& a, const vec3& b)
{ return !(a == b); }

ostream& operator << (ostream& s, vec3& v)
{ return s << "| " << v.n[VX] << ' ' << v.n[VY] << ' ' << v.n[VZ] << " |"; }

istream& operator >> (istream& s, vec3& v) {
    vec3        v_tmp;
    char        c = ' ';

    while (isspace(c))
        s >> c;
    // The vectors can be formatted either as x y z or as | x y z |
    if (c == '|') {
        s >> v_tmp[VX] >> v_tmp[VY] >> v_tmp[VZ];
        while (s >> c && isspace(c)) ;
        if (c != '|')
            s.set(_bad);
        }
    else {
        s.putback(c);
        s >> v_tmp[VX] >> v_tmp[VY] >> v_tmp[VZ];
        }
    if (s)
        v = v_tmp;
    return s;
}

void swap(vec3& a, vec3& b)
{ vec3 tmp(a); a = b; b = tmp; }

vec3 min(const vec3& a, const vec3& b)
{ return vec3(MIN(a.n[VX], b.n[VX]), MIN(a.n[VY], b.n[VY]), MIN(a.n[VZ],
  b.n[VZ])); }

vec3 max(const vec3& a, const vec3& b)
{ return vec3(MAX(a.n[VX], b.n[VX]), MAX(a.n[VY], b.n[VY]), MAX(a.n[VZ],
  b.n[VZ])); }
```

```
vec3 prod(const vec3& a, const vec3& b)
{ return vec3(a.n[VX] * b.n[VX], a.n[VY] * b.n[VY], a.n[VZ] * b.n[VZ]); }

/*****************************************************************
 *                                                               *
 *                   vec4 member functions                       *
 *                                                               *
 *****************************************************************/

// Constructors

vec4::vec4() {}

vec4::vec4(const double x, const double y, const double z, const double w)
{ n[VX] = x; n[VY] = y; n[VZ] = z; n[VW] = w; }

vec4::vec4(const double d)
{   n[VX] = n[VY] = n[VZ] = n[VW] = d; }

vec4::vec4(const vec4& v)
{ n[VX] = v.n[VX]; n[VY] = v.n[VY]; n[VZ] = v.n[VZ]; n[VW] = v.n[VW]; }

vec4::vec4(const vec3& v)
{ n[VX] = v.n[VX]; n[VY] = v.n[VY]; n[VZ] = v.n[VZ]; n[VW] = 1.0; }

vec4::vec4(const vec3& v, const double d)
{ n[VX] = v.n[VX]; n[VY] = v.n[VY]; n[VZ] = v.n[VZ];   n[VW] = d; }

// Assignment operators
vec4& vec4::operator = (const vec4& v)
{ n[VX] = v.n[VX]; n[VY] = v.n[VY]; n[VZ] = v.n[VZ]; n[VW] = v.n[VW];
return *this; }

vec4& vec4::operator += ( const vec4& v )
{ n[VX] += v.n[VX]; n[VY] += v.n[VY]; n[VZ] += v.n[VZ]; n[VW] += v.n[VW];
return *this; }

vec4& vec4::operator -= ( const vec4& v )
{ n[VX] -= v.n[VX]; n[VY] -= v.n[VY]; n[VZ] -= v.n[VZ]; n[VW] -= v.n[VW];
return *this; }

vec4& vec4::operator *= ( const double d )
{ n[VX] *= d; n[VY] *= d; n[VZ] *= d; n[VW] *= d; return *this; }

vec4& vec4::operator /= ( const double d )
{ double d_inv = 1./d; n[VX] *= d_inv; n[VY] *= d_inv; n[VZ] *= d_inv;
  n[VW] *= d_inv; return *this; }

double& vec4::operator [] ( int i) {
    if (i < VX || i > VW)
        V_ERROR("vec4 [] operator: illegal access; index = " << i << '\n')
    return n[i];
}
```

```
// Special functions

double vec4::length()
{ return sqrt(length2()); }

double vec4::length2()
{ return n[VX]*n[VX] + n[VY]*n[VY] + n[VZ]*n[VZ] + n[VW]*n[VW]; }

vec4& vec4::normalize() // it is up to caller to avoid divide-by-zero
{ *this /= length(); return *this; }

vec4& vec4::apply(V_FCT_PTR fct)
{ n[VX] = (*fct)(n[VX]); n[VY] = (*fct)(n[VY]); n[VZ] = (*fct)(n[VZ]);
n[VW] = (*fct)(n[VW]); return *this; }


// Friends

vec4 operator - (const vec4& a)
{ return vec4(-a.n[VX],-a.n[VY],-a.n[VZ],-a.n[VW]); }

vec4 operator + (const vec4& a, const vec4& b)
{ return vec4(a.n[VX] + b.n[VX], a.n[VY] + b.n[VY], a.n[VZ] + b.n[VZ],
  a.n[VW] + b.n[VW]); }

vec4 operator - (const vec4& a, const vec4& b)
{  return vec4(a.n[VX] - b.n[VX], a.n[VY] - b.n[VY], a.n[VZ] - b.n[VZ],
   a.n[VW] - b.n[VW]); }

vec4 operator * (const vec4& a, const double d)
{ return vec4(d*a.n[VX], d*a.n[VY], d*a.n[VZ], d*a.n[VW] ); }

vec4 operator * (const double d, const vec4& a)
{ return a*d; }

vec4 operator * (const mat4& a, const vec4& v) {
    #define ROWCOL(i) a.v[i].n[0]*v.n[VX] + a.v[i].n[1]*v.n[VY] \
    + a.v[i].n[2]*v.n[VZ] + a.v[i].n[3]*v.n[VW]
    return vec4(ROWCOL(0), ROWCOL(1), ROWCOL(2), ROWCOL(3));
    #undef ROWCOL(i)
}

vec4 operator * (const vec4& v, mat4& a)
{ return a.transpose() * v; }

double operator * (const vec4& a, const vec4& b)
{ return (a.n[VX]*b.n[VX] + a.n[VY]*b.n[VY] + a.n[VZ]*b.n[VZ] +
  a.n[VW]*b.n[VW]); }

vec4 operator / (const vec4& a, const double d)
{ double d_inv = 1./d; return vec4(a.n[VX]*d_inv, a.n[VY]*d_inv, a.n[VZ]*d_inv,
  a.n[VW]*d_inv); }
```

```
int operator == (const vec4& a, const vec4& b)
{ return (a.n[VX] == b.n[VX]) && (a.n[VY] == b.n[VY]) && (a.n[VZ] == b.n[VZ])
  && (a.n[VW] == b.n[VW]); }

int operator != (const vec4& a, const vec4& b)
{ return !(a == b); }

ostream& operator << (ostream& s, vec4& v)
{ return s << "| " << v.n[VX] << ' ' << v.n[VY] << ' ' << v.n[VZ] << ' '
  << v.n[VW] << " |"; }

istream& operator >> (istream& s, vec4& v) {
    vec4        v_tmp;
    char        c = ' ';

    while (isspace(c))
        s >> c;
    // The vectors can be formatted either as x y z w or as | x y z w |
    if (c == '|') {
        s >> v_tmp[VX] >> v_tmp[VY] >> v_tmp[VZ] >> v_tmp[VW];
        while (s >> c && isspace(c)) ;
        if (c != '|')
            s.set(_bad);
        }
    else {
        s.putback(c);
        s >> v_tmp[VX] >> v_tmp[VY] >> v_tmp[VZ] >> v_tmp[VW];
        }
    if (s)
        v = v_tmp;
    return s;
}

void swap(vec4& a, vec4& b)
{ vec4 tmp(a); a = b; b = tmp; }

vec4 min(const vec4& a, const vec4& b)
{ return vec4(MIN(a.n[VX], b.n[VX]), MIN(a.n[VY], b.n[VY]), MIN(a.n[VZ],
  b.n[VZ]), MIN(a.n[VW], b.n[VW])); }

vec4 max(const vec4& a, const vec4& b)
{ return vec4(MAX(a.n[VX], b.n[VX]), MAX(a.n[VY], b.n[VY]), MAX(a.n[VZ],
  b.n[VZ]), MAX(a.n[VW], b.n[VW])); }

vec4 prod(const vec4& a, const vec4& b)
{ return vec4(a.n[VX] * b.n[VX], a.n[VY] * b.n[VY], a.n[VZ] * b.n[VZ],
  a.n[VW] * b.n[VW]); }
```

```
/******************************************************************
*                                                                *
*                     mat3 member functions                      *
*                                                                *
******************************************************************/

// Constructors

mat3::mat3() {}

mat3::mat3(const vec3& v0, const vec3& v1, const vec3& v2)
{ v[0] = v0; v[1] = v1; v[2] = v2; }

mat3::mat3(const double d)
{ v[0] = v[1] = v[2] = vec3(d); }

mat3::mat3(const mat3& m)
{ v[0] = m.v[0]; v[1] = m.v[1]; v[2] = m.v[2]; }

// Assignment operators

mat3& mat3::operator = ( const mat3& m )
{ v[0] = m.v[0]; v[1] = m.v[1]; v[2] = m.v[2]; return *this; }

mat3& mat3::operator += ( const mat3& m )
{ v[0] += m.v[0]; v[1] += m.v[1]; v[2] += m.v[2]; return *this; }

mat3& mat3::operator -= ( const mat3& m )
{ v[0] -= m.v[0]; v[1] -= m.v[1]; v[2] -= m.v[2]; return *this; }

mat3& mat3::operator *= ( const double d )
{ v[0] *= d; v[1] *= d; v[2] *= d; return *this; }

mat3& mat3::operator /= ( const double d )
{ v[0] /= d; v[1] /= d; v[2] /= d; return *this; }

vec3& mat3::operator [] ( int i) {
    if (i < VX || i > VZ)
        V_ERROR("mat3 [] operator: illegal access; index = " << i << '\n')
    return v[i];
}

// Special functions

mat3 mat3::transpose() {
    return mat3(vec3(v[0][0], v[1][0], v[2][0]),
                vec3(v[0][1], v[1][1], v[2][1]),
                vec3(v[0][2], v[1][2], v[2][2]));
}

mat3 mat3::inverse()          // Gauss-Jordan elimination with partial pivoting
    {
    mat3 a(*this),            // As a evolves from original mat into identity
```

```
        b(identity2D());    // b evolves from identity into inverse(a)
    int   i, j, i1;

    // Loop over cols of a from left to right, eliminating above and below diag
    for (j=0; j<3; j++) {   // Find largest pivot in column j among rows j..2
    i1 = j;                 // Row with largest pivot candidate
    for (i=j+1; i<3; i++)
        if (fabs(a.v[i].n[j]) > fabs(a.v[i1].n[j]))
            i1 = i;

    // Swap rows i1 and j in a and b to put pivot on diagonal
    swap(a.v[i1], a.v[j]);
    swap(b.v[i1], b.v[j]);

    // Scale row j to have a unit diagonal
    if (a.v[j].n[j]==0.)
        V_ERROR("mat3::inverse: singular matrix; can't invert\n")
    b.v[j] /= a.v[j].n[j];
    a.v[j] /= a.v[j].n[j];

    // Eliminate off-diagonal elems in col j of a, doing identical ops to b
    for (i=0; i<3; i++)
        if (i!=j) {
        b.v[i] -= a.v[i].n[j]*b.v[j];
        a.v[i] -= a.v[i].n[j]*a.v[j];
        }
    }
    return b;
}

mat3& mat3::apply(V_FCT_PTR fct) {
    v[VX].apply(fct);
    v[VY].apply(fct);
    v[VZ].apply(fct);
    return *this;
}


// Friends

mat3 operator - (const mat3& a)
{ return mat3(-a.v[0], -a.v[1], -a.v[2]); }

mat3 operator + (const mat3& a, const mat3& b)
{ return mat3(a.v[0] + b.v[0], a.v[1] + b.v[1], a.v[2] + b.v[2]); }

mat3 operator - (const mat3& a, const mat3& b)
{ return mat3(a.v[0] - b.v[0], a.v[1] - b.v[1], a.v[2] - b.v[2]); }

mat3 operator * (mat3& a, mat3& b) {
    #define ROWCOL(i, j) \
    a.v[i].n[0]*b.v[0][j] + a.v[i].n[1]*b.v[1][j] + a.v[i].n[2]*b.v[2][j]
    return mat3(vec3(ROWCOL(0,0), ROWCOL(0,1), ROWCOL(0,2)),
```

```
                vec3(ROWCOL(1,0), ROWCOL(1,1), ROWCOL(1,2)),
                vec3(ROWCOL(2,0), ROWCOL(2,1), ROWCOL(2,2)));
    #undef ROWCOL(i, j)
}

mat3 operator * (const mat3& a, const double d)
{ return mat3(a.v[0] * d, a.v[1] * d, a.v[2] * d); }

mat3 operator * (const double d, const mat3& a)
{ return a*d; }

mat3 operator / (const mat3& a, const double d)
{ return mat3(a.v[0] / d, a.v[1] / d, a.v[2] / d); }

int operator == (const mat3& a, const mat3& b)
{ return (a.v[0] == b.v[0]) && (a.v[1] == b.v[1]) && (a.v[2] == b.v[2]); }

int operator != (const mat3& a, const mat3& b)
{ return !(a == b); }

ostream& operator << (ostream& s, mat3& m)
{ return s << m.v[VX] << '\n' << m.v[VY] << '\n' << m.v[VZ]; }

istream& operator >> (istream& s, mat3& m) {
    mat3    m_tmp;

    s >> m_tmp[VX] >> m_tmp[VY] >> m_tmp[VZ];
    if (s)
        m = m_tmp;
    return s;
}

void swap(mat3& a, mat3& b)
{ mat3 tmp(a); a = b; b = tmp; }


/******************************************************************
 *                                                                *
 *                  mat4 member functions                         *
 *                                                                *
 ******************************************************************/

// Constructors

mat4::mat4() {}

mat4::mat4(const vec4& v0, const vec4& v1, const vec4& v2, const vec4& v3)
{ v[0] = v0; v[1] = v1; v[2] = v2; v[3] = v3; }

mat4::mat4(const double d)
{ v[0] = v[1] = v[2] = v[3] = vec4(d); }

mat4::mat4(const mat4& m)
```

```
{ v[0] = m.v[0]; v[1] = m.v[1]; v[2] = m.v[2]; v[3] = m.v[3]; }


// Assignment operators

mat4& mat4::operator = ( const mat4& m )
{ v[0] = m.v[0]; v[1] = m.v[1]; v[2] = m.v[2]; v[3] = m.v[3];
return *this; }

mat4& mat4::operator += ( const mat4& m )
{ v[0] += m.v[0]; v[1] += m.v[1]; v[2] += m.v[2]; v[3] += m.v[3];
return *this; }

mat4& mat4::operator -= ( const mat4& m )
{ v[0] -= m.v[0]; v[1] -= m.v[1]; v[2] -= m.v[2]; v[3] -= m.v[3];
return *this; }

mat4& mat4::operator *= ( const double d )
{ v[0] *= d; v[1] *= d; v[2] *= d; v[3] *= d; return *this; }

mat4& mat4::operator /= ( const double d )
{ v[0] /= d; v[1] /= d; v[2] /= d; v[3] /= d; return *this; }

vec4& mat4::operator [] ( int i) {
    if (i < VX || i > VW)
        V_ERROR("mat4 [] operator: illegal access; index = " << i << '\n')
    return v[i];
}

// Special functions;

mat4 mat4::transpose() {
    return mat4(vec4(v[0][0], v[1][0], v[2][0], v[3][0]),
                vec4(v[0][1], v[1][1], v[2][1], v[3][1]),
                vec4(v[0][2], v[1][2], v[2][2], v[3][2]),
                vec4(v[0][3], v[1][3], v[2][3], v[3][3])));
}

mat4 mat4::inverse()            // Gauss-Jordan elimination with partial pivoting
{
    mat4 a(*this),              // As a evolves from original mat into identity
        b(identity3D());        // b evolves from identity into inverse(a)
    int i, j, i1;

    // Loop over cols of a from left to right, eliminating above and below diag
    for (j=0; j<4; j++) {       // Find largest pivot in column j among rows j..3
        i1 = j;                 // Row with largest pivot candidate
        for (i=j+1; i<4; i++)
            if (fabs(a.v[i].n[j]) > fabs(a.v[i1].n[j]))
                i1 = i;

        // Swap rows i1 and j in a and b to put pivot on diagonal
        swap(a.v[i1], a.v[j]);
```

```
        swap(b.v[i1], b.v[j]);

        // Scale row j to have a unit diagonal
        if (a.v[j].n[j]==0.)
            V_ERROR("mat4::inverse: singular matrix; can't invert\n");
        b.v[j] /= a.v[j].n[j];
        a.v[j] /= a.v[j].n[j];

        // Eliminate off-diagonal elems in col j of a, doing identical ops to b
        for (i=0; i<4; i++)
            if (i!=j) {
            b.v[i] -= a.v[i].n[j]*b.v[j];
            a.v[i] -= a.v[i].n[j]*a.v[j];
            }
    }
    return b;
}

mat4& mat4::apply(V_FCT_PTR fct)
{ v[VX].apply(fct); v[VY].apply(fct); v[VZ].apply(fct); v[VW].apply(fct);
return *this; }


// Friends

mat4 operator - (const mat4& a)
{ return mat4(-a.v[0], -a.v[1], -a.v[2], -a.v[3]); }

mat4 operator + (const mat4& a, const mat4& b)
{ return mat4(a.v[0] + b.v[0], a.v[1] + b.v[1], a.v[2] + b.v[2],
  a.v[3] + b.v[3]);
}

mat4 operator - (const mat4& a, const mat4& b)
{ return mat4(a.v[0] - b.v[0], a.v[1] - b.v[1], a.v[2] - b.v[2], a.v[3] - b.v[3]); }

mat4 operator * (mat4& a, mat4& b) {
    #define ROWCOL(i, j) a.v[i].n[0]*b.v[0][j] + a.v[i].n[1]*b.v[1][j] + \
    a.v[i].n[2]*b.v[2][j] + a.v[i].n[3]*b.v[3][j]
    return mat4(
    vec4(ROWCOL(0,0), ROWCOL(0,1), ROWCOL(0,2), ROWCOL(0,3)),
    vec4(ROWCOL(1,0), ROWCOL(1,1), ROWCOL(1,2), ROWCOL(1,3)),
    vec4(ROWCOL(2,0), ROWCOL(2,1), ROWCOL(2,2), ROWCOL(2,3)),
    vec4(ROWCOL(3,0), ROWCOL(3,1), ROWCOL(3,2), ROWCOL(3,3))
    );
}

mat4 operator * (const mat4& a, const double d)
{ return mat4(a.v[0] * d, a.v[1] * d, a.v[2] * d, a.v[3] * d); }

mat4 operator * (const double d, const mat4& a)
{ return a*d; }
```

```
mat4 operator / (const mat4& a, const double d)
{ return mat4(a.v[0] / d, a.v[1] / d, a.v[2] / d, a.v[3] / d); }

int operator == (const mat4& a, const mat4& b)
{ return ((a.v[0] == b.v[0]) && (a.v[1] == b.v[1]) && (a.v[2] == b.v[2]) &&
  (a.v[3] == b.v[3])); }

int operator != (const mat4& a, const mat4& b)
{ return !(a == b); }

ostream& operator << (ostream& s, mat4& m)
{ return s << m.v[VX] << '\n' << m.v[VY] << '\n' << m.v[VZ] << '\n' << m.v[VW]; }

istream& operator >> (istream& s, mat4& m)
{
    mat4    m_tmp;

    s >> m_tmp[VX] >> m_tmp[VY] >> m_tmp[VZ] >> m_tmp[VW];
    if (s)
        m = m_tmp;
    return s;
}

void swap(mat4& a, mat4& b)
{ mat4 tmp(a); a = b; b = tmp; }


/******************************************************************
*                                                                *
*               2D functions and 3D functions                    *
*                                                                *
******************************************************************/

mat3 identity2D()
{   return mat3(vec3(1.0, 0.0, 0.0),
                vec3(0.0, 1.0, 0.0),
                vec3(0.0, 0.0, 1.0)); }

mat3 translation2D(vec2& v)
{   return mat3(vec3(1.0, 0.0, v[VX]),
                vec3(0.0, 1.0, v[VY]),
                vec3(0.0, 0.0, 1.0)); }

mat3 rotation2D(vec2& Center, const double angleDeg) {
    double  angleRad = angleDeg * M_PI / 180.0,
            c = cos(angleRad),
            s = sin(angleRad);

    return mat3(vec3(c, -s, Center[VX] * (1.0-c) + Center[VY] * s),
                vec3(s, c, Center[VY] * (1.0-c) - Center[VX] * s),
                vec3(0.0, 0.0, 1.0));
}
```

```
mat3 scaling2D(vec2& scaleVector)
{   return mat3(vec3(scaleVector[VX], 0.0, 0.0),
                vec3(0.0, scaleVector[VY], 0.0),
                vec3(0.0, 0.0, 1.0)); }

mat4 identity3D()
{   return mat4(vec4(1.0, 0.0, 0.0, 0.0),
                vec4(0.0, 1.0, 0.0, 0.0),
                vec4(0.0, 0.0, 1.0, 0.0),
                vec4(0.0, 0.0, 0.0, 1.0)); }

mat4 translation3D(vec3& v)
{   return mat4(vec4(1.0, 0.0, 0.0, v[VX]),
                vec4(0.0, 1.0, 0.0, v[VY]),
                vec4(0.0, 0.0, 1.0, v[VZ]),
                vec4(0.0, 0.0, 0.0, 1.0)); }

mat4 rotation3D(vec3& Axis, const double angleDeg) {
    double  angleRad = angleDeg * M_PI / 180.0,
            c = cos(angleRad),
            s = sin(angleRad),
            t = 1.0 - c;

    Axis.normalize();
    return mat4(vec4(t * Axis[VX] * Axis[VX] + c,
                     t * Axis[VX] * Axis[VY] - s * Axis[VZ],
                     t * Axis[VX] * Axis[VZ] + s * Axis[VY],
                     0.0),
                vec4(t * Axis[VX] * Axis[VY] + s * Axis[VZ],
                     t * Axis[VY] * Axis[VY] + c,
                     t * Axis[VY] * Axis[VZ] - s * Axis[VX],
                     0.0),
                vec4(t * Axis[VX] * Axis[VZ] - s * Axis[VY],
                     t * Axis[VY] * Axis[VZ] + s * Axis[VX],
                     t * Axis[VZ] * Axis[VZ] + c,
                     0.0),
                vec4(0.0, 0.0, 0.0, 1.0));
}

mat4 scaling3D(vec3& scaleVector)
{   return mat4(vec4(scaleVector[VX], 0.0, 0.0, 0.0),
                vec4(0.0, scaleVector[VY], 0.0, 0.0),
                vec4(0.0, 0.0, scaleVector[VZ], 0.0),
                vec4(0.0, 0.0, 0.0, 1.0)); }

mat4 perspective3D(const double d)
{   return mat4(vec4(1.0, 0.0, 0.0, 0.0),
                vec4(0.0, 1.0, 0.0, 0.0),
                vec4(0.0, 0.0, 1.0, 0.0),
                vec4(0.0, 0.0, 1.0/d, 0.0)); }
```

X.4

C Header File and Vector Library

Andrew Glassner
Xerox PARC
3333 Coyote Hill Road
Palo Alto, CA 94304
glassner@parc.xerox.com

Eric Haines
3D/Eye Inc.
2359 N. Triphammer Road
Ithaca, NY 14850
erich@eye.com

The following are C definitions and subroutines that are useful for graphics, particularly for manipulating 2-vectors, 3-vectors, and for root-finding.[1]

◇   GraphicsGems.h   ◇

```
/*
 * GraphicsGems.h
 * Version 1.0 - Andrew Glassner
 * from "Graphics Gems", Academic Press, 1990
 */

#ifndef GG_H

#define GG_H 1

/*********************/
/* 2d geometry types */
/*********************/

typedef struct Point2Struct {   /* 2d point */
        double x, y;
        } Point2;
typedef Point2 Vector2;

typedef struct IntPoint2Struct {        /* 2d integer point */
        int x, y;
        } IntPoint2;

typedef struct Matrix3Struct {  /* 3-by-3 matrix */
        double element[3][3];
        } Matrix3;

typedef struct Box2dStruct {            /* 2d box */
```

[1]Earlier versions of these routines, written by Andrew Glassner, appeared in *Graphics Gems I–III*. Eric Haines collected the corrections that appear here.

```
        Point2 min, max;
        } Box2;


/*********************/
/* 3d geometry types */
/*********************/

typedef struct Point3Struct {    /* 3d point */
        double x, y, z;
        } Point3;
typedef Point3 Vector3;

typedef struct IntPoint3Struct {        /* 3d integer point */
        int x, y, z;
        } IntPoint3;


typedef struct Matrix4Struct {  /* 4-by-4 matrix */
        double element[4][4];
        } Matrix4;

typedef struct Box3dStruct {            /* 3d box */
        Point3 min, max;
        } Box3;



/**********************/
/* one-argument macros */
/**********************/

/* absolute value of a */
#define ABS(a)          (((a)<0) ? -(a) : (a))

/* round a to nearest int */
#define ROUND(a)        floor((a)+0.5)

/* take sign of a, either -1, 0, or 1 */
#define ZSGN(a)         (((a)<0) ? -1 : (a)>0 ? 1 : 0)

/* take binary sign of a, either -1, or 1 if >= 0 */
#define SGN(a)          (((a)<0) ? -1 : 1)

/* shout if something that should be true isn't */
#define ASSERT(x) \
if (!(x)) fprintf(stderr," Assert failed: x\n");

/* square a */
#define SQR(a)          ((a)*(a))


/**********************/
```

```
/* two-argument macros */
/**********************/

/* find minimum of a and b */
#define MIN(a,b)         (((a)<(b))?(a):(b))

/* find maximum of a and b */
#define MAX(a,b)         (((a)>(b))?(a):(b))

/* swap a and b (see Gem by Wyvill) */
#define SWAP(a,b)        { a^=b; b^=a; a^=b; }

/* linear interpolation from l (when a=0) to h (when a=1)*/
/* (equal to (a*h)+((1-a)*l) */
#define LERP(a,l,h)      ((l)+(((h)-(l))*(a)))

/* clamp the input to the specified range */
#define CLAMP(v,l,h)    ((v)<(l) ? (l) : (v) > (h) ? (h) : v)


/***************************/
/* memory allocation macros */
/***************************/

/* create a new instance of a structure (see Gem by Hultquist) */
#define NEWSTRUCT(x)    (struct x *)(malloc((unsigned)sizeof(struct x)))

/* create a new instance of a type */
#define NEWTYPE(x)      (x *)(malloc((unsigned)sizeof(x)))


/*******************/
/* useful constants */
/*******************/

#define PI              3.141592        /* the venerable pi */
#define PITIMES2        6.283185        /* 2 * pi */
#define PIOVER2         1.570796        /* pi / 2 */
#define E               2.718282        /* the venerable e */
#define SQRT2           1.414214        /* sqrt(2) */
#define SQRT3           1.732051        /* sqrt(3) */
#define GOLDEN          1.618034        /* the golden ratio */
#define DTOR            0.017453        /* convert degrees to radians */
#define RTOD            57.29578        /* convert radians to degrees */


/************/
/* booleans */
/************/

#define TRUE            1
#define FALSE           0
#define ON              1
```

```
#define OFF            0
typedef int boolean;                    /* boolean data type */
typedef boolean flag;                   /* flag data type */

extern double V2SquaredLength(), V2Length();
extern double V2Dot(), V2DistanceBetween2Points();
extern Vector2 *V2Negate(), *V2Normalize(), *V2Scale(), *V2Add(), *V2Sub();
extern Vector2 *V2Lerp(), *V2Combine(), *V2Mul(), *V2MakePerpendicular();
extern Vector2 *V2New(), *V2Duplicate();
extern Point2 *V2MulPointByProjMatrix();
extern Matrix3 *V2MatMul(), *TransposeMatrix3();

extern double V3SquaredLength(), V3Length();
extern double V3Dot(), V3DistanceBetween2Points();
extern Vector3 *V3Normalize(), *V3Scale(), *V3Add(), *V3Sub();
extern Vector3 *V3Lerp(), *V3Combine(), *V3Mul(), *V3Cross();
extern Vector3 *V3New(), *V3Duplicate();
extern Point3 *V3MulPointByMatrix(), *V3MulPointByProjMatrix();
extern Matrix4 *V3MatMul();

extern double RegulaFalsi(), NewtonRaphson(), findroot();

#endif
```

◇ **GraphicsGems.c** ◇

```c
/*
2d and 3d Vector C Library
by Andrew Glassner
from "Graphics Gems", Academic Press, 1990
*/


#include <math.h>
#include "GraphicsGems.h"

/*******************/
/*   2d Library   */
/*******************/

/* returns squared length of input vector */
double V2SquaredLength(a)
Vector2 *a;
{       return((a->x * a->x)+(a->y * a->y));
        }

/* returns length of input vector */
double V2Length(a)
Vector2 *a;
{
        return(sqrt(V2SquaredLength(a)));
        }

/* negates the input vector and returns it */
Vector2 *V2Negate(v)
Vector2 *v;
{
        v->x = -v->x;   v->y = -v->y;
        return(v);
        }

/* normalizes the input vector and returns it */
Vector2 *V2Normalize(v)
Vector2 *v;
{
double len = V2Length(v);
        if (len != 0.0) { v->x /= len;   v->y /= len; }
        return(v);
        }


/* scales the input vector to the new length and returns it */
Vector2 *V2Scale(v, newlen)
Vector2 *v;
double newlen;
{
double len = V2Length(v);
        if (len != 0.0) { v->x *= newlen/len;   v->y *= newlen/len; }
```

```
                return(v);
                }

/* return vector sum c = a+b */
Vector2 *V2Add(a, b, c)
Vector2 *a, *b, *c;
{
        c->x = a->x+b->x;   c->y = a->y+b->y;
        return(c);
        }

/* return vector difference c = a-b */
Vector2 *V2Sub(a, b, c)
Vector2 *a, *b, *c;
{
        c->x = a->x-b->x;   c->y = a->y-b->y;
        return(c);
        }

/* return the dot product of vectors a and b */
double V2Dot(a, b)
Vector2 *a, *b;
{
        return((a->x*b->x)+(a->y*b->y));
        }

/* linearly interpolate between vectors by an amount alpha */
/* and return the resulting vector. */
/* When alpha=0, result=lo.  When alpha=1, result=hi. */
Vector2 *V2Lerp(lo, hi, alpha, result)
Vector2 *lo, *hi, *result;
double alpha;
{
        result->x = LERP(alpha, lo->x, hi->x);
        result->y = LERP(alpha, lo->y, hi->y);
        return(result);
        }


/* make a linear combination of two vectors and return the result. */
/* result = (a * ascl) + (b * bscl) */
Vector2 *V2Combine (a, b, result, ascl, bscl)
Vector2 *a, *b, *result;
double ascl, bscl;
{
        result->x = (ascl * a->x) + (bscl * b->x);
        result->y = (ascl * a->y) + (bscl * b->y);
        return(result);
        }

/* multiply two vectors together component-wise */
Vector2 *V2Mul (a, b, result)
Vector2 *a, *b, *result;
```

```
{
        result->x = a->x * b->x;
        result->y = a->y * b->y;
        return(result);
        }

/* return the distance between two points */
double V2DistanceBetween2Points(a, b)
Point2 *a, *b;
{
double dx = a->x - b->x;
double dy = a->y - b->y;
        return(sqrt((dx*dx)+(dy*dy)));
        }

/* return the vector perpendicular to the input vector a */
Vector2 *V2MakePerpendicular(a, ap)
Vector2 *a, *ap;
{
        ap->x = -a->y;
        ap->y = a->x;
        return(ap);
        }

/* create, initialize, and return a new vector */
Vector2 *V2New(x, y)
double x, y;
{
Vector2 *v = NEWTYPE(Vector2);
        v->x = x;   v->y = y;
        return(v);
        }


/* create, initialize, and return a duplicate vector */
Vector2 *V2Duplicate(a)
Vector2 *a;
{
Vector2 *v = NEWTYPE(Vector2);
        v->x = a->x;   v->y = a->y;
        return(v);
        }

/* multiply a point by a projective matrix and return the transformed point */
Point2 *V2MulPointByProjMatrix(pin, m, pout)
Point2 *pin, *pout;
Matrix3 *m;
{
double w;
        pout->x = (pin->x * m->element[0][0]) +
            (pin->y * m->element[1][0]) + m->element[2][0];
        pout->y = (pin->x * m->element[0][1]) +
            (pin->y * m->element[1][1]) + m->element[2][1];
```

```
        w    = (pin->x * m->element[0][2]) +
             (pin->y * m->element[1][2]) + m->element[2][2];
        if (w != 0.0) { pout->x /= w;  pout->y /= w; }
        return(pout);
        }

/* multiply together matrices c = ab */
/* note that c must not point to either of the input matrices */
Matrix3 *V2MatMul(a, b, c)
Matrix3 *a, *b, *c;
{
int i, j, k;
        for (i=0; i<3; i++) {
                for (j=0; j<3; j++) {
                        c->element[i][j] = 0;
                        for (k=0; k<3; k++) c->element[i][j] +=
                                a->element[i][k] * b->element[k][j];
                        }
                }
        return(c);
        }

/* transpose matrix a, return b */
Matrix3 *TransposeMatrix3(a, b)
Matrix3 *a, *b;
{
int i, j;
        for (i=0; i<3; i++) {
                for (j=0; j<3; j++)
                        b->element[i][j] = a->element[j][i];
                }
        return(b);
        }




/******************/
/*   3d Library   */
/******************/

/* returns squared length of input vector */
double V3SquaredLength(a)
Vector3 *a;
{
        return((a->x * a->x)+(a->y * a->y)+(a->z * a->z));
        }

/* returns length of input vector */
double V3Length(a)
Vector3 *a;
{
        return(sqrt(V3SquaredLength(a)));
```

```
        }

/* negates the input vector and returns it */
Vector3 *V3Negate(v)
Vector3 *v;
{
        v->x = -v->x;   v->y = -v->y;   v->z = -v->z;
        return(v);
        }

/* normalizes the input vector and returns it */
Vector3 *V3Normalize(v)
Vector3 *v;
{
double len = V3Length(v);
        if (len != 0.0) { v->x /= len;   v->y /= len; v->z /= len; }
        return(v);
        }

/* scales the input vector to the new length and returns it */
Vector3 *V3Scale(v, newlen)
Vector3 *v;
double newlen;
{
double len = V3Length(v);
        if (len != 0.0) {
        v->x *= newlen/len;   v->y *= newlen/len;   v->z *= newlen/len;
        }
        return(v);
        }


/* return vector sum c = a+b */
Vector3 *V3Add(a, b, c)
Vector3 *a, *b, *c;
{
        c->x = a->x+b->x;   c->y = a->y+b->y;   c->z = a->z+b->z;
        return(c);
        }

/* return vector difference c = a-b */
Vector3 *V3Sub(a, b, c)
Vector3 *a, *b, *c;
{
        c->x = a->x-b->x;   c->y = a->y-b->y;   c->z = a->z-b->z;
        return(c);
        }

/* return the dot product of vectors a and b */
double V3Dot(a, b)
Vector3 *a, *b;
{
        return((a->x*b->x)+(a->y*b->y)+(a->z*b->z));
```

```
        }

/* linearly interpolate between vectors by an amount alpha */
/* and return the resulting vector. */
/* When alpha=0, result=lo.  When alpha=1, result=hi. */
Vector3 *V3Lerp(lo, hi, alpha, result)
Vector3 *lo, *hi, *result;
double alpha;
{
        result->x = LERP(alpha, lo->x, hi->x);
        result->y = LERP(alpha, lo->y, hi->y);
        result->z = LERP(alpha, lo->z, hi->z);
        return(result);
        }

/* make a linear combination of two vectors and return the result. */
/* result = (a * ascl) + (b * bscl) */
Vector3 *V3Combine (a, b, result, ascl, bscl)
Vector3 *a, *b, *result;
double ascl, bscl;
{
        result->x = (ascl * a->x) + (bscl * b->x);
        result->y = (ascl * a->y) + (bscl * b->y);
        result->z = (ascl * a->z) + (bscl * b->z);
        return(result);
        }


/* multiply two vectors together component-wise and return the result */
Vector3 *V3Mul (a, b, result)
Vector3 *a, *b, *result;
{
        result->x = a->x * b->x;
        result->y = a->y * b->y;
        result->z = a->z * b->z;
        return(result);
        }

/* return the distance between two points */
double V3DistanceBetween2Points(a, b)
Point3 *a, *b;
{
double dx = a->x - b->x;
double dy = a->y - b->y;
double dz = a->z - b->z;
        return(sqrt((dx*dx)+(dy*dy)+(dz*dz)));
        }

/* return the cross product c = a cross b */
Vector3 *V3Cross(a, b, c)
Vector3 *a, *b, *c;
{
        c->x = (a->y*b->z) - (a->z*b->y);
```

```
          c->y = (a->z*b->x) - (a->x*b->z);
          c->z = (a->x*b->y) - (a->y*b->x);
          return(c);
          }

/* create, initialize, and return a new vector */
Vector3 *V3New(x, y, z)
double x, y, z;
{
Vector3 *v = NEWTYPE(Vector3);
          v->x = x;  v->y = y;  v->z = z;
          return(v);
          }

/* create, initialize, and return a duplicate vector */
Vector3 *V3Duplicate(a)
Vector3 *a;
{
Vector3 *v = NEWTYPE(Vector3);
          v->x = a->x;  v->y = a->y;  v->z = a->z;
          return(v);
          }


/* multiply a point by a matrix and return the transformed point */
Point3 *V3MulPointByMatrix(pin, m, pout)
Point3 *pin, *pout;
Matrix3 *m;
{
          pout->x = (pin->x * m->element[0][0]) + (pin->y * m->element[1][0]) +
                    (pin->z * m->element[2][0]);
          pout->y = (pin->x * m->element[0][1]) + (pin->y * m->element[1][1]) +
                    (pin->z * m->element[2][1]);
          pout->z = (pin->x * m->element[0][2]) + (pin->y * m->element[1][2]) +
                    (pin->z * m->element[2][2]);
          return(pout);
          }

/* multiply a point by a projective matrix and return the transformed point */
Point3 *V3MulPointByProjMatrix(pin, m, pout)
Point3 *pin, *pout;
Matrix4 *m;
{
double w;
          pout->x = (pin->x * m->element[0][0]) + (pin->y * m->element[1][0]) +
                    (pin->z * m->element[2][0]) + m->element[3][0];
          pout->y = (pin->x * m->element[0][1]) + (pin->y * m->element[1][1]) +
                    (pin->z * m->element[2][1]) + m->element[3][1];
          pout->z = (pin->x * m->element[0][2]) + (pin->y * m->element[1][2]) +
                    (pin->z * m->element[2][2]) + m->element[3][2];
          w =      (pin->x * m->element[0][3]) + (pin->y * m->element[1][3]) +
                    (pin->z * m->element[2][3]) + m->element[3][3];
          if (w != 0.0) { pout->x /= w;  pout->y /= w;  pout->z /= w; }
```

```
        return(pout);
        }

/* multiply together matrices c = ab */
/* note that c must not point to either of the input matrices */
Matrix4 *V3MatMul(a, b, c)
Matrix4 *a, *b, *c;
{
int i, j, k;
        for (i=0; i<4; i++) {
                for (j=0; j<4; j++) {
                        c->element[i][j] = 0;
                        for (k=0; k<4; k++) c->element[i][j] +=
                                a->element[i][k] * b->element[k][j];
                        }
                }
        return(c);
        }

/* binary greatest common divisor by Silver and Terzian.  See Knuth */
/* both inputs must be >= 0 */
gcd(u, v)
int u, v;
{
int t, f;
        if ((u<0) || (v<0)) return(1); /* error if u<0 or v<0 */
        f = 1;
        while ((0 == (u%2)) && (0 == (v%2))) {
                u>>=1;  v>>=1,   f*=2;
                }
        if (u&01) { t = -v;  goto B4; } else { t = u; }
        B3: if (t > 0) { t >>= 1; } else { t = -((-t) >> 1); }
        B4: if (0 == (t%2)) goto B3;

        if (t > 0) u = t; else v = -t;
        if (0 != (t = u - v)) goto B3;
        return(u*f);
        }

/***********************/
/*    Useful Routines    */
/***********************/

/* return roots of ax^2+bx+c */
/* stable algebra derived from Numerical Recipes by Press et al.*/
int quadraticRoots(a, b, c, roots)
double a, b, c, *roots;
{
double d, q;
int count = 0;
        d = (b*b)-(4*a*c);
        if (d < 0.0) { *roots = *(roots+1) = 0.0;  return(0); }
        q =  -0.5 * (b + (SGN(b)*sqrt(d)));
```

```
        if (a != 0.0)  { *roots++ = q/a; count++; }
        if (q != 0.0) { *roots++ = c/q; count++; }
        return(count);
        }


/* generic 1d regula-falsi step.  f is function to evaluate */
/* interval known to contain root is given in left, right */
/* returns new estimate */
double RegulaFalsi(f, left, right)
double (*f)(), left, right;
{
double d = (*f)(right) - (*f)(left);
        if (d != 0.0) return (right - (*f)(right)*(right-left)/d);
        return((left+right)/2.0);
        }

/* generic 1d Newton-Raphson step. f is function, df is derivative */
/* x is current best guess for root location. Returns new estimate */
double NewtonRaphson(f, df, x)
double (*f)(), (*df)(), x;
{
double d = (*df)(x);
        if (d != 0.0) return (x-((*f)(x)/d));
        return(x-1.0);
        }


/* hybrid 1d Newton-Raphson/Regula Falsi root finder. */
/* input function f and its derivative df, an interval */
/* left, right known to contain the root, and an error tolerance */
/* Based on Blinn */
double findroot(left, right, tolerance, f, df)
double left, right, tolerance;
double (*f)(), (*df)();
{
double newx = left;
        while (ABS((*f)(newx)) > tolerance) {
                newx = NewtonRaphson(f, df, newx);
                if (newx < left || newx > right)
                        newx = RegulaFalsi(f, left, right);
                if ((*f)(newx) * (*f)(left) <= 0.0) right = newx;
                        else left = newx;
                }
        return(newx);
        }
```

◊ Index

LIMITED WARRANTY AND DISCLAIMER OF LIABILITY